GAY RIGHTS AND THE CONSTITUTION

JAMES E. FLEMING
THE HONORABLE PAUL J. LIACOS PROFESSOR OF LAW
BOSTON UNIVERSITY

SOTIRIOS A. BARBER
PROFESSOR OF POLITICAL SCIENCE
UNIVERSITY OF NOTRE DAME

STEPHEN MACEDO
LAURANCE S. ROCKEFELLER PROFESSOR OF POLITICS AND HUMAN VALUES
PRINCETON UNIVERSITY

LINDA C. McCLAIN
PROFESSOR OF LAW AND PAUL M. SISKIND RESEARCH SCHOLAR
BOSTON UNIVERSITY

FOUNDATION PRESS

© 2016 LEG, Inc. d/b/a West Academic
    444 Cedar Street, Suite 700
    St. Paul, MN 55101
    1-877-888-1330

West, West Academic Publishing, and West Academic are trademarks of West Publishing Corporation, used under license.

Printed in the United States of America

ISBN: 978-1-63460-268-6

Preface

Despite dramatic changes in American constitutional law regarding sexual orientation over the last two decades, and despite the general public's keen interest in these changes, a brief collection of the leading judicial opinions has yet to be published. We have prepared this book, *Gay Rights and the Constitution* (GRC), to fill this need.

We present GRC as a casebook for law students, undergraduates, teachers, scholars, and the general public. As a casebook, GRC shows the evolution of judicial doctrine in a particular area of the law. But GRC also looks beyond judicial doctrine and asks whether the current constitutional status of gay rights is consistent with principles that trace back to the American Founding and the Civil War Amendments and that continue to animate American politics. In pursuing this aim we connect the gay rights debate to issues of longstanding importance about the best conception of the form of democracy embodied in the Constitution, the Constitution's basic normative properties, the principles of individual liberty and equality, and the role of the judiciary.

We have tried to make GRC accessible to a wide range of students, scholars, and educated citizens with no specialized background in constitutional law. We offer it as the main text in a course on gay rights or as a supplementary text in a much wider range of courses for students in law, the social sciences, and the humanities. Questions surrounding gay rights under the Constitution are embedded in broader questions of different kinds. Some of these broader questions are structural in nature, like the best understanding of American federalism and judicial power in a constitutional democracy. The gay rights debate also involves a broad range of substantive issues, like the jurisprudence of personal liberty, equal protection, freedom of association, free exercise of religion, and freedom from establishment of religion. These issues are explored in interesting ways in the opinions in the various cases included, and our introductory chapters and editors' notes to the cases will help fill in the picture. Our challenge is an adequate treatment of the gay rights debate that displays its connections to broader questions.

The book is considerably shorter than currently available law-school casebooks. Instead of exploring the whole range of legal controversies addressed in casebooks on sexuality and the law, GRC focuses on the controversies over constitutional interpretation leading up to the Supreme Court's holdings in

Lawrence v. Texas (2003) and Obergefell v. Hodges (2015): that the Constitution's commitments to liberty and equal protection encompass rights of same-sex intimacy and marriage.

We begin, in Chapter 1, with an introductory essay on the gay rights revolution in the U.S. and the *Obergefell* decision. The majority opinion, by Justice Kennedy, and the four dissenting opinions raise, in compact and vivid prose, the major debates that have run through the debates over gay rights and civil rights and personal liberties more broadly for many decades. Our introductory essay, along with our editors' notes concerning the various opinions, preview the issues taken up in the remaining chapters.

One central question of the gay rights debate, to which we turn in Chapter 2, is what counts as a reason for denying some group of people the freedoms and/or tax-supported benefits enjoyed by persons generally. Constitutional arguments against gay rights usually appeal to tradition and represent a so-called originalist approach to constitutional interpretation. On the other side, defenders of gay rights usually appeal to the idea of a living constitution. This chapter explores those alternatives and suggests a third possibility. We review material from *The Federalist* and standard interpretations of the Founding (both classic and more recent) to show that historical sources lend support to what we now understand to be a principle of public reasonableness that is very strongly present in the recent debates over gay rights. For most of American history, including the founding period, this principle ruled out appeals to sectarian doctrine and clerical authority as a basis for public policy. This has proved to be a crucial factor in the recognition of gay rights.

Chapter 3 discusses important cases and constitutional developments protecting personal liberties and securing equal protection. We discuss the cases that were the building blocks for the Supreme Court decisions protecting rights to intimate association and marriage for same-sex couples. These cases elaborated the legal terms and categories (like "equal protection" and "due process") and the "levels of scrutiny" (or stringency of protection) through which the courts have located and shaped gay rights.

Chapter 4 reprints and discusses the leading gay rights cases themselves. We analyze the development of both the due process and the equal protection grounds for justifying the rights protected in these cases, showing how these grounds are intertwined. We also trace the trajectory of the due process inquiry—for deciding whether rights to intimate association and to marry extend to gay men and lesbians—from Roe v. Wade (1973) to *Obergefell*, bringing out the fundamentally differing conceptions of constitutional interpretation that divide the majority from the dissenters in *Lawrence* and *Obergefell*.

Chapter 5 sketches emerging conflicts between protection of constitutional rights for gay men and lesbians, on the one hand, and First Amendment claims of freedom of association and religious liberty, on the other. Does freedom of association entail freedom to exclude gay men and lesbians from civic organizations and the services and employment of commercial enterprises? Does liberty of conscience entail rights to religious exemptions for clerks, business people, and religious organizations opposed to same-sex marriage? May schools teach the virtues of tolerance and respect toward gay men and lesbians and their families even if doing so conflicts with parents' and students' views that sex or marriage between same-sex couples is immoral or sinful? We also consider the warning, in Chief Justice Roberts's dissent in *Obergefell*, that recognizing the right of same-sex couples to marry puts us on a slippery slope to recognizing the right to plural marriage or polygamy.

We conclude with an epilogue asking, "What's next?" We also raise possible future developments concerning transgender rights.

We greatly appreciate the diligent and intelligent research assistance of Michael DiMaio, Jessica Lees, Jaime Margolis, Ashley Novak, and Sarah Schimmel, all students at Boston University School of Law. We especially appreciate Michael and Jessica for their capable and cheerful help at every stage from beginning to end. Thanks also to Laura Brown for invaluable assistance.

We thank Ryan Pfeiffer of Foundation Press for his encouragement of and enthusiasm concerning our preparation of this book. We gratefully acknowledge Foundation's permission to reprint several edited versions of cases from Walter F. Murphy, James E. Fleming, Sotirios A. Barber, and Stephen Macedo, *American Constitutional Interpretation* (5th edition, Foundation Press, 2014).

JEF
Boston, MA

SAB
Notre Dame, IN

SM
Princeton, NJ

LCM
Boston, MA

May 2016

Table of Contents

Table of Cases

GAY RIGHTS AND THE CONSTITUTION

The Gay Rights Revolution in America: Triumph of Constitutional Justice or Judicial Coup d'État?

On June 26, 2015, the Supreme Court of the United States made history by holding that the Constitution's guarantees of liberty and equality require that states extend the right to marry to two persons of the same sex. In one sense, the Court's decision in Obergefell v. Hodges was no surprise. Just two years before, in United States v. Windsor, the Court had held that the federal government must recognize the validity of civil marriages between two women or two men performed in those states that permitted gay and lesbian couples to wed. And in the wake of that decision, a cascade of federal and state court rulings—and law reform in several state legislatures—had extended marriage rights across most of the United States.[1] Thus, while in 2013, the year the Court decided *Windsor*, approximately 21 percent of all same-sex couples were married, when the Court decided *Obergefell* that number had grown to 38 percent.[2] By the time the *Obergefell* Court reviewed the only federal appeals court ruling to the contrary, only thirteen states still had laws or constitutional amendments that prohibited marriage by same-sex couples or refused to recognize such marriages.

If we take a longer view, however, the speed with which same-sex marriage came to the United States seems astonishing. Fewer than thirty years ago, a majority of justices of the Supreme Court voted to uphold state laws that criminalized same-sex sexual acts, even by consenting adults in the privacy of the home. The case was Bowers v. Hardwick (1986). Seventeen years later, in

---

[1] For a list, see Obergefell v. Hodges, 135 S.Ct. 2584 (2015), Appendix A: State and Federal Judicial Decisions Addressing Same-Sex Marriage, and Appendix B: State Legislation and Judicial Decisions Legalizing Same-Sex Marriage.

[2] Gary J. Gates and Taylor N.T. Brown, "Marriage and Same-Sex Couples After *Obergefell*," Williams Institute, UCLA School of Law, Nov. 2015. http://williamsinstitute.law.ucla.edu/research/census-lgbt-demographics-studies/marriage-and-same-sex-couples-after-obergefell/.

Lawrence v. Texas (2003), the Court overturned *Bowers*. Also in 2003, the Massachusetts Supreme Judicial Court, in Goodridge v. Department of Public Health, drew on *Lawrence* and ruled that its state constitution protected the right of same-sex couples to marry. After its legislature responded in 2004, Massachusetts became the first state to allow such marriages. The developments in Massachusetts intensified calls by conservative lawmakers for a federal constitutional amendment that would define marriage in every state as between one man and one woman. National opinion polls conducted after *Goodridge* showed that opponents of same-sex marriage outnumbered supporters by roughly two-to-one. Some scholars also contend that the decision prompted a political backlash that helped elect George W. Bush to a second term as President.[3] Very few observers would have predicted a decade ago that same-sex marriage would be constitutionally mandated across the United States any time soon. And if we look back sixty years, as we will do shortly, the idea of a constitutional right to same-sex marriage would have seemed preposterous. Even those who link judicial rulings like *Goodridge* to electoral backlash acknowledge that, without such high profile constitutional litigation making the issue salient for Americans, public support for gay marriage would not have grown as it did.[4]

We begin our analysis of gay rights and the Constitution with the case that consummated one important component of the revolution in gay rights in America, the U.S. Supreme Court's decision in Obergefell v. Hodges. In the chapters that follow, we reprint other cases and furnish additional materials to help readers critically assess and weigh for themselves the conflicting arguments over gay rights and the Constitution. These questions go to the very heart of our constitutional project and concern the very nature of the Constitution, the grounds for constitutional rights, and the kind of democracy that our Constitution establishes. We will see deep and heated disagreements about the nature of liberty and how to distinguish liberties that warrant special judicial protection from those that don't. We will see disagreements about the respective roles of unelected judges and elected legislatures in protecting personal liberties in a constitutional democracy. We will see profound conflicts over the right approach to constitutional interpretation. The subject of gay rights and the Constitution thus serves as a unique window onto many of the most

---

[3]   *See* Michael J. Klarman, *From the Closet to the Altar: Courts, Backlash, and the Struggle for Same-Sex Marriage* (New York: Oxford University Press, 2012), 97–98, 116–17, 174–76. *But see* Thomas M. Keck, "Beyond Backlash: Assessing the Impact of LGBT Decisions on LGBT Rights," 43 *Law & Society Rev.* 151 (2009) (challenging the backlash thesis).

[4]   *See* Klarman, *Closet to Altar*, 208.

fundamental constitutional, political, moral, and religious questions that divide Americans.

Obergefell is "the culmination of a series of opinions that began with the dissents in *Bowers* in 1986."[5] The *Bowers* dissenters insisted that longstanding disapproval of homosexual sexual conduct and moral convictions rooted in religious beliefs were insufficient reasons for depriving people of rights and liberties enjoyed by other Americans, like the right to intimate association. The dissenting side became a majority in Romer v. Evans (1996), and again in *Lawrence* (2003), *Windsor* (2013), and *Obergefell* (2015). In all of the cases from *Romer* on, Justice Anthony M. Kennedy wrote for the majority. In each of his gay rights opinions, Justice Kennedy emphasized that our understanding of constitutional liberty and equality, human dignity, and the nature and importance of basic institutions of society, such as marriage, change over time. Judges, as much as other constitutional interpreters, learn from and draw upon these evolving insights in understanding and applying constitutional rights. For a capsule statement of both the substance and the spirit of his position, consider the closing lines of his opinion of the Court in *Obergefell*:

> No union is more profound than marriage, for it embodies the highest ideals of love, fidelity, devotion, sacrifice, and family. In forming a marital union, two people become something greater than once they were. As some of the petitioners in these cases demonstrate, marriage embodies a love that may endure even past death. It would misunderstand these men and women to say they disrespect the idea of marriage. Their plea is that they do respect it, respect it so deeply that they seek to find its fulfillment for themselves. Their hope is not to be condemned to live in loneliness, excluded from one of civilization's oldest institutions. They ask for equal dignity in the eyes of the law. The Constitution grants them that right.

In each of the gay rights cases, conservative justices excoriated their colleagues for undemocratic willfulness and, in effect, legislating from the bench. Chief Justice John Roberts, dissenting in *Obergefell*, acknowledged that same-sex marriage proponents "make strong arguments rooted in social policy and considerations of fairness. . . . But this is a Court, not a legislature."[6] "Many people will rejoice in this decision, and I begrudge none their celebration," he

---

[5] The language of this paragraph is indebted to Stanley Fish, "Justice Scalia Gets it Pretty Much Right," Huffington Post Politics (Jul. 27, 2015), http://www.huffingtonpost.com/stanley-fish/scalia-gets-it-pretty-muc_b_7880118.html.

[6] *Obergefell*, 135 S.Ct. at 2611 (Roberts, C.J., dissenting).

added, but, "[fi]ve lawyers have closed the debate and offered their own vision of marriage as a matter of constitutional law," "stealing this issue from the people," and casting "a cloud over same-sex marriage." The states are entitled if they wish to "maintain the meaning of marriage that has persisted in every culture throughout human history."[7]

Marriage has been a relationship between man and woman (or, as we will see, between man and *women*) since the time of Genesis and even before. In addition, conservative judges and commentators often point out that sexual relations among men and among women have been deeply disapproved of by most cultures and religious traditions for millennia. Such conservatives hold these facts of historical practice to constitute sufficient reasons for judges to turn aside the fairness arguments for marriage equality. A further basis asserted by some conservative justices is the "channeling" or "responsible reproduction" rationale frequently invoked in defense of restrictive state and federal marriage laws (discussed later in this chapter and in Chapter 2). According to the channeling argument, marriage arose as a universal social institution to ensure that men and women who conceive children together stay together and invest in those children.[8]

Central to the controversies around gay rights and the U.S. Constitution has been the question whether longstanding forms of discrimination against homosexuals, like excluding them from the military, governmental employment, and civil marriage, have an adequate justification. Do they reflect old prejudices that are ebbing away and religious convictions that a pluralist democracy rules out as an inadequate basis for public policy?

Before turning to the cases and the debates they have provoked, we should review the political circumstances out of which today's controversies emerged.

---

[7]   Ibid., 2611–12.

[8]   An influential source for this argument is James Q. Wilson, *The Marriage Problem: How Our Culture Has Weakened Families* (New York: HarperCollins, 2002), 41. From this alleged anthropological fact it follows, or so say conservatives of the "New Natural Law" persuasion, that a couple that can't perform coitus (the baby-making act) can't really be married in the only correct sense of the term "marriage." *See* Ryan T. Anderson, *Truth Overruled: The Future of Marriage and Religious Freedom* (Washington, DC: Regnery, 2015), 24–26, 33–34. For an analysis and trenchant criticism of the New Natural Law theory of marriage and its emphasis on coitus, see Stephen Macedo, *Just Married: Same-Sex Couples, Monogamy, and the Future of Marriage* (Princeton, NJ: Princeton University Press, 2015), 41–43.

I. AMERICA THEN AND NOW

A. A Brave Few: Gays and Lesbians in the 1950s and 60s

A widespread popular movement in favor of marriage equality for same-sex couples was inconceivable in the U.S. in the 1950s and 60s, when today's older Americans were coming to maturity. A few individuals were brave enough to publicly identify as homosexual in the 1950s and early 60s, and they founded "homophile" groups: the predominantly male Mattachine Society, founded in 1950, and the lesbian group, Daughters of Bilitis, founded in 1955. These pioneers sought to secure some of the most basic rights of equal citizenship: curbing police harassment, ending the blanket exclusion of "out" homosexuals from public employment, and combating other harsh forms of discrimination.[9]

An influential amicus curiae ("friend of the court") brief submitted in *Obergefell* by the Organization of American Historians, cited by the majority opinion in *Obergefell*, describes the period from the late nineteenth century into the 1960s as one of widespread and intensifying discrimination, harassment, policing, prosecution, and demonization of those suspected of homosexual inclinations and behavior.[10] Persecution "dramatically increased at every level of government after the Second World War," spurred in part by Senator Joseph McCarthy's denunciations of the State Department for harboring communist sympathizers and "sexual perverts."[11] A special Senate Committee, set up to investigate "the employment of homosexuals and other sex perverts in government," reported that, "between January 1, 1947, and August 1, 1950, approximately 1700 applicants for federal positions were denied employment because they had a record of homosexuality or other sex perversions."[12] Homosexuals, said the report, lack "emotional stability," because "indulgence in acts of sex perversion weakens the moral fiber of an individual to a degree that

---

[9]   *See* William N. Eskridge, Jr., *Gaylaw: Challenging the Apartheid of the Closet* (Cambridge, MA: Harvard University Press, 1999), chs. 1 and 2; William N. Eskridge, Jr., *Equality Practice: Civil Unions and the Future of Gay Rights* (New York: Routledge, 2002), 17; David K. Johnson, *The Lavender Scare: The Cold War Persecution of Gays and Lesbians in the Federal Government* (Chicago, IL: University of Chicago Press, 2004); John D'Emilio and Estelle B. Freedman, *Intimate Matters: A History of Sexuality in America*, 3rd ed. (Chicago, IL: University of Chicago Press, 3rd ed., 2012); and Dudley Clendinen and Adam Nagourney, *Out For Good: The Struggle to Build a Gay Rights Movement in America* (New York: Simon and Schuster, 1999).

[10]   *See* Brief of the Organization of American Historians as Amicus Curiae in Support of Petitioners (hereinafter OAH Brief), Obergefell v. Hodges, 135 U.S. 2584 (2015), 8–11.

[11]   "McCarthy Probe Chronology," in CQ Almanac 1950, 6th ed., 456–57 (Washington, DC: Congressional Quarterly, 1951), http://library.cqpress.com/cqalmanac/cqal50–1378518 (entry for Oct. 16).

[12]   Senate Report No. 81–241 (1950), 9; OAH Brief, 11–12.

he is not suitable for a position of responsibility." The committee report warned that just one "sex pervert in a Government agency"

> tends to have a corrosive influence upon his fellow employees. These perverts will frequently attempt to entice normal individuals to engage in perverted practices. This is particularly true in the case of young and impressionable people who might come under the influence of a pervert. . . . One homosexual can pollute a Government office.[13]

Note the language of "pollution." Scholars such as William Eskridge, Martha Nussbaum, and Andrew Koppelman have amply documented the extent to which gays have been the objects of others' feelings of disgust.[14]

In 1953, President Dwight Eisenhower signed an Executive Order declaring that "the interests of national security require" the exclusion from federal employment of those found to have engaged in "any criminal, infamous, dishonest, immoral, or notoriously disgraceful conduct, habitual use of intoxicants to excess, drug addiction, sexual perversion."[15] The order was understood to include homosexuals. Defense contractors and all corporations with federal contracts were required to seek out and discharge homosexual employees, and many private employers with no federal contracts followed suit.[16] State governments similarly sought to "ferret out and fire their gay employees; countless state employees, teachers, hospital workers, and others lost their jobs as a result"; local police forces also "sharply escalated" the "policing of gay life," stepping up enforcement actions against "sexual deviants."[17] Between the late 1930s and 1950s, "police and press campaigns" promoting "vicious stereotypes of homosexuals as child molesters" prompted a "public hysteria" and wave of state laws "empowering the police or courts to force people convicted of certain sexual offenses"—or, in some states, even people "merely suspected of being 'sexual deviants' "—to undergo psychiatric examinations.

---

[13] Senate Report No. 81–241 (1950), 4; *see* Andrew Koppelman, "Are the Boy Scouts Being as Bad as Racists?" *Public Affairs Quarterly*, vol. 18, no. 4 (Oct., 2004), 363–86 (discussing the Senate Report); Thomas A. Foster, ed., *Documenting Intimate Matters: Primary Sources for a History of Sexuality in America* (Chicago, IL: University of Chicago Press, 2012), 146 (reprint of the Senate Report).

[14] *See* Eskridge, *Gaylaw*; Koppelman, "Boy Scouts"; Martha C. Nussbaum, *From Disgust to Humanity: Sexual Orientation and Constitutional Law* (New York: Oxford University Press, 2010).

[15] Executive Order 10450, 3 C.F.R. 1949–1953 (1953) (security requirements for Government employment).

[16] David K. Johnson, " 'Homosexual Citizens': Washington's Gay Community Confronts the Civil Service," *Washington History* 6 (Fall/Winter 1994–95), 45–63; *see also* OAH Brief, 12.

[17] OAH Brief, 13–15 (citing D'Emilio and Freedman, *Intimate Matters*, and John D'Emilio, "The Homosexual Menace: The Politics of Sexuality in Cold War America," in Kathy Peiss and Christina Simmons, eds., *Passion and Power: Sexuality in History* (Philadelphia, PA: Temple University Press, 1989), 226–240); Eskridge, *Gaylaw*.

The latter could lead to "indeterminate civilian confinements" if people were "deemed in need of a 'cure' for their homosexual 'pathology.' "[18]

The case of Dr. Franklin Kameny is instructive and proved consequential. A veteran of World War II, Kameny was fired from his job with the Army map service in 1957 because he was gay. He did not go quietly. At a time when same-sex sexual relations were criminalized in all fifty states, and "even the American Civil Liberties Union declared it had no interest in challenging laws 'aimed at the suppression or elimination of homosexuals,' "[19] Kameny called his treatment "an affront to human dignity." He helped found a Washington, DC chapter of the Mattachine Society and, in 1961, prepared his own appeal petition to the Supreme Court, the first for a violation of civil rights based on sexual orientation.[20] An astonishing document for its forward-looking eloquence, Kameny invoked America's founding principles:

> Not only are the government's present policies on homosexuality irrational in themselves, but they are unreasonable in that they are grossly inconsistent with the fundamental precepts upon which this government is based. . . . [W]e may commence with the Declaration of Independence, and its affirmation, as an "inalienable right," that of the "pursuit of happiness." Surely a most fundamental, unobjectionable, and unexceptionable element in human happiness is the right to bestow affection upon and to receive affection from whom one wishes. Yet, upon pain of severe penalty, the government itself would abridge this right for the homosexual.[21]

After the Supreme Court refused to take his case, Kameny and a handful of other brave souls began picketing the White House and the Pentagon in 1965 to protest the federal government's exclusion of gays from employment.

---

[18] OAH Brief, 15 (citing, among other sources, Estelle Freedman, " 'Uncontrolled Desires': The Response to the Sexual Psychopath, 1920–1960," *The Journal of American History,* vol. 74, no. 1 (June 1987), 83–106; George Chauncey, "The Postwar Sex Crime Panic," in *True Stories from the American Past,* William Greener, ed. (New York: McGraw-Hill, 1993)).

[19] Dale Carpenter, "How the Law Accepted Gays," *New York Times,* April 28, 2011.

[20] "Library of Congress Exhibits Gay Rights History," http://www.washingtonpost.com/blogs/the-buzz/post/library-of-congress-exhibits-gay-rights-history/2011/05/09/AFklNtYG_blog.html.

[21] Kameny's Petition for a Writ of Certiorari to the United States Supreme Court, January, 1961, Charles Francis, "50th Anniversary of a Legal Revolution," www.huffingtonpost.com/charles-francis/frank-karmeny-supreme-court_b_840659.html; *see also* Eskridge, *Gaylaw,* 97, 125–6.

In 1966, the Johnson Administration rejected a request from Mattachine to modify the ban on federal employment.[22] John W. Macy, Jr., Chairman of the Civil Service Commission, issued a "landmark policy statement on homosexuals":

> Pertinent considerations here [for maintaining the ban on homosexuals in government] are the revulsion of other employees by homosexual conduct and the consequent disruption of service efficiency, the apprehension caused other employees by homosexual advances, solicitations or assaults, the unavoidable subjection of the sexual deviate to erotic stimulation through on the job use of common toilet, shower and living facilities, the offense to members of the public who are required to deal with a known or admitted sexual deviate.[23]

President Lyndon Johnson, whose special assistant and chief of staff, Walter Jenkins, had been arrested on morals charges not long before in the men's restroom of the local YMCA, ordered renewed investigations of executive branch appointees for suspected homosexuality. In a "curious exchange" with the man who led that investigation, J. Edgar Hoover, Johnson confided: "I swear I can't recognize them. I don't know anything about them." To which Hoover replied, in part, "It's a thing you just can't tell sometimes. . . . There are some people who walk kind of funny. That you might think a little bit off or queer." But Jenkins exhibited no such obvious signs, said the FBI Director. And nor, apparently, did Hoover himself.[24]

Medical science reinforced the hostility toward gays. In 1952, the *Diagnostic and Statistical Manual* of the American Psychiatric Association (APA) listed homosexuality as a sociopathic personality disorder. Ten years later, the *Manual* pronounced that this disorder resulted "from a pathological hidden fear of the opposite sex caused by traumatic parent-child relationships."[25] Kameny lobbied the APA for a change in its policies, joined by lesbian rights pioneer Barbara Gittings and others. The APA eventually removed homosexuality from its list of mental disorders in 1973, followed in 1975 by a similar stance taken by the American Psychological Association, which also urged "all mental health

---

[22] David Boies and Theodore B. Olson, *Redeeming the Dream: The Case for Marriage Equality* (New York: Penguin, 2014), 36. *But see* Cole v. Young, 351 U.S. 536 (1955), in which the Supreme Court narrowed the application of the order for an FDA employee thought to have associates with Communist sympathies.

[23] Charles Francis, "Kameny Papers Expose a Dark Legacy: How a civil servant's 'revulsion letter' doomed a generation," *The Gay and Lesbian Review* (January 2011), http://www.kamenypapers.org/images/KamenyPapersDarkLegacyPackageV5.pdf.

[24] Ibid.

[25] Boies and Olson, *Redeeming the Dream*, 33.

professionals to help dispel the stigma of mental illness that had long been associated with homosexual orientation."[26] Other major medical and psychological professional associations eventually did the same, and all have issued further statements condemning discrimination against gay and lesbian people.[27] Notably, the APA, the American Psychological Association, and other major health organizations have filed friend of the court briefs *in support* of gay men and lesbians in the Court's major cases involving discrimination, most recently arguing, in *Obergefell*, that there is "no scientific justification for excluding same-sex couples from marriage."[28] With growing understanding of sexual orientation as a basic—even immutable—feature of human personality, some states have now banned licensed professionals from offering "sexual orientation change effort" therapy (also called conversion therapy) to minors.[29] However, the labeling of gays as psychologically disordered or as amenable to conversion or reparative therapy continues to this day, at least on the fringes of psychology.[30]

"In the face of government, religious, and academic condemnations" of homosexuals as "criminal, deviant, and dangerous," attorneys David Boies and Theodore B. Olson point out that violence against them was inevitable, though of course no statistics were compiled until much later.[31] One study in the early 1990s found that 89 percent of American males aged 15–19 thought that homosexual sexual activity was "disgusting," and only 12 percent were sure they would befriend an openly gay male.[32] Even today, reported hate crimes number

---

[26] Brief of the American Psychological Ass'n et al. as Amicus Curiae in Support of Respondents, Romer v. Evans, 517 U.S. 620 (1996), 7–8.

[27] D'Emilio and Freedman, *Intimate Matters*, 320.

[28] Brief of the American Psychological Ass'n et al. as Amicus Curiae in Support of Petitioners, in Obergefell v. Hodges, 135 S. Ct. 2584 (2015), 5. For an earlier brief condemning laws discriminating on the basis of sexual orientation, see Brief of the American Psychological Ass'n et al. as Amicus Curiae in Support of Respondents, Romer v. Evans, 517 U.S. 620 (1996).

[29] Some parents, minor children, and therapists, for example, have brought unsuccessful challenges to California's and New Jersey's bans on "sexual orientation change effort" therapy, asserting infringement of their First Amendment rights to free speech and free exercise of religion. *See* King v. Christie, 981 F. Supp. 2d 296 (D. N.J. 2013), *aff'd*, 767 F. 3d 216 (3d Cir. 2014); Pickup v. Brown, 42 F. Supp. 3d 1347 (E.D. Cal. 2012), *aff'd*, 740 F.3d 1208 (9th Cir. 2013).

[30] The idea that same-sex attraction is a psychological disorder that can be "cured" or successfully treated by "reparative therapy" continues to be defended by a dwindling number of fringe characters. See the moving account in Gabriel Arana, "My So-Called Ex-Gay Life: A deep look at the fringe movement that just lost its only shred of scientific support," http://prospect.org/article/my-so-called-ex-gay-life. Reparative therapy has been advocated by religious communities and figures, including Mormonism, http://www.lds-mormon.com/hldsss.shtml. Leading organizations such as Exodus have now abandoned it.

[31] Boies and Olson, *Redeeming the Dream*, 34.

[32] William Marsiglio, "Attitudes Toward Homosexual Activity and Gays as Friends: A National Survey of Heterosexual 15 to 19-Year-Old Males," *Journal of Sex Research*, vol. 30 (1993), 12–17, discussed in Koppelman, "Boy Scouts," 371.

in the thousands every year, according to the FBI, though there is no requirement that they be reported.[33] And hate crimes against gays are frequently extremely brutal, involving torture and mutilation.[34]

General social surveys in the 1990s found hostility toward gay men and lesbians to be widespread and intensely felt. Americans participating in a national "Feelings Thermometer," repeated four times by the American National Election Study over a ten-year period, consistently assigned the lowest score, zero, to gays and lesbians; next in order were illegal immigrants, people on welfare, and Christian fundamentalists. (In 1994, 28.2 percent assigned gays the very coldest zero ranking, as compared with 24.2 percent for the next most unpopular group, illegal immigrants, and 9.1 percent for the third most unpopular group, people on welfare. The figure for blacks was 2.0 percent.) As Kenneth Sherrill observes, "only lesbians and gay men were the objects of cold feelings from a majority of Americans."[35]

All of these factors led the great majority of gay, lesbian, and bisexual people to conceal their sexual identities, making them invisible to the rest of society, and facilitating "the persistence of antigay prejudice."[36] Federal judge Richard Posner observes that when he grew up in the 1950s, "I knew . . . that there were homosexuals," but, "if asked I would have truthfully said that as far as I knew I had never met one, or expected ever to meet one, any more than I had ever met or expected to meet an Eskimo."[37] No doubt most Americans would have said the same thing until recently.

Given such widespread and frequently expressed hostility toward homosexuality issuing from the government, churches, family, and friends, one must also consider the toll of the anxiety and self-doubt among those with same-sex attractions. One study found that lesbian, gay, and bisexual young people are more than twice as likely as their heterosexual peers to have attempted suicide.[38]

---

[33] Federal Bureau of Investigation, *Hate Crime Statistics*, 2012 (Nov. 25, 2013), http://www.fbi.gov/news/pressrel/press-releases/fbi-releases–2012–hate-crime-statistics.

[34] *See* Koppelman, "Boy Scouts."

[35] Kenneth Sherrill, "The Political Power of Lesbians, Gays, and Bisexuals," *PS: Political Science and Politics* (1996), 469–73, 470; *see also* Koppelman, "Boy Scouts," 370 & 381 n. 45.

[36] Boies and Olson, *Redeeming the Dream*, 35.

[37] Richard Posner, "Homosexual Marriage," Becker-Posner blog (May 13, 2012), http://www.becker-posner-blog.com/2012/05/homosexual-marriageposner.html.

[38] S.T. Russell and K. Joyner, "Adolescent sexual orientation and suicide risk: Evidence from a national study," *American Journal of Public Health*, vol. 91 (2001): 1276–1281; *see also* Centers for Disease Control and Prevention, "Lesbian, Gay, Bisexual, and Transgender Health," (Nov. 12, 2014), http://www.cdc.gov/lgbthealth/youth.htm.

B. The Early Push for Marriage Rights

In the 1970s, the "gay rights" agenda was to secure basic protections from harassment by the police, decriminalization of gay sex, hate crimes legislation, and anti-discrimination rights in employment and housing. Though marriage was rarely discussed, it was pushed briefly to the fore by a few activists emboldened by the revolutionary advances of the Civil Rights Movement and the Women's Movement of the 1960s and 70s.[39] Significant developments in constitutional law limiting the state's ability to regulate sex in marriage also encouraged gay activists. In 1965, in Griswold v. Connecticut, the Supreme Court struck down a Connecticut law prohibiting use of contraception by married couples, in an opinion with rhetorical flourishes not only about keeping police out of the "sacred precincts" of the marital bedroom but also about the "noble" purposes of the marital union. Two years later, in Loving v. Virginia (1967), a case in which police literally did invade the marital bedroom to challenge an interracial marriage that violated Virginia's antimiscegenation law, the Court relied on both Due Process liberty and Equal Protection to strike down the law. Although both *Griswold* and *Loving* would prove to play central roles in the many judicial opinions ruling in favor of same-sex couples, including *Obergefell*, those precedents did not help Jack Baker and Michael McConnell in their early challenge to Minnesota's marriage law.[40]

Jack Baker and Michael McConnell met at a party in 1966, and they soon fell in love. They were both convinced that gay people deserved equal rights, including marriage rights. Not long after, Baker, a veteran, was fired from a job at Tinker Air Force Base for being gay. They moved to Minnesota so Baker could attend the state's flagship university to study law and McConnell could take up a job as a university librarian. When university officials learned McConnell was gay, he was fired from his library job, and the men began a lawsuit. Baker also ran for student body president as an openly gay man: He was pictured in a campaign ad in the student newspaper sitting on the floor, arms curled around his knees, looking—with long hair and sideburns—like the typical early 70s college student, except for his high-heels.[41]

Noticing that Minnesota law did not explicitly prohibit same-sex marriage, Baker and McConnell applied for a marriage license in Hennepin County,

---

[39] Eskridge, *Gaylaw*; Clendinen and Nagourney, *Out for Good*.

[40] Baker v. Nelson, 191 N.W.2d 185 (Minn. 1971).

[41] Thomas Kraemer, "Jack Baker & Michael McConnell: Lunatics or Geniuses?" GayToday.com (June 21, 2004), http://gaytoday.com/people/062104pe.asp; Clendinen and Nagourney, *Out for Good*.

Minnesota, in 1970. The clerk asked, "Who's going to be the wife?" "We don't play those kinds of roles," the men replied.[42] This reported exchange is telling because it hints at how central gender-differentiated roles were to marriage. Without what has come to be called the gender revolution both in constitutional law and family law, marriage between two men or two women would be unimaginable.

In 1971, however, as Mary Anne Case observes, "legally enforced sex-role differentiation" was "firmly entrenched in law and not yet seen as constitutionally problematic."[43] Although states had moved away from the legal model of marriage articulated by William Blackstone, under which women's very civil existence was suspended in marriage as husband and wife become one person—namely, the husband—vestiges of coverture and of the ideology of men's and women's separate spheres remained. Legal rules reinforced husbands' roles as breadwinners/heads of households and wives' roles as dependents/homemakers. As recently as 1961, for example, the Supreme Court upheld the exclusion of women from jury rolls in Florida (unless they expressly put their names on the list) on the premise that, despite some social change in recent years, "Woman is still regarded as the center of home and family life. We cannot say that it is constitutionally impermissible for a State . . . to conclude that a woman should be relieved from the civil duty of jury service unless she determines that such service is consistent with her own special responsibilities."[44] It was only in 1971 that the Supreme Court for the first time struck down a sex-based classification, a Florida law giving men priority over women as administrators of an estate.[45]

In 1973, Frontiero v. Richardson, the Court came within one vote of ruling that sex-based classifications must be subject to "strict scrutiny" to determine whether the state had a compelling interest that could be served in no less restrictive ways. The four justices emphasized the parallels between race discrimination and the nation's "long and unfortunate history of sex discrimination." They noted parallels between slave codes and rules regulating the status of wives.[46] In a series of cases, several of which were orchestrated by law professor—and future Supreme Court justice—Ruth Bader Ginsburg at the ACLU Women's Rights Project, the Court began to dismantle the unequal

---

[42]   Kay Tobin and Randy Wicker, *The Gay Crusaders* (New York: Paperback Library, 1972), 145 (quoted in Mary Anne Case, "Marriage Licenses," 89 *Minnesota Law Review* 1758 (2005), 1784).

[43]   Case, "Marriage Licenses," 1785.

[44]   Hoyt v. Florida, 368 U.S. 57, 62 (1961).

[45]   Reed v. Reed, 404 U.S. 71 (1971).

[46]   411 U.S. 677, 684–86 (1973).

entitlements of husbands and wives, and fathers and mothers.[47] In 1976, the Court finally settled on an "intermediate scrutiny" standard for evaluating sex-based classifications—a standard more exacting than the "rational basis scrutiny" applied to laws in general but less demanding than the "strict scrutiny" applied to race-based classifications.[48] Under such a heightened standard, the Court struck down, in 1977, a state law that child support should be paid for boys until age 21, but for girls, only until 18, and, in 1979, a state law that only wives could receive alimony upon divorce and only husbands must pay it, regardless of the actual financial needs or resources of the spouses.[49] It was only in 1981 that the Court ruled that Louisiana's "head and master" law, which granted husbands exclusive control over the couple's community property, violated the Equal Protection Clause.[50]

A basic premise of this gender revolution was that notions of sex roles within marriage—and in the broader society—that once seemed natural and just were now seen to reflect outmoded and ancient stereotypes that denied men's and women's actual capacities to participate in society. Although the effort to ratify the federal Equal Rights Amendment, long a feminist goal, narrowly failed, a number of states enacted ERAs, often requiring strict scrutiny for laws that classified on the basis of sex.

These developments, which would transform the law of marriage in subsequent decades and pave the way for reconsidering the one-man-one-woman definition of marriage, were all in the future when the intrepid duo of Baker and McConnell sued for marriage rights in 1971. At that time, "The fear ... wasn't that you'd be discriminated against, that was a given," according to Jean Tretter, another Minnesota activist. "You were a lot more afraid that someone might come after you with a shotgun."[51] Other gay rights activists in Minnesota reportedly regarded the two as "lunatics" for pressing the marriage issue at the time, and some opposed monogamous marriage as "a trap."[52] In the

---

[47] For an entertaining account of Ginsburg's efforts and the social climate in which she brought these cases, see Irin Carmon and Shana Knizhnik, *Notorious RBG: The Life and Times of Ruth Bader Ginsburg* (New York: Dey Street Books, 2015), 43–73.

[48] Craig v. Boren, 429 U.S. 190, 197–204 (1976).

[49] Stanton v. Stanton, 421 U.S. 7, 17 (1975) (child support); Orr v. Orr, 440 U.S. 268, 279–80 (1979) (alimony).

[50] 450 U.S. 455, 460 (1981). We draw here on Case, "Marriage Licenses," 1786.

[51] Patrick Condon, "Four Decades Ago, This Gay Couple Sued for Right to Marry—and the Supreme Court Rejected Them," *Associated Press* (Dec. 10, 2012), http://usnews.nbcnews.com/_news/2012/12/10/15 817378-four-decades-ago-this-gay-couple-sued-for-right-to-marry-and-the-supreme-court-rejected-them?lite.

[52] Kraemer, "Lunatics or Geniuses."

course of the litigation the couple was featured in *Look* magazine and appeared on the Phil Donohue Show, but they eventually moved on with their lives.[53]

Hennepin County Attorney George M. Scott observed that, "The distinction between a husband and wife, a man and a woman, and the rights and duties which are placed upon each . . . are too numerous to set forth." The law, he said, "is replete with references to the distinction of husband and wife as being male and female with different rights, duties and obligations accorded to each." He warned that, "if one were to permit the marriage of two male persons, it would result in a complete confusion as to the rights and duties of husband and wife, man and woman, in the numerous other sections of our law which govern the rights and duties of married persons." The result would be no less than the "destruction of the entire legal concept of our family structure in all areas of law."[54]

The Minnesota Supreme Court eventually agreed with Scott, ruling that "The institution of marriage as a union of man and woman, uniquely involving the procreation and rearing of children within a family, is as old as the Book of Genesis."[55] The court concluded that the U.S. Supreme Court's precedents establishing the fundamental right to marry simply did not apply because such cases involved marriage between husband and wife. Further, the Minnesota court read *Loving* as confined solely to the "patent racial discrimination" in that case, and reasoned that "in common sense and in a constitutional sense, there is a clear distinction between a marital distinction based merely upon race and one based on the fundamental difference of sex."[56] In 1972 the U.S. Supreme Court declined to hear arguments in Baker v. Nelson, "for want of a substantial federal question."[57]

In 1975, Clela Rorex, a county clerk in Colorado, noticed that the law was silent on the question of whether a same-sex couple could file for a marriage license, and issued six marriage licenses to gay and lesbian couples on her own discretion.[58] The Colorado Attorney General quickly stepped in to prevent the clerk's office from issuing further licenses to same-sex couples and voided the

---

[53] Condon, "Four Decades Ago."

[54] Appellees motion to Dismiss Appeal and Brief, 12–13, Baker v. Nelson, 191 N.W.2d 185 (Minn. 1971) (No. 71–978) (quoted in Case, "Marriage Licenses," 1787).

[55] Baker v. Nelson, 191 N.W.2d 185, 186 (Minn. 1971).

[56] Ibid., 187.

[57] 410 U.S. 810 (1972).

[58] NPR Staff, "Colo. Clerk Recalls Issuing Same-Sex-Marriage Licenses—In 1975," *NPR Morning Edition* (July 18, 2014, 3:35 AM), http://www.npr.org/2014/07/18/332344999/colo-clerk-recalls-issuing-same-sex-marriage-licenses-in-1975.

unions, though at least one license was never legally voided.[59] Similar scenarios played out elsewhere.

What happened to Jack Baker and Michael McConnell? They remain together after 45 years of marriage. Wait, marriage? How so? A Methodist minister performed a marriage ceremony for them in 1971 and, after being turned down in Hennepin County, they traveled to Minnesota's Blue Earth County "where they obtained a marriage license on which Baker was listed with an altered, gender-neutral name." Though challenged in court, says Baker, the license was never actually invalidated by a judge.[60]

C. The Beginnings of a Wider Movement: From Stonewall Through the 1980s

In June 1969 the New York City police raided the Stonewall Inn, a hangout for the gay community of the city's Greenwich Village. The community reacted with a series of violent demonstrations. The Stonewall riots helped radicalize an emerging gay activism on college campuses and in cities like New York and San Francisco. Gay pride parades began in June 1970 on the first anniversary of Stonewall. Thousands came out of the closet and hundreds of gay rights and gay liberation groups were formed in cities and on college campuses across the country, often in the face of considerable hostility. In 1973, the Lambda Legal Defense and Education Fund filed an application for non-profit status in New York State. A panel of judges ruled its mission was "neither benevolent nor charitable,"[61] a decision later overturned by New York's highest court. Similarly, the IRS turned down San Francisco's Pride Foundation's application for charitable status in 1974, on the ground that promoting "the alleged normalcy of homosexuality" was offensive and contrary to public policy.[62]

After Stonewall, many gay and lesbian activists adopted the kind of radical agenda embraced by many in the civil rights and women's movements of the early 1970s. The traditional family and its gendered roles of husband and wife was a central target. Complaining of insufficient militancy, a committee spilt off from the Mattachine Society and the parallel women's homophile group, the Daughters of Bilitis. The Gay Liberation Front "adopted much of the

---

[59] Margalit Fox, "Richard Adams, Same-Sex Spouse Who Sued U.S., Dies at 65," *New York Times,* Dec. 24, 2012, http://www.nytimes.com/2012/12/25/us/richard-adams-who-sued-us-after-1975-gay-marriage-dies-at-65.html; Carol Taylor, "Boulder was Trendsetter for Same-Sex Marriage," *Daily Camera* (May 26, 2013, 1:00 AM), http://www.dailycamera.com/ci_23316471/boulder-acknowleged-same-sex-marriage-1975.

[60] Condon, "Four Decades Ago."

[61] Lambda Legal website, "Lambda Legal History," http://www.lambdalegal.org/about-us/history.

[62] Eskridge, *Gaylaw,* 115; Boies and Olson, *Redeeming the Dream,* 38.

revolutionary rhetoric of the New Left,"[63] opposing capitalism as well as patriarchy, with slogans like: "Smash phallic tyranny," and "We oppose the family and support the living collective."[64] The National Coalition of Gay Organizations published a list of legal reforms in 1972: "Repeal of all legislative provisions that restrict the sex or number of persons entering into a marriage unit and extension of legal benefits of marriage to all persons who cohabit regardless of sex or numbers."[65]

In the wake of Stonewall and for decades after, many activists saw marriage equality as an unimaginably distant goal, and some regarded it with profound ambivalence. Many considered marriage the enemy, a patriarchal bastion of male supremacy and sexual repression, and certainly not a cause to be fought for. Radicals called "husband-wife marriage with children . . . 'the microcosm of oppression.' "[66] An early gay tract denounced the " 'rotten, oppressive institution' " of traditional marriage. "Marriage is a great institution," quipped Paula Ettelbrick (riffing on Mae West), "if you like living in institutions." For two decades she argued against placing marriage equality high on the LGBT agenda. Marriage rights "would force our assimilation into the mainstream" and sap efforts to transform society more radically. Along with other marriage opponents, such as Nancy Polikoff, Ettelbrick worried that gay marriage would further stigmatize those who chose not to marry, diminish a distinctive gay and lesbian identity, and privilege the concerns of middle class gays over the needs of the most vulnerable in the movement. Why, they argued, should basic benefits like health insurance depend on one's marital status rather than be a universal entitlement?[67]

Making marriage equality a central aim of the LGBT agenda would, it was feared, sell out the broader and more radical goals of early 1970s gay and feminist activism: ending "heterosexual supremacy and oppression" and "sex-determined gender and familial roles."[68] "It is white gay men who seem to be

[63] D'Emilio and Freedman, *Intimate Matters*, 321.

[64] Sewell Chan, "Revisiting 1969 and the Start of Gay Liberation," *New York Times*, June 8, 2009 10:47 AM, http://cityroom.blogs.nytimes.com/2009/06/08/nypl-stonewall-post/.

[65] William N. Eskridge, Jr., *The Case for Same-Sex Marriage: From Sexual Liberty to Civilized Commitment* (New York: Free Press, 1996), 54.

[66] Eskridge, *Equality Practice*, 4.

[67] Ibid. 208–09; Klarman, *Closet to Altar*, 48–49. For the classic debate on this issue, compare Paula L. Ettelbrick, "Since When Is Marriage A Path to Liberation?," in Suzanne Sherman, ed., *Lesbian and Gay Marriage* (Philadelphia, PA: Temple University Press, 1992), 20, with Thomas B. Stoddard, "Why Gay People Should Seek the Right to Marry," in Sherman, *Lesbian and Gay Marriage*, 13.

[68] Paula Ettelbrick, "Legal Marriage Is Not the Answer," *The Gay and Lesbian Review* vol. 19, issue 6: Issue #100 (Nov. 1, 2012).

most vociferous in promoting the same-sex marriage philosophy," Ettelbrick observed in 1997, and "these activists ignore the history of women's experience with marriage."[69] Nonetheless, some feminist theorists within the LGBT movement contended that same-sex marriage had the potential to further erode gendered marriage by denaturalizing and calling into question the "spousal roles of husband and wife."[70]

In the 1980s, things got worse, not better, in many respects, as gay and lesbian Americans confronted AIDS along with the rise of the Religious Right and the Moral Majority. From the late 1970s to the late 1980s, the percentage of Americans who thought that homosexual sexual relations were always wrong rose from around 70 percent to nearly 80 percent. And whereas 40 percent of Americans "opposed legalization of consensual sodomy" in 1982, it was 55 percent in 1986 (the year the Court decided *Bowers*).[71] In a Kansas telephone survey in the late 1980s, it took 1650 calls—or "55 hours of random dialing— before pollsters found the first person willing to admit being lesbian or gay."[72] Progress toward anti-discrimination laws was halted or reversed.

Fear of contagion with AIDS by gay men using the same water fountain or public telephone or toilet seat led some to call for the quarantine of AIDS carriers. Republican Congressman William Dannemeyer, running for a California Senate seat, charged that "AIDS carriers emitted deadly spores and that they might be engaged in 'blood terrorism.' "[73] *National Review* editor William F. Buckley, Jr., proposed: "Everyone detected with AIDS should be tattooed in the upper forearm, to protect common-needle users, and on the buttocks, to prevent the victimization of other homosexuals."[74]

A more lasting consequence of AIDS was that it encouraged many gays to come out of the closet, and forced out others. As coming out spread beyond the hard core of urban activists, openly gay people came to include a wider cross-section of society. The percentage of Americans who reported knowing someone gay doubled between 1985 and 1992. Moreover, the example of gay

---

[69] Ibid.

[70] Nan Hunter, "Marriage, Law, and Gender: A Feminist Inquiry," 1 *Law & Sexuality* 9 (1991); Klarman, *Closet to Altar,* 49; *see generally* Eskridge, *Equality Practice,* 206–29.

[71] Klarman, *Closet to Altar,* 35–41 (explaining that the wording of the question changed).

[72] David L. Chambers, "What If? The Legal Consequences of Marriage and the Legal Needs of Lesbian and Gay Male Couples." 95 *Michigan Law Review* 447 (1996), 449 n.3 (citing Larry Hatfield, "Methods of Polling," *S.F. Examiner,* June 5, 1989, A20).

[73] *See* Klarman, *Closet to Altar,* 34; Eskridge, *Equality Practice,* 66.

[74] William F. Buckley, Jr., "Crucial Steps in Combating the Aids Epidemic; Identify All the Carriers," *New York Times,* Op-Ed, Mar. 18, 1986, http://www.nytimes.com/books/00/07/16/specials/buckley-aids.html.

men caring for each other and forming various types of family ties and support networks in the face of crisis also likely helped counteract some of the stigma associated with the disease.[75] The Americans with Disabilities Act, which took effect in 1992, was interpreted by courts to require employers to accommodate those with AIDS and to bar discrimination against those who were HIV positive, unless they posed a clear risk to others.[76]

It was in the inauspicious climate of the mid 1980s that Lambda Legal sought to overturn existing state anti-sodomy laws. In 1986, the Supreme Court granted review in Bowers v. Hardwick. In the justices' conference, after oral argument, Justice Lewis Powell, who was widely seen as the swing vote, at first sided with the four liberal justices in favor of decriminalizing gay sex. After further deliberation, however, including discussions with a closeted gay law clerk in which Powell volunteered that he had never known anyone who was gay, the Justice switched sides and joined the conservatives in upholding the criminal statute, noting only that actual incarceration for private, consensual sodomy might amount to cruel and unusual punishment.[77]

Bowers was a sobering defeat, yet many reacted against it. A Gallup poll conducted shortly after the decision found that more people opposed it than supported it.[78] The language and reasoning employed by the conservative majority was condemned by a number of major newspapers. Justice Byron White's opinion of the Court termed the attempt to locate support for a "fundamental right to engage in homosexual sodomy" in the Constitution's guarantees of liberty and equality as "at best, facetious."[79] Chief Justice Warren Burger summoned what he called the "millennia of moral teaching" that homosexuality was wrong. Burger's citations of authority included William Blackstone's judgment that homosexual sodomy was a crime of "deeper malignity" than rape.[80] *Bowers* energized gay rights activists and produced a mini-backlash in public opinion.

Beginning in the 1980s, a significant advance was that some municipalities created new legal statuses, such as domestic partnerships, that accorded some recognition to nonmarital (including same-sex) adult relationships. The San Francisco Board of Supervisors passed the first major domestic partnership bill

---

[75]   Klarman, *Closet to Altar*, 39–40.

[76]   Ibid., 40.

[77]   Ibid., 37; Eskridge, *Gaylaw*, 150, 166–67.

[78]   Klarman, *Closet to Altar*, 37.

[79]   478 U.S. 186, 192–94 (1986).

[80]   *Bowers*, 478 U.S. at 197 (Burger, C.J., dissenting).

in 1982, but Mayor Diane Feinstein vetoed it on the ground that it too closely "mimics a marriage license."[81] In 1984, Berkeley, California became the first city in the United States to enact a domestic partnership law, in the late 80s, West Hollywood and Madison, Wisconsin followed, and San Francisco and New York, in 1990 and 1993, by which time around 25 cities had enacted such laws, though they remained unpopular with most Americans.[82] Such ordinances typically recited a governmental interest in "strengthening and supporting all caring, committed, and responsible family forms."[83] California established the first statewide domestic partnership in 1999. Just one year later, California voters approved a "defense of marriage act," limiting marriage to the union of one man and one woman, but the legislature worked around that law to expand the domestic partnership law to afford domestic partners more of the rights, protections, and duties of married couples. Some other states also enacted domestic partnership laws, allowing some formal recognition of and protection for the intimate relationships of same-sex couples. And in 1992, the first American universities—Iowa, Stanford, and the University of Chicago—provided partnership benefits to same-sex employees.[84]

Another positive development was the turn, by some state courts, toward a more functional definition of family. For example, in 1989, the New York state court of appeals ruled that same-sex partners could qualify as "family members" "for purposes of inheriting a rent-controlled apartment."[85] In the 1990s and early 21st century, other state courts adopted a more functional definition of "family," beyond biology and marriage.

On the other hand, same-sex relationships remained unrecognized and unprotected in law. In 1983, Sharon Kowalski was in a serious auto accident that left her paralyzed, with brain injuries, and unable to speak. Kowalski and her partner, Sharon Thompson, had lived together for four years. They jointly owned "a home, had exchanged rings, and considered themselves married, but had not yet come out to their families, friends, or colleagues."[86]

After the accident, Sharon Kowalski's parents denied that she was a lesbian and, when her father was appointed guardian by a court, he denied even visitation rights to his daughter's partner. The court battle dragged on until 1991,

---

[81] Eskridge, *Equality Practice*, 13.

[82] Klarman, *Closet to Altar*, 45.

[83] Ann Arbor Code ch. 110, Sect. 9:86 (2015).

[84] Klarman, *Closet to Altar*, 46, 59, 77.

[85] Braschi v. Stahl Associates Co., 543 N.E.2d 49 (N.Y. 1989).

[86] *See* In re Guardianship of Kowalski, 478 N.W.2d 790 (Minn. Ct. App. 1991).

when a Minnesota court of appeals described the two women as a "family of affinity, which ought to be accorded respect," and ruled that Sharon Kowalski had been "competent to make her own choice of a guardian," and had chosen Thompson.[87]

Many gay and lesbian baby boomers wanted rights beyond visitation and care, especially the right to become parents. Their control over their own children was quite vulnerable to the discretion of judges. Consider, for example, the Sharon Bottoms case from Virginia in 1993. When a judge decided that it was not in her son's best interests to be raised by an open lesbian, Bottoms lost custody of the child to her mother.[88] At that time, Virginia, like many other states, viewed homosexuality as evidence of immorality and, therefore, of parental unfitness. However, a growing number of states began to move away from such an approach and to require a showing that a parent's sexual orientation had a concrete harmful impact on a child. Since many gay men and lesbians of an earlier era had married straight partners, had children, and divorced, this move away from an assumption of parental unfitness was critically important.

Adoption also became an important pathway to parenthood, both when a gay or lesbian partner was permitted, under state law, to adopt a partner's child and when a gay or lesbian couple was allowed to adopt children. As Michael Klarman puts it, "once same-sex couples were permitted to adopt children, explaining why those couples should not be permitted to marry became much harder."[89] States were hard pressed to justify excluding same-sex couples from marriage—lauded as a child-protective institution—when other state laws facilitated such couples becoming parents. These sorts of considerations would later resonate powerfully with Justice Anthony M. Kennedy of the U.S. Supreme Court.[90]

D. Toward Marriage Rights: The 1990s Through *Obergefell*

In the early 1990s, serious discussion of same-sex marriage was still a long way off, with opinion polls showing support for gay marriage between 11 and 23 percent. Same-sex marriage was not on the agenda of major gay rights organizations, and the gay community itself "remained deeply divided over

---

[87] Klarman, *Closet to Altar*, 50; *see also* Eskridge, *Same-Sex Marriage*, 69–70.

[88] Klarman, *Closet to Altar*, 51.

[89] Ibid.

[90] *See* Obergefell v. Hodges, 135 S.Ct. 2584, 2600 (2015).

whether to pursue gay marriage." Polls showed that gay Americans were much more interested in "securing equal rights in employment, housing, and health care," not to mention AIDS research, sodomy law reform, and hate crimes legislation. Nevertheless, younger gays were much more supportive of gay marriage than older gays and lesbians: "One opinion poll showed that 18-year old gays were 31 percentage points more likely to support gay marriage than were 65-year old gays."[91]

Despite the fact that same-sex marriage remained extremely unpopular with the general public in the early 1990s, same-sex marriage was thrust onto the national agenda when, in 1993, the Hawaii Supreme Court held that bans on same-sex marriage discriminated on the basis of sex in violation of the state constitution's Equal Rights Amendment.[92] In the political contest that followed this decision, an amendment to Hawaii's constitution took the issue away from state courts and derailed same-sex marriage in Hawaii. Nevertheless, a panic gripped much of the country, based on the fear that the U.S. Constitution's "Full Faith and Credit" Clause would force other states to recognize Hawaiian gay marriages.[93] A backlash ensued and it resulted in passage—by overwhelming majorities in the U.S. House and Senate—of the federal Defense of Marriage Act (DOMA), signed by President Bill Clinton in 1996. DOMA had two key provisions: Section 2 provided that no state "shall be required to give effect" to any marriage between a same-sex couple permitted in another state and Section 3 (at issue in *Windsor*) declared that, for purposes of all federal laws, marriage would mean "only a legal union between one man and one woman as husband and wife" and "spouse" would refer "only to a person of the opposite sex who is a husband or a wife."[94] In support of DOMA, lawmakers and witnesses invoked many considerations, ranging from Judeo-Christian morality and the procreative functions of the human body to the need to stop "an orchestrated legal assault ... against traditional marriage by gay rights groups and their lawyers" and the need to stop judges in Hawaii from "foist[ing] the newly-coined institution of homosexual 'marriage' upon an unwilling Hawaiian public" and, ultimately, on other states.[95] Many state legislatures passed "mini-DOMAs,"

---

[91] Klarman, *Closet to Altar*, 45, 48, 50–51, and see his discussion of the debate within the gay community over pressing for marriage equality at that time, 5–55; *see also* Eskridge, *Equality Practice*, 15–17.

[92] Baehr v. Lewin, 74 Haw. 645, 852 P.2d 44 (Haw. 1993).

[93] Article IV, Section 1: "Full faith and credit shall be given in each state to the public acts, records, and judicial proceedings of every other state. And the Congress may by general laws prescribe the manner in which such acts, records, and proceedings shall be proved, and the effect thereof."

[94] Defense of Marriage Act of 1996, 28 U.S.C. Section 1738C (1996).

[95] H.R. Rep. No. 104–664 (1996).

defining marriage in state law as the relation of one man and one woman and barring recognition of out-of-state marriages contrary to that definition.[96]

As the gay rights movement made halting gains in the late 1990s and 2000s, it frequently precipitated popular backlash. When the Vermont legislature enacted legislation creating same-sex civil unions in 1999, in response to the Vermont Supreme Court's ruling in Baker v. State that same-sex couples are entitled to "the same benefits and protections afforded by Vermont law to married opposite-sex couples," many supporters of the bill lost their seats in the state legislature.[97] The Massachusetts Supreme Judicial Court decision, in 2003, requiring same-sex marriage under that state's constitution, unleashed a more ferocious nationwide response that (as noted above) may well have tipped the 2004 presidential election in favor of George W. Bush over John Kerry, the U.S. Senator from Massachusetts. Although Democratic presidential candidates opposed a federal constitutional amendment supported by Bush and many Republicans, Al Gore, in 2004, and Barack Obama and many other Democrats, in 2008, declined to support same-sex marriage, preferring civil unions instead and letting states decide for themselves.[98] It was only in 2012 that the Democratic party for the first time embraced marriage by same-sex couples as part of their platform and that President Obama declared his support for such marriage, drawing analogies among Seneca Falls, Selma, and Stonewall.[99]

It is against this background that we should weigh the significance of *Obergefell*. Public attitudes toward and moral judgments about gay and lesbian Americans have changed with astonishing speed. We know of no similar issue on which public opinion has shifted so strikingly and speedily. An obvious comparison is with the question of abortion, which is the other issue that has done most to energize and mobilize the Religious Right. American public opinion has seen no comparable shift on abortion and, in fact, Americans (including younger Americans) have become somewhat more "pro-life" on the abortion issue since the late 1970s.[100]

---

[96] Eskridge, *Equality Practice*, 17–85; Klarman, *Closet to Altar*, ch. 3.

[97] Baker v. State, 744 A.2d 864 (Vt. 1999); Klarman, *Closet to Altar* 82, 78–83.

[98] Klarman, *Closet to Altar*, 111–12, 126, and *passim*; Gerald N. Rosenberg, *The Hollow Hope: Can Courts Bring About Social Change?* (Chicago, IL: University of Chicago Press, 2nd ed., 2008), Part IV: "Same-Sex Marriage."

[99] For an account of this evolution on marriage, see Linda C. McClain, "Federal Family Policy and Family Values from Clinton to Obama, 1992–2012 and Beyond," 2013 *Mich. St. L. Rev.* 1621, 1653–1668, 1709–1715.

[100] "Abortion," *Gallup,* http://www.gallup.com/poll/1576/abortion.aspx (reviewing public opinion from 1975 to 2015).

The nine justices of the Supreme Court who decided *Obergefell* in June 2015 lived through the episodes just described. The questions they faced were whether the Constitution, fairly interpreted, requires states to grant equal marriage rights to same-sex couples seeking to marry and to recognize such couples' valid out-of-state marriages. Constitutional requirements range from the very specific to the very abstract, and the latter raise special interpretive challenges. At the specific end of the spectrum are many of the constitutional provisions setting out the terms and structures of the three branches of the federal government. Thus, the President must be at least thirty-five years old, with no judgment required as to her or his maturity. At the other end of the spectrum, provisions guaranteeing basic liberties are set out in abstract terms that often require judges and other interpreters to make controversial value judgments. The Eighth Amendment to the U.S. Constitution prohibits "cruel and unusual punishments," without specifying which punishments are cruel. The Fourth Amendment prohibits "unreasonable searches and seizures," setting out an even more abstract principle that appears to require interpreters to consider the sorts of searches and seizures that should be judged unreasonable, given the competing imperatives of law enforcement and the value of personal privacy.

Of central importance are two provisions of the Fourteenth Amendment, ratified in the wake of the Civil War, which declare that "no state shall . . . deprive any person of life, liberty or property, without due process of law," "nor deny to any person within its jurisdiction the equal protection of the laws." The guarantee of liberty in the Due Process Clause has long been held to have "substantive" as well as procedural implications. The reasons for this will be explored at greater length in Chapter 3, and we only note here that the language of other provisions of the Fourteenth Amendment suggest even more clearly that certain basic rights and liberties require more than merely procedural protections ("[n]o state shall make or enforce any law which shall abridge the privileges or immunities of citizens of the United States").

Interpreters of the U.S. Constitution, including the justices, are deeply divided on the question whether those abstractly worded constitutional provisions furnish a warrant for, and indeed require, judges to decide which punishments really are cruel, which searches are properly regarded as unreasonable, which liberties are important enough to be protected, and which forms of unequal treatment are genuinely invidious—or morally objectionable. The individual authors of this book have argued in other works that interpreters can't avoid making moral judgments when applying constitutional provisions of these kinds.[101] But many scholars and jurists argue that inviting unelected judges to make such judgments is inconsistent with their proper role in our constitutional democracy, and that it involves judges usurping the role of legislators.

Many politically conservative jurists and scholars, and some progressive ones as well, argue that judges ought to avoid making moral judgments, and instead should give meaning to abstractly worded constitutional guarantees by looking to the past: to history and past authoritative court decisions (understood narrowly as confined to their facts rather than as expressing general principles). These mainly conservative (and typically "originalist") constitutional commentators oppose the idea of a "living constitution," which gains fresh meaning from the moral and practical insights of rising generations. More generally, they oppose the idea of a moral reading of the Constitution, which conceives the Constitution's commitments to liberty and equality to be abstract moral principles to be elaborated or built out over time on the basis of experience and moral learning about the best understanding of those principles. There are many varieties of originalism, but originalists typically argue that the Constitution's meaning is to be determined from the relatively specific understandings and expectations of the historical framers and ratifiers at the time the provision in question was adopted.

On the other side, many mainly liberal jurists and scholars argue that is altogether proper for interpreters to draw on improved understandings of liberty, equality, and justice based upon new insights into the human condition, including sexual orientation. This impulse is amply on display in the opinion for the Court in *Obergefell* penned by Justice Kennedy. Though a lifelong Republican and an appointee of one of America's most celebrated conservative Presidents, Ronald Reagan, Kennedy (because he has been the "swing vote") has consistently proven to be the most important judicial voice in the landmark opinions vindicating the basic rights of gay and lesbian Americans.

———

[101] *See, e.g.,* Sotirios A. Barber & James E. Fleming, *Constitutional Interpretation: The Basic Questions* (New York: Oxford University Press, 2007); James E. Fleming, *Fidelity to Our Imperfect Constitution: For Moral Readings and Against Originalisms* (New York: Oxford University Press, 2015).

II. THE CULMINATION FOR MARRIAGE EQUALITY

"The nature of injustice is that we may not always see it in our own times. The generations that wrote and ratified the Bill of Rights and the Fourteenth Amendment did not presume to know the extent of freedom in all of its dimensions, and so they entrusted to future generations a charter protecting the right of all persons to enjoy liberty as we learn its meaning. When new insight reveals discord between the Constitution's central protections and a received legal stricture, a claim to liberty must be addressed."—JUSTICE KENNEDY

"The majority's decision is an act of will, not legal judgment. The right it announces has no basis in the Constitution or this Court's precedent. . . . [T]he Court invalidates the marriage laws of more than half the States and orders the transformation of a social institution that has formed the basis of human society for millennia, for the Kalahari Bushmen and the Han Chinese, the Carthaginians and the Aztecs. Just who do we think we are?"
—CHIEF JUSTICE ROBERTS

"When the Fourteenth Amendment was ratified in 1868, every State limited marriage to one man and one woman, and no one doubted the constitutionality of doing so. That resolves these cases."—JUSTICE SCALIA

"As a philosophical matter, liberty is only freedom from governmental action, not an entitlement to governmental benefits. And as a constitutional matter, it is likely even narrower . . ., encompassing only freedom from physical restraint and imprisonment. . . ."—JUSTICE THOMAS

"Today's decision . . . will be used to vilify Americans who are unwilling to assent to the new orthodoxy. [T]he majority compares traditional marriage laws to laws that denied equal treatment for African-Americans and women. The implications of this analogy will be exploited by those who are determined to stamp out every vestige of dissent."—JUSTICE ALITO

OBERGEFELL V. HODGES

576 U.S. ___, 135 S.Ct. 2584, 192 L.Ed.2d 609 (2015)

■ JUSTICE KENNEDY delivered the opinion of the Court.

The Constitution promises liberty to all within its reach, a liberty that includes certain specific rights that allow persons, within a lawful realm, to define and express their identity. The petitioners . . . seek to find that liberty by marrying someone of the same sex and having their marriages deemed lawful on the same terms and conditions as marriages between persons of the opposite sex.

I

These cases come from Michigan, Kentucky, Ohio, and Tennessee, States that define marriage as a union between one man and one woman. The petitioners are 14 same-sex couples and two men whose same-sex partners are deceased. The respondents are state officials responsible for enforcing the laws in question. The petitioners claim the respondents violate the Fourteenth Amendment by denying them the right to marry or to have their marriages, lawfully performed in another State, given full recognition. . . .

II . . .

A

[T]he annals of human history reveal the transcendent importance of marriage. The lifelong union of a man and a woman always has promised nobility and dignity to all persons, without regard to their station in life. Marriage is sacred to those who live by their religions and offers unique fulfillment to those who find meaning in the secular realm. Its dynamic allows two people to find a life that could not be found alone, for a marriage becomes greater than just the two persons. Rising from the most basic human needs, marriage is essential to our most profound hopes and aspirations.

The centrality of marriage to the human condition makes it unsurprising that the institution has existed for millennia and across civilizations. Since the dawn of history, marriage has transformed strangers into relatives, binding families and societies together. . . . There are untold references to the beauty of marriage in religious and philosophical texts spanning time, cultures, and faiths, as well as in art and literature in all their forms. It is fair and necessary to say these references were based on the understanding that marriage is a union between two persons of the opposite sex.

That history is the beginning of these cases. The respondents say it should be the end as well. To them, it would demean a timeless institution if the concept and lawful status of marriage were extended to two persons of the same sex. Marriage, in their view, is by its nature a gender-differentiated union of man and woman. This view long has been held—and continues to be held—in good faith by reasonable and sincere people here and throughout the world.

The petitioners acknowledge this history but contend that these cases cannot end there. Were their intent to demean the revered idea and reality of marriage, the petitioners' claims would be of a different order. . . . To the contrary, it is the enduring importance of marriage that underlies the petitioners' contentions. . . . Far from seeking to devalue marriage, the petitioners seek it for themselves because of their respect—and need—for its privileges and responsibilities. And their immutable nature dictates that same-sex marriage is their only real path to this profound commitment.

. . . Petitioner James Obergefell, a plaintiff in the Ohio case, met John Arthur over two decades ago. They fell in love and started a life together, establishing a lasting, committed relation. In 2011, . . . Arthur was diagnosed with amyotrophic lateral sclerosis, or ALS. . . . Two years ago, Obergefell and Arthur . . . resolv[ed] to marry before Arthur died. [T]hey traveled from Ohio to Maryland, where same-sex marriage was legal. It was difficult for Arthur to move, and so the couple were wed inside a medical transport plane as it remained on the tarmac in Baltimore. Three months later, Arthur died. Ohio law does not permit Obergefell to be listed as the surviving spouse on Arthur's death certificate. By statute, they must remain strangers even in death, a state-imposed separation Obergefell deems "hurtful for the rest of time." He brought suit to be shown as the surviving spouse on Arthur's death certificate.

April DeBoer and Jayne Rowse are co-plaintiffs in the case from Michigan. They celebrated a commitment ceremony to honor their permanent relation in 2007. They both work as nurses. . . . In 2009, DeBoer and Rowse fostered and then adopted a baby boy. Later that same year, they welcomed another son into their family. The new baby, born prematurely and abandoned by his biological mother, required around-the-clock care. The next year, a baby girl with special needs joined their family. Michigan, however, permits only opposite-sex married couples or single individuals to adopt, so each child can have only one woman as his or her legal parent. If an emergency were to arise, schools and hospitals may treat the three children as if they had only one parent. And, were tragedy to befall either DeBoer or Rowse, the other would have no legal rights over the children she had not been permitted to adopt. This couple seeks relief from the continuing uncertainty their unmarried status creates in their lives.

Army Reserve Sergeant First Class Ijpe DeKoe and his partner Thomas Kostura, co-plaintiffs in the Tennessee case, fell in love. In 2011, DeKoe received orders to deploy to Afghanistan. Before leaving, he and Kostura married in New York. A week later, DeKoe began his deployment, which lasted for almost a year. When he returned, the two settled in Tennessee, where DeKoe works full-time for the Army Reserve. Their lawful marriage is stripped from them whenever they reside in Tennessee, returning and disappearing as they travel across state lines. DeKoe, who served this Nation to preserve the freedom the Constitution protects, must endure a substantial burden.

The cases now before the Court involve other petitioners as well, each with their own experiences. Their stories reveal that they seek not to denigrate marriage but rather to live their lives, or honor their spouses' memory, joined by its bond.

B

The ancient origins of marriage confirm its centrality, but it has not stood in isolation from developments in law and society. The history of marriage is one of both continuity and change. That institution . . . has evolved over time.

For example, marriage was once viewed as an arrangement by the couple's parents based on political, religious, and financial concerns; but by the time of the Nation's founding it was understood to be a voluntary contract between a man and a woman. See N. Cott, *Public Vows: A History of Marriage and the Nation* 9–17 (2000); S. Coontz, *Marriage, A History* 15–16 (2005). As the role and status of women changed, the institution further evolved. Under the centuries-old doctrine of coverture, a married man and woman were treated by the State as a single, male-dominated legal entity. See 1 W. Blackstone, *Commentaries on the Laws of England* 430 (1765). As women gained legal, political, and property rights, and as society began to understand that women have their own equal dignity, the law of coverture was abandoned. These and other developments in the institution of marriage . . . were not mere superficial changes. Rather, they worked deep transformations in its structure, affecting aspects of marriage long viewed by many as essential. See generally N. Cott, *Public Vows*; S. Coontz, *Marriage*; H. Hartog, *Man & Wife in America: A History* (2000).

These new insights have strengthened, not weakened, the institution of marriage. Indeed, changed understandings of marriage are characteristic of a Nation where new dimensions of freedom become apparent to new generations, often through perspectives that begin in pleas or protests and then are considered in the political sphere and the judicial process.

This dynamic can be seen in the Nation's experiences with the rights of gays and lesbians. Until the mid-20th century, same-sex intimacy long had been condemned as immoral by the state itself in most Western nations, a belief often embodied in the criminal law. . . . A truthful declaration by same-sex couples of what was in their hearts had to remain unspoken. . . . Gays and lesbians were prohibited from most government employment, barred from military service, excluded under immigration laws, targeted by police, and burdened in their rights to associate. . . .

For much of the 20th century, moreover, homosexuality was treated as an illness. When the American Psychiatric Association published the first Diagnostic and Statistical Manual of Mental Disorders in 1952, homosexuality was classified as a mental disorder, a position adhered to until 1973. Only in more recent years have psychiatrists and others recognized that sexual orientation is both a normal expression of human sexuality and immutable.

In the late 20th century, following substantial cultural and political developments, same-sex couples began to lead more open and public lives and to establish families. This development was followed by a quite extensive discussion of the issue in both governmental and private sectors and by a shift in public attitudes toward greater tolerance. . . .

This Court first gave detailed consideration to the legal status of homosexuals in Bowers v. Hardwick (1986). There it upheld the constitutionality of a Georgia law deemed to criminalize certain homosexual acts. Ten years later, in Romer v. Evans (1996), the Court invalidated an amendment to Colorado's Constitution that sought to foreclose any branch or political subdivision of the State from protecting persons against discrimination based on sexual orientation. Then, in 2003, the Court overruled *Bowers*, holding that laws making same-sex intimacy a crime "demea[n] the lives of homosexual persons." Lawrence v. Texas.

Against this background, the legal question of same-sex marriage arose. In 1993, the Hawaii Supreme Court held Hawaii's law restricting marriage to opposite-sex couples constituted a classification on the basis of sex and was therefore subject to strict scrutiny under the Hawaii Constitution. Baehr v. Lewin. Although this decision did not mandate that same-sex marriage be allowed, some States were concerned by its implications and reaffirmed in their laws that marriage is defined as a union between opposite-sex partners. So too in

1996, Congress passed the Defense of Marriage Act (DOMA), defining marriage for all federal-law purposes as "only a legal union between one man and one woman as husband and wife."

The new and widespread discussion of the subject led other States to a different conclusion. In 2003, the Supreme Judicial Court of Massachusetts held the State's Constitution guaranteed same-sex couples the right to marry. See Goodridge v. Department of Public Health. After that ruling, some additional States granted marriage rights to same-sex couples, either through judicial or legislative processes. [I]n United States v. Windsor (2013), this Court invalidated DOMA to the extent it barred the Federal Government from treating same-sex marriages as valid even when they were lawful in the State where they were licensed. . . .

Numerous cases about same-sex marriage have reached the United States Courts of Appeals in recent years. In accordance with the judicial duty to base their decisions on principled reasons and neutral discussions, without scornful or disparaging commentary, courts have written a substantial body of law considering all sides of these issues. That case law helps to explain and formulate the underlying principles this Court now must consider. With the exception of the opinion here under review and one other, see Citizens for Equal Protection v. Bruning (CA8 2006), the Courts of Appeals have held that excluding same-sex couples from marriage violates the Constitution. There also have been many thoughtful District Court decisions addressing same-sex marriage—and most of them, too, have concluded same-sex couples must be allowed to marry. In addition the highest courts of many States have contributed to this ongoing dialogue in decisions interpreting their own State Constitutions. . . .

III

Under the Due Process Clause of the Fourteenth Amendment, no State shall "deprive any person of life, liberty, or property, without due process of law." The fundamental liberties protected by this Clause include most of the rights enumerated in the Bill of Rights. In addition these liberties extend to certain personal choices central to individual dignity and autonomy, including intimate choices that define personal identity and beliefs. See, *e.g.,* Eisenstadt v. Baird (1972); Griswold v. Connecticut (1965).

The identification and protection of fundamental rights is an enduring part of the judicial duty to interpret the Constitution. That responsibility, however, "has not been reduced to any formula." Poe v. Ullman (1961) (Harlan, J., dissenting). Rather, it requires courts to exercise reasoned judgment in identifying interests of the person so fundamental that the State must accord them its respect. See *ibid.* That process is guided by many of the same considerations relevant to analysis of other constitutional provisions that set forth broad principles rather than specific requirements. History and tradition guide and discipline this inquiry but do not set its outer boundaries. See *Lawrence.* That method respects our history and learns from it without allowing the past alone to rule the present.

The nature of injustice is that we may not always see it in our own times. The generations that wrote and ratified the Bill of Rights and the Fourteenth Amendment did not presume to know the extent of freedom in all of its dimensions, and so they entrusted to future generations a charter protecting the right of all persons to enjoy liberty as we learn its meaning. When new insight reveals discord between the Constitution's central protections and a received legal stricture, a claim to liberty must be addressed. Applying these established tenets, the Court has long held the right to marry is protected by the Constitution. In Loving v. Virginia (1967), which invalidated bans on interracial unions, a unanimous Court held marriage is "one of the vital personal rights essential to the orderly pursuit of happiness by free men." The Court reaffirmed that holding in Zablocki v. Redhail (1978), which held the right to marry was burdened by a law prohibiting fathers who were behind on child support from marrying. The Court again applied this principle in Turner v. Safley (1987), which held the right to marry was abridged by regulations limiting the privilege of prison inmates to marry.

Over time and in other contexts, the Court has reiterated that the right to marry is fundamental under the Due Process Clause. It cannot be denied that this Court's cases describing the right to marry presumed a relationship involving opposite-sex partners. The Court, like many institutions, has made assumptions defined by the world and time of which it is a part. This was evident in Baker v. Nelson, a one-line summary decision issued in 1972, holding the exclusion of same-sex couples from marriage did not present a substantial federal question.

Still, there are other, more instructive precedents. This Court's cases have expressed constitutional principles of broader reach. In defining the right to marry these cases have identified essential attributes of that right based in history, tradition, and other constitutional liberties inherent in this intimate bond. See, *e.g., Lawrence; Turner; Zablocki; Loving; Griswold.* And in assessing whether the force and rationale of its cases apply to same-sex couples, the Court must respect the basic reasons why the right to marry has been long protected. See, *e.g., Poe* (Harlan, J., dissenting).

This analysis compels the conclusion that same-sex couples may exercise the right to marry. [F]our principles and traditions ... demonstrate that the reasons marriage is fundamental under the Constitution apply with equal force to same-sex couples.

A first premise of the Court's relevant precedents is that the right to personal choice regarding marriage is inherent in the concept of individual autonomy. This abiding connection between marriage and liberty is why *Loving* invalidated interracial marriage bans under the Due Process Clause. Like choices concerning contraception, family relationships, procreation, and childrearing, all of which are protected by the Constitution, decisions concerning marriage are among the most intimate that an individual can make. See *Lawrence*. ...

Choices about marriage shape an individual's destiny. As the Supreme Judicial Court of Massachusetts has explained, because "it fulfils yearnings for security, safe haven, and connection that express our common humanity, civil marriage is an esteemed institution, and the decision whether and whom to marry is among life's momentous acts of self-definition." *Goodridge*. ...

A second principle in this Court's jurisprudence is that the right to marry is fundamental because it supports a two-person union unlike any other in its importance to the committed individuals. ... Suggesting that marriage is a right "older than the Bill of Rights," *Griswold* described marriage this way:

> Marriage is a coming together for better or for worse, hopefully enduring, and intimate to the degree of being sacred. It is an association that promotes a way of life, not causes; a harmony in living, not political faiths; a bilateral loyalty, not commercial or social projects. Yet it is an association for as noble a purpose as any involved in our prior decisions.

... Marriage ... offers the hope of companionship and understanding and assurance that while both still live there will be someone to care for the other.

As this Court held in *Lawrence*, same-sex couples have the same right as opposite-sex couples to enjoy intimate association. ... But while *Lawrence* confirmed a dimension of freedom that allows individuals to engage in intimate association without criminal liability, it does not follow that freedom stops there. Outlaw to outcast may be a step forward, but it does not achieve the full promise of liberty.

A third basis for protecting the right to marry is that it safeguards children and families and thus draws meaning from related rights of childrearing, procreation, and education. See Pierce v. Society of Sisters (1925); Meyer v. Nebraska (1923). The Court has recognized these connections by describing the varied rights as a unified whole: "[T]he right to 'marry, establish a home and bring up children' is a central part of the liberty protected by the Due Process Clause." *Zablocki* (quoting *Meyer*). . . . By giving recognition and legal structure to their parents' relationship, marriage allows children "to understand the integrity and closeness of their own family and its concord with other families in their community and in their daily lives." *Windsor*. Marriage also affords the permanency and stability important to children's best interests. . . .

Excluding same-sex couples from marriage thus conflicts with a central premise of the right to marry. Without the recognition, stability, and predictability marriage offers, their children suffer the stigma of knowing their families are somehow lesser. They also suffer the significant material costs of being raised by unmarried parents, relegated through no fault of their own to a more difficult and uncertain family life. The marriage laws at issue here thus harm and humiliate the children of same-sex couples. See *Windsor*.

That is not to say the right to marry is less meaningful for those who do not or cannot have children. An ability, desire, or promise to procreate is not and has not been a prerequisite for a valid marriage in any State. . . .

Fourth and finally, this Court's cases and the Nation's traditions make clear that marriage is a keystone of our social order. Alexis de Tocqueville recognized this truth on his travels through the United States almost two centuries ago. . . . 1 *Democracy in America* 309 (H. Reeve transl., rev. ed. 1990).

In Maynard v. Hill (1888), the Court echoed de Tocqueville, explaining that marriage is "the foundation of the family and of society, without which there would be neither civilization nor progress." Marriage . . . has long been " 'a great public institution, giving character to our whole civil polity.' " *Id.* This idea has been reiterated even as the institution has evolved in substantial ways over time, superseding rules related to parental consent, gender, and race once thought by many to be essential. See generally N. Cott, *Public Vows*. Marriage remains a building block of our national community.

For that reason, just as a couple vows to support each other, so does society pledge to support the couple, offering symbolic recognition and material benefits to protect and nourish the union. Indeed, while the States are in general free to vary the benefits they confer on all married couples, they have throughout our history made marriage the basis for an expanding list of governmental rights, benefits, and responsibilities. . . . Valid marriage under state law is also a significant status for over a thousand provisions of federal law. See *Windsor.* The States have contributed to the fundamental character of the marriage right by placing that institution at the center of so many facets of the legal and social order.

There is no difference between same-and opposite-sex couples with respect to this principle. Yet by virtue of their exclusion from that institution, same-sex couples are denied the constellation of benefits that the States have linked to marriage. This harm results in more than just material burdens. Same-sex couples are consigned to an instability many opposite-sex couples would deem intolerable in their own lives. As the State itself makes marriage all the more precious by the significance it attaches to it, exclusion from that status has the effect of teaching that gays and lesbians are unequal in important respects. It demeans gays and lesbians for the State to lock them out of a central institution of the Nation's society. Same-sex couples, too, may aspire to the transcendent purposes of marriage and seek fulfillment in its highest meaning.

The limitation of marriage to opposite-sex couples may long have seemed natural and just, but its inconsistency with the central meaning of the fundamental right to marry is now manifest. With that knowledge must come the recognition that laws excluding same-sex couples from the marriage right impose stigma and injury of the kind prohibited by our basic charter.

Objecting that this does not reflect an appropriate framing of the issue, the respondents refer to Washington v. Glucksberg (1997), which called for a " 'careful description' " of fundamental rights. They assert the petitioners do not seek to exercise the right to marry but rather a new and nonexistent "right to same-sex marriage." *Glucksberg* did insist that liberty under the Due Process Clause must be defined in a most circumscribed manner, with central reference to specific historical practices. Yet while that approach may have been appropriate for the asserted right there involved (physician-assisted suicide), it is inconsistent with the approach this Court has used in discussing other fundamental rights, including marriage and intimacy. *Loving* did not ask about a "right to interracial marriage"; *Turner* did not ask about a "right of inmates to marry"; and *Zablocki* did not ask about a "right of fathers with unpaid child support duties to marry." Rather, each case inquired about the right to marry in its comprehensive sense, asking if there was a sufficient justification for excluding the relevant class from the right. See also *Glucksberg* (Souter, J., concurring in judgment); *id.* (Breyer, J., concurring in judgments).

That principle applies here. If rights were defined by who exercised them in the past, then received practices could serve as their own continued justification and new groups could not invoke rights once denied. This Court has rejected that approach, both with respect to the right to marry and the rights of gays and lesbians. See *Loving; Lawrence.*

The right to marry is fundamental as a matter of history and tradition, but rights come not from ancient sources alone. They rise, too, from a better informed understanding of how constitutional imperatives define a liberty that remains urgent in our own era. Many who deem same-sex marriage to be wrong reach that conclusion based on decent and honorable religious or philosophical premises, and neither they nor their beliefs are disparaged here. But when that sincere, personal opposition becomes enacted law and public policy, the necessary consequence is to put the imprimatur of the State itself on an exclusion that soon demeans or stigmatizes those whose own liberty is then denied. Under the Constitution, same-sex couples seek in marriage the same legal treatment as opposite-sex couples, and it would disparage their choices and diminish their personhood to deny them this right.

The right of same-sex couples to marry that is part of the liberty promised by the Fourteenth Amendment is derived, too, from that Amendment's guarantee of the equal protection of the laws. The Due Process Clause and the Equal Protection Clause are connected in a profound way, though they set forth independent principles. Rights implicit in liberty and rights secured by equal protection may rest on different precepts and are not always coextensive, yet in some instances each may be instructive as to the meaning and reach of the other. In any particular case one Clause may be thought to capture the essence of the right in a more accurate and comprehensive way, even as the two Clauses may converge in the identification and definition of the right. . . .

The Court's cases touching upon the right to marry reflect this dynamic. In *Loving* the Court invalidated a prohibition on interracial marriage under both the Equal Protection Clause and the Due Process Clause. The Court first declared the prohibition invalid because of its unequal treatment of interracial couples. . . . [T]he Court proceeded to hold . . . : "To deny this fundamental freedom on so unsupportable a basis as the racial classifications embodied in these statutes, classifications so directly subversive of the principle of equality at the heart of the Fourteenth Amendment, is surely to deprive all the State's citizens of liberty without due process of law." The reasons why marriage is a fundamental right became more clear and compelling from a full awareness and understanding of the hurt that resulted from laws barring interracial unions. . . .

Indeed, in interpreting the Equal Protection Clause, the Court has recognized that new insights and societal understandings can reveal unjustified inequality within our most fundamental institutions that once passed unnoticed and unchallenged. [T]his occurred with respect to marriage in the 1970s and 1980s. Notwithstanding the gradual erosion of the doctrine of coverture, invidious sex-based classifications in marriage remained common through the mid-20th century. These classifications denied the equal dignity of men and women. One State's law, for example, provided in 1971 that "the husband is the head of the family and the wife is subject to him; her legal civil existence is merged in the husband, except so far as the law recognizes her separately, either for her own protection, or for her benefit." Ga. Code Ann. § 53–501 (1935). Responding to a new awareness, the Court invoked equal protection principles to invalidate laws imposing sex-based inequality on marriage. See, *e.g.,* Frontiero v. Richardson (1973). Like *Loving* . . . , these precedents show the Equal Protection Clause can help to identify and correct inequalities in the institution of marriage, vindicating precepts of liberty and equality under the Constitution. . . .

In *Lawrence* the Court acknowledged the interlocking nature of these constitutional safeguards in the context of the legal treatment of gays and lesbians. Although *Lawrence* elaborated its holding under the Due Process Clause, it acknowledged, and sought to remedy, the continuing inequality that resulted from laws making intimacy in the lives of gays and lesbians a crime. . . . *Lawrence* therefore drew upon principles of liberty and equality to define and protect the rights of gays and lesbians. . . .

This dynamic also applies to same-sex marriage. It is now clear that the challenged laws burden the liberty of same-sex couples, and it must be further acknowledged that they abridge central precepts of equality . . . : same-sex couples are denied all the benefits afforded to opposite-sex couples and are barred from exercising a fundamental right. Especially against a long history of disapproval of their relationships, this denial to same-sex couples of the right to marry works a grave and continuing harm. The imposition of this disability on gays and lesbians serves to disrespect and subordinate them. And the Equal Protection Clause, like the Due Process Clause, prohibits this unjustified infringement of the fundamental right to marry. See, *e.g., Zablocki*; Skinner v. Oklahoma (1942).

These considerations lead to the conclusion that the right to marry is a fundamental right inherent in the liberty of the person, and under the Due Process and Equal Protection Clauses of the Fourteenth Amendment couples of the same-sex may not be deprived of that right and that liberty. The Court now holds that same-sex couples may exercise the fundamental right to marry. . . . *Baker* . . . is overruled, and the State laws challenged by Petitioners in these cases are . . . invalid to the extent they exclude same-sex couples from civil marriage on the same terms and conditions as opposite-sex couples.

IV

There may be an initial inclination in these cases to proceed with caution—to await further legislation, litigation, and debate. The respondents warn there has been insufficient democratic discourse before deciding an issue so basic as the definition of marriage. . . .

Yet there has been far more deliberation than this argument acknowledges. There have been referenda, legislative debates, and grassroots campaigns, as well as countless studies, papers, books, and other popular and scholarly writings. There has been extensive litigation in state and federal courts. . . . As more than 100 *amici* make clear in their filings, many of the central institutions in American life . . . have devoted substantial attention to the question. This has led to an enhanced understanding of the issue—an understanding reflected in the arguments now presented for resolution as a matter of constitutional law.

Of course, the Constitution contemplates that democracy is the appropriate process for change, so long as that process does not abridge fundamental rights. . . . The dynamic of our constitutional system is that individuals need not await legislative action before asserting a fundamental right. The Nation's courts are open to injured individuals who come to them to vindicate their own direct, personal stake in our basic charter. An individual can invoke a right to constitutional protection when he or she is harmed, even if the broader public disagrees and even if the legislature refuses to act. The idea of the Constitution "was to withdraw certain subjects from the vicissitudes of political controversy, to place them beyond the reach of majorities and officials and to establish them as legal principles to be applied by the courts." West Virginia Bd. of Ed. v. Barnette (1943). This is why "fundamental rights may not be submitted to a vote; they depend on the outcome of no elections." *Ibid.* . . .

This is not the first time the Court has been asked to adopt a cautious approach to recognizing and protecting fundamental rights. In *Bowers*, a bare majority upheld a law criminalizing same-sex intimacy. That approach might have been viewed as a cautious endorsement of the democratic process, which had only just begun to consider the rights of gays and lesbians. Yet, in effect, *Bowers* upheld state action that denied gays and lesbians a fundamental right and caused them pain and humiliation. ... Although *Bowers* was eventually repudiated in *Lawrence*, men and women were harmed in the interim, and the substantial effects of these injuries no doubt lingered long after *Bowers* was overruled. Dignitary wounds cannot always be healed with the stroke of a pen.

A ruling against same-sex couples would have the same effect—and, like *Bowers*, would be unjustified under the Fourteenth Amendment. The petitioners' stories make clear the urgency of the issue they present to the Court. ... Properly presented with the petitioners' cases, the Court has a duty to address these claims and answer these questions.

... Were the Court to stay its hand to allow slower, case-by-case determination of the required availability of specific public benefits to same-sex couples, it still would deny gays and lesbians many rights and responsibilities intertwined with marriage.

The respondents also argue allowing same-sex couples to wed will harm marriage as an institution by leading to fewer opposite-sex marriages. This may occur, the respondents contend, because licensing same-sex marriage severs the connection between natural procreation and marriage. That argument, however, rests on a counterintuitive view of opposite-sex couple's decisionmaking processes regarding marriage and parenthood. Decisions about whether to marry and raise children are based on many personal, romantic, and practical considerations; and it is unrealistic to conclude that an opposite-sex couple would choose not to marry simply because same-sex couples may do so. The respondents have not shown a foundation for the conclusion that allowing same-sex marriage will cause the harmful outcomes they describe. Indeed, ... these cases involve only the rights of two consenting adults whose marriages would pose no risk of harm to themselves or third parties.

Finally, it must be emphasized that religions, and those who adhere to religious doctrines, may continue to advocate with utmost, sincere conviction that, by divine precepts, same-sex marriage should not be condoned. The First Amendment ensures that religious organizations and persons are given proper protection as they seek to teach the principles that are so fulfilling and so central to their lives and faiths, and to their own deep aspirations to continue the family structure they have long revered. The same is true of those who oppose same-sex marriage for other reasons. In turn, those who believe allowing same-sex marriage is proper or indeed essential, whether as a matter of religious conviction or secular belief, may engage those who disagree with their view in an open and searching debate. The Constitution, however, does not permit the

State to bar same-sex couples from marriage on the same terms as accorded to couples of the opposite sex.

V

. . . The Court, in this decision, holds same-sex couples may exercise the fundamental right to marry in all States. It follows that the Court also must hold . . . that there is no lawful basis for a State to refuse to recognize a lawful same-sex marriage performed in another State on the ground of its same-sex character.

* * *

No union is more profound than marriage, for it embodies the highest ideals of love, fidelity, devotion, sacrifice, and family. In forming a marital union, two people become something greater than once they were. As some of the petitioners in these cases demonstrate, marriage embodies a love that may endure even past death. It would misunderstand these men and women to say they disrespect the idea of marriage. Their plea is that they do respect it, respect it so deeply that they seek to find its fulfillment for themselves. Their hope is not to be condemned to live in loneliness, excluded from one of civilization's oldest institutions. They ask for equal dignity in the eyes of the law. The Constitution grants them that right. . . .

■ CHIEF JUSTICE ROBERTS, with whom JUSTICE SCALIA and JUSTICE THOMAS join, dissenting.

Petitioners make strong arguments rooted in social policy and considerations of fairness. They contend that same-sex couples should be allowed to affirm their love and commitment through marriage, just like opposite-sex couples. That position has undeniable appeal; over the past six years, voters and legislators in eleven States and the District of Columbia have revised their laws to allow marriage between two people of the same sex.

But this Court is not a legislature. Whether same-sex marriage is a good idea should be of no concern to us. Under the Constitution, judges have power to say what the law is, not what it should be. The people who ratified the Constitution authorized courts to exercise "neither force nor will but merely judgment." *The Federalist* No. 78, p. 465 (C. Rossiter ed. 1961) (A. Hamilton).

Although the policy arguments for extending marriage to same-sex couples may be compelling, the legal arguments for requiring such an extension are not. The fundamental right to marry does not include a right to make a State change its definition of marriage. And a State's decision to maintain the meaning of marriage that has persisted in every culture throughout human history can hardly be called irrational. In short, our Constitution does not enact any one theory of marriage. The people of a State are free to expand marriage to include same-sex couples, or to retain the historic definition.

Today, however, the Court takes the extraordinary step of ordering every State to license and recognize same-sex marriage. Many people will rejoice at this decision, and I begrudge none their celebration. But for those who believe in a government of laws, not of men, the majority's approach is deeply disheartening. Supporters of same-sex marriage have achieved considerable success persuading their fellow citizens—through the democratic process—to adopt their view. That ends today. Five lawyers have closed the debate and enacted their own vision of marriage as a matter of constitutional law. Stealing this issue from the people will for many cast a cloud over same-sex marriage, making a dramatic social change that much more difficult to accept.

The majority's decision is an act of will, not legal judgment. The right it announces has no basis in the Constitution or this Court's precedent. . . . [T]he Court invalidates the marriage laws of more than half the States and orders the transformation of a social institution that has formed the basis of human society for millennia, for the Kalahari Bushmen and the Han Chinese, the Carthaginians and the Aztecs. Just who do we think we are?

It can be tempting for judges to confuse our own preferences with the requirements of the law. But as this Court has been reminded throughout our history, the Constitution "is made for people of fundamentally differing views." Lochner v. New York (1905) (Holmes, J., dissenting). Accordingly, "courts are not concerned with the wisdom or policy of legislation." *Id.* (Harlan, J., dissenting). The majority today neglects that restrained conception of the judicial role. It seizes for itself a question the Constitution leaves to the people, at a time when the people are engaged in a vibrant debate on that question. And it answers that question based not on neutral principles of constitutional law, but on its own "understanding of what freedom is and must become." . . .

I

Petitioners and their *amici* base their arguments on the "right to marry" and the imperative of "marriage equality." There is no serious dispute that, under our precedents, the Constitution protects a right to marry and requires States to apply their marriage laws equally. The real question in these cases is what constitutes "marriage," or—more precisely—*who decides* what constitutes "marriage"? . . .

Th[e] universal definition of marriage as the union of a man and a woman is no historical coincidence. Marriage . . . arose in the nature of things to meet a vital need: ensuring that children are conceived by a mother and father committed to raising them in the stable conditions of a lifelong relationship.

The premises supporting this concept of marriage are so fundamental that they rarely require articulation. The human race must procreate to survive. Procreation occurs through sexual relations between a man and a woman. When sexual relations result in the conception of a child, that child's prospects are generally better if the mother and father stay together rather than going their separate ways. Therefore, for the good of children and society, sexual relations that can lead to procreation should occur only between a man and a woman committed to a lasting bond.

Society has recognized that bond as marriage. And by bestowing a respected status and material benefits on married couples, society encourages men and women to conduct sexual relations within marriage rather than without. As one prominent scholar put it, "Marriage is a socially arranged solution for the problem of getting people to stay together and care for children that the mere desire for children, and the sex that makes children possible, does not solve." J. Q. Wilson, *The Marriage Problem* 41 (2002).

This singular understanding of marriage has prevailed in the United States throughout our history. . . . To those who drafted and ratified the Constitution, this conception of marriage and family "was a given: its structure, its stability, roles, and values accepted by all." Forte, "The Framers' Idea of Marriage and Family," in *The Meaning of Marriage* 100, 102 (R. George & J. Elshtain eds. 2006).

The Constitution itself says nothing about marriage, and the Framers thereby entrusted the States with "[t]he whole subject of the domestic relations of husband and wife." *Windsor*. There is no dispute that every State at the founding—and every State throughout our history until a dozen years ago—defined marriage in the traditional, biologically rooted way. . . . This Court's precedents have repeatedly described marriage in ways that are consistent only with its traditional meaning. . . .

As the majority notes, some aspects of marriage have changed over time. . . . [It] observes that these developments "were not mere superficial changes" in marriage, but rather "worked deep transformations in its structure." They did not, however, work any transformation in the core structure of marriage as the union between a man and a woman. . . .

II . . .

The majority purports to identify four "principles and traditions" in this Court's due process precedents that support a fundamental right for same-sex couples to marry. In reality, however, the majority's approach has no basis in principle or tradition, except for the unprincipled tradition of judicial policymaking that characterized discredited decisions such as *Lochner*. . . .

A

. . . Petitioners do not contend that their States' marriage laws violate an *enumerated* constitutional right, such as the freedom of speech protected by the First Amendment. . . . They argue instead that the laws violate a right *implied* by the Fourteenth Amendment's requirement that "liberty" may not be deprived without "due process of law."

This Court has interpreted the Due Process Clause to include a "substantive" component that protects certain liberty interests against state deprivation "no matter what process is provided." Reno v. Flores (1993). The theory is that some liberties are "so rooted in the traditions and conscience of our people as to be ranked as fundamental," and therefore cannot be deprived without compelling justification. Snyder v. Massachusetts (1934).

. . . Our precedents have . . . insisted that judges "exercise the utmost care" in identifying implied fundamental rights, "lest the liberty protected by the Due Process Clause be subtly transformed into the policy preferences of the Members of this Court." *Glucksberg*.

The need for restraint in administering the strong medicine of substantive due process is a lesson this Court has learned the hard way. The Court first applied substantive due process to strike down a statute in Dred Scott v. Sandford (1857). There the Court invalidated the Missouri Compromise on the ground that legislation restricting the institution of slavery violated the implied rights of slaveholders. The Court relied on its own conception of liberty and property in doing so. It asserted that "an act of Congress which deprives a citizen of the United States of his liberty or property, merely because he came himself or brought his property into a particular Territory of the United States . . . could hardly be dignified with the name of due process of law." . . .

Dred Scott's holding was overruled on the battlefields of the Civil War and by constitutional amendment after Appomattox, but its approach to the Due Process Clause reappeared. In a series of early 20th-century cases, most prominently *Lochner*, this Court invalidated state statutes that presented "meddlesome interferences with the rights of the individual," and "undue interference with liberty of person and freedom of contract." In *Lochner* itself, the Court struck down a New York law setting maximum hours for bakery employees, because there was "in our judgment, no reasonable foundation for holding this to be necessary or appropriate as a health law."

The dissenting Justices in *Lochner* explained that the New York law could be viewed as a reasonable response to legislative concern about the health of bakery employees, an issue on which there was at least "room for debate and for an honest difference of opinion." *Id.* (opinion of Harlan, J.). The majority's contrary conclusion required adopting as constitutional law "an economic theory which a large part of the country does not entertain." *Id.* (opinion of Holmes, J.). As Justice Holmes memorably put it, "The Fourteenth Amendment does not enact Mr. Herbert Spencer's *Social Statics*," a leading work on the philosophy of Social Darwinism. The Constitution "is not intended to embody a particular economic theory. . . . It is made for people of fundamentally differing views. . . ."

In the decades after *Lochner*, the Court struck down nearly 200 laws as violations of individual liberty, often over strong dissents. . . . Eventually, the Court recognized its error and vowed not to repeat it. . . . Thus, it has become an accepted rule that the Court will not hold laws unconstitutional simply because we find them "unwise, improvident, or out of harmony with a particular school of thought." Williamson v. Lee Optical of Okla., Inc. (1955).

Rejecting *Lochner* does not require disavowing the doctrine of implied fundamental rights, and this Court has not done so. But to avoid repeating *Lochner*'s error of converting personal preferences into constitutional mandates, our modern substantive due process cases have stressed the need for "judicial self-restraint." Collins v. Harker Heights (1992). Our precedents have required that implied fundamental rights be "objectively, deeply rooted in this Nation's history and tradition," and "implicit in the concept of ordered liberty, such that neither liberty nor justice would exist if they were sacrificed." *Glucksberg*.

[G]iven the few "guideposts for responsible decisionmaking in this unchartered area," *Collins*, "an approach grounded in history imposes limits on the judiciary that are more meaningful than any based on [an] abstract formula," Moore v. East Cleveland (1977) (plurality opinion). Expanding a right suddenly and dramatically is likely to require tearing it up from its roots. Even a sincere profession of "discipline" in identifying fundamental rights does not provide a meaningful constraint on a judge, for "what he is really likely to be 'discovering,' whether or not he is fully aware of it, are his own values," J. Ely, *Democracy and*

Distrust 44 (1980). The only way to ensure restraint in this delicate enterprise is "continual insistence upon respect for the teachings of history, solid recognition of the basic values that underlie our society, and wise appreciation of the great roles [of] the doctrines of federalism and separation of powers." *Griswold* (Harlan, J., concurring in judgment).

B

The majority['s] aggressive application of substantive due process breaks sharply with decades of precedent and returns the Court to the unprincipled approach of *Lochner.*

1

The majority[] ... relies primarily on precedents discussing the fundamental "right to marry." These cases do not hold, of course, that anyone who wants to get married has a constitutional right to do so. They instead require a State to justify barriers to marriage as that institution has always been understood. In *Loving*, the Court held that racial restrictions on the right to marry lacked a compelling justification. In *Zablocki*, restrictions based on child support debts did not suffice. In *Turner*, restrictions based on status as a prisoner were deemed impermissible.

None of the laws at issue in those cases purported to change the core definition of marriage as the union of a man and a woman. . . . In short, the "right to marry" cases stand for the important but limited proposition that particular restrictions on access to marriage *as traditionally defined* violate due process. These precedents say nothing at all about a right to make a State change its definition of marriage, which is the right petitioners actually seek here. . . .

2

The majority suggests that "there are other, more instructive precedents" informing the right to marry. [T]his reference seems to correspond to a line of cases discussing an implied fundamental "right of privacy." In [*Griswold*], the Court invalidated a criminal law that banned the use of contraceptives. The Court stressed the invasive nature of the ban, which threatened the intrusion of "the police to search the sacred precincts of marital bedrooms." In the Court's view, such laws infringed the right to privacy in its most basic sense: the "right to be let alone." [S]ee Olmstead v. United States (1928) (Brandeis, J., dissenting).

The Court also invoked the right to privacy in *Lawrence*, which . . . relied on the position that criminal sodomy laws, like bans on contraceptives, invaded privacy by inviting "unwarranted government intrusions" that "touc[h] upon the most private human conduct, sexual behavior . . . in the most private of places, the home."

. . . Unlike criminal laws banning contraceptives and sodomy, the marriage laws at issue here involve no government intrusion. They create no crime and impose no punishment. Same-sex couples remain free to live together, to engage in intimate conduct, and to raise their families as they see fit. No one is "condemned to live in loneliness" by the laws. . . . [T]he laws in no way interfere with the "right to be let alone." . . .

In sum, the privacy cases provide no support for the majority's position, because petitioners do not seek privacy. Quite the opposite, they seek public recognition of their relationships, along with corresponding government benefits. Our cases have consistently refused to allow litigants to convert the shield provided by constitutional liberties into a sword to demand positive entitlements from the State. See DeShaney v. Winnebago County Dept. of Social Servs. (1989); San Antonio Independent School Dist. v. Rodriguez (1973); *post* (Thomas, J., dissenting). Thus, although the right to privacy recognized by our precedents certainly plays a role in protecting the intimate conduct of same-sex couples, it provides no affirmative right to redefine marriage and no basis for striking down the laws at issue here.

3

[T]he majority . . . jettison[s] the "careful" approach to implied fundamental rights taken by this Court in *Glucksberg*. It[s] position requires it to effectively overrule *Glucksberg*, the leading modern case setting the bounds of substantive due process. . . .

Ultimately, only one precedent offers any support for the majority's methodology: *Lochner*. . . . [Its] freewheeling notion of individual autonomy echoes nothing so much as "the general right of an individual to be *free in his person* and in his power to contract in relation to his own labor." *Lochner* (emphasis added).

. . . The truth is that today's decision rests on nothing more than the majority's own conviction that same-sex couples should be allowed to marry because they want to, and that "it would disparage their choices and diminish their personhood to deny them this right." Whatever force that belief may have as a matter of moral philosophy, it has no more basis in the Constitution than did the naked policy preferences adopted in *Lochner*.

. . . Today, the majority casts caution aside and revives the grave errors of that period.

One immediate question invited by the majority's position is whether States may retain the definition of marriage as a union of two people. Cf. Brown v. Buhman, 947 F. Supp. 2d 1170 (Utah 2013), appeal pending, No. 14–4117 (CA10). [The majority] offers no reason at all why the two-person element of the core definition of marriage may be preserved while the man-woman element may not. Indeed, from the standpoint of history and tradition, a leap from opposite-sex marriage to same-sex marriage is much greater than one from a two-person union to plural unions, which have deep roots in some cultures around the world. If the majority is willing to take the big leap, it is hard to see how it can say no to the shorter one.

It is striking how much of the majority's reasoning would apply with equal force to the claim of a fundamental right to plural marriage. . . . If a same-sex couple has the constitutional right to marry because their children would otherwise "suffer the stigma of knowing their families are somehow lesser," why wouldn't the same reasoning apply to a family of three or more persons raising children? If not having the opportunity to marry "serves to disrespect and subordinate" gay and lesbian couples, why wouldn't the same "imposition of this disability," serve to disrespect and subordinate people who find fulfillment in polyamorous relationships? See Otter, "Three May Not Be a Crowd: The Case for a Constitutional Right to Plural Marriage," 64 *Emory L. J.* 1977 (2015). . . .

4

Near the end of its opinion, the majority offers perhaps the clearest insight into its decision. Expanding marriage to include same-sex couples, the majority insists, would "pose no risk of harm to themselves or third parties." This argument again echoes *Lochner*, which relied on its assessment that "we think that a law like the one before us involves neither the safety, the morals nor the welfare of the public, and that the interest of the public is not in the slightest degree affected by such an act."

Then and now, this assertion of the "harm principle" sounds more in philosophy than law. The elevation of the fullest individual self-realization over the constraints that society has expressed in law may or may not be attractive moral philosophy. But a Justice's commission does not confer any special moral, philosophical, or social insight sufficient to justify imposing those perceptions on fellow citizens under the pretense of "due process." There is indeed a process due the people on issues of this sort—the democratic process. . . . As

Judge Henry Friendly once put it, echoing Justice Holmes's dissent in *Lochner*, the Fourteenth Amendment does not enact John Stuart Mill's *On Liberty* any more than it enacts Herbert Spencer's *Social Statics*. See Randolph, "Before *Roe v. Wade*: Judge Friendly's Draft Abortion Opinion," 29 *Harv. J. L. & Pub. Pol'y* 1035, 1036–1037, 1058 (2006). And it certainly does not enact any one concept of marriage. . . .

III

In addition to their due process argument, petitioners contend that the Equal Protection Clause requires their States to license and recognize same-sex marriages. . . . Absent from this portion of the opinion, however, is anything resembling our usual framework for deciding equal protection cases. . . .

The majority . . . fails to provide even a single sentence explaining how the Equal Protection Clause supplies independent weight for its position. . . . In any event, the marriage laws at issue here do not violate the Equal Protection Clause, because distinguishing between opposite-sex and same-sex couples is rationally related to the States' "legitimate state interest" in "preserving the traditional institution of marriage." *Lawrence* (O'Connor, J., concurring in judgment). . . .

IV

. . . Over and over, the majority exalts the role of the judiciary in delivering social change. . . . The Court's accumulation of power . . . comes at the expense of the people. . . . Here and abroad, people are in the midst of a serious and thoughtful public debate on the issue of same-sex marriage. They see voters carefully considering same-sex marriage, casting ballots in favor or opposed, and sometimes changing their minds. They see political leaders similarly reexamining their positions, and either reversing course or explaining adherence to old convictions confirmed anew. They see governments and businesses modifying policies and practices with respect to same-sex couples, and participating actively in the civic discourse. They see countries overseas democratically accepting profound social change, or declining to do so. This deliberative process is making people take seriously questions that they may not have even regarded as questions before. . . .

But today the Court puts a stop to all that. By deciding this question under the Constitution, the Court removes it from the realm of democratic decision. There will be consequences to shutting down the political process on an issue of such profound public significance. Closing debate tends to close minds. People denied a voice are less likely to accept the ruling of a court on an issue that does not seem to be the sort of thing courts usually decide. As a thoughtful commentator observed about another issue, "The political process was moving . . . , not swiftly enough for advocates of quick, complete change, but majoritarian institutions were listening and acting. Heavy-handed judicial intervention was difficult to justify and appears to have provoked, not resolved, conflict." Ginsburg, "Some Thoughts on Autonomy and Equality in Relation to *Roe v. Wade*," 63 *N. C. L. Rev.* 375, 385–386 (1985). Indeed, however heartened the proponents of same-sex marriage might be on this day, it is worth acknowledging what they have lost, and lost forever: the opportunity to win the true acceptance that comes from persuading their fellow citizens of the justice of their cause. And they lose this just when the winds of change were freshening at their backs.

Federal courts are blunt instruments when it comes to creating rights. They have constitutional power only to resolve concrete cases or controversies; they do not have the flexibility of legislatures to address concerns of parties not before the court or to anticipate problems that may arise from the exercise of a new right. Today's decision, for example, creates serious questions about religious liberty. . . .

Respect for sincere religious conviction has led voters and legislators in every State that has adopted same-sex marriage democratically to include accommodations for religious practice. The majority's decision imposing same-sex marriage cannot, of course, create any such accommodations. The majority graciously suggests that religious believers may continue to "advocate" and "teach" their views of marriage. The First Amendment guarantees, however, the freedom to "*exercise*" religion. Ominously, that is not a word the majority uses. . . .

. . . The majority offers a cursory assurance that it does not intend to disparage people who, as a matter of conscience, cannot accept same-sex marriage. That disclaimer is hard to square with the very next sentence, in which the majority explains that "the necessary consequence" of laws codifying the traditional definition of marriage is to "demea[n] or stigmatiz[e]" same-sex couples. . . . These apparent assaults on the character of fairminded people will have an effect, in society and in court. Moreover, they are entirely gratuitous. It is one thing for the majority to conclude that the Constitution protects a right to same-sex marriage; it is something else to portray everyone who does not share the majority's "better informed understanding" as bigoted.

In the face of all this, a much different view of the Court's role is possible. That view is more modest and restrained. It is more skeptical that the legal abilities of judges also reflect insight into moral and philosophical issues. It is more sensitive to the fact that judges are unelected and unaccountable, and that the legitimacy of their power depends on confining it to the exercise of legal judgment. It is more attuned to the lessons of history, and what it has meant for the country and Court when Justices have exceeded their proper bounds. And it is less pretentious than to suppose that while people around the world have viewed an institution in a particular way for thousands of years, the present generation and the present Court are the ones chosen to burst the bonds of that history and tradition.

* * *

If you are among the many Americans—of whatever sexual orientation—who favor expanding same-sex marriage, by all means celebrate today's decision. Celebrate the achievement of a desired goal. Celebrate the opportunity for a new expression of commitment to a partner. Celebrate the availability of new benefits. But do not celebrate the Constitution. It had nothing to do with it.

I respectfully dissent.

■ JUSTICE SCALIA, with whom JUSTICE THOMAS joins, dissenting.

I join THE CHIEF JUSTICE's opinion in full. I write separately to call attention to this Court's threat to American democracy.

The substance of today's decree is not of immense personal importance to me. The law can recognize as marriage whatever sexual attachments and living arrangements it wishes, and can accord them favorable civil consequences, from tax treatment to rights of inheritance. Those civil consequences—and the public approval that conferring the name of marriage evidences—can perhaps have adverse social effects, but no more adverse than the effects of many other controversial laws. . . . It is of overwhelming importance, however, who it is that rules me. Today's decree says that my Ruler, and the Ruler of 320 million Americans coast-to-coast, is a majority of the nine lawyers on the Supreme Court. The opinion in these cases is the furthest extension in fact—and the furthest extension one can even imagine—of the Court's claimed power to create "liberties" that the Constitution and its Amendments neglect to mention. This practice of constitutional revision by an unelected committee of nine, always accompanied . . . by extravagant praise of liberty, robs the People of the most important liberty they asserted in the Declaration of Independence and won in the Revolution of 1776: the freedom to govern themselves.

I . . .

The Constitution places some constraints on self-rule—constraints adopted *by the People themselves* when they ratified the Constitution and its Amendments. . . . Aside from these limitations, those powers "reserved to the States respectively, or to the people" can be exercised as the States or the People desire. These cases ask us to decide whether the Fourteenth Amendment contains a limitation that requires the States to license and recognize marriages between two people of the same sex. Does it remove *that* issue from the political process?

Of course not. . . . When the Fourteenth Amendment was ratified in 1868, every State limited marriage to one man and one woman, and no one doubted the constitutionality of doing so. That resolves these cases. When it comes to determining the meaning of a vague constitutional provision—such as "due process of law" or "equal protection of the laws"—it is unquestionable that the People who ratified that provision did not understand it to prohibit a practice that remained both universal and uncontroversial in the years after ratification. We have no basis for striking down a practice that is not expressly prohibited by the Fourteenth Amendment's text, and that bears the endorsement of a long tradition of open, widespread, and unchallenged use dating back to the Amendment's ratification. Since there is no doubt whatever that the People never decided to prohibit the limitation of marriage to opposite-sex couples, the public debate over same-sex marriage must be allowed to continue.

But the Court ends this debate, in an opinion lacking even a thin veneer of law. Buried beneath the mummeries and straining-to-be-memorable passages of the opinion is a candid and startling assertion: No matter *what* it was the People ratified, the Fourteenth Amendment protects those rights that the Judiciary, in its "reasoned judgment," thinks the Fourteenth Amendment ought to protect. . . . [R]ather than focusing on *the People's* understanding of "liberty"—at the time of ratification or even today—the majority focuses on four "principles and traditions" that, *in the majority's view*, prohibit States from defining marriage as an institution consisting of one man and one woman.

This is a naked judicial claim to legislative—indeed, *super*-legislative—power; a claim fundamentally at odds with our system of government. Except as limited by a constitutional prohibition agreed to by the People, the States are free to adopt whatever laws they like, even those that offend the esteemed Justices' "reasoned judgment." A system of government that makes the People subordinate to a committee of nine unelected lawyers does not deserve to be called a democracy.

. . . The strikingly unrepresentative character of the body voting on today's social upheaval would be irrelevant if they were functioning as *judges*, answering the legal question whether the American people had ever ratified a constitutional provision that was understood to proscribe the traditional definition of marriage. But of course the Justices in today's majority are not voting on that basis; *they say they are not*. And to allow the policy question of same-sex marriage to be considered and resolved by a select, patrician, highly unrepresentative panel of nine is to violate a principle even more fundamental than no taxation without representation: no social transformation without representation.

II

But what really astounds is the hubris reflected in today's judicial Putsch. The five Justices who compose today's majority are entirely comfortable concluding that every State violated the Constitution for all of the 135 years between the Fourteenth Amendment's ratification and Massachusetts' permitting of same-sex marriages in 2003. They have discovered in the Fourteenth Amendment a "fundamental right" overlooked by every person alive at the time of ratification, and almost everyone else in the time since. . . . They are certain that the People ratified the Fourteenth Amendment to bestow on them the power to remove questions from the democratic process when that is called for by their "reasoned judgment." These Justices *know* that limiting marriage to one man and one woman is contrary to reason; they *know* that an institution as old as government itself, and accepted by every nation in history until 15 years ago, cannot possibly be supported by anything other than ignorance or bigotry. And they are willing to say that any citizen who does not agree with that, who adheres to what was, until 15 years ago, the unanimous judgment of all generations and all societies, stands against the Constitution.

The opinion is couched in a style that is as pretentious as its content is egotistic. It is one thing for separate concurring or dissenting opinions to contain extravagances . . . of thought and expression; it is something else for the official opinion of the Court to do so.[22] Of course the opinion's showy profundities are often profoundly incoherent. "The nature of marriage is that,

---

[22] If, even as the price to be paid for a fifth vote, I ever joined an opinion for the Court that began: "The Constitution promises liberty to all within its reach, a liberty that includes certain specific rights that allow persons, within a lawful realm, to define and express their identity," I would hide my head in a bag. The Supreme Court of the United States has descended from the disciplined legal reasoning of John Marshall and Joseph Story to the mystical aphorisms of the fortune cookie. [Footnote by Justice Scalia.]

through its enduring bond, two persons together can find other freedoms, such as expression, intimacy, and spirituality." (Really? Who ever thought that intimacy and spirituality [whatever that means] were freedoms? And if intimacy is, one would think Freedom of Intimacy is abridged rather than expanded by marriage. Ask the nearest hippie. . . .) . . . The world does not expect logic and precision in poetry or inspirational pop-philosophy; it demands them in the law. The stuff contained in today's opinion has to diminish this Court's reputation for clear thinking and sober analysis.

* * *

. . . With each decision of ours that takes from the People a question properly left to them—with each decision that is unabashedly based not on law, but on the "reasoned judgment" of a bare majority of this Court—we move one step closer to being reminded of our impotence.

■ JUSTICE THOMAS, with whom JUSTICE SCALIA joins, dissenting. . . .

<h2 align="center">I</h2>

The majority's decision today [is] largely based on a constitutional provision guaranteeing "due process" before a person is deprived of his "life, liberty, or property." I have elsewhere explained the dangerous fiction of treating the Due Process Clause as a font of substantive rights. McDonald v. Chicago (2010) (Thomas, J., concurring in part and concurring in judgment). It distorts the constitutional text, which guarantees only whatever "process" is "due" before a person is deprived of life, liberty, and property. . . .

<h2 align="center">II . . .</h2>

<h3 align="center">A</h3>

<h3 align="center">1</h3>

As used in the Due Process Clauses, "liberty" most likely refers to "the power of loco-motion, of changing situation, or removing one's person to whatsoever place one's own inclination may direct; without imprisonment or restraint, unless by due course of law." 1 W. Blackstone, *Commentaries on the Laws of England* 130 (1769). That definition is drawn from the historical roots of the Clauses and is consistent with our Constitution's text and structure.

Both of the Constitution's Due Process Clauses reach back to Magna Carta. . . .

If the Fifth Amendment uses "liberty" in this narrow sense [of "freedom from physical restraint"], then the Fourteenth Amendment likely does as well.

See Hurtado v. California (1884). . . . That the Court appears to have lost its way in more recent years does not justify deviating from the original meaning of the Clauses.

2

Even assuming that the "liberty" in those Clauses encompasses something more than freedom from physical restraint, it would not include the types of rights claimed by the majority. In the American legal tradition, liberty has long been understood as individual freedom *from* governmental action, not as a right *to* a particular governmental entitlement. . . .

B

Whether we define "liberty" as locomotion or freedom from governmental action more broadly, petitioners have in no way been deprived of it.

Petitioners cannot claim . . . that they have been imprisoned or physically restrained by the States for participating in same-sex relationships. To the contrary, they have been able to cohabitate and raise their children in peace. They have been able to hold civil marriage ceremonies in States that recognize same-sex marriages and private religious ceremonies in all States. They have been able to travel freely around the country, making their homes where they please. Far from being incarcerated or physically restrained, petitioners have been left alone to order their lives as they see fit.

. . . Nor have the States prevented petitioners from approximating a number of incidents of marriage through private legal means, such as wills, trusts, and powers of attorney.

Instead, the States have refused to grant them governmental entitlements. Petitioners claim that as a matter of "liberty," they are entitled to access privileges and benefits that exist solely *because of* the government. . . . But receiving governmental recognition and benefits has nothing to do with any understanding of "liberty" that the Framers would have recognized.

To the extent that the Framers would have recognized a natural right to marriage that fell within the broader definition of liberty, it would not have included a right to governmental recognition and benefits. Instead, it would have included a right to engage in the very same activities that petitioners have been left free to engage in—making vows, holding religious ceremonies celebrating those vows, raising children, and otherwise enjoying the society of one's spouse—without governmental interference. At the founding, such conduct was understood to predate government, not to flow from it. . . . Petitioners misunderstand the institution of marriage when they say that it would "mean little" absent governmental recognition.

Petitioners' misconception of liberty carries over into their discussion of our precedents identifying a right to marry, not one of which has expanded the concept of "liberty" beyond the concept of negative liberty. Those precedents all involved absolute prohibitions on private actions associated with marriage. . . .[5] In *none* of those cases were individuals denied solely governmental recognition and benefits associated with marriage.

. . . As a philosophical matter, liberty is only freedom from governmental action, not an entitlement to governmental benefits. And as a constitutional matter, it is likely even narrower . . . , encompassing only freedom from physical restraint and imprisonment. . . .

III . . .

Aside from undermining the political processes that protect our liberty, the majority's decision threatens the religious liberty our Nation has long sought to protect. . . .

Numerous *amici* . . . have cautioned the Court that its decision here will "have unavoidable and wide-ranging implications for religious liberty." In our society, marriage is not simply a governmental institution; it is a religious institution as well. Today's decision might change the former, but it cannot change the latter. It appears all but inevitable that the two will come into conflict, particularly as individuals and churches are confronted with demands to participate in and endorse civil marriages between same-sex couples.

The majority appears unmoved by that inevitability. It makes only a weak gesture toward religious liberty. . . . And even that gesture indicates a misunderstanding of religious liberty in our Nation's tradition. Religious liberty is about more than just the protection for "religious organizations and persons . . . as they seek to teach the principles that are so fulfilling and so central to their

---

[5]   The suggestion . . . that antimiscegenation laws are akin to laws defining marriage as between one man and one woman is both offensive and inaccurate. "America's earliest laws against interracial sex and marriage were spawned by slavery." P. Pascoe, *What Comes Naturally: Miscegenation Law and the Making of Race in America* 19 (2009). . . .

Laws defining marriage as between one man and one woman do not share this sordid history. The traditional definition of marriage has prevailed in every society that has recognized marriage throughout history. It arose not out of a desire to shore up an invidious institution like slavery, but out of a desire "to increase the likelihood that children will be born and raised in stable and enduring family units by both the mothers and the fathers who brought them into this world." And it has existed in civilizations containing all manner of views on homosexuality. See Brief for Ryan T. Anderson as *Amicus Curiae* 11–12. [Footnote by Justice Thomas.]

lives and faiths." Religious liberty is about freedom of action in matters of religion generally, and the scope of that liberty is directly correlated to the civil restraints placed upon religious practice.

Although our Constitution provides some protection against such governmental restrictions on religious practices, the People have long elected to afford broader protections than this Court's constitutional precedents mandate. Had the majority allowed the definition of marriage to be left to the political process—as the Constitution requires—the People could have considered the religious liberty implications of deviating from the traditional definition as part of their deliberative process. Instead, the majority's decision short-circuits that process, with potentially ruinous consequences for religious liberty. . . .

* * *

Our Constitution—like the Declaration of Independence before it—was predicated on a simple truth: One's liberty, not to mention one's dignity, was something to be shielded from—not provided by—the State. Today's decision casts that truth aside. In its haste to reach a desired result, the majority misapplies a clause focused on "due process" to afford substantive rights, disregards the most plausible understanding of the "liberty" protected by that clause, and distorts the principles on which this Nation was founded. Its decision will have inestimable consequences for our Constitution and our society. I respectfully dissent.

■ JUSTICE ALITO, with whom JUSTICE SCALIA and JUSTICE THOMAS join, dissenting.

Until the federal courts intervened, the American people were engaged in a debate about whether their States should recognize same-sex marriage. The question in these cases, however, is not what States *should* do about same-sex marriage but whether the Constitution answers that question for them. It does not. The Constitution leaves that question to be decided by the people of each State. . . .

II

. . . Noting that marriage is a fundamental right, the majority argues that a State has no valid reason for denying that right to same-sex couples. This reasoning is dependent upon a particular understanding of the purpose of civil marriage. Although the Court expresses the point in loftier terms, its argument is that the fundamental purpose of marriage is to promote the well-being of those who choose to marry. Marriage provides emotional fulfillment and the promise of support in times of need. And by benefiting persons who choose to wed, marriage indirectly benefits society because persons who live in stable, fulfilling, and supportive relationships make better citizens. It is for these reasons, the argument goes, that States encourage and formalize marriage, confer special benefits on married persons, and also impose some special obligations. This understanding of the States' reasons for recognizing marriage enables the majority to argue that same-sex marriage serves the States' objectives in the same way as opposite-sex marriage.

This understanding of marriage . . . is shared by many people today, but it is not the traditional one. For millennia, marriage was inextricably linked to the one thing that only an opposite-sex couple can do: procreate.

. . . Here, the States defending their adherence to the traditional understanding of marriage [argue] that States formalize and promote marriage . . . in order to encourage potentially procreative conduct to take place within a lasting unit that has long been thought to provide the best atmosphere for raising children. They thus argue that there are reasonable secular grounds for restricting marriage to opposite-sex couples.

If this traditional understanding of the purpose of marriage does not ring true to all ears today, that is probably because the tie between marriage and procreation has frayed. Today, for instance, more than 40 percent of all children in this country are born to unmarried women. This development undoubtedly is both a cause and a result of changes in our society's understanding of marriage.

While, for many, the attributes of marriage in 21st century America have changed, those States that do not want to recognize same-sex marriage have not yet given up on the traditional understanding. They worry that by officially abandoning the older understanding, they may contribute to marriage's further decay. It is far beyond the outer reaches of this Court's authority to say that a State may not adhere to the understanding of marriage that has long prevailed, not just in this country and others with similar cultural roots, but also in a great variety of countries and cultures all around the globe.

As I wrote in *Windsor* [dissenting]:

The family is an ancient and universal human institution. Family structure reflects the characteristics of a civilization, and changes in family structure and in the popular understanding of marriage and the family can have profound effects. Past changes in the understanding of marriage—for example, the gradual ascendance of the idea that romantic love is a prerequisite to marriage—have had far-reaching consequences. But the process by which such consequences come about is complex, involving the interaction of numerous factors, and tends to occur over an extended period of time.

We can expect something similar to take place if same-sex marriage becomes widely accepted. The long-term consequences of this change are not now known and are unlikely to be ascertainable for some time to come. There are those who think that allowing same-sex marriage will seriously undermine the institution of marriage. Others think that recognition of same-sex marriage will fortify a now-shaky institution.

At present, no one—including social scientists, philosophers, and historians—can predict with any certainty what the long-term ramifications of widespread acceptance of same-sex marriage will be. And judges are certainly not equipped to make such an assessment. The Members of this Court have the authority and the responsibility to interpret and apply the Constitution. Thus, if the Constitution contained a provision guaranteeing the right to marry a person of the same sex, it would be our duty to enforce that right. But the Constitution simply does not speak to the issue of same-sex marriage. In our system of government, ultimate sovereignty rests with the people, and the people have the right to control their own destiny. Any change on a question so fundamental should be made by the people through their elected officials.

III

Today's decision . . . will be used to vilify Americans who are unwilling to assent to the new orthodoxy. [T]he majority compares traditional marriage laws to laws that denied equal treatment for African-Americans and women. The implications of this analogy will be exploited by those who are determined to stamp out every vestige of dissent.

[T]he majority attempts . . . to reassure those who oppose same-sex marriage that their rights of conscience will be protected. We will soon see whether this proves to be true. I assume that those who cling to old beliefs will be able to whisper their thoughts in the recesses of their homes, but if they repeat those views in public, they will risk being labeled as bigots and treated as such by governments, employers, and schools.

The system of federalism established by our Constitution provides a way for people with different beliefs to live together in a single nation. If the issue of same-sex marriage had been left to the people of the States, it is likely that some

States would recognize same-sex marriage and others would not. It is also possible that some States would tie recognition to protection for conscience rights. The majority today makes that impossible. By imposing its own views on the entire country, the majority facilitates the marginalization of the many Americans who have traditional ideas. Recalling the harsh treatment of gays and lesbians in the past, some may think that turnabout is fair play. But if that sentiment prevails, the Nation will experience bitter and lasting wounds.

Today's decision will also have a fundamental effect on this Court and its ability to uphold the rule of law. . . . A lesson that some will take from today's decision is that preaching about the proper method of interpreting the Constitution or the virtues of judicial self-restraint and humility cannot compete with the temptation to achieve what is viewed as a noble end by any practicable means. I do not doubt that my colleagues in the majority sincerely see in the Constitution a vision of liberty that happens to coincide with their own. But this sincerity is cause for concern, not comfort. What it evidences is the deep and perhaps irremediable corruption of our legal culture's conception of constitutional interpretation. . . .

EDITORS' NOTES

(1) Justice Kennedy's majority opinion grounded its holding on both the Due Process Clause and the Equal Protection Clause. What is his due process/liberty argument? What is his equal protection argument? What is the relationship between the two? Does one of these clauses provide a firmer basis for the holding than the other? Or are both equally persuasive? Put another way, is the denial of the right to marry here fundamentally a denial of a basic liberty, a denial of equal dignity, or both?

(2) What is Justice Kennedy's conception of history and tradition in constitutional interpretation? How does his conception differ from those of the dissenters? As historian Nancy Cott observes: "more than one version of the history of marriage is operating" in the majority and dissenting opinions in *Obergefell*. Nancy F. Cott, "Which History in *Obergefell v. Hodges?*," *Perspectives on History* (American Historical Association, July 2015). What is Justice Kennedy's conception of the institution of marriage and its history and how does it shape his reasoning? What are the conceptions of the dissenting justices? Which is more persuasive?

(3) Justice Kennedy refers to a "substantial body of law" growing out of federal appellate court decisions about same-sex marriage as helping "to explain

and formulate the underlying principles" the Court develops in *Obergefell*. In emphasizing liberty and the fundamental right to marry, however, Kennedy did not explicitly pursue two constitutional paths taken in some of those appellate court decisions and explored in Chapter 4: (1) a holding that sexual orientation is a "suspect" classification warranting "strict judicial scrutiny" and that the discriminatory marriage bans fail that test, or (2) a holding that the one man-one woman definition of marriage discriminated on the basis of gender and could not survive "intermediate judicial scrutiny." With respect to the former, one unanswered question is whether the majority's focus on the significance of exclusion from marriage has implications for "the larger goal of eliminating discrimination" based on sexual orientation "throughout American law and society." Serena Mayeri, "Marriage (In)equality and the Historical Legacies of Feminism," 6 *Calif. L. Rev. Circuit* 126, 131 (2015). With respect to the latter, Justice Ginsburg, an obvious candidate to write a concurring opinion advancing the gender discrimination argument, reportedly believed that it was "more powerful to have the same, single opinion." Ibid., n. 32 (quoting interview with Neil Siegel).

(4)   Some have criticized the United States Supreme Court decisions protecting a right of autonomy for exalting "choice" over the good of what is chosen and for "bracketing" moral arguments about goods or virtues promoted by protecting freedoms. See, e.g., Michael J. Sandel, "Moral Argument and Liberal Toleration: Abortion and Homosexuality," 77 *Cal. L. Rev.* 521 (1989). Is *Obergefell* vulnerable to this criticism? Justice Kennedy's majority opinion stresses the "transcendent purposes of marriage" and its "highest ideals of love, fidelity, devotion, sacrifice, and family." Should courts seek to justify protecting rights on the ground that they promote such moral goods? See James E. Fleming and Linda C. McClain, *Ordered Liberty: Rights, Responsibilities, and Virtues* (Cambridge: Harvard University Press, 2013), ch. 7.

(5)   In emphasizing the exalted status of marriage in our society, the dignity and respectability attached to that status, and the harm and humiliation suffered by same-sex couples and their children due to restrictive marriage laws, does the majority opinion suggest that those who choose *not* to marry and to form nonmarital family relationships lack dignity or are less worthy? *See* Nan Hunter, "Interpreting Liberty and Equality Through the Lens of Marriage," 6 *Calif. L. Rev. Circuit* 107, 111 (2015).

(6)   What are we to make of Chief Justice Roberts's argument in dissent that Justice Kennedy's majority opinion has "no basis in the Constitution or this Court's precedent"? Whether it does depends upon our conceptions of (a) the

Constitution and (b) precedent. The clash between Kennedy and the dissenters is between two competing understandings of *the Constitution*: Is it a basic charter of abstract principles like liberty and equality? Or a code of specific, enumerated rights whose meaning is determined by the deposit of concrete historical practices extant at the time of the adoption of the Fourteenth Amendment in 1868? The clash is also between two competing understandings of how abstractly or concretely we conceive *precedents and traditions*: do we limit precedents to specific holdings and traditions to concrete historical practices, or do we build upon them through making recourse to the basic reasons underlying precedents and the aspirational principles embodied in traditions? Who holds the more defensible view of the Constitution and precedent?

(7)   Does Justice Kennedy's majority opinion really read John Stuart Mill's "harm principle" from *On Liberty* into the Fourteenth Amendment's protection of liberty, as Chief Justice Roberts charges in dissent? Or is Kennedy simply rebutting the argument that extending marriage to gay men and lesbians will harm the institution of marriage, with the result that straight couples might decide not to marry?

(8)   Does Justice Kennedy's majority opinion repeat the "grave errors" of Lochner v. New York (1905), as Chief Justice Roberts argues in dissent? What was it that the Supreme Court did in *Lochner* that was so horrible? Did the majority do the same horrible thing in *Obergefell*, or can we distinguish the two cases? We will examine *Lochner* in Chapter 3.

(9)   Chief Justice Roberts quotes Justice Ruth Bader Ginsburg's famous critique of the Court in Roe v. Wade (1973) for its "heavy-handed judicial intervention" just as the people through the democratic process were considering whether and how to liberalize abortion laws, and he contends that her critique applies to *Obergefell* as well. Is his analogy between *Obergefell* and *Roe* sound? Is the Supreme Court really in the vanguard of social change with respect to same-sex marriage? Or is it following and consolidating social change that has been occurring through the democratic and judicial processes throughout the nation for more than 40 years (since Baker v. Nelson (1972))?

(10) More generally, Chief Justice Roberts criticizes the majority opinion for being undemocratic (in the sense that its protection of rights puts limits on what the majorities in the states may legislate concerning access to marriage). The majority opinion retorts: "Of course, the Constitution contemplates that democracy is the appropriate process for change, so long as that process does not abridge fundamental rights." To what extent is the disagreement between

the majority and the dissenters a disagreement about the basic character of the form of democracy embodied in the Constitution? What are their contrasting understandings of democracy?

(11) Chief Justice Roberts and the other dissenters express worries about *Obergefell* threatening the religious liberty of opponents of same-sex marriage. Are these worries well founded? Roberts acknowledges that every state that has recognized same-sex marriage has created religious exemptions for those who oppose such marriage. Is there any reason to believe that, after *Obergefell*, the political process will not continue to operate as before in creating religious exemptions and accommodations? Is there anything in the majority opinion that would prohibit or preclude state legislatures from creating religious exemptions?

(12) Chief Justice Roberts and the other dissenters accuse the majority opinion of tarring opponents of same-sex marriage with the brush of "bigotry." Are these accusations well-founded? Justice Kennedy's opinion avoids holding that discrimination on the basis of sexual orientation is analogous to discrimination on the basis of race (a holding that might imply that discrimination on the basis of sexual orientation is analogous to racial bigotry). Kennedy also stresses that the majority does not doubt the sincerity or the conscientiousness of opponents of same-sex marriage. Does he successfully deflect Roberts's and the other dissenters' accusations?

(13) Is Chief Justice Roberts sound in suggesting that protecting the right of gay men and lesbians to marry puts us on the slippery slope toward protecting a right to plural marriage or polygamy? Or are there significant distinctions between the two? In support of the claim that *Obergefell* does put us on such a slippery slope, Roberts cites Ronald C. Den Otter, "Three May Not Be a Crowd: The Case for a Constitutional Right to Plural Marriage," 64 *Emory L. J.* 1977 (2015). For a sustained argument to the contrary, see Stephen Macedo, *Just Married: Same-Sex Couples, Monogamy, and the Future of Marriage* (Princeton, NJ: Princeton University Press, 2015), 145–203. We discuss this issue further in Chapter 5.

(14) On October 8, 2015, a group of conservative scholars "and informed citizens" affiliated with the American Principles Project (founded by Professor Robert P. George) released a "Statement Calling for Constitutional Resistance to Obergefell v. Hodges." https://americanprinciplesproject.org/founding-principles/statement-calling-for-constitutional-resistance-to-obergefell-v-hodges%E2%80%AF/. Invoking James Madison and Abraham Lincoln for recognizing that "the

Constitution is not whatever a majority of Supreme Court justices say it is," the Statement contends that:

> The Court's majority eschewed reliance on the text, logic, structure, or original understanding of the Constitution, as well as the Court's own interpretive doctrines and precedents, and supplied no compelling reasoning to show why it is unjustified for the laws of the states to sustain marriage as it has been understood for millennia as the union of husband and wife. The opinion for the Court substitutes for traditional—and sound—methods of constitutional interpretation a new and ill-defined jurisprudence of identity—one that abused the moral concept of human dignity.

The Statement quotes extensively (and favorably) from the dissenting opinions and asserts that "the consequences will be grave" if "*Obergefell* is accepted as binding law." The signatories to the Statement call upon "all federal and state officeholders" to, among other things, "refuse to accept *Obergefell* as binding precedent for all but the specific plaintiffs in that case," "recognize the authority of states to define marriage" and of officeholders "to act in accordance with those definitions," and "pledge full and mutual legal assistance to anyone who refuses to follow *Obergefell* for constitutionally protected reasons." As Chapter 5 will discuss, some state legislatures have considered bills that would, in a similar spirit of resistance, claim to "nullify" *Obergefell*.

CHAPTER 2

The American Founding and What Should Count as a Reason in Public Debate

In Romer v. Evans (1996), the U.S. Supreme Court held that the voters of Colorado could not amend the state's constitution to impose special political burdens on homosexuals, burdens that don't apply to others. In Lawrence v. Texas (2003), the Court held that Texas could not criminalize homosexual sexual acts. In Obergefell v. Hodges (2015), the Court declared that same-sex couples have a constitutional right to marry and have that right recognized for all governmental purposes, state and federal. We have discussed *Obergefell* in Chapter 1, and we will discuss *Romer*, *Lawrence*, and other gay rights cases in Chapter 4. This chapter asks whether constitutional status for gay rights, including marriage equality, is consistent with the Constitution's founding principles. Chapter 3 takes up these questions in light of constitutional developments after the founding.

Constitutional arguments against gay rights usually appeal to "tradition" and represent a so-called originalist approach to constitutional interpretation.[1] On the other side, defenders of gay rights usually appeal to the idea of a living constitution. This chapter suggests a third possibility. We review material from the founding era to show that historical sources support a practice of justifying

---

[1]   The originalist approach either seeks the original definition of a constitutional idea (assuming that some original definition differs from some current definition) or it derives a definition from how the generation that ratified the constitutional provision in question applied that provision. A true originalist would say, for example, that since the schools of the District of Columbia were segregated by law in 1868, the Fourteenth Amendment's Equal Protection Clause neither bans racial classifications in the law nor guarantees equal educational opportunity, and therefore the Supreme Court erred in Brown v. Board of Education (1954). For analyses and criticism of "originalism" in its various forms, see Sotirios A. Barber and James E. Fleming, *Constitutional Interpretation: The Basic Questions* (New York: Oxford University Press, 2007), chs. 6–7; James E. Fleming, *Fidelity to Our Imperfect Constitution: For Moral Readings and Against Originalisms* (New York: Oxford University Press, 2015), chs. 1–3.

political decisions with reasons that appeal to widely supported moral values, such as liberty, equality, and justice, and widely shared "public purposes," like national security and prosperity, as well as common experiences about causes and consequences and ways and means. For brevity's sake, we call this practice the practice of "public reasonableness"; when we focus on the normative aspect of this practice, we'll refer to the "principle of public reasonableness."[2]

The principle of public reasonableness has positive and negative implications. It positively requires that public officials and citizens should seek to justify their preferred political outcomes by appealing to reasons and evidence accessible to all. On the negative side, it excludes appeals to special interests and sectarian religious authority. That a policy would benefit General Motors is no reason to adopt it unless it can be argued with some plausibility that what benefits General Motors benefits America as a whole. That Romans 1:26–28 condemns gay sex as unnatural is no reason to criminalize gay sex unless medical science confirms it as harmful and unless we're prepared to criminalize similar sex acts when performed by straight couples. The principle of public reasonableness has proven a controlling presence in the recent debates over gay rights because it rules out appeals to sectarian doctrine and clerical authority as a basis for public policy. Moreover, the principle is accepted by leading advocates on both sides of the gay rights debate, including, for example, conservative moral philosopher John Finnis, who observed two decades ago that while "embarrassment" makes "most people more than usually inarticulate" with respect to homosexuality, "public policies should indeed be based on reasons, not merely emotions, prejudices, and biases."[3]

This chapter argues that leading figures of the founding generation were centrally committed to public reasonableness as a governing political principle. They gave priority to securing equal liberty (including religious freedom) and promoting this-worldly goods such as physical security and economic plenty. Though the Constitution originally permitted the states to establish official religions, Article VI of the Constitution bans religious tests for national office, the First Amendment bans the establishment of a national religion, and Article VI gives national policy supremacy over state laws when the latter clash with the former. The Constitution thus overrides any religiously-based state law that might conflict with Congress's view of national prosperity or security. The

---

2   This principle and its pivotal role in the contemporary debate over same-sex marriage are explained in Stephen Macedo, *Just Married: Same-Sex Couples, Monogamy, and the Future of Marriage* (2015), chs. 1–3.

3   John Finnis, "Is Natural Law Theory Compatible with Limited Government?," in *Natural Law, Liberalism, and Morality: Contemporary Essays*, Robert P. George, ed. (New York: Oxford University Press, 1996), 12.

Constitution ensures *complete* freedom of religious exercise only for those religions whose teachings are compatible with ends like religious freedom itself—that is, different religions living peacefully with each other and with non-believers under a government that reserves coercive power for worldly ends. Though Americans have long been more of a "religious people" than their Western European counterparts, American political and judicial leaders today exclude direct appeals to biblical or clerical authority as acceptable reasons for controversial public choices. This essentially secular understanding of what counts as a reason in public and judicial deliberation traces back to the American founding.

I.   REASONS IN PUBLIC DEBATE

Sexual morality and family law were not areas of national political debate in late 18th century America. (Nor were they areas of national political debate in 1868, at the time of ratification of the Fourteenth Amendment.) For better or worse, participants in the founding debates assumed that invoking the Bible or other religious authority was an inappropriate way to settle disagreements about the arrangement of governmental institutions and the distribution of governmental powers and individual rights. In no part of its argument for ratifying the proposal of the Philadelphia Convention did *The Federalist* say that the American people should do something because the Bible says so. Nor did the Antifederalist opponents of the Constitution claim that ratification would sin against God in some way. Though the Antifederalists did stress the importance of religion for cultivating the virtues needed in a democratic society, and though they feared the Federalists' emphasis on commerce would weaken religion, the Antifederalist arguments *for* religion were not religious arguments. They were arguments for religion *as means* to secular ends like courage, moderation, patriotism, public-spiritedness, and public decency.[4] What's true of the founding period remains true today: Most of the country's leadership communities (political, business, journalistic, academic, and even clerical) take it for granted that in U.S. constitutional debate, public, non-sectarian arguments should prevail.

This principle of public reasonableness has had a decisive bearing on the gay rights issues. One reason is that much of today's opposition to gay rights comes from religious sources. The very diversity of religious beliefs in America requires believers to make secular arguments in court. That is, believers must

---

⁴   For a summary of the Antifederalist position, see Herbert J. Storing, *What the Anti-Federalists Were For* (Chicago, IL: University of Chicago Press, 1981), 21–22.

couch their religious beliefs in terms that are acceptable to people who might not share their religious convictions. But faith-based reasons formulated in secular terms tend either to fall short of or to exceed the values and beliefs that motivate them. These secular arguments motivated by religious beliefs thus quickly prove vulnerable to obvious counter instances, and these counter instances defeat the arguments.

The leading example of this phenomenon in the gay rights debate is what we can call "the procreation argument." This popular argument against marriage equality begins with a non-controversial premise, namely, that as a matter of historical fact marriage has been linked to procreation. As we've seen in Chapter 1, Justice Kennedy and the *Obergefell* majority give this historical fact their unqualified acknowledgment. Chief Justice Roberts, on the other hand, wants to take a further step. He takes the historical practice to establish the true meaning of marriage, what marriage essentially is. He refers to the "universal definition of marriage" as an institution that "arose in the nature of things to meet a vital need: ensuring that children are conceived by a mother and father committed to raising them in the stable conditions of a lifelong relationship."[5] From this presumed historical fact[6] it is said to follow that declaring a right of same-sex marriage "changes the definition of marriage." Ryan Anderson picks up this argument and develops its further implications. Because he assumes that the traditional definition of marriage captures the truth about marriage, he says same-sex marriage denies the true "essence of marriage" and "teaches a falsehood about marriage."[7] So goes the procreation argument.

Even if one puts aside the logical and broader philosophic defects of the procreation argument,[8] it has failed the test of common sense and is evidently a

---

[5]   Obergefell v. Hodges, 135 S.Ct. 2584, 2613 (2013) (Roberts, C.J., dissenting).

[6]   Somewhat bizarrely, Chief Justice Roberts chastised the *Obergefell* majority for ordering "the transformation of a social institution that has formed the basis of human society for millennia, for the Kalahari Bushmen and the Han Chinese, the Carthaginians and the Aztecs." But the practices of these societies concerning marriage and sex were, in varying ways, radically different from what Americans would find acceptable or that the Constitution would permit; the Han Chinese, the Bushmen, and the Aztecs all practiced polygamy, for example.

[7]   Ryan T. Anderson, *Truth Overruled: The Future of Marriage and Religious Freedom* (Washington, DC: Regnery Publishing, 2015), 2. For a lengthier discussion, see Macedo, *Just Married*, ch. 2.

[8]   Logically, no normative conclusion follows from a historical fact. Just because Jane has long abused her husband and he has gotten used to it is no reason that she should continue to abuse him or that he should continue to take her abuse. Also, as a matter of usage, the conventional definition of a thing is a theory of that thing and theories of a thing are generally understood as revisable in light of better theories of the thing. It's entirely possible that some culture would define frogs as messengers of the Devil. This definition would not capture the essence of frogs; frogs would not be messengers of the Devil even if all of the world's people, past present, and future believed them to be so. *See* Barber and Fleming, *Constitutional Interpretation*, 87–88. To this one might respond that the referent of "frog" is different from the referent of

"marriage," the latter being a human convention. One might therefore say that the conventional view of a convention (e.g., what people generally believe about marriage) does constitute the convention's essence and therefore to change the definition of the conventional thing is to change the thing itself.

But from this it would not follow that (as Anderson holds about marriage) to change the thing's definition is to abandon *the truth* about it or to lie about it. If an institution like marriage is purely conventional—not based on some unchanging good or natural need—then marriage itself can provide no real reason for opposing changed conceptions of it. We might want to change some conception of marriage for the sake of some other good, like political unity (*see* Plato's *Republic*, 457c–461e). But we couldn't judge one conception of marriage better than another on the basis of the truth about marriage itself because there would be no "marriage itself." There would be only different conceptions of marriage, different marriage conventions or practices. In this case one could only report that conservatives oppose or favor a particular change that progressives favor or oppose. Those who think they oppose same-sex marriage for a reason— i.e., a real reason, one that all reasonable people can see, should see, and would see if they could think straight—assume that marriage has an unchanging nature and that this unchanging nature serves as a basis for evaluating social conventions about marriage. Only on the basis of this assumption could one speak (rationally) of "the truth about marriage."

But if there is a "truth about marriage" one can't (rationally) oppose new definitions of marriage per se, for in light of the truth, any given historical definition could be mistaken. A definition of marriage established everywhere for millennia could be wrong when measured against the truth, just as a universal and long-held view of frogs as the Devil's messengers could be wrong in light of the truth. If there is a truth about marriage, then that truth can't depend on what this or that social convention might hold about marriage. If there is a truth about marriage then, other factors permitting, traditional definitions of marriage should stand or fall as that truth comes progressively in view. If there is a truth about marriage, that truth can't be disclosed by pointing to this or that or even to all historical practices, for we would judge all historical marriage practices by the truth about marriage. This truth about marriage would have to be pursued in a manner analogous to the experimental processes through which humankind pursues the truth about frogs: a process of advancing and testing hypotheses against evidence that can be confirmed by all persons blessed with normal powers of perception and thought and who strive to understand things for themselves independently of hearsay and social convention (which, remember, can always be wrong). If it's true that marriage just is one man and one woman, that fact can be confirmed only through an argument—only through appeals to values held in common and facts evident to all independently of hearsay and coercive authority. Again, the requisite argument can't just point to historical practices or "tradition" as magically self-confirming. It can't just report that marriage has been one-man-one-woman; it must also show why our deepest values and perceptions of the world presently indicate that marriage ought to be nothing but one-man-one-woman. And this is precisely the showing that opponents of same-sex marriage have (so far) failed to make.

Opponents of marriage equality can escape the burden they've been unable to meet only if they can point to the conventional view of marriage and simply declare (without argument) that the conventional view is the truth about marriage. This strategy fails, ironically enough, because of our conventional understanding of conventions. Changing the conventional view of a thing isn't abandoning the truth about that thing because the conventional view of social conventions allows conventions to change—conventions change and differ from each other without ceasing to be conventions. Thus, no one in the present debate about marriage claims that it is always wrong for social conventions to change. And everyone in the present debate would agree that, in general, social conventions can be morally wrong and should be changed for the moral better where feasible.

The question in the American debate is whether the federal judiciary should assume the power to change a state's legal definition of marriage for the moral better. This question comes too late for the gay rights debate, for virtually no one questions the Court's decision in Loving v. Virginia (1967), which rejected a state's ban on interracial marriage as inconsistent with the Fourteenth Amendment. That leaves us asking for two reasons, one about personal rights, and the other about institutional duties: Why should same-sex couples be denied the benefits of marriage that their tax dollars help pay for? And why should courts be responsible for deciding whether bans on interracial marriage are consistent with constitutional principles, but not whether bans on same-sex marriage are consistent with constitutional principles? The two big problems faced by opponents of marriage equality are, first, that longstanding political practice in the United pretext for religious claims. The pretextual character of the procreation argument is exposed by the fact that no one supports its plainest logical consequences. No one will say (in court or anywhere in the broader public sphere) that the law should compel unmarried women past 55 (who are presumed infertile) to stay single or that, if they do marry, their marriages aren't real marriages. Nor would we say this of married couples who choose to use contraceptives to avoid pregnancy. No one would require the country's men and women to declare their fertility or intent to procreate before issuing them marriage licenses. We can't say that no one would outlaw contraception or criminalize non-procreative sex (straight and gay), but no more than around 10% of adult Americans would do so,[9] and the Supreme Court's major holdings protecting the right to use contraceptives (Griswold v. Connecticut (1965) and Eisenstadt v. Baird (1972)) seem safely beyond the reach of the most determined culture warriors.

This doesn't mean that there's no argument against marriage equality. Contrast the unsuccessful procreation argument with the one advanced by Roy S. Moore, Chief Justice of the Alabama Supreme Court, in a very public letter to the governor of Alabama, urging him to remember that the state constitution recognizes marriage as a "sacred covenant, solemnized between a man and a woman." Chief Justice Moore further opined that, "The laws of this state have always recognized the Biblical admonition stated by our Lord," namely that, " 'God made them male and female. For this cause shall a man leave father and mother, and cleave to his wife; And they twain shall be one flesh. . . .' (Mark 10:6–9)."[10] True believers who happen to share the same faith often need no reason beyond a quotation or inference from scripture. They wouldn't have to justify opening marriage to older and infertile heterosexual couples while closing it to gay couples, beyond citing scripture's condemnation of homosexuality. If the Bible or other holy writing says something, the true believer believes it, period. The very fact that opponents of gay rights persist in secular arguments that have long proved to be unsuccessful suggests that these secular arguments

---

States—longstanding tradition, if you will—addresses both of these questions to the federal judiciary and, second, that the judges require answers in terms of non-sectarian values and secular views of whatever social facts might be in question. Maybe biblical principles do oppose American-style judicial review along with marriage equality. But biblical principles as such don't count as reasons in American courts.

   [9] For relevant statistics, see Frank Newport, "Americans, Including Catholics, Say Birth Control is Morally OK," *Gallup* (May 22, 2012), http://www.gallup.com/poll/154799/Americans–Including–Catholics –Say–Birth–Control–Morally.aspx?g_source=birthcontrol&g_medium=search&g_campaign=tiles.

   [10] Roy S. Moore, Chief Justice, Alabama Supreme Court, Letter to Hon. Robert Bentley, Governor of Alabama, Jan. 27, 2015, http://media.al.com/news_impact/other/Read%20Chief%20Justice%20Moore%20 letter.pdf.

are often covers for religious arguments—arguments that do work or that would work in a different place, the community of believers that the believers yearn to achieve. Whether a nation governed by the word of God would be a better place than the present United States is certainly an open question. It is the same question as whether Americans would be better off under a constitution different from their present constitution. We, your very fallible authors, are very far from either closing these questions or wanting them closed. But these are not our questions in this book. This book takes the American constitutional order for granted. Our questions here center on what the present U.S. Constitution provides with respect to gay rights.

Because the goodness and/or rightness of the U.S. Constitution is beyond our purview here, a corollary question is also out of bounds: whether, for constitutional purposes, the United States is one community. We mention this issue because opponents of gay rights have implicitly raised it. The dissenting justices in *Obergefell* claim that the Constitution lets each state "define marriage" as its voters will. Before *Obergefell*, two of these justices said (in *Lawrence*) the same thing about criminalizing same-sex sex: It should be up to each state. This states'-rights approach to gay sex and marriage implicitly questions any but the narrowest consequences of the American Civil War. Only one who denied the personhood of homosexuals could deny that the Fourteenth Amendment declares homosexuals born in the United States to be citizens of the United States and the state in which they choose to reside. The dissenting justices in *Obergefell* and *Lawrence* implicitly deny this last right, the rights of homosexual persons to reside where they will and to enjoy the rights enjoyed by other residents of their states. A states'-rights approach to same-sex marriage and sex would mean that a class of U.S. citizens would not be free (or as free as others) to move from state to state, for moving to some states would mean loss of either their liberty (including loss of voting rights in states that criminalize gay sex and disfranchise persons convicted of crimes) or their property (like marriage benefits under state and federal tax and pension laws, for which homosexuals, along with everyone else, work and pay). A states'-rights approach thus cancels the full meaning of the Fourteenth Amendment by permitting some states to deny some of their citizens the right to be treated equally with others.

One might try to square a states'-rights approach to gay rights with the Civil War Amendments by denying that homosexuals are a natural class of persons. One might analogize homosexuals to burglars. Burglars don't belong to a natural kind of thing; people who are burglars are born people, not burglars. Psychologically compulsive burglars aside, almost all burglars are persons who don't have to be burglars, but instead persons who *choose* to burgle. At least some of the dissenting justices in *Obergefell* and *Lawrence* would permit each state to say the same about homosexuals. A state's voters would have the constitutional authority to ignore the scientific community cited by Justice Kennedy in *Obergefell* and declare that some homosexuals are straights who elect to be gay and others are persons with a mental illness that inclines them toward a specific criminal activity. But the Civil War Amendments would lose much of their effectiveness if public opinion in each state were free to decide questions like what constitutes mental illness and the attributes of personhood. The dissenting justices in *Lawrence* and *Obergefell* would hardly let the states declare that members of any race lacked the attributes of personhood. Nor would the dissenting justices let the states treat any political creed as a sure sign of insanity. Why then leave the states free to declare homosexuality a mental illness—an abnormal condition that inclines its victims to a specific variety of criminal activity, namely, gay sex?

To this argument, one might respond that the generation of Americans that proposed and ratified the Civil War Amendments sought to protect not persons generally but only Americans of sub-Saharan African descent. But whatever else one might say about this argument, it would come far too late. Since 1886 when the Supreme Court declared business corporations persons protected by the Fourteenth Amendment (Santa Clara v. Southern Pacific), protections of that amendment have steadily expanded to include persons of all races, ethnicities, political persuasions, religions, and genders. The Court had not protected homosexuals as such until 1996 in *Romer*, but even before *Romer*, the Court assumed that the states needed reasons, however weak, for denying that homosexuals, as such, had rights. In Bowers v. Hardwick (1986), reprinted in Chapter 4, a 5–4 Court held that "the presumed belief of a majority of the electorate in Georgia that homosexual sodomy is immoral and unacceptable" constituted sufficient reason to allow the state to criminalize gay sex.[11] Later, in *Romer*, the Court began to change its opinion; preserving traditional sexual morality was now seen as "animus" against and "a bare . . . desire to harm a politically unpopular group."[12] But traditional morality was a reason in *Bowers*, and the question even in *Bowers* was why exclude homosexuals from protection under the Civil War Amendments given the many kinds of persons, artificial and natural, that those amendments now protected? By answering this question *Bowers* assumed it was a meaningful question, one that required an answer. That

---

11 Bowers v. Hardwick, 478 U.S. 186, 195 (1986).

12 Romer v. Evans, 517 U.S. 620, 632, 634 (1996).

is, *Bowers* took for granted the personhood of homosexuals, their membership in the community of persons assumed by the Civil War Amendments, and their right to challenge state governments under those amendments.

In view of the cultural divisions of which the gay rights debate is a major part, the question whether the United States ought to remain one nation may be reopened at some future point. But the culture war in America has yet to reach that point. No social movement of any consequence in America today (save perhaps the movement to end "birthright citizenship" for the children of undocumented immigrants) demands repeal of the Civil War Amendments, which ensure that all persons born in the United States are equally franchised and mobile members of one political community—all are free to relocate and exercise full and equal rights of citizenship wherever they want (and can afford) in the 50 states. Until there's a movement to repeal these rights of national citizenship or to exchange them for the right to establish enclaves that exclude other kinds of people, calls for states'-rights responses to issues like abortion and gay rights should be seen for what they are: fallback positions of those who are losing the national debate.

Fallback positions often fall short of what their advocates actually want. Pro-life forces who call for letting each state decide the abortion question have proved to be pro-lifers, not states' righters. They might be less unhappy with different abortion policies in different states, but they'll remain unhappy as long as any state permits abortions. One can see this in their support of the national Partial Birth Abortion Act of 2003, upheld by five erstwhile states'-rights justices in Gonzales v. Carhart (2007).[13] The same holds for opponents of gay rights. If they actually believed in a states'-rights approach to gay marriage, they would have opposed the federal Defense of Marriage Act that Congress enacted in 1996. To preclude Social Security and other federal benefits for same-sex couples married in the states, Section 3 of this act defined marriage as a legal union of one man and one woman. The Supreme Court declared this act unconstitutional, partly on states'-rights grounds, in U.S. v. Windsor (2013)[14] over the dissents of the same justices who would later call for a states'-rights approach in *Obergefell*.

Now to the central question of this chapter. As we've said, gay rights in America have advanced chiefly because opponents of gay rights have proved unable to make the kind of argument that would be required for denying gay

---

[13]   550 U.S. 124 (2007).

[14]   133 S.Ct. 2675, 2695–96 (2013).

rights. The requisite argument is comprised of value premises and factual premises (descriptive and causal) that are widely shared, not on narrowly held religious values and beliefs. And the usual arguments against gay rights, e.g., the procreation argument against same-sex marriage, are evidently pretextual arguments—covers for faith-based arguments. Our question in this chapter is whether the American practice of giving and exchanging non-sectarian reasons has a basis in the American founding. We shall show that it does.

II. COMMERCE AND RELIGION IN THE EARLY DECADES

Gordon Wood, the renowned historian of the American Founding, paints a mixed picture of the place of religion in the political thought of late eighteenth century America. On the one hand, the elites who led the move to a new constitution took for granted that commerce would be the nation's foundation. They considered no other alternative because the rampant commercialism of American society presented no other alternative. On the other hand, the masses of the founding period were deeply religious, and their faith asserted itself in two "Great Awakenings," one around the 1750s and the other around the turn of the 19th century. Yet, according to Wood, these Great Awakenings were expressions of an evangelical Protestantism that undermined the authority of religious establishments and mainstream denominations in favor of a more "individualistic faith." The Second Great Awakening was fused with a democratic and commercial ethic that elevated money-making ("trade") to social respectability and lowered the claims of non-economic distinctions like family lineage, elegant manners, and refined tastes. "Trade" also inspired a depreciation of ideas like "gentleman" and "honor" ("except of course in the South," says Wood). All levels of society, despite their pretentions, were increasingly seen as interested in the same thing: wealth, "the grand leveling principle."[15]

The Second Great Awakening spawned many private associations seeking moral reforms that ranged from ending slavery to ending poverty, drinking, and horse racing. These associations generally sought to make men and women moral by appealing ultimately to " 'that which gives the keenest edge to human ingenuity—self interest.' " The savings bank provided the model for this strategy. As men and women saved their money bit by bit and began to see the "progressive increase of the[ir] little capital," their "acquisitive instincts would be aroused," and once aroused they would prove "stronger than their instincts for

---

[15]   Gordon S. Wood, *The Radicalism of the American Revolution* (New York: Vintage, 1993), 342–44.

vice," proving self-interest to be "the best means of binding the nation together".[16]

This last observation is the most telling for our purposes. Americans who didn't subordinate religion to commerce (self-interest) inclined toward those faiths that minimized conflict between religion and commerce. Thus, elites like the Founding Fathers did subordinate religion to commerce in public affairs,[17] while ordinary Americans generally belonged to Protestant denominations that treated religion as a private matter of the individual's conscience and minimized conflict between salvation and the lawful pursuit of gain. The U.S. Constitution as written reflects this accommodation of religion to commerce. An examination of the constitutional text reveals the following:

(1) The Constitution grants no power to impose religious orthodoxy through law.

(2) The First Amendment prohibits Congress from (a) establishing a religion and (b) abridging the free exercise of religion.

(3) Article VI says that no religious test shall ever be required for any office or public trust under the authority of the United States (i.e., the national government).

(4) Article I gives Congress the power "to regulate commerce with foreign nations, and among the several states, and with the Indian tribes."

(5) Article VI also provides that federal laws pursuant to the Constitution shall be the supreme law of the land notwithstanding conflicts with the constitutions and laws of the several states.

With these features of the Constitution in mind, imagine a state banning "R" and "PG" movies on the strength of hard scientific evidence that movies with "R" and "PG" ratings weaken religious commitments that the state believes crucial to true well-being (i.e., the salvation) of her people. Hollywood film producers could claim that this law violates a federal policy of an open national market in "R" and "PG" films. This would be an example of commerce subordinating religion on those occasions when religious beliefs clashed with the government's secular aims, in this case a national entertainment market. The constitutional priority of economic values would not affect faiths that might be

---

[16] Ibid., 334–35.

[17] As Thomas Jefferson put it, "it does me no injury for my neighbor to say there are twenty gods or no God. It neither picks my pocket nor breaks my leg," *Notes on the State of Virginia,* Query 17 (1954), 159.

indifferent to what happens in the world outside the private beliefs of their members, for they would "not be of this world," so to speak. Nor would the constitutional priority of economic values affect faiths that might believe that God wills unrestrained capitalism or that wealth signifies God's favor. In any case, the constitutional priority of earthly goods affects only those religions that would use the criminal law to enforce their beliefs and call for a less fair, or a less secure, or a less prosperous nation in the name of God's will. It is these religions that invoke God's will as sufficient reason to criminalize gay sex and force homosexuals to work and pay taxes for the benefit of others while not themselves receiving the benefits afforded others.

III. EARTH-BOUND REASONING AND *THE FEDERALIST*

A quick tour through *The Federalist* will show that even though the Founding debate featured no issues of sexual morality, *Obergefell* and the other gay rights cases of recent years are consistent with the thinking of the framers about the nature of the Constitution as a whole, the importance of reason in public affairs, and the federal judiciary's role in protecting fundamental rights.

A. Introduction: The First *Federalist*

Hamilton, Madison, and Jay used the nom de plume "Publius" in authoring *The Federalist*, where they made arguments in support of ratifying the proposed constitution. By following their usage we can assume that they coauthored a coherent argument. We can also take our bearings from that argument, not their biographies or private motives. For no one can deliberate about reasons that people keep to themselves; nor can anyone ratify private motives as law. And we can test the relevance of that argument to the gay rights debate by including present-day phenomena and issues within its general terms and propositions. Thus, when Publius says a large republic is better than a small republic for handling the problem of faction, we can test that generalization by applying it to problems Publius didn't face, like the problems of racial and economic polarization.

The main points of the First *Federalist* for our purposes begin with Publius's positive understanding of what the Constitution is: the charter of a government established to work as a set of means for pursuing good things like the people's "liberty," "dignity," and "happiness."[18] In *Federalist* No. 40, Publius urges that constitutional provisions be construed as means to the ends for which constitutions are established (259–60). "Liberty" is among these good things, says Publius in the First *Federalist*, where he warns against forgetting that "the vigour of government is essential to the security of liberty" and that the interests of liberty and vigorous government "can never be separated." He calls for a new constitution precisely because the old constitution (the Articles of Confederation) was too weak to secure the people's liberty, dignity, and happiness (5–6). He assumes readers motivated by considerations that range from their private interest to patriotism (love of one's own people) and even philanthropy (love of humankind). He assumes readers who want to prove to all humanity that it's possible to establish good government from "reflection and choice," as opposed to being governed by "accident and force" (1, 6). These features of the First *Federalist*—an emphasis on "reflection and choice" and a view of strong government as means to "liberty"—will influence our judgment on whether the Constitution can admit a place for gay rights. Publius's emphasis on reason in government and his understanding of liberty should be contrasted with the dissents in *Obergefell* that ridicule "reasoned judgment" (Justice Scalia's) and reject the idea of liberty as a provision of government (Justice Thomas's).

B. The Ninth and Tenth *Federalist*

In *Federalist* Nos. 2–8 Publius argues mostly that a firm union of thirteen states will enable the country either to avoid foreign wars or to win them should they prove unavoidable. He argues also that a union of the thirteen states will make wars between the states less likely. In the Ninth *Federalist* he turns to the problem of domestic faction and insurrection. Looking at the history of Greece and Italy, he finds a tendency to domestic faction that condemns democracy to a "perpetual vibration between the extremes of tyranny and anarchy." He also says—note well—that if democracy can't avoid this fate, then the friends of liberty must abandon democracy as "indefensible" (51). This is a most important statement; it implies that for Publius (strikingly unlike the dissenting justices in *Obergefell*), democracy is not an end in itself—that a people's "liberty," "dignity," and "happiness" are higher values than majoritarian democracy.

---

[18] Alexander Hamilton, John Jay, and James Madison, *The Federalist*, Jacob E. Cooke, ed. (Middletown, CT: Wesleyan University Press, 1961), 6. We indicate citations to this edition of *The Federalist* with page numbers in parentheses. For analysis of the principal features of the American constitutional order as seen in *The Federalist*, see Barber and Fleming, *Constitutional Interpretation*, 35–55. We draw from that analysis here.

Publius goes on to maintain that hope for saving democracy from the ravages of domestic faction lies in the discoveries of a new science of politics. These discoveries include separation of powers, checks and balances, "courts composed of judges holding their offices during good behavior," and legislatures composed of elected representatives of the people. To this list he adds a further discovery of the new science of politics: the enlargement of the orbit of popular government (51–52). We see in the Tenth *Federalist* that this further discovery is especially important, for it is the necessary condition for the successful operation of checks and balances, representative legislatures, and the other institutions on Publius's list of new means for saving democracy. We see, in other words, that checks and balances and the rest can be expected to work only in a large republic, not in a small republic (63–64). Publius's move from several small republics to one large republic has implications for the kind of arguments that count in national political decision, including judicial decisions about constitutional meaning: The grounds of decision must be something that Americans in general can understand and appreciate. The very size of the country undermines religion as the foundation of civic morality because a big country means many religious denominations, leaving liberty, equality, security, and prosperity as the commitments that Americans generally share.[19] We note also that unlike the dissenting justices in *Obergefell*, Publius sees no conflict between democracy (i.e., democracy of the kind that's worth defending) and strong and politically independent courts.

Publius's famous Tenth *Federalist* picks up the theme of the Ninth *Federalist*: how to "break and control the violence of faction." This project is crucial, he says, because factious politics "have, in truth, been the mortal diseases under which popular governments have everywhere perished." By "faction" he means a group that pursues policies that are contrary either to the rights of individuals or to the permanent and aggregate interests of the community at large. And, he says, a faction can consist of either a minority or a majority of the community (56–57). This all-important definition of faction implies a crucial point: the ultimate standard for good government is not majority will. Publius is a friend of popular government, but popular government is not his highest political good. He is prepared to abandon popular government if it fails to avoid the injustices and disorders of historical democracies. As a friend of popular government, Publius seeks a government that will control the violence of faction at the same time that it conforms to the basic principles of popular government. For him conformity to majority will is not a sufficient condition for good government.

---

19   Storing, *What the Anti-Federalists Were For*, 23.

Then Publius sets forth his famous theory of how a large republic can control the violence of faction. An outline of the key points follows:

Control the violence of faction by either (1) curing the causes of faction or (2) controlling the effects of faction. We might:

I.   Cure the causes of faction by

     A.   destroying liberty or

     B.   destroying diversity ("giving to every citizen the same opinions, the same passions, and the same interests," 58).

Because (1) destroying liberty is worse than the disease and (2) destroying diversity is "impracticable," we can't hope to cure the causes of faction. We therefore turn to:

II.   Controlling the effects of faction

     A.   To control minority faction, we rely mainly on the "republican principle" (i.e., majority rule and a political culture suspicious of elites).

     B.   To control majority faction, we must prevent the impulse and/or the opportunity to form majority faction.

         (1)   Preventing the impulse and the opportunity to form majority faction is more likely in a republic rather than a pure democracy, and in a large republic rather than a small republic.

         (2)   Because it's much easier to form majority coalitions among a small number of interest groups, it's much easier to form majority faction in a small republic.

         (3)   Avoiding majority faction is more likely in a large rather than a small republic because the large republic will have a greater number of interest groups, and it's less likely that unjust policies can gain the support of a large number of interest groups.

         (4)   The large republic has the additional advantage of making more likely the election of competent and public-spirited representatives.

C. Interpreting the Tenth *Federalist*: The Large Commercial Republic

Martin Diamond observed some 50 years ago that, in the Tenth *Federalist*, Publius cannot just assume that movement from a small country to a large one will automatically produce the political pluralism that his solution to the problem of majority faction assumes.[20] A large territory with a large population could be the setting for political polarization along any number of lines, including race, wealth, and religion. Whether a nation's interest groups are sufficiently numerous or few will depend on how people see themselves politically. How will Americans think of themselves when they step into the voting booth? Will they vote as Catholics versus Protestants or as whites versus blacks or as rich versus poor? Or will they vote as members of the retail industry, or the transportation industry, or as physicians, or engineers, or autoworkers, or teachers? What makes Publius so sure Americans will see themselves chiefly in terms of narrow economic interests (of which there are many) and not in bi-polar terms like Catholics against Protestants, blacks against whites, and rich against poor?

A related problem is Publius's view of modern government's "principal task," which he says is regulating economic conflict. Economic conflict arises from "the various and unequal distribution of property," which constitutes "the most common and durable source of faction." But he also recognizes sources of social division other than economic conflict, like "a zeal for different opinions concerning religion, concerning government, and many other points." Class conflict, sectarian conflict, ideological conflict—any of these things can tear a society apart. Why doesn't Publius recognize the need to regulate them all? How can a government adequate to the people's liberty, dignity, and happiness regulate only economic conflict? Does Publius assume that, while the proposed national government will regulate economic conflict, the state governments will regulate sectarian and ideological conflict? This assumption would need explaining. If the states could handle the problem of majority religious and ideological factions, why couldn't they deal with majority economic factions? Does Publius contradict himself by implicitly relying on the states for major problems of social division while claiming they can't handle the problem of majority faction? And if he's right about the destructive potential of sectarian and ideological as well as economic conflict, his theory seems inadequate to the

---

[20] The following interpretation of Diamond's position is based on Martin Diamond, "The Federalist," in Leo Strauss and Joseph Cropsey, eds., *History of Political Philosophy* (Chicago, IL: University of Chicago Press, 1987), 659–79.

full range of problems that the nation may well face and that he himself identifies—problems of non-economic as well as economic conflict.

At this point we could either declare Publius's theory a failure or ask from what point of view or under what conditions it would be likely that (1) the large republic would be pluralist and not polarized and (2) regulating economic conflict at the national level would ameliorate non-economic divisions nationwide.

The state of affairs that Publius envisions in the Tenth *Federalist* is one in which political interest groups form and reform different social and legislative coalitions that exclude no stable minority for long. Diamond proposed that the people who belong in this picture must live in

(1) an urban-industrial society, for our picture is one of many political interest groups, and an urban-industrial society features many ways to make a living and pursue economic advancement. Where there are few paths to security and wealth, as in an agrarian society, there can't be many economic groups and therefore there can't be many political interest groups that define themselves in economic terms. A people who see their political interests in terms of their economic interests are more-or-less

(2) a materialistic people. They want coercive government to secure their physical security and promote their material well-being. If they care for the salvation of their souls as individuals, they won't insist that the government facilitate or compel the salvation of their neighbors' souls. This makes them appear

(3) religiously and ideologically tolerant. These people will be

(4) a democratic people in several ways. They will support the idea of **(a) equal economic opportunity** regardless of race, class, religion, and gender, lest the society polarize along these lines. They will value **(b) equal political opportunity** for the same reason. And because political power and economic power are largely in private hands, they will eventually value **(c) equal social opportunity**.

To avoid polarization and the politics of resentment, the typical citizen of this large commercial republic must have evidence that his or her achievements reflect more-or-less what he or she has been willing to work for. This evidence can only take the form of

(5) upward (or downward) mobility for people who start poor (or rich) and a fair distribution of wealth and status across lines of race, religion, and gender. A poor man who is black must know many blacks who are not poor in order to believe that racism isn't a major cause of his poverty. He must see poor people become rich and rich people become poor in order to feel that people generally have what they deserve to have by virtue of their personal efforts and talents. Such a society would also have to be

(6) a wealthy society, for much wealth would be needed to feed the economic ambition of everyone willing to work and to convince people that the system is basically fair in practice, not just theory. To this Diamond cautiously added that perhaps the wealth of this society would have to increase more-or-less indefinitely—that the society had to be committed to

(7) ever-expanding personal and national wealth. Diamond seemed less comfortable than some of his associates about this condition of the large commercial republic. Influenced by Nietzsche and Tocqueville, he wasn't sure a "growth" mentality was compatible with independent-minded and public-spirited citizenship. And Diamond may well have worried that a commitment to unending economic growth would eventually mean a global market whose institutions were beyond the control of any government, economic polarization at home (a growing income gap) caused by rampant technological change and capital flight to cheaper labor markets first at home and then abroad, and the violent resentment of anti-Western cultures targeted as markets for western goods and the ideas that come with them. This last prospect would be especially dangerous as technological innovation and interdependence created the profoundly vulnerable homeland revealed to Americans on September 11, 2001.

D. Beyond the Large Commercial Republic

We note a matter of the utmost importance. Though Diamond might not have agreed, the Constitution is not necessarily committed to the large commercial republic. The ends listed in the Preamble are not reducible to the features of the large commercial republic. The features of the large commercial republic may be necessary if the system outlined in the Tenth *Federalist* is to work, and these features can serve as conceptions of preambular ends like justice and the general welfare. But these would be mere conceptions of justice and the general welfare; and as mere conceptions, they may be false conceptions. Many of us will deny, for example, that well-being can be conceived mostly in terms of wealth and the faculties and opportunities for acquiring it. Have people been better off, and may they again be better off, in settings that define well-being largely in terms of spiritual achievement? Would people be happier, as recent studies suggest, with less economic mobility and more stable families, friendships, and communities?[21]

Optimism that a large commercial republic can serve peoples' interests and aspirations while promoting opportunity and advancement for all seems increasingly questionable. In recent decades, the gains of economic globalization have flowed overwhelmingly to the richest and best educated Americans, while many working class and middle income citizens have seen their prospects decline. Upward and downward mobility is not nearly as great as Americans have thought.[22] Political divisions now seem deeper, and the level of partisan discourse lower, than in many decades.

Assume the Constitution is what it says it is, an instrument designed to promote things like the peoples' welfare, and acknowledge the gap between any conception of well-being and the real thing, and you may conclude that people who are really well-off are people with the capacity to do what the founding generation did: assess their problems and fashion new institutions accordingly. Precisely because we can always be wrong in our conceptions of real goods and the means thereto, a constitution adequate to real ends will preserve the capacity for constructive social and governmental change—the very capacity on display for the world to see at the American Founding. Whether Americans still have this capacity for constitutional change is something we can seriously doubt, and we won't say more about this problem here.[23] But we will say that this element of national well-being—the capacity for constructive change—amends our understanding of the ends of government to include freedoms, conditions, practices, and attitudes incident to the processes of collective "reflection and choice"—i.e., some freedoms of speech, press, political association, religious association, academic inquiry and all that accompanies them, like political and social diversity and commitments to toleration and a politics of public reasonableness. Seen in this light, freedoms of speech, religion, and the rest are

---

[21] *See* Robert E. Lane, *The Loss of Happiness in Market Democracies* (New Haven, CT: Yale University Press, 2000).

[22] *See, e.g.,* Roland Bénabou and Jean Tirole, "Belief in a Just World and Redistributive Politics," *The Quarterly Journal of Economics*, vol. 121, no. 2 (May 2006), 699–746.

[23] For analysis of this problem, see Sotirios A. Barber, *Constitutional Failure* (Lawrence, KS: University Press of Kansas, 2014).

not mere limitations on our collective power as a people; they are elements of that power, for without them we can't pursue the ends of the Constitution, nor can we pursue real as opposed to merely apparent goods.

The American Constitution reflects this general view of the world and humans' place in it. An artifact of the Western tradition, the Constitution preserves an appreciation of human fallibility in the presence of higher authority (either God or nature), which is common to both the biblical and pagan branches of that tradition. An element of that tradition has been pride in a people's ability to acknowledge and provide for the fact that its beliefs and practices may be wrong. The larger community typically becomes aware of that fact through the agency of some dissenting individual or unpopular minority. Justice Kennedy makes the point in *Obergefell*: "[N]ew dimensions of freedom become apparent to new generations, often through perspectives that begin in pleas or protests and then are considered in the political sphere and the judicial process."[24] To this, he adds that the framers of the Constitution and the Fourteenth Amendment "did not presume to know the extent of freedom in all its dimensions, and so they entrusted to future generations a charter protecting the right of all persons to enjoy liberty as we learn its meaning."[25] Publius dramatizes the point: When individuals or minorities brave "the perils of the community's displeasure" and change the public's mind, the community honors them as benefactors or even heroes. Thus Publius alludes to Socrates in several places (see 63:425; 71:483). Because the West from the beginning has valued truth over convention and associated the dissenting individual with truth, the individual has had a potential for dignity. Recognition of this potential is reflected in American law, especially the Bill of Rights and the Civil War Amendments.

In sum, as listed in the Preamble, the ends of government are provisionally conceived as aspects of the large commercial republic (i.e., growth, equal opportunity, prosperity, fair distribution of wealth and opportunity, upward mobility, etc.). They include security for rights associated with truth seeking in political decision (like freedom of speech) and the administration of criminal and civil justice (like procedural due process). They involve respect for potential agents of the truth: individuals and minorities who can stand apart from conventional wisdom and teach the community something new and better.

---

[24] *Obergefell*, 135 S.Ct. at 2596.

[25] Ibid., 2628.

IV. JUDICIAL POWER IN A CONSTITUTIONAL DEMOCRACY

Publius's conception of judicial power is part of his understanding of what constitutional government seeks to accomplish: the reconciliation of popular government to objective standards of the common good and human rights. Publius presents himself as a "friend of popular government" or, as we would say, a friend of democracy. But he seeks much more than a democracy. He seeks a democracy that does the right and good thing more often than not, with the right and good thing determined by objective standards of rightness and goodness. This call for responsibility to objective standards is clear in several places in *The Federalist*. We've seen it in *Federalist* No. 9, where Publius is prepared to abandon democracy if it can't avoid its historical injustices and disorder. We've seen it in *Federalist* No. 10's famous definition of faction. We can see it also in the definition of "responsible government" that emerges in Publius's discussion of the Senate and the presidency. On occasions when "the interests of the people are at variance with their inclinations," he says, "it is the duty of the persons whom they have appointed to be the guardians of those interests, to withstand the temporary delusion, in order to give them time and opportunity for more cool and sedate reflection" (482–83). Elsewhere he says that on critical occasions when the people call for illicit measures that they will later regret, "how salutary will be the interference of some temperate and respectable body of citizens, in order to check the misguided career, and to suspend the blow meditated by the people against themselves, until reason, justice, and truth can regain their authority over the public mind" (425).

Publius says essentially the same thing in *Federalist* No. 78 when defending a strong and independent judiciary with the power of judicial review. Independent courts should not only maintain the Constitution's supremacy over ordinary acts of legislation, says Publius, they should also:

> guard the constitution and the rights of individuals from the effects of those ill humours which the arts of designing men, or the influence of particular conjunctures, sometimes disseminate among the people themselves, and which, though they speedily give place to better information and more deliberate reflection, have a tendency in the mean time to occasion dangerous innovations in the government, and serious oppressions of the minor party in the community (527).

A telling passage of *Federalist* No. 49 rejects an alternative to judicial review: Thomas Jefferson's proposal for convening constitutional conventions to decide constitutional controversies among the branches of the national government. These conventions "would inevitably be connected with the spirit of preexisting parties," says Publius, and this would ensure that the "passions" of the public would decide the issue, not "the reason of the public," though "the reason of the public alone ought to control and regulate the government" (342–43). This passage prefigures Publius's contention in *Federalist* No. 78 that in maintaining constitutional supremacy over ordinary legislation, the Court speaks for the public (525). Justices Kennedy, Souter, and O'Connor made basically the same claim in Planned Parenthood v. Casey (1992). There, they said that Americans' belief in themselves as "a Nation of people who aspire to live according to the rule of law . . . is not readily separable from their understanding of the Court invested with the authority to decide their constitutional cases and speak before all others for their constitutional ideals."[26]

Justice Scalia excoriated this statement as expressing a "Nietzschean vision" of judicial imperialism. He contrasted it with what he calls "the somewhat more modest role" that Publius envisions for the judiciary when he says in *Federalist* No. 78 that courts should exercise "neither FORCE nor WILL, but merely judgment."[27] But Scalia saw a modest role for the judiciary only because he ignored the message of *The Federalist* as a whole and because he implicitly distinguished Publius's "judgment" from *Casey*'s and *Obergefell*'s "reasoned judgment" and adopted a skeptical stance toward values like "liberty." Scalia denied that "liberty" refers to an idea whose nature can be progressively disclosed through reasoned judgment. For him, "liberty" meant no more than what the framers and ratifiers of the Fourteenth Amendment thought it meant and, he assumed, that meaning is found through historical research into the framers' and ratifiers' expectations, not reasoned judgment concerning the best understanding of the principles to which they committed us. That Publius holds otherwise is evident from his theory of responsible government and what he says about the standards for judicial decision.

Publius's theory of judicial power is thus part of his theory of responsible government. He sees the federal judiciary as one of the instruments for educating the public to its true interests. (*The Federalist* at 527; cf. 482, 424–25) Though he may well have disapproved specific decisions of the Court over the years—for he recognizes that judges often disagree among themselves and that they might sometimes overstep their boundaries and err about justice and other constitutional standards (see 22:143; 78:523, 526; 81:545)—he argues for a

---

26   505 U.S. 833, 868 (1992) (joint opinion).

27   Ibid., 996 (Scalia, J., dissenting).

strong judiciary with the power to declare legislative enactments unconstitutional (see 22:142–43 and No. 78 generally). And, as we have seen, in *Federalist* No. 9, Publius lists a strong judiciary as one of the institutions that would save popular government from its historical swings between anarchy and tyranny (51; see also 22:143–44; 64:436).

As for the sources of judicial criteria—i.e., where the courts should look for guidance when deciding cases—Publius says that "it is not with a view to the infractions of the Constitution only, that the independence of the judges may be an essential safeguard against the effects of occasional ill humors in the society." A strong judiciary is also "of vast importance in mitigating the severity and confining the operation" of "unjust and partial laws" that "injur[e] the private rights of particular classes of citizens" (78:528). Publius says this even before the adoption of a bill of rights (an action he warns against in *Federalist* No. 84). He thus looks beyond the written law to the principles of justice and reason themselves.

Publius's look to broader principles of political morality comes as no surprise given his general view of the Constitution as a means for reconciling public opinion to objective standards of political morality—standards antecedent to and above the written law and to which the legal system is responsible. As he says in a famous passage of *Federalist* No. 51: "Justice is the end of government. It is the end of civil society. It ever has been and ever will be pursued until it be obtained, or until liberty be lost in the pursuit. In a society under the forms of which [like majority rule] the stronger faction can readily unite and oppress the weaker, anarchy may as truly be said to reign as in a state of nature" (352). For a markedly different view of both the Constitution and the responsibility of judges, consider the opening thought of Chief Justice Roberts's dissent in *Obergefell*: "Petitioners make strong arguments rooted in social policy and considerations of fairness. They contend that same-sex couples should be allowed to affirm their love and commitment through marriage, just like opposite-sex couples. That position has undeniable appeal. . . . But this Court is not a legislature."[28]

V. CONCLUSION

We noted at the outset that issues of sexual morality and family law made up no part of the founding debate (or of the debate surrounding the adoption of the Fourteenth Amendment). Yet the Constitution does contain ideas that the

---

[28] *Obergefell*, 135 S.Ct. at 2611 (Roberts, C.J., dissenting).

Supreme Court has applied to issues of sexual morality and family law. Leading among these are the Fourteenth Amendment ideas of "liberty" and "equal protection." Liberty, said the Court almost a century ago, includes parents' right to direct the upbringing and education of their children, including sending their children to a parochial school and having them taught German. Liberty and equality, said the Court more recently, embrace the rights of married and unmarried couples to use contraceptives and the right of a black woman to marry a white man. And the Court said these things despite the complete lack of evidence that the framers of either the Constitution or the Fourteenth Amendment had parochial schools, the German language, contraceptives, or interracial marriage in mind. So a recent question has been whether liberty and equality guarantee gay rights, notwithstanding the fact that the framers of the Fourteenth Amendment had other things in mind. The Supreme Court has answered yes chiefly because opponents of gay rights have been unable to give the Court a good reason for denying such rights. This chapter has asked whether (1) the requirement of a reason, (2) the nature of the reason required, and (3) the Court's authority to assess the reason proffered—whether these things fairly represent the philosophy of the American Founding. To the extent that *The Federalist* speaks for the Founding, the answer is clearly yes. Opponents of gay rights may have compelling arguments, but they have yet to produce them, and they won't find them in the Constitution's origins.

CHAPTER 3

The Constitution's Protection of Fundamental Rights

A constitutional case arises when some individual, group, or corporation claims that some state or federal government has violated a constitutional right. The court hearing this claim will decide whether courts have given or should have given special protection to the claimed right and, if they have, whether the government has a sufficient reason for abridging the right. If the courts have given special protection to the claimed right in the past, or if the court concludes the judiciary should give the claimed right special protection, the court will require that the government give a strong reason for abridging the right. Reasons justifying acts of racial and religious discrimination have to be so strong that courts rarely uphold them. (Such acts are subject, in constitutional law jargon, to "strict scrutiny.") Not so with reasons justifying age discrimination, for example. Though many 18-year olds are far more responsible than many 21-year olds, states may forbid 18-year olds from drinking because it's not totally arbitrary to believe that 21-year olds are generally more responsible. (Such laws are subject to "rational basis scrutiny.") The question in gay rights cases is how strong the reason must be for laws that deny homosexuals the privileges and immunities, due process, and equal protection (in the form of antidiscrimination laws, marriage benefits and subsidies, and police-protected privacy) that others enjoy.

Gay rights have emerged in a historical context comprised of judicial decisions involving economic liberties, racial discrimination, and federalism; and judicial thinking in these other areas has influenced judicial thought about gay rights. Thus, one way to deny a federal constitutional right to gay marriage is to claim that the Constitution leaves family law (and the definition of marriage) to the states. Another way is to claim that courts should treat gay rights as they now treat some economic liberties: allow the states to regulate for reasons that may be unconvincing but not altogether beyond plausibility (see Williamson v. Lee Optical, discussed in this chapter). Thus, John Finnis, a leading moral philosopher of our era, fears that gay marriage will lead to an industry that employs surrogates to produce babies for sale to gay couples.[1] Though this result is far-fetched and, indeed, forbidden under existing law, no one will claim that it's inconceivable. A baby industry could materialize, and that's enough for Finnis to deny homosexuals the enjoyment of rights (like marriage subsidies) that their tax dollars help pay for. Alternatively, one way to argue for a federal constitutional right of gays and lesbians to marry is to compare discrimination against gays and lesbians to discrimination on the basis of race.

To understand the gay rights cases, therefore, we must first attend to some of the Supreme Court's decisions regarding economic liberties, racial discrimination, and federalism. Then we must consider some of the Court's decisions protecting personal liberties besides economic liberties, like the right to intimate association, the right to decide whether to terminate a pregnancy, and the right to marry.

The Fourteenth Amendment includes three clauses that serve as textual bases for protecting fundamental liberties: the Privileges or Immunities Clause, the Due Process Clause, and the Equal Protection Clause:

> No State shall make or enforce any law which shall abridge the privileges or immunities of citizens of the United States; nor shall any State deprive any person of life, liberty, or property, without due process of law; nor deny to any person within its jurisdiction the equal protection of the laws.

The Privileges or Immunities Clause might seem to be the most promising textual basis for protecting fundamental liberties of a substantive nature, like the freedoms of speech and religion. The Due Process Clause speaks of "due process of law," which might seem to be limited to guaranteeing that the government must follow processes established under existing law, whatever the law is. That is, it might permit the government to deprive anyone of liberty, provided that it follows prescribed processes for doing so. Finally, the Equal Protection Clause speaks of "equal protection of the laws," which might appear to be limited to assuring equal protection under existing laws, whatever they are. That is, it might permit the government to treat everyone equally badly.

We shall discuss two topics related to the federal judiciary's protection of fundamental rights: first, the "incorporation" of liberties specified (or "enumerated") in the Bill of Rights so that they apply not only to the national

---

government but also to the states, and second, the protection of "unenumerated" substantive liberties against encroachment by either the national government or the state governments.

I. NATIONALIZATION OF THE BILL OF RIGHTS

Shocking as it may seem, before the 1930s a local sheriff could hire and fire deputies and office workers solely on the basis of their religion or political affiliation without fear of being sued in federal court. Once upon a time, in other words, Americans had no federal constitutional rights of speech and religion against *all* of their governments; federal constitutional rights applied only against the *national* government. The Supreme Court case that established this principle was Barron v. Baltimore (1833), and the reason, essentially, was that the framers of the Bill of Rights did not intend it to limit the state governments. As a technical matter, *Barron* has never been overruled, yet almost all of the Bill of Rights now applies to the states. The Court accomplished this result step-by-step over a period of several generations through a process called "incorporation." Most of the Bill of Rights now limits state governments because the Due Process Clause of the Fourteenth Amendment limits state governments, and the Court has *incorporated* the specific rights of the Bill of Rights *into* the Due Process Clause of the Fourteenth Amendment. Strictly speaking, therefore, we have no federally secured freedom of religion against the local sheriff. What we have is a federally secured right of *due process* against the sheriff, *and* that right of due process *incorporates* the religious freedoms listed in the First Amendment. A nationalized bill of rights comports with the framers' view—set forth in *Federalist* No. 10 and discussed in Chapter 2—that the national government is a better government for protecting rights than the state governments. The superiority of the national government in this respect remains the generally received moral of the Civil War and the Civil War Amendments, along with the subsequent movements for Civil Rights, Women's Rights, and now Gay Rights.

Support for a nationalized bill of rights doesn't mean support for each and every Supreme Court decision regarding the nature and meaning of any particular right. The case for nationalizing the Bill of Rights leaves many claims unsettled. Consider the claim that married couples have a right to use contraceptives (see Griswold v. Connecticut (1965), discussed in this chapter). The secular nature of the American Founding (see Chapter 2) would favor such a right *if* the reason for outlawing contraception were sectarian in nature, but not for an honest secular reason. Evidence that non-procreative sex caused moral and psychological harm might not be a dispositive reason for banning contraception, but it would be a *constitutionally admissible reason*, one the federal courts would weigh against reasons on the other side. Thus, you can believe that there is one set of basic rights that all Americans should enjoy against all of their governments without committing yourself to one position on what specific rights we have and the scope of each and every right.

If the slavery controversy and the Civil War proved anything, however, they proved the contention of *The Federalist* that the national government was a better repository of individual rights than the states. Yet states' rights continued to have a powerful hold on the American constitutional consciousness, even in the generation after the Civil War, and a 5–4 majority of the Court in *The Slaughterhouse Cases* (1873) ignored the larger message of the War and eviscerated the Privileges or Immunities Clause of the Fourteenth Amendment. "Privileges or immunities" of U.S. citizenship should have meant—was intended by the Reconstruction Congress to embrace—important human rights like speech, religion, and property, arguably of the kind claimed by the Butchers Benevolent Association in *Slaughterhouse*. The Court held otherwise, however, on states'- rights grounds. In later years the Court repaired most of the damage by using the Due Process Clause of the Fourteenth Amendment to protect substantive rights that should have fallen under the Privileges or Immunities Clause. Economic liberties were the first to be incorporated into the Due Process Clause. Before we discuss cases involving economic liberties, let's examine the distinction between *substantive due process* and *procedural due process*.

II. ARGUMENTS FOR SUBSTANTIVE DUE PROCESS

The Due Process Clause appears in two places: the Fifth Amendment and the Fourteenth Amendment. When Justice Miller addressed the due process claim of the butchers in *Slaughterhouse*, he alluded to the Due Process Clause of the Fifth Amendment. The Fifth Amendment clause applies only to the national government, as Chief Justice Marshall said some 40 years earlier in *Barron*, but Miller assumed that the *meaning* of "due process of law" was the same wherever it appeared. Thus, he consulted the meaning of the Fifth Amendment right in determining the meaning of the Fourteenth Amendment right. And, said Miller in effect, "due process" is a *procedural* guarantee, not a substantive guarantee. It doesn't say the government can't take something from you; it just indicates *how* government must go about such deprivations. Government must reach such decisions in certain ways, and those ways constitute "due process."

At that point in the nation's history (with the possible exception of Dred Scott v. Sandford (1857), which we don't discuss in this book) the Due Process Clause was seen as addressed to the executive and judicial departments of government, not to the legislative department. It instructed executive officials not to arrest people without reason to believe they had violated pre-existing law. It instructed courts not to convict people without fair trials. The Due Process Clause was *not* thought to be addressed to the legislatures. It didn't say that they had to pass reasonable laws. It didn't forbid passage of arbitrary laws—laws unconnected to any reasonable view of the public interest. The butchers in *Slaughterhouse* were using the Due Process Clause in this unconventional way. They charged that the legislature of Louisiana had reached an unjust result—that it had established an unjust monopoly, a monopoly without reasonable justification in the public interest. Note well that the Court in *Slaughterhouse* didn't decide whether the Louisiana legislature had an adequate reason for granting the monopoly. The Court didn't address that question because the Court felt that the Due Process Clause didn't require the legislature to justify its policies. The butchers had a different view; they were saying that whenever a legislature restricts someone's liberty—as laws regulating conduct do—the legislature has to have a reason. The butchers were also saying that the legislature must *satisfy a court* that the law serves some reasonable view of the public interest. The butchers' view is now called "substantive due process": the requirement that government show a court that there's *a reason*, respectable and even sometimes compelling, to believe that the law will benefit the community as a whole.

Justice Miller dismissed this understanding of the Due Process Clause with little comment; he'd simply never seen it before. And since his day, many judges and scholars have dismissed substantive due process as an intellectual and even a moral mistake, useful, they say, mainly to judges who would manipulate the law to their liking, contrary to the will of democratically-elected legislatures. Justice Clarence Thomas takes this position in his dissent in *Obergefell*. Despite Miller's opinion, substantive due process was to return in cases after *Slaughterhouse*. At first it protected the liberty to contract, as in Lochner v. New York (1905); then it protected the rights of parents to direct the upbringing and education of their children, as in Meyer v. Nebraska (1923) and Pierce v. Society of Sisters (1925). It went on to protect the substantive liberties of the First Amendment, like freedoms of speech and religion. And more recently, as we'll see below, courts have used substantive due process to protect a group of rights connected to matters of personal autonomy, including intimate association, abortion, and marriage (for both opposite-sex and same-sex couples).

The controversial nature of many of these decisions, the apparent illogic of finding substantive rights in an ostensibly procedural guarantee, and resentment over judicial impositions on democratic choice have combined to condemn substantive due process in many quarters, progressive as well as conservative. But good arguments support using the Due Process Clause to protect substantive rights. These are general arguments. They have little bearing on whether any particular claim of substantive right is a valid one. You can hold *for* substantive due process rights in general and still hold that there is no valid right to decide whether to terminate a pregnancy, for example. But if you hold *against* substantive due process rights in general, you have no federal constitutional complaint against an anti-Catholic legislature that would close parochial schools, as the democratically-elected government of Oregon once tried to do (see *Pierce*).

The first argument for substantive due process is limited to American constitutional law and assumes that *Slaughterhouse* was wrongly decided. The argument is that substantive due process enabled the Court to correct *Slaughterhouse*'s mistaken theory of the Privileges or Immunities Clause. Instead of overruling *Slaughterhouse* and restoring the Privileges or Immunities Clause as a guarantee of important substantive rights against the states, the Court has largely achieved the same result by incorporating substantive liberties into the Due Process Clause.[2]

Stronger arguments for finding substantive rights in the Due Process Clause begin by noting that the guarantee of due process is a guarantee of due process *of law*. As we go through these arguments, keep in mind what's involved in a substantive claim under the Due Process Clause. The right in question is not simply a right, say, to use contraceptives or liberty to contract; it's a right to a reason from the government for restricting these liberties—a weak but possible reason, a plausible reason, or even a compelling reason, depending on the liberty in question. The Supreme Court has never held any substantive liberty to be absolutely beyond restriction; it has always held that under some circumstances

---

[2]   Dissenting in Saenz v. Roe (1999), Justice Thomas hints that he would reject Miller's theory of the Privileges or Immunities Clause to revive that clause and thus to eliminate the need to use the Due Process Clause to protect substantive rights. Thomas would then cite Corfield v. Coryell (1825) and limit substantive rights to those that the framers had concretely in mind as "fundamental." This strategy would enable Thomas to exclude the expanded right to travel that *Saenz* declared. It would also enable him to exclude rights that protect contraception, abortion, and gay sex and marriage. Concurring alone in McDonald v. Chicago (2010), Thomas found handgun ownership in the home a fundamental right protected by the Privileges or Immunities Clause.

or for some reasons any liberty can be abridged. So, due process has everything to do with *giving reasons*. Procedural due process would guarantee that government will not take a person's life, liberty, or property without sufficient reasons to believe that he or she has in fact violated some validly enacted, pre-existing, and generally applicable law.

Substantive due process would guarantee that a generally applicable law is not an arbitrary enactment, but one that reasonable people can believe is in the public interest. There's nothing strange about this guarantee. In the West since before the time of Socrates, *law* has been connected with *justifying reason*—that is, reason to believe that some rule is in the *public interest, not some mere special interest.* And this connection with reason is one justification for substantive due process: a law that is clearly arbitrary—admittedly not in the public interest—is not constitutional. An enactment clearly not in the public interest is not a law under our Constitution because the law-making power of our Constitution explicitly serves the purposes set forth in the Preamble, and these purposes are *public purposes.* The Constitution thus grants power to regulate commerce for such things as *the general welfare*, not the partial welfare. It authorizes the powers to declare and wage war for the *common defense*, not for the advancement of some part of the community at the expense of others. Of course, power can always be used to advance some group or class at the expense of others, but that's just another way of saying that power can be abused, and no one claims that power can be *legitimately* abused. Moreover, few exercises of power are beyond controversy, and belief in some objective "public interest" may be a fairy tale. But these considerations don't alter the principle of no power—that is, no legitimate power—to serve anything but the public interest, and if the public interest is truly a fairy tale, constitutionalism and constitutional democracy are parts of that fairy tale.

A closely related justification for charging the courts with reviewing the reasonableness of legislative enactments is the Constitution's instrumental nature. American constitutionalists believe that the people establish governments for ends like those listed in the Preamble of the Constitution: the common defense, the general welfare, the blessings of liberty, and so forth. *The Federalist* defended the Constitution as an instrument of its ends, and the Declaration of Independence describes popular government generally in instrumental terms. If instrumentalism is a correct view of our institutions, then we can say that laws that clearly defeat their justifying ends are not constitutional because no democratic constitution would authorize such laws, and the U.S. Constitution is no exception.

Of course, the problem with this kind of thinking is that people regularly disagree about whether a given enactment or policy is likely to succeed or even whether its purported aim is its real aim. Was the motivation for the Second Iraq War really security from terrorism or was it oil or cover for a domestic agenda, including privatized Social Security, that couldn't make it politically on its own? Is Obamacare designed to reform the present system of private health insurance, or is it a calculated step toward socialized medicine in the form of Medicare for all? Would either privatized Social Security or Medicare for all be better for all of our people or just some of them? Given disputes like these, if a law must be supportable by reasons everyone can respect, there will be very few real laws. One way to mitigate this difficulty is to say that law must generally be seen not necessarily as a good law but as a law enacted in good faith—that is, as a good-faith, if wrong-headed, pursuit of the common defense or the general welfare. When the community begins to divide into partisan camps that are unable to see each other's policies as good-faith (if wrongheaded) attempts to serve public purposes, the political culture is changing from one that can support constitutional democracy to one that can't—for the Constitution does seem to guarantee that restraints on liberty will flow only from good-faith attempts to serve the public interest.

III. *SLAUGHTERHOUSE*'S EVISCERATION OF THE PRIVILEGES OR IMMUNITIES CLAUSE

Most constitutional scholars think *Slaughterhouse* a mistake. But maybe the Fourteenth Amendment was a mistake—a well-intentioned but overreaching attempt to change a federal system that is essential to freedom in America—and *Slaughterhouse* was an attempt to mitigate *that* mistake. This evidently was what Justice Miller thought. Was he right? Let's see:

Slaughterhouse answered four constitutional questions. Did the monopoly violate the butchers' rights under:

(1) the Thirteenth Amendment (which abolished slavery)?

(2) the Privileges or Immunities Clause of the Fourteenth Amendment?

(3) the Equal Protection Clause of the Fourteenth Amendment?

(4) the Due Process Clause of the Fourteenth Amendment?

The Court dismissed claims (1) and (3) as related claims. It argued not from an extended reflection on the nature of freedom and equal rights but from the concrete intentions behind the Civil War Amendments, the subjects of which were the plight of recently freed African-Americans in the southern states. The Court's narrow view of the Equal Protection and Due Process Clauses has not survived in American constitutional law, as we've seen in the incorporation debate and as we'll see further in cases involving so-called "unenumerated rights," like the liberties to contract and to use contraceptives.

What has survived is Miller's view of the Privileges or Immunities Clause. Via a strained theory of "dual citizenship," Miller tried to minimize the impact of the Civil War on the constitutional system by declaring the states answerable in federal court only for a limited set of relatively uncontroversial rights regarding the public's access to the national government and its facilities (ports, post offices, etc.) and agencies.[3] In dissent, Justice Field saw the Civil War and the constitutional amendments in its aftermath as changing the system that Marshall had described in *Barron*; henceforth, Field believed, the national government should secure the important civil rights and liberties of Americans generally against their state and local governments. Our government today is to a large extent what Field envisioned, thanks to the nationalization of the Bill of Rights and the social and economic changes that made a nationalized bill of rights a compelling idea.

Justice Miller saw this potential in the Fourteenth Amendment, but he rejected it as a mistake. To avoid this mistake he effectively read the Privileges or Immunities Clause out of the amendment, for, as Justice Field pointed out, the rights that Miller would have protected needed no new amendment. These so-called "rights of national citizenship" were implicit in the very existence of the national government and in the supremacy of its laws over those of the states. To some extent Field may have exaggerated the status of these rights prior to the Fourteenth Amendment, but his basic point remains untouched: the people who debated the Fourteenth Amendment in Congress and the country thought that more was involved than the narrow "rights of national citizenship" that Miller described. According to Field, the majority's interpretation reduced the Fourteenth Amendment to a "vain and idle enactment, which accomplished nothing, and most unnecessarily excited Congress and the people on its passage." Whether Miller or Field was right is largely the same question as that of the incorporation debate. The logical, cultural, and constitutional considerations that support a nationalized bill of rights support Field's view of the Privileges or Immunities Clause.

---

[3] "*Relatively* uncontroversial" doesn't always mean unimportant, as the right to travel affirmed in *Saenz* proves.

IV. SUBSTANTIVE DUE PROCESS FROM *LOCHNER* TO THE PRESENT

Having gutted the Privileges or Immunities Clause in (appropriately) *Slaughterhouse*, the Court soon began to use the Due Process Clause as the basis for protecting fundamental rights. As noted above, the text of this clause might make it seem a problematic basis for protecting substantive rights. The joint opinion of Justices O'Connor, Kennedy, and Souter in Planned Parenthood v. Casey (1992) begins by acknowledging that "a literal reading of the [Due Process] Clause might suggest that it governs only the procedures by which a State may deprive persons of liberty." On that reading, the controlling word in the Clause would be "process." But, *Casey* continues: "at least since Mugler v. Kansas (1887), the Clause has been understood to contain a substantive component as well." On this reading, as *Casey* puts it, "[t]he controlling word in the case before us is 'liberty.' "[4] And so it is today.

We shall distinguish three phases in judicial protection of fundamental rights or liberties: (1) from 1887 to 1937; (2) from 1937 to 1973; and (3) from 1973 to the present.[5]

A.   1887 to 1937: From the *Lochner* Era to *Parrish*

During the first phase, the era of Lochner v. New York (1905), the Court aggressively protected economic liberties—such as liberty to contract—along with personal liberties—such as the liberty of parents to direct the upbringing and education of their children—without distinguishing between the two. Both were seen as essential liberties to be protected under the Due Process Clauses. Meyer v. Nebraska (1923) gave a classic formulation concerning liberty during the *Lochner* era:

> While this Court has not attempted to define with exactness the liberty thus guaranteed, the term has received much consideration and some of the included things have been definitely stated. Without doubt, it denotes not merely freedom from bodily restraint but also the right of the individual to contract, to engage in any of the common occupations of life, to acquire useful knowledge, to marry, establish a home and bring up children, to worship God according to the dictates

---

[4]   505 U.S. 833, 846 (1992).

[5]   In this section, we draw from James E. Fleming and Linda C. McClain, "Liberty," in *The Oxford Handbook of the U.S. Constitution,* Mark Tushnet, Mark A. Graber, and Sanford Levinson, eds. (New York: Oxford University Press, 2015), 479, 484–89.

of his own conscience, and generally to enjoy those privileges long recognized at common law as essential to the orderly pursuit of happiness by free men. Slaughter-House Cases [1873]; Yick Wo v. Hopkins [1886]; Minnesota v. Barber [1890]; Allgeyer v. Louisiana [1897]; Lochner v. New York [1905]; Twining v. New Jersey [1908]; Truax v. Raich [1915]; Adams v. Tanner [1917]; Truax v. Corrigan [1921]; Adkins v. Children's Hospital [1923].[6]

Note that most of the liberties listed in the paragraph above are not "enumerated" in the text of the Constitution. Most of the liberties that are enumerated—freedom of speech and freedom of religion—are listed in the first eight amendments (the Bill of Rights) and as such (according to *Barron*) are secured only against the national government. Most of these liberties have now been "incorporated" into the Due Process Clause of the Fourteenth Amendment and made applicable to the state governments.

But *Meyer* conceived liberty more generally as including not only the things that have been either enumerated somewhere in the Constitution or "definitely stated" in the Court's precedents, but also "those privileges long recognized at common law as essential to the orderly pursuit of happiness by free men."[7] Here the *Meyer* Court prefigured later formulations of the due process inquiry such as those in Palko v. Connecticut (1937) ("implicit in the concept of ordered liberty") and Loving v. Virginia (1967) ("essential to the orderly pursuit of happiness by free men").[8] Still more abstractly, *Meyer* intimated a fundamental theory of liberty—of "the relation between the individual and the state"—as prohibiting the state from "submerg[ing] the individual and develop[ing] ideal citizens."[9] Two years later, Pierce v. Society of Sisters (1925) articulated this theory of liberty as forbidding the state to "standardize" its children by treating them as "the mere creature[s] of the state" to be molded into its vision of ideal citizens.[10] Here the Court clearly conceived liberty as an abstract principle, not a concrete historical practice or a list of specific historical applications.

Meyer and *Pierce* upheld the right of parents to direct the upbringing and education of their children by striking down, respectively, a state statute prohibiting the teaching of any modern language other than English in any public or private grammar school and a state statute requiring parents to send

---

[6] 262 U.S. 390, 399 (1923).

[7] Ibid., 399.

[8] Palko v. Connecticut, 302 U.S. 319, 325 (1937); Loving v. Virginia, 388 U.S. 1, 12 (1967).

[9] 262 U.S. at 401–02.

[10] 268 U.S. 510, 534–35 (1925).

their children between the ages of eight and sixteen, with limited exceptions, to public schools rather than private schools.

Justice Rufus Peckham's opinion for the majority in *Lochner* ranks as one of the most infamous opinions in Supreme Court history. This explains Chief Justice Roberts's strenuous attempt to portray the majority opinion in *Obergefell* as a reprise of *Lochner*. The question in *Lochner* was whether New York could impose a maximum ten-hour day and sixty-hour week on bakers without violating the liberty to contract that the Court held guaranteed by the Due Process Clause of the Fourteenth Amendment. The New York law was probably motivated by the desire to achieve for the bakers the sixty-hour week they were unable to achieve for themselves at the bargaining table with management. The reason the bakers couldn't achieve a sixty-hour week by themselves was that management had greater bargaining power. Peckham let it be known at the outset of his opinion that the Court would not accept a "mere labor law"—that is, an act of the state legislature giving the bakers what they couldn't get on their own at the bargaining table. Peckham took this position because he believed with the free-marketeers of his day (and ours) that bargaining power amounted to property lawfully earned, and that using law to equalize bargaining power was using force to steal property from one party and give it to another. Peckham also recognized, however, that even if a "mere labor law" was a kind of theft, private property could be regulated if the state had a legitimate reason—that is, if the state could show that the regulation served a good that was important to the general public. So the state gave the Court its reasons—mainly, to protect the health of bakers—and Peckham looked at the evidence and pronounced this reason a "pretext" for "other motives," that is, *a phony reason*. The Court seemed to fear that upholding such legislation under the police power would put the nation on a slippery slope that would ultimately permit "the supreme sovereignty of the State to be exercised free from constitutional restraint."[11]

In dissent, Justice Harlan argued that the Court was wrong to doubt the state's motive. He contended that since a reasonable person could see the law as a good-faith effort to protect the bakers from overexposure to the dirty air of bakeries, the Court should uphold the law. In a separate dissent, Justice Holmes said, in effect, that the Court was wrong to see the Constitution as committed to a free-market philosophy that regarded "mere labor laws" as a form of theft. He said the Constitution enacted no particular economic theory, that the Constitution was "made for people of fundamentally differing views," and that

---

[11]   198 U.S. 45, 56, 64 (1905).

the Court should leave economic policy to popularly elected legislatures, as long as they acted within traditionally reasonable limits.

Notwithstanding Holmes and his many followers (like Chief Justice Roberts in dissent in *Obergefell*), the Constitution may *not* be made for people with fundamentally differing views. Many people, from Social Darwinists and classical Marxists to some fundamentalist Christians, Jews, and Muslims reject the American Constitution for different reasons, like the Constitution's separation of church and state. Moreover, notwithstanding Harlan and his followers, the Constitution does seem to promise restrictions on liberty only for good-faith reasons, and one can reasonably doubt that New York's reason was a good-faith reason. Judges who won't examine the stated reasons of legislatures invite transparently phony reasons or "pretexts" (as *Lee Optical*, to be discussed, arguably shows).

Whether Holmes and Harlan were right in their criticisms, Peckham was wrong in his failure to see the legitimacy of "mere labor legislation." Recalling our analysis of *Federalist* No. 10, we can see that the Constitution can't work if the nation is economically polarized, or if people lack equal economic opportunity, upward economic mobility, and a general sense that their economic station more-or-less fairly reflects the effort they've been willing to make. These conditions are impossible if government sees "labor legislation" as theft and permits the greater bargaining power of the few to truncate the life chances of the many.

In West Coast Hotel v. Parrish (1937), at the height of the confrontation between President Franklin Roosevelt and the Supreme Court concerning the constitutionality of the New Deal, the Court repudiated the *Lochner* era and therewith aggressive judicial protection of economic liberties under the Due Process Clauses. The Court instead began to apply what has come to be known as "rational basis scrutiny" in deciding the constitutionality of economic regulations: "regulation which is reasonable in relation to its subject and is adopted in the interests of the community is due process."[12] Applying this standard, the Court upheld a state minimum wage law against the challenge that it violated liberty of contract. In justifying this shift, the Court took judicial notice of "recent economic experience" during the Great Depression. It stated that "the liberty safeguarded [by the Constitution] is liberty in a social organization which requires the protection of law against the evils which menace the health, safety, morals and welfare of the people," and it concluded that

---

[12]   300 U.S. 379, 391–92 (1937).

"[e]ven if the wisdom of [legislative] policy be regarded as debatable and its effects uncertain, still the Legislature is entitled to its judgment."[13]

Despite *Parrish*'s repudiation of the *Lochner* era, Peckham was hardly a zealous free-marketeer. He assumed that, indeed, the state *could* regulate property when such regulation was in the public interest. Read fairly, the message of *Lochner* is that the property to which we are entitled—property that government actively protects with taxes extracted from the entire community—is property whose possession and use contributes to the community's benefit. *Lochner* implies further that the state can legitimately regulate property when used in ways that harm the public. This part of *Lochner* (at least on its face) resonates with the opinion of Chief Justice Hughes in *Parrish:* that the liberty we have is "liberty in a social organization which requires the protection of law against the evils which menace the health, safety, morals, and welfare of the people."

Hughes and Peckham disagreed in two key respects, however. One involved unequal bargaining power. Hughes assumed that the economy left Elsie Parrish few opportunities for employment at a decent wage and that the West Coast Hotel was using its unequal bargaining power to force a choice on her: either starve or work for bare subsistence or even less than bare subsistence. Hughes assumed that many other women of Oregon were in the same situation as Elsie Parrish. Under this circumstance, he concluded, Oregon could pass what Peckham would have called a "mere labor law."

The second point of disagreement between Hughes and Peckham was who was to decide the need for such legislation. Peckham had insisted on the Court's careful review of the law to determine whether the legislature had a good reason, ruling out the redress of unequal bargaining power as a reason. Hughes, by contrast, argued that the Court should give the legislature benefit of all reasonable doubts, that the Court should relax its understanding of what counted as an admissible reason to regulate business, and that redressing unequal bargaining power was an admissible reason.

Although it may not have been clear from *Parrish* in 1937, the Court left undisturbed the cases from the *Lochner* era protecting personal liberties (such as the right to direct the upbringing and education of children in *Meyer* and *Pierce*) as distinguished from economic liberties (such as liberty to contract in *Lochner*). Ultimately the Court built upon the former cases from 1965 to the present in protecting substantive personal liberties, including those of gay men and lesbians.

---

[13] Ibid., 391, 399.

B. 1937 to 1973: From *Parrish* to *Roe*

We turn now to the second phase, from 1937 (*Parrish*) to 1973 (*Roe*). *Parrish* was decided at a time when the Great Depression had discredited the free-market thinking behind decisions like *Lochner*. So it's understandable how future courts could have settled on an even more deferential version of what Hughes said in *Parrish*. The high-water mark of this judicial deference came eighteen years after *Parrish* in Justice Douglas's opinion for the Court in Williamson v. Lee Optical (1955). *Lee Optical* is a case of special importance in the gay rights debate because the approach to economic liberties in that case is the model of due process analysis for opponents of gay rights, as we saw in Chief Justice Roberts's *Obergefell* dissent.

In *Lee Optical*, Justice Douglas strained to formulate legitimate governmental interests that legislators might have thought would be served by what evidently was a naked case of special-interest legislation demanded by a powerful lobby in Oklahoma to ensure profits that they didn't deserve, i.e., profits at the expense of competitors who could legitimately produce and repair eyeglasses at a lower cost to consumers. The trial court in this case held that it was unreasonable on grounds of health for the Oklahoma legislature to forbid opticians from replacing broken lenses without prescriptions from either ophthalmologists or optometrists. The Supreme Court rejected the trial court's reasoning. Douglas came close to announcing that the Court would no longer review the reasonableness of economic legislation even if the laws seemed as needless, wasteful, and logically inconsistent as this one. Abuses of legislative power must be left to the electorate to remedy, not the courts, said Douglas.

But Douglas (at least officially) did not altogether abandon the old principle that restraints on economic liberty required justifying reasons—the principle that constitutional government has no power not dedicated to the common good. So he came up with hypotheses concerning the legitimate governmental interests that the legislature conceivably might have thought the law served: maybe the Oklahoma legislature wanted to encourage frequent vision examinations, or maybe it wanted frequent checks to catch unsuspected diseases of the eyes. It didn't matter that the state didn't give these reasons or even that these reasons didn't actually motivate the Oklahoma legislation. They were *possible* reasons for the legislation, and the existence of *any possible* reason, albeit weak, was enough to uphold the law. This is the approach of Chief Justice Roberts, Justice Scalia, Professor Finnis, and other opponents of gay marriage. If there is any reason for denying gay marriage, whether the "reason" actually moves the legislature, or however speculative the reason might be—if there's any possible reason, the courts must uphold legislation banning gay marriage.

In assessing *Lee Optical*, remember that the ends of constitutional government are formulated in the Preamble as public purposes and that there are good reasons to read the Due Process Clause as a guarantee that legislation will be good-faith and reasonable efforts to serve the public interest. In spite of himself, Douglas couldn't completely suppress this assumption in *Lee Optical*, for the possible reasons he offered for the legislation were formulated as public purposes. He couldn't bring himself to say that the legislature was free to act in admittedly arbitrary ways. He said that Oklahoma might have a public purpose in mind, and that the Court would presume that it did, even though the Court would make no effort to ensure that it did.

Our question at this point is whether the Court should review economic legislation to see if the legislature has the kind of good-faith reason that the Constitution requires. We ask this question to see whether a defensible view of the Constitution can admit any class of legislation that categorically excludes the need for a reason in the public interest. If the Constitution leaves economic rights at the mercy of popular prejudices, why not other kinds of rights, including the right to procreate or the rights of gay men and lesbians to intimate association and to marry?

From 1937 to 1973, the Court eschewed protecting fundamental rights or liberties on the basis of the Due Process Clauses alone. In Skinner v. Oklahoma (1942), the Court considered the constitutionality of an Oklahoma statute requiring sterilization of "habitual criminals"—persons convicted two or more times for felonies involving "moral turpitude." The statute excepted certain "white collar" crimes: "offenses arising out of the violation of the prohibitory laws, revenue acts, embezzlement, or political offenses."[14] Jack Skinner, who had been convicted of stealing chickens and of robbery with firearms, challenged the law under which a state court had ordered his sterilization.

The Supreme Court opened its opinion by waxing eloquent about "important . . . human rights." It called "the right to have offspring" or to procreate a "fundamental" or "basic civil right."[15] But the Court did not hold that the state may not sterilize anyone on the ground that there is a fundamental right to procreate rooted in the Due Process Clause. The ghost of *Lochner* foreclosed that straightforward option so soon after *Parrish*. Instead, the Court

---

[14]   316 U.S. 535, 537 (1942).

[15]   Ibid., 536, 541.

protected the right to procreate by establishing what came to be known as the "fundamental rights or interests" strand of Equal Protection doctrine (as distinguished from the "suspect classifications" strand that the Court employs to combat racial and ethnic discrimination). The Court held the Oklahoma statute unconstitutional on the ground that equal protection requires that the state must either (1) sterilize embezzlers along with larceners or (2) sterilize neither class of "habitual criminals."[16] All or none. Retrospectively, though, the Court has sometimes cited *Skinner* as if it were a substantive due process case involving the fundamental right to procreate—which the state may not deny to anyone— rather than an equal protection case merely holding that the state must treat everyone equally.[17]

Over the next three decades, the Court developed the fundamental rights and interests strand of Equal Protection doctrine—sometimes called "substantive equal protection"—and largely avoided substantive due process. The two most celebrated cases that might seem to be counterexamples, but which in fact confirm the point, are Griswold v. Connecticut (1965) (protecting a right of privacy by invalidating a law prohibiting the use of contraceptives by married couples), and Loving v. Virginia (1967) (protecting a right to marry by invalidating a law prohibiting interracial marriage).

Writing for the Court in *Griswold*, Justice Douglas, a veteran of the New Deal critique of *Lochner* (and the author of the opinions of the Court in *Lee Optical* and *Skinner*) officially avoided reviving substantive due process as the basis for protecting the right of privacy. Rather than deriving "unenumerated" rights from the word "liberty,"[18] he grounded the right in the language and the "penumbras" or "emanations" of "specific guarantees in the Bill of Rights," namely, the First, Third, Fourth, and Fifth Amendments.[19] Douglas invoked the command of the Ninth Amendment—"The enumeration in the Constitution, of certain rights, shall not be construed to deny or disparage others retained by the people"—to justify going beyond the bare enumeration of the foregoing rights so as not to exclude the protection of the penumbras or emanations that were not explicitly enumerated.[20] Finally, gathering the several guarantees and emanations into one general right to personal privacy, Douglas stated that this

---

[16]   Ibid., 542.

[17]   *See, e.g., Loving*, 388 U.S. at 12; Roe v. Wade, 410 U.S. 113, 152 (1973).

[18]   381 U.S. 479, 481–82 (1965).

[19]   Ibid., 482–85.

[20]   Ibid., 484.

case "concerns a relationship lying within the zone of privacy created by several fundamental constitutional guarantees."[21]

Loving held that Virginia's statute prohibiting and punishing interracial marriage violated both the Equal Protection and Due Process Clauses. For a unanimous Court Chief Justice Warren held first that the law reflected invidious racial discrimination that denied equal protection.[22] Warren then added that the law denied the fundamental right to marry in violation of the Due Process Clause. "The freedom to marry," he said, "has long been recognized as one of the vital personal rights essential to the orderly pursuit of happiness by free men." He continued:

> To deny this fundamental freedom on so unsupportable a basis as the racial classifications embodied in these statutes, classifications so directly subversive of the principle of equality at the heart of the Fourteenth Amendment, is surely to deprive all the State's citizens of liberty without due process of law. The Fourteenth Amendment requires that the freedom of choice to marry not be restricted by invidious racial discriminations.[23]

This passage demonstrates the overlap between the Court's due process holding and its equal protection holding concerning invidious racial discrimination.

Bruce Ackerman reports that Warren's first draft of the opinion in *Loving* cited *Meyer*, the substantive due process precedent from the era of *Lochner*, but that Justice Black, an adamant opponent of substantive due process, objected.[24] Warren deleted the specific citation to *Meyer*, and instead intertwined the due process holding with the equal protection holding concerning invidious racial discrimination. But Warren still managed to insert into *Loving* a formulation straight out of *Meyer*—characterizing the fundamental right to marry as "essential to the orderly pursuit of happiness by free men."[25] The stage was set for reviving substantive due process.

---

[21] Ibid., 485.

[22] 388 U.S. at 12.

[23] Ibid.

[24] Bruce Ackerman, *We the People: The Civil Rights Revolution* (Cambridge, MA: Harvard University Press, 2014), 305.

[25] 388 U.S. at 12.

C. From *Roe* (1973) to the Present

In Roe v. Wade (1973), the Supreme Court officially revived substantive due process: protecting a substantive liberty—the right of a woman to decide whether to terminate a pregnancy—under the Due Process Clause alone.[26] The Court stated generally that the Due Process Clause's guarantee of "personal privacy" protects "personal rights" "implicit in the concept of ordered liberty," citing *Palko*.[27] The Court has recognized at least the following substantive liberties under the categories of privacy, autonomy, or substantive due process:

(1) liberty of conscience and freedom of thought;

(2) freedom of association, including both expressive association and intimate association;

(3) the right to live with one's family, whether nuclear or extended;

(4) the right to travel or relocate;

(5) the right to marry;

(6) the right to decide whether to bear or beget children, including the rights to procreate, to use contraceptives, and to terminate a pregnancy;

(7) the right to direct the education and rearing of children, including the right to make decisions concerning their care, custody, and control; and

(8) the right to exercise dominion over one's body, including the right to bodily integrity and ultimately the right to die (at least to the extent of the right to refuse unwanted medical treatment).[28]

---

[26] 410 U.S. at 152–53.

[27] Ibid., 152.

[28] *See, e.g.*, West Virginia State Bd. of Educ. v. Barnette, 319 U.S. 624, 630, 642 (1943) (liberty of conscience, freedom of thought, and right to self-determination); Roberts v. United States Jaycees, 468 U.S. 609, 617–18 (1984) (freedom of association, including both expressive association and intimate association); Lawrence v. Texas, 539 U.S. 558, 574–75 (2003) (right to privacy or autonomy for gays and lesbians to engage in intimate association); Moore v. City of E. Cleveland, 431 U.S. 494, 503–4 (1977) (right to live with one's family, whether nuclear or extended); Crandall v. Nevada, 73 U.S. (6 Wall.) 35, 49 (1868) (right to travel); Shapiro v. Thompson, 394 U.S. 618, 629–30 (1969) (right to travel or relocate); Turner v. Safley, 482 U.S. 78, 95–96 (1987) (right to marry); Loving v. Virginia, 388 U.S. 1, 12 (1967) (right to marry); Skinner v. Oklahoma, 316 U.S. 535, 541 (1942) (right to procreate); Griswold v. Connecticut, 381 U.S. 479, 485–86 (1965) (right within marital association to use contraceptives); Eisenstadt v. Baird, 405 U.S. 438, 453 (1972) (right of individual, married or single, to use contraceptives); Carey v. Population Servs. Int'l, 431 U.S. 678, 694 (1977) (right to distribute contraceptives); Roe v. Wade, 410 U.S. 113, 153 (1973) (right of a woman to decide whether to terminate a pregnancy); Planned Parenthood v. Casey, 505 U.S. 833, 846, 857 (1992) (reaffirming "central holding" of *Roe* and emphasizing personal autonomy and bodily integrity); Meyer v.

There are two radically different views concerning this practice of substantive due process and this list of substantive fundamental rights or liberties. One view is that it is a subjective, lawless product of judicial fiat and that the whole enterprise is indefensibly indeterminate and irredeemably undemocratic.[29] The other view is that the list represents a "rational continuum" of basic liberties stemming from "the individual's right to make certain unusually important decisions that will affect his own, or his family's, destiny."[30] The rational continuum view holds that the list of substantive rights has been developed through a common-law process of "reasoned judgment" about liberties basic for personal self-government.[31] This latter view has now yielded the rights of gay men and lesbians to intimate association (*Lawrence*) and to marry (*Obergefell*), with the dissenters in these cases taking the former view.

V. THE "DOUBLE STANDARD" CONCERNING ECONOMIC LIBERTIES VERSUS PERSONAL LIBERTIES AND CIVIL RIGHTS

Cases like *Lee Optical* raised the specter of a "double standard" between economic liberties and other rights, such as the personal liberties protected in *Meyer, Pierce,* and later in *Roe, Lawrence*, and *Obergefell*. By the early 1940s, the Supreme Court had abandoned meaningful review of economic regulations under the Due Process Clause. The Court then faced the problem of justifying greater judicial protection for personal liberties than for economic liberties. Why the difference? Does the Due Process Clause not expressly refer to "property" as well as "life" and "liberty"? Observers sought a justification for this

---

Nebraska, 262 U.S. 390, 400 (1923) (right to direct the education of children); Pierce v. Society of Sisters, 268 U.S. 510, 534–35 (1925) (right to direct the upbringing and education of children); Troxel v. Granville, 530 U.S. 57, 66 (2000) (right of parents to make decisions concerning the care, custody, and control of children);Washington v. Harper, 494 U.S. 210, 221–22 (1990) (right to bodily integrity, in particular, to avoid unwanted administration of antipsychotic drugs); Rochin v. California, 342 U.S. 165, 172–73 (1952) (right to bodily integrity, in particular, to be protected against the extraction of evidence obtained by "breaking into the privacy" of a person's mouth or stomach); Cruzan v. Director, Mo. Dep't of Health, 497 U.S. 261, 279 (1990) (assuming for purposes of the case a "right to die" that includes the "right to refuse lifesaving hydration and nutrition"); Stanley v. Georgia, 394 U.S. 557, 564 (1969) (right to receive ideas and to be free from unwanted governmental intrusions into the privacy of one's home). For discussion of this list of substantive liberties, see James E. Fleming, *Securing Constitutional Democracy: The Case of Autonomy* (Chicago, IL: University of Chicago Press, 2006), 92–98.

[29] *See, e.g., Casey*, 505 U.S. at 979–80, 982–84 (Scalia, J., dissenting); John Hart Ely, *Democracy and Distrust* (Cambridge, MA: Harvard University Press, 1980), 43–72.

[30] Poe v. Ullman, 367 U.S. 497, 543 (1961) (Harlan, J., dissenting); Bowers v. Hardwick, 478 U.S. 186, 217 (1986) (Stevens, J., dissenting); *see also Casey*, 505 U.S. at 848, 851 (joint opinion).

[31] For a defense of the latter position, see Fleming, *Securing Constitutional Democracy*, 89–111. For a defense of *Roe* as a product of common law constitutional interpretation, see David A. Strauss, *The Living Constitution* (New York: Oxford University Press, 2010), 92–97.

distinction among different classes of rights because it was hard to say in this country (of all countries) that economic liberties were of less concern to the framers and the constitutional tradition than personal liberties—or, better, other personal liberties, since economic liberties are personal liberties too. One explanation for the double standard—a causal explanation, not a moral justification—was the moral skepticism that, in the 1940s and 50s, was consolidating its grip on legal thought and American intellectual life generally. As you might learn in a course in constitutional interpretation, judges who uphold constitutional rights against popular or legislative opinion presuppose that moral truth favors those rights. If judges increasingly believe that there is no "moral truth"—that justice and fairness are in the eye of the beholder—they have no firm reason for saying the legislature is wrong.

While they professed skepticism about moral truth, however, many of the nation's legal intellectuals held on to their assumption that, in doubtful cases, it was morally right for judges to defer to democratic opinion. The thinking was that because one person's values are as good or bad as another's, there can be no reason for excluding anyone from a say in community affairs; ergo, democracy. And thus a certain vision of democracy came to "justify" a double standard between economic liberties and civil rights. Freedom from discrimination was claimed most often by members of racial, ethnic, and religious minorities whom the majority's prejudices had regularly excluded from shifting legislative coalitions. Rights of criminal defendants were disproportionately claimed by racial and economic minorities. Freedoms of speech, press, and political association were essential to democratic decision. The same held for the rights to vote and have one's vote counted equally. So democracy was thought to justify judicial protection for these specific classes of rights.

By contrast, economic liberties were typically asserted by the middle and upper economic classes, and these elements had more than enough influence on elected officials at all levels—the middle and upper economic classes lacked the discreteness, insularity, and general powerlessness that could justify active judicial concern for their interests. The legal expression of this general view was the famous footnote 4 of United States v. Carolene Products Co. (1938). The Court in *Carolene Products* took an approach to reviewing the constitutionality of statutes that in general resembled its approach in *Parrish*, but in footnote 4 of the decision Justice Stone suggested three exceptions in which a "more searching" judicial scrutiny is warranted:

(1)   "when legislation appears on its face to be within a specific prohibition of the Constitution," like the First Amendment freedoms of speech and press;

(2)   when legislation "restricts those political processes which can ordinarily be expected to bring about repeal of undesirable legislation," like the right to vote; and

(3)   when statutes are "directed at particular religious . . . or national . . . or racial minorities" or reflect "prejudice against discrete and insular minorities," "which tends seriously to curtail the operation of those political processes ordinarily to be relied upon to protect minorities."[32]

But, for several reasons, *Carolene Products* footnote 4 failed to solve the problem of the double standard. First, it's hard to say why, if all values are equal, anyone should favor democracy or some particular version of democracy, which are themselves values in competition with other values. Second, a concern for democracy can't diminish a concern for property if property and democracy are linked. And property is linked with democracy because people who are needy or who fear economic reprisal can't be counted on to be the active and independent-minded citizens of democracy at its ideal best. Third, the Constitution doesn't mention "democracy"; it does mention "liberty" and "property," and it's hard either to exclude economic liberties from "liberty" or to deny that democratic majorities can treat those liberties in arbitrary ways (remember *Lee Optical*). It was only a matter of time before economic liberties began to make a comeback or before the Court began to restore the requirement of a minimally good-faith and sound reason—as opposed to any old reason, however speculative.

The partial restoration of concern for property rights is beyond the scope of this book. But an early indication that the Court might restore some teeth to its requirement of a reason was the Court's decision in Cleburne v. Cleburne Living Center (1985).[33] *Cleburne* raised a question under the Equal Protection Clause: Could a municipality deny a special-use permit to establish a home for "mentally retarded" (or developmentally disabled) persons in a neighborhood where other care and multiple dwelling facilities were freely permitted? Since the Court had not declared that "mentally retarded" persons warranted special judicial protection under the Equal Protection Clause, all the city needed was a

---

[32]   304 U.S. 144, 152–53 n.4 (1938).

[33]   473 U.S. 432 (1985).

reason, and up to that point in cases like this a reason meant any old reason. But the Court now changed its approach: the reason had to be more than the "mere negative attitudes of the majority of property owners" in the vicinity of the planned home toward developmentally disabled persons. In fact, the Court rejected such reasons as "animus" against and "a bare . . . desire to harm a politically unpopular group," which are not legitimate governmental interests or reasons. A decade later, the Court applied this no-animus standard under the Equal Protection Clause—putting some teeth into the requirement of a rational basis for the law—in the watershed gay-rights case of Romer v. Evans (1996). And in 2003, the Court applied a similar standard under the Due Process Clause in protecting the right of intimate association for gay men and lesbians in Lawrence v. Texas (2003).

The standard in *Cleburne, Romer,* and *Lawrence* amounts to a middle level of review in two contexts. It is in the middle of (1) the due process framework between the "double standards" of highly deferential "rational basis scrutiny" of laws affecting economic liberties and relatively searching scrutiny of laws infringing on personal liberties. It is also in the middle of (2) the equal protection framework between deferential "rational basis" scrutiny for classifications like those based on age and "strict scrutiny" for racial classifications (not to mention "intermediate scrutiny" for gender classifications). A middling position between any old reason and a strong reason, this standard represents "rational basis scrutiny with bite." It applies under the Due Process and Equal Protection Clauses to secure the several gay rights that we will discuss in Chapter 4: unburdened citizenship (*Romer*), sexual intimacy (*Lawrence*), and marriage (*Obergefell*).

Gay Rights

In Chapter 3 we discussed developments in areas of the law that came together to provide the constitutional basis for the gay-rights victories that began in Romer v. Evans (1996) and Lawrence v. Texas (2003) and culminated in Obergefell v. Hodges (2015). This chapter reprints and discusses the gay-rights cases themselves. Before we get started, however, we should remember that the Fourteenth Amendment protects three kinds of rights:

(1) The privileges and immunities of U.S. citizenship (Slaughterhouse Cases (1873) killed this clause as a basis for most civil rights, including gay rights).

(2) Due process rights, substantive as well as procedural (the "liberty" protected under this clause includes the freedom of intimate association that now shelters same-sex sexual conduct from criminal prosecution and secures the right to marry that same-sex couples now enjoy).

(3) Equal protection of the laws (the right to which overlaps with due process guarantees to support gay rights).

We shall begin by showing the intertwining of due process and equal protection in the cases protecting gay rights, before discussing the trajectory of the due process inquiry from Roe v. Wade (1973) to *Obergefell*, and finally considering the stringency of the protection of basic liberties under the Fourteenth Amendment.

I. THE INTERTWINING OF DUE PROCESS AND EQUAL PROTECTION

To see how the rights of due process and equal protection work together, consider again the Supreme Court's approach in the 1960s to the Virginia law against interracial marriage. The Court found that this law deprived the persons

111

involved of liberty—the liberty to marry—and, by treating them differently from couples of the same race, deprived them of the equal protection of the laws, Loving v. Virginia (1967). Recall also a point in Chapter 3 about the nature of substantive due process rights and the strength of all individual rights under the U.S. Constitution. These rights are not absolute; governments can abridge them *if* there's an adequate reason in the public interest. So the question in *Loving* was whether Virginia had a reason for denying marriage to interracial couples. How strong a reason Virginia needed depended on the status of the right to marry, and the Supreme Court had held as far back as 1888 that the right to marry was a fundamental right protected against state laws by the Fourteenth Amendment. Maynard v. Hill (1888).[1] Since marriage was a fundamental right and the Virginia statute discriminated on the basis of race, Virginia needed a very strong reason or, in the jargon of the Court, a "compelling governmental interest." As it turned out, Virginia's reason was not only not compelling, it was constitutionally forbidden. Virginia sought to "preserve the racial integrity of its citizens," which, said Chief Justice Warren for a unanimous court, was no more than the perpetuation of white supremacy, an end forbidden by the Civil War Amendments. Had Virginia offered an admissible reason that did not discriminate on the basis of race, the Court would have scrutinized it "strictly" to determine if the state could have pursued its aim through means that didn't deny or burden the right to marry.[2]

Had the right in question been other than a fundamental right, the state, in theory, would still have needed a reason in the public interest, but in practice, any old reason would have sufficed, even a reason hypothesized or presumed by the court itself to rationalize the challenged state action. Prior to Cleburne v. Cleburne Living Center (1985; discussed in Chapter 3), Williamson v. Lee Optical (1955; discussed in Chapter 3) was the undisputed paradigm case for controversies involving rights other than fundamental rights, and for the majority in Bowers v. Hardwick (1986) and the dissenting justices in the subsequent gay-rights cases, *Lee Optical* remains the controlling precedent. Opponents of gay rights favor *Lee Optical* because the Supreme Court has never held gay sex to be a fundamental right. Thus, in *Bowers*, Justice White described the right claimed by the defendant as "a fundamental right to engage in homosexual sodomy," and applied the doctrinal criterion of Palko v. Connecticut (1937)—whether the asserted right was "implicit in the concept of ordered liberty"—to deny fundamental status to homosexual sodomy. The

---

[1]   125 U.S. 190 (1888).

[2]   388 U.S. 1, 7 (1967).

Court then applied a *Lee Optical* approach to conclude that "the presumed belief of a majority of the electorate in Georgia that homosexual sodomy is immoral and unacceptable" provided a sufficient reason to uphold Georgia's anti-sodomy law as applied to same-sex couples.[3]

Though the Supreme Court decriminalized gay sex in *Lawrence* and constitutionalized same-sex marriage in *Obergefell*, it has managed to do so without declaring a fundamental right to gay sex as such. In *Lawrence*, Justice Kennedy (following Justice Blackmun's prescient dissent in *Bowers*) conceived the right asserted by the defendant not as "homosexual sodomy" but as the liberty to decide questions of intimate association for oneself. And whereas the majority in *Bowers* had stated that "none of the rights" protected in the Court's precedents (like intimate association for straights) "bears any resemblance" to the right asserted by gays, Kennedy in *Lawrence* concluded that gays were similar to straights with respect to these rights: "Persons in a homosexual relationship may seek autonomy for the[ ] purposes . . . heterosexual persons do."[4] Justice Kennedy's point was that everyone in the community, regardless of sexual orientation, has a stake in this right. In this way, he treated gays and straights as comprising one community, not separate communities. For their part, the majority in *Bowers* and the dissenters in the subsequent gay-rights cases saw the issues in terms of specific kinds of sexual activity ("homosexual sodomy") and kinds of union (male-male, female-female) that deviate from the community norm (male-female). Where Justice Kennedy sees one community, the dissenters in *Lawrence* and *Obergefell* imply two communities. So, the due process issues in the cases of this chapter take the form of competing descriptions of the rights at stake, whether they meet previously announced criteria of fundamentality, whether the precedents support recognition of the right, and how strong a reason the states need to deny the right.

Most of the cases that follow also raise problems under the Fourteenth Amendment's Equal Protection Clause. Under this clause, laws imposing special disabilities on any group must be justified by a reason. For example, laws excluding persons under eighteen from voting are justified by the state's interest in informed and mature voters, and it's not unreasonable to assume that persons under eighteen are not as mature and informed as older persons. Denying this assumption would cut no ice, for the Court has not regarded age groups (the young, the middle aged, the old) as warranting special judicial protection from

---

3   Bowers v. Hardwick, 478 U.S. 186, 191–94, 196 (1986) (applying Palko v. Connecticut, 302 U.S. 319, 325 (1937)).

4   539 U.S. 558 (2003).

legislative majorities. Or, in the Court's doctrinal formulation, age is not a "suspect classification," so the courts will not "strictly scrutinize" laws classifying persons by age to ensure that governments can find no other, less restrictive way to serve a compelling public interest.

Laws imposing special disabilities on homosexuals must also be justified by reasons in the public interest. But the question has been how strong these reasons must be. In light of an ugly history of violence and discrimination against homosexuals, many have argued that they come within what footnote 4 of United States v. Carolene Products Co. (1938; discussed in Chapter 3) calls "discrete and insular minorities" or that the Court should recognize sexual orientation as a "suspect classification" analogous to race. If the Court had so classified LGBT persons, laws naming them or affecting them unequally would be subject to "more exacting judicial scrutiny" or "strict scrutiny" and would usually be found unconstitutional. But the Court has managed to decriminalize gay sex and secure marriage equality without declaring gays and lesbians members of a class specially protected against majoritarian prejudice. Some lower federal courts have taken these routes, however. For example, in Baskin v. Bogan (2014; reprinted below), Circuit Judge Richard Posner's majority opinion for the Seventh Circuit Court of Appeals held that laws prohibiting same-sex couples from marrying discriminated against homosexuals "along suspect lines" in violation of the Equal Protection Clause, and in Latta v. Otter (2014; reprinted below), Circuit Judge Marsha Berzon of the Ninth Circuit Court of Appeals argued in a concurring opinion that bans on same-sex marriage unconstitutionally discriminate on the basis of gender.

To protect gays and lesbians without holding sexual orientation to be a "suspect classification" (analogous to race) or even a somewhat suspicious classification (analogous to gender), the Supreme Court has made a significant shift from the approach of *Lee Optical* to the approach of *Cleburne* (recall the discussion in Chapter 3), putting some "bite" into its review of the reasons proffered to justify the law being challenged. Under *Lee Optical*'s highly deferential approach, a reason could be any old reason, even one fabricated by the Court and lacking any quality that could make "reason" connote "justification": A law could pass judicial scrutiny even if it was "a needless, wasteful requirement . . . not in every respect consistent with its aims."[5] Under *Cleburne*, by contrast, a reason has to be worthy of the name, something other than a flimsy pretext or an after-the-fact rationalization. In *Cleburne*, a Texas city denied the Cleburne Living Center a permit to establish a home for "mentally

---

5   348 U.S. 483, 487 (1955).

retarded" or developmentally disabled persons in a residential neighborhood. A unanimous court found that the city had acted from "an irrational prejudice against the mentally retarded" or a "bare desire to harm a politically unpopular group," and that there was no reason "to believe the proposed home posed any threat to the city's legitimate interest."[6] Accordingly, the Court concluded that the city's action lacked a justification that could satisfy the reasonableness required by the Fourteenth Amendment under the form of review that we have called rational basis scrutiny with "bite" (as distinguished from *Lee Optical*'s toothless review). *Cleburne* thus drew from an ancient tradition (discussed in Chapter 3) linking law and reason and attaching moral force to both. The Supreme Court's decisions from *Romer* to *Obergefell* have done the same under both the Equal Protection Clause and the Due Process Clause.

We should emphasize that state supreme courts have played a vital role in the movement toward recognizing gay rights, including marriage equality. The two leading state supreme court decisions concerning same-sex marriage took approaches to scrutinizing reasons that are similar to that taken by the U.S. Supreme Court in *Cleburne*. Not long after *Romer* (1996), the Vermont Supreme Court held that Vermont, which "exclude[d] same-sex couples from the benefits and protections that its laws provide to opposite-sex married couples," had violated the Common Benefits Clause of the state's constitution, its analogue to the Equal Protection Clause; see Baker v. State (Vt. 1999; reprinted below). Shortly after *Lawrence* (2003), the Massachusetts Supreme Judicial Court held that Massachusetts, whose laws "den[ied] the protections, benefits, and obligations conferred by civil marriage to two individuals of the same sex who wish to marry," had violated both the Due Process Clause and the Equal Protection Clause of the state's constitution; see Goodridge v. Department of Public Health (Ma. 2003; reprinted below).

II. THE TRAJECTORY OF THE DUE PROCESS INQUIRY FROM *ROE* TO *OBERGEFELL*

Officially, the criterion for deciding what liberties the Due Process Clause protects against both the federal government and state governments is whether the asserted liberty is "implicit in the concept of ordered liberty," *Palko*. This was the test stated in Roe v. Wade (1973).[7] In some cases since *Roe*, the Supreme Court has applied an alternative test: whether the asserted liberty is "deeply rooted in this Nation's history and tradition," Moore v. City of East Cleveland

---

6   473 U.S. 432, 447, 450 (1985).

7   410 U.S. 113, 152 (1973) (citing *Palko*, 302 U.S. at 325).

(1977). In some cases before *Roe*, the Court had asked whether the asserted liberty comes within a "principle of justice so rooted in the traditions and conscience of our people as to be ranked as fundamental," Snyder v. Massachusetts (1934). Yet another well-known formulation was: "fundamental principles of liberty and justice which lie at the base of all our civil and political institutions," Hebert v. Louisiana (1926).[8] These several formulations raise the question of what constitutes a tradition and therefore the baseline for what liberties are protected by the Due Process Clauses.

From *Roe* (1973) to *Lawrence* (2003) and beyond to *Obergefell* (2015), the justices have debated the foundations for fundamental liberties. Three conceptions of what constitutes a tradition stand out:[9]

(1)   *abstract aspirational principles* (for example, Justice Cardozo's opinions of the Court in *Palko* and *Snyder*, and Justice Brennan's dissenting opinion in Michael H. v. Gerald D. (1989))—abstract principles to which we as a people aspire, and for which we as a people stand, whether or not we have always realized them in our historical practices, statute books, or common law;[10]

(2)   *concrete historical practices* (for example, Justice White's majority opinion in *Bowers*, Justice Scalia's plurality opinion in *Michael H.*, and Chief Justice Rehnquist's majority opinion in Washington v. Glucksberg (1997))—liberty includes whatever liberties were protected specifically in the statute books or recognized concretely in the common law when the Fourteenth Amendment was adopted in 1868;[11] and

(3)   a *"rational continuum"* and a *"living thing"* or evolving consensus (for example, Justice Harlan's dissenting opinion in Poe v. Ullman (1961) and the joint opinion of Justices O'Connor, Kennedy, and Souter in Planned Parenthood v. Casey (1973))—liberty is a "rational continuum," a "balance struck by this country, having

---

[8]   Moore v. City of East Cleveland, 431 U.S. 494, 503 (1977); Snyder v. Massachusetts, 291 U.S. 97, 105 (1934); Hebert v. Louisiana, 272 U.S. 312, 316 (1926).

[9]   For fuller analysis, see James E. Fleming, *Securing Constitutional Democracy: The Case of Autonomy* (Chicago: University of Chicago Press, 2006), 112–27. In this section, we draw upon that analysis as well as from James E. Fleming and Linda C. McClain, "Liberty," in *The Oxford Handbook of the U.S. Constitution*, Mark Tushnet, Mark A. Graber, and Sanford Levinson, eds. (New York: Oxford University Press, 2015), 479, 489–93.

[10]   491 U.S. 110, 141 (1989) (Brennan, J., dissenting).

[11]   Michael H. v. Gerald D., 491 U.S. 110, 127 n.6 (1989) (Scalia, J., plurality); Washington v. Glucksberg, 521 U.S. 702, 720–23 (1997).

regard to what history teaches are the traditions from which it developed as well as the traditions from which it broke. That tradition is a living thing."[12]

The third conception for all practical purposes is similar to the first, although the first contemplates a more philosophical inquiry in elaborating abstract principles, and the third a more historical inquiry in articulating an evolving consensus.

In the period between *Roe* (1973) and *Bowers* (1986), an important change occurred in the Supreme Court's conception of the due process inquiry. The Court moved from (1) considering whether an asserted right is "of the very essence of a scheme of ordered liberty," or is required by a "principle of justice so rooted in the traditions and conscience of our people as to be ranked as fundamental," to (2) considering only whether, as a historical matter, it has been protected against governmental interference. The former formulations call for an inquiry into traditions conceived as *abstract aspirational principles*, while the latter makes an inquiry into traditions understood as *concrete historical practices*.

Roe conceived due process as encompassing the basic liberties implicit in a scheme of ordered liberty embodied in our Constitution—or again, the fundamental principles of justice to which we as a people aspire and for which we as a people stand—whether or not we actually have realized them in our historical practices, common law, and statute books. On this view, our aspirational principles may be critical of our historical practices, and our basic liberties and traditions are not merely the deposits of those practices. Cases such as *Roe* and *Loving*, not to mention subsequent cases such as *Lawrence* and *Obergefell*, broke from historical practices in pursuit of due process and traditions in the sense of aspirational principles.

In *Bowers*, by contrast, the Court per Justice White narrowly conceived the due process inquiry as a backward-looking question concerning historical practices, stripped of virtually any aspirational force or critical bite with respect to the status quo. White simply recounted our nation's historical practices disapproving of sodomy and dismissed the claim that the Due Process Clause protects "a fundamental right of homosexuals to engage in acts of consensual sodomy" as, "at best, facetious."[13]

Justice Scalia's plurality opinion in *Michael H.* (1989) was an attempt to narrow the *Bowers* due process inquiry even further, limiting substantive due

---

[12] Poe v. Ullman, 367 U.S. 497, 542–43 (1961) (Harlan, J., dissenting); Planned Parenthood v. Casey, 505 U.S. 833, 848–50 (1992).

[13] 478 U.S. at 192–94.

process to include only those rights that actually have been protected through historical practices, common law, and statutes. Scalia argued against conceiving protected rights abstractly, insisting on framing them at "the most specific level [of generality] at which a relevant tradition protecting, or denying protection to, the asserted right can be identified."[14] For example, in *Michael H.*, in rejecting an unwed biological father's assertion of parental visitation rights, Scalia framed the right at issue not in abstract terms of rights of parenthood (as Justice Brennan did in dissent), but in highly specific terms as the right of "the natural father to assert parental rights over a child born into a woman's existing marriage with another man," or the right to have a state "award substantive parental rights to the natural father of a child conceived within, and born into, an extant marital union that wishes to embrace the child."[15] That same year, concurring in Cruzan v. Director, Missouri Dept. of Health (1989), Scalia warned that if the Court used the Due Process Clause to try to protect the citizenry from "irrationality and oppression" through recognizing substantive liberties, "it will destroy itself."[16] For Scalia, the ghost of Lochner v. New York (1905; discussed in Chapter 3) lurked. We should note, however, that in *Cruzan*, the majority took a broader view of liberty than did Scalia; it expressly "assum[ed]" that the Due Process Clause protected the right to refuse unwanted medical treatment.[17]

In *Casey* (1992), which affirmed the central holding of *Roe* (with qualifications noted below), the joint opinion of Justices O'Connor, Kennedy, and Souter rejected Scalia's *Michael H.* jurisprudence as "inconsistent with our law," namely, the line of decisions protecting substantive liberties under the Due Process Clause (discussed in Chapter 3).[18] *Casey* instead accepted the third approach identified above: Justice Harlan's approach in dissent in *Poe*. We note four characteristics of Harlan's substantive due process jurisprudence.

First, Harlan conceived the liberty guaranteed by the Due Process Clause as a "rational continuum" of ordered liberty, not a "series of isolated points pricked out" here and there in the constitutional document. Liberty is an abstract concept, comprised, as *Casey* put it, of "ideas and aspirations"; it is not a list of concrete, enumerated rights. Second, Harlan conceived interpretation of abstract commitments like liberty as a "rational process" of "reasoned judgment," not a quest for a formula, code, or bright-line rule framework that enables judges to

---

14   491 U.S. at 123–27 & 127 n.6. Only Chief Justice Rehnquist joined the quoted formulation from n.6 of Justice Scalia's plurality opinion.

15   Ibid., 125, 127.

16   497 U.S. 261, 300–01 (1989) (Scalia, J., concurring).

17   497 U.S. at 279.

18   505 U.S. 833, 847–48 (1992).

avoid judgment. Third, Harlan believed that applying the commitment to liberty in concrete cases requires judgment about the balance between liberty and order ("ordered liberty") and reasoning by analogy from case to case. Finally, while Harlan agreed with Scalia that judgments about liberties must be grounded in history and tradition, unlike Scalia, Harlan conceived tradition as a "living thing" or an evolving consensus, not a set of historical practices fixed at the time the Due Process Clause was ratified in 1868.[19]

In sum, the joint opinion in *Casey* followed Harlan's approach in *Poe* and conceived the due process inquiry as requiring "reasoned judgment" in interpreting the Constitution, understood as a "covenant" or "coherent succession" whose "written terms embody ideas and aspirations that must survive more ages than one" and guarantee "the promise of liberty." The joint opinion concluded: "We accept our responsibility not to retreat from interpreting the full meaning of the covenant in light of all of our precedents."[20] *Casey* clearly conceived liberty as an abstract aspirational principle, not a concrete historical practice.

In *Glucksberg* (1997), in which the Court declined to extend the right to refuse unwanted medical treatment to include the right to physician-assisted suicide, Chief Justice Rehnquist sought to rein in the *Poe-Casey* formulation of the due process inquiry. Rehnquist wrote that the Court's "established method of substantive due process analysis has two primary features":

> First, we have regularly observed that the Due Process Clause specially protects those fundamental rights and liberties which are, objectively, "deeply rooted in this Nation's history and tradition" . . . and "implicit in the concept of ordered liberty." . . . Second, we have required . . . a "careful description" of the asserted fundamental liberty interest.[21]

In calling for a "careful description" of the asserted right and an "objective[ ]" inquiry into "[o]ur Nation's history, legal traditions, and practices," Rehnquist called to mind Scalia's formulation of the due process inquiry in his plurality opinion in *Michael H.* and in his concurring opinion in *Cruzan*, along with White's understanding in *Bowers*.

---

[19] Ibid., 848–50, 901; *Poe*, 367 U.S. at 542–43 (Harlan, J., dissenting). For fuller discussion, see James E. Fleming and Linda C. McClain, *Ordered Liberty: Rights, Responsibilities, and Virtues* (Cambridge, MA: Harvard University Press, 2013), 241–43.

[20] 505 U.S. at 849, 901.

[21] 521 U.S. 702, 720–21 (1997).

In *Lawrence* (2003), however, Justice Kennedy's opinion of the Court repudiated the framework of *Glucksberg* in favor of an understanding like that in *Casey*. (*Lawrence* overruled *Bowers*, holding that the Due Process Clause protects "homosexual persons' " right to privacy regarding consensual sexual conduct.) It signaled a return to a conception of liberty as a rational continuum or evolving consensus of aspirational principles. In fact, one reason Scalia was so indignant in dissent in *Lawrence* was his belief that *Glucksberg* had "eroded" *Casey*'s conception of the due process inquiry.[22] Kennedy wrote in *Lawrence*:

> Had those who drew and ratified the Due Process Clauses of the Fifth Amendment or the Fourteenth Amendment known the components of liberty in its manifold possibilities, they might have been more specific. They did not presume to have this insight. They knew times can blind us to certain truths and later generations can see that laws once thought necessary and proper in fact serve only to oppress. As the Constitution endures, persons in every generation can invoke its principles in their own search for greater freedom.[23]

This passage underscores that the *Lawrence* Court conceived the Constitution as an abstract scheme of principles such as liberty to be elaborated over time—in a "search for greater freedom"—not as a specific code of historical practices and enumerated rights (or an expression of the founders' intentions, understandings, and meanings to be discovered and preserved).

If Kennedy did not claim to ground the right to privacy or autonomy in original understanding or concrete historical practices, where did he ground it? The answer is in the line of privacy or autonomy cases beginning with *Griswold* and running through *Roe* and *Casey* and in an understanding of tradition as an evolving consensus of aspirational principles.[24] Kennedy conceived tradition not as a positivist, historicist, or traditionalist deposit of "millennia of moral teaching" (to quote Chief Justice Burger's concurrence in *Bowers*),[25] but as an evolving consensus about how best to realize liberty (and by implication equality) as an aspirational principle.

Since 2003, the Supreme Court has not retreated from *Lawrence*. In fact, in United States v. Windsor (2013), the Court drew upon *Lawrence*'s understanding of liberty together with *Romer*'s understanding of equality in striking down

---

[22]   539 U.S. 558, 588 (2003) (Scalia, J., dissenting).

[23]   539 U.S. 558, 578–79 (2003).

[24]   Ibid., 564–66, 573–76.

[25]   478 U.S. at 197 (Burger, C.J., concurring).

Section 3 of the Defense of Marriage Act, which had defined marriage for purposes of federal law as "only a legal union between one man and one woman."[26] And in *Obergefell* (2015), the Court likewise applied *Casey's* and *Lawrence's* understanding of liberty in holding that the right to marry extends to same-sex unions along with opposite-sex unions. Chief Justice Roberts in dissent protested that the majority was rejecting *Glucksberg's* approach to due process.[27] Yet *Lawrence* and *Obergefell* may not be the last word concerning the due process inquiry. Competing understandings of what liberties are embodied in our traditions may be on a pendulum that swings back and forth.

III. THE STRINGENCY OF THE PROTECTION OF LIBERTY UNDER THE DUE PROCESS CLAUSES

We come finally to the question of the stringency of the protection of basic liberties under the Due Process Clauses, including the liberties protected in *Lawrence* and *Obergefell*.[28] In constitutional law, it is commonplace to say that the Supreme Court applies absolutist "strict scrutiny" in protecting fundamental rights or liberties under the Due Process Clauses. Dissenting in *Lawrence*, Justice Scalia stated that, under the Due Process Clauses, if an asserted liberty is a "fundamental right," it triggers "strict scrutiny" that almost automatically invalidates any statute restricting it. For strict scrutiny requires that the challenged statute, to be upheld, (1) must further a "compelling governmental interest" or reason and (2) must be "necessary" or "narrowly tailored" to do so. Scalia also wrote that if an asserted liberty is not a fundamental right, it is merely a "liberty interest" that triggers rational basis scrutiny that is so deferential to the political processes that the Court all but automatically upholds the statute in question (the approach exemplified by *Lee Optical*). For deferential rational basis scrutiny requires merely that the challenged statute, to be valid, (1) might conceivably further a "legitimate governmental interest" and (2) need only be "rationally related" to doing so.[29] In attempting to limit the protection of substantive liberties under the Due Process Clauses, Scalia argued for a narrow approach to what constitutes a "fundamental right" and a broad approach to what constitutes a mere "liberty interest."

---

[26]   133 S.Ct. 2675, 2692, 2694, 2695–96 (2013) (citing *Lawrence* and Romer v. Evans, 517 U.S. 620, 633 (1996)).

[27]   135 S.Ct. 2584, 2597–2602 (2015); 135 S.Ct. 2584, 2620–21 (Roberts, C.J., dissenting).

[28]   For further development of the analysis of this section, see Fleming and McClain, *Ordered Liberty*, 237–72. In this section, we draw upon that analysis.

[29]   539 U.S. at 593–94 (Scalia, J., dissenting).

Lawrence deviated from this regime. The Court did not hold that gays' and lesbians' right to autonomy or intimate association was a fundamental right requiring strict scrutiny. Nor, on the other hand, did it hold that their right was merely a liberty interest calling for highly deferential rational basis scrutiny. Instead, the Court applied a middle standard—what we have called "rational basis scrutiny with bite"—and struck down the statute criminalizing same-sex sexual conduct. Instead of deferring to the state's proffered "legitimate governmental interest" in preserving traditional sexual morality, the Court (explicitly in *Romer* and implicitly in *Lawrence*) put some bite into its scrutiny of the legitimacy of the reason and found illegitimate "animosity" toward and a "bare desire to harm" a "politically unpopular group." (Thus did the *Lawrence* Court abandon the *Lee Optical* approach for the approach exemplified by *Cleburne*.)[30]

Justice Scalia chastised the Court for not following the rigid two-tier framework that all but automatically decides rights questions one way or the other.[31] Many scholars and judges have questioned whether the Court's actual practice has followed or should follow this framework.[32] Indeed, a careful reading of the cases shows that the only substantive due process case ever to recognize a "fundamental right" implicating "strict scrutiny"—requiring that the statute further a compelling governmental interest and be necessary to doing so—was *Roe*.[33] And those aspects of *Roe* were overruled in *Casey*, which avoided calling the right of a woman to decide whether to terminate a pregnancy a "fundamental right" and substituted an "undue burden" standard for strict scrutiny. Under the less stringent test of *Casey*, the Court instead inquires whether a state regulation "has the purpose or effect of placing a substantial obstacle" to or undue burden upon a woman's exercise of the right to make the "ultimate decision" whether to have an abortion.[34]

Moreover, the leading due process cases *protecting* liberty and autonomy—from Meyer v. Nebraska (1923)[35] and Pierce v. Society of Sisters (1925)[36]

---

30 *Romer*, 517 U.S. at 632–34; *Lawrence*, 539 U.S. at 574; 539 U.S. at 580, 582–83 (O'Connor, J., concurring).

31 539 U.S. at 593–94 (Scalia, J., dissenting).

32 Adam Winkler, "Fatal in Theory and Strict in Fact: An Empirical Analysis of Strict Scrutiny in the Federal Courts," 59 *Vanderbilt Law Review* 793 (2006); Richard H. Fallon, J., "Strict Judicial Scrutiny," 54 *UCLA Law Review* 1267 (2007). Two of us argue along these lines in Fleming and McClain, *Ordered Liberty*, 237–72.

33 410 U.S. at 155–56.

34 505 U.S. at 851–53, 877.

35 262 U.S. 390 (1923).

36 268 U.S. 510 (1925).

through *Moore* (1977) on up through *Casey* (1992), *Lawrence* (2003), and *Obergefell* (2015)—have not applied the framework that Scalia propounds: the Court has not maintained two rigidly-policed tiers of scrutiny, with strict scrutiny automatically invalidating laws and deferential rational basis scrutiny automatically upholding them. Instead, actual practice in the leading cases protecting liberties maps onto a "rational continuum" evincing "reasoned judgment," with several intermediate levels of review.[37] These levels include the undue burden standard exemplified in *Casey* and the rational basis scrutiny "with bite" illustrated by *Lawrence* and *Obergefell*. Early cases like *Meyer* and *Pierce* reflect a form of review resembling that in *Lawrence* and *Obergefell*. Thus, the cases *protecting* substantive liberties reflect a continuum of judgmental responses, not a framework with two rigidly-policed tiers.[38] The cases that have applied Scalia's framework have been the cases *refusing to recognize* asserted rights: *Bowers*, *Michael H.*, and *Glucksberg*. In these cases, the Court was attempting to narrow the protection of substantive liberties under the Due Process Clauses (as were the dissenters in *Lawrence* and *Obergefell*).

* * *

The cases reprinted in this chapter, from *Bowers* to *Obergefell*, represent a struggle between the two approaches to the due process inquiry we have sketched—the *Casey-Lawrence* conception of liberty as an abstract aspirational principle or evolving consensus and the *Glucksberg* conception of it as a deposit of concrete historical practices—and the two approaches to the due process doctrinal framework we have distinguished—a "rational continuum" evincing "reasoned judgment," with several intermediate levels of review, versus a rigidly policed two-tier framework that almost automatically either invalidates or upholds the statutes being challenged. As you read the cases, ask yourself which approach to the due process inquiry, and which approach to the due process doctrinal framework, better fits and justifies the cases that make up our actual constitutional practice.

---

[37] See Fleming and McClain, *Ordered Liberty*, 238–72.

[38] Compare Justice Stevens's and Justice Marshall's well-known analyses of actual practice under the Equal Protection Clause. *See* City of Cleburne v. Cleburne Living Center, 473 U.S. 432, 451 (1985) (Stevens, J., concurring) ("continuum of judgmental responses"); San Antonio v. Rodriguez, 411 U.S. 1, 98 (1973) (Marshall, J., dissenting) ("spectrum of standards").

IV. TRADITIONAL MORAL DISAPPROVAL VERSUS SECURING LIBERTY AND EQUALITY FOR GAYS AND LESBIANS

"The Court is most vulnerable and comes nearest to illegitimacy when it deals with judge-made constitutional law having little or no cognizable roots in the language or design of the Constitution."—JUSTICE WHITE

"[T]his case is about 'the most comprehensive of rights and the right most valued by civilized men,' namely, 'the right to be let alone.' "—JUSTICE BLACKMUN

BOWERS V. HARDWICK

478 U.S. 186, 106 S.Ct. 2841, 92 L.Ed.2d 140 (1986)

[In 1982, police charged Michael Hardwick with engaging in oral sex in his own bedroom with a consenting, adult male. Georgia Code Ann. § 16–6–2 (1984) provided, in pertinent part:

(a)   "A person commits the offense of sodomy when he performs or submits to any sexual act involving the sex organs of one person and the mouth or anus of another. . . . [and] (b) A person convicted of the offense of sodomy shall be punished by imprisonment for not less than one nor more than 20 years. . . ."

The district attorney decided not to prosecute. Hardwick then brought suit in federal district court, seeking an injunction forbidding Georgia to enforce the statute. He asserted that, as a practicing homosexual, he was in imminent danger of arrest for violating this statute—a threat which deprived him of the liberty guaranteed by the Due Process Clause of the Fourteenth Amendment.

The district court dismissed the suit, but a divided panel of the Court of Appeals for the Eleventh Circuit reversed, holding that the Georgia statute violated Hardwick's fundamental rights because his homosexual sexual activity was a private and intimate association beyond the reach of state regulation. The Court of Appeals stated: "For some, the sexual activity in question here serves the same purpose as the intimacy of marriage." The judges invoked the Ninth Amendment as well as the Due Process Clause. Georgia then obtained review from the U.S. Supreme Court.]

■ JUSTICE WHITE delivered the opinion of the Court. . . .

This case does not require a judgment on whether laws against sodomy between consenting adults in general, or between homosexuals in particular, are wise or desirable. It raises no question about the right or propriety of state legislative decisions to repeal their laws that criminalize homosexual sodomy, or of state-court decisions invalidating those laws on state constitutional grounds. The issue presented is whether the Federal Constitution confers a fundamental right upon homosexuals to engage in sodomy and hence invalidates the laws of [many] States. . . .[2] The case also calls for some judgment about the limits of the Court's role in carrying out its constitutional mandate.

We first register our disagreement . . . that the Court's prior cases have construed the Constitution to confer a right of privacy that extends to homosexual sodomy. . . . The reach of this line of cases was sketched in Carey v. Population Services Int'l (1977). Pierce v. Society of Sisters (1925) and Meyer v. Nebraska (1923) were described as dealing with child rearing and education; Prince v. Massachusetts (1944) with family relationships; Skinner v. Oklahoma (1942) with procreation; Loving v. Virginia (1967) with marriage; Griswold v. Connecticut (1965) and Eisenstadt v. Baird (1972) with contraception; and Roe v. Wade (1973) with abortion. . . .

. . . [W]e think it evident that none of the rights announced in those cases bears any resemblance to the claimed constitutional right of homosexuals to engage in acts of sodomy. . . . No connection between family, marriage, or procreation on the one hand and homosexual activity on the other has been demonstrated. . . . Moreover, any claim that these cases nevertheless stand for the proposition that any kind of private sexual conduct between consenting adults is constitutionally insulated from state proscription is unsupportable. Indeed, the Court's opinion in *Carey* twice asserted that the privacy right, which the *Griswold* line of cases found to be one of the protections provided by the Due Process Clause, did not reach so far.

Precedent aside, however, respondent would have us announce . . . a fundamental right to engage in homosexual sodomy. This we are quite unwilling to do. It is true that despite the language of the Due Process Clauses of the Fifth and Fourteenth Amendments, which appears to focus only on the processes by which life, liberty, or property is taken, the cases are legion in which those

---

[2] . . . The only claim properly before the Court . . . is Hardwick's challenge to the Georgia statute as applied to consensual homosexual sodomy. We express no opinion on the constitutionality of the Georgia statute as applied to other acts of sodomy. [Footnote by the Court (moved by Editors).]

Clauses have been interpreted to have substantive content. . . . Among such cases are those recognizing rights that have little or no textual support in the constitutional language. *Meyer, Prince*, and *Pierce* fall in this category, as do the privacy cases from *Griswold* to *Carey*.

Striving to assure itself and the public that announcing rights not readily identifiable in the Constitution's text involves much more than the imposition of the Justices' own choice of values on the States and the Federal Government, the Court has sought to identify the nature of the rights qualifying for heightened judicial protection. In Palko v. Connecticut (1937), it was said that this category includes those fundamental liberties that are "implicit in the concept of ordered liberty," such that "neither liberty nor justice would exist if [they] were sacrificed." A different description of fundamental liberties appeared in Moore v. East Cleveland (1977) (opinion of Powell, J.), where they are characterized as those liberties that are "deeply rooted in this Nation's history and tradition." See also *Griswold*.

It is obvious to us that neither of these formulations would extend a fundamental right to homosexuals to engage in acts of consensual sodomy. Proscriptions against that conduct have ancient roots. Sodomy was a criminal offense at common law and was forbidden by the laws of the original 13 States when they ratified the Bill of Rights. In 1868, when the Fourteenth Amendment was ratified, all but 5 of the 37 States in the Union had criminal sodomy laws. In fact, until 1961, all 50 States outlawed sodomy, and today, 24 States and the District of Columbia continue to provide criminal penalties for sodomy performed in private and between consenting adults. Against this background, to claim that a right to engage in such conduct is "deeply rooted in this Nation's history and tradition" or "implicit in the concept of ordered liberty" is, at best, facetious.

Nor are we inclined to take a more expansive view of our authority to discover new fundamental rights imbedded in the Due Process Clause. The Court is most vulnerable and comes nearest to illegitimacy when it deals with judge-made constitutional law having little or no cognizable roots in the language or design of the Constitution. That this is so was painfully demonstrated by the face-off between the Executive and the Court in the 1930s, which resulted in the repudiation of much of the substantive gloss that the Court had placed on the Due Process Clauses of the Fifth and Fourteenth Amendments. There should be, therefore, great resistance to expand the substantive reach of those Clauses, particularly if it requires redefining the category of rights deemed to be fundamental. Otherwise, the Judiciary necessarily takes to itself further authority to govern the country without express constitutional authority. . . .

Respondent, however, asserts that the result should be different where the homosexual conduct occurs in the privacy of the home. He relies on Stanley v. Georgia (1969), where the Court held that the First Amendment prevents conviction for possessing and reading obscene material in the privacy of one's home. . . .

Stanley did protect conduct that would not have been protected outside the home, and it partially prevented the enforcement of state obscenity laws; but the decision was firmly grounded in the First Amendment. The right pressed upon us here has no similar support in the text of the Constitution, and it does not qualify for recognition under the prevailing principles for construing the Fourteenth Amendment. Its limits are also difficult to discern. Plainly enough, otherwise illegal conduct is not always immunized whenever it occurs in the home. Victimless crimes, such as the possession and use of illegal drugs, do not escape the law where they are committed at home. *Stanley* itself recognized that its holding offered no protection for the possession in the home of drugs, firearms, or stolen goods. And if respondent's submission is limited to the voluntary sexual conduct between consenting adults, it would be difficult, except by fiat, to limit the claimed right to homosexual conduct while leaving exposed to prosecution adultery, incest, and other sexual crimes even though they are committed in the home. We are unwilling to start down that road.

Even if the conduct at issue here is not a fundamental right, respondent asserts that there must be a rational basis for the law and that there is none in this case other than the presumed belief of a majority of the electorate in Georgia that homosexual sodomy is immoral and unacceptable. This is said to be an inadequate rationale to support the law. The law, however, is constantly based on notions of morality, and if all laws representing essentially moral choices are to be invalidated under the Due Process Clause, the courts will be very busy indeed. Even respondent makes no such claim, but insists that majority sentiments about the morality of homosexuality should be declared inadequate. We do not agree, and are unpersuaded that the sodomy laws of some 25 States should be invalidated on this basis.

Reversed.

■ CHIEF JUSTICE BURGER, concurring. . . .

. . . [T]he proscriptions against sodomy have very "ancient roots." Decisions of individuals relating to homosexual conduct have been subject to state intervention throughout the history of Western civilization. Condemnation of those practices is firmly rooted in Judeao-Christian moral and ethical standards. Homosexual sodomy was a capital crime under Roman law. During the English Reformation . . . the first English statute criminalizing sodomy was passed. Blackstone described "the infamous crime against nature" as an offense of "deeper malignity" than rape, a heinous act "the very mention of which is a disgrace to human nature," and "a crime not fit to be named." 4 W. Blackstone, *Commentaries* at 215. The common law of England, including its prohibition of sodomy, became the received law of Georgia and the other Colonies. In 1816 the Georgia Legislature passed the statute at issue here, and that statute has been continuously in force in one form or another since that time. To hold that the act of homosexual sodomy is somehow protected as a fundamental right would be to cast aside millennia of moral teaching. . . .

■ JUSTICE POWELL, concurring.

. . . I agree with the Court that there is no fundamental right—*i.e.*, no substantive right under the Due Process Clause—such as that claimed by respondent Hardwick. . . . This is not to suggest, however, that respondent may not be protected by the Eighth Amendment. . . . The Georgia statute . . . authorizes a court to imprison a person for up to 20 years for a single private, consensual act of sodomy. In my view, a prison sentence for such conduct—certainly a sentence of long duration—would create a serious Eighth Amendment issue. . . .

In this case, however, respondent has not been tried, much less convicted and sentenced. Moreover, respondent has not raised the Eighth Amendment issue below. For these reasons this constitutional argument is not before us.

■ JUSTICE BLACKMUN, with whom JUSTICE BRENNAN, JUSTICE MARSHALL, and JUSTICE STEVENS join, dissenting.

This case is no more about "a fundamental right to engage in homosexual sodomy" . . . than *Stanley* was about a fundamental right to watch obscene movies, or Katz v. United States (1967) was about a fundamental right to place interstate bets from a telephone booth. Rather, this case is about "the most comprehensive of rights and the right most valued by civilized men," namely, "the right to be let alone." Olmstead v. United States (1928) (Brandeis, J., dissenting).

The statute . . . denies individuals the right to decide for themselves whether to engage in particular forms of private, consensual sexual activity. The Court concludes that § 16–6–2 is valid essentially because "the laws of . . . many

States . . . still make such conduct illegal and have done so for a very long time." But the fact that the moral judgments expressed by statutes like § 16–6–2 may be " 'natural and familiar . . . ought not to conclude our judgment upon the question whether statutes embodying them conflict with the Constitution of the United States.' " *Roe*, quoting Lochner v. New York (1905) (Holmes, J., dissenting). Like Justice Holmes, I believe that "[it] is revolting to have no better reason for a rule of law than that so it was laid down in the time of Henry IV. It is still more revolting if the grounds upon which it was laid down have vanished long since, and the rule simply persists from blind imitation of the past." Holmes, The Path of the Law, 10 *Harv.L.Rev.* 457, 469 (1897). I believe we must analyze respondent Hardwick's claim in the light of the values that underlie the constitutional right to privacy. If that right means anything, it means that, before Georgia can prosecute its citizens for making choices about the most intimate aspects of their lives, it must do more than assert that the choice they have made is an " 'abominable crime not fit to be named among Christians.' "

I

. . . A fair reading of the statute and of the complaint clearly reveals that the majority has distorted the question this case presents. First, the Court's almost obsessive focus on homosexual activity is particularly hard to justify in light of the broad language Georgia has used. Unlike the Court, the Georgia Legislature has not proceeded on the assumption that homosexuals are so different from other citizens that their lives may be controlled in a way that would not be tolerated if it limited the choices of those other citizens. Rather, Georgia has provided that "[a] person commits the offense of sodomy when he performs or submits to any sexual act involving the sex organs of one person to the mouth or anus of another." The sex or status of the persons who engage in the act is irrelevant. . . . [T]o the extent I can discern a legislative purpose for Georgia's 1968 enactment of § 16–6–2, that purpose seems to have been to broaden the coverage of the law to reach heterosexual as well as homosexual activity. I therefore see no basis for the Court's decision to treat this case as an "as applied" challenge to § 16–6–2, or for Georgia's attempt . . . to defend § 16–6–2 solely on the grounds that it prohibits homosexual activity. Michael Hardwick's . . . claim that § 16–6–2 involves an unconstitutional intrusion into his privacy and his right of intimate association does not depend in any way on his sexual orientation.

Second, I disagree with the Court's refusal to consider whether § 16–6–2 runs afoul of the Eighth or Ninth Amendments or the Equal Protection Clause of the Fourteenth Amendment. Respondent's complaint expressly invoked the

Ninth Amendment, and he relied heavily before this Court on *Griswold*, which identifies that Amendment as one of the specific constitutional provisions giving "life and substance" to our understanding of privacy. . . . [N]either the Eighth Amendment nor the Equal Protection Clause is so clearly irrelevant that a claim resting on either provision should be peremptorily dismissed.[2] The Court's cramped reading of the issue before it makes for a short opinion, but it does little to make for a persuasive one.

II

"Our cases long have recognized that the Constitution embodies a promise that a certain private sphere of individual liberty will be kept largely beyond the reach of government." Thornburgh v. American College of Obstetricians & Gynecologists (1986). In construing the right to privacy, the Court has proceeded along two somewhat distinct, albeit complementary, lines. First, it has recognized a privacy interest with reference to certain decisions that are properly for the individual to make. *E.g.*, *Roe*; *Pierce*. Second, it has recognized a privacy interest with reference to certain places without regard for the particular activities in which the individuals who occupy them are engaged. *E.g.*, United States v. Karo (1984); Payton v. New York (1980); Rios v. United States (1960). The case before us implicates both the decisional and the spatial aspects of the right to privacy.

---

2   In Robinson v. California (1962), the Court held that the Eighth Amendment barred convicting a defendant due to his "status" as a narcotics addict, since that condition was "apparently an illness which may be contracted innocently or involuntarily." . . .

Despite historical views of homosexuality, it is no longer viewed by mental health professionals as a "disease" or disorder. But, obviously, neither is it simply a matter of deliberate personal election. Homosexual orientation may well form part of the very fiber of an individual's personality. Consequently, under Justice White's analysis in Powell [v. Texas (1968)], the Eighth Amendment may pose a constitutional barrier to sending an individual to prison for acting on that attraction regardless of the circumstances. An individual's ability to make constitutionally protected "decisions concerning sexual relations," *Carey* (Powell, J., concurring in part and concurring in judgment), is rendered empty indeed if he or she is given no real choice but a life without any physical intimacy.

With respect to the Equal Protection Clause's applicability to § 16–6–2, I note that Georgia's exclusive stress before this Court on its interest in prosecuting homosexual activity despite the gender-neutral terms of the statute may raise serious questions of discriminatory enforcement, questions that cannot be disposed of before this Court on a motion to dismiss. See Yick Wo v. Hopkins (1886). The legislature having decided that the sex of the participants is irrelevant to the legality of the acts, I do not see why the State can defend § 16–6–2 on the ground that individuals singled out for prosecution are of the same sex as their partners. Thus . . . a claim under the Equal Protection Clause may well be available without having to reach the more controversial question whether homosexuals are a suspect class. *See, e.g.,* Rowland v. Mad River Local School Dist. (1985) (Brennan, J., dissenting from denial of cert.); Note, "The Constitutional Status of Sexual Orientation: Homosexuality as a Suspect Classification," 98 *Harv.L.Rev.* 1285 (1985). [Footnote by Justice Blackmun.]

A

. . . While . . . [our earlier] cases may be characterized by their connection to protection of the family, the Court's conclusion that they extend no further than this boundary ignores the warning in *Moore* (plurality opinion), against "[closing] our eyes to the basic reasons why certain rights associated with the family have been accorded shelter under the Fourteenth Amendment's Due Process Clause." We protect those rights not because they contribute, in some direct and material way, to the general public welfare, but because they form so central a part of an individual's life. "[The] concept of privacy embodies the 'moral fact that a person belongs to himself and not others nor to society as a whole.'" *Thornburgh* (Stevens, J., concurring), quoting Fried, Correspondence, 6 *Phil. & Pub. Affrs* 288–289 (1977). And so we protect the decision whether to marry precisely because marriage "is an association that promotes a way of life, not causes; a harmony in living, not political faiths; a bilateral loyalty, not commercial or social projects." *Griswold*. We protect the decision whether to have a child because parenthood alters so dramatically an individual's self-definition, not because of demographic considerations or the Bible's command to be fruitful and multiply. And we protect the family because it contributes so powerfully to the happiness of individuals, not because of a preference for stereotypical households. Cf. *Moore* (plurality opinion). The Court recognized in *Roberts* [v. U.S. Jaycees (1984)] that the "ability independently to define one's identity that is central to any concept of liberty" cannot truly be exercised in a vacuum; we all depend on the "emotional enrichment from close ties with others."

Only the most willful blindness could obscure the fact that sexual intimacy is "a sensitive, key relationship of human existence, central to family life, community welfare, and the development of human personality," Paris Adult Theatre I v. Slaton (1973); see also *Carey*. The fact that individuals define themselves in a significant way through their intimate sexual relationships with others suggests, in a Nation as diverse as ours, that there may be many "right" ways of conducting those relationships, and that much of the richness of a relationship will come from the freedom an individual has to choose the form and nature of these intensely personal bonds. See Karst, The Freedom of Intimate Association, 89 *Yale L.J.* 624, 637 (1980); cf. *Eisenstadt*; *Roe*.

In a variety of circumstances we have recognized that a necessary corollary of giving individuals freedom to choose how to conduct their lives is acceptance of the fact that different individuals will make different choices. For example, in holding that the clearly important state interest in public education should give way to a competing claim by the Amish to the effect that extended formal schooling threatened their way of life, the Court declared: "There can be no assumption that today's majority is 'right' and the Amish and others like them are 'wrong.' A way of life that is odd or even erratic but interferes with no rights or interests of others is not to be condemned because it is different." Wisconsin v. Yoder (1972). The Court claims that its decision today merely refuses to recognize a fundamental right to engage in homosexual sodomy; what the Court really has refused to recognize is the fundamental interest all individuals have in controlling the nature of their intimate associations with others.

B

The behavior for which Hardwick faces prosecution occurred in his own home, a place to which the Fourth Amendment attaches special significance. The Court's treatment of this aspect of the case is symptomatic of its overall refusal to consider the broad principles that have informed our treatment of privacy in specific cases. Just as the right to privacy is more than the mere aggregation of a number of entitlements to engage in specific behavior, so too, protecting the physical integrity of the home is more than merely a means of protecting specific activities that often take place there. . . .

The Court's interpretation of the pivotal case of *Stanley* is entirely unconvincing. . . . According to the majority here, *Stanley* relied entirely on the First Amendment, and thus . . . sheds no light on cases not involving printed materials. But . . . the *Stanley* Court anchored its holding in the Fourth Amendment's special protection for the individual in his home. . . .

The central place that *Stanley* gives Justice Brandeis' dissent in *Olmstead*, a case raising *no* First Amendment claim, shows that *Stanley* rested as much on the Court's understanding of the Fourth Amendment as it did on the First. . . . "The right of the people to be secure in their . . . houses," expressly guaranteed by the Fourth Amendment, is perhaps the most "textual" of the various constitutional provisions that inform our understanding of the right to privacy, and thus I cannot agree with the Court's statement that "[the] right pressed upon us here has no . . . support in the text of the Constitution." Indeed, the right of an individual to conduct intimate relationships in the intimacy of his or her own home seems to me to be the heart of the Constitution's protection of privacy.

III

The Court's failure to comprehend the magnitude of the liberty interests at stake in this case leads it to slight the question whether . . . [Georgia] has justified [its] infringement on these interests. . . .[4]

The core of petitioner's defense of § 16–6–2 . . . is that respondent and others who engage in the conduct prohibited by § 16–6–2 interfere with Georgia's exercise of the " 'right of the Nation and of the States to maintain a decent society,' " *Paris Adult Theatre I*, quoting Jacobellis v. Ohio (1964) (Warren, C. J., dissenting). Essentially, petitioner argues, and the Court agrees, that the fact that the acts described in § 16–6–2 "for hundreds of years, if not thousands, have been uniformly condemned as immoral" is a sufficient reason to permit a State to ban them today.

I cannot agree that either the length of time a majority has held its convictions or the passions with which it defends them can withdraw legislation from this Court's scrutiny. See, *e.g., Roe; Loving*; Brown v. Bd. of Ed. (1954).[5] As Justice Jackson wrote so eloquently for the Court in West Virginia Bd. of Ed. v. Barnette (1943), "we apply the limitations of the Constitution with no fear that freedom to be intellectually and spiritually diverse or even contrary will disintegrate the social organization. . . . [Freedom] to differ is not limited to things that do not matter much. That would be a mere shadow of freedom. The test of its substance is the right to differ as to things that touch the heart of the existing order." It is precisely because the issue raised by this case touches the

---

[4] . . . [I]t does seem to me that a court could find simple, analytically sound distinctions between certain private, consensual sexual conduct, on the one hand, and adultery and incest (the only two vaguely specific "sexual crimes" to which the majority points), on the other. . . . A State might define the contractual commitment necessary to become eligible for [mutual] benefits to include a commitment of fidelity and then punish individuals for breaching that contract. Moreover, a State might conclude that adultery is likely to injure third persons, in particular, spouses and children of persons who engage in extramarital affairs. With respect to incest, a court might well agree with respondent that the nature of familial relationships renders true consent to incestuous activity sufficiently problematical that a blanket prohibition of such activity is warranted. Notably, the Court makes no effort to explain why it has chosen to group private, consensual homosexual activity with adultery and incest rather than with private, consensual heterosexual activity by unmarried persons or, indeed, with oral or anal sex within marriage. [Footnote by Justice Blackmun.]

[5] The parallel between *Loving* and this case is almost uncanny. There, too, the State relied on a religious justification for its law. . . . There, too, defenders of the challenged statute relied heavily on the fact that when the Fourteenth Amendment was ratified, most of the States had similar prohibitions. There, too, at the time the case came before the Court, many of the States still had criminal statutes concerning the conduct at issue. Yet the Court held, not only that the invidious racism of Virginia's law violated the Equal Protection Clause, but also that the law deprived the Lovings of due process by denying them the "freedom of choice to marry" that had "long been recognized as one of the vital personal rights essential to the orderly pursuit of happiness by free men." [Footnote by Justice Blackmun.]

heart of what makes individuals what they are that we should be especially sensitive to the rights of those whose choices upset the majority.

The assertion that "traditional Judeo-Christian values proscribe" the conduct involved cannot provide an adequate justification for § 16–6–2. That certain, but by no means all, religious groups condemn the behavior at issue gives the State no license to impose their judgments on the entire citizenry. The legitimacy of secular legislation depends instead on whether the State can advance some justification for its law beyond its conformity to religious doctrine. See, *e.g.*, McGowan v. Maryland (1961); Stone v. Graham (1980). Thus, far from buttressing his case, petitioner's invocation of Leviticus, Romans, St. Thomas Aquinas, and sodomy's heretical status during the Middle Ages undermines his suggestion that § 16–6–2 represents a legitimate use of secular coercive power. A State can no more punish private behavior because of religious intolerance than it can punish such behavior because of racial animus. "The Constitution cannot control such prejudices, but neither can it tolerate them. Private biases may be outside the reach of the law, but the law cannot, directly or indirectly, give them effect." Palmore v. Sidoti (1984). No matter how uncomfortable a certain group may make the majority of this Court, we have held that "[mere] public intolerance or animosity cannot constitutionally justify the deprivation of a person's physical liberty." O'Connor v. Donaldson (1975). See also Cleburne v. Cleburne Living Center, Inc. (1985).

Nor can § 16–6–2 be justified as a "morally neutral" exercise of Georgia's power to "protect the public environment," *Paris Adult Theatre I*. Certainly, some private behavior can affect the fabric of society as a whole. Reasonable people may differ about whether particular sexual acts are moral or immoral, but "we have ample evidence for believing that people will not abandon morality, will not think any better of murder, cruelty and dishonesty, merely because some private sexual practice which they abominate is not punished by the law." H. L. A. Hart, Immorality and Treason, reprinted in *The Law as Literature* 220, 225 (L. Blom-Cooper ed. 1961). Petitioner and the Court fail to see the difference between laws that protect public sensibilities and those that enforce private morality. [T]hat intimate behavior may be punished when it takes place in public cannot dictate how States can regulate intimate behavior that occurs in intimate places. . . .

This case involves no real interference with the rights of others, for the mere knowledge that other individuals do not adhere to one's value system cannot be a legally cognizable interest, cf. Diamond v. Charles (1986), let alone an interest that can justify invading the houses, hearts, and minds of citizens who choose to live their lives differently.

IV

It took but three years for the Court to see the error in its analysis in Minersville v. Gobitis (1940), and to recognize that the threat to national cohesion posed by a refusal to salute the flag was vastly outweighed by the threat to those same values posed by compelling such a salute. See West Virginia v. Barnette (1943). I can only hope that here, too, the Court soon will reconsider its analysis and conclude that depriving individuals of the right to choose for themselves how to conduct their intimate relationships poses a far greater threat to the values most deeply rooted in our Nation's history than tolerance of nonconformity could ever do. Because I think the Court today betrays those values, I dissent.

■ JUSTICE STEVENS, with whom JUSTICE BRENNAN and JUSTICE MARSHALL join, dissenting.

Like the statute that is challenged in this case, the rationale of the Court's opinion applies equally to the prohibited conduct regardless of whether the parties who engage in it are married or unmarried, or are of the same or different sexes. . . . The history of the Georgia statute before us clearly reveals this traditional prohibition of heterosexual, as well as homosexual, sodomy. Indeed, at one point in the 20th century, Georgia's law was construed to permit certain sexual conduct between homosexual women even though such conduct was prohibited between heterosexuals. The history of the statutes cited by the majority as proof for the proposition that sodomy is not constitutionally protected, similarly reveals a prohibition on heterosexual, as well as homosexual, sodomy.[8]

Because the Georgia statute expresses the traditional view that sodomy is an immoral kind of conduct regardless of the identity of the persons who engage in it, I believe that a proper analysis of its constitutionality requires consideration of two questions: First, may a State totally prohibit the described conduct by means of a neutral law applying without exception to all persons subject to its jurisdiction? If not, may the State save the statute by announcing that it will only enforce the law against homosexuals? . . .

---

[8]   A review of the statutes cited by the majority discloses that, in 1791, in 1868, and today, the vast majority of sodomy statutes do not differentiate between homosexual and heterosexual sodomy. [Footnote by Justice Stevens.]

I

Our prior cases make two propositions abundantly clear. First, the fact that the governing majority in a State has traditionally viewed a particular practice as immoral is not a sufficient reason for upholding a law prohibiting the practice; neither history nor tradition could save a law prohibiting miscegenation from constitutional attack.[9] Second, individual decisions by married persons, concerning the intimacies of their physical relationship, even when not intended to produce offspring, are a form of "liberty" protected by the Due Process Clause of the Fourteenth Amendment. *Griswold.* Moreover, this protection extends to intimate choices by unmarried as well as married persons. *Carey; Eisenstadt.*

In consideration of claims of this kind, the Court has emphasized the individual interest in privacy, but its decisions have actually been animated by an even more fundamental concern. As I wrote some years ago:

> These cases . . . [deal] with the individual's right to make certain unusually important decisions that will affect his own, or his family's, destiny. The Court has referred to such decisions as implicating "basic values," as being "fundamental," and as being dignified by history and tradition. The . . . Court's language in these cases brings to mind the origins of the American heritage of freedom—the abiding interest in individual liberty that makes certain state intrusions on the citizen's right to decide how he will live his own life intolerable. Guided by history, our tradition of respect for the dignity of individual choice in matters of conscience . . . federal judges have accepted the responsibility for recognition and protection of these rights in appropriate cases. Fitzgerald v. Porter Memorial Hospital (7th Cir.1975), cert. denied (1976).

Society has every right to encourage its individual members to follow particular traditions in expressing affection for one another and in gratifying their personal desires. It, of course, may prohibit an individual from imposing his will on another to satisfy his own selfish interests. It also may prevent an individual from interfering with, or violating, a legally sanctioned and protected relationship, such as marriage. And it may explain the relative advantages and disadvantages of different forms of intimate expression. But when individual married couples are isolated from observation by others, the way in which they

---

[9]   See *Loving.* Interestingly, miscegenation was once treated as a crime similar to sodomy. [Footnote by Justice Stevens.]

voluntarily choose to conduct their intimate relations is a matter for them—not the State—to decide. The essential "liberty" that animated the development of the law in cases like *Griswold, Eisenstadt*, and *Carey* surely embraces the right to engage in nonreproductive, sexual conduct that others may consider offensive or immoral.

. . . [O]ur prior cases thus establish that a State may not prohibit sodomy within "the sacred precincts of marital bedrooms," *Griswold*, or, indeed, between unmarried heterosexual adults. *Eisenstadt*. In all events, it is perfectly clear that the State of Georgia may not totally prohibit the conduct proscribed by § 16–6–2.

II

If the Georgia statute cannot be enforced as it is written . . . the State must assume the burden of justifying a selective application of its law. Either the persons to whom Georgia seeks to apply its statute do not have the same interest in "liberty" that others have, or there must be a reason why the State may be permitted to apply a generally applicable law to certain persons that it does not apply to others. The first possibility is plainly unacceptable. Although the meaning of the principle that "all men are created equal" is not always clear, it surely must mean that every free citizen has the same interest in "liberty" that the members of the majority share. From the standpoint of the individual, the homosexual and the heterosexual have the same interest in deciding how he will live his own life. . . .

The second possibility is similarly unacceptable. A policy of selective application must be supported by a neutral and legitimate interest—something more substantial than a habitual dislike for, or ignorance about, the disfavored group. Neither the State nor the Court has identified any such interest in this case. The Court has posited as a justification for the Georgia statute "the presumed belief of a majority of the electorate in Georgia that homosexual sodomy is immoral and unacceptable." But the Georgia electorate has expressed no such belief—instead, its representatives enacted a law that presumably reflects the belief that all sodomy is immoral and unacceptable. Unless the Court is prepared to conclude that such a law is constitutional, it may not rely on the work product of the Georgia Legislature to support its holding. For the Georgia statute does not single out homosexuals as a separate class meriting special disfavored treatment. . . .

EDITORS' NOTES

(1)   To what extent was the disagreement between Justices White and Blackmun a disagreement about WHAT the Constitution is? In particular, do they disagree about whether we should conceive the constitutional right of liberty specifically or abstractly? Was Michael Hardwick urging the Court to "discover new fundamental rights" or simply asking it to extend a fundamental right already protected for heterosexuals to homosexuals?

(2)   What was White's (and Burger's) conception of constitutionally relevant "tradition"? Was it merely a notion of concrete historical practices embodied in statute books and the common law as of 1868, without regard for whether those practices have changed over time? Contrast their understanding with two other conceptions of tradition discussed above: as a "living thing" or as abstract moral principles to which we as a people aspire (whether or not we have realized them in our historical practices)?

(3)   Do the "traditions" that White and Burger invoked condemn only homosexual sodomy or all sodomy (as Stevens suggested)? Did the majority's analyses imply that a statute criminalizing sodomy between married heterosexuals would be constitutional? In *Bowers* itself, Georgia conceded at oral argument that such a statute would be unconstitutional under the principles of Griswold v. Connecticut (1965; discussed above). What would White and Burger have said?

(4)   White is clearly worried that protecting the right asserted here will put the Court on a slippery slope. Are his fears warranted? Is there really no distinction between the right Hardwick claims and (1) use of illegal drugs at home and (2) adultery, incest, and other sexual crimes committed in the home?

(5)   The Papers of Justice Thurgood Marshall indicate that in *Bowers*, Powell initially voted to affirm the decision below on the basis of the Eighth Amendment's prohibition of cruel and unusual punishment, but subsequently changed his vote. (The Library of Congress, Manuscripts Division, Case File 393.) Several years later, after he had retired, Powell publicly remarked, "I think I probably made a mistake" in voting with the majority in *Bowers*. See Linda Greenhouse, "When Second Thoughts In Case Come Too Late," *N.Y. Times*, Nov. 5, 1990, p. A14. He had come to believe the majority opinion in *Bowers* "was inconsistent in a general way" with Roe v. Wade (1973). Were Powell's second thoughts about a conflict between *Bowers* and *Roe* sound?

At the time Powell cast his decisive vote in *Bowers*, he stated to one of his clerks that he had never met a homosexual. See John C. Jeffries, Jr., *Justice Lewis F. Powell, Jr.* (New York: Charles Scribner's Sons, 1994), pp. 511–30. In fact, Jeffries reports, the clerk to whom Powell was speaking was gay, as were many of his other previous clerks. Powell simply was not aware of this. Had he been aware of this, might it have changed his perceptions concerning homosexuality and whether there was any resemblance or analogy between heterosexual intimate association (safeguarded in *Griswold*) and that of homosexuals? Are such considerations regarding the real life knowledge and experience of justices appropriate in constitutional interpretation?

(6) Did *Bowers* leave open the possibility of challenges to discrimination against homosexuals under the Equal Protection Clause? See Romer v. Evans (1996; reprinted as the next case).

(7) Between 1986 and 2003, some state courts construed their state constitutions to invalidate criminal sodomy statutes notwithstanding the Supreme Court's interpretation of the U.S. Constitution in *Bowers*. Notably, the Georgia Supreme Court invalidated, on state constitutional grounds, the very Georgia law upheld in *Bowers*. Powell v. State (Ga. 1998). It ruled that private consensual sodomy between adults is protected within the right of privacy guaranteed by the Georgia Constitution's due process clause. These cases illustrate a basic feature of the U.S. federal system: the independent jurisprudence of state constitutional law. This feature becomes important in the movement toward protection of marriage equality. See Baker v. State (1999; reprinted below) and Goodridge v. Department of Public Health (2003; reprinted below), two landmark state supreme court decisions under state constitutions.

(8) Lawrence v. Texas (2003; reprinted below), overruled *Bowers*.

———

"We must conclude that Amendment 2 classifies homosexuals not to further a proper legislative end but to make them unequal to everyone else. This Colorado cannot do. A State cannot so deem a class of persons a stranger to its laws."—JUSTICE KENNEDY

"The Court has mistaken a Kulturkampf for a fit of spite. The constitutional amendment before us here is not the manifestation of a 'bare . . . desire to harm' homosexuals, but is rather a modest attempt by seemingly tolerant Coloradans to

preserve traditional sexual mores against the efforts of a politically powerful minority to revise those mores through use of the laws."—JUSTICE SCALIA

ROMER V. EVANS
517 U.S. 620, 116 S.Ct. 1620, 134 L.Ed.2d 855 (1996)

■ JUSTICE KENNEDY delivered the opinion of the Court.

One century ago, the first Justice Harlan admonished this Court that the Constitution "neither knows nor tolerates classes among citizens." Plessy v. Ferguson (1896) (dissenting opinion). Unheeded then, those words now are understood to state a commitment to the law's neutrality where the rights of persons are at stake. The Equal Protection Clause enforces this principle and today requires us to hold invalid a provision of Colorado's Constitution.

I

The enactment challenged in this case is an amendment to the Constitution of the State of Colorado, adopted in a 1992 statewide referendum. The parties and the state courts refer to it as "Amendment 2," its designation when submitted to the voters. The impetus for the amendment and the contentious campaign that preceded its adoption came in large part from ordinances that had been passed in various Colorado municipalities. For example, the cities of Aspen and Boulder and the City and County of Denver each had enacted ordinances which banned discrimination in many transactions and activities, including housing, employment, education, public accommodations, and health and welfare services. What gave rise to the statewide controversy was the protection the ordinances afforded to persons discriminated against by reason of their sexual orientation. Amendment 2 repeals these ordinances to the extent they prohibit discrimination on the basis of "homosexual, lesbian or bisexual orientation, conduct, practices or relationships." Colo. Const., Art. II, § 30b.

Yet Amendment 2, in explicit terms, does more than repeal or rescind these provisions. It prohibits all legislative, executive or judicial action at any level of state or local government designed to protect the named class, a class we shall refer to as homosexual persons or gays and lesbians. The amendment reads:

No Protected Status Based on Homosexual, Lesbian, or Bisexual Orientation. Neither the State of Colorado, through any of its branches or departments, nor any of its agencies, political subdivisions, municipalities or school districts, shall enact, adopt or enforce any statute, regulation, ordinance or policy whereby homosexual, lesbian or bisexual orientation, conduct, practices or relationships shall constitute or otherwise be the basis of or entitle any person or class of persons to have or claim any minority status, quota preferences, protected status or claim of discrimination. This Section of the Constitution shall be in all respects self-executing.

. . . [T]he State Supreme Court held that Amendment 2 was subject to strict scrutiny under the Fourteenth Amendment because it infringed the fundamental right of gays and lesbians to participate in the political process. To reach this conclusion, the state court relied on our voting rights cases, e.g., Reynolds v. Sims (1964); Harper v. Virginia Bd. of Elections (1966); Williams v. Rhodes (1968), and on our precedents involving discriminatory restructuring of governmental decision making. On remand, the State advanced various arguments in an effort to show that Amendment 2 was narrowly tailored to serve compelling interests, but the trial court found none sufficient. It enjoined enforcement of Amendment 2, and the Supreme Court of Colorado affirmed the ruling. We granted certiorari and now affirm the judgment, but on a rationale different from that adopted by the State Supreme Court.

II

The State's principal argument in defense of Amendment 2 is that it puts gays and lesbians in the same position as all other persons. So, the State says, the measure does no more than deny homosexuals special rights. This reading of the amendment's language is implausible. We rely not upon our own interpretation of the amendment but upon the authoritative construction of Colorado's Supreme Court . . . :

The immediate objective of Amendment 2 is, at a minimum, to repeal existing statutes, regulations, ordinances, and policies of state and local entities that barred discrimination based on sexual orientation and various provisions prohibiting discrimination based on sexual orientation at state colleges.

The "ultimate effect" of Amendment 2 is to prohibit any governmental entity from adopting similar, or more protective statutes, regulations, ordinances, or policies in the future unless the state constitution is first amended to permit such measures.

Sweeping and comprehensive is the change in legal status effected by this law. So much is evident from the ordinances that the Colorado Supreme Court declared would be void by operation of Amendment 2. Homosexuals, by state decree, are put in a solitary class with respect to transactions and relations in both the private and governmental spheres. The amendment withdraws from homosexuals, but no others, specific legal protection from the injuries caused by discrimination, and it forbids reinstatement of these laws and policies.

The change that Amendment 2 works in the legal status of gays and lesbians in the private sphere is far-reaching, both on its own terms and when considered in light of the structure and operation of modern anti-discrimination laws. That structure is well illustrated by contemporary statutes and ordinances prohibiting discrimination by providers of public accommodations. "At common law, innkeepers, smiths, and others who 'made profession of a public employment,' were prohibited from refusing, without good reason, to serve a customer." Hurley v. Irish-American Gay, Lesbian and Bisexual Group of Boston, Inc. (1995). The duty was a general one and did not specify protection for particular groups. The common law rules, however, proved insufficient in many instances, and it was settled early that the Fourteenth Amendment did not give Congress a general power to prohibit discrimination in public accommodations, Civil Rights Cases (1883). In consequence, most States have chosen to counter discrimination by enacting detailed statutory schemes.

Colorado's state and municipal laws typify this emerging tradition of statutory protection and follow a consistent pattern. The laws first enumerate the persons or entities subject to a duty not to discriminate. The list goes well beyond the entities covered by the common law. The Boulder ordinance, for example, has a comprehensive definition of entities deemed places of "public accommodation." They include "any place of business engaged in any sales to the general public and any place that offers services, facilities, privileges, or advantages to the general public or that receives financial support through solicitation of the general public or through governmental subsidy of any kind."...

These statutes and ordinances also depart from the common law by enumerating the groups or persons within their ambit of protection. Enumeration is the essential device used to make the duty not to discriminate concrete and to provide guidance for those who must comply. In following this approach, Colorado's state and local governments have not limited anti-discrimination laws to groups that have so far been given the protection of heightened equal protection scrutiny under our cases. Rather, they set forth an extensive catalogue of traits which cannot be the basis for discrimination, including age, military status, marital status, pregnancy, parenthood, custody of a minor child, political affiliation, physical or mental disability of an individual or of his or her associates—and, in recent times, sexual orientation.

Amendment 2 bars homosexuals from securing protection against the injuries that these public-accommodations laws address. That in itself is a severe consequence, but there is more. Amendment 2, in addition, nullifies specific legal protections for this targeted class in all transactions in housing, sale of real estate, insurance, health and welfare services, private education, and employment.

Not confined to the private sphere, Amendment 2 also operates to repeal and forbid all laws or policies providing specific protection for gays or lesbians from discrimination by every level of Colorado government. . . .

Amendment 2's reach may not be limited to specific laws passed for the benefit of gays and lesbians. It is a fair, if not necessary, inference from the broad language of the amendment that it deprives gays and lesbians even of the protection of general laws and policies that prohibit arbitrary discrimination in governmental and private settings. At some point in the systematic administration of these laws, an official must determine whether homosexuality is an arbitrary and thus forbidden basis for decision. Yet a decision to that effect would itself amount to a policy prohibiting discrimination on the basis of homosexuality, and so would appear to be no more valid under Amendment 2 than the specific prohibitions against discrimination the state court held invalid.

[T]he state court did not decide whether the amendment has this effect, however, and neither need we. . . . In any event, even if, as we doubt, homosexuals could find some safe harbor in laws of general application, we cannot accept the view that Amendment 2's prohibition on specific legal protections does no more than deprive homosexuals of special rights. To the contrary, the amendment imposes a special disability upon those persons alone. Homosexuals are forbidden the safeguards that others enjoy or may seek without constraint. They can obtain specific protection against discrimination only by enlisting the citizenry of Colorado to amend the state constitution or perhaps, on the State's view, by trying to pass helpful laws of general applicability. This is so no matter how local or discrete the harm, no matter how public and widespread the injury. We find nothing special in the protections Amendment 2 withholds. These are protections taken for granted by most people either because they already have them or do not need them; these are protections against exclusion from an almost limitless number of transactions and endeavors that constitute ordinary civic life in a free society.

III

The Fourteenth Amendment's promise that no person shall be denied the equal protection of the laws must co-exist with the practical necessity that most legislation classifies for one purpose or another, with resulting disadvantage to various groups or persons. We have attempted to reconcile the principle with the reality by stating that, if a law neither burdens a fundamental right nor targets a suspect class, we will uphold the legislative classification so long as it bears a rational relation to some legitimate end.

Amendment 2 fails, indeed defies, even this conventional inquiry. First, the amendment has the peculiar property of imposing a broad and undifferentiated disability on a single named group, an exceptional and . . . invalid form of legislation. Second, its sheer breadth is so discontinuous with the reasons offered for it that the amendment seems inexplicable by anything but animus toward the class that it affects; it lacks a rational relationship to legitimate state interests.

Taking the first point, even in the ordinary equal protection case calling for the most deferential of standards, we insist on knowing the relation between the classification adopted and the object to be attained. . . . In the ordinary case, a law will be sustained if it can be said to advance a legitimate government interest, even if the law seems unwise or works to the disadvantage of a particular group, or if the rationale for it seems tenuous. See Williamson v. Lee Optical of Okla., Inc. (1955); Railway Express Agency, Inc. v. New York (1949). . . . By requiring that the classification bear a rational relationship to an independent and legitimate legislative end, we ensure that classifications are not drawn for the purpose of disadvantaging the group burdened by the law. See United States Railroad Retirement Bd. v. Fritz (1980) (Stevens, J., concurring) ("If the adverse impact on the disfavored class is an apparent aim of the legislature, its impartiality would be suspect.").

Amendment 2 confounds this normal process of judicial review. It is at once too narrow and too broad. It identifies persons by a single trait and then denies them protection across the board. The resulting disqualification of a class of persons from the right to seek specific protection from the law is unprecedented in our jurisprudence. . . .

It is not within our constitutional tradition to enact laws of this sort. Central both to the idea of the rule of law and to our own Constitution's guarantee of equal protection is the principle that government and each of its parts remain open on impartial terms to all who seek its assistance. Respect for this principle explains why laws singling out a certain class of citizens for disfavored legal status or general hardships are rare. A law declaring that in general it shall be more difficult for one group of citizens than for all others to seek aid from the government is itself a denial of equal protection of the laws in the most literal sense.

Davis v. Beason (1890), not cited by the parties but relied upon by the dissent, is not evidence that Amendment 2 is within our constitutional tradition, and any reliance upon it as authority for sustaining the amendment is misplaced. In *Davis*, the Court approved an Idaho territorial statute denying Mormons, polygamists, and advocates of polygamy the right to vote and to hold office because, as the Court construed the statute, it "simply excludes from the privilege of voting, or of holding any office of honor, trust or profit, those who have been convicted of certain offences, and those who advocate a practical resistance to the laws of the Territory and justify and approve the commission of crimes forbidden by it." To the extent *Davis* held that persons advocating a certain practice may be denied the right to vote, it is no longer good law. Brandenburg v. Ohio (1969) (per curiam). To the extent it held that the groups designated in the statute may be deprived of the right to vote because of their status, its ruling could not stand without surviving strict scrutiny, a most doubtful outcome. To the extent *Davis* held that a convicted felon may be denied the right to vote, its holding is not implicated by our decision and is unexceptionable.

A second and related point is that laws of the kind now before us raise the inevitable inference that the disadvantage imposed is born of animosity toward the class of persons affected. "[I]f the constitutional conception of 'equal protection of the laws' means anything, it must at the very least mean that a bare . . . desire to harm a politically unpopular group cannot constitute a legitimate governmental interest." Department of Agriculture v. Moreno (1973). Even laws enacted for broad and ambitious purposes often can be explained by reference to legitimate public policies which justify the incidental disadvantages they impose on certain persons. Amendment 2, however, in making a general announcement that gays and lesbians shall not have any particular protections from the law, inflicts on them immediate, continuing, and real injuries that outrun and belie any legitimate justifications that may be claimed for it. We conclude that, in addition to the far-reaching deficiencies of Amendment 2 that we have noted, the principles it offends, in another sense, are conventional and venerable; a law must bear a rational relationship to a legitimate governmental purpose, and Amendment 2 does not.

The primary rationale the State offers for Amendment 2 is respect for other citizens' freedom of association, and in particular the liberties of landlords or employers who have personal or religious objections to homosexuality. Colorado also cites its interest in conserving resources to fight discrimination against other groups. The breadth of the Amendment is so far removed from these particular justifications that we find it impossible to credit them. We cannot say that Amendment 2 is directed to any identifiable legitimate purpose or discrete objective. It is a status-based enactment divorced from any factual context from which we could discern a relationship to legitimate state interests; it is a classification of persons undertaken for its own sake, something the Equal Protection Clause does not permit. "[C]lass legislation . . . [is] obnoxious to the prohibitions of the Fourteenth Amendment. . . ." *Civil Rights Cases.*

We must conclude that Amendment 2 classifies homosexuals not to further a proper legislative end but to make them unequal to everyone else. This Colorado cannot do. A State cannot so deem a class of persons a stranger to its laws. Amendment 2 violates the Equal Protection Clause, and the judgment of the Supreme Court of Colorado is affirmed.

■ JUSTICE SCALIA, with whom THE CHIEF JUSTICE [REHNQUIST] and JUSTICE THOMAS join, dissenting.

The Court has mistaken a Kulturkampf for a fit of spite. The constitutional amendment before us here is not the manifestation of a " 'bare . . . desire to harm' " homosexuals, but is rather a modest attempt by seemingly tolerant Coloradans to preserve traditional sexual mores against the efforts of a politically powerful minority to revise those mores through use of the laws. That objective, and the means chosen to achieve it, are not only unimpeachable under any constitutional doctrine hitherto pronounced (hence the opinion's heavy reliance upon principles of righteousness rather than judicial holdings); they have been specifically approved by the Congress and by this Court.

In holding that homosexuality cannot be singled out for disfavorable treatment, the Court contradicts a decision, unchallenged here, pronounced only 10 years ago, see Bowers v. Hardwick (1986), and places the prestige of this institution behind the proposition that opposition to homosexuality is as reprehensible as racial or religious bias. Whether it is or not is precisely the cultural debate that gave rise to the Colorado constitutional amendment (and to the preferential laws against which the amendment was directed). Since the Constitution of the United States says nothing about this subject, it is left to be resolved by normal democratic means, including the democratic adoption of provisions in state constitutions. This Court has no business imposing upon all Americans the resolution favored by the elite class from which the Members of this institution are selected, pronouncing that "animosity" toward homosexuality is evil. I vigorously dissent.

I

[The court rejects as "implausible"] the State's arguments that Amendment 2 "puts gays and lesbians in the same position as all other persons," and "does no more than deny homosexuals special rights." . . .

In reaching this conclusion, the Court considers it unnecessary to decide the validity of the State's argument that Amendment 2 does not deprive homosexuals of the "protection [afforded by] general laws and policies that prohibit arbitrary discrimination in governmental and private settings." I agree that we need not resolve that dispute, because the Supreme Court of Colorado has resolved it for us:

> [I]t is significant to note that Colorado law currently proscribes discrimination against persons who are not suspect classes, including discrimination based on age, marital or family status, veterans' status, and for any legal, off-duty conduct such as smoking tobacco. *Of course Amendment 2 is not intended to have any effect on this legislation, but seeks only to prevent the adoption of antidiscrimination laws intended to protect gays, lesbians, and bisexuals.* (emphasis added).

. . . The clear import of the Colorado court's conclusion . . . is that "general laws and policies that prohibit arbitrary discrimination" would continue to prohibit discrimination on the basis of homosexual conduct as well. This analysis . . . lays to rest such horribles, raised in the course of oral argument, as the prospect that assaults upon homosexuals could not be prosecuted. The amendment prohibits special treatment of homosexuals, and nothing more. It would not affect, for example, a requirement of state law that pensions be paid to all retiring state employees with a certain length of service; homosexual employees, as well as others, would be entitled to that benefit. But it would prevent the State or any municipality from making death-benefit payments to the "life partner" of a homosexual when it does not make such payments to the long-time roommate of a nonhomosexual employee. . . .

Despite all of its hand-wringing about the potential effect of Amendment 2 on general antidiscrimination laws, the Court's opinion ultimately does not dispute all this, but assumes it to be true. The only denial of equal treatment it contends homosexuals have suffered is this: They may not obtain preferential treatment without amending the state constitution. That is to say, the principle underlying the Court's opinion is that one who is accorded equal treatment under the laws, but cannot as readily as others obtain preferential treatment under the laws, has been denied equal protection of the laws. If merely stating this alleged "equal protection" violation does not suffice to refute it, our constitutional jurisprudence has achieved terminal silliness.

The central thesis of the Court's reasoning is that any group is denied equal protection when, to obtain advantage (or, presumably, to avoid disadvantage), it must have recourse to a more general and hence more difficult level of political decision making than others. The world has never heard of such a principle, which is why the Court's opinion is so long on emotive utterance and so short on relevant legal citation. . . .

. . . The Court's entire novel theory rests upon the proposition that there is something special—something that cannot be justified by normal "rational basis" analysis—in making a disadvantaged group (or a nonpreferred group) resort to a higher decision making level. That proposition finds no support in law or logic.

II

I turn next to whether there was a legitimate rational basis for the substance of the constitutional amendment—for the prohibition of special protection for homosexuals.[1] It is unsurprising that the Court avoids discussion of this question, since the answer is so obviously yes. The case most relevant to the issue before us today is not even mentioned in the Court's opinion: In Bowers v. Hardwick (1986), we held that the Constitution does not prohibit what virtually all States had done from the founding of the Republic until very recent years—making homosexual conduct a crime. That holding is unassailable, except by those who think that the Constitution changes to suit current fashions. But in any event it is a given in the present case: Respondents' briefs did not urge overruling *Bowers*, and at oral argument respondents' counsel expressly disavowed any intent to seek such overruling. If it is constitutionally permissible for a State to make homosexual conduct criminal, surely it is constitutionally permissible for a State to enact other laws merely disfavoring homosexual

---

1   The Court evidently agrees that "rational basis"—the normal test for compliance with the Equal Protection Clause—is the governing standard. The trial court rejected respondents' argument that homosexuals constitute a "suspect" or "quasi-suspect" class, and respondents elected not to appeal that ruling to the Supreme Court of Colorado. And the Court implicitly rejects the Supreme Court of Colorado's holding that Amendment 2 infringes upon a "fundamental right" of "independently identifiable class[es]" to "participate equally in the political process." [Footnote by Justice Scalia.]

conduct. (As the Court of Appeals for the District of Columbia Circuit has aptly put it: "If the Court [in *Bowers*] was unwilling to object to state laws that criminalize the behavior that defines the class, it is hardly open . . . to conclude that state sponsored discrimination against the class is invidious. After all, there can hardly be more palpable discrimination against a class than making the conduct that defines the class criminal." Padula v. Webster (1987).) And a fortiori it is constitutionally permissible for a State to adopt a provision not even disfavoring homosexual conduct, but merely prohibiting all levels of state government from bestowing special protections upon homosexual conduct. Respondents (who, unlike the Court, cannot afford the luxury of ignoring inconvenient precedent) counter *Bowers* with the argument that a greater-includes-the-lesser rationale cannot justify Amendment 2's application to individuals who do not engage in homosexual acts, but are merely of homosexual "orientation." Some courts of appeals [including apparently the Supreme Court of Colorado] have concluded that . . . that is a distinction without a difference.

But assuming that, in Amendment 2, a person of homosexual "orientation" is someone who does not engage in homosexual conduct but merely has a tendency or desire to do so, *Bowers* still suffices to establish a rational basis for the provision. If it is rational to criminalize the conduct, surely it is rational to deny special favor and protection to those with a self-avowed tendency or desire to engage in the conduct. Indeed, where criminal sanctions are not involved, homosexual "orientation" is an acceptable stand-in for homosexual conduct. A State "does not violate the Equal Protection Clause merely because the classifications made by its laws are imperfect." Dandridge v. Williams (1970). [A]mendment 2 is not constitutionally invalid simply because it could have been drawn more precisely so as to withdraw special antidiscrimination protections only from those of homosexual "orientation" who actually engage in homosexual conduct. . . .

III

The foregoing suffices to establish what the Court's failure to cite any case remotely in point would lead one to suspect: No principle set forth in the Constitution, nor even any imagined by this Court in the past 200 years, prohibits what Colorado has done here. . . . What it has done is not only unprohibited, but eminently reasonable, with close, congressionally approved precedent in earlier constitutional practice.

First, as to its eminent reasonableness. The Court's opinion contains grim, disapproving hints that Coloradans have been guilty of "animus" or "animosity" toward homosexuality, as though that has been established as Un-American. Of course it is our moral heritage that one should not hate any human being or class of human beings. But I had thought that one could consider certain conduct reprehensible—murder, for example, or polygamy, or cruelty to animals—and could exhibit even "animus" toward such conduct. Surely that is the only sort of "animus" at issue here: moral disapproval of homosexual conduct, the same sort of moral disapproval that produced the centuries-old criminal laws that we held constitutional in *Bowers*. . . .

But though Coloradans are, as I say, entitled to be hostile toward homosexual conduct, the fact is that the degree of hostility reflected by Amendment 2 is the smallest conceivable. The Court's portrayal of Coloradans as a society fallen victim to pointless, hate-filled "gay-bashing" is so false as to be comical. Colorado not only is one of the 25 States that have repealed their antisodomy laws, but was among the first to do so. But the society that eliminates criminal punishment for homosexual acts does not necessarily abandon the view that homosexuality is morally wrong and socially harmful; often, abolition simply reflects the view that enforcement of such criminal laws involves unseemly intrusion into the intimate lives of citizens.

There is a problem, however, which arises when criminal sanction of homosexuality is eliminated but moral and social disapprobation of homosexuality is meant to be retained. The Court cannot be unaware of that problem; it is evident in many cities of the country, and occasionally bubbles to the surface of the news, in heated political disputes over such matters as the introduction into local schools of books teaching that homosexuality is an optional and fully acceptable "alternate life style." The problem (a problem, that is, for those who wish to retain social disapprobation of homosexuality) is that, because those who engage in homosexual conduct tend to reside in disproportionate numbers in certain communities, have high disposable income, and of course care about homosexual-rights issues much more ardently than the public at large, they possess political power much greater than their numbers, both locally and statewide. Quite understandably, they devote this political power to achieving not merely a grudging social toleration, but full social acceptance, of homosexuality. See, e.g., Jacobs, The Rhetorical Construction of Rights: The Case of the Gay Rights Movement, 1969–1991, 72 *Neb. L.Rev.* 723, 724 (1993) ("[T]he task of gay rights proponents is to move the center of public discourse along a continuum from the rhetoric of disapprobation, to rhetoric of tolerance, and finally to affirmation").

By the time Coloradans were asked to vote on Amendment 2, their exposure to homosexuals' quest for social endorsement was not limited to newspaper accounts of happenings in places such as New York, Los Angeles, San Francisco, and Key West. Three Colorado cities—Aspen, Boulder, and Denver—had enacted ordinances that listed "sexual orientation" as an impermissible ground for discrimination, equating the moral disapproval of homosexual conduct with racial and religious bigotry. The phenomenon had even appeared statewide: the Governor of Colorado had signed an executive order pronouncing that "in the State of Colorado we recognize the diversity in our pluralistic society and strive to bring an end to discrimination in any form," and directing state agency-heads to "ensure non-discrimination" in hiring and promotion based on, among other things, "sexual orientation." I do not mean to be critical of these legislative successes; homosexuals are as entitled to use the legal system for reinforcement of their moral sentiments as are the rest of society. But they are subject to being countered by lawful, democratic countermeasures as well.

That is where Amendment 2 came in. It sought to counter both the geographic concentration and the disproportionate political power of homosexuals by (1) resolving the controversy at the statewide level, and (2) making the election a single-issue contest for both sides. It put directly, to all the citizens of the State, the question: Should homosexuality be given special protection? They answered no. The Court today asserts that this most democratic of procedures is unconstitutional. Lacking any cases to establish that facially absurd proposition, it simply asserts that it must be unconstitutional, because it has never happened before. . . .

But there is a [close] analogy, one that involves precisely the effort by the majority of citizens to preserve its view of sexual morality statewide, against the efforts of a geographically concentrated and politically powerful minority to undermine it. The constitutions of the States of Arizona, Idaho, New Mexico, Oklahoma, and Utah to this day contain provisions stating that polygamy is "forever prohibited." Polygamists, and those who have a polygamous "orientation," have been "singled out" by these provisions for much more severe treatment than merely denial of favored status; and that treatment can only be changed by achieving amendment of the state constitutions. The Court's disposition today suggests that these provisions are unconstitutional, and that polygamy must be permitted in these States on a state-legislated, or perhaps even local-option, basis—unless, of course, polygamists for some reason have fewer constitutional rights than homosexuals.

The United States Congress, by the way, required the inclusion of these antipolygamy provisions in the constitutions of Arizona, New Mexico, Oklahoma, and Utah, as a condition of their admission to statehood. Thus, this "singling out" of the sexual practices of a single group for statewide, democratic vote—so utterly alien to our constitutional system, the Court would have us believe—has not only happened, but has received the explicit approval of the United States Congress.

I cannot say that this Court has explicitly approved any of these state constitutional provisions; but it has approved a territorial statutory provision that went even further, depriving polygamists of the ability even to achieve a constitutional amendment, by depriving them of the power to vote. . . . [T]he proposition that polygamy can be criminalized, and those engaging in that crime deprived of the vote, remains good law. [Davis v.] Beason (1890) rejected the argument that "such discrimination is a denial of the equal protection of the laws." . . .

This Court cited *Beason* with approval as recently as 1993, in an opinion authored by the same Justice who writes for the Court today. That opinion said: "[A]dverse impact will not always lead to a finding of impermissible targeting. For example, a social harm may have been a legitimate concern of government for reasons quite apart from discrimination. . . . See, e.g., . . . Davis v. Beason." Church of Lukumi Babalu Aye, Inc. v. Hialeah. It remains to be explained how § 501 of the Idaho Revised Statutes was not an "impermissible targeting" of polygamists, but (the much more mild) Amendment 2 is an "impermissible targeting" of homosexuals. Has the Court concluded that the perceived social harm of polygamy is a "legitimate concern of government," and the perceived social harm of homosexuality is not?

IV

I strongly suspect that the answer to the last question is yes, which leads me to the last point I wish to make: The Court today . . . employs a constitutional theory heretofore unknown to frustrate Colorado's reasonable effort to preserve traditional American moral values. The Court's stern disapproval of "animosity" towards homosexuality might be compared with what an earlier Court (including the revered Justices Harlan and Bradley) said in Murphy v. Ramsey (1885), rejecting a constitutional challenge to a United States statute that denied the franchise in federal territories to those who engaged in polygamous cohabitation:

[C]ertainly no legislation can be supposed more wholesome and necessary in the founding of a free, self-governing commonwealth, fit to take rank as one of the co-ordinate States of the Union, than that which seeks to establish it on the basis of the idea of the family, as consisting in and springing from the union for life of one man and one woman in the holy estate of matrimony; the sure foundation of all that is stable and noble in our civilization; the best guaranty of that reverent morality which is the source of all beneficent progress in social and political improvement.

I would not myself indulge in such official praise for heterosexual monogamy, because I think it no business of the courts (as opposed to the political branches) to take sides in this culture war.

But the Court today has done so, not only by inventing a novel and extravagant constitutional doctrine to take the victory away from traditional forces, but even by verbally disparaging as bigotry adherence to traditional attitudes. To suggest, for example, that this constitutional amendment springs from nothing more than " 'a bare . . . desire to harm a politically unpopular group' " is nothing short of insulting. (It is also nothing short of preposterous to call "politically unpopular" a group which enjoys enormous influence in American media and politics, and which, as the trial court here noted, though composing no more than 4% of the population had the support of 46% of the voters on Amendment 2.)

When the Court takes sides in the culture wars, it tends to be with the knights rather than the villeins—and more specifically with the Templars, reflecting the views and values of the lawyer class from which the Court's Members are drawn. How that class feels about homosexuality will be evident to anyone who wishes to interview job applicants at virtually any of the Nation's law schools. The interviewer may refuse to offer a job because the applicant is a Republican; because he is an adulterer; because he went to the wrong prep school or belongs to the wrong country club; because he eats snails; because he is a womanizer; because she wears real-animal fur; or even because he hates the Chicago Cubs. But if the interviewer should wish not to be an associate or partner of an applicant because he disapproves of the applicant's homosexuality, then he will have violated the pledge which the Association of American Law Schools requires all its member-schools to exact from job interviewers: "assurance of the employer's willingness" to hire homosexuals. This law-school view of what "prejudices" must be stamped out may be contrasted with the more plebeian attitudes that apparently still prevail in the United States

Congress, which has been unresponsive to repeated attempts to extend to homosexuals the protections of federal civil rights laws, and which took the pains to exclude them specifically from the Americans With Disabilities Act of 1990.

Today's opinion has no foundation in American constitutional law, and barely pretends to. The people of Colorado have adopted an entirely reasonable provision which does not even disfavor homosexuals in any substantive sense, but merely denies them preferential treatment. Amendment 2 is designed to prevent piecemeal deterioration of the sexual morality favored by a majority of Coloradans, and is not only an appropriate means to that legitimate end, but a means that Americans have employed before. Striking it down is an act, not of judicial judgment, but of political will. I dissent.

EDITORS' NOTES

(1)   The Court rejects Colorado's argument (accepted by Justice Scalia) that Amendment 2 "does no more than deny homosexuals special rights." To the contrary, the majority contends, the protections that Amendment 2 withholds are "taken for granted by most people either because they already have them or do not need them." The Court held that Colorado had violated the Equal Protection Clause by "deem[ing] a class of persons a stranger to its laws." Who has the better argument concerning whether Amendment 2 "does no more than deny homosexuals special rights," the majority or Justice Scalia? If a law protecting homosexuals from discrimination confers upon them special rights, could the same be said of civil rights laws protecting African Americans from discrimination on the basis of race? Indeed, does the objection to "special rights" entail that every civil rights law protecting against discrimination on every basis confers "special rights" and is for that reason unconstitutional? If not, which "special rights" are constitutionally objectionable and which constitutionally permissible?

(2)   What is the relationship between the Court's equal protection holding in *Romer* and its due process holding in Bowers v. Hardwick (1986; reprinted above)? (Even though Lawrence v. Texas [2003; reprinted below] overruled *Bowers*, it is worth considering this question.) Would *Romer* reject, as "animus" and a "bare . . . desire to harm a politically unpopular group," what *Bowers* readily presumed was a legitimate governmental objective, namely, the attempt to preserve traditional sexual morality? Does *Romer* imply that *Bowers* was wrongly decided? Is Scalia right to suggest that *Bowers* is "unassailable" and to argue from

this presupposition that *Romer* is wrongly decided? Or can the two cases be distinguished?

(3) Analytically, it is important to recognize that the Court does not consider certain familiar equal protection arguments. First, the Court does not consider the question whether discrimination against homosexuals constitutes a suspect classification that, like racial classifications, would trigger strict scrutiny. Second, the Court does not address whether such discrimination is an impermissible discrimination on the basis of gender that would invoke intermediate scrutiny. What, then, does the case hold? Does it, like Cleburne v. Cleburne Living Center (1985; discussed above), apply rational basis "with bite" in scrutinizing both the legitimacy of the governmental objective and the fit between the measure in question and that objective?

(4) What is the basis for Scalia's objection that the Court "places the prestige of this institution behind the proposition that opposition to homosexuality is as reprehensible as racial or religious bias"? Is this objection sound?

(5) As Scalia sees it, there is a "culture war" between "seemingly tolerant Coloradans," who have made a "modest attempt . . . to preserve traditional sexual mores," and gays and lesbians, "a politically powerful minority" who "devote this political power to achieving not merely a grudging social toleration, but full social acceptance, of homosexuality." What is the relevance for constitutional interpretation of Scalia's characterization of gays and lesbians as "a politically powerful minority"? Of his claim that "they devote this political power to achieving not merely a grudging social toleration, but full social acceptance, of homosexuality"? See Linda C. McClain, "Toleration, Autonomy, and Governmental Promotion of Good Lives: Beyond 'Empty' Toleration to Toleration as Respect," 59 *Ohio St. L.J.* 19 (1998); James E. Fleming and Linda C. McClain, *Ordered Liberty: Rights, Responsibilities, and Virtues* (Cambridge: Harvard University Press, 2013), chap. 7; Michael J. Sandel, "Moral Argument and Liberal Toleration: Abortion and Homosexuality," 77 *Cal. L. Rev.* 521 (1989).

"The central holding of *Bowers* has been brought in question by this case, and it should be addressed. Its continuance as precedent demeans the lives of homosexual persons."—JUSTICE KENNEDY

"*Bowers'* conclusion that homosexual sodomy is not a fundamental right 'deeply rooted in this Nation's history and tradition' is utterly unassailable."—JUSTICE SCALIA

LAWRENCE V. TEXAS

539 U.S. 558, 123 S.Ct. 2472, 156 L.Ed.2d 508 (2003)

■ JUSTICE KENNEDY delivered the opinion of the Court.

Liberty protects the person from unwarranted government intrusions into a dwelling or other private places. In our tradition the State is not omnipresent in the home. And there are other spheres of our lives and existence, outside the home, where the State should not be a dominant presence. Freedom extends beyond spatial bounds. Liberty presumes an autonomy of self that includes freedom of thought, belief, expression, and certain intimate conduct. The instant case involves liberty of the person both in its spatial and more transcendent dimensions.

I

The question before the Court is the validity of a Texas statute making it a crime for two persons of the same sex to engage in certain intimate sexual conduct.

In Houston, Texas, officers of the Harris County Police Department were dispatched to a private residence in response to a reported weapons disturbance. They entered an apartment where one of the petitioners, John Geddes Lawrence, resided. The right of the police to enter does not seem to have been questioned. The officers observed Lawrence and another man, Tyron Garner, engaging in a sexual act. The two petitioners were arrested, held in custody over night, and charged and convicted before a Justice of the Peace.

The complaints described their crime as "deviate sexual intercourse, namely anal sex, with a member of the same sex (man)." The applicable state law is Tex. Penal Code Ann. § 21.06(a) (2003). It provides: "A person commits an offense if he engages in deviate sexual intercourse with another individual of the same sex." The statute defines "[d]eviate sexual intercourse" as follows:

(A) any contact between any part of the genitals of one person and the mouth or anus of another person; or

(B) the penetration of the genitals or the anus of another person with an object. § 21.01(1).

The petitioners exercised their right to a trial *de novo* in Harris County Criminal Court. They challenged the statute as a violation of the Equal Protection Clause of the Fourteenth Amendment and of a like provision of the Texas Constitution. Tex. Const., Art. 1, § 3a. Those contentions were rejected. The petitioners, having entered a plea of *nolo contendere*, were each fined $200 and assessed court costs of $141.25.

The Court of Appeals for the Texas Fourteenth District considered the petitioners' federal constitutional arguments under both the Equal Protection and Due Process Clauses of the Fourteenth Amendment. After hearing the case en banc the court, in a divided opinion, rejected the constitutional arguments and affirmed the convictions. . . .

The petitioners were adults at the time of the alleged offense. Their conduct was in private and consensual.

II

We conclude the case should be resolved by determining whether the petitioners were free as adults to engage in the private conduct in the exercise of their liberty under the Due Process Clause of the Fourteenth Amendment to the Constitution. For this inquiry we deem it necessary to reconsider the Court's holding in Bowers v. Hardwick (1986).

There are broad statements of the substantive reach of liberty under the Due Process Clause in earlier cases, including Pierce v. Society of Sisters (1925), and Meyer v. Nebraska (1923); but the most pertinent beginning point is our decision in Griswold v. Connecticut (1965).

In *Griswold* the Court invalidated a state law prohibiting the use of drugs or devices of contraception and counseling or aiding and abetting the use of contraceptives. The Court described the protected interest as a right to privacy and placed emphasis on the marriage relation and the protected space of the marital bedroom.

After *Griswold* it was established that the right to make certain decisions regarding sexual conduct extends beyond the marital relationship. In Eisenstadt v. Baird (1972), the Court invalidated a law prohibiting the distribution of contraceptives to unmarried persons [under the Equal Protection Clause] . . . :

It is true that in *Griswold* the right of privacy in question inhered in the marital relationship. . . . If the right of privacy means anything, it is the right of the *individual*, married or single, to be free from unwarranted governmental intrusion into matters so fundamentally affecting a person as the decision whether to bear or beget a child.

The opinions in *Griswold* and *Eisenstadt* were part of the background for the decision in Roe v. Wade (1973). . . . Although the Court held the woman's rights were not absolute, her right to elect an abortion did have real and substantial protection as an exercise of her liberty under the Due Process Clause. The Court cited cases that protect spatial freedom and cases that go well beyond it. *Roe* recognized the right of a woman to make certain fundamental decisions affecting her destiny and confirmed once more that the protection of liberty under the Due Process Clause has a substantive dimension of fundamental significance in defining the rights of the person.

. . . Both *Eisenstadt* and . . . the holding and rationale in *Roe* confirmed that the reasoning of *Griswold* could not be confined to the protection of rights of married adults. This was the state of the law with respect to some of the most relevant cases when the Court considered *Bowers.*

The facts in *Bowers* had some similarities to the instant case. A police officer . . . observed Hardwick, in his own bedroom, engaging in intimate sexual conduct with another adult male. The conduct was in violation of a Georgia statute making it a criminal offense to engage in sodomy. One difference between the two cases is that the Georgia statute prohibited the conduct whether or not the participants were of the same sex, while the Texas statute, as we have seen, applies only to participants of the same sex. . . . The Court, in an opinion by Justice White, sustained the Georgia law. . . .

The Court began its substantive discussion in *Bowers* as follows: "The issue presented is whether the Federal Constitution confers a fundamental right upon homosexuals to engage in sodomy and hence invalidates the laws of the many States that still make such conduct illegal and have done so for a very long time." That statement, we now conclude, discloses the Court's own failure to appreciate the extent of the liberty at stake. To say that the issue in *Bowers* was simply the right to engage in certain sexual conduct demeans the claim the individual put forward, just as it would demean a married couple were it to be said marriage is simply about the right to have sexual intercourse. The laws involved in *Bowers* and here are, to be sure, statutes that purport to do no more than prohibit a particular sexual act. Their penalties and purposes, though, have more far-reaching consequences, touching upon the most private human conduct, sexual behavior, and in the most private of places, the home. The statutes do seek to control a personal relationship that, whether or not entitled to formal recognition in the law, is within the liberty of persons to choose without being punished as criminals.

This, as a general rule, should counsel against attempts by the State, or a court, to define the meaning of the relationship or to set its boundaries absent injury to a person or abuse of an institution the law protects. It suffices for us to acknowledge that adults may choose to enter upon this relationship in the confines of their homes and their own private lives and still retain their dignity as free persons. When sexuality finds overt expression in intimate conduct with another person, the conduct can be but one element in a personal bond that is more enduring. The liberty protected by the Constitution allows homosexual persons the right to make this choice.

Having misapprehended the claim of liberty there presented to it, and thus stating the claim to be whether there is a fundamental right to engage in consensual sodomy, the *Bowers* Court said: "Proscriptions against that conduct have ancient roots." In academic writings, and in many of the scholarly amicus briefs filed to assist the Court in this case, there are fundamental criticisms of the historical premises relied upon by the majority and concurring opinions in *Bowers.* Brief for Cato Institute as *Amicus Curiae*; Brief for American Civil Liberties Union et al. as *Amici Curiae*; Brief for Professors of History et al. as *Amici Curiae.* We need not enter this debate in the attempt to reach a definitive historical judgment, but the following considerations counsel against adopting the definitive conclusions upon which *Bowers* placed such reliance.

At the outset it should be noted that there is no longstanding history in this country of laws directed at homosexual conduct as a distinct matter. Beginning in colonial times there were prohibitions of sodomy derived from the English criminal laws passed in the first instance by the Reformation Parliament of 1533. The English prohibition was understood to include relations between men and women as well as relations between men and men. Nineteenth-century commentators similarly read American sodomy, buggery, and crime-against-nature statutes as criminalizing certain relations between men and women and between men and men. See, e.g., J. Chitty, *Criminal Law* 47–50 (5th Am. ed. 1847). The absence of legal prohibitions focusing on homosexual conduct may be explained in part by noting that according to some scholars the concept of the homosexual as a distinct category of person did not emerge until the late 19th century. See, e.g., J. Katz, *The Invention of Heterosexuality* 10 (1995); J. D'Emilio & E. Freedman, *Intimate Matters: A History of Sexuality in America* 121 (2d ed. 1997) ("The modern terms homosexuality and heterosexuality do not apply to an era that had not yet articulated these distinctions"). Thus early

American sodomy laws were not directed at homosexuals as such but instead sought to prohibit nonprocreative sexual activity more generally. This does not suggest approval of homosexual conduct. It does tend to show that this particular form of conduct was not thought of as a separate category from like conduct between heterosexual persons.

Laws prohibiting sodomy do not seem to have been enforced against consenting adults acting in private. A substantial number of sodomy prosecutions and convictions for which there are surviving records were for predatory acts against those who could not or did not consent, as in the case of a minor or the victim of an assault. . . . Instead of targeting relations between consenting adults in private, 19th-century sodomy prosecutions typically involved relations between men and minor girls or minor boys, relations between adults involving force, relations between adults implicating disparity in status, or relations between men and animals.

. . . In all events that infrequency [of prosecutions] makes it difficult to say that society approved of a rigorous and systematic punishment of the consensual acts committed in private and by adults. The longstanding criminal prohibition of homosexual sodomy upon which the *Bowers* decision placed such reliance is as consistent with a general condemnation of nonprocreative sex as it is with an established tradition of prosecuting acts because of their homosexual character.

[F]ar from possessing "ancient roots," *Bowers*, American laws targeting same-sex couples did not develop until the last third of the 20th century. The reported decisions concerning the prosecution of consensual, homosexual sodomy between adults for the years 1880–1995 are not always clear in the details, but a significant number involved conduct in a public place.

It was not until the 1970s that any State singled out same-sex relations for criminal prosecution, and only nine States have done so. Post-*Bowers* even some of these States did not adhere to the policy of suppressing homosexual conduct. Over the course of the last decades, States with same-sex prohibitions have moved toward abolishing them.

In summary, the historical grounds relied upon in *Bowers* are more complex than the majority opinion and the concurring opinion by Chief Justice Burger indicate. Their historical premises are not without doubt and, at the very least, are overstated.

It must be acknowledged, of course, that the Court in *Bowers* was making the broader point that for centuries there have been powerful voices to condemn homosexual conduct as immoral. The condemnation has been shaped by religious beliefs, conceptions of right and acceptable behavior, and respect for the traditional family. For many persons these are not trivial concerns but profound and deep convictions accepted as ethical and moral principles to which they aspire and which thus determine the course of their lives. These considerations do not answer the question before us, however. The issue is whether the majority may use the power of the State to enforce these views on the whole society through operation of the criminal law. "Our obligation is to define the liberty of all, not to mandate our own moral code." Planned Parenthood of Southeastern Pa. v. Casey (1992).

Chief Justice Burger joined the opinion for the Court in *Bowers* and further explained his views as follows: "Decisions of individuals relating to homosexual conduct have been subject to state intervention throughout the history of Western civilization. Condemnation of those practices is firmly rooted in Judeao-Christian moral and ethical standards." As with Justice White's assumptions about history, scholarship casts some doubt on the sweeping nature of the statement by Chief Justice Burger as it pertains to private homosexual conduct between consenting adults. See, e.g., Eskridge, Hardwick and Historiography, 1999 *U. Ill. L. Rev.* 631, 656. In all events we think that our laws and traditions in the past half century are of most relevance here. These references show an emerging awareness that liberty gives substantial protection to adult persons in deciding how to conduct their private lives in matters pertaining to sex. "[H]istory and tradition are the starting point but not in all cases the ending point of the substantive due process inquiry." County of Sacramento v. Lewis (1998) (Kennedy, J., concurring).

This emerging recognition should have been apparent when *Bowers* was decided. In 1955 the American Law Institute promulgated the Model Penal Code and made clear that it did not recommend or provide for "criminal penalties for consensual sexual relations conducted in private." It justified its decision on three grounds: (1) The prohibitions undermined respect for the law by penalizing conduct many people engaged in; (2) the statutes regulated private conduct not harmful to others; and (3) the laws were arbitrarily enforced and thus invited the danger of blackmail. ALI, Model Penal Code, Commentary 277–280 (Tent. Draft No. 4, 1955). . . .

In *Bowers* the Court referred to the fact that before 1961 all 50 States had outlawed sodomy, and that at the time of the Court's decision 24 States and the District of Columbia had sodomy laws. Justice Powell pointed out that these prohibitions often were being ignored, however. Georgia, for instance, had not sought to enforce its law for decades. ("The history of nonenforcement suggests the moribund character today of laws criminalizing this type of private, consensual conduct").

The sweeping references by Chief Justice Burger to the history of Western civilization and to Judeo-Christian moral and ethical standards did not take account of other authorities pointing in an opposite direction. A committee advising the British Parliament recommended in 1957 repeal of laws punishing homosexual conduct. The Wolfenden Report: Report of the Committee on Homosexual Offenses and Prostitution (1963). Parliament enacted the substance of those recommendations 10 years later. Sexual Offences Act 1967, § 1.

Of even more importance, almost five years before *Bowers* was decided the European Court of Human Rights considered a case with parallels to *Bowers* and to today's case. An adult male resident in Northern Ireland alleged he was a practicing homosexual who desired to engage in consensual homosexual conduct. The laws of Northern Ireland forbade him that right. He alleged that he had been questioned, his home had been searched, and he feared criminal prosecution. The court held that the laws proscribing the conduct were invalid under the European Convention on Human Rights. Dudgeon v. United Kingdom, 45 Eur. Ct. H. R. (1981). Authoritative in all countries that are members of the Council of Europe (21 nations then, 45 nations now), the decision is at odds with the premise in *Bowers* that the claim put forward was insubstantial in our Western civilization.

In our own constitutional system the deficiencies in *Bowers* became even more apparent in the years following its announcement. The 25 States with laws prohibiting the relevant conduct referenced in the *Bowers* decision are reduced now to 13, of which 4 enforce their laws only against homosexual conduct. In those States where sodomy is still proscribed, whether for same-sex or heterosexual conduct, there is a pattern of nonenforcement with respect to consenting adults acting in private. The State of Texas admitted in 1994 that as of that date it had not prosecuted anyone under those circumstances.

Two principal cases decided after *Bowers* cast its holding into even more doubt. In *Casey*, the Court reaffirmed the substantive force of the liberty protected by the Due Process Clause. The *Casey* decision again confirmed that our laws and tradition afford constitutional protection to personal decisions relating to marriage, procreation, contraception, family relationships, child rearing, and education. In explaining the respect the Constitution demands for the autonomy of the person in making these choices, we stated as follows:

These matters, involving the most intimate and personal choices a person may make in a lifetime, choices central to personal dignity and autonomy, are central to the liberty protected by the Fourteenth Amendment. At the heart of liberty is the right to define one's own concept of existence, of meaning, of the universe, and of the mystery of human life. Beliefs about these matters could not define the attributes of personhood were they formed under compulsion of the State.

Persons in a homosexual relationship may seek autonomy for these purposes, just as heterosexual persons do. The decision in *Bowers* would deny them this right.

The second post-*Bowers* case of principal relevance is Romer v. Evans (1996). There the Court struck down class-based legislation directed at homosexuals as a violation of the Equal Protection Clause. *Romer* invalidated an amendment to Colorado's constitution which named as a solitary class persons who were homosexuals, lesbians, or bisexual either by "orientation, conduct, practices or relationships," and deprived them of protection under state antidiscrimination laws. We concluded that the provision was "born of animosity toward the class of persons affected" and further that it had no rational relation to a legitimate governmental purpose.

As an alternative argument in this case, counsel for the petitioners and some *amici* contend that *Romer* provides the basis for declaring the Texas statute invalid under the Equal Protection Clause. That is a tenable argument, but we conclude the instant case requires us to address whether *Bowers* itself has continuing validity. Were we to hold the statute invalid under the Equal Protection Clause some might question whether a prohibition would be valid if drawn differently, say, to prohibit the conduct both between same-sex and different-sex participants.

Equality of treatment and the due process right to demand respect for conduct protected by the substantive guarantee of liberty are linked in important respects, and a decision on the latter point advances both interests. If protected conduct is made criminal and the law which does so remains unexamined for its substantive validity, its stigma might remain even if it were not enforceable as drawn for equal protection reasons. When homosexual conduct is made criminal by the law of the State, that declaration in and of itself is an invitation to subject homosexual persons to discrimination both in the public and in the private spheres. The central holding of *Bowers* has been brought in question by this case, and it should be addressed. Its continuance as precedent demeans the lives of homosexual persons.

The stigma this criminal statute imposes, moreover, is not trivial. The offense, to be sure, is but a class C misdemeanor, a minor offense in the Texas legal system. Still, it remains a criminal offense with all that imports for the dignity of the persons charged. The petitioners will bear on their record the history of their criminal convictions. . . . We are advised that if Texas convicted an adult for private, consensual homosexual conduct under the statute here in question the convicted person would come within the registration [of sex offenders] laws of a least four States were he or she to be subject to their jurisdiction. This underscores the consequential nature of the punishment and the state-sponsored condemnation attendant to the criminal prohibition. Furthermore, the Texas criminal conviction carries with it the other collateral consequences always following a conviction, such as notations on job application forms, to mention but one example.

The foundations of *Bowers* have sustained serious erosion from our recent decisions in *Casey* and *Romer*. When our precedent has been thus weakened, criticism from other sources is of greater significance. In the United States criticism of *Bowers* has been substantial and continuing, disapproving of its reasoning in all respects, not just as to its historical assumptions. See, e.g., C. Fried, *Order and Law: Arguing the Reagan Revolution—A Firsthand Account* 81–84 (1991); R. Posner, *Sex and Reason* 341–350 (1992). The courts of five different States have declined to follow it in interpreting provisions in their own state constitutions parallel to the Due Process Clause of the Fourteenth Amendment, see Jegley v. Picado (Ark. 2002); Powell v. State (Ga. 1998); Gryczan v. State (Mont. 1997); Campbell v. Sundquist (Tenn. App. 1996); Commonwealth v. Wasson (Ky. 1992).

To the extent *Bowers* relied on values we share with a wider civilization, it should be noted that the reasoning and holding in *Bowers* have been rejected elsewhere. The European Court of Human Rights has followed not *Bowers* but its own decision in *Dudgeon v. United Kingdom*. . . . Other nations, too, have taken action consistent with an affirmation of the protected right of homosexual adults to engage in intimate, consensual conduct. The right the petitioners seek in this case has been accepted as an integral part of human freedom in many other countries. There has been no showing that in this country the governmental interest in circumscribing personal choice is somehow more legitimate or urgent.

The doctrine of *stare decisis* is essential to the respect accorded to the judgments of the Court and to the stability of the law. It is not, however, an inexorable command. In *Casey* we noted that when a Court is asked to overrule a precedent recognizing a constitutional liberty interest, individual or societal reliance on the existence of that liberty cautions with particular strength against reversing course. The holding in *Bowers*, however, has not induced detrimental reliance comparable to some instances where recognized individual rights are involved. Indeed, there has been no individual or societal reliance on *Bowers* of the sort that could counsel against overturning its holding once there are compelling reasons to do so. *Bowers* itself causes uncertainty, for the precedents before and after its issuance contradict its central holding.

The rationale of *Bowers* does not withstand careful analysis. In his dissenting opinion in *Bowers* Justice Stevens came to these conclusions:

> Our prior cases make two propositions abundantly clear. First, the fact that the governing majority in a State has traditionally viewed a particular practice as immoral is not a sufficient reason for upholding a law prohibiting the practice; neither history nor tradition could save a law prohibiting miscegenation from constitutional attack. Second, individual decisions by married persons, concerning the intimacies of their physical relationship, even when not intended to produce offspring, are a form of "liberty" protected by the Due Process Clause of the Fourteenth Amendment. Moreover, this protection extends to intimate choices by unmarried as well as married persons.

Justice Stevens's analysis, in our view, should have been controlling in *Bowers* and should control here.

Bowers was not correct when it was decided, and it is not correct today. It ought not to remain binding precedent. *Bowers* should be and now is overruled.

The present case does not involve minors. It does not involve persons who might be injured or coerced or who are situated in relationships where consent might not easily be refused. It does not involve public conduct or prostitution. It does not involve whether the government must give formal recognition to any relationship that homosexual persons seek to enter. The case does involve two adults who, with full and mutual consent from each other, engaged in sexual practices common to a homosexual lifestyle. The petitioners are entitled to respect for their private lives. The State cannot demean their existence or control their destiny by making their private sexual conduct a crime. Their right to liberty under the Due Process Clause gives them the full right to engage in their conduct without intervention of the government. "It is a promise of the Constitution that there is a realm of personal liberty which the government may not enter." *Casey.* The Texas statute furthers no legitimate state interest which can justify its intrusion into the personal and private life of the individual.

Had those who drew and ratified the Due Process Clauses of the Fifth Amendment or the Fourteenth Amendment known the components of liberty in its manifold possibilities, they might have been more specific. They did not presume to have this insight. They knew times can blind us to certain truths and later generations can see that laws once thought necessary and proper in fact serve only to oppress. As the Constitution endures, persons in every generation can invoke its principles in their own search for greater freedom.

[*Reversed.*]

■ JUSTICE O'CONNOR, concurring in the judgment.

The Court today overrules *Bowers.* I joined *Bowers*, and do not join the Court in overruling it. Nevertheless, I agree with the Court that Texas' statute banning same-sex sodomy is unconstitutional. Rather than relying on the substantive component of the Fourteenth Amendment's Due Process Clause, as the Court does, I base my conclusion on the Fourteenth Amendment's Equal Protection Clause.

The Equal Protection Clause of the Fourteenth Amendment "is essentially a direction that all persons similarly situated should be treated alike." Cleburne v. Cleburne Living Center, Inc. (1985); see also Plyler v. Doe (1982). Under our rational basis standard of review, "legislation is presumed to be valid and will be sustained if the classification drawn by the statute is rationally related to a legitimate state interest." *Cleburne*; see also Department of Agriculture v. Moreno (1973); *Romer.*

Laws such as economic or tax legislation that are scrutinized under rational basis review normally pass constitutional muster, since "the Constitution presumes that even improvident decisions will eventually be rectified by the democratic processes." *Cleburne*; see also Williamson v. Lee Optical of Okla., Inc. (1955). We have consistently held, however, that some objectives, such as "a bare . . . desire to harm a politically unpopular group," are not legitimate state interests. *Moreno.* See also *Cleburne; Romer.* When a law exhibits such a desire to harm a politically unpopular group, we have applied a more searching form of rational basis review to strike down such laws under the Equal Protection Clause.

We have been most likely to apply rational basis review to hold a law unconstitutional under the Equal Protection Clause where, as here, the challenged legislation inhibits personal relationships. . . .

The statute at issue here makes sodomy a crime only if a person "engages in deviate sexual intercourse with another individual of the same sex." Sodomy between opposite-sex partners, however, is not a crime in Texas. That is, Texas treats the same conduct differently based solely on the participants. Those harmed by this law are people who have a same-sex sexual orientation and thus are more likely to engage in behavior prohibited by [the law]. . . .

And the effect of Texas' sodomy law is not just limited to the threat of prosecution or consequence of conviction. Texas' sodomy law brands all homosexuals as criminals, thereby making it more difficult for homosexuals to be treated in the same manner as everyone else. Indeed, Texas itself has previously acknowledged the collateral effects of the law, stipulating in a prior challenge to this action that the law "legally sanctions discrimination against [homosexuals] in a variety of ways unrelated to the criminal law," including in the areas of "employment, family issues, and housing." State v. Morales (Tex. App. 1992).

Texas attempts to justify its law, and the effects of the law, by arguing that the statute satisfies rational basis review because it furthers the legitimate governmental interest of the promotion of morality. . . .

This case raises a different issue than *Bowers*: whether, under the Equal Protection Clause, moral disapproval is a legitimate state interest to justify by itself a statute that bans homosexual sodomy, but not heterosexual sodomy. It is not. Moral disapproval of this group, like a bare desire to harm the group, is an interest that is insufficient to satisfy rational basis review under the Equal Protection Clause. See, e.g., *Moreno*; *Romer*. Indeed, we have never held that moral disapproval, without any other asserted state interest, is a sufficient rationale under the Equal Protection Clause to justify a law that discriminates among groups of persons.

Moral disapproval of a group cannot be a legitimate governmental interest under the Equal Protection Clause because legal classifications must not be "drawn for the purpose of disadvantaging the group burdened by the law." *Romer*. Texas' invocation of moral disapproval as a legitimate state interest proves nothing more than Texas' desire to criminalize homosexual sodomy. But the Equal Protection Clause prevents a State from creating "a classification of persons undertaken for its own sake." *Id.* And because Texas so rarely enforces its sodomy law as applied to private, consensual acts, the law serves more as a statement of dislike and disapproval against homosexuals than as a tool to stop criminal behavior. The Texas sodomy law "raise[s] the inevitable inference that the disadvantage imposed is born of animosity toward the class of persons affected." *Id.* . . .

. . . The State has admitted that because of the sodomy law, *being* homosexual carries the presumption of being a criminal. See *State v. Morales* ("[T]he statute brands lesbians and gay men as criminals and thereby legally sanctions discrimination against them in a variety of ways unrelated to the criminal law"). . . . In *Romer*, we refused to sanction a law that singled out homosexuals "for disfavored legal status." The same is true here. The Equal Protection Clause " 'neither knows nor tolerates classes among citizens.' " *Id.* (quoting Plessy v. Ferguson (1896) (Harlan, J. dissenting)).

. . . Whether a sodomy law that is neutral both in effect and application, see Yick Wo v. Hopkins (1886), would violate the substantive component of the Due Process Clause is an issue that need not be decided today. I am confident, however, that so long as the Equal Protection Clause requires a sodomy law to apply equally to the private consensual conduct of homosexuals and heterosexuals alike, such a law would not long stand in our democratic society. In the words of Justice Jackson:

> The framers of the Constitution knew, and we should not forget today, that there is no more effective practical guaranty against arbitrary and unreasonable government than to require that the principles of law which officials would impose upon a minority be imposed generally. Conversely, nothing opens the door to arbitrary action so effectively as to allow those officials to pick and choose only a few to whom they will apply legislation and thus to escape the political retribution that might be visited upon them if larger numbers were affected. Railway Express Agency, Inc. v. New York (1949) (concurring opinion).

That this law as applied to private, consensual conduct is unconstitutional under the Equal Protection Clause does not mean that other laws distinguishing between heterosexuals and homosexuals would similarly fail under rational basis review. Texas cannot assert any legitimate state interest here, such as national security or preserving the traditional institution of marriage. Unlike the moral disapproval of same-sex relations—the asserted state interest in this case—other reasons exist to promote the institution of marriage beyond mere moral disapproval of an excluded group.

A law branding one class of persons as criminal solely based on the State's moral disapproval of that class and the conduct associated with that class runs contrary to the values of the Constitution and the Equal Protection Clause, under any standard of review. I therefore concur in the Court's judgment that Texas' sodomy law banning "deviate sexual intercourse" between consenting adults of the same sex, but not between consenting adults of different sexes, is unconstitutional.

■ JUSTICE SCALIA, with whom THE CHIEF JUSTICE [REHNQUIST] and JUSTICE THOMAS join, dissenting.

"Liberty finds no refuge in a jurisprudence of doubt." *Casey.* That was the Court's sententious response, barely more than a decade ago, to those seeking to overrule *Roe.* The Court's response today, to those who have engaged in a 17-year crusade to overrule *Bowers,* is very different. The need for stability and certainty presents no barrier. . . .

I

I begin with the Court's surprising readiness to reconsider . . . *Bowers.* . . .

. . . It seems to me that the "societal reliance" on the principles confirmed in *Bowers* and discarded today has been overwhelming. Countless judicial decisions and legislative enactments have relied on the ancient proposition that a governing majority's belief that certain sexual behavior is "immoral and unacceptable" constitutes a rational basis for regulation. . . . State laws against bigamy, same-sex marriage, adult incest, prostitution, masturbation, adultery, fornication, bestiality, and obscenity are likewise sustainable only in light of *Bowers'* validation of laws based on moral choices. Every single one of these laws is called into question by today's decision; the Court makes no effort to cabin the scope of its decision to exclude them from its holding. The impossibility of distinguishing homosexuality from other traditional "morals" offenses is precisely why *Bowers* rejected the rational-basis challenge. "The law," it said, "is constantly based on notions of morality, and if all laws representing essentially moral choices are to be invalidated under the Due Process Clause, the courts will be very busy indeed."

What a massive disruption of the current social order, therefore, the overruling of *Bowers* entails. Not so the overruling of *Roe,* which would simply have restored the regime that existed for centuries before 1973, in which the permissibility of and restrictions upon abortion were determined legislatively State-by-State. . . .

To tell the truth, it does not surprise me, and should surprise no one, that the Court has chosen today to revise the standards of *stare decisis* set forth in *Casey*. It has thereby exposed *Casey*'s extraordinary deference to precedent for the result-oriented expedient that it is.

II

Having decided that it need not adhere to *stare decisis*, the Court still must establish that *Bowers* was wrongly decided and that the Texas statute, as applied to petitioners, is unconstitutional.

Texas Penal Code Ann. § 21.06(a) (2003) undoubtedly imposes constraints on liberty. So do laws prohibiting prostitution, recreational use of heroin, and, for that matter, working more than 60 hours per week in a bakery. But there is no right to "liberty" under the Due Process Clause, though today's opinion repeatedly makes that claim. The Fourteenth Amendment *expressly allows* States to deprive their citizens of "liberty," *so long as "due process of law" is provided*: "No state shall . . . deprive any person of life, liberty, or property, *without due process of law*." (emphasis added).

Our opinions applying the doctrine known as "substantive due process" hold that the Due Process Clause prohibits States from infringing *fundamental* liberty interests, unless the infringement is narrowly tailored to serve a compelling state interest. Washington v. Glucksberg (1997). We have held repeatedly, in cases the Court today does not overrule, that *only* fundamental rights qualify for this so-called "heightened scrutiny" protection—that is, rights which are " 'deeply rooted in this Nation's history and tradition,' " *ibid*. See Reno v. Flores (1993) (fundamental liberty interests must be "so rooted in the traditions and conscience of our people as to be ranked as fundamental"). See also Michael H. v. Gerald D. (1989) ("[W]e have insisted not merely that the interest denominated as a 'liberty' be 'fundamental' . . . but also that it be an interest traditionally protected by our society"); Moore v. East Cleveland (1977) (plurality opinion); Meyer v. Nebraska (1923) (Fourteenth Amendment protects "those privileges *long recognized at common law* as essential to the orderly pursuit of happiness by free men" (emphasis added)). All other liberty interests may be abridged or abrogated pursuant to a validly enacted state law if that law is rationally related to a legitimate state interest.

Bowers held, first, that criminal prohibitions of homosexual sodomy are not subject to heightened scrutiny because they do not implicate a "fundamental right" under the Due Process Clause. Noting that "[p]roscriptions against that conduct have ancient roots," that "[s]odomy was a criminal offense at common law and was forbidden by the laws of the original 13 States when they ratified the Bill of Rights," and that many States had retained their bans on sodomy, *Bowers* concluded that a right to engage in homosexual sodomy was not " 'deeply rooted in this Nation's history and tradition.' "

The Court today does not overrule this holding. Not once does it describe homosexual sodomy as a "fundamental right" or a "fundamental liberty interest," nor does it subject the Texas statute to strict scrutiny. Instead, having failed to establish that the right to homosexual sodomy is " 'deeply rooted in this Nation's history and tradition,' " the Court concludes that the application of Texas's statute to petitioners' conduct fails the rational-basis test, and overrules *Bowers'* holding to the contrary. . . .

I shall address that rational-basis holding presently. First, however, I address some aspersions that the Court casts upon *Bowers'* conclusion that homosexual sodomy is not a "fundamental right"—even though, as I have said, the Court does not have the boldness to reverse that conclusion.

III . . .

After discussing the history of antisodomy laws, the Court proclaims that, "it should be noted that there is no longstanding history in this country of laws directed at homosexual conduct as a distinct matter." This observation in no way casts into doubt the "definitive [historical] conclusion," on which *Bowers* relied: that our Nation has a longstanding history of laws prohibiting *sodomy in general*—regardless of whether it was performed by same-sex or opposite-sex couples. . . . It is (as *Bowers* recognized) entirely irrelevant whether the laws in our long national tradition criminalizing homosexual sodomy were "directed at homosexual conduct as a distinct matter." Whether homosexual sodomy was prohibited by a law targeted at same-sex sexual relations or by a more general law prohibiting both homosexual and heterosexual sodomy, the only relevant point is that it *was* criminalized—which suffices to establish that homosexual sodomy is not a right "deeply rooted in our Nation's history and tradition." The Court today agrees that homosexual sodomy was criminalized and thus does not dispute the facts on which *Bowers actually* relied.

. . . *Bowers'* conclusion that homosexual sodomy is not a fundamental right "deeply rooted in this Nation's history and tradition" is utterly unassailable.

Realizing that fact, the Court instead says: "[W]e think that our laws and traditions in the past half century are of most relevance here. These references show *an emerging awareness* that liberty gives substantial protection to adult persons in deciding how to conduct their private lives *in matters pertaining to sex*."

(emphasis added). Apart from the fact that such an "emerging awareness" does not establish a "fundamental right," the statement is factually false. States continue to prosecute all sorts of crimes by adults "in matters pertaining to sex": prostitution, adult incest, adultery, obscenity, and child pornography. Sodomy laws, too, have been enforced "in the past half century," in which there have been 134 reported cases involving prosecutions for consensual, adult, homosexual sodomy. W. Eskridge, *Gaylaw: Challenging the Apartheid of the Closet* 375 (1999). In relying, for evidence of an "emerging recognition," upon the American Law Institute's 1955 recommendation not to criminalize " 'consensual sexual relations conducted in private,' " the Court ignores the fact that this recommendation was "a point of resistance in most of the states that considered adopting the Model Penal Code." *Gaylaw* 159.

In any event, an "emerging awareness" is by definition not "deeply rooted in this Nation's history and tradition[s]," as we have said "fundamental right" status requires. Constitutional entitlements do not spring into existence because some States choose to lessen or eliminate criminal sanctions on certain behavior. Much less do they spring into existence, as the Court seems to believe, because *foreign nations* decriminalize conduct. The *Bowers* majority opinion *never* relied on "values we share with a wider civilization," but rather rejected the claimed right to sodomy on the ground that such a right was not " 'deeply rooted in *this Nation's* history and tradition,' " (emphasis added). *Bowers'* rational-basis holding is likewise devoid of any reliance on the views of a "wider civilization." The Court's discussion of these foreign views (ignoring, of course, the many countries that have retained criminal prohibitions on sodomy) is therefore meaningless dicta. Dangerous dicta, however, since "this Court . . . should not impose foreign moods, fads, or fashions on Americans." Foster v. Florida (2002) (Thomas, J., concurring in denial of certiorari).

IV

I turn now to the ground on which the Court squarely rests its holding: the contention that there is no rational basis for the law here under attack. This proposition is so out of accord with our jurisprudence—indeed, with the jurisprudence of *any* society we know—that it requires little discussion.

The Texas statute undeniably seeks to further the belief of its citizens that certain forms of sexual behavior are "immoral and unacceptable," *Bowers*—the same interest furthered by criminal laws against fornication, bigamy, adultery, adult incest, bestiality, and obscenity. *Bowers* held that this *was* a legitimate state interest. The Court today reaches the opposite conclusion. The Texas statute, it says, "furthers *no legitimate state interest* which can justify its intrusion into the personal and private life of the individual" (emphasis added). The Court embraces instead Justice Stevens' declaration in his *Bowers* dissent, that "the fact that the governing majority in a State has traditionally viewed a particular practice as immoral is not a sufficient reason for upholding a law prohibiting the practice." This effectively decrees the end of all morals legislation. If, as the Court asserts, the promotion of majoritarian sexual morality is not even a *legitimate* state interest, none of the above-mentioned laws can survive rational-basis review.

V

Finally, I turn to petitioners' equal-protection challenge, which no Member of the Court save Justice O'Connor embraces: On its face § 21.06(a) applies equally to all persons. Men and women, heterosexuals and homosexuals, are all subject to its prohibition of deviate sexual intercourse with someone of the same sex. To be sure, § 21.06 does distinguish between the sexes insofar as concerns the partner with whom the sexual acts are performed: men can violate the law only with other men, and women only with other women. But this cannot itself be a denial of equal protection, since it is precisely the same distinction regarding partner that is drawn in state laws prohibiting marriage with someone of the same sex while permitting marriage with someone of the opposite sex.

The objection is made, however, that the antimiscegenation laws invalidated in Loving v. Virginia (1967), similarly were applicable to whites and blacks alike, and only distinguished between the races insofar as the *partner* was concerned. In *Loving*, however, we correctly applied heightened scrutiny, rather than the usual rational-basis review, because the Virginia statute was "designed to maintain White Supremacy." A racially discriminatory purpose is always sufficient to subject a law to strict scrutiny, even a facially neutral law that makes no mention of race. See Washington v. Davis (1976). No purpose to discriminate against men or women as a class can be gleaned from the Texas law, so rational-basis review applies. That review is readily satisfied here by the same rational basis that satisfied it in *Bowers*—society's belief that certain forms of sexual behavior are "immoral and unacceptable." This is the same justification that supports many other laws regulating sexual behavior that make a distinction based upon the identity of the partner—for example, laws against adultery, fornication, and adult incest, and laws refusing to recognize homosexual marriage.

Justice O'Connor argues that the discrimination in this law which must be justified is not its discrimination with regard to the sex of the partner but its discrimination with regard to the sexual proclivity of the principal actor.

While it is true that the law applies only to conduct, the conduct targeted by this law is conduct that is closely correlated with being homosexual. Under such circumstances, Texas' sodomy law is targeted at more than conduct. It is instead directed toward gay persons as a class.

. . . Even if the Texas law *does* deny equal protection to "homosexuals as a class," that denial *still* does not need to be justified by anything more than a rational basis, which our cases show is satisfied by the enforcement of traditional notions of sexual morality. . . .

Today's opinion is the product of a Court, which is the product of a law-profession culture, that has largely signed on to the so-called homosexual agenda, by which I mean the agenda promoted by some homosexual activists directed at eliminating the moral opprobrium that has traditionally attached to homosexual conduct. . . .

One of the most revealing statements in today's opinion is the Court's grim warning that the criminalization of homosexual conduct is "an invitation to subject homosexual persons to discrimination both in the public and in the private spheres." It is clear from this that the Court has taken sides in the culture war, departing from its role of assuring, as neutral observer, that the democratic rules of engagement are observed. Many Americans do not want persons who openly engage in homosexual conduct as partners in their business, as scoutmasters for their children, as teachers in their children's schools, or as boarders in their home. They view this as protecting themselves and their families from a lifestyle that they believe to be immoral and destructive. The Court views it as "discrimination" which it is the function of our judgments to deter. So imbued is the Court with the law profession's anti-anti-homosexual culture, that it is seemingly unaware that the attitudes of that culture are not obviously "mainstream"; that in most States what the Court calls "discrimination" against those who engage in homosexual acts is perfectly legal; that proposals to ban such "discrimination" under Title VII have repeatedly been rejected by Congress . . . ; that in some cases such "discrimination" is *mandated* by federal statute, see 10 U.S.C. § 654(b)(1) (mandating discharge from the armed forces of any service member who engages in or intends to engage in homosexual acts); and that in some cases such "discrimination" is a constitutional right, see Boy Scouts of America v. Dale (2000).

Let me be clear that I have nothing against homosexuals, or any other group, promoting their agenda through normal democratic means. Social perceptions of sexual and other morality change over time, and every group has the right to persuade its fellow citizens that its view of such matters is the best. That homosexuals have achieved some success in that enterprise is attested to by the fact that Texas is one of the few remaining States that criminalize private, consensual homosexual acts. But persuading one's fellow citizens is one thing, and imposing one's views in absence of democratic majority will is something else. I would no more *require* a State to criminalize homosexual acts—or, for that matter, display any moral disapprobation of them—than I would *forbid* it to do so. What Texas has chosen to do is well within the range of traditional democratic action, and its hand should not be stayed through the invention of a brand-new "constitutional right" by a Court that is impatient of democratic change. It is indeed true that "later generations can see that laws once thought necessary and proper in fact serve only to oppress;" and when that happens, later generations can repeal those laws. But it is the premise of our system that those judgments are to be made by the people, and not imposed by a governing caste that knows best.

One of the benefits of leaving regulation of this matter to the people rather than to the courts is that the people, unlike judges, need not carry things to their logical conclusion. The people may feel that their disapprobation of homosexual conduct is strong enough to disallow homosexual marriage, but not strong enough to criminalize private homosexual acts—and may legislate accordingly. The Court today pretends that it possesses a similar freedom of action, so that that we need not fear judicial imposition of homosexual marriage, as has recently occurred in Canada (in a decision that the Canadian Government has chosen not to appeal). See Halpern v. Toronto, 2003 WL 34950 (Ontario Ct. App.). At the end of its opinion—after having laid waste the foundations of our rational-basis jurisprudence—the Court says that the present case "does not involve whether the government must give formal recognition to any relationship that homosexual persons seek to enter." Do not believe it. More illuminating than this bald, unreasoned disclaimer is the progression of thought displayed by an earlier passage in the Court's opinion, which notes the constitutional protections afforded to "personal decisions relating to *marriage*, procreation, contraception, family relationships, child rearing, and education," and then declares that "[p]ersons in a homosexual relationship may seek autonomy for these purposes, just as heterosexual persons do" (emphasis added).

Today's opinion dismantles the structure of constitutional law that has permitted a distinction to be made between heterosexual and homosexual unions, insofar as formal recognition in marriage is concerned. If moral disapprobation of homosexual conduct is "no legitimate state interest" for purposes of proscribing that conduct; and if, as the Court coos (casting aside all pretense of neutrality), "[w]hen sexuality finds overt expression in intimate conduct with another person, the conduct can be but one element in a personal bond that is more enduring;" what justification could there possibly be for denying the benefits of marriage to homosexual couples exercising "[t]he liberty protected by the Constitution"? Surely not the encouragement of procreation, since the sterile and the elderly are allowed to marry. This case "does not involve" the issue of homosexual marriage only if one entertains the belief that principle and logic have nothing to do with the decisions of this Court. Many will hope that, as the Court comfortingly assures us, this is so.

The matters appropriate for this Court's resolution are only three: Texas's prohibition of sodomy neither infringes a "fundamental right" (which the Court does not dispute), nor is unsupported by a rational relation to what the Constitution considers a legitimate state interest, nor denies the equal protection of the laws. I dissent.

■ JUSTICE THOMAS, dissenting.

I join Justice Scalia's dissenting opinion. I write separately to note that the law before the Court today "is . . . uncommonly silly." *Griswold* (Stewart, J., dissenting). If I were a member of the Texas Legislature, I would vote to repeal it. Punishing someone for expressing his sexual preference through noncommercial consensual conduct with another adult does not appear to be a worthy way to expend valuable law enforcement resources.

Notwithstanding this, I recognize that as a member of this Court I am not empowered to help petitioners and others similarly situated. My duty, rather, is to "decide cases 'agreeably to the Constitution and laws of the United States.'" *Id.* And, just like Justice Stewart, I "can find [neither in the Bill of Rights nor any other part of the Constitution a] general right of privacy," *ibid.*, or as the Court terms it today, the "liberty of the person both in its spatial and more transcendent dimensions."

EDITORS' NOTES

(1)   What is the majority opinion's conception of "history and tradition" in interpreting the Due Process Clause? How does it differ from Justice White's notion in his majority opinion in Bowers v. Hardwick (1986; reprinted above)? From Justice Harlan's conception of history and tradition as a "living thing" in dissent in Poe v. Ullman (1961; discussed above)? Is the majority's conception an understanding of evolving consensus more than of backward-looking historical practice as of 1868?

(2)   What role do the Court's references to a "wider civilization" play in justifying the decision here? Historically, the Court has been reluctant to engage in comparative constitutional analysis. Does Justice Scalia give good reasons for such reluctance? Note here that the Court not only refers to decisions of courts and legislatures in other countries but also to decisions of state supreme courts interpreting state constitutions in this country.

(3)   The Court states that the present decision "does not involve whether the government must give formal recognition to any relationship that homosexual persons seek to enter." Yet Justice O'Connor in concurrence and Justice Scalia in dissent are clearly worried about the implications of the Court's decision for same-sex marriage. What, if anything, are those implications? Is Scalia right to state that "[t]oday's opinion dismantles the structure of constitutional law that has permitted a distinction to be made between heterosexual and homosexual unions, insofar as formal recognition in marriage is concerned"?

(4)   What, if anything, are the implications of the decision here for "morals legislation" generally? Is Scalia right to charge that the decision "effectively decrees the end of all morals legislation"? Is there really no moral distinction between homosexual intimate association, on the one hand, and, to quote Scalia's list, "fornication, bigamy, adultery, adult incest, bestiality, and obscenity"? Can the Court avoid drawing moral distinctions among these activities? Does *Lawrence* presuppose a liberty to choose to do whatever traditionally immoral things one wishes to do? Or does it presuppose simply that the rights of spatial privacy and personal autonomy already recognized for heterosexuals extend to homosexuals? If the former, is Scalia right about the slippery slope? If the latter, is he wrong about it?

(5)   Which clause provides a firmer ground for striking down the Texas law, the Due Process Clause (as held by the majority) or the Equal Protection Clause (as argued by O'Connor in concurrence)? Does the majority's liberty

holding reflect an implicit concern for protecting the equality of gays and lesbians? (Subsequently, in Obergefell v. Hodges (2015; reprinted in Chapter 1), Justice Kennedy for the majority wrote that "*Lawrence* therefore drew upon principles of liberty and equality to define and protect the rights of gays and lesbians.") Assume that O'Connor's opinion was not a concurrence but the opinion of the Court. In what sense would her opinion, based on the Equal Protection Clause alone, leave *Bowers* standing? The majority clearly viewed *Bowers* as a pox upon the Court and an insult to homosexuals: "Its continuance as precedent demeans the lives of homosexual persons." Hence, it vigorously overruled *Bowers* rather than seeking an alternative equal protection ground that would have left it standing officially but gutted for all practical purposes.

———

V. THE FUNDAMENTAL RIGHT TO MARRY UNDER STATE CONSTITUTIONS: SECURING EQUALITY AND LIBERTY FOR GAYS AND LESBIANS

"We hold only that plaintiffs are entitled under Chapter I, Article 7, of the Vermont Constitution to obtain the same benefits and protections afforded by Vermont law to married opposite-sex couples. We do not purport to infringe upon the prerogatives of the Legislature to craft an appropriate means of addressing this constitutional mandate, other than to note that the record here refers to a number of potentially constitutional statutory schemes from other jurisdictions."—CHIEF JUSTICE AMESTOY

"I concur with the majority's holding, but I respectfully dissent from its novel and truncated remedy, which in my view abdicates this Court's constitutional duty to redress violations of constitutional rights. . . . We should simply enjoin the State from denying marriage licenses to plaintiffs based on sex or sexual orientation."—JUSTICE JOHNSON

BAKER V. STATE OF VERMONT
170 Vt. 194, 744 A.2d 864 (Supreme Court of Vermont, 1999)

■ AMESTOY, C.J.

May the State of Vermont exclude same-sex couples from the benefits and protections that its laws provide to opposite-sex married couples? That is the fundamental question we address in this appeal, a question that the Court well knows arouses deeply-felt religious, moral, and political beliefs. Our constitutional responsibility to consider the legal merits of issues properly before us provides no exception for the controversial case. The issue before the Court, moreover, does not turn on the religious or moral debate over intimate same-sex relationships, but rather on the statutory and constitutional basis for the exclusion of same-sex couples from the secular benefits and protections offered married couples.

We conclude that under the Common Benefits Clause of the Vermont Constitution, which, in pertinent part, reads,

> That government is, or ought to be, instituted for the common benefit, protection, and security of the people, nation, or community, and not for the particular emolument or advantage of any single person, family, or set of persons, who are a part only of that community . . . ,

Vt. Const., ch. I, art 7., plaintiffs may not be deprived of the statutory benefits and protections afforded persons of the opposite sex who choose to marry. We hold that the State is constitutionally required to extend to same-sex couples the common benefits and protections that flow from marriage under Vermont law. Whether this ultimately takes the form of inclusion within the marriage laws themselves or a parallel "domestic partnership" system or some equivalent statutory alternative, rests with the Legislature. Whatever system is chosen, however, must conform with the constitutional imperative to afford all Vermonters the common benefit, protection, and security of the law.

Plaintiffs are three same-sex couples who have lived together in committed relationships for periods ranging from four to twenty-five years. Two of the couples have raised children together. Each couple applied for a marriage license from their respective town clerk, and each was refused a license as ineligible under the applicable state marriage laws. Plaintiffs thereupon filed this lawsuit against defendants—the State of Vermont, the Towns of Milton and Shelburne, and the City of South Burlington—seeking a declaratory judgment that the refusal to issue them a license violated the marriage statutes and the Vermont Constitution.

. . . The [trial] court ruled that the marriage statutes could not be construed to permit the issuance of a license to same-sex couples. The court further ruled that the marriage statutes were constitutional because they rationally furthered the State's interest in promoting "the link between procreation and child rearing." This appeal followed. . . .

II. The Constitutional Claim

... [P]laintiffs contend that the exclusion violates their right to the common benefit and protection of the law guaranteed by Chapter I, Article 7 of the Vermont Constitution. They note that in denying them access to a civil marriage license, the law effectively excludes them from a broad array of legal benefits and protections incident to the marital relation, including access to a spouse's medical, life, and disability insurance, hospital visitation and other medical decisionmaking privileges, spousal support, intestate succession, homestead protections, and many other statutory protections. They claim the trial court erred in upholding the law on the basis that it reasonably served the State's interest in promoting the "link between procreation and child rearing." They argue that the large number of married couples without children, and the increasing incidence of same-sex couples with children, undermines the State's rationale. They note that Vermont law affirmatively guarantees the right to adopt and raise children regardless of the sex of the parents, see 15A V.S.A. § 1–102, and challenge the logic of a legislative scheme that recognizes the rights of same-sex partners as parents, yet denies them—and their children—the same security as spouses. . . .

In considering this issue, it is important to emphasize at the outset that it is the Common Benefits Clause of the Vermont Constitution we are construing, rather than its counterpart, the Equal Protection Clause of the Fourteenth Amendment to the United States Constitution. . . . As we explain in the discussion that follows, the Common Benefits Clause of the Vermont Constitution differs markedly from the federal Equal Protection Clause in its language, historical origins, purpose, and development. While the federal amendment may thus supplement the protections afforded by the Common Benefits Clause, it does not supplant it as the first and primary safeguard of the rights and liberties of all Vermonters. See *id.* (Court is free to "provide more generous protection to rights under the Vermont Constitution than afforded by the federal charter"); see generally H. Linde, First Things First, Rediscovering the States' Bill of Rights, 9 *U. Balt. L.Rev.* 379, 381–82 (1980); S. Pollock, State Constitutions as Separate Sources of Fundamental Rights, 35 *Rutgers L.Rev.* 707, 717–19 (1983).

A. *Historical Development*

In understanding the import of the Common Benefits Clause, this Court has often referred to principles developed by the federal courts in applying the Equal Protection Clause. At the same time, however, we have recognized that "[a]lthough the provisions have some similarity of purpose, they are not identical." Indeed, recent Vermont decisions reflect a very different approach from current federal jurisprudence. That approach may be described as broadly deferential to the legislative prerogative to define and advance governmental *ends*, while vigorously ensuring that the *means* chosen bear a just and reasonable relation to the governmental objective.

Although our decisions over the last few decades have routinely invoked the rhetoric of suspect class favored by the federal courts, there are notable exceptions. The principal decision in this regard is the landmark case of State v. Ludlow Supermarkets, Inc. (1982) . . . *Ludlow* . . . did not alter the traditional requirement under Article 7 that legislative classifications must "reasonably relate to a legitimate public purpose." . . . It did establish that Article 7 would require a "more stringent" reasonableness inquiry than was generally associated with rational basis review under the federal constitution. *Ludlow* . . . signaled that Vermont courts—having "access to specific legislative history and all other proper resources" to evaluate the object and effect of state laws—would engage in a meaningful, case-specific analysis to ensure that any exclusion from the general benefit and protection of the law would bear a just and reasonable relation to the legislative goals. . . .

B.   *Text*

We typically look to a variety of sources in construing our Constitution, including the language of the provision in question, historical context, case-law development, the construction of similar provisions in other state constitutions, and sociological materials. The Vermont Constitution was adopted with little recorded debate and has undergone remarkably little revision in its 200-year history. Recapturing the meaning of a particular word or phrase as understood by a generation more than two centuries removed from our own requires, in some respects, an immersion in the culture and materials of the past more suited to the work of professional historians than courts and lawyers. See generally H. Powell, Rules for Originalists, 73 *Va. L.Rev.* 659, 659–61 (1987); P. Brest, The Misconceived Quest for the Original Understanding, 60 *B.U. L.Rev.* 204, 204–09 (1980). The responsibility of the Court, however, is distinct from that of the historian, whose interpretation of past thought and actions necessarily informs our analysis of current issues but cannot alone resolve them. See Powell, *supra*, at 662–68; Brest, *supra*, at 237. As we observed in State v. Kirchoff (1991), "our duty is to discover . . . the *core value* that gave life to Article [7]." (Emphasis added.) Out of the shifting and complicated kaleidoscope of events, social forces, and ideas that culminated in the Vermont Constitution of 1777, our task is to distill the essence, the motivating ideal of the framers. The challenge is to remain faithful to that historical ideal, while addressing contemporary issues that the framers undoubtedly could never have imagined.

We first focus on the words of the Constitution themselves, for, as Chief Justice Marshall observed, "although the spirit of an instrument, especially of a constitution, is to be respected not less than its letter, yet the spirit is to be collected chiefly from its words." Sturges v. Crowninshield (1819). One of the fundamental rights included in Chapter I of the Vermont Constitution of 1777, entitled "A Declaration of Rights of the Inhabitants of the State of Vermont," the Common Benefits Clause as originally written provided:

> That government is, or ought to be, instituted for the common benefit, protection, and security of the people, nation or community; and not for the particular emolument or advantage of any single man, family or set of men, who are a part only of that community; and that the community hath an indubitable, unalienable and indefeasible right, to reform, alter or abolish government, in such manner as shall be, by that community, judged most conducive to the public weal. Vt. Const. of 1777, ch. I, art. VI.

The first point to be observed about the text is the affirmative and unequivocal mandate of the first section, providing that government is established for the common benefit of the people and community as a whole. Unlike the Fourteenth Amendment, whose origin and language reflect the solicitude of a dominant white society for an historically-oppressed African-American minority (no state shall "deny" the equal protection of the laws), the Common Benefits Clause mirrors the confidence of a homogeneous, eighteenth-century group of men aggressively laying claim to the same rights as their peers in Great Britain or, for that matter, New York, New Hampshire, or the Upper Connecticut River Valley. The same assumption that all the people should be afforded all the benefits and protections bestowed by government is also reflected in the second section, which prohibits not the denial of rights to the oppressed, but rather the conferral of advantages or emoluments upon the privileged.

. . . The affirmative right to the "common benefits and protections" of government and the corollary proscription of favoritism in the distribution of public "emoluments and advantages" reflect the framers' overarching objective "not only that everyone enjoy equality before the law or have an equal voice in government but also that everyone have *an equal share in the fruits of the common enterprise*." W. Adams, *The First American Constitutions* 188 (1980) (emphasis added). Thus, at its core the Common Benefits Clause expressed a vision of government that afforded every Vermonter its benefit and protection and provided no Vermonter particular advantage.

C. *Historical Context*

Although historical research yields little direct evidence of the framers' intentions, an examination of the ideological origins of the Common Benefits Clause casts a useful light upon the inclusionary principle at its textual core. . . .

The historical origins of the Vermont Constitution . . . reveal that the framers, although enlightened for their day, were not principally concerned with civil rights for African-Americans and other minorities, but with equal access to public benefits and protections for the community as a whole. The concept of equality at the core of the Common Benefits Clause was not the eradication of racial or class distinctions, but rather the elimination of artificial governmental preferments and advantages. The Vermont Constitution would ensure that the law uniformly afforded every Vermonter its benefit, protection, and security so that social and political preeminence would reflect differences of capacity, disposition, and virtue, rather than governmental favor and privilege.

D. *Analysis Under Article 7*

The language and history of the Common Benefits Clause thus reinforce the conclusion that a relatively uniform standard, reflective of the inclusionary principle at its core, must govern our analysis of laws challenged under the Clause. Accordingly, we conclude that this approach, rather than the rigid, multi-tiered analysis evolved by the federal courts under the Fourteenth Amendment, shall direct our inquiry under Article 7. As noted, Article 7 is intended to ensure that the benefits and protections conferred by the state are for the common benefit of the community and are not for the advantage of persons "who are a part only of that community." When a statute is challenged under Article 7, we first define that "part of the community" disadvantaged by the law. We examine the statutory basis that distinguishes those protected by the law from those excluded from the state's protection. Our concern here is with delineating, not with labelling the excluded class as "suspect," "quasi-suspect," or "non-suspect" for purposes of determining different levels of judicial scrutiny.

We look next to the government's purpose in drawing a classification that includes some members of the community within the scope of the challenged law but excludes others. Consistent with Article 7's guiding principle of affording the protection and benefit of the law to all members of the Vermont community, we examine the nature of the classification to determine whether it is reasonably necessary to accomplish the State's claimed objectives.

We must ultimately ascertain whether the omission of a part of the community from the benefit, protection and security of the challenged law bears a reasonable and just relation to the governmental purpose. Consistent with the core presumption of inclusion, factors to be considered in this determination may include: (1) the significance of the benefits and protections of the challenged law; (2) whether the omission of members of the community from the benefits and protections of the challenged law promotes the government's stated goals; and (3) whether the classification is significantly underinclusive or overinclusive. As Justice Souter has observed in a different context, this approach necessarily "calls for a court to assess the relative 'weights' or dignities of the contending interests." Washington v. Glucksberg (1997) (Souter, J., concurring). What keeps that assessment grounded and objective, and not based upon the private sensitivities or values of individual judges, is that in assessing the relative weights of competing interests courts must look to the history and " 'traditions from which [the State] developed' " as well as those " 'from which it broke,' " *id.* (quoting Poe v. Ullman (1961) (Harlan, J., dissenting)), and not to merely personal notions. Moreover, the process of review is necessarily "one of close criticism going to the *details* of the opposing interests and to their relationships with the historically recognized principles that lend them weight or value." *Id.* (emphasis added). . . .

Ultimately, the answers to these questions, however useful, cannot substitute for " '[t]he inescapable fact . . . that adjudication of . . . claims may call upon the Court in interpreting the Constitution to exercise that same capacity which by tradition courts always have exercised: reasoned judgment.' " *Id.* (quoting Planned Parenthood of Southeastern Pa. v. Casey (1992)). The balance between individual liberty and organized society which courts are continually called upon to weigh does not lend itself to the precision of a scale. It is, indeed, a recognition of the imprecision of "reasoned judgment" that compels both judicial restraint and respect for tradition in constitutional interpretation.

E. *The Standard Applied*

With these general precepts in mind, we turn to the question of whether the exclusion of same-sex couples from the benefits and protections incident to marriage under Vermont law contravenes Article 7. The first step in our analysis is to identify the nature of the statutory classification. As noted, the marriage statutes apply expressly to opposite-sex couples. Thus, the statutes exclude anyone who wishes to marry someone of the same sex.[13]

Next, we must identify the governmental purpose or purposes to be served by the statutory classification. The principal purpose the State advances in support of the excluding same-sex couples from the legal benefits of marriage is the government's interest in "furthering the link between procreation and child rearing." The State has a strong interest, it argues, in promoting a permanent commitment between couples who have children to ensure that their offspring are considered legitimate and receive ongoing parental support. The State contends, further, that the Legislature could reasonably believe that sanctioning same-sex unions "would diminish society's perception of the link between procreation and child rearing . . . [and] advance the notion that fathers or mothers . . . are mere surplusage to the functions of procreation and child rearing." . . .

It is . . . undisputed that many *opposite*-sex couples marry for reasons unrelated to procreation, that some of these couples never intend to have children, and that others are incapable of having children. Therefore, if the purpose of the statutory exclusion of same-sex couples is to "further [ ] the link between procreation and child rearing," it is significantly underinclusive. The law

---

[13] Relying largely on federal precedents, our colleague in her concurring and dissenting opinion suggests that the statutory exclusion of same-sex couples from the benefits and protections of marriage should be subject to heightened scrutiny as a "suspect" or "quasi-suspect" classification based on sex. All of the seminal sex-discrimination decisions, however, have invalidated statutes that single out men or women as a discrete class for unequal treatment. See, e.g., United States v. Virginia (1996); Mississippi Univ. for Women v. Hogan (1982); Craig v. Boren (1976); Frontiero v. Richardson (1973). . . . The difficulty here is that the marriage laws are facially neutral; they do not single out men or women as a class for disparate treatment, but rather prohibit men and women equally from marrying a person of the same sex. . . . Indeed, most appellate courts that have addressed the issue have rejected the claim that defining marriage as the union of one man and one woman discriminates on the basis of sex. But see Baehr v. Lewin (Haw. 1993) (plurality opinion holding that state's marriage laws discriminated on basis of sex).

Although the concurring and dissenting opinion invokes the United States Supreme Court decision in Loving v. Virginia (1967), the reliance is misplaced. There the high court had little difficulty in looking behind the superficial neutrality of Virginia's anti-miscegenation statute to hold that its real purpose was to maintain the pernicious doctrine of white supremacy. Our colleague argues, by analogy, that the effect, if not the purpose, of the exclusion of same-sex partners from the marriage laws is to maintain certain male and female stereotypes to the detriment of both. To support the claim, she cites a number of antiquated statutes that denied married women a variety of freedoms, including the right to enter into contracts and hold property. The test to evaluate whether a facially gender-neutral statute discriminates on the basis of sex is whether the law "can be traced to a discriminatory purpose." The evidence does not demonstrate such a purpose. It is one thing to show that long-repealed marriage statutes subordinated women to men within the marital relation. It is quite another to demonstrate that the authors of the marriage laws excluded same-sex couples because of incorrect and discriminatory assumptions about gender roles or anxiety about gender-role confusion. That evidence is not before us. Accordingly, we are not persuaded that sex discrimination offers a useful analytic framework for determining plaintiffs' rights under the Common Benefits Clause. [Footnote by the Court.]

extends the benefits and protections of marriage to many persons with no logical connection to the stated governmental goal.

Furthermore, . . . a significant number of children today are actually being raised by same-sex parents, and increasing numbers of children are being conceived by such parents through a variety of assisted-reproductive techniques. . . .

. . . The Vermont Legislature has not only recognized this reality, but has acted affirmatively to remove legal barriers so that same-sex couples may legally adopt and rear the children conceived through such efforts. See 15A V.S.A. § 1–102(b) (allowing partner of biological parent to adopt if in child's best interest without reference to sex). The state has also acted to expand the domestic relations laws to safeguard the interests of same-sex parents and their children when such couples terminate their domestic relationship. See 15A V.S.A. § 1–112 (vesting family court with jurisdiction over parental rights and responsibilities, parent-child contact, and child support when unmarried persons who have adopted minor child "terminate their domestic relationship").

Therefore, to the extent that the state's purpose in licensing civil marriage was, and is, to legitimize children and provide for their security, the statutes plainly exclude many same-sex couples who are no different from opposite-sex couples with respect to these objectives. . . .

The State also argues that because same-sex couples cannot conceive a child on their own, their exclusion promotes "a perception of the link between procreation and child rearing," and that to discard it would "advance the notion that mothers and fathers . . . are mere surplusage to the functions of procreation and child rearing." Apart from the bare assertion, the State offers no persuasive reasoning to support these claims. Indeed, it is undisputed that most of those who utilize nontraditional means of conception are infertile *married* couples, and that many assisted-reproductive techniques involve only one of the married partner's genetic material, the other being supplied by a third party through sperm, egg, or embryo donation. The State does not suggest that the use of these technologies undermines a married couple's sense of parental responsibility, or fosters the perception that they are "mere surplusage" to the conception and parenting of the child so conceived. Nor does it even remotely suggest that access to such techniques ought to be restricted as a matter of public policy to "send a public message that procreation and child rearing are intertwined." Accordingly, there is no reasonable basis to conclude that a same-sex couple's use of the same technologies would undermine the bonds of parenthood, or society's perception of parenthood. . . .

The State asserts that a number of additional rationales could support a legislative decision to exclude same-sex partners from the statutory benefits and protections of marriage. The most substantive of the State's remaining claims relates to the issue of childrearing. It is conceivable that the Legislature could conclude that opposite-sex partners offer advantages in this area, although we note that child-development experts disagree and the answer is decidedly uncertain. The argument, however, contains a more fundamental flaw, and that is the Legislature's endorsement of a policy diametrically at odds with the State's claim. In 1996, the Vermont General Assembly enacted, and the Governor signed, a law removing all prior legal barriers to the adoption of children by same-sex couples. See 15A V.S.A. § 1–102. At the same time, the Legislature provided additional legal protections in the form of court-ordered child support and parent-child contact in the event that same-sex parents dissolved their "domestic relationship." *Id.* § 1–112. . . .

Similarly, the State's argument that Vermont's marriage laws serve a substantial governmental interest in maintaining uniformity with other jurisdictions cannot be reconciled with Vermont's recognition of unions, such as first-cousin marriages, not uniformly sanctioned in other states. In an analogous context, Vermont has sanctioned adoptions by same-sex partners, see 15A V.S.A. § 1–102, notwithstanding the fact that many states have not.

Finally, it is suggested that the long history of official intolerance of intimate same-sex relationships cannot be reconciled with an interpretation of Article 7 that would give state-sanctioned benefits and protection to individuals of the same sex who commit to a permanent domestic relationship. We find the argument to be unpersuasive. . . . [T]o the extent that state action historically has been motivated by an animus against a class, that history cannot provide a legitimate basis for continued unequal application of the law. . . .

Thus . . . none of the interests asserted by the State provides a reasonable and just basis for the continued exclusion of same-sex couples from the benefits incident to a civil marriage license under Vermont law. Accordingly, in the faith that a case beyond the imagining of the framers of our Constitution may, nevertheless, be safely anchored in the values that infused it, we find a constitutional obligation to extend to plaintiffs the common benefit, protection, and security that Vermont law provides opposite-sex married couples. It remains only to determine the appropriate means and scope of relief compelled by this constitutional mandate.

F.   *Remedy*

It is important to state clearly the parameters of today's ruling. . . .

We hold only that plaintiffs are entitled under Chapter I, Article 7, of the Vermont Constitution to obtain the same benefits and protections afforded by Vermont law to married opposite-sex couples. We do not purport to infringe upon the prerogatives of the Legislature to craft an appropriate means of addressing this constitutional mandate, other than to note that the record here refers to a number of potentially constitutional statutory schemes from other jurisdictions. These include what are typically referred to as "domestic partnership" or "registered partnership" acts, which generally establish an alternative legal status to marriage for same-sex couples, impose similar formal requirements and limitations, create a parallel licensing or registration scheme, and extend all or most of the same rights and obligations provided by the law to married partners. . . . We do not intend specifically to endorse any one or all of the referenced acts, particularly in view of the significant benefits omitted from several of the laws.

Further, while the State's prediction of "destabilization" cannot be a ground for denying relief, it is not altogether irrelevant. A sudden change in the marriage laws or the statutory benefits traditionally incidental to marriage may have disruptive and unforeseen consequences. Absent legislative guidelines defining the status and rights of same-sex couples, consistent with constitutional requirements, uncertainty and confusion could result. Therefore, we hold that the current statutory scheme shall remain in effect for a reasonable period of time to enable the Legislature to consider and enact implementing legislation in an orderly and expeditious fashion. In the event that the benefits and protections in question are not statutorily granted, plaintiffs may petition this Court to order the remedy they originally sought.

Our colleague asserts that granting the relief requested by plaintiffs—an injunction prohibiting defendants from withholding a marriage license—is our "constitutional duty." (Johnson, J., concurring in part and dissenting in part). We believe the argument is predicated upon a fundamental misinterpretation of our opinion. It appears to assume that we hold plaintiffs are entitled to a marriage license. We do not. We hold that the State is constitutionally required to extend to same-sex couples the common benefits and protections that flow from marriage under Vermont law. That the State could do so through a marriage license is obvious. But it is not required to do so, and the mandate proposed by our colleague is inconsistent with the Court's holding. . . .

The concurring and dissenting opinion further claims that our mandate represents an "abdicat[ion]" of the constitutional duty to decide, and an inexplicable failure to implement "the most straightforward and effective remedy." First, our opinion provides greater recognition of—and protection for—same sex relationships than has been recognized by any court of final jurisdiction in this country with the instructive exception of the Hawaii Supreme Court in *Baehr*. See Hawaii Const., art. I, § 23 (state constitutional amendment overturned same-sex marriage decision in *Baehr* by returning power to legislature "to reserve marriage to opposite-sex couples"). Second, the dissent's suggestion that her mandate would avoid the "political caldron" of public debate is—even allowing for the welcome lack of political sophistication of the judiciary—significantly insulated from reality. See Hawaii Const., art. I, § 23; see also Alaska Const., art. I, § 25 (state constitutional amendment reversed trial court decision in favor of same-sex marriage, Brause v. Bureau of Vital Statistics (Alaska Super.Ct. Feb. 27, 1998), by providing that "a marriage may exist only between one man and one woman").

The concurring and dissenting opinion confuses decisiveness with wisdom and judicial authority with finality. Our mandate is predicated upon a fundamental respect for the ultimate source of constitutional authority, not a fear of decisiveness. No court was ever more decisive than the United States Supreme Court in Dred Scott v. Sandford (1857). Nor more wrong. Ironically it was a Vermonter, Stephen Douglas, who in defending the decision said—as the dissent in essence does here—"I never heard before of an appeal being taken from the Supreme Court." See A. Bickel, *The Morality of Consent* 101 (1975). But it was a profound understanding of the law and the "unruliness of the human condition," *id.* at 11, that prompted Abraham Lincoln to respond that the Court does not issue Holy Writ. See *id.* at 101.* [I]t cannot be doubted that judicial authority is not ultimate authority. It is certainly not the only repository of wisdom.

When a democracy is in moral flux, courts may not have the best or the final answers. Judicial answers may be wrong. They may be counterproductive even if they are right. Courts do best by proceeding in a way that is catalytic rather than preclusive, and that is closely attuned to the fact that courts are participants in the system of

---

* See Abraham Lincoln's First Inaugural Address.—**Eds.**

democratic deliberation. C. Sunstein, Foreword: Leaving Things Undecided, 110 *Harv. L.Rev.* 4, 101 (1996).

The implementation by the Vermont Legislature of a constitutional right expounded by this Court pursuant to the Vermont Constitution for the common benefit and protection of the Vermont community is not an abdication of judicial duty, it is the fulfillment of constitutional responsibility.

III. Conclusion

While many have noted the symbolic or spiritual significance of the marital relation, it is plaintiffs' claim to the secular benefits and protections of a singularly human relationship that, in our view, characterizes this case. The State's interest in extending official recognition and legal protection to the professed commitment of two individuals to a lasting relationship of mutual affection is predicated on the belief that legal support of a couple's commitment provides stability for the individuals, their family, and the broader community. Although plaintiffs' interest in seeking state recognition and protection of their mutual commitment may—in view of divorce statistics—represent "the triumph of hope over experience," the essential aspect of their claim is simply and fundamentally for inclusion in the family of state-sanctioned human relations.

The past provides many instances where the law refused to see a human being when it should have. See, e.g., *Dred Scott* (concluding that African slaves and their descendants had "no rights which the white man was bound to respect"). . . . The extension of the Common Benefits Clause to acknowledge plaintiffs as Vermonters who seek nothing more, nor less, than legal protection and security for their avowed commitment to an intimate and lasting human relationship is simply, when all is said and done, a recognition of our common humanity.

The judgment of the superior court upholding the constitutionality of the Vermont marriage statutes under Chapter I, Article 7 of the Vermont Constitution is reversed. The effect of the Court's decision is suspended, and jurisdiction is retained in this Court, to permit the Legislature to consider and enact legislation consistent with the constitutional mandate described herein.

■ DOOLEY, J., concurring. . . .

■ JOHNSON, J., concurring in part and dissenting in part.

. . . I concur with the majority's holding, but I respectfully dissent from its novel and truncated remedy, which in my view abdicates this Court's constitutional duty to redress violations of constitutional rights. . . . We should simply enjoin the State from denying marriage licenses to plaintiffs based on sex or sexual orientation. That remedy would provide prompt and complete relief to plaintiffs and create reliable expectations that would stabilize the legal rights and duties of all couples.

I

. . . [A]bsent "compelling" reasons that dictate otherwise, it is not only the prerogative but the duty of courts to provide prompt relief for violations of individual civil rights. This basic principle is designed to assure that laws enacted through the will of the majority do not unconstitutionally infringe upon the rights of a disfavored minority. . . .

The majority declines to provide plaintiffs with a marriage license, however, because a sudden change in the marriage laws "may have disruptive and unforeseen consequences," and "uncertainty and confusion could result." Thus, within a few pages of rejecting the State's doomsday speculations as a basis for upholding the unconstitutionally discriminatory classification, the majority relies upon those same speculations to deny plaintiffs the relief to which they are entitled as the result of the discrimination.

During the civil rights movement of the 1960s, state and local governments defended segregation or gradual desegregation on the grounds that mixing the races would lead to interracial disturbances. The Supreme Court's "compelling answer" to that contention was "that constitutional rights may not be denied simply because of hostility to their assertion or exercise." See Watson v. City of Memphis (1963). Here, too, we should not relinquish our duty to redress the unconstitutional discrimination that we have found merely because of "personal speculations" or "vague disquietudes." While the laudatory goals of preserving institutional credibility and public confidence in our government may require elected bodies to wait for changing attitudes concerning public morals, those same goals require courts to act independently and decisively to protect civil rights guaranteed by our Constitution. . . .

Today's decision, which is little more than a declaration of rights, abdicates that responsibility. The majority declares that plaintiffs have been unconstitutionally deprived of the benefits of marriage, but does not hold that the marriage laws are unconstitutional, does not hold that plaintiffs are entitled to the license that triggers those benefits, and does not provide plaintiffs with any other specific or direct remedy for the constitutional violation that the Court has found to exist. By suspending its judgment and allowing the Legislature to choose a remedy, the majority, in effect, issues an advisory opinion that leaves plaintiffs without redress and sends the matter to an uncertain fate in the Legislature. . . .

No decision of this Court will abate the moral and political debate over same-sex marriage. My view as to the appropriateness of granting plaintiffs the license they seek is not based on any overestimate (or *any* estimate) of its effectiveness, nor on a miscalculation (or *any* calculation) as to its likely permanence, were it to have received the support of a majority of this Court. Rather, it is based on what I believe are the commands of our Constitution.

II

Although I concur with the majority's conclusion that Vermont law unconstitutionally excludes same-sex couples from the benefits of marriage, I write separately to state my belief that this is a straightforward case of sex discrimination.

As the majority states, the marriage "statutes, read as a whole, reflect the common understanding that marriage under Vermont law consists of a union between a man and a woman." Thus, the statutes impose a sex-based classification. A woman is denied the right to marry another woman because her would-be partner is a woman, not because one or both are lesbians. Similarly, a man is denied the right to marry another man because his would-be partner is a man, not because one or both are gay. Thus, an individual's right to marry a person of the same sex is prohibited solely on the basis of sex, not on the basis of sexual orientation. Indeed, sexual orientation does not appear as a qualification for marriage under the marriage statutes. The State makes no inquiry into the sexual practices or identities of a couple seeking a license.

The State advances two arguments in support of its position that Vermont's marriage laws do not establish a sex-based classification. The State first contends that the marriage statutes merely acknowledge that marriage, by its very nature, cannot be comprised of two persons of the same sex. Thus, in the State's view, it is the *definition* of marriage, not the statutes, that restricts marriage to two people of the opposite sex. This argument is circular. It is the State that defines civil marriage under its statute. The issue before us today is whether the State may continue to deprive same-sex couples of the benefits of marriage. This question is not resolved by resorting to a historical definition of marriage; it is that very definition that is being challenged in this case.

The State's second argument, also propounded by the majority, is that the marriage statutes do not discriminate on the basis of sex because they treat similarly situated males the same as similarly situated females. Under this argument, there can be no sex discrimination here because "[i]f a man wants to marry a man, he is barred; a woman seeking to marry a woman is barred in precisely the same way. For this reason, women and men are not treated differently." C. Sunstein, Homosexuality and the Constitution, 70 *Ind. L.J.* 1, 19 (1994). But consider the following example. Dr. A and Dr. B both want to marry Ms. C, an X-ray technician. Dr. A may do so because Dr. A is a man. Dr. B may not because Dr. B is a woman. Dr. A and Dr. B are people of opposite sexes who are similarly situated in the sense that they both want to marry a person of their choice. The statute disqualifies Dr. B from marriage solely on the basis of her sex and treats her differently from Dr. A, a man. This is sex discrimination.

I recognize, of course, that although the classification here is sex-based on its face, its most direct impact is on lesbians and gay men, the class of individuals most likely to seek same-sex marriage. Viewing the discrimination as sex-based, however, is important. Although the *original* purpose of the marriage statutes was not to exclude same-sex couples, for the simple reason that same-sex marriage was very likely not on the minds of the Legislature when it passed the licensing statute, the *preservation* of the sex-based classification deprives lesbians and gay men of the right to marry the life partner of their choice. If . . . the sex-based classification contained in the marriage laws is unrelated to any valid purpose, but rather is a vestige of sex-role stereotyping that applies to both men and women, the classification is still unlawful sex discrimination even if it applies equally to men and women. See MacCallum v. Seymour's Adm'r (1996) (Constitution does not permit law to give effect, either directly or indirectly, to private biases; when government itself makes the classification, it is obliged to afford all persons equal protection of the law); Loving v. Virginia (1967) (statute prohibiting racial intermarriage violates Equal Protection Clause although it applies equally to Whites and Blacks because classification was designed to maintain White Supremacy.) . . .

EDITORS' NOTES

(1) How does the Vermont Supreme Court's interpretation of the Common Benefits Clause of the Vermont Constitution differ from the United States Supreme Court's interpretation of the Equal Protection Clause of the United States Constitution? How does the Vermont Supreme Court's form of scrutiny compare with the rational basis scrutiny "with bite" that we have seen, e.g., in Cleburne v. Cleburne Living Center (1985; discussed above) and Romer v. Evans (1996; reprinted above)?

(2) Who has the better argument concerning whether laws denying marriage to same-sex couples discriminate on the basis of gender, Chief Justice Amestoy (rejecting the argument) or Justice Johnson (accepting the argument)? Is the analogy to Loving v. Virginia (1967) "misplaced" or cogent?

(3) Is the majority's disposition regarding the remedy—leaving it to the Vermont Legislature to implement the constitutional mandate by choosing a statutory scheme that will afford common benefits to same-sex couples—a "fulfillment of constitutional responsibility," as Chief Justice Amestoy claims, or an "abdication of judicial duty," as Justice Johnson claims? Put another way, should it be celebrated as a prudential act of judicial statesmanship or condemned for declaring a right without recognizing a remedy?

(4) Presumably one of the prudential reasons for Chief Justice Amestoy's decision to leave it to the Vermont Legislature to implement a statutory scheme was his aim to avoid what he saw as the fate of the Hawaii Supreme Court in Baehr v. Lewin (1993). In that case, a plurality opinion held that the state's marriage laws denying marriage to same-sex couples discriminated on the basis of sex, only to be overturned by a state constitutional amendment returning the power to the legislature "to reserve marriage to opposite-sex couples." Hawaii Const., art. I, § 23. That was not the end of the story in Hawaii, however. Subsequently, the Hawaii Legislature passed a "reciprocal beneficiaries statute"—basically a civil union statute. Same-sex couples could enter into a reciprocal beneficiary relationship and thus become entitled to many, but not all, of the rights and benefits accorded to married couples. Haw. Rev. Stat. § 572C–1 et seq.

(5) At the beginning of the majority opinion, Chief Justice Amestoy purports to bracket the "religious or moral debate over intimate same-sex relationships." Does he succeed in doing so? Should he seek to do so?

(6) Soon after the decision, the Vermont Legislature enacted a statute recognizing same-sex civil unions while not recognizing same-sex marriage. Nonetheless, it afforded all of the benefits of marriage (except the name "marriage") to such civil unions. Would civil unions be a sufficient remedy? Or a regime of "second-class citizenship"? In 2009, before *Obergefell*, the Vermont Legislature enacted a statute recognizing same-sex marriage. What might have prompted Vermont to move from civil unions to marriage?

———

"The Massachusetts Constitution affirms the dignity and equality of all individuals. It forbids the creation of second-class citizens."—CHIEF JUSTICE MARSHALL

"The plaintiffs are members of our community, our neighbors, our coworkers, our friends. . . . We share a common humanity and participate together in the social contract that is the foundation of our Commonwealth. Simple principles of decency dictate that we extend to the plaintiffs, and to their new status, full acceptance, tolerance, and respect. We should do so because it is the right thing to do."—JUSTICE GREANEY

"Because a conceivable rational basis exists upon which the Legislature could conclude that the marriage statute furthers the legitimate State purpose of ensuring, promoting, and supporting an optimal social structure for the bearing and raising of children, it is a valid exercise of the State's police power."
—JUSTICE CORDY

GOODRIDGE V. DEPARTMENT OF PUBLIC HEALTH

440 Mass. 309, 798 N.E.2d 941 (Supreme Judicial Court of Massachusetts, 2003)

■ MARSHALL, C.J.

Marriage is a vital social institution. The exclusive commitment of two individuals to each other nurtures love and mutual support; it brings stability to our society. For those who choose to marry, and for their children, marriage provides an abundance of legal, financial, and social benefits. In return it imposes weighty legal, financial, and social obligations. The question before us is whether, consistent with the Massachusetts Constitution, the Commonwealth may deny the protections, benefits, and obligations conferred by civil marriage to two individuals of the same sex who wish to marry. We conclude that it may not. The Massachusetts Constitution affirms the dignity and equality of all individuals. It forbids the creation of second-class citizens. In reaching our conclusion we have given full deference to the arguments made by the Commonwealth. But it has failed to identify any constitutionally adequate reason for denying civil marriage to same-sex couples.

We are mindful that our decision marks a change in the history of our marriage law. Many people hold deep-seated religious, moral, and ethical convictions that marriage should be limited to the union of one man and one woman, and that homosexual conduct is immoral. Many hold equally strong religious, moral, and ethical convictions that same-sex couples are entitled to be married, and that homosexual persons should be treated no differently than their heterosexual neighbors. Neither view answers the question before us. Our concern is with the Massachusetts Constitution as a charter of governance for every person properly within its reach. "Our obligation is to define the liberty of all, not to mandate our own moral code." Lawrence v. Texas (2003), quoting Planned Parenthood v. Casey (1992).

Whether the Commonwealth may use its formidable regulatory authority to bar same-sex couples from civil marriage is a question not previously addressed by a Massachusetts appellate court. It is a question the United States Supreme Court left open as a matter of Federal law in *Lawrence*, where it was not an issue. There, the Court affirmed that the core concept of common human dignity protected by the Fourteenth Amendment to the United States Constitution precludes government intrusion into the deeply personal realms of consensual adult expressions of intimacy and one's choice of an intimate partner. The Court also reaffirmed the central role that decisions whether to marry or have children bear in shaping one's identity. The Massachusetts Constitution is, if anything, more protective of individual liberty and equality than the Federal Constitution; it may demand broader protection for fundamental rights; and it is less tolerant of government intrusion into the protected spheres of private life.

Barred access to the protections, benefits, and obligations of civil marriage, a person who enters into an intimate, exclusive union with another of the same sex is arbitrarily deprived of membership in one of our community's most rewarding and cherished institutions. That exclusion is incompatible with the constitutional principles of respect for individual autonomy and equality under law.

I

The plaintiffs are fourteen individuals from five Massachusetts counties. As of April 11, 2001, the date they filed their complaint, the plaintiffs Gloria Bailey, sixty years old, and Linda Davies, fifty-five years old, had been in a committed relationship for thirty years; the plaintiffs Maureen Brodoff, forty-nine years old, and Ellen Wade, fifty-two years old, had been in a committed relationship for twenty years and lived with their twelve year old daughter; the plaintiffs Hillary Goodridge, forty-four years old, and Julie Goodridge, forty-three years old, had been in a committed relationship for thirteen years and lived with their five year old daughter; the plaintiffs Gary Chalmers, thirty-five years old, and Richard Linnell, thirty-seven years old, had been in a committed relationship for thirteen years and lived with their eight year old daughter and Richard's mother; the plaintiffs Heidi Norton, thirty-six years old, and Gina Smith, thirty-six years old, had been in a committed relationship for eleven years and lived with their two sons, ages five years and one year; the plaintiffs Michael Horgan, forty-one years old, and Edward Balmelli, forty-one years old, had been in a committed relationship for seven years; and the plaintiffs David Wilson, fifty-seven years old, and Robert Compton, fifty-one years old, had been in a committed relationship for four years and had cared for David's mother in their home after a serious illness until she died.

The plaintiffs include business executives, lawyers, an investment banker, educators, therapists, and a computer engineer. Many are active in church, community, and school groups. They have employed such legal means as are available to them—for example, joint adoption, powers of attorney, and joint ownership of real property—to secure aspects of their relationships. Each plaintiff attests a desire to marry his or her partner in order to affirm publicly their commitment to each other and to secure the legal protections and benefits afforded to married couples and their children.

In March and April, 2001, each of the plaintiff couples attempted to obtain a marriage license from a city or town clerk's office. . . . In each case, the clerk either refused to accept the notice of intention to marry or denied a marriage license to the couple on the ground that Massachusetts does not recognize same-sex marriage. . . .

On April 11, 2001, the plaintiffs filed suit in the Superior Court against the [Department of Public Health] . . . alleg[ing] violation of the laws of the Commonwealth, including but not limited to their rights under . . . the Massachusetts Constitution[7]. . . .

A Superior Court judge ruled for the department. . . . [P]laintiffs appealed. Both parties requested direct appellate review, which we granted. . . .

---

[7] Article 1, as amended by art. 106 of the Amendments to the Massachusetts Constitution, provides: "All people are born free and equal and have certain natural, essential and unalienable rights; among which may be reckoned the right of enjoying and defending their lives and liberties; that of acquiring, possessing and protecting property; in fine, that of seeking and obtaining their safety and happiness. Equality under the law shall not be denied or abridged because of sex, race, color, creed or national origin." . . . Article 10 provides, in relevant part: "Each individual of the society has a right to be protected by it in the enjoyment of his life, liberty and property, according to standing laws. . . ." . . . [Footnote by the Court.]

III

A

The larger question is whether, as the department claims, government action that bars same-sex couples from civil marriage constitutes a legitimate exercise of the State's authority to regulate conduct, or whether, as the plaintiffs claim, this categorical marriage exclusion violates the Massachusetts Constitution. We have recognized the long-standing statutory understanding, derived from the common law, that "marriage" means the lawful union of a woman and a man. But that history cannot and does not foreclose the constitutional question.

The plaintiffs' claim that the marriage restriction violates the Massachusetts Constitution can be analyzed in two ways. Does it offend the Constitution's guarantees of equality before the law? Or do the liberty and due process provisions . . . secure the plaintiffs' right to marry their chosen partner? In matters implicating marriage, family life, and the upbringing of children, the two constitutional concepts frequently overlap, as they do here. See *Lawrence* ("Equality of treatment and the due process right to demand respect for conduct protected by the substantive guarantee of liberty are linked in important respects, and a decision on the latter point advances both interests"); Bolling v. Sharpe (1954) (racial segregation in District of Columbia public schools violates the Due Process Clause of Fifth Amendment to United States Constitution), decided the same day as Brown v. Board of Educ. of Topeka (1954) (holding that segregation of public schools in States violates Equal Protection Clause of Fourteenth Amendment). Much of what we say concerning one standard applies to the other.

We begin by considering the nature of civil marriage itself. Simply put, the government creates civil marriage. In Massachusetts, civil marriage is, and since pre-Colonial days has been, precisely what its name implies: a wholly secular institution. No religious ceremony has ever been required to validate a Massachusetts marriage.

In a real sense, there are three partners to every civil marriage: two willing spouses and an approving State. . . . Civil marriage is created and regulated through exercise of the police power. . . . In broad terms, it is the Legislature's power to enact rules to regulate conduct, to the extent that such laws are "necessary to secure the health, safety, good order, comfort, or general welfare of the community."

Without question, civil marriage enhances the "welfare of the community." It is a "social institution of the highest importance." Civil marriage anchors an ordered society by encouraging stable relationships over transient ones. It is central to the way the Commonwealth identifies individuals, provides for the orderly distribution of property, ensures that children and adults are cared for and supported whenever possible from private rather than public funds, and tracks important epidemiological and demographic data.

Marriage also bestows enormous private and social advantages on those who choose to marry. Civil marriage is at once a deeply personal commitment to another human being and a highly public celebration of the ideals of mutuality, companionship, intimacy, fidelity, and family. "It is an association that promotes a way of life, not causes; a harmony in living, not political faiths; a bilateral loyalty, not commercial or social projects." Griswold v. Connecticut (1965). Because it fulfils yearnings for security, safe haven, and connection that express our common humanity, civil marriage is an esteemed institution, and the decision whether and whom to marry is among life's momentous acts of self-definition. . . .

The benefits accessible only by way of a marriage license are enormous, touching nearly every aspect of life and death. The department states that "hundreds of statutes" are related to marriage and to marital benefits. With no attempt to be comprehensive, we note that some of the statutory benefits conferred by the Legislature on those who enter into civil marriage include, as to property: joint Massachusetts income tax filing; tenancy by the entirety; extension of the benefit of the homestead protection to one's spouse and children; automatic rights to inherit the property of a deceased spouse who does not leave a will; entitlement to wages owed to a deceased employee; the right to share the medical policy of one's spouse; thirty-nine week continuation of health coverage for the spouse of a person who is laid off or dies; preferential options under the Commonwealth's pension system; preferential benefits in the Commonwealth's medical program; access to veterans' spousal benefits and preferences; the equitable division of marital property on divorce; temporary and permanent alimony rights; the right to separate support on separation of the parties that does not result in divorce; and the right to bring claims for wrongful death and loss of consortium, and for funeral and burial expenses and punitive damages resulting from tort actions.

Exclusive marital benefits . . . not directly tied to property rights include the presumptions of legitimacy and parentage of children born to a married couple;

and evidentiary rights, such as the prohibition against spouses testifying against one another about their private conversations. . . .

Where a married couple has children, their children are also directly or indirectly . . . the recipients of the special legal and economic protections obtained by civil marriage. Notwithstanding the Commonwealth's strong public policy to abolish legal distinctions between marital and nonmarital children in providing for the support and care of minors, the fact remains that marital children reap a measure of family stability and economic security based on their parents' legally privileged status that is largely inaccessible, or not as readily accessible, to nonmarital children. Some of these benefits are social, such as the enhanced approval that still attends the status of being a marital child. Others are material, such as the greater ease of access to family-based State and Federal benefits that attend the presumptions of one's parentage.

It is undoubtedly for these concrete reasons, as well as for its intimately personal significance, that civil marriage has long been termed a "civil right." See, e.g., Loving v. Virginia (1967) ("Marriage is one of the 'basic civil rights of man,' fundamental to our very existence and survival"), quoting Skinner v. Oklahoma (1942); see also Baehr v. Lewin (Haw. 1993) (identifying marriage as "civil right[ ]"); Baker v. State (Vt. 1999) (Johnson, J., concurring in part and dissenting in part) (same). The United States Supreme Court has described the right to marry as "of fundamental importance for all individuals" and as "part of the fundamental 'right of privacy' implicit in the Fourteenth Amendment's Due Process Clause." Zablocki v. Redhail (1978). See *Loving* ("The freedom to marry has long been recognized as one of the vital personal rights essential to the orderly pursuit of happiness by free men").[14]

Without the right to marry—or more properly, the right to choose to marry—one is excluded from the full range of human experience and denied full protection of the laws for one's "avowed commitment to an intimate and lasting human relationship." *Baker*. Because civil marriage is central to the lives of individuals and the welfare of the community, our laws assiduously protect the individual's right to marry against undue government incursion. Laws may not "interfere directly and substantially with the right to marry." *Zablocki*. . . .

---

[14] Civil marriage enjoys a dual and in some sense paradoxical status as both a State-conferred benefit (with its attendant obligations) and a multi-faceted personal interest of "fundamental importance." *Zablocki*. As a practical matter, the State could not abolish civil marriage without chaotic consequences. The "right to marry" is different from rights deemed "fundamental" for equal protection and due process purposes because the State could, in theory, abolish all civil marriage while it cannot, for example, abolish all private property rights. [Footnote by the Court.]

B

For decades, indeed centuries, in much of this country (including Massachusetts) no lawful marriage was possible between white and black Americans. That long history availed not when the Supreme Court of California held in 1948 that a legislative prohibition against interracial marriage violated the due process and equality guarantees of the Fourteenth Amendment, Perez v. Sharpe (Ca. 1948), or when, nineteen years later, the United States Supreme Court also held that a statutory bar to interracial marriage violated the Fourteenth Amendment, *Loving*.[16] As both *Perez* and *Loving* make clear, the right to marry means little if it does not include the right to marry the person of one's choice, subject to appropriate government restrictions in the interests of public health, safety, and welfare. In this case, as in *Perez* and *Loving*, a statute deprives individuals of access to an institution of fundamental legal, personal, and social significance—the institution of marriage—because of a single trait: skin color in *Perez* and *Loving*, sexual orientation here. As it did in *Perez* and *Loving*, history must yield to a more fully developed understanding of the invidious quality of the discrimination.[17]

The Massachusetts Constitution protects matters of personal liberty against government incursion as zealously, and often more so, than does the Federal Constitution, even where both Constitutions employ essentially the same language. That the Massachusetts Constitution is in some instances more protective of individual liberty interests than is the Federal Constitution is not surprising. Fundamental to the vigor of our Federal system of government is that "state courts are absolutely free to interpret state constitutional provisions to accord greater protection to individual rights than do similar provisions of the United States Constitution." Arizona v. Evans (1995).

---

[16] The department argues that the *Loving* decision did not profoundly alter the by-then common conception of marriage because it was decided at a time when antimiscegenation statutes were in "full-scale retreat." But the relationship the department draws between popular consensus and the constitutionality of a statute oppressive to a minority group ignores the successful constitutional challenges to an antimiscegenation statute, initiated some twenty years earlier. When the Supreme Court of California decided *Perez*, a precursor to *Loving*, racial inequality was rampant and normative, segregation in public and private institutions was commonplace, the civil rights movement had not yet been launched, and the "separate but equal" doctrine of Plessy v. Ferguson (1896) was still good law. The lack of popular consensus favoring integration (including interracial marriage) did not deter the Supreme Court of California from holding that that State's antimiscegenation statute violated the plaintiffs' constitutional rights. Neither the *Perez* court nor the *Loving* Court was content to permit an unconstitutional situation to fester because the remedy might not reflect a broad social consensus. [Footnote by the Court.]

[17] Recently, the United States Supreme Court has reaffirmed that the Constitution prohibits a State from wielding its formidable power to regulate conduct in a manner that demeans basic human dignity, even though that statutory discrimination may enjoy broad public support. The Court struck down a statute criminalizing sodomy. See *Lawrence*. [Footnote by the Court.]

The individual liberty and equality safeguards of the Massachusetts Constitution protect both "freedom from" unwarranted government intrusion into protected spheres of life and "freedom to" partake in benefits created by the State for the common good. Both freedoms are involved here. Whether and whom to marry, how to express sexual intimacy, and whether and how to establish a family—these are among the most basic of every individual's liberty and due process rights. See, e.g., *Lawrence; Casey; Zablocki*; Roe v. Wade (1973); *Loving*. And central to personal freedom and security is the assurance that the laws will apply equally to persons in similar situations. The liberty interest in choosing whether and whom to marry would be hollow if the Commonwealth could, without sufficient justification, foreclose an individual from freely choosing the person with whom to share an exclusive commitment in the unique institution of civil marriage. . . .

The plaintiffs challenge the marriage statute on both equal protection and due process grounds. With respect to each such claim, we must first determine the appropriate standard of review. Where a statute implicates a fundamental right or uses a suspect classification, we employ "strict judicial scrutiny." For all other statutes, we employ the " 'rational basis' test." For due process claims, rational basis analysis requires that statutes "bear[ ] a real and substantial relation to the public health, safety, morals, or some other phase of the general welfare." For equal protection challenges, the rational basis test requires that "an impartial lawmaker could logically believe that the classification would serve a legitimate public purpose that transcends the harm to the members of the disadvantaged class." Cleburne v. Cleburne Living Ctr., Inc. (1985) (Stevens, J., concurring).[20]

The department argues that no fundamental right or "suspect" class is at issue here,[21] and rational basis is the appropriate standard of review. [W]e conclude that the marriage ban does not meet the rational basis test for either due process or equal protection. [W]e do not consider the plaintiffs' arguments that this case merits strict judicial scrutiny.

The department posits three legislative rationales for prohibiting same-sex couples from marrying: (1) providing a "favorable setting for procreation"; (2) ensuring the optimal setting for child rearing, which the department defines

---

[20] Not every asserted rational relationship is a "conceivable" one, and rationality review is not "toothless." Statutes have failed rational basis review even in circumstances where no fundamental right or "suspect" classification is implicated. . . . [Footnote by the Court.]

[21] Article 1 of the Massachusetts Constitution specifically prohibits sex-based discrimination. We have not previously considered whether "sexual orientation" is a "suspect" classification. Our resolution of this case does not require that inquiry here. [Footnote by the Court.]

as "a two-parent family with one parent of each sex"; and (3) preserving scarce State and private financial resources. . . .

The judge in the Superior Court endorsed the first rationale, holding that "the state's interest in regulating marriage is based on the traditional concept that marriage's primary purpose is procreation." This is incorrect. Our laws of civil marriage do not privilege procreative heterosexual intercourse between married people above every other form of adult intimacy and every other means of creating a family. General Laws c. 207 contains no requirement that the applicants for a marriage license attest to their ability or intention to conceive children by coitus. Fertility is not a condition of marriage, nor is it grounds for divorce. People who have never consummated their marriage, and never plan to, may be and stay married. People who cannot stir from their deathbed may marry. While it is certainly true that many, perhaps most, married couples have children together (assisted or unassisted), it is the exclusive and permanent commitment of the marriage partners to one another, not the begetting of children, that is the sine qua non of civil marriage.[23]

Moreover, the Commonwealth affirmatively facilitates bringing children into a family regardless of whether the intended parent is married or unmarried, whether the child is adopted or born into a family, whether assistive technology was used to conceive the child, and whether the parent or her partner is heterosexual, homosexual, or bisexual. If procreation were a necessary component of civil marriage, our statutes would draw a tighter circle around the permissible bounds of nonmarital child bearing and the creation of families by noncoital means. . . .

The "marriage is procreation" argument singles out the one unbridgeable difference between same-sex and opposite-sex couples, and transforms that difference into the essence of legal marriage. Like "Amendment 2" to the Constitution of Colorado, which effectively denied homosexual persons equality under the law and full access to the political process, the marriage restriction impermissibly "identifies persons by a single trait and then denies them protection across the board." Romer v. Evans (1996). In so doing, the State's

---

[23] It is hardly surprising that civil marriage developed historically as a means to regulate heterosexual conduct and to promote child rearing, because until very recently unassisted heterosexual relations were the only means short of adoption by which children could come into the world, and the absence of widely available and effective contraceptives made the link between heterosexual sex and procreation very strong indeed. Punitive notions of illegitimacy, and of homosexual identity, see *Lawrence*, further cemented the common and legal understanding of marriage as an unquestionably heterosexual institution. But it is circular reasoning, not analysis, to maintain that marriage must remain a heterosexual institution because that is what it historically has been. . . . [Footnote by the Court.]

action confers an official stamp of approval on the destructive stereotype that same-sex relationships are inherently unstable and inferior to opposite-sex relationships and are not worthy of respect.

The department's first stated rationale, equating marriage with unassisted heterosexual procreation, shades imperceptibly into its second: that confining marriage to opposite-sex couples ensures that children are raised in the "optimal" setting. Protecting the welfare of children is a paramount State policy. Restricting marriage to opposite-sex couples, however, cannot plausibly further this policy. "The demographic changes of the past century make it difficult to speak of an average American family. The composition of families varies greatly from household to household." Troxel v. Granville (2000). Massachusetts has responded supportively to "the changing realities of the American family," *id.*, and has moved vigorously to strengthen the modern family in its many variations. Moreover, we have repudiated the common-law power of the State to provide varying levels of protection to children based on the circumstances of birth. The "best interests of the child" standard does not turn on a parent's sexual orientation or marital status.

The department has offered no evidence that forbidding marriage to people of the same sex will increase the number of couples choosing to enter into opposite-sex marriages in order to have and raise children. There is thus no rational relationship between the marriage statute and the Commonwealth's proffered goal of protecting the "optimal" child rearing unit. Moreover, the department readily concedes that people in same-sex couples may be "excellent" parents. These couples (including four of the plaintiff couples) have children for the reasons others do—to love them, to care for them, to nurture them. But the task of child rearing for same-sex couples is made infinitely harder by their status as outliers to the marriage laws. While establishing the parentage of children as soon as possible is crucial to the safety and welfare of children, same-sex couples must undergo the sometimes lengthy and intrusive process of second-parent adoption to establish their joint parentage. While the enhanced income provided by marital benefits is an important source of security and stability for married couples and their children, those benefits are denied to families headed by same-sex couples. While the laws of divorce provide clear and reasonably predictable guidelines for child support, child custody, and property division on dissolution of a marriage, same-sex couples who dissolve their relationships find themselves and their children in the highly unpredictable terrain of equity jurisdiction. Given the wide range of public benefits reserved only for married couples, we do not credit the department's contention that the absence of access to civil marriage amounts to little more than an inconvenience to same-sex couples and their children. Excluding same-sex couples from civil marriage will not make children of opposite-sex marriages more secure, but it does prevent children of same-sex couples from enjoying the immeasurable advantages that flow from the assurance of "a stable family structure in which children will be reared, educated, and socialized." (Cordy, J., dissenting).

No one disputes that the plaintiff couples are families, that many are parents, and that the children they are raising, like all children, need and should have the fullest opportunity to grow up in a secure, protected family unit. Similarly, no one disputes that, under the rubric of marriage, the State provides a cornucopia of substantial benefits to married parents and their children. The preferential treatment of civil marriage reflects the Legislature's conclusion that marriage "is the foremost setting for the education and socialization of children" precisely because it "encourages parents to remain committed to each other and to their children as they grow." (Cordy, J., dissenting).

In this case, we are confronted with an entire, sizeable class of parents raising children who have absolutely no access to civil marriage and its protections because they are forbidden from procuring a marriage license. It cannot be rational under our laws, and indeed it is not permitted, to penalize children by depriving them of State benefits because the State disapproves of their parents' sexual orientation.

The third rationale advanced by the department is that limiting marriage to opposite-sex couples furthers the Legislature's interest in conserving scarce State and private financial resources. The marriage restriction is rational, it argues, because the General Court logically could assume that same-sex couples are more financially independent than married couples and thus less needy of public marital benefits, such as tax advantages, or private marital benefits, such as employer-financed health plans that include spouses in their coverage.

An absolute statutory ban on same-sex marriage bears no rational relationship to the goal of economy. First, the department's conclusory generalization . . . ignores that many same-sex couples, such as many of the plaintiffs in this case, have children and other dependents (here, aged parents) in their care. . . . Second, Massachusetts marriage laws do not condition receipt of public and private financial benefits to married individuals on a demonstration of financial dependence on each other. . . .

The department suggests additional rationales. . . . It argues that broadening civil marriage to include same-sex couples will trivialize or destroy the institution of marriage as it has historically been fashioned. Certainly our decision today marks a significant change in the definition of marriage as it has been inherited from the common law, and understood by many societies for centuries. But it does not disturb the fundamental value of marriage in our society.

Here, the plaintiffs seek only to be married, not to undermine the institution of civil marriage. They do not want marriage abolished. They do not attack the binary nature of marriage, the consanguinity provisions, or any of the other gate-keeping provisions of the marriage licensing law. Recognizing the right of an individual to marry a person of the same sex will not diminish the validity or dignity of opposite-sex marriage, any more than recognizing the right of an individual to marry a person of a different race devalues the marriage of a person who marries someone of her own race.[28] If anything, extending civil marriage to same-sex couples reinforces the importance of marriage to individuals and communities. That same-sex couples are willing to embrace marriage's solemn obligations of exclusivity, mutual support, and commitment to one another is a testament to the enduring place of marriage in our laws and in the human spirit.[29]

It has been argued that, due to the State's strong interest in the institution of marriage as a stabilizing social structure, only the Legislature can control and define its boundaries. . . . These arguments miss the point. The Massachusetts Constitution requires that legislation meet certain criteria and not extend beyond certain limits. It is the function of courts to determine whether these criteria are met and whether these limits are exceeded. . . . The Legislature in the first instance, and the courts in the last instance, must ascertain whether . . . a rational basis exists. To label the court's role as usurping that of the Legislature (Cordy, J., dissenting) is to misunderstand the nature and purpose of judicial review. We owe great deference to the Legislature to decide social and policy issues, but it is the traditional and settled role of courts to decide constitutional issues.

---

[28] Justice Cordy suggests that we have "transmuted the 'right' to marry into a right to change the institution of marriage itself" (Cordy, J., dissenting), because marriage is intimately tied to the reproductive systems of the marriage partners and to the "optimal" mother and father setting for child rearing. That analysis hews perilously close to the argument, long repudiated by the Legislature and the courts, that men and women are so innately and fundamentally different that their respective "proper spheres" can be rigidly and universally delineated. An abundance of legislative enactments and decisions of this court negate any such stereotypical premises. [Footnote by the Court.]

[29] We are concerned only with the withholding of the benefits, protections, and obligations of civil marriage from a certain class of persons for invalid reasons. Our decision in no way limits the rights of individuals to refuse to marry persons of the same sex for religious or any other reasons. It in no way limits the personal freedom to disapprove of, or to encourage others to disapprove of, same-sex marriage. Our concern, rather, is whether historical, cultural, religious, or other reasons permit the State to impose limits on personal beliefs concerning whom a person should marry. [Footnote by the Court.]

The history of constitutional law "is the story of the extension of constitutional rights and protections to people once ignored or excluded." United States v. Virginia (1996) (construing Equal Protection Clause of Fourteenth Amendment to prohibit categorical exclusion of women from public military institute). This statement is as true in the area of civil marriage as in any other area of civil rights. See, e.g., *Loving; Perez.* As a public institution and a right of fundamental importance, civil marriage is an evolving paradigm. The common law was exceptionally harsh toward women who became wives: a woman's legal identity all but evaporated into that of her husband. . . . But since at least the middle of the Nineteenth Century, both the courts and the Legislature have acted to ameliorate the harshness of the common-law regime. . . . Alarms about the imminent erosion of the "natural" order of marriage were sounded over the demise of antimiscegenation laws, the expansion of the rights of married women, and the introduction of "no-fault" divorce. Marriage has survived all of these transformations, and we have no doubt that marriage will continue to be a vibrant and revered institution.

We also reject the argument suggested by the department . . . that expanding the institution of civil marriage in Massachusetts to include same-sex couples will lead to interstate conflict. We would not presume to dictate how another State should respond to today's decision. But neither should considerations of comity prevent us from according Massachusetts residents the full measure of protection available under the Massachusetts Constitution. The genius of our Federal system is that each State's Constitution has vitality specific to its own traditions, and that, subject to the minimum requirements of the Fourteenth Amendment, each State is free to address difficult issues of individual liberty in the manner its own Constitution demands.

Several amici suggest that prohibiting marriage by same-sex couples reflects community consensus that homosexual conduct is immoral. Yet Massachusetts has a strong affirmative policy of preventing discrimination on the basis of sexual orientation. . . .

The marriage ban works a deep and scarring hardship on a very real segment of the community for no rational reason. The absence of any reasonable relationship between, on the one hand, an absolute disqualification of same-sex couples who wish to enter into civil marriage and, on the other, protection of public health, safety, or general welfare, suggests that the marriage restriction is rooted in persistent prejudices against persons who are (or who are believed to be) homosexual. "The Constitution cannot control such prejudices but neither can it tolerate them. Private biases may be outside the reach of the law, but the law cannot, directly or indirectly, give them effect." Palmore v. Sidoti (1984) (construing Fourteenth Amendment). Limiting the protections, benefits, and obligations of civil marriage to opposite-sex couples violates the basic premises of individual liberty and equality under law protected by the Massachusetts Constitution.

IV

We consider next the plaintiffs' request for relief. . . .[34] We face a problem similar to one that recently confronted the Court of Appeal for Ontario, the highest court of that Canadian province, when it considered the constitutionality of the same-sex marriage ban under Canada's Federal Constitution, the Charter of Rights and Freedoms (Charter). See Halpern v. Toronto (City) (2003). Canada, like the United States, adopted the common law of England that civil marriage is "the voluntary union for life of one man and one woman, to the exclusion of all others." *Id.* In holding that the limitation of civil marriage to opposite-sex couples violated the Charter, the Court of Appeal refined the common-law meaning of marriage. We concur with this remedy, which is entirely consonant with established principles of jurisprudence empowering a court to refine a common-law principle in light of evolving constitutional standards.

We construe civil marriage to mean the voluntary union of two persons as spouses, to the exclusion of all others. This reformulation redresses the plaintiffs' constitutional injury and furthers the aim of marriage to promote stable, exclusive relationships. It advances the two legitimate State interests the department has identified: providing a stable setting for child rearing and conserving State resources. It leaves intact the Legislature's broad discretion to regulate marriage.

. . . We declare that barring an individual from the protections, benefits, and obligations of civil marriage solely because that person would marry a person of the same sex violates the Massachusetts Constitution. . . . We remand this case to the Superior Court for entry of judgment consistent with this opinion. Entry of judgment shall be stayed for 180 days to permit the Legislature to take such action as it may deem appropriate in light of this opinion.

---

[34] [N]o one argues that the restrictions on incestuous or polygamous marriages are so dependent on the marriage restriction that they too should fall if the marriage restriction falls. Nothing in our opinion today should be construed as relaxing or abrogating the consanguinity or polygamy prohibitions of our marriage laws. [Footnote by the Court.]

■ GREANEY, J. (concurring).

I agree with the result reached by the court, the remedy ordered, and much of the reasoning in the court's opinion. In my view, however, the case is more directly resolved using traditional equal protection analysis.

(a) ... Because our marriage statutes intend, and state, the ordinary understanding that marriage under our law consists only of a union between a man and a woman, they create a statutory classification based on the sex of the two people who wish to marry. See *Baehr* (plurality opinion) (Hawaii marriage statutes created sex-based classification); *Baker* (Johnson, J., concurring in part and dissenting in part) (same). That the classification is sex based is self-evident. The marriage statutes prohibit some applicants, such as the plaintiffs, from obtaining a marriage license, and that prohibition is based solely on the applicants' gender. As a factual matter, an individual's choice of marital partner is constrained because of his or her own sex. Stated in particular terms, Hillary Goodridge cannot marry Julie Goodridge because she (Hillary) is a woman. Likewise, Gary Chalmers cannot marry Richard Linnell because he (Gary) is a man. Only their gender prevents Hillary and Gary from marrying their chosen partners under the present law.

A classification may be gender based whether or not the challenged government action apportions benefits or burdens uniformly along gender lines. This is so because constitutional protections extend to individuals and not to categories of people. Thus, when an individual desires to marry, but cannot marry his or her chosen partner because of the traditional opposite-sex restriction, a violation of art. 1 has occurred. I find it disingenuous, at best, to suggest that such an individual's right to marry has not been burdened at all, because he or she remains free to choose another partner, who is of the opposite sex.

The equal protection infirmity at work here is strikingly similar to (although, perhaps, more subtle than) the invidious discrimination perpetuated by Virginia's antimiscegenation laws and unveiled in the decision of *Loving*. In its landmark decision striking down Virginia's ban on marriages between Caucasians and members of any other race on both equal protection and substantive due process grounds, the United States Supreme Court soundly rejected the proposition that the equal application of the ban (i.e., that it applied equally to whites and blacks) made unnecessary the strict scrutiny analysis traditionally required of statutes drawing classifications according to race. ... That our marriage laws, unlike antimiscegenation laws, were not enacted purposely to discriminate in no way neutralizes their present discriminatory character. . . .

The rights of couples to have children, to adopt, and to be foster parents, regardless of sexual orientation and marital status, are firmly established. [T]he State's refusal to accord legal recognition to unions of same-sex couples has had the effect of creating a system in which children of same-sex couples are unable to partake of legal protections and social benefits taken for granted by children in families whose parents are of the opposite sex. The continued maintenance of this caste-like system is irreconcilable with, indeed, totally repugnant to, the State's strong interest in the welfare of all children and its primary focus, in the context of family law where children are concerned, on "the best interests of the child." . . .

A comment is in order with respect to the insistence of some that marriage is, as a matter of definition, the legal union of a man and a woman. To define the institution of marriage by the characteristics of those to whom it always has been accessible, in order to justify the exclusion of those to whom it never has been accessible, is conclusory and bypasses the core question we are asked to decide. This case calls for a higher level of legal analysis. Precisely, the case requires that we confront ingrained assumptions with respect to historically accepted roles of men and women within the institution of marriage and requires that we reexamine these assumptions in light of the unequivocal language of art. 1, in order to ensure that the governmental conduct challenged here conforms to the supreme charter of our Commonwealth. . . . I do not doubt the sincerity of deeply held moral or religious beliefs that make inconceivable to some the notion that any change in the common-law definition of what constitutes a legal civil marriage is now, or ever would be, warranted. But, as matter of constitutional law, neither the mantra of tradition, nor individual conviction, can justify the perpetuation of a hierarchy in which couples of the same sex and their families are deemed less worthy of social and legal recognition than couples of the opposite sex and their families. See *Lawrence* (O'Connor, J., concurring) (moral disapproval, with no other valid State interest, cannot justify law that discriminates against groups of persons); *Casey* ("Our obligation is to define the liberty of all, not to mandate our own moral code").

(b) I am hopeful that our decision will be accepted by those thoughtful citizens who believe that same-sex unions should not be approved by the State. I am not referring here to acceptance in the sense of grudging acknowledgment of the court's authority to adjudicate the matter. My hope is more liberating. The plaintiffs are members of our community, our neighbors, our coworkers, our friends. As pointed out by the court, their professions include investment advisor, computer engineer, teacher, therapist, and lawyer. The plaintiffs volunteer in our schools, worship beside us in our religious houses, and have children who play with our children, to mention just a few ordinary daily contacts. We share a common humanity and participate together in the social contract that is the foundation of our Commonwealth. Simple principles of decency dictate that we extend to the plaintiffs, and to their new status, full acceptance, tolerance, and respect. We should do so because it is the right thing to do. The union of two people contemplated by G.L. c. 207 "is a coming together for better or for worse, hopefully enduring, and intimate to the degree of being sacred. It is an association that promotes a way of life, not causes; a harmony in living, not political faiths; a bilateral loyalty, not commercial or social projects. Yet it is an association for as noble a purpose as any involved in our prior decisions." *Griswold.* Because of the terms of art. 1, the plaintiffs will no longer be excluded from that association.

■ SPINA, J. (dissenting, with whom SOSMAN and CORDY, JJ., join). . . .

1. *Equal protection* . . . G.L. c. 207 does not unconstitutionally discriminate on the basis of gender. A claim of gender discrimination will lie where it is shown that differential treatment disadvantages one sex over the other. G.L. c. 207 . . . creates no distinction between the sexes, but applies to men and women in precisely the same way. It does not create any disadvantage identified with gender, as both men and women are similarly limited to marrying a person of the opposite sex.

Similarly, the marriage statutes do not discriminate on the basis of sexual orientation. . . . The[y] do not disqualify individuals on the basis of sexual orientation from entering into marriage. All individuals, with certain exceptions not relevant here, are free to marry. Whether an individual chooses not to marry because of sexual orientation or any other reason should be of no concern to the court. . . .

. . . This court should not have invoked even the most deferential standard of review within equal protection analysis because no individual was denied access to the institution of marriage.

2. *Due process.* The marriage statutes do not impermissibly burden a right protected by our constitutional guarantee of due process. . . . There is no restriction on the right of any plaintiff to enter into marriage. Each is free to marry a willing person of the opposite sex. . . .

. . . Same-sex marriage, or the "right to marry the person of one's choice" as the court today defines that right, does not fall within the fundamental right to marry. Same-sex marriage is not "deeply rooted in this Nation's history," and the court does not suggest that it is. Except for the occasional isolated decision in recent years, see, e.g., *Baker*, same-sex marriage is not a right, fundamental or otherwise, recognized in this country. . . . In this Commonwealth and in this country, the roots of the institution of marriage are deeply set in history as a civil union between a single man and a single woman. There is no basis for the court to recognize same-sex marriage as a constitutionally protected right. . . .

. . . The purpose of substantive due process is to protect existing rights, not to create new rights. Its aim is to thwart government intrusion, not invite it. The court asserts that the Massachusetts Declaration of Rights serves to guard against government intrusion into each individual's sphere of privacy. . . . The statute in question does not seek to regulate intimate activity within an intimate relationship, but merely gives formal recognition to a particular marriage. The State has respected the private lives of the plaintiffs, and has done nothing to intrude in the relationships that each of the plaintiff couples enjoy. *Cf. Lawrence* (case "does not involve whether the government must give formal recognition to any relationship that homosexual persons seek to enter"). Ironically, by extending the marriage laws to same-sex couples the court has turned substantive due process on its head and used it to interject government into the plaintiffs' lives.

■ Sosman, J. (dissenting, with whom Spina and Cordy, JJ., join).

. . . Reduced to its essence, the court's opinion concludes that, because same-sex couples are now raising children, and withholding the benefits of civil marriage from their union makes it harder for them to raise those children, the State must therefore provide the benefits of civil marriage to same-sex couples just as it does to opposite-sex couples. Of course, many people are raising children outside the confines of traditional marriage, and, by definition, those children are being deprived of the various benefits that would flow if they were being raised in a household with married parents. That does not mean that the Legislature must accord the full benefits of marital status on every household raising children. Rather, the Legislature need only have some rational basis for concluding that, at present, those alternate family structures have not yet been conclusively shown to be the equivalent of the marital family structure that has established itself as a successful one over a period of centuries. People are of course at liberty to raise their children in various family structures, as long as they are not literally harming their children by doing so. That does not mean that the State is required to provide identical forms of encouragement, endorsement, and support to all of the infinite variety of household structures that a free society permits. . . .

. . . Conspicuously absent from the court's opinion today is any acknowledgment that the attempts at scientific study of the ramifications of raising children in same-sex couple households are themselves in their infancy and have so far produced inconclusive and conflicting results. . . . The Legislature can rationally view the state of the scientific evidence as unsettled on the critical question it now faces: are families headed by same-sex parents equally successful in rearing children from infancy to adulthood as families headed by parents of opposite sexes? Our belief that children raised by same-sex couples *should* fare the same as children raised in traditional families is just that: a passionately held but utterly untested belief. The Legislature is not required to share that belief but may, as the creator of the institution of civil marriage, wish to see the proof before making a fundamental alteration to that institution.

Although ostensibly applying the rational basis test to the civil marriage statutes, it is abundantly apparent that the court is in fact applying some undefined stricter standard to assess the constitutionality of the marriage statutes' exclusion of same-sex couples. . . .

As a matter of social history, today's opinion may represent a great turning point that many will hail as a tremendous step toward a more just society. As a matter of constitutional jurisprudence, however, the case stands as an aberration. To reach the result it does, the court has tortured the rational basis test beyond recognition. I fully appreciate the strength of the temptation to find this particular law unconstitutional—there is much to be said for the argument that excluding gay and lesbian couples from the benefits of civil marriage is cruelly unfair and hopelessly outdated; the inability to marry has a profound impact on the personal lives of committed gay and lesbian couples (and their children) to whom we are personally close (our friends, neighbors, family members, classmates, and co-workers); and our resolution of this issue takes place under the intense glare of national and international publicity. . . . In my view, however, such factors make it all the more imperative that we adhere precisely and scrupulously to the established guideposts of our constitutional jurisprudence, a jurisprudence that makes the rational basis test an extremely deferential one that focuses on the rationality, not the persuasiveness, of the potential justifications for the classifications in the legislative scheme. . . . Applying that deferential test in the manner it is customarily applied, the exclusion of gay and lesbian couples from the institution of civil marriage passes constitutional muster. I respectfully dissent.

■ CORDY, J. (dissenting, with whom SPINA and SOSMAN, JJ., join). . . .

The Massachusetts marriage statute does not impair the exercise of a recognized fundamental right, or discriminate on the basis of sex in violation of the equal rights amendment to the Massachusetts Constitution. Consequently, it is subject to review only to determine whether it satisfies the rational basis test. Because a conceivable rational basis exists upon which the Legislature could conclude that the marriage statute furthers the legitimate State purpose of ensuring, promoting, and supporting an optimal social structure for the bearing and raising of children, it is a valid exercise of the State's police power.

A.   *Limiting marriage to the union of one man and one woman does not impair the exercise of a fundamental right.* . . . As the court notes in its opinion, the institution of marriage is "the legal union of a man and woman as husband and wife," and it has always been so under Massachusetts law, colonial or otherwise.

The plaintiffs contend that because the right to choose to marry is a "fundamental" right, the right to marry the person of one's choice, including a member of the same sex, must also be a "fundamental" right. While the court stops short of deciding that the right to marry someone of the same sex is "fundamental" such that strict scrutiny must be applied to any statute that impairs it, it nevertheless agrees with the plaintiffs that the right to choose to marry is of fundamental importance and would be "hollow" if an individual was foreclosed from "freely choosing the person with whom to share . . . the . . . institution of civil marriage." Hence, it concludes that a marriage license cannot be denied to an individual who wishes to marry someone of the same sex. In reaching this result the court has transmuted the "right" to marry into a right to change the institution of marriage itself. This feat of reasoning succeeds only if one accepts the proposition that the definition of the institution of marriage as a union between a man and a woman is merely "conclusory" rather than the basis on which the "right" to partake in it has been deemed to be of fundamental importance. In other words, only by assuming that "marriage" includes the union of two persons of the same sex does the court conclude that restricting marriage to opposite-sex couples infringes on the "right" of same-sex couples to "marry." . . .

Supreme Court cases that have described marriage or the right to marry as "fundamental" have focused primarily on the underlying interest of every individual in procreation, which, historically, could only legally occur within the construct of marriage because sexual intercourse outside of marriage was a criminal act. . . . Because same-sex couples are unable to procreate on their own, any right to marriage they may possess cannot be based on their interest in procreation. . . .

The marriage statute, which regulates only the act of obtaining a marriage license, does not implicate privacy in the sense that it has found constitutional protection under Massachusetts and Federal law. It does not intrude on any right that the plaintiffs have to privacy in their choices regarding procreation, an intimate partner or sexual relations. The plaintiffs' right to privacy in such matters does not require that the State officially endorse their choices in order for the right to be constitutionally vindicated. . . .

While the institution of marriage is deeply rooted in the history and traditions of our country and our State, the right to marry someone of the same sex is not. No matter how personal or intimate a decision to marry someone of the same sex might be, the right to make it is not guaranteed by the right of personal autonomy.

Finally, the constitutionally protected interest in child rearing . . . is not implicated or infringed by the marriage statute here. The fact that the plaintiffs cannot marry has no bearing on their independently protected constitutional rights as parents which, as with opposite-sex parents, are limited only by their continued fitness and the best interests of their children. . . .

This is not to say that a statute that has no rational basis must nevertheless be upheld as long as it is of ancient origin. However, "[t]he long history of a certain practice . . . and its acceptance as an uncontroversial part of our national and State tradition do suggest that [the court] should reflect carefully before striking it down." As this court has recognized, the "fact that a challenged practice is followed by a large number of states . . . is plainly worth considering in determining whether the practice 'offends some principle of justice so rooted in the traditions and conscience of our people as to be ranked as fundamental.'"

Although public attitudes toward marriage in general and same-sex marriage in particular have changed and are still evolving, "the asserted contemporary concept of marriage and societal interests for which [plaintiffs] contend" are "manifestly [less] deeply founded" than the "historic institution" of marriage. Indeed, it is not readily apparent to what extent contemporary values have embraced the concept of same-sex marriage. Perhaps the "clearest and most reliable objective evidence of contemporary values is the legislation enacted by the country's legislatures," Atkins v. Virginia (2002). No State Legislature has enacted laws permitting same-sex marriages; and a large majority of States, as well as the United States Congress, have affirmatively prohibited the recognition of such marriages for any purpose. . . .

Given this history and the current state of public opinion, as reflected in the actions of the people's elected representatives, it cannot be said that "a right to same-sex marriage is so rooted in the traditions and collective conscience of our people that failure to recognize it would violate the fundamental principles of liberty and justice that lie at the base of all our civil and political institutions. Neither . . . [is] a right to same-sex marriage . . . implicit in the concept of ordered liberty, such that neither liberty nor justice would exist if it were sacrificed." In such circumstances, the law with respect to same-sex marriages must be left to develop through legislative processes, subject to the constraints of rationality, lest the court be viewed as using the liberty and Due Process Clauses as vehicles merely to enforce its own views regarding better social policies, a role that the strongly worded separation of powers principles in art. 30 of the Declaration of Rights of our Constitution forbids, and for which the court is particularly ill suited.

B. *The marriage statute, in limiting marriage to heterosexual couples, does not constitute discrimination on the basis of sex in violation of the Equal Rights Amendment to the Massachusetts Constitution.* In his concurrence, Justice Greaney contends that the marriage statute constitutes discrimination on the basis of sex in violation of . . . the Equal Rights Amendment (ERA). Such a conclusion is analytically unsound and inconsistent with the legislative history of the ERA.

The central purpose of the ERA was to eradicate discrimination against women and in favor of men or vice versa. Consistent with this purpose, we have construed the ERA to prohibit laws that advantage one sex at the expense of the other, but not laws that treat men and women equally. The Massachusetts marriage statute does not subject men to different treatment from women; each is equally prohibited from precisely the same conduct. . . .

[T]here is no evidence that limiting marriage to opposite-sex couples was motivated by sexism in general or a desire to disadvantage men or women in particular. Moreover, no one has identified any harm, burden, disadvantage, or advantage accruing to either gender as a consequence of the Massachusetts marriage statute. In the absence of such effect, the statute limiting marriage to couples of the opposite sex does not violate the ERA's prohibition of sex discrimination. . . .

C. *The marriage statute satisfies the rational basis standard.* . . .

Paramount among its many important functions, the institution of marriage has systematically provided for the regulation of heterosexual behavior, brought order to the resulting procreation, and ensured a stable family structure in which children will be reared, educated, and socialized. Admittedly, heterosexual intercourse, procreation, and child care are not necessarily conjoined (particularly in the modern age of widespread effective contraception and supportive social welfare programs), but an orderly society requires some mechanism for coping with the fact that sexual intercourse commonly results in pregnancy and childbirth. The institution of marriage is that mechanism.

The institution of marriage provides the important legal and normative link between heterosexual intercourse and procreation on the one hand and family responsibilities on the other. The partners in a marriage are expected to engage in exclusive sexual relations, with children the probable result and paternity presumed. Whereas the relationship between mother and child is demonstratively and predictably created and recognizable through the biological process of pregnancy and childbirth, there is no corresponding process for creating a relationship between father and child. Similarly, aside from an act of heterosexual intercourse nine months prior to childbirth, there is no process for creating a relationship between a man and a woman as the parents of a particular child. The institution of marriage fills this void by formally binding the husband-father to his wife and child, and imposing on him the responsibilities of fatherhood. The alternative, a society without the institution of marriage, in which heterosexual intercourse, procreation, and child care are largely disconnected processes, would be chaotic.

The marital family is also the foremost setting for the education and socialization of children. . . . The institution of marriage encourages parents to remain committed to each other and to their children as they grow, thereby encouraging a stable venue for the education and socialization of children. . . .

It is undeniably true that dramatic historical shifts in our cultural, political, and economic landscape have altered some of our traditional notions about marriage. . . . Nevertheless, the institution of marriage remains the principal weave of our social fabric. A family defined by heterosexual marriage continues to be the most prevalent social structure into which the vast majority of children are born, nurtured, and prepared for productive participation in civil society.

It is difficult to imagine a State purpose more important and legitimate than ensuring, promoting, and supporting an optimal social structure within which to bear and raise children. At the very least, the marriage statute continues to serve this important State purpose.

. . . The question we must turn to next is whether the statute . . . remains a rational way to further that purpose. Stated differently, we ask whether a conceivable rational basis exists on which the Legislature could conclude that continuing to limit the institution of civil marriage to members of the opposite sex furthers the legitimate purpose of ensuring, promoting, and supporting an optimal social structure for the bearing and raising of children.

In considering whether such a rational basis exists, we defer to the decision-making process of the Legislature, and must make deferential assumptions about the information that it might consider and on which it may rely.

We must assume that the Legislature (1) might conclude that the institution of civil marriage has successfully and continually provided this structure over several centuries; (2) might consider and credit studies that document negative consequences that too often follow children either born outside of marriage or raised in households lacking either a father or a mother figure, and scholarly commentary contending that children and families develop best when mothers and fathers are partners in their parenting; and (3) would be familiar with many recent studies that variously support the proposition that children raised in intact families headed by same-sex couples fare as well on many measures as children raised in similar families headed by opposite-sex couples; support the proposition that children of same-sex couples fare worse on some measures; or reveal notable differences between the two groups of children that warrant further study.

Taking all of this available information into account, the Legislature could rationally conclude that a family environment with married opposite-sex parents remains the optimal social structure in which to bear children, and that the raising of children by same-sex couples . . . presents an alternative structure for child rearing that has not yet proved itself beyond reasonable scientific dispute to be as optimal as the biologically based marriage norm. Working from the assumption that a recognition of same-sex marriages will increase the number of children experiencing this alternative, the Legislature could conceivably conclude that declining to recognize same-sex marriages remains prudent until empirical questions about its impact on the upbringing of children are resolved.

The fact that the Commonwealth currently allows same-sex couples to adopt does not affect the rationality of this conclusion. The eligibility of a child for adoption presupposes that at least one of the child's biological parents is unable or unwilling, for some reason, to participate in raising the child. In that sense, society has "lost" the optimal setting in which to raise that child. . . . In these circumstances, the principal and overriding consideration is the "best interests of the child." . . . The objective is an individualized determination of the best environment for a particular child, where the normative social structure—a home with both the child's biological father and mother—is not an option. That such a focused determination may lead to the approval of a same-sex couple's adoption of a child does not mean that it would be irrational for a legislator, in fashioning statutory laws that cannot make such individualized determinations, to conclude generally that being raised by a same-sex couple has not yet been shown to be the absolute equivalent of being raised by one's married biological parents.

That the State does not preclude different types of families from raising children does not mean that it must view them all as equally optimal and equally deserving of State endorsement and support. For example, . . . the fact that the Legislature permits single-parent adoption does not mean that it has endorsed single parenthood as an optimal setting in which to raise children or views it as the equivalent of being raised by both of one's biological parents. The same holds true with respect to same-sex couples. . . . The Legislature may rationally permit adoption by same-sex couples yet harbor reservations as to whether parenthood by same-sex couples should be affirmatively encouraged to the same extent as parenthood by the heterosexual couple whose union produced the child.

In addition, the Legislature could conclude that redefining the institution of marriage to permit same-sex couples to marry would impair the State's interest in promoting and supporting heterosexual marriage as the social institution that it has determined best normalizes, stabilizes, and links the acts of procreation and child rearing. While the plaintiffs argue that they only want to take part in the same stabilizing institution, the Legislature conceivably could conclude that permitting their participation would have the unintended effect of undermining to some degree marriage's ability to serve its social purpose.

As long as marriage is limited to opposite-sex couples who can at least theoretically procreate, society is able to communicate a consistent message to its citizens that marriage is a (normatively) necessary part of their procreative endeavor; that if they are to procreate, then society has endorsed the institution of marriage as the environment for it and for the subsequent rearing of their children; and that benefits are available explicitly to create a supportive and conducive atmosphere for those purposes. If society proceeds similarly to recognize marriages between same-sex couples who cannot procreate, it could be perceived as an abandonment of this claim, and might result in the mistaken view that civil marriage has little to do with procreation: just as the potential of procreation would not be necessary for a marriage to be valid, marriage would not be necessary for optimal procreation and child rearing to occur. In essence, the Legislature could conclude that the consequence of such a policy shift would be a diminution in society's ability to steer the acts of procreation and child rearing into their most optimal setting.

The court recognizes this concern, but brushes it aside with the assumption that permitting same-sex couples to marry "will not diminish the validity or dignity of opposite-sex marriage," and that "we have no doubt that marriage will continue to be a vibrant and revered institution." Whether the court is correct in its assumption is irrelevant. What is relevant is that such predicting is not the business of the courts. A rational Legislature, given the evidence, could conceivably come to a different conclusion, or could at least harbor rational concerns about possible unintended consequences of a dramatic redefinition of marriage.

There is no question that many same-sex couples are capable of being good parents, and should be (and are) permitted to be so. The policy question that a legislator must resolve is a different one, and turns on an assessment of whether the marriage structure proposed by the plaintiffs will, over time, if endorsed and supported by the State, prove to be as stable and successful a model as the one that has formed a cornerstone of our society since colonial times, or prove to be less than optimal, and result in consequences, perhaps now unforeseen, adverse to the State's legitimate interest in promoting and supporting the best possible social structure in which children should be born and raised. Given the critical importance of civil marriage as an organizing and stabilizing institution of society, it is eminently rational for the Legislature to postpone making fundamental changes to it until such time as there is unanimous scientific evidence, or popular consensus, or both, that such changes can safely be made.

There is no reason to believe that legislative processes are inadequate to effectuate legal changes in response to evolving evidence, social values, and views of fairness on the subject of same-sex relationships. Deliberate consideration of, and incremental responses to rapidly evolving scientific and social understanding is the norm of the political process—that it may seem painfully slow to those who are already persuaded by the arguments in favor of change is not a sufficient basis to conclude that the processes are constitutionally infirm. The advancement of the rights, privileges, and protections afforded to homosexual members of our community in the last three decades has been significant, and there is no reason to believe that that evolution will not continue. Changes of attitude in the civic, social, and professional communities have been even more profound. Thirty years ago, The Diagnostic and Statistical Manual, the seminal handbook of the American Psychiatric Association, still listed homosexuality as a mental disorder. Today, the Massachusetts Psychiatric Society, the American Psychoanalytic Association, and many other psychiatric, psychological, and social science organizations have joined in an amicus brief on behalf of the plaintiffs' cause. A body of experience and evidence has provided the basis for change, and that body continues to mount. The Legislature is the appropriate branch, both constitutionally and practically, to consider and respond to it. It is not enough that we as Justices might be personally of the view that we have learned enough to decide what is best. So long as the question is at all debatable, it must be the Legislature that decides. The marriage statute thus meets the requirements of the rational basis test.

EDITORS' NOTES

(1) What is the relationship between *Lawrence* (reprinted above) and *Goodridge?* In *Lawrence,* the United States Supreme Court avoided any implications for same-sex marriage. In *Goodridge,* though, the Massachusetts Supreme Judicial Court interprets *Lawrence* as affirming "the core concept of common human dignity" and "the central role that decisions whether to marry or have children bear in shaping one's identity." Thus, the Supreme Judicial Court interprets *Lawrence* as supporting, if not paving the way for, its holding.

(2) The Massachusetts Supreme Judicial Court here, like the Vermont Supreme Court in *Baker* (reprinted above), illustrates an independent jurisprudence of state constitutional law. The Court interprets the Massachusetts Constitution to give broader protection to both individual liberty and equality than the United States Constitution. But the Court here, unlike the Vermont Supreme Court, held in a subsequent advisory opinion that same-sex civil unions as distinguished from same-sex marriage would not be an adequate remedy, but instead would be a form of "second-class citizenship." Which court is more persuasive with respect to remedy? Beyond the remedy, what are the main differences between *Baker* and *Goodridge* as a matter of constitutional interpretation?

(3) The Massachusetts Supreme Judicial Court characterizes marriage as "a vital social institution": "simply put, the government creates civil marriage,"

which is "a wholly secular institution." Is this understanding obviously true or deeply controversial? Do some opponents of extending marriage to same-sex couples hold a different conception of marriage?

(4) Some have criticized the United States Supreme Court decisions protecting a right of privacy or autonomy for exalting "choice" over the good of what is chosen and for "bracketing" moral arguments about goods or virtues promoted by protecting freedoms. See, e.g., Michael J. Sandel, "Moral Argument and Liberal Toleration: Abortion and Homosexuality," 77 *Cal. L. Rev.* 521 (1989). Is *Goodridge* vulnerable to this criticism? The Massachusetts Supreme Judicial Court waxes eloquent about such goods or virtues: commitment to another human being, along with "the ideals of mutuality, companionship, intimacy, fidelity, and family" and "yearnings for security, safe haven, and connection that express our common humanity." Should courts seek to justify protecting rights on the ground that they promote moral goods? See James E. Fleming and Linda C. McClain, *Ordered Liberty: Rights, Responsibilities, and Virtues* (Cambridge: Harvard University Press, 2013), Chapter 7.

(5) What standard of review does the Supreme Judicial Court apply to both the due process and equal protection challenges? Rational basis scrutiny with "bite" both as to ends and as to fit between means and ends? Compare this standard with those of Cleburne v. Cleburne Living Center (1985; discussed above) and Romer v. Evans (1996; reprinted above).

(6) The Supreme Judicial Court states: "The individual liberty and equality safeguards of the Massachusetts Constitution protect both 'freedom from' unwarranted government intrusion into protected spheres of life and 'freedom to' partake in benefits created by the State for the common good." It thus sets its face against the United States Supreme Court's conception of the United States Constitution as a charter of "negative liberties" or "freedom from" instead of as a charter of positive benefits or "freedom to." Contrast DeShaney v. Winnebago County (1989). In dissent in Obergefell v. Hodges (2015; reprinted in Chapter 1), Chief Justice Roberts and Justice Thomas invoke *DeShaney* in opposing the majority's recognition of the right of gay men and lesbians to marry.

———

VI. THE FUNDAMENTAL RIGHT TO MARRY UNDER THE U.S. CONSTITUTION: SECURING EQUALITY AND LIBERTY FOR GAYS AND LESBIANS

"After careful consideration, including a review of my recommendation, the President has concluded that given a number of factors, including a documented history of discrimination, classifications based on sexual orientation should be subject to a heightened standard of scrutiny. The President has also concluded that Section 3 of DOMA, as applied to legally married same-sex couples, fails to meet that standard and is therefore unconstitutional."—ATTORNEY GENERAL HOLDER

LETTER FROM THE ATTORNEY GENERAL TO CONGRESS ON LITIGATION INVOLVING THE DEFENSE OF MARRIAGE ACT

Office of the Attorney General

Washington, D.C. 20530

February 23, 2011

The Honorable John A. Boehner
Speaker
U.S. House of Representatives
Washington, DC 20515

Re: Defense of Marriage Act

Dear Mr. Speaker:

After careful consideration, including review of a recommendation from me, the President of the United States has made the determination that Section 3 of the Defense of Marriage Act ("DOMA"), as applied to same-sex couples who are legally married under state law, violates the equal protection component of the Fifth Amendment. . . . I am writing to advise you of the Executive Branch's determination and to inform you of the steps the Department will take in two pending DOMA cases to implement that determination.

While the Department has previously defended DOMA against legal challenges involving legally married same-sex couples, recent lawsuits that challenge the constitutionality of DOMA Section 3 have caused the President and the Department to conduct a new examination of the defense of this provision. In particular, in November 2010, plaintiffs filed two new lawsuits challenging the constitutionality of Section 3 of DOMA in jurisdictions without precedent on whether sexual-orientation classifications are subject to rational basis review or whether they must satisfy some form of heightened scrutiny. Windsor v. United States (S.D.N.Y.); Pedersen v. OPM (D. Conn.). Previously, the Administration has defended Section 3 in jurisdictions where circuit courts have already held that classifications based on sexual orientation are subject to rational basis review, and it has advanced arguments to defend DOMA Section 3 under the binding standard that has applied in those cases.

These new lawsuits, by contrast, will require the Department to take an affirmative position on the level of scrutiny that should be applied to DOMA Section 3 in a circuit without binding precedent on the issue. As described more fully below, the President and I have concluded that classifications based on sexual orientation warrant heightened scrutiny and that, as applied to same-sex couples legally married under state law, Section 3 of DOMA is unconstitutional.

Standard of Review

The Supreme Court has yet to rule on the appropriate level of scrutiny for classifications based on sexual orientation. It has, however, rendered a number of decisions that set forth the criteria that should inform this and any other judgment as to whether heightened scrutiny applies: (1) whether the group in question has suffered a history of discrimination; (2) whether individuals "exhibit obvious, immutable, or distinguishing characteristics that define them as a discrete group"; (3) whether the group is a minority or is politically powerless; and (4) whether the characteristics distinguishing the group have little relation to legitimate policy objectives or to an individual's "ability to perform or contribute to society." See Bowen v. Gilliard (1987); City of Cleburne v. Cleburne Living Ctr. (1985).

Each of these factors counsels in favor of being suspicious of classifications based on sexual orientation. First and most importantly, there is, regrettably, a significant history of purposeful discrimination against gay and lesbian people, by governmental as well as private entities, based on prejudice and stereotypes that continue to have ramifications today. Indeed, until very recently, states have "demean[ed] the[] existence" of gays and lesbians "by making their private sexual conduct a crime." Lawrence v. Texas (2003).

Second, while sexual orientation carries no visible badge, a growing scientific consensus accepts that sexual orientation is a characteristic that is immutable, see Richard A. Posner, *Sex and Reason* 101 (1992); it is undoubtedly unfair to require sexual orientation to be hidden from view to avoid discrimination, see Don't Ask, Don't Tell Repeal Act of 2010.

Third, the adoption of laws like those at issue in Romer v. Evans (1996), and *Lawrence*, the longstanding ban on gays and lesbians in the military, and the absence of federal protection for employment discrimination on the basis of sexual orientation show the group to have limited political power and "ability to attract the [favorable] attention of the lawmakers." *Cleburne*. And while the enactment of the Matthew Shepard Act and pending repeal of Don't Ask, Don't Tell indicate that the political process is not closed entirely to gay and lesbian people, that is not the standard by which the Court has judged "political powerlessness." Indeed, when the Court ruled that gender-based classifications were subject to heightened scrutiny, women already had won major political victories such as the Nineteenth Amendment (right to vote) and protection under Title VII (employment discrimination).

Finally, there is a growing acknowledgment that sexual orientation "bears no relation to ability to perform or contribute to society." Frontiero v. Richardson (1973) (plurality). Recent evolutions in legislation (including the pending repeal of Don't Ask, Don't Tell), in community practices and attitudes, in case law (including the Supreme Court's holdings in Lawrence and Romer), and in social science regarding sexual orientation all make clear that sexual orientation is not a characteristic that generally bears on legitimate policy objectives. See, e.g., Statement by the President on the Don't Ask, Don't Tell Repeal Act of 2010 ("It is time to recognize that sacrifice, valor and integrity are no more defined by sexual orientation than they are by race or gender, religion or creed.")

To be sure, there is substantial circuit court authority applying rational basis review to sexual-orientation classifications. We have carefully examined each of those decisions. Many of them reason only that if consensual same-sex sodomy may be criminalized under Bowers v. Hardwick, then it follows that no heightened review is appropriate—a line of reasoning that does not survive the overruling of *Bowers* in *Lawrence*. Others rely on claims regarding "procreational responsibility" that the Department has disavowed already in litigation as unreasonable, or claims regarding the immutability of sexual orientation that we do not believe can be reconciled with more recent social science understandings. And none engages in an examination of all the factors that the Supreme Court has identified as relevant to a decision about the appropriate level of scrutiny. Finally, many of the more recent decisions have relied on the fact that the Supreme Court has not recognized that gays and lesbians constitute a suspect class or the fact that the Court has applied rational basis review in its most recent decisions addressing classifications based on sexual orientation, *Lawrence* and *Romer*. But neither of those decisions reached, let alone resolved, the level of scrutiny issue because in both the Court concluded that the laws could not even survive the more deferential rational basis standard.

Application to Section 3 of DOMA

In reviewing a legislative classification under heightened scrutiny, the government must establish that the classification is "substantially related to an important government objective.". . . Under heightened scrutiny, "a tenable justification must describe actual state purposes, not rationalizations for actions in fact differently grounded." United States v. Virginia (1996). "The justification must be genuine, not hypothesized or invented post hoc in response to litigation." Id.

In other words, under heightened scrutiny, the United States cannot defend Section 3 by advancing hypothetical rationales, independent of the legislative record, as it has done in circuits where precedent mandates application of rational basis review. Instead, the United States can defend Section 3 only by invoking Congress' actual justifications for the law.

Moreover, the legislative record underlying DOMA's passage contains discussion and debate that undermines any defense under heightened scrutiny. The record contains numerous expressions reflecting moral disapproval of gays and lesbians and their intimate and family relationships—precisely the kind of stereotype-based thinking and animus the Equal Protection Clause is designed to guard against. See *Cleburne* ("mere negative attitudes, or fear" are not permissible bases for discriminatory treatment); see also *Romer* (rejecting rationale that law was supported by "the liberties of landlords or employers who have personal or religious objections to homosexuality"); Palmore v. Sidoti (1984) ("Private biases may be outside the reach of the law, but the law cannot, directly or indirectly, give them effect.").

Application to Second Circuit Cases

After careful consideration, including a review of my recommendation, the President has concluded that given a number of factors, including a documented history of discrimination, classifications based on sexual orientation should be subject to a heightened standard of scrutiny. The President has also concluded that Section 3 of DOMA, as applied to legally married same-sex couples, fails to meet that standard and is therefore unconstitutional. Given that conclusion, the President has instructed the Department not to defend the statute in *Windsor* and *Pedersen*, now pending in the Southern District of New York and the District of Connecticut. I concur in this determination.

Notwithstanding this determination, the President has informed me that Section 3 will continue to be enforced by the Executive Branch. To that end, the President has instructed Executive agencies to continue to comply with Section 3 of DOMA, consistent with the Executive's obligation to take care that the laws be faithfully executed, unless and until Congress repeals Section 3 or the judicial branch renders a definitive verdict against the law's constitutionality. This course of action respects the actions of the prior Congress that enacted DOMA, and it recognizes the judiciary as the final arbiter of the constitutional claims raised.

As you know, the Department has a longstanding practice of defending the constitutionality of duly-enacted statutes if reasonable arguments can be made in their defense, a practice that accords the respect appropriately due to a coequal branch of government. However, the Department in the past has declined to defend statutes despite the availability of professionally responsible arguments, in part because the Department does not consider every plausible argument to be a "reasonable" one. "[D]ifferent cases can raise very different issues with respect to statutes of doubtful constitutional validity," and thus there are "a variety of factors that bear on whether the Department will defend the constitutionality of a statute." Letter to Hon. Orrin G. Hatch from Assistant Attorney General Andrew Fois at 7 (Mar. 22, 1996). This is the rare case where the proper course is to forgo the defense of this statute. Moreover, the Department has declined to defend a statute "in cases in which it is manifest that the President has concluded that the statute is unconstitutional," as is the case here. . . .

[P]ursuant to the President's instructions, and upon further notification to Congress, I will instruct Department attorneys to advise courts in other pending DOMA litigation of the President's and my conclusions that a heightened standard should apply, that Section 3 is unconstitutional under that standard and that the Department will cease defense of Section 3. . . .

Sincerely yours,

Eric H. Holder, Jr.

Attorney General

EDITORS' NOTES

(1)   There is a long tradition of "departmentalism" that rejects the idea that the U.S. Supreme Court is the exclusive interpreter of the U.S. Constitution. To what extent does the President (and the Attorney General) share in the authority to interpret the Constitution? Is the Attorney General in this letter simply offering his interpretation of the Supreme Court's decisions interpreting the Constitution? Or is he is offering his own independent interpretations of what the Constitution means and requires concerning the rights of gay men and lesbians?

(2)   What is the Attorney General's argument for "heightened scrutiny" of laws embodying classifications based on sexual orientation? Is this argument persuasive as an interpretation of the judicial precedents? Or is the Attorney General arguing for recasting the precedents to support "heightened scrutiny."?

(3)   Although the President believed firmly that DOMA Section 3 was unconstitutional, he ordered federal agencies to apply it until the Supreme Court agreed, citing respect for Congress and acknowledging the Court as the Constitution's final interpreter. Was this order consistent with the President's oath of office?

(4)   The Attorney General's opinion on the constitutionality of DOMA Section 3 contains propositions of law—regarding, for example, what criteria determine whether a legal classification warrants heightened scrutiny—and questions of fact to which the law applies—regarding, for example, whether the legislative record in DOMA evinces prejudice toward same-sex couples to which the law may not give effect. Virtually all of the Attorney General's legal propositions remain safely within established precedents. A crucial factual

proposition is essentially a scientific finding, namely, the "immutability" of sexual orientation. This proposition is crucial to the Attorney General's conclusion, and he attributes it to "a growing scientific consensus." Yet the Attorney General takes the trouble to confirm this proposition by citing not a scientist but a jurist, Richard Posner, a judge of the Seventh Circuit Court of Appeals. How then would you describe the Attorney General's approach to constitutional meaning? For Posner's own subsequent analysis of the relevant science, see his opinion in Baskin v. Bogan (7th Cir. 2014; reprinted below). Subsequently, in *Obergefell*, the Supreme Court referred to sexual orientation as "immutable."

(5)   In United States v. Windsor (2013; reprinted as the next case), the Supreme Court held that Section 3 of DOMA was unconstitutional.

———

"**DOMA undermines both the public and private significance of state-sanctioned same-sex marriages; for it tells those couples, and all the world, that their otherwise valid marriages are unworthy of federal recognition. This places same-sex couples in an unstable position of being in a second-tier marriage. The differentiation demeans the couple, whose moral and sexual choices the Constitution protects, see *Lawrence*, and whose relationship the State has sought to dignify. And it humiliates tens of thousands of children now being raised by same-sex couples.**"—JUSTICE KENNEDY

"**[T]he majority says that the supporters of this Act acted with malice—with the "purpose" "to disparage and to injure" same-sex couples. . . . I am sure these accusations are quite untrue. To be sure . . . , the legislation is called the Defense of Marriage Act. But to defend traditional marriage is not to condemn, demean, or humiliate those who would prefer other arrangements. . . .**"
—JUSTICE SCALIA

UNITED STATES V. WINDSOR

570 U.S. ___, 133 S.Ct. 2675, 186 L.Ed.2d 808 (2013)

■ JUSTICE KENNEDY delivered the opinion of the Court. . . .

I

In 1996, as some States were beginning to consider the concept of same-sex marriage, see, *e.g.*, Baehr v. Lewin (1993), and before any State had acted to permit it, Congress enacted the Defense of Marriage Act (DOMA). DOMA contains two operative sections: Section 2, which has not been challenged here, allows States to refuse to recognize same-sex marriages performed under the laws of other States.

Section 3 is at issue here. It . . . provides as follows:

> In determining the meaning of any Act of Congress, or of any ruling, regulation, or interpretation of the various administrative bureaus and agencies of the United States, the word 'marriage' means only a legal union between one man and one woman as husband and wife, and the word 'spouse' refers only to a person of the opposite sex who is a husband or a wife.

The definitional provision does not by its terms forbid States from enacting laws permitting same-sex marriages or civil unions or providing state benefits to residents in that status. The enactment's comprehensive definition of marriage for purposes of all federal statutes and other regulations or directives covered by its terms, however, does control over 1,000 federal laws in which marital or spousal status is addressed as a matter of federal law.

Edith Windsor and Thea Spyer met in New York City in 1963 and began a long-term relationship. Windsor and Spyer registered as domestic partners when New York City gave that right to same-sex couples in 1993. Concerned about Spyer's health, the couple made the 2007 trip to Canada for their marriage, but they continued to reside in New York City. The State of New York deems their Ontario marriage to be a valid one.

Spyer died in February 2009, and left her entire estate to Windsor. Because DOMA denies federal recognition to same-sex spouses, Windsor did not qualify for the marital exemption from the federal estate tax, which excludes from taxation "any interest in property which passes or has passed from the decedent to his surviving spouse." Windsor paid $363,053 in estate taxes and sought a refund. The Internal Revenue Service denied the refund, concluding that, under DOMA, Windsor was not a "surviving spouse." Windsor commenced this refund suit in the United States District Court for the Southern District of New York. She contended that DOMA violates the guarantee of equal protection, as applied to the Federal Government through the Fifth Amendment.

While the tax refund suit was pending, the Attorney General of the United States notified the Speaker of the House of Representatives that the Department of Justice would no longer defend the constitutionality of DOMA's § 3. [T]he Attorney General informed Congress that "the President has concluded that given a number of factors, including a documented history of discrimination, classifications based on sexual orientation should be subject to a heightened standard of scrutiny." . . .

Although "the President . . . instructed the Department not to defend the statute in *Windsor*," he also decided "that Section 3 will continue to be enforced by the Executive Branch" and that the United States had an "interest in providing Congress a full and fair opportunity to participate in the litigation of those cases." The stated rationale for this dual-track procedure (determination of unconstitutionality coupled with ongoing enforcement) was to "recogniz[e] the judiciary as the final arbiter of the constitutional claims raised."

In response to the notice from the Attorney General, the Bipartisan Legal Advisory Group (BLAG) of the House of Representatives voted to intervene in the litigation to defend the constitutionality of § 3 of DOMA. The Department of Justice did not oppose limited intervention by BLAG. . . .

On the merits of the tax refund suit, the District Court . . . held that § 3 of DOMA is unconstitutional and ordered the Treasury to refund the tax with interest. [T]he Court of Appeals for the Second Circuit affirmed. . . . It applied heightened scrutiny to classifications based on sexual orientation, as both the Department and Windsor had urged. The United States has not complied with the judgment. Windsor has not received her refund, and the Executive Branch continues to enforce § 3 of DOMA. . . .

III

[U]ntil recent years, many citizens had not even considered the possibility that two persons of the same sex might aspire to occupy the same status and dignity as that of a man and woman in lawful marriage. For marriage between a man and a woman no doubt had been thought of by most people as essential to the very definition of that term and to its role and function throughout the history of civilization. That belief, for many who long have held it, became even more urgent, more cherished when challenged. For others, however, came the beginnings of a new perspective, a new insight. Accordingly some States concluded that same-sex marriage ought to be given recognition and validity in the law for those same-sex couples who wish to define themselves by their commitment to each other. The limitation of lawful marriage to heterosexual couples, which for centuries had been deemed both necessary and fundamental, came to be seen in New York and certain other States as an unjust exclusion.

Slowly at first and then in rapid course, the laws of New York came to acknowledge the urgency of this issue for same-sex couples who wanted to affirm their commitment to one another before their children, their family, their friends, and their community. And so New York recognized same-sex marriages performed elsewhere; and then it later amended its own marriage laws to permit same-sex marriage. New York, in common with, as of this writing, 11 other States and the District of Columbia, decided that same-sex couples should have the right to marry and so live with pride in themselves and their union and in a status of equality with all other married persons. After a statewide deliberative process that enabled its citizens to discuss and weigh arguments for and against same-sex marriage, New York acted to enlarge the definition of marriage to correct what its citizens and elected representatives perceived to be an injustice that they had not earlier known or understood. See Marriage Equality Act, 2011 N.Y. Laws 749.

Against this background of lawful same-sex marriage in some States, the design, purpose, and effect of DOMA should be considered as the beginning point in deciding whether it is valid under the Constitution. By history and tradition the definition and regulation of marriage . . . has been treated as being within the authority and realm of the separate States. Yet it is further established that Congress, in enacting discrete statutes, can make determinations that bear on marital rights and privileges. . . . This is one example of the general principle that when the Federal Government acts in the exercise of its own proper authority, it has a wide choice of the mechanisms and means to adopt. See McCulloch v. Maryland (1819). Congress has the power both to ensure efficiency in the administration of its programs and to choose what larger goals and policies to pursue. . . .

Though [d]iscrete examples establish the constitutionality of limited federal laws that regulate the meaning of marriage in order to further federal policy, DOMA has a far greater reach; for it enacts a directive applicable to over 1,000 federal statutes and the whole realm of federal regulations. And its operation is directed to a class of persons that the laws of New York, and of 11 other States, have sought to protect.

In order to assess the validity of that intervention it is necessary to discuss the extent of the state power and authority over marriage as a matter of history and tradition. State laws defining and regulating marriage, of course, must respect the constitutional rights of persons, see, *e.g.,* Loving v. Virginia (1967); but, subject to those guarantees, "regulation of domestic relations" is "an area that has long been regarded as a virtually exclusive province of the States." Sosna v. Iowa (1975).

The recognition of civil marriages is central to state domestic relations law applicable to its residents and citizens. The definition of marriage is the foundation of the State's broader authority to regulate the subject of domestic relations with respect to the "[p]rotection of offspring, property interests, and the enforcement of marital responsibilities."

Consistent with this allocation of authority, the Federal Government, through our history, has deferred to state-law policy decisions with respect to domestic relations.

The significance of state responsibilities for the definition and regulation of marriage dates to the Nation's beginning; for "when the Constitution was adopted the common understanding was that the domestic relations of husband and wife and parent and child were matters reserved to the States." Ohio ex rel. Popovici v. Agler (1930). Marriage laws vary in some respects from State to State. . . . But these rules are in every event consistent within each State.

Against this background DOMA rejects the long-established precept that the incidents, benefits, and obligations of marriage are uniform for all married couples within each State, though they may vary, subject to constitutional guarantees, from one State to the next. Despite these considerations, it is unnecessary to decide whether this federal intrusion on state power is a violation of the Constitution because it disrupts the federal balance. The State's power in defining the marital relation is of central relevance in this case quite apart from principles of federalism. Here the State's decision to give this class of persons the right to marry conferred upon them a dignity and status of immense import. When the State used its historic and essential authority to define the marital relation in this way, its role and its power in making the decision enhanced the recognition, dignity, and protection of the class in their own community. DOMA, because of its reach and extent, departs from this history and tradition of reliance on state law to define marriage. " '[D]iscriminations of an unusual character especially suggest careful consideration to determine whether they are obnoxious to the constitutional provision.' " Romer v. Evans (1996) (quoting Louisville Gas & Elec. Co. v. Coleman (1928)).

The Federal Government uses this state-defined class for the opposite purpose—to impose restrictions and disabilities. That result requires this Court now to address whether the resulting injury and indignity is a deprivation of an essential part of the liberty protected by the Fifth Amendment. . . .

The States' interest in defining and regulating the marital relation, subject to constitutional guarantees, stems from the understanding that marriage is more than a routine classification for purposes of certain statutory benefits. Private, consensual sexual intimacy between two adult persons of the same sex may not be punished by the State, and it can form "but one element in a personal bond that is more enduring." Lawrence v. Texas (2003). . . . New York sought to give further protection and dignity to that bond. For same-sex couples who wished to be married, the State acted to give their lawful conduct a lawful status. This status is a far-reaching legal acknowledgment of the intimate relationship between two people, a relationship deemed by the State worthy of dignity in the community equal with all other marriages. It reflects both the community's considered perspective on the historical roots of the institution of marriage and its evolving understanding of the meaning of equality.

IV

DOMA seeks to injure the very class New York seeks to protect. By doing so it violates basic due process and equal protection principles applicable to the Federal Government. See U. S. Const., Amdt. 5; Bolling v. Sharpe (1954). The Constitution's guarantee of equality "must at the very least mean that a bare congressional desire to harm a politically unpopular group cannot" justify disparate treatment of that group. Department of Agriculture v. Moreno (1973). In determining whether a law is motived by an improper animus or purpose, " '[d]iscriminations of an unusual character' " especially require careful consideration. *Supra* (quoting *Romer*). DOMA cannot survive under these principles. . . . DOMA's unusual deviation from the usual tradition of recognizing and accepting state definitions of marriage here operates to deprive same-sex couples of the benefits and responsibilities that come with the federal recognition of their marriages. . . . The avowed purpose and practical effect of the law here in question are to impose a disadvantage, a separate status, and so a stigma upon all who enter into same-sex marriages made lawful by the unquestioned authority of the States.

The history of DOMA's enactment and its own text demonstrate that interference with the equal dignity of same-sex marriages, a dignity conferred by the States in the exercise of their sovereign power, was more than an incidental effect of the federal statute. It was its essence. The House Report announced its conclusion that "it is both appropriate and necessary for Congress to do what it can to defend the institution of traditional heterosexual marriage. . . ." The House concluded that DOMA expresses "both moral disapproval of homosexuality, and a moral conviction that heterosexuality better comports with traditional (especially Judeo-Christian) morality." Were there any doubt of this far-reaching purpose, the title of the Act confirms it: The Defense of Marriage.

The arguments put forward by BLAG are just as candid about the congressional purpose to influence or interfere with state sovereign choices about who may be married. As the title and dynamics of the bill indicate, its purpose is to discourage enactment of state same-sex marriage laws and to restrict the freedom and choice of couples married under those laws if they are enacted. . . . The Act's demonstrated purpose is to ensure that if any State decides to recognize same-sex marriages, those unions will be treated as second-class marriages for purposes of federal law. This raises a most serious question under the Constitution's Fifth Amendment.

DOMA's operation in practice confirms this purpose. When New York adopted a law to permit same-sex marriage, it sought to eliminate inequality; but DOMA frustrates that objective through a system-wide enactment with no identified connection to any particular area of federal law. DOMA writes inequality into the entire United States Code. . . .

DOMA's principal effect is to identify a subset of state-sanctioned marriages and make them unequal. The principal purpose is to impose inequality, not for other reasons like governmental efficiency. Responsibilities, as well as rights, enhance the dignity and integrity of the person. And DOMA contrives to deprive some couples married under the laws of their State, but not other couples, of both rights and responsibilities. By creating two contradictory marriage regimes within the same State, DOMA forces same-sex couples to live as married for the purpose of state law but unmarried for the purpose of federal law, thus diminishing the stability and predictability of basic personal relations the State has found it proper to acknowledge and protect. By this dynamic DOMA undermines both the public and private significance of state-sanctioned same-sex marriages; for it tells those couples, and all the world, that their otherwise valid marriages are unworthy of federal recognition. This places same-sex couples in an unstable position of being in a second-tier marriage. The differentiation demeans the couple, whose moral and sexual choices the Constitution protects, see *Lawrence*, and whose relationship the State has sought to dignify. And it humiliates tens of thousands of children now being raised by same-sex couples. The law in question makes it even more difficult for the children to understand the integrity and closeness of their own family and its concord with other families in their community and in their daily lives.

Under DOMA, same-sex married couples have their lives burdened, by reason of government decree, in visible and public ways. By its great reach, DOMA touches many aspects of married and family life, from the mundane to the profound. It prevents same-sex married couples from obtaining government healthcare benefits they would otherwise receive. It deprives them of the Bankruptcy Code's special protections for domestic-support obligations. It forces them to follow a complicated procedure to file their state and federal taxes jointly. It prohibits them from being buried together in veterans' cemeteries. . . .

DOMA also brings financial harm to children of same-sex couples. It raises the cost of health care for families by taxing health benefits provided by employers to their workers' same-sex spouses. And it denies or reduces benefits allowed to families upon the loss of a spouse and parent, benefits that are an integral part of family security. . . .

DOMA divests married same-sex couples of the duties and responsibilities that are an essential part of married life and that they in most cases would be honored to accept were DOMA not in force. . . .

* * *

The power the Constitution grants it also restrains. And though Congress has great authority to design laws to fit its own conception of sound national policy, it cannot deny the liberty protected by the Due Process Clause of the Fifth Amendment.

What has been explained to this point should more than suffice to establish that the principal purpose and the necessary effect of this law are to demean those persons who are in a lawful same-sex marriage. This requires the Court to hold . . . that DOMA is unconstitutional as a deprivation of the liberty of the person protected by the Fifth Amendment of the Constitution.

The liberty protected by the Fifth Amendment's Due Process Clause contains within it the prohibition against denying to any person the equal protection of the laws. See *Bolling*. While the Fifth Amendment itself withdraws from Government the power to degrade or demean in the way this law does, the equal protection guarantee of the Fourteenth Amendment makes that Fifth Amendment right all the more specific and all the better understood and preserved.

The class to which DOMA directs its restrictions and restraints are those persons who are joined in same-sex marriages made lawful by the State. DOMA singles out a class of persons deemed by a State entitled to recognition and protection to enhance their own liberty. It imposes a disability on the class by refusing to acknowledge a status the State finds to be dignified and proper. DOMA instructs all federal officials, and indeed all persons with whom same-sex couples interact, including their own children, that their marriage is less worthy than the marriages of others. The federal statute is invalid, for no legitimate purpose overcomes the purpose and effect to disparage and to injure those whom the State, by its marriage laws, sought to protect in personhood and dignity. By seeking to displace this protection and treating those persons as living in marriages less respected than others, the federal statute is in violation of the Fifth Amendment. This opinion and its holding are confined to those lawful marriages.

The judgment of the Court of Appeals for the Second Circuit is affirmed.

■ CHIEF JUSTICE ROBERTS, dissenting.

I agree with Justice Scalia that this Court lacks jurisdiction. . . . I also agree with Justice Scalia that Congress acted constitutionally in passing DOMA. Interests in uniformity and stability amply justified Congress's decision to retain the definition of marriage that, at that point, had been adopted by every State in our Nation, and every nation in the world.

The majority sees a more sinister motive, . . . a bare desire to harm. . . . At least without some more convincing evidence that the Act's principal purpose was to codify malice, and that it furthered *no* legitimate government interests, I would not tar the political branches with the brush of bigotry.

[T]he Court does not have before it, and the logic of its opinion does not decide, the distinct question whether the States, in the exercise of their "historic and essential authority to define the marital relation," may continue to utilize the traditional definition of marriage.

The majority goes out of its way to make this explicit in the penultimate sentence of its opinion. It states that "[t]his opinion and its holding are confined to those lawful marriages" . . . that a State has already recognized. . . . Justice

Scalia believes this is a " 'bald, unreasoned disclaime[r].' " In my view, though, the disclaimer is a logical and necessary consequence of the argument the majority has chosen to adopt. [I]t is undeniable that its judgment is based on federalism. . . .

It is not just this central feature of the majority's analysis that is unique to DOMA, but many considerations on the periphery as well. For example, the majority focuses on the legislative history and title of this particular Act; those statute-specific considerations will, of course, be irrelevant in future cases about different statutes. . . .

We may in the future have to resolve challenges to state marriage definitions affecting same-sex couples. That issue, however, is not before us in this case, and we hold today that we lack jurisdiction to consider it in the particular context of Hollingsworth v. Perry (2013). I write only to highlight the limits of the majority's holding and reasoning today, lest its opinion be taken to resolve . . . a question that all agree, and the Court explicitly acknowledges, is not at issue.

■ JUSTICE SCALIA, with whom JUSTICE THOMAS joins, and with whom THE CHIEF JUSTICE [ROBERTS] joins as to Part I, dissenting.

This case is about . . . the power of our people to govern themselves, and the power of this Court to pronounce the law. . . . We have no power to decide this case [and] we have no power under the Constitution to invalidate this democratically adopted legislation. The Court's errors on both points spring forth from the same diseased root: an exalted conception of the role of this institution in America. . . .

II . . .

A

There are many remarkable things about the majority's merits holding. The first is how rootless and shifting its justifications are. For example, the opinion starts with seven full pages about the traditional power of States to define domestic relations—initially fooling many readers, I am sure, into thinking that this is a federalism opinion. But we are eventually told that "it is unnecessary to decide whether this federal intrusion on state power is a violation of the Constitution," and that "[t]he State's power in defining the marital relation is of central relevance in this case quite apart from principles of federalism" because "the State's decision to give this class of persons the right to marry conferred upon them a dignity and status of immense import." . . . What to make of this?

The opinion never explains. My guess is that the majority, while reluctant to suggest that defining the meaning of "marriage" in federal statutes is unsupported by any of the Federal Government's enumerated powers, nonetheless needs some rhetorical basis to support its pretense that today's prohibition of laws excluding same-sex marriage is confined to the Federal Government (leaving the second, state-law shoe to be dropped later, maybe next Term). But I am only guessing.

Equally perplexing are the opinion's references to "the Constitution's guarantee of equality." Near the end of the opinion, we are told that although the "equal protection guarantee of the Fourteenth Amendment makes [the] Fifth Amendment [due process] right all the more specific and all the better understood and preserved"—what can *that* mean?—"the Fifth Amendment itself withdraws from Government the power to degrade or demean in the way this law does." The only possible interpretation of this statement is that the Equal Protection Clause, even the Equal Protection Clause as incorporated in the Due Process Clause, is not the basis for today's holding. But the portion of the majority opinion that explains why DOMA is unconstitutional (Part IV) begins by citing *Bolling, Moreno,* and *Romer*—*all* of which are equal-protection cases. And those three cases are the *only* authorities that the Court cites in Part IV about the Constitution's meaning, except for its citation of *Lawrence* (not an equal-protection case) to support its passing assertion that the Constitution protects the "moral and sexual choices" of same-sex couples.

Moreover, if this is meant to be an equal-protection opinion, it is a confusing one. The opinion does not resolve and indeed does not even mention what had been the central question in this litigation: whether, under the Equal Protection Clause, laws restricting marriage to a man and a woman are reviewed for more than mere rationality. That is the issue that divided the parties and the court below . . . In accord with my previously expressed skepticism about the Court's "tiers of scrutiny" approach, I would review this classification only for its rationality. See United States v. Virginia (1996) (Scalia, J., dissenting). As nearly as I can tell, the Court agrees with that; its opinion does not apply strict scrutiny, and its central propositions are taken from rational-basis cases like *Moreno*. But the Court certainly does not *apply* anything that resembles that deferential framework. See Heller v. Doe (1993) (a classification " 'must be upheld . . . if there is any reason-ably conceivable state of facts' " that could justify it).

The majority opinion need not get into the strict-vs.-rational-basis scrutiny question, and need not justify its holding under either, because it says that

DOMA is unconstitutional as "a deprivation of the liberty of the person protected by the Fifth Amendment of the Constitution"; that it violates "basic due process" principles; and that it inflicts an "injury and indignity" of a kind that denies "an essential part of the liberty protected by the Fifth Amendment." The majority never utters the dread words "substantive due process," perhaps sensing the disrepute into which that doctrine has fallen, but that is what those statements mean. Yet the opinion does not argue that same-sex marriage is "deeply rooted in this Nation's history and tradition," Washington v. Glucksberg (1997), a claim that would of course be quite absurd. So would the further suggestion (also necessary, under our substantive-due-process precedents) that a world in which DOMA exists is one bereft of " 'ordered liberty.' " *Id.* (quoting Palko v. Connecticut (1937)).

[T]he sum of all the Court's nonspecific hand-waving is that this law is invalid (maybe on equal-protection grounds, maybe on substantive-due-process grounds, and perhaps with some amorphous federalism component playing a role) because it is motivated by a " 'bare . . . desire to harm' " couples in same-sex marriages. It is this proposition with which I will therefore engage.

B

As I have observed before, the Constitution does not forbid the government to enforce traditional moral and sexual norms. See *Lawrence* (Scalia, J., dissenting). . . . [T]he Constitution neither requires nor forbids our society to approve of same-sex marriage, much as it neither requires nor forbids us to approve of no-fault divorce, polygamy, or the consumption of alcohol.

However, even setting aside traditional moral disapproval of same-sex marriage (or indeed same-sex sex), there are many perfectly valid . . . justifying rationales for this legislation. Their existence ought to be the end of this case. . . .

The majority concludes that the only motive for this Act was the "bare . . . desire to harm a politically unpopular group." Bear in mind that the object of this condemnation is . . . our respected coordinate branches, the Congress and Presidency of the United States. Laying such a charge against them should require the most extraordinary evidence, and I would have thought that every attempt would be made to indulge a more anodyne explanation for the statute. The majority . . . makes only a passing mention of the "arguments put forward" by the Act's defenders, and does not even trouble to paraphrase or describe them. I imagine that this is because it is harder to maintain the illusion of the Act's supporters as unhinged members of a wild-eyed lynch mob when one first describes their views as *they* see them.

To choose just one of these defenders' arguments, DOMA avoids difficult choice-of-law issues that will now arise absent a uniform federal definition of marriage. Imagine a pair of women who marry in Albany and then move to Alabama, which does not "recognize as valid any marriage of parties of the same sex." When the couple files their next federal tax return, may it be a joint one? Which State's law controls, for federal-law purposes: their State of celebration (which recognizes the marriage) or their State of domicile (which does not)? (Does the answer depend on whether they were just visiting in Albany?) Are these questions to be answered as a matter of federal common law, or perhaps by borrowing a State's choice-of-law rules? If so, *which* State's? And what about States where the status of an out-of-state same-sex marriage is an unsettled question under local law? DOMA avoided all of this uncertainty by specifying which marriages would be recognized for federal purposes. That is a classic purpose for a definitional provision. . . .

The Court mentions none of this. Instead, it accuses the Congress that enacted this law and the President who signed it of something much worse than, for example, having acted in excess of enumerated federal powers—or even having drawn distinctions that prove to be irrational. Those legal errors may be made in good faith. . . . But the majority says that the supporters of this Act acted with *malice*—with *the "purpose"* "to disparage and to injure" same-sex couples. It says that the motivation for DOMA was to "demean"; to "impose inequality"; to "impose . . . a stigma"; to deny people "equal dignity"; to brand gay people as "unworthy"; and to "*humiliat[e]*" their children (emphasis added).

I am sure these accusations are quite untrue. To be sure . . . , the legislation is called the Defense of Marriage Act. But to defend traditional marriage is not to condemn, demean, or humiliate those who would prefer other arrangements. . . . To question its high-handed invalidation of a presumptively valid statute is to act (the majority is sure) with *the purpose* to "disparage," "injure," "degrade," "demean," and "humiliate" our fellow human beings, our fellow citizens, who are homosexual. All that, simply for supporting an Act that did no more than codify an aspect of marriage that had been unquestioned in our society for most of its existence—indeed, had been unquestioned in virtually all societies for virtually all of human history. It is one thing for a society to elect change; it is another for a court of law to impose change by adjudging those who oppose it *hostes humani generis*, enemies of the human race.

* * *

The penultimate sentence of the majority's opinion is a naked declaration that "[t]his opinion and its holding are confined" to those couples "joined in same-sex marriages made lawful by the State." I have heard such "bald, unreasoned disclaimer[s]" before. *Lawrence*. When the Court declared a constitutional right to homosexual sodomy, we were assured that the case had nothing, nothing at all to do with "whether the government must give formal recognition to any relationship that homosexual persons seek to enter." *Id.* Now we are told that DOMA is invalid because it "demeans the couple, whose moral and sexual choices the Constitution protects"—with an accompanying citation of *Lawrence*. It takes real cheek for today's majority to assure us, as it is going out the door, that a constitutional requirement to give formal recognition to same-sex marriage is not at issue here—when what has preceded that assurance is a lecture on how superior the majority's moral judgment in favor of same-sex marriage is to the Congress's hateful moral judgment against it. I promise you this: The only thing that will "confine" the Court's holding is its sense of what it can get away with.

I do not mean to suggest disagreement with The Chief Justice's view, that lower federal courts and state courts can distinguish today's case when the issue before them is state denial of marital status to same-sex couples—or even that this Court could *theoretically* do so. Lord, an opinion with such scatter-shot rationales as this one (federalism noises among them) can be distinguished in many ways. . . .

In my opinion, however, the view that *this* Court will take of state prohibition of same-sex marriage is indicated beyond mistaking by today's opinion. [T]he real rationale of today's opinion, whatever disappearing trail of its legalistic argle-bargle one chooses to follow, is that DOMA is motivated by " 'bare . . . desire to harm' " couples in same-sex marriages. How easy it is, indeed how inevitable, to reach the same conclusion with regard to state laws denying same-sex couples marital status.

[T]hat Court which finds it so horrific that Congress irrationally and hatefully robbed same-sex couples of the "personhood and dignity" which state legislatures conferred upon them, will of a certitude be similarly appalled by state legislatures' irrational and hateful failure to acknowledge that "personhood and dignity" in the first place. [N]o one should be fooled; it is just a matter of listening and waiting for the other shoe.

[F]ew public controversies touch an institution so central to the lives of so many, and few inspire such attendant passion by good people on all sides. Few public controversies will ever demonstrate so vividly the beauty of what our Framers gave us, a gift the Court pawns today to buy its stolen moment in the spotlight: a system of government that permits us to rule *ourselves*. Since DOMA's passage, citizens on all sides of the question have seen victories and they have seen defeats. There have been plebiscites, legislation, persuasion, and loud voices—in other words, democracy. Victories in one place for some . . . are offset by victories in other places for others. . . . Even in a *single State*, the question has come out differently on different occasions. . . .

In the majority's telling, this story is black-and-white: Hate your neighbor or come along with us. The truth is more complicated. It is hard to admit that one's political opponents are not monsters, especially in a struggle like this one. . . . A reminder that disagreement over something so fundamental as marriage can still be politically legitimate would have been a fit task for what in earlier times was called the judicial temperament. We might have covered ourselves with honor today, by promising all sides of this debate that it was theirs to settle and that we would respect their resolution. We might have let the People decide.

But that the majority will not do. Some will rejoice in today's decision, and some will despair at it. . . . But the Court has cheated both sides, robbing the winners of an honest victory, and the losers of the peace that comes from a fair defeat. We owed both of them better. I dissent.

■ JUSTICE ALITO, with whom JUSTICE THOMAS joins as to Parts II and III, dissenting.

Our Nation is engaged in a heated debate about same-sex marriage. That debate is, at bottom, about the nature of the institution of marriage. [W]hat [respondent Edith Windsor] seeks is a holding that enshrines in the Constitution a particular understanding of marriage under which the sex of the partners makes no difference. The Constitution, however, does not dictate that choice. It leaves the choice to the people, acting through their elected representatives at both the federal and state levels. I would therefore hold that Congress did not violate Windsor's constitutional rights by enacting § 3 of DOMA. . . .

II

[T]he family is an ancient and universal human institution. Family structure reflects the characteristics of a civilization, and changes in family structure and in the popular understanding of marriage and the family can have profound effects. Past changes in the understanding of marriage—for example, the gradual ascendance of the idea that romantic love is a prerequisite to marriage—have had far-reaching consequences. But the process by which such consequences come about is complex, involving the interaction of numerous factors, and tends to occur over an extended period of time.

We can expect something similar to take place if same-sex marriage becomes widely accepted. The long-term consequences of this change are not now known and are unlikely to be ascertainable for some time to come. There are those who think that allowing same-sex marriage will seriously undermine the institution of marriage. See, *e.g.,* S. Girgis, R. Anderson, & R. George, *What is Marriage? Man and Woman: A Defense* 53–58 (2012); Finnis, Marriage: A Basic and Exigent Good, 91 *The Monist* 388, 398 (2008). Others think that recognition of same-sex marriage will fortify a now-shaky institution. See, *e.g.,* A. Sullivan, *Virtually Normal: An Argument About Homosexuality* 202–203 (1996); J. Rauch, *Gay Marriage: Why It Is Good for Gays, Good for Straights, and Good for America* 94 (2004).

At present, no one—including social scientists, philosophers, and historians—can predict with any certainty what the long-term ramifications of widespread acceptance of same-sex marriage will be. And judges are certainly not equipped to make such an assessment. The Members of this Court have the authority and the responsibility to interpret and apply the Constitution. Thus, if the Constitution contained a provision guaranteeing the right to marry a person of the same sex, it would be our duty to enforce that right. But the Constitution simply does not speak to the issue of same-sex marriage. In our system of government, ultimate sovereignty rests with the people, and the people have the right to control their own destiny. Any change on a question so fundamental should be made by the people through their elected officials.

III

[Windsor and the United States] argue that § 3 of DOMA discriminates on the basis of sexual orientation, that classifications based on sexual orientation should trigger a form of "heightened" scrutiny, and that § 3 cannot survive such scrutiny. . . . The Court's holding, too, seems to rest on "the equal protection guarantee of the Fourteenth Amendment"—although the Court is careful not to adopt most of Windsor's and the United States' argument.

In my view, the approach that Windsor and the United States advocate is misguided. Our equal protection framework . . . is a judicial construct that provides a useful mechanism for analyzing a certain universe of equal protection cases. But that framework is ill suited for use in evaluating the constitutionality of laws based on the traditional understanding of marriage, which fundamentally turn on what marriage is. . . .

In asking the Court to determine that § 3 of DOMA is subject to and violates heightened scrutiny, Windsor and the United States . . . ask us to rule that the presence of two members of the opposite sex is as rationally related to marriage as white skin is to voting or a Y-chromosome is to the ability to administer an estate. That is a striking request and one that unelected judges should pause before granting. Acceptance of the argument would cast all those who cling to traditional beliefs about the nature of marriage in the role of bigots or superstitious fools.

[W]indsor and the United States are really seeking to have the Court resolve a debate between two competing views of marriage.

The first and older view, which I will call the "traditional" or "conjugal" view, sees marriage as an intrinsically opposite-sex institution. BLAG notes that virtually every culture, including many not influenced by the Abrahamic religions, has limited marriage to people of the opposite sex. And BLAG attempts to explain this phenomenon by arguing that the institution of marriage was created for the purpose of channeling heterosexual intercourse into a structure that supports child rearing. Others explain the basis for the institution in more philosophical terms. They argue that marriage is essentially the solemnizing of a comprehensive, exclusive, permanent union that is intrinsically ordered to producing new life, even if it does not always do so. See, *e.g.*, Girgis, Anderson, & George, *What is Marriage? Man and Woman: A Defense*, at 23–28. . . .

The other, newer view is what I will call the "consent-based" vision of marriage, a vision that primarily defines marriage as the solemnization of mutual commitment—marked by strong emotional attachment and sexual attraction— between two persons. . . . Proponents of same-sex marriage argue that because gender differentiation is not relevant to this vision, the exclusion of same-sex couples from the institution of marriage is rank discrimination.

The Constitution does not codify either of these views of marriage (although I suspect it would have been hard at the time of the adoption of the Constitution or the Fifth Amendment to find Americans who did not take the traditional view for granted). The silence of the Constitution on this question should be enough to end the matter as far as the judiciary is concerned. Yet, Windsor and the United States implicitly ask us to endorse the consent-based view of marriage and to reject the traditional view, thereby arrogating to ourselves the power to decide a question that philosophers, historians, social scientists, and theologians are better qualified to explore. Because our constitutional order assigns the resolution of questions of this nature to the people, I would not presume to enshrine either vision of marriage in our constitutional jurisprudence.

Legislatures, however, have little choice but to decide between the two views. We have long made clear that neither the political branches of the Federal Government nor state governments are required to be neutral between competing visions of the good, provided that the vision of the good that they adopt is not countermanded by the Constitution. See, *e.g.,* Rust v. Sullivan (1991) ("[T]he government 'may make a value judgment favoring childbirth over abortion' "). Accordingly, both Congress and the States are entitled to enact laws recognizing either of the two understandings of marriage. . . .

To the extent that the Court takes the position that the question of same-sex marriage should be resolved primarily at the state level, I wholeheartedly agree. . . . Unless the Court is willing to allow this to occur, the whiffs of federalism in the today's opinion of the Court will soon be scattered to the wind.

In any event, § 3 of DOMA, in my view, does not encroach on the prerogatives of the States. . . . [I]t does not prevent any State from recognizing same-sex marriage or from extending to same-sex couples any right, privilege, benefit, or obligation stemming from state law. All that § 3 does is to define a class of persons to whom federal law extends certain special benefits and upon whom federal law imposes certain special burdens. In these provisions, Congress used marital status as a way of defining this class—in part, I assume, because it viewed marriage as a valuable institution to be fostered and in part because it viewed married couples as comprising a unique type of economic unit that merits special regulatory treatment. Assuming that Congress has the power under the Constitution to enact the laws affected by § 3, Congress has the power to define the category of persons to whom those laws apply. . . .

EDITORS' NOTES

(1) In *Windsor,* the United States had argued, and the lower court had held, that "heightened" scrutiny should apply to classifications on the basis of sexual orientation. (See also the Letter from Attorney General Holder to Congress on Litigation Involving the Defense of Marriage Act [reprinted above].) The Supreme Court did not officially address or adopt this argument and holding. Does its application of *Romer*-style "careful consideration"—or rational basis scrutiny with "bite"—nonetheless amount to "heightened" scrutiny? Did *Windsor* simply apply a *Romer*-style analysis—concerned to protect against "animus," a "bare desire to harm a politically unpopular group," and

classifications that "demean" on the basis of sexual orientation—or did *Windsor* add anything new to *Romer*?

(2) Officially, the basis for the Court's holding that DOMA is unconstitutional is the Due Process Clause of the Fifth Amendment. The Equal Protection Clause of the Fourteenth Amendment applies only to the states, and the Court has held that the Due Process Clause of the Fifth Amendment "incorporates" an "equal protection component" that applies to the federal government. See Bolling v. Sharpe (1954), where Chief Justice Warren wrote: "But the concepts of equal protection and due process, both stemming from our American ideal of fairness, are not mutually exclusive." Is the Court's holding under the Due Process Clause of the Fifth Amendment only (1) a holding that DOMA denies equal protection or also (2) a holding that DOMA denies liberty as a matter of substantive due process? Both Justices Scalia and Alito in dissent interpret Kennedy's opinion as making these two separate holdings, and they criticize his opinion for not clearly delineating these two holdings. Are their readings sound? Or are they failing to grasp that for Kennedy (as for Warren in *Bolling*), due process and equal protection overlap and are intertwined? Kennedy's intertwining of due process and equal protection here foreshadows his intertwining of them in the majority opinion in Obergefell v. Hodges (2015; reprinted in Chapter 1).

(3) What role do principles of federalism play in Kennedy's opinion? Consider the following two scenarios. (A) What if, after 26 states recognized same-sex marriage, the federal government passed a "Marriage Equality Act" that provided that, for purposes of federal law, " 'marriage' is a union between two adults as spouses" without regard to the sex of the two spouses? Would Kennedy's opinion imply that such a law violated principles of federalism? (B) Does *Windsor* imply, notwithstanding Kennedy's stated concern for principles of federalism, that states' "mini-DOMAs" are unconstitutional for the same reasons that the federal DOMA is unconstitutional: that they reflect a "bare desire to harm a politically unpopular group" and "demean" and "humiliate" same-sex couples?

(4) What are the implications, if any, of *Windsor* for the constitutionality of state laws that deny recognition to same-sex marriage? Kennedy's opinion officially did not address this question—stating that "[t]his opinion and its holding are confined" to those couples "joined in same-sex marriages made lawful by the State." Was Scalia right to argue nevertheless that Kennedy's opinion clearly implies that such laws are unconstitutional for the same reasons that DOMA is unconstitutional? Between *Windsor* and *Obergefell*, a number of

federal courts drew upon *Windsor* in striking down state laws that did not recognize marriage between same-sex couples. See, for example, Baskin v. Bogan (7th Cir. 2014; reprinted as the next case). Some federal courts even invoked Scalia's dissent in support of their holdings that *Windsor* implied that such laws were unconstitutional! See, for example, Kitchen v. Herbert (D. Utah 2013).

(5)   The same day that the Supreme Court decided *Windsor*, the DOMA case, it also decided Hollingsworth v. Perry (2013), the Proposition 8 case. There the federal district court had held Proposition 8—a ballot initiative amending the California Constitution to define marriage as the union between a man and a woman after the California Supreme Court had held that the state constitution required recognition of same-sex marriage—unconstitutional under both the Due Process and Equal Protection Clauses of the Fourteenth Amendment. The state of California decided not to appeal the district court's decision. But the official proponents of the ballot initiative appealed. The Ninth Circuit Court of Appeals, after concluding that the official proponents had standing under federal law to defend the constitutionality of Proposition 8, affirmed the district court's decision on the ground of equal protection. The United States Supreme Court, though, held that in these circumstances the proponents of Proposition 8 did not have standing to appeal the district court's decision. The Court stated: "We have never before upheld the standing of a private party to defend the constitutionality of a state statute when state officials have chosen not to. We decline to do so for the first time here." Accordingly, the Court vacated the judgment of the Ninth Circuit with the result that the district court's judgment was in force.

(6)   Two years after *Windsor*, in *Obergefell*, the U.S. Supreme Court held that the right to marry extended to same-sex couples.

———

"[T]he governments of Indiana and Wisconsin have given us no reason to think they have a "reasonable basis" for forbidding same-sex marriage. And more than a reasonable basis is required because this is a case in which the challenged discrimination is . . . 'along suspect lines.' "

Baskin v. Bogan

766 F.3d 648 (7th Cir. 2014)

■ Before Posner, Williams, and Hamilton, Circuit Judges.

Opinion

■ Posner, Circuit Judge.

Indiana and Wisconsin are among the shrinking majority of states that do not recognize the validity of same-sex marriages, whether contracted in these states or in states (or foreign countries) where they are lawful. The states have appealed from district court decisions invalidating the states' laws that ordain such refusal.

Formally these cases are about discrimination against the small homosexual minority in the United States. But at a deeper level . . . they are about the welfare of American children. The argument that the states press hardest in defense of their prohibition of same-sex marriage is that the only reason government encourages marriage is to induce heterosexuals to marry so that there will be fewer "accidental births," which when they occur outside of marriage often lead to abandonment of the child to the mother (unaided by the father) or to foster care. Overlooked by this argument is that many of those abandoned children are adopted by homosexual couples, and those children would be better off both emotionally and economically if their adoptive parents were married.

We are mindful of the Supreme Court's insistence that "whether embodied in the Fourteenth Amendment or inferred from the Fifth, equal protection is not a license for courts to judge the wisdom, fairness, or logic of legislative choices. In areas of social and economic policy, a statutory classification that neither proceeds *along suspect lines* nor infringes fundamental constitutional rights must be upheld against equal protection challenge if there is any reasonably conceivable state of facts that could provide a rational basis for the classification." FCC v. Beach Communications, Inc. (1993) (emphasis added). The phrase we've italicized is the exception applicable to this pair of cases.

We hasten to add that even when the group discriminated against is not a "suspect class," courts examine, and sometimes reject, the rationale offered by government for the challenged discrimination. See, e.g., City of Cleburne v. Cleburne Living Center (1985). . . .

We'll see that the governments of Indiana and Wisconsin have given us no reason to think they have a "reasonable basis" for forbidding same-sex marriage. And more than a reasonable basis is required because this is a case in which the challenged discrimination is . . . "along suspect lines." Discrimination by a state or the federal government against a minority, when based on an immutable characteristic of the members of that minority (most familiarly skin color and gender), and occurring against an historical background of discrimination against the persons who have that characteristic, makes the discriminatory law or policy constitutionally suspect. These circumstances create a presumption that the discrimination is a denial of the equal protection of the laws. . . . The presumption is rebuttable, if at all, only by a compelling showing that the benefits of the discrimination to society as a whole clearly outweigh the harms to its victims. See, e.g., Grutter v. Bollinger (2003); United States v. Virginia (1996).

The approach is straightforward but comes wrapped, in many of the decisions applying it, in a formidable doctrinal terminology—the terminology of rational basis, of strict, heightened, and intermediate scrutiny, of narrow tailoring, fundamental rights, and the rest. We'll be invoking in places the conceptual apparatus that has grown up around this terminology, but our main focus will be on the states' arguments, which are based largely on the assertion that banning same-sex marriage is justified by the state's interest in channeling procreative sex into (necessarily heterosexual) marriage. We will engage the states' arguments on their own terms, enabling us to decide our brace of cases on the basis of a sequence of four questions:

(1) Does the challenged practice involve discrimination, rooted in a history of prejudice, against some identifiable group of persons, resulting in unequal treatment harmful to them?

(2) Is the unequal treatment based on some immutable or at least tenacious characteristic of the people discriminated against . . . ? The characteristic must be one that isn't relevant to a person's ability to participate in society. . . .

(3) Does the discrimination, even if based on an immutable characteristic, nevertheless confer an important offsetting benefit on society as a whole? Age is an immutable characteristic, but a rule prohibiting persons over 70 to pilot airliners might reasonably be thought to confer an essential benefit in the form of improved airline safety.

(4) Though it does confer an offsetting benefit, is the discriminatory policy overinclusive because the benefit . . . could be achieved in a way less harmful to the discriminated-against group, or underinclusive because the government's purported rationale for the

policy implies that it should equally apply to other groups as well? One way to decide whether a policy is overinclusive is to ask whether unequal treatment is *essential* to attaining the desired benefit. [I]n a same-sex marriage case the issue is not whether heterosexual marriage is a socially beneficial institution but whether the benefits to the state from discriminating against same-sex couples clearly outweigh the harms that this discrimination imposes.

Our questions go to the heart of equal protection doctrine. Questions 1 and 2 are consistent with the various formulas for what entitles a discriminated-against group to heightened scrutiny of the discrimination, and questions 3 and 4 capture the essence of the Supreme Court's approach in heightened-scrutiny cases: "To succeed, the defender of the challenged action must show 'at least that the classification serves important governmental objectives and that the discriminatory means employed are substantially related to the achievement of those objectives.' " *Virginia*.

The difference between the approach we take in these two cases and the more conventional approach is semantic rather than substantive. The conventional approach doesn't purport to balance the costs and benefits of the challenged discriminatory law. Instead it evaluates the importance of the state's objective in enacting the law and the extent to which the law is suited ("tailored") to achieving that objective. It asks whether the statute actually furthers the interest that the state asserts and whether there might be some less burdensome alternative. The analysis thus focuses not on "costs" and "benefits" as such, but on "fit." That is why the briefs in these two cases overflow with debate over whether prohibiting same-sex marriage is "over-or underinclusive"—for example, overinclusive in ignoring the effect of the ban on the children adopted by same-sex couples, underinclusive in extending marriage rights to other non-procreative couples. But to say that a discriminatory policy is overinclusive is to say that the policy does more harm to the members of the discriminated-against group than necessary to attain the legitimate goals of the policy, and to say that the policy is underinclusive is to say that its exclusion of other, very similar groups is indicative of arbitrariness. . . .

Our pair of cases is rich in detail but ultimately straightforward to decide. The challenged laws discriminate against a minority defined by an immutable characteristic, and the only rationale that the states put forth with any conviction—that same-sex couples and their children don't *need* marriage because same-sex couples can't *produce* children, intended or unintended—is so full of holes that it cannot be taken seriously. To the extent that children are better off in families in which the parents are married, they are better off whether they are raised by their biological parents or by adoptive parents. The discrimination against same-sex couples is irrational, and therefore unconstitutional even if the discrimination is not subjected to heightened scrutiny, which is why we can largely elide the more complex analysis found in more closely balanced equal-protection cases.

It is also why we can avoid engaging with the plaintiffs' further argument that the states' prohibition of same-sex marriage violates a fundamental right protected by the due process clause of the Fourteenth Amendment. The plaintiffs rely on cases such as Zablocki v. Redhail (1978) that hold that the right to choose whom to marry is indeed a fundamental right. . . . In light of the compelling alternative grounds that we'll be exploring for allowing same-sex marriage, we won't have to engage with the parties' "fundamental right" debate; we can confine our attention to equal protection.

We begin our detailed analysis of whether prohibiting same-sex marriage denies equal protection of the laws by noting that Indiana and Wisconsin . . . are discriminating against homosexuals by denying them a right that these states grant to heterosexuals, namely the right to marry an unmarried adult of their choice. And there is little doubt that sexual orientation, the ground of the discrimination, is an immutable (and probably an innate, in the sense of in-born) characteristic rather than a choice. Wisely, neither Indiana nor Wisconsin argues otherwise. The American Psychological Association has said that "most people experience little or no sense of choice about their sexual orientation." APA, "Answers to Your Questions: For a Better Understanding of Sexual Orientation & Homosexuality" 2 (2008), www.apa.org/topics/lgbt/orientation.pdf. That homosexual orientation is not a choice is further suggested by the absence of evidence (despite extensive efforts to find it) that psychotherapy is effective in altering sexual orientation in general and homosexual orientation in particular. APA, "Answers to Your Questions," *id.* at 3; *Report of the American Psychological Association Task Force on Appropriate Therapeutic Responses to Sexual Orientation* 35–41 (2009).

The leading scientific theories of the causes of homosexuality are genetic and neuroendocrine theories, the latter being theories that sexual orientation is shaped by a fetus's exposure to certain hormones. See, e.g., J. Michael Bailey, "Biological Perspectives on Sexual Orientation," in *Lesbian, Gay, and Bisexual Identities Over the Lifespan: Psychological Perspectives* 102–30 (Anthony R. D'Augelli and Charlotte J. Patterson eds.1995); Barbara L. Frankowski, "Sexual Orientation and Adolescents," 113 *Pediatrics* 1827, 1828 (2004). [H]omosexuality may, like menopause, by reducing procreation by some members of society free them to provide child-caring assistance to their procreative relatives, thus increasing the survival and hence procreative prospects of these relatives. This is called the "kin selection hypothesis" or the "helper in the nest theory."

The harm to homosexuals (and, as we'll emphasize, to their adopted children) of being denied the right to marry is considerable. Marriage confers respectability on a sexual relationship; to exclude a couple from marriage is thus to deny it a coveted status. Because homosexuality is not a voluntary condition and homosexuals are among the most stigmatized, misunderstood, and discriminated-against minorities in the history of the world, the disparagement of their sexual orientation, implicit in the denial of marriage rights to same-sex couples, is a source of continuing pain to the homosexual community. Not that allowing same-sex marriage will change in the short run the negative views that many Americans hold of same-sex marriage. But it will enhance the status of these marriages in the eyes of other Americans, and in the long run it may convert some of the opponents of such marriage by demonstrating that homosexual married couples are in essential respects, notably in the care of their adopted children, like other married couples.

The tangible as distinct from the psychological benefits of marriage, which . . . enure directly or indirectly to the children of the marriage, whether biological or adopted, are also considerable. In Indiana they include the right to file state tax returns jointly; the marital testimonial privilege; spousal-support obligations; survivor benefits for the spouse of a public safety officer killed in the line of duty; the right to inherit when a spouse dies intestate; custodial rights to and child support obligations for children of the marriage, and protections for marital property upon the death of a spouse. Because Wisconsin allows domestic partnerships, some spousal benefits are available to same-sex couples in that state. But others are not, such as the right to adopt children jointly; spousal-support obligations; the presumption that all property of married couples is marital property; and state-mandated access to enrollment in a spouse's health insurance plan.

Of great importance are the extensive *federal* benefits to which married couples are entitled: the right to file income taxes jointly; social security spousal and surviving-spouse benefits; death benefits for surviving spouse of a military veteran; the right to transfer assets to one's spouse during marriage or at divorce without additional tax liability; exemption from federal estate tax of property that passes to the surviving spouse; the tax exemption for employer-provided healthcare to a spouse; and healthcare benefits for spouses of federal employees.

The denial of these federal benefits to same-sex couples brings to mind the Supreme Court's opinion in United States v. Windsor (2013), which held unconstitutional the denial of all federal marital benefits to same-sex marriages recognized by state law. The Court's criticisms of such denial apply with even greater force to Indiana's law. The denial "tells those couples, and all the world, that their otherwise valid marriages are unworthy of federal recognition. [*No same-sex marriages are valid in Indiana.*] This places same-sex couples in an unstable position of being in a second-tier marriage [in Indiana, in the lowest—the *unmarried*—tier]. The differentiation demeans the couple . . . [and] humiliates tens of thousands of children now being raised by same-sex couples. The law . . . makes it even more difficult for the children to understand the integrity and closeness of their own family and its concord with other families in their community and in their daily lives." *Id.*

The Court went on to describe at length the federal marital benefits denied by the Defense of Marriage Act to married same-sex couples. Of particular relevance to our two cases is the Court's finding that denial of those benefits causes economic harm to children of same-sex couples. . . .

Of course there are costs to marriage as well as benefits. . . . But those are among "the duties and responsibilities that are an essential part of married life and that [the spouses] in most cases would be honored to accept." That marriage continues to predominate over cohabitation as a choice of couples indicates that on average the sum of the tangible and intangible benefits of marriage outweighs the costs.

In light of the foregoing analysis it is apparent that *groundless* rejection of same-sex marriage by government must be a denial of equal protection of the laws, and therefore that Indiana and Wisconsin must to prevail establish a clearly offsetting governmental interest in that rejection. [B]efore addressing [that issue] we must address the states' argument that . . . we are bound by Baker v. Nelson (mem.). For there the Supreme Court, without issuing an opinion, dismissed "for want of a substantial federal question" an appeal from a state court that had held that prohibiting same-sex marriage did not violate the Constitution. . . . *Baker* was decided in 1972–42 years ago and the dark ages so far as litigation over discrimination against homosexuals is concerned. Subsequent decisions such as Romer v. Evans (1996); Lawrence v. Texas (2003), and *Windsor* are distinguishable from the present two cases but make clear that *Baker* is no longer authoritative. . . .

First up to bat is Indiana, which defends its refusal to allow same-sex marriage on a single ground, namely that government's sole purpose . . . in making marriage a legal relation (unlike cohabitation, which is purely contractual) is to enhance child welfare. Notably the state does not argue that recognizing same-sex marriage undermines conventional marriage.

When a child is conceived intentionally, the parents normally intend to raise the child together. But pregnancy, and the resulting birth (in the absence of abortion), are sometimes accidental, unintended; and often in such circumstances the mother is stuck with the baby—the father, not having wanted to become a father, refuses to take any responsibility for the child's welfare. The sole reason for Indiana's marriage law, the state's argument continues, is to try to channel unintentionally procreative sex into a legal regime in which the biological father is required to assume parental responsibility. . . . Government has no interest in recognizing and protecting same-sex marriage, Indiana argues, because homosexual sex cannot result in unintended births.

As for the considerable benefits that marriage confers on the married couple, these in the state's view are a part of the regulatory regime: the carrot supplementing the stick. Marital benefits for homosexual couples would not serve the regulatory purpose of marital benefits for heterosexual couples because homosexual couples don't produce babies. . . .

In short, Indiana argues that homosexual relationships are created and dissolved without legal consequences because they don't create family-related regulatory concerns. Yet encouraging marriage is less about forcing fathers to take responsibility for their unintended children—state law has mechanisms for determining paternity and requiring the father to contribute to the support of his children—than about enhancing child welfare by encouraging parents to commit to a stable relationship in which they will be raising the child together. Moreover, if channeling procreative sex into marriage were the only reason that Indiana recognizes marriage, the state would not allow an infertile person to marry. Indeed it would make marriage licenses expire when one of the spouses (fertile upon marriage) became infertile because of age or disease. The state treats married homosexuals as would-be "free riders" on heterosexual marriage, unreasonably reaping benefits intended by the state for fertile couples. But infertile couples are free riders too. Why are they allowed to reap the benefits accorded marriages of fertile couples, and homosexuals are not? . . .

At oral argument the state's lawyer was asked whether "Indiana's law is about successfully raising children," and since "you agree same-sex couples can successfully raise children, why shouldn't the ban be lifted as to them?" The lawyer answered that "the assumption is that with opposite-sex couples there is very little thought given during the sexual act, sometimes, to whether babies may be a consequence." In other words, Indiana's government thinks that straight couples tend to be sexually irresponsible, producing unwanted children by the carload, and so must be pressured (in the form of governmental encouragement of marriage through a combination of sticks and carrots) to marry, but that gay couples, unable as they are to produce children wanted or unwanted, are model parents—model citizens really—so have no need for marriage. Heterosexuals get drunk and pregnant, producing unwanted children; their reward is to be allowed to marry. Homosexual couples do not produce unwanted children; their reward is to be denied the right to marry. Go figure.

Which brings us to Indiana's weakest defense of its distinction among different types of infertile couple: its assumption that same-sex marriage cannot contribute to alleviating the problem of "accidental births," which the state contends is the sole governmental interest in marriage. . . . In advancing this as *the* reason to forbid same-sex marriage, Indiana has ignored adoption—an extraordinary oversight. Unintentional offspring are the children most likely to be put up for adoption, and if not adopted, to end up in a foster home. Accidental pregnancies are the major source of unwanted children, and unwanted children are a major problem for society, which is doubtless the reason homosexuals are permitted to adopt in most states—including Indiana and Wisconsin.

It's been estimated that more than 200,000 American children (some 3000 in Indiana and about the same number in Wisconsin) are being raised by homosexuals, mainly homosexual couples. Gary J. Gates, "LGBT Parenting in the United States" 3 (Williams Institute, UCLA School of Law, Feb. 2013). Gary Gates's demographic surveys find that among couples who have children, homosexual couples are five times as likely to be raising an adopted child as heterosexual couples in Indiana, and two and a half times as likely as heterosexual couples in Wisconsin.

If the fact that a child's parents are married enhances the child's prospects for a happy and successful life, as Indiana believes not without reason, this should be true whether the child's parents are natural or adoptive. The state's lawyers tell us that "the point of marriage's associated benefits and protections is to encourage child-rearing environments where parents care for their biological children in tandem." Why the qualifier "biological"? The state recognizes that family is about raising children and not just about producing them. It does not explain why the "point of marriage's associated benefits and protections" is inapplicable to a couple's adopted as distinct from biological children.

Married homosexuals are more likely to want to adopt than unmarried ones if only because of the many state and federal benefits to which married people are entitled. And so same-sex marriage improves the prospects of unintended children by increasing the number and resources of prospective adopters. Notably, same-sex couples are *more* likely to adopt foster children than opposite-sex couples are. Gates, "LGBT Parenting in the United States," *supra,* at 3. . . .

Also, the more willing adopters there are, not only the fewer children there will be in foster care or being raised by single mothers but also the fewer abortions there will be. Carrying a baby to term and putting the baby up for adoption is an alternative to abortion for a pregnant woman who thinks that as a single mother she could not cope with the baby. The pro-life community recognizes this. . . .

Indiana permits joint adoption by homosexuals (Wisconsin does not). But an unmarried homosexual couple is less stable than a married one, or so at least the state's insistence that marriage is better for children implies. If marriage is better for children who are being brought up by their biological parents, it must be better for children who are being brought up by their adoptive parents. The state should *want* homosexual couples who adopt children—as, to repeat, they are permitted to do—to be married, if it is serious in arguing that the only governmental interest in marriage derives from the problem of accidental births. (We doubt that it is serious.)

The state's claim that conventional marriage is the solution to that problem is belied by the state's experience with births out of wedlock. . . . [I]f the state's policy of trying to channel procreative sex into marriage were succeeding, we would expect a drop in the percentage of children born to an unmarried woman, or at least not an increase in that percentage. Yet in fact that percentage has been rising even since Indiana in 1997 reenacted its prohibition of same-sex marriage and for the first time declared that it would not recognize same-sex marriages contracted in other states or abroad. . . .

In 1997, the year of the enactment, 33 percent of births in Indiana were to unmarried women; in 2012 (the latest year for which we have statistics) the percentage was 43 percent. The corresponding figures for Wisconsin are 28 percent and 37 percent and for the nation as a whole 32 percent and 41 percent. (The source of all these data is Kids Count Data Center, "Births to Unmarried Women," http://datacenter.kidscount.org/data/tables/7–births–to–unmarried-women#detailed/2/16,51/false/868,867,133,38,35/any/257,258.) There is no indication that these states' laws, ostensibly aimed at channeling procreation into marriage, have had any such effect.

A degree of arbitrariness is inherent in government regulation, but when there is no justification for government's treating a traditionally discriminated-against group significantly worse than the dominant group in the society, doing so denies equal protection of the laws. One wouldn't know, reading Wisconsin's brief, that there is or ever has been discrimination against homosexuals anywhere in the United States. The state either is oblivious to, or thinks irrelevant, that until quite recently homosexuality was anathematized by the vast majority of heterosexuals . . . , including by most Americans who were otherwise quite liberal. Homosexuals had, as homosexuals, no rights; homosexual sex was criminal . . . ; homosexuals were formally banned from the armed forces and many other types of government work . . . ; and there were no laws prohibiting employment discrimination against homosexuals. Because homosexuality is more easily concealed than race, homosexuals did not experience the same economic and educational discrimination, and public humiliation, that African-Americans experienced. But to avoid discrimination and ostracism they had to conceal their homosexuality and so were reluctant to participate openly in homosexual relationships or reveal their homosexuality to the heterosexuals with whom they associated. Most of them stayed "in the closet." Same-sex marriage was out of the question, even though interracial marriage was legal in most states. Although discrimination against homosexuals has diminished greatly, it remains widespread. It persists in statutory form in Indiana and in Wisconsin's constitution.

At the very least, "a [discriminatory] law must bear a rational relationship to a legitimate governmental purpose." *Romer.* Indiana's ban flunks this undemanding test.

Wisconsin's prohibition of same-sex marriage . . . is found in a 2006 amendment to the state's constitution . . . : "Only a marriage between one man and one woman shall be valid or recognized as a marriage in this state. A legal status identical or substantially similar to that of marriage for unmarried individuals shall not be valid or recognized in this state." . . .

Wisconsin's brief in defense of its prohibition of same-sex marriage adopts Indiana's ground ("accidental births") but does not amplify it. . . .

[W]isconsin . . . makes four arguments of its own against such marriage: First, limiting marriage to heterosexuals is traditional and tradition is a valid basis for limiting legal rights. Second, the consequences of allowing same-sex marriage cannot be foreseen and therefore a state should be permitted to move cautiously—that is, to do nothing, for Wisconsin does not suggest that it plans to take any steps in the direction of eventually authorizing such marriage. Third, the decision whether to permit or forbid same-sex marriage should be left to the democratic process, that is, to the legislature and the electorate. And fourth, same-sex marriage is analogous in its effects to no-fault divorce, which, the state argues, makes marriage fragile and unreliable—though of course Wisconsin *has* no-fault divorce, and it's surprising that the state's assistant attorney general, who argued the state's appeal, would trash his own state's law. The contention, built on the analogy to no-fault divorce . . . is that . . . allowing same-sex marriage creates a danger of "shifting the public understanding of marriage away from a largely child-centric institution to an adult-centric institution focused on emotion." No evidence is presented that same-sex marriage is on average less "child-centric" and more emotional than an infertile marriage of heterosexuals, or for that matter that no-fault divorce has rendered marriage less "child-centric."

The state's argument from tradition runs head on into Loving v. Virginia (1967), since the limitation of marriage to persons of the same race was traditional in a number of states when the Supreme Court invalidated it. Laws forbidding black-white marriage dated back to colonial times and were found in northern as well as southern colonies and states. See Peggy Pascoe, *What Comes Naturally: Miscegenation Law and the Making of Race in America* (2009). Tradition per se has no positive or negative significance. There are good traditions, bad traditions pilloried in such famous literary stories as Franz Kafka's "In the Penal Colony" and Shirley Jackson's "The Lottery," bad traditions that are historical realities such as cannibalism, foot-binding, and suttee, and traditions that from a public-policy standpoint are neither good nor bad (such as trick-or-treating on Halloween). Tradition per se therefore cannot be a lawful ground for discrimination—regardless of the age of the tradition. Holmes thought it "revolting to have no better reason for a rule of law than that so it was laid down in the time of Henry IV." Oliver Wendell Holmes, Jr., "The Path of the Law," 10 *Harv. L.Rev.* 457, 469 (1897). Henry IV died in 1413. Criticism of homosexuality is far older. In Leviticus 18:22 we read that "thou shalt not lie with mankind, as with womankind: it is abomination." . . .

Wisconsin points out that many venerable customs appear to rest on nothing more than tradition—one might even say on mindless tradition. Why do men wear ties? Why do people shake hands (thus spreading germs) or give a peck on the cheek (ditto) when greeting a friend? Why does the President at Thanksgiving spare a brace of turkeys . . . from the butcher's knife? But these traditions, while to the fastidious they may seem silly, are at least harmless. If no social benefit is conferred by a tradition *and* it is written into law *and* it discriminates against a number of people and does them harm beyond just offending them, it is not just a harmless anachronism; it is a violation of the equal protection clause, as in *Loving*. . . .

The state elaborates its argument from the wonders of tradition by asserting that "thousands of years of collective experience has [*sic*] established traditional marriage, between one man and one woman, as optimal for the family, society, and civilization." No evidence in support of the claim of optimality is offered, and there is no acknowledgment that a number of countries permit polygamy— Syria, Yemen, Iraq, Iran, Egypt, Sudan, Morocco, and Algeria—and that it flourishes in many African countries that do not actually authorize it, as well as in parts of Utah. (Indeed it's been said that "polygyny, whereby a man can have multiple wives, is the marriage form found in more places and at more times than any other." Stephanie Coontz, *Marriage, a History: How Love Conquered Marriage* 10 (2006).) But suppose the assertion is correct. How does that bear on same-sex marriage? Does Wisconsin want to push homosexuals to marry persons of the opposite sex because opposite-sex marriage is "optimal"? Does it think that allowing same-sex marriage will cause heterosexuals to convert to homosexuality? Efforts to convert homosexuals to heterosexuality have been a bust; is the opposite conversion more feasible?

Arguments from tradition must be distinguished from arguments based on morals. Many unquestioned laws are founded on moral principles that cannot be reduced to cost-benefit analysis. Laws forbidding gratuitous cruelty to animals, and laws providing public assistance for poor and disabled persons, are examples. There is widespread moral opposition to homosexuality. The opponents are entitled to their opinion. But neither Indiana nor Wisconsin make a moral argument against permitting same-sex marriage.

The state's second argument is: "go slow": maintaining the prohibition of same-sex marriage is the "prudent, cautious approach," and the state should therefore be allowed "to act deliberately and with prudence—or, at the very least, to gather sufficient information—before transforming this cornerstone of civilization and society." There is no suggestion that the state has any interest in gathering information, for notice the assumption in the quoted passage that the state already *knows* that allowing same-sex marriage would transform a "cornerstone of civilization and society," namely monogamous heterosexual marriage. One would expect the state to have provided *some* evidence, *some* reason to believe, however speculative and tenuous, that allowing same-sex marriage will or may "transform" marriage. At the oral argument the state's lawyer conceded that he had no knowledge of any study underway to determine the possible effects on heterosexual marriage in Wisconsin of allowing same-sex marriage. He did say that same-sex marriage might somehow devalue marriage, thus making it less attractive to opposite-sex couples. But he quickly acknowledged that he hadn't studied how same-sex marriage might harm marriage for heterosexuals and wasn't prepared to argue the point. Massachusetts, the first state to legalize same-sex marriage, did so a decade ago. Has heterosexual marriage in Massachusetts been "transformed"? Wisconsin's lawyer didn't suggest it has been.

He may have been gesturing toward the concern expressed by some that same-sex marriage is likely to cause the heterosexual marriage rate to decline because heterosexuals who are hostile to homosexuals, or who . . . think that allowing them to marry degrades the institution of marriage . . . might decide not to marry. Yet the only study that we've discovered, a reputable statistical study, finds that allowing same-sex marriage has no effect on the heterosexual marriage rate. Marcus Dillender, "The Death of Marriage? The Effects of New Forms of Legal Recognition on Marriage Rates in the United States," 51 *Demography* 563 (2014). . . .

No one knows exactly how many Americans are homosexual. Estimates vary from about 1.5 percent to about 4 percent. The estimate for Wisconsin is 2.8 percent, which includes bisexual and transgendered persons. Gary J. Gates & Frank Newport, "LGBT Percentage Highest in D.C., Lowest in North Dakota," *Gallup* (Feb. 15, 2013), www.gallup.com/poll/160517/lgbt-percentage-highest-lowest-north-dakota.aspx. Given how small the percentage is, it is sufficiently implausible that allowing same-sex marriage would cause palpable harm to family, society, or civilization to require the state to tender evidence justifying its fears; it has provided none.

The state falls back on Justice Alito's statement in dissent in *Windsor*, that "at present, no one—including social scientists, philosophers, and historians—can predict with any certainty what the long-term ramifications of widespread acceptance of same-sex marriage will be. And judges are certainly not equipped to make such an assessment." What follows, if prediction is impossible? Justice Alito thought what follows is that the Supreme Court should not interfere with Congress's determination in the Defense of Marriage Act that "marriage," for purposes of entitlement to federal marital benefits, excludes same-sex marriage even if lawful under state law. But can the "long-term ramifications" of *any* constitutional decision be predicted with certainty at the time the decision is rendered?

The state does not mention Justice Alito's invocation of a moral case against same-sex marriage, when he states in his dissent that "others explain the basis for the institution in more philosophical terms. They argue that marriage is essentially the solemnizing of a comprehensive, exclusive, permanent union that is intrinsically ordered to producing new life, even if it does not always do so." *Id.* That is a moral argument for limiting marriage to heterosexuals. . . .

We know that many people want to enter into a same-sex marriage . . . , and that forbidding them to do so imposes a heavy cost, financial and emotional, on them and their children. What Wisconsin has not told us is whether any heterosexuals have been harmed by same-sex marriage. Obviously many people are distressed by the idea or reality of such marriage; otherwise these two cases wouldn't be here. But there is a difference, famously emphasized by John Stuart Mill in *On Liberty* (1869), between the distress that is caused by an assault, or a theft of property, or an invasion of privacy, or for that matter discrimination, and the distress that is caused by behavior that disgusts some people but does no (other) harm to them. Mill argued that neither law (government regulation) nor morality (condemnation by public opinion) has any proper concern with acts that, unlike a punch in the nose, inflict no temporal harm on another person without consent or justification. The qualification *temporal* is key. To be the basis of legal or moral concern, Mill argued, the harm must be tangible, secular, material—physical or financial, or, if emotional, focused and direct—rather than moral or spiritual. Mill illustrated nontemporal harm with revulsion against polygamy in Utah. . . . The English people were fiercely critical of polygamy wherever it occurred. As they were entitled to be. But there was no way polygamy in Utah could have adverse effects in England, 4000 miles away. Mill didn't think that polygamy, however offensive, was a proper political concern of England.

Similarly, while many heterosexuals (though in America a rapidly diminishing number) disapprove of same-sex marriage, there is no way they are going to be hurt by it in a way that the law would take cognizance of. Wisconsin doesn't argue otherwise. Many people strongly disapproved of interracial marriage, and, more to the point, many people strongly disapproved (and still strongly disapprove) of homosexual sex, yet *Loving* invalidated state laws banning interracial marriage, and *Lawrence* invalidated state laws banning homosexual sex acts.

Though these decisions are in the spirit of Mill, Mill is not the last word on public morality. But Wisconsin like Indiana does not base its prohibition of same-sex marriage on morality, perhaps because it believes plausibly that *Lawrence* rules out moral objections to homosexuality as legitimate grounds for discrimination.

In passing, Wisconsin in its opening brief notes that it "recogniz[es] domestic partnerships." And the domestic partners must be of the same sex. But the preamble to the statute states: "The legislature . . . finds that the legal status of domestic partnership as established in this chapter is not substantially similar to that of marriage,". . . . [T]he rights and obligations of domestic partners are far more limited than those of married persons. (For example, only spouses may jointly adopt a child.) They *have* to be far more limited, because of the state's constitutional provision quoted above that "a legal status identical or substantially similar to that of marriage for unmarried individuals shall not be valid or recognized." Wis. Const. Art. XIII, § 13. Domestic partnership in Wisconsin is not and cannot be marriage by another name. . . .

So look what the state has done: it has thrown a crumb to same-sex couples, denying them not only many of the rights and many of the benefits of marriage but also of course the name. Imagine if in the 1960s the states that forbade interracial marriage had said to interracial couples: "you can have domestic partnerships that create the identical rights and obligations of marriage, but you can call them only 'civil unions' or 'domestic partnerships.' The term 'marriage' is reserved for same-race unions." This would give interracial couples much more than Wisconsin's domestic partnership statute gives same-sex couples. Yet withholding the term "marriage" would be considered deeply offensive, and, having no justification other than bigotry, would be invalidated as a denial of equal protection. . . .

Wisconsin's remaining argument is that the ban on same-sex marriage is the outcome of a democratic process—the enactment of a constitutional ban by popular vote. But homosexuals are only a small part of the state's population—2.8 percent, we said, grouping transgendered and bisexual persons with homosexuals. Minorities trampled on by the democratic process have recourse to the courts; the recourse is called constitutional law.

In its reply brief Indiana adopts Wisconsin's democracy argument, adding that "homosexuals are politically powerful out of proportion to their numbers." No evidence is presented by the state to support this contention. It is true that an increasing number of heterosexuals support same-sex marriage; otherwise 11 states would not have changed their laws to permit such marriage (the other 8 states that allow same-sex marriage do so as a result of judicial decisions invalidating the states' bans). No inference of manipulation of the democratic process by homosexuals can be drawn, however, any more than it could be inferred from the enactment of civil rights laws that African-Americans "are politically powerful out of proportion to their numbers." It is to the credit of American voters that they do not support only laws that are in their palpable self-interest. They support laws punishing cruelty to animals, even though not a single animal has a vote.

To return to where we started . . . more than unsupported conjecture that same-sex marriage will harm heterosexual marriage or children or any other valid and important interest of a state is necessary to justify discrimination on the basis of sexual orientation. [T]he grounds advanced by Indiana and Wisconsin for their discriminatory policies are not only conjectural; they are totally implausible.

For completeness we note the ultimate convergence of our simplified four-step analysis with the more familiar, but also more complex, approach found in many cases. In SmithKline Beecham Corp. v. Abbott Laboratories, 740 F.3d 471, 483 (9th Cir.2014), the Ninth Circuit concluded, based on a reading of the Supreme Court's decisions in *Lawrence* and *Windsor,* that statutes that discriminate on the basis of sexual orientation are subject to "heightened scrutiny"—and in doing so noted that *Windsor,* in invalidating the Defense of Marriage Act, had balanced the Act's harms and offsetting benefits: . . . "*Windsor's* balancing is not the work of rational basis review." . . .

The district court judgments invalidating and enjoining these two states' prohibitions of same-sex marriage are

AFFIRMED.

EDITORS' NOTES

(1) What is Judge Posner's argument that bans on same-sex marriage violate the Equal Protection Clause? Is he right that there is no reasonable basis for such bans? Is he right that previous cases had established that discrimination on the basis of sexual orientation is "constitutionally suspect"? How does Posner's equal protection justification for the right of gay men and lesbians to marry differ from the justification subsequently offered by Justice Kennedy for the majority in *Obergefell?*

(2)   What role do science and social science play in Posner's opinion? How, for example, does empirical information about family formation shape his evaluation of Indiana and Wisconsin's channeling/responsible procreation argument? How does his evaluation of that argument differ from that of Chief Justice Roberts's dissent in *Obergefell* (in Chapter 1)? With Justice Cordy's dissent in *Goodridge* (in this chapter)? What place should empirical evidence of this sort have in constitutional interpretation?

(3)   What role does *Windsor* play in Posner's analysis? Does he read *Windsor* as implying that laws banning same-sex marriage are unconstitutional under the Equal Protection Clause? Which framework is more cogent in analyzing the reasons offered to support these bans, that of *Windsor* or Posner's proposed four-question analysis?

(4)   How does Posner reply to the argument that courts should defer to the "democratic process" and uphold the ban on same-sex marriage? How does his understanding of democracy differ from that offered in Chief Justice Roberts's dissent in *Obergefell*?

(5)   What is Posner's reply to the state's argument that "tradition is a valid basis for limiting legal rights" (understanding tradition here as referring to concrete historical practices rather than abstract moral principles)? Is his analysis cogent? Is his discussion of *Loving* and tradition persuasive?

(6)   Is Posner persuasive in suggesting that the states may "believe[ ] plausibly that *Lawrence* rules out moral objections to homosexuality as legitimate grounds for discrimination"? Is he right to suggest that *Loving* and *Lawrence* are "in the spirit of Mill," who famously argued that the only justification for government to restrict liberty is to prevent harm to others? Compare Posner's views concerning Mill with Chief Justice Roberts's objection in dissent in *Obergefell* that the majority in that case interprets the Constitution to incorporate the "harm principle" of Mill's *On Liberty*.

(7)   By framing these cases as "at a deeper level . . . about the welfare of American children" and emphasizing that gay couples are "model parents" and "model citizens" because they are more likely than straight couples to adopt unwanted children, does Posner premise same-sex couples' couples' right to marry upon their altruism or their instrumental value to the state? Would Posner's opinion equally support the right to marry of couples who became parents through the use of assisted reproductive technology? Couples who did not intend to become parents?

"I agree that Idaho and Nevada's same-sex marriage prohibitions fail because they discriminate on the basis of sexual orientation. . . . I write separately because I am persuaded that [those] bans are also unconstitutional for another reason: They are classifications on the basis of gender that do not survive the level of scrutiny applicable to such classifications."—CIRCUIT JUDGE BERZON

LATTA V. OTTER
771 F.3d 456 (9th Cir. 2014)

■ Before REINHARDT, GOULD, and BERZON, CIRCUIT JUDGES.

[Idaho and Nevada passed statutes and enacted constitutional amendments preventing same-sex couples from marrying and refusing to recognize same-sex marriages validly performed elsewhere. The Ninth Circuit Court of Appeals, in an opinion by Judge Stephen Reinhardt, invalidated the bans on the ground that they violated the Equal Protection Clause of the Fourteenth Amendment. Specifically, the Court of Appeals held that such bans discriminated on the basis of sexual orientation, that they were subject to "heightened scrutiny," and that they were unconstitutional under that test. Judge Reinhardt wrote separately "to add that [he] would also hold that the fundamental right to marriage [includes] the right to marry an individual of one's choice" protected by the Due Process Clause.

We include below Judge Berzon's concurrence because she makes a different equal protection argument: that bans on same-sex marriage unconstitutionally discriminate on the basis of gender.]

■ BERZON, CIRCUIT JUDGE, concurring:

I agree that Idaho and Nevada's same-sex marriage prohibitions fail because they discriminate on the basis of sexual orientation . . . I write separately because I am persuaded that [those] bans are also unconstitutional for another reason: They are classifications on the basis of gender that do not survive the level of scrutiny applicable to such classifications.

I.   The Same-Sex Marriage Prohibitions Facially Classify on the Basis of Gender

"[S]tatutory classifications that distinguish between males and females are 'subject to scrutiny under the Equal Protection Clause.' " Craig v. Boren (1976) (quoting Reed v. Reed (1971)). "To withstand constitutional challenge, . . .

classifications by gender must serve important governmental objectives and must be substantially related to achievement of those objectives." *Id.* "The burden of justification" the state shoulders under this intermediate level of scrutiny is "demanding": the state must convince the reviewing court that the law's "proffered justification" for the gender classification "is 'exceedingly persuasive.'" United States v. Virginia (1996) ("*VMI*"). Idaho and Nevada's same-sex marriage bans discriminate on the basis of sex and so are invalid unless they meet this "demanding" standard.

A. Idaho and Nevada's same-sex marriage prohibitions facially classify on the basis of sex.[1] Only women may marry men, and only men may marry women. Susan Latta may not marry her partner Traci Ehlers for the sole reason that Latta is a woman; Latta could marry Ehlers if Latta were a man. Theodore Small may not marry his partner Antioco Carillo for the sole reason that Small is a man; Small could marry Carillo if Small were a woman. But for their gender, plaintiffs would be able to marry the partners of their choice. Their rights under the states' bans on same-sex marriage are wholly determined by their sex.

A law that facially dictates that a man may do X while a woman may not, or vice versa, constitutes, without more, a gender classification. . . . Thus, plaintiffs challenging policies that facially discriminate on the basis of sex need not separately show either "intent" or "purpose" to discriminate. Personnel Adm'r of Massachusetts v. Feeney (1979).

Some examples help to illuminate these fundamental precepts. Surely, a law providing that women may enter into business contracts only with other women would classify on the basis of gender. And that would be so whether or not men were similarly restricted to entering into business relationships only with other men.

Likewise, a prison regulation that requires correctional officers be the same sex as the inmates in a prison "explicitly discriminates . . . on the basis of . . . sex." Dothard v. Rawlinson (1977). Again, that is so whether women alone are affected or whether men are similarly limited to serving only male prisoners.

Further, it can make no difference to the existence of a sex-based classification whether the challenged law imposes gender homogeneity, as in the

---

1 "Sex" and "gender" are not necessarily coextensive concepts; the meanings of these terms and the difference between them are highly contested. *See, e.g.,* Katherine Franke, "The Central Mistake of Sex Discrimination Law: The Disaggregation of Sex from Gender," 144 *U. Pa. L. Rev.* 1 (1995). For present purposes, I will use the terms "sex" and "gender" interchangeably, to denote the social and legal categorization of people into the generally recognized classes of "men" and "women." [Footnote by Judge Berzon.]

business partner example or *Dothard,* or gender heterogeneity. Either way, the *classification* is one that limits the affected individuals' opportunities based on their sex, as compared to the sex of the other people involved in the arrangement or transaction.

As Justice Johnson of the Vermont Supreme Court noted, the same-sex marriage prohibitions, if anything, classify *more* obviously on the basis of sex than they do on the basis of sexual orientation: "A woman is denied the right to marry another woman because her would-be partner is a woman, not because one or both are lesbians.... [S]exual orientation does not appear as a qualification for marriage" under these laws; sex does. Baker v. State (1999) (Johnson, J., concurring in part and dissenting in part).

The statutes' gender focus is also borne out by the experience of one of the Nevada plaintiff couples:

> When Karen Goody and Karen Vibe went to the Washoe County Marriage Bureau to obtain a marriage license, the security officer asked, "Do you have a man with you?" When Karen Vibe said they did not, and explained that she wished to marry Karen Goody, she was told she could not even obtain or complete a marriage license application . . . [because] "[t]wo women can't apply" . . . [and] marriage is "between a man and a woman."

Notably, Goody and Vibe were not asked about their sexual orientation; Vibe was told she was being excluded because of her gender and the gender of her partner.

Of course, the reason Vibe wants to marry Goody, one presumes, is due in part to their sexual orientations. But that does not mean the classification at issue is not sex-based. . . .

B. In concluding that these laws facially classify on the basis of gender, it is of no moment that the prohibitions "treat men as a class and women as a class equally" and in that sense give preference to neither gender, as the defendants fervently maintain. That argument revives the long-discredited reasoning of Pace v. Alabama (1883), which upheld an anti-miscegenation statute on the ground that "[t]he punishment of each offending person, whether white or black, is the same," *overruled by* McLaughlin v. Florida (1964). Plessy v. Ferguson (1896), *overruled by* Brown v. Board of Education (1954), similarly upheld racial segregation on the reasoning that segregation laws applied equally to black and white citizens.

This narrow view of the reach of the impermissible classification concept is, of course, no longer the law after *Brown*. Loving v. Virginia (1967) reinforced the post-*Brown* understanding of impermissible classification under the Fourteenth Amendment in a context directly analogous to the present one. Addressing the constitutionality of anti-miscegenation laws banning interracial marriage, *Loving* firmly "reject[ed] the notion that the mere 'equal application' of a statute containing racial classifications is enough to remove the classifications from the Fourteenth Amendment's proscription of all invidious racial discrimination." . . .

Under all these precedents, it is simply irrelevant that the same-sex marriage prohibitions privilege neither gender as a whole or on average. Laws that strip *individuals* of their rights or restrict personal choices or opportunities solely on the basis of the individuals' gender are sex discriminatory and must be subjected to intermediate scrutiny. *See* J.E.B. [v. Alabama ex rel. T.B. (1994)]. Accordingly, I would hold that Idaho and Nevada's same-sex marriage prohibitions facially classify on the basis of gender, and that the "equal application" of these laws to men and women as a class does not remove them from intermediate scrutiny.[7] . . .

II. Same-Sex Marriage Bars Are Based in Gender Stereotypes

Idaho and Nevada's same sex marriage laws not only classify on the basis of sex but also, implicitly and explicitly, draw on "archaic and stereotypic notions" about the purportedly distinctive roles and abilities of men and women. Eradicating the legal impact of such stereotypes has been a central concern of constitutional sex-discrimination jurisprudence for the last several decades. *See, e.g.,* Mississippi Univ. for Women v. Hogan (1982). The same-sex marriage bans thus share a key characteristic with many other sex-based classifications, one that underlay the Court's adoption of intermediate scrutiny for such classifications.

The Supreme Court has consistently emphasized that "gender-based classifications . . . may be reflective of 'archaic and overbroad' generalizations about gender, or based on 'outdated misconceptions concerning the role of females in the home rather than in the marketplace and world of ideas.' " *J.E.B.* (quoting Schlesinger v. Ballard (1975); *Craig*). Laws that rest on nothing more than "the 'baggage of sexual stereotypes,' that presume [ ] the father has the 'primary responsibility to provide a home and its essentials,' while the mother is the 'center of home and family life' " have been declared constitutionally invalid

---

[7] Several courts have so held. See Perry v. Schwarzenegger, 704 F.Supp.2d 921, 996 (N.D.Cal.2010) *aff'd sub nom.,* Perry v. Brown, 671 F.3d 1052 (9th Cir.2012), *vacated and remanded sub nom.,* Hollingsworth v. Perry (2013); Baehr v. Lewin, 74 Haw. 530, 852 P.2d 44, 59 (1993) (plurality op.); *Baker,* 744 A.2d at 905 (Johnson, J., concurring in part and dissenting in part). [Footnote by Judge Berzon.]

time after time. Califano v. Westcott (1979) (quoting Orr v. Orr (1979); Stanton v. Stanton (1975); Taylor v. Louisiana (1975)). Moreover, "gender classifications that rest on impermissible stereotypes violate the Equal Protection Clause, even when some statistical support can be conjured up for the generalization." *J.E.B.*. And hostility toward nonconformance with gender stereotypes also constitutes impermissible gender discrimination. *See generally* Price Waterhouse v. Hopkins (1989); accord Nichols v. Azteca Rest. Enters., Inc. (9th Cir.2001) (harassment against a person for "failure to conform to [sex] stereotypes" is gender-based discrimination).

The notion underlying the Supreme Court's anti-stereotyping doctrine in both Fourteenth Amendment and Title VII cases is simple, but compelling: "[n]obody should be forced into a predetermined role on account of sex," or punished for failing to conform to prescriptive expectations of what behavior is appropriate for one's gender. *See* Ruth Bader Ginsburg, *Gender and the Constitution,* 44 U. Cin.L.Rev. 1, 1 (1975). In other words, laws that give effect to "pervasive sex-role stereotype[s]" about the behavior appropriate for men and women are damaging because they restrict individual choices by punishing those men and women who do not fit the stereotyped mold. Nev. Dep't of Human Resources v. Hibbs (2003).

Idaho and Nevada's same-sex marriage prohibitions, as the justifications advanced for those prohibitions in this Court demonstrate, patently draw on "archaic and stereotypic notions" about gender. *Hogan.* These prohibitions, the defendants have emphatically argued, communicate the state's view of what is both "normal" and preferable with regard to the romantic preferences, relationship roles, and parenting capacities of men and women. By doing so, the laws enforce the state's view that men and women "naturally" behave differently from one another in marriage and as parents.

The defendants, for example, assert that "gender diversity or complementarity among parents . . . provides important benefits" to children, because "mothers and fathers tend on average to parent differently and thus make unique contributions to the child's overall development." The defendants similarly assert that "[t]he man-woman meaning at the core of the marriage institution, reinforced by the law, has always recognized, valorized, and made normative the roles of 'mother' and 'father' and their uniting, complementary roles in raising their offspring."

Viewed through the prism of the Supreme Court's contemporary anti-stereotyping sex discrimination doctrine, these proffered justifications simply underscore that the same-sex marriage prohibitions discriminate on the basis of sex, not only in their form . . . but also in reviving the very infirmities that led the Supreme Court to adopt an intermediate scrutiny standard for sex classifications in the first place. I so conclude for two, somewhat independent, reasons.

A.   First, and more obviously, the gender stereotyping at the core of the same-sex marriage prohibitions clarifies that those laws affect men and women in basically the same way as, not in a fundamentally different manner from, a wide range of laws and policies that have been viewed consistently as discrimination based on sex. [L]egislating on the basis of such stereotypes limits, and is meant to limit, the choices men and women make about the trajectory of their own lives, choices about work, parenting, dress, driving—and yes, marriage. This focus in modern sex discrimination law on the preservation of the ability freely to make individual life choices regardless of one's sex confirms that sex discrimination operates at, and must be justified at, the level of individuals, not at the broad class level of all men and women. Because the same-sex marriage prohibitions restrict individuals' choices on the basis of sex, they discriminate based on sex for purposes of constitutional analysis precisely to the same degree as other statutes that infringe on such choices—whether by distributing benefits or by restricting behavior—on that same ground.

B.   Second, the long line of cases since 1971 invalidating various laws and policies that categorized by sex have been part of a transformation that has altered the very institution at the heart of this case, marriage. Reviewing that transformation, including the role played by constitutional sex discrimination challenges in bringing it about, reveals that the same sex marriage prohibitions seek to preserve an outmoded, sex-role-based vision of the marriage institution, and in that sense as well raise the very concerns that gave rise to the contemporary constitutional approach to sex discrimination.

(i)   Historically, marriage was a profoundly unequal institution, one that imposed distinctly different rights and obligations on men and women. The law of coverture, for example, deemed the "the husband and wife . . . one person," such that "the very being or legal existence of the woman [was] suspended . . . or at least [was] incorporated and consolidated into that of the husband" during the marriage. 1 William Blackstone, *Commentaries on the Laws of England* 441 (3d rev. ed.1884). Under the principles of coverture, "a married woman [was] incapable, without her husband's consent, of making contracts . . . binding on her or him." Bradwell v. Illinois (1872) (Bradley, J., concurring). She could not sue or be sued without her husband's consent. *See, e.g.,* Nancy F. Cott, *Public Vows: A History of*

Marriage and the Nation 11–12 (2000). Married women also could not serve as the legal guardians of their children. Frontiero v. Richardson (1973) (plurality op.).

Marriage laws further dictated economically disparate roles for husband and wife. In many respects, the marital contract was primarily understood as an economic arrangement between spouses, whether or not the couple had or would have children. "Coverture expressed the legal essence of marriage as reciprocal: a husband was bound to support his wife, and in exchange she gave over her property and labor." Cott, *Public Vows,* at 54. That is why "married women traditionally were denied the legal capacity to hold or convey property. . . ." *Frontiero.* Notably, husbands owed their wives support even if there were no children of the marriage. *See, e.g.,* Hendrik Hartog, *Man and Wife in America: A History* 156 (2000).

There was also a significant disparity between the rights of husbands and wives with regard to physical intimacy. At common law, "a woman was the sexual property of her husband; that is, she had a duty to have intercourse with him." John D'Emilio & Estelle B. Freedman, *Intimate Matters: A History of Sexuality in America* 79 (3d ed.2012). Quite literally, a wife was legally "the possession of her husband, . . . [her] husband's property." Hartog, Man and Wife in America, at 137. Accordingly, a husband could sue his wife's lover in tort for "entic[ing]" her or "alienat[ing]" her affections and thereby interfering with his property rights in her body and her labor. *Id.* A husband's possessory interest in his wife was undoubtedly also driven by the fact that, historically, marriage was the only legal site for licit sex; sex outside of marriage was almost universally criminalized. *See, e.g.,* Ariela R. Dubler, "Immoral Purposes: Marriage and the Genus of Illicit Sex," 115 *Yale L.J.* 756, 763–64 (2006).

Notably, although sex was strongly presumed to be an essential part of marriage, the ability to procreate was generally not. *See, e.g.,* Chester Vernier, American Family Laws: A Comparative Study of the Family Law of the Forty-Eight American States, Alaska, the District of Columbia, and Hawaii (to Jan. 1, 1931) (1931) I § 50, 239–46.

The common law also dictated that it was legally impossible for a man to rape his wife. . . . A husband's "incapacity" to rape his wife was justified by the theory that " 'the marriage constitute[d] a blanket consent to sexual intimacy which the woman [could] revoke only by dissolving the marital relationship.' " *See, e.g.,* Jill Elaine Hasday, "Contest and Consent: A Legal History of Marital Rape," 88 *Calif. L. Rev.* 1373, 1376 n.9 (2000) (quoting Model Penal Code and

Commentaries, § 213.1 cmt. 8(c), at 342 (Official Draft and Revised Comments 1980)).

Concomitantly, dissolving the marital partnership via divorce was exceedingly difficult. Through the mid-twentieth century, divorce could be obtained only on a limited set of grounds, if at all. . . .

Perhaps unsurprisingly, the profoundly unequal status of men and women in marriage was frequently cited as justification for denying women equal rights in other arenas, including the workplace. "[S]tate courts made clear that the basis, and validity, of such laws lay in stereotypical beliefs about the appropriate roles of men and women." Hibbs v. Dep't of Human Res., 273 F.3d 844, 864 (9th Cir.2001), aff'd sub nom., Nevada Dep't of Human Res. v. Hibbs (2003). Justice Bradley infamously opined in 1887 that "the civil law, as well as nature herself, has always recognized a wide difference in the respective spheres and destinies of man and woman." Bradwell (Bradley, J., concurring). On this view, women could be excluded from various professions because "[t]he natural and proper timidity and delicacy which belongs to the female sex evidently unfits it for many of the occupations of civil life." Id. Instead, the law gave effect to the belief that "[t]he paramount destiny and mission of woman are to fulfill the noble and benign offices of wife and mother." Id.

As a result of this separate-spheres regime, " '[h]istorically, denial or curtailment of women's employment opportunities has been traceable directly to the pervasive presumption that women are mothers first, and workers second.' . . . Stereotypes about women's domestic roles [we]re reinforced by parallel stereotypes presuming a lack of domestic responsibilities for men." Hibbs. Likewise, social benefits programs historically distinguished between men and women on the assumption, grounded in the unequal marital status of men and women, that women were more likely to be homemakers, supported by their working husbands. See, e.g., Califano v. Goldfarb (1977); Weinberger v. Wiesenfeld (1975).

(ii) This asymmetrical regime began to unravel slowly in the nineteenth century, starting with the advent of Married Women's Property Acts, which allowed women to possess property in their own right for the first time. See, e.g., Reva B. Siegel, "The Modernization of Marital Status Law: Adjudicating Wives' Rights to Earnings, 1860–1930," 82 Geo. L.Rev. 2127 (1994). Eventually, state legislatures revised their laws. Today, of course, a married woman may enter contracts, sue and be sued without her husband's participation, and own and convey property. The advent of "no fault" divorce regimes in the late 1960s and early 1970s made marital dissolutions more common, and legislatures also directed family courts to impose child and spousal support obligations on divorcing couples without regard to gender. *See* Cott, *Public Vows,* at 205–06. As these legislative reforms were taking hold, "in 1971 . . . the Court f[ou]nd for the first time that a state law violated the Equal Protection Clause because it arbitrarily discriminated on the basis of sex." [*Reed.*]

This same legal transformation extended into the marital (and nonmarital) bedroom. Spousal rape has been criminalized in all states since 1993. *See, e.g.,* Sarah M. Harless, "From the Bedroom to the Courtroom: The Impact of Domestic Violence Law on Marital Rape Victims," 35 *Rutgers L.J.* 305, 318 (2003). Griswold v. Connecticut (1965), held that married couples have a fundamental privacy right to use contraceptives, and Eisenstadt v. Baird (1972), later applied equal protection principles to extend this right to single persons. More recently, Lawrence [v. Texas (2003)] clarified that licit, consensual sexual behavior is no longer confined to marriage, but is protected when it occurs, in private, between two consenting adults, regardless of their gender.

In the child custody context, mothers and fathers today are generally presumed to be equally fit parents. *See, e.g.,* Cott, *Public Vows,* at 206. Stanley v. Illinois (1972), for example, held invalid as an equal protection violation a state law that presumed unmarried fathers, but not unwed mothers, unfit as parents. Later, the Supreme Court expressly "reject[ed] . . . the claim that . . . [there is] any universal difference between maternal and paternal relations at every phase of a child's development." Caban v. Mohammed (1979). Likewise, both spouses in a marriage are now entitled to economic support without regard to gender. *See* Cott, at 206–07. Once again, equal protection adjudication contributed to this change: *Orr* struck down a state statutory scheme imposing alimony obligations on husbands but not wives.

In short, a combination of constitutional sex-discrimination adjudication, legislative changes, and social and cultural transformation has, in a sense, already rendered contemporary marriage "genderless," to use the phrase favored by the defendants. For, as a result of these transformative social, legislative, and doctrinal developments, "[g]ender no longer forms an essential part of marriage; marriage under law is a union of equals." *Perry,* 704 F.Supp.2d at 993. As a result, in the states that currently ban same-sex marriage, the legal norms that currently govern the institution of marriage are "genderless" in every respect *except* the requirement that would-be spouses be of different genders. With that exception, Idaho and Nevada's marriage regimes have jettisoned the rigid roles marriage as an institution once prescribed for men and women. In sum, "the sex-based classification contained in the[se] marriage laws," as the *only* gender classification that persists in some states' marriage statutes, is, at best, "a vestige of sex-role stereotyping" that long plagued marital regimes before the modern era, *see Baker,* 744 A.2d at 906 (Johnson, J., concurring in part and dissenting in part), and, at worst, an attempt to reintroduce gender roles.

The same-sex marriage bars constitute gender discrimination both facially and when recognized, in their historical context, both as resting on sex stereotyping and as a vestige of the sex-based legal rules once imbedded in the institution of marriage. They must be subject to intermediate scrutiny.

III. Idaho and Nevada's Same-Sex Marriage Prohibitions Fail Under Intermediate Scrutiny

For Idaho and Nevada's same-sex marriage prohibitions to survive the intermediate scrutiny applicable to sex discriminatory laws, it must be shown that these laws "serve important governmental objectives and [are] substantially related to achievement of those objectives." *Craig.* "The purpose of requiring that close relationship is to assure that the validity of a classification is determined through reasoned analysis rather than through the mechanical application of traditional, often inaccurate, assumptions about the proper roles of men and women." *Hogan.*

In part, the interests advanced by the defendants fail because they are interests in promoting and enforcing gender stereotyping and so simply are not legitimate governmental interests. And even if we assume that the other governmental objectives cited by the defendants are legitimate and important, the defendants have not shown that the same-sex marriage prohibitions are substantially related to achieving any of them.

The asserted interests fall into roughly three categories: (1) ensuring children are raised by parents who provide them with the purported benefits of "gender complementarity," also referred to as "gender diversity"; (2) "furthering the stability of family structures through benefits targeted at couples possessing biological procreative capacity," and/or discouraging "motherlessness" or "fatherlessness in the home"; and (3) promoting a "child-centric" rather than "adult-centric" model of marriage.[8] The defendants insist that "genderless

---

[8] The defendants also assert that the state has an interest in "accommodating religious freedom and reducing the potential for civic strife." But . . . even if allowing same-sex marriage were likely to lead to religious strife, which is highly doubtful, to say the least, that fact would not justify the denial of equal protection inherent in the gender-based classification of the same-sex marriage bars. See Watson v. City of Memphis (1963) (rejecting the city's proffered justification that delay in desegregating park facilities was

marriage run[s] counter to . . . [these] norms and ideals," which is why "man-woman marriage" must be preserved.

The Opinion of the Court thoroughly demonstrates why all of these interests are without merit as justifications for sexual orientation discrimination. [T]he justifications are likewise wholly insufficient under intermediate scrutiny to support the sex-based classifications at the core of these laws.

A. The Idaho defendants assert that the state has an interest in ensuring children have the benefit of parental "gender complementarity." There must be "space in the law for the distinct role of 'mother' [and] the distinct role of 'father' and therefore of their united, complementary role in raising offspring," the Idaho defendants insist. On a slightly different tack, the Nevada intervenors similarly opine that "[s]ociety has long recognized that diversity in education brings a host of benefits to students," and ask, "[i]f that is true in education, why not in parenting?"

Under the constitutional sex-discrimination jurisprudence of the last forty years, neither of these purported justifications can possibly pass muster as a justification for sex discrimination. Indeed, these justifications are laden with the very " 'baggage of sexual stereotypes' " the Supreme Court has repeatedly disavowed. *Califano v. Westcott* (quoting *Orr*).

(i) It should be obvious that the stereotypic notion "that the two sexes bring different talents to the parenting enterprise," runs directly afoul of the Supreme Court's repeated disapproval of "generalizations about 'the way women are,' " *VMI*, or "the way men are," as a basis for legislation. Just as *Orr* rejected gender-disparate alimony statutes "as effectively announcing the State's preference for an allocation of family responsibilities under which the wife plays a dependent role," so a state preference for supposed gender-specific parenting styles cannot serve as a legitimate reason for a sex-based classification.

This conclusion would follow "[e]ven [if] some statistical support can be conjured up for the generalization" that men and women behave differently as marital partners and/or parents, because laws that rely on gendered stereotypes about how men and women behave (or should behave) must be reviewed under intermediate scrutiny. *See J.E.B..* It has even greater force where, as here, the supposed difference in parenting styles lacks reliable empirical support, even "on

---

necessary to avoid interracial "turmoil," and explaining "constitutional rights may not be denied simply because of hostility to their assertion or exercise"). [Footnote by Judge Berzon.]

average."[9] Communicating such archaic gender-role stereotypes to children, or to parents and potential parents, is not a legitimate governmental interest, much less a substantial one.

(ii) The assertion that preserving "man-woman marriage" is permissible because the state has a substantial interest in promoting "diversity" has no more merit than the "gender complementarity" justification. . . .

[E]ven if it were true that, on average, women and men have different perspectives on some issues because of different life experiences, individual couples are at least as likely to exhibit conformity as diversity of personal characteristics. Sociological research suggests that individual married couples are more likely to be *similar* to each other in terms of political ideology, educational background, and economic background than they are to be dissimilar; despite the common saying that "opposites attract," in actuality it appears that "like attracts like." *See, e.g.,* John R. Alford et al., "The Politics of Mate Choice," 73:2 *J. Politics* 362, 376 (2011); Jeremy Greenwood et al., *Marry Your Like: Assortative Mating and Income Inequality* (Population Studies Ctr., Univ. Of Penn., Working Paper No. 14–1, at 1, 2014). Further, there is no evidence of which I am aware that gender is a better predictor of diversity of viewpoints or of parenting styles than other characteristics. . . .

In short, the defendants' asserted state interests in "gender complementarity" and "gender diversity" are not legitimate "important governmental objectives." *See Craig.* Accordingly, I do not address whether excluding same-sex couples from marriage is substantially related to this goal.

B. The defendants also argue that their states have an important interest in "encouraging marriage between opposite-sex partners" who have biological children, so that those children are raised in an intact marriage rather than in a cohabiting or single-parent household. Assuming that this purpose is in fact a "important governmental objective," the defendants have entirely failed to explain how excluding same-sex couples from marriage is substantially related to achieving the objective of furthering family stability.

(i) I will interpret the asserted state goal in preventing "fatherlessness" and "motherlessness" broadly. That is, I shall assume that the states want to discourage parents from abandoning their children by encouraging dual parenting over single parenting. If the asserted purpose were instead read

---

[9] As one of the plaintiffs' expert psychologists, Dr. Michael Lamb, explained, "[t]here . . . is no empirical support for the notion that the presence of both male and female role models in the home enhances the adjustment of children and adolescents." [Footnote by Judge Berzon.]

narrowly, as an interest in ensuring that a child has both a mother and a father in the home (rather than two mothers or two fathers), the justification would amount to the same justification as the asserted interest in "gender complementarity," and would fail for the same reason. That is, the narrower version of the family stability justification rests on impermissible gender stereotypes about the relative capacities of men and women.

Discouraging single parenting by excluding same-sex couples from marriage is oxymoronic, in the sense that it will likely achieve exactly the opposite of what the states say they seek to accomplish. The defendants' own evidence suggests that excluding same-sex couples from marriage renders their unions less stable, increasing the risk that the children of those couples will be raised by one parent rather than two.

True, an increasing number of children are now born and raised outside of marriage, a development that may well be undesirable. But that trend began apace well before the advent of same-sex marriage and has been driven by entirely different social and legal developments. The trend can be traced to declines in marriage rates, as well as to the rise in divorce rates after the enactment of "no fault" divorce regimes in the late 1960s and early 1970s. "The proportion of adults who declined to marry at all rose substantially between 1972 and 1998. . . . [In the same period,] [t]he divorce rate rose more furiously, to equal more than half the marriage rate, portending that at least one in two marriages would end in divorce." Cott, *Public Vows,* at 203. The defendants' assertion that excluding same-sex couples from marriage will do anything to reverse these trends is utterly unsubstantiated.

(ii) The defendants' appeal to biology is similarly without merit. Their core assertion is that the states have a substantial interest in channeling opposite-sex couples into marriage, so that any accidentally produced children are more likely to be raised in a two-parent household. But the exclusion of same-sex couples from the benefits and obligations of state-sanctioned marriage is assuredly not "substantially related," *Craig,* to achieving that goal.

The reason only opposite-sex couples should be allowed to marry, we are told by the defendants, is that they "possess the unique ability to create new life." But both same-sex and opposite-sex couples can and do produce children biologically related only to one member of the couple, via assisted reproductive technology or otherwise. And both same-sex and opposite-sex couples adopt children, belying the notion that the two groups necessarily differ as to their biological connection to the children they rear.

More importantly, the defendants "cannot explain how the failure of *opposite-sex* couples to accept responsibility for the children they create relates at all to the exclusion of same-sex couples from the benefits of marriage." *Baker,* 744 A.2d at 911 (Johnson, J., concurring in part and dissenting in part). For one thing, marriage has never been restricted to opposite-sex couples able to procreate; as noted earlier, the spousal relationship, economic and otherwise, has always been understood as a sufficient basis for state approval and regulation. For another, to justify sex discrimination, the state must explain why the *discriminatory feature* is closely related to the state interest. *See Hogan.* The states thus would have to explain, without reliance on sex-stereotypical notions, why the bans on same-sex marriage advance their interests in inducing more biological parents to marry each other. No such showing has been or can be made.

Biological parents' inducements to marry will remain exactly what they have always been if same-sex couples can marry. The legal benefits of marriage—taxation, spousal support, inheritance rights, familial rights to make decisions concerning the illness and death of a spouse, and so on—will not change. *See, e.g.* Turner v. Safley (1987). The only change will be that now-excluded couples will enjoy the same rights. As the sex-based exclusion of same-sex couples from marrying does not in any way enhance the marriage benefits available to opposite-sex couples, that exclusion does not substantially advance—or advance at all—the state interest in inducing opposite-sex couples to raise their biological children within a stable marriage.

(iii) Finally, the defendants argue that "the traditional marriage institution" or "man-woman marriage . . . is relatively but decidedly more child-centric" than "genderless marriage," which they insist is "relatively but decidedly more adult-centric."

These assertions are belied by history. As I have noted, "traditional marriage" was in fact quite "adult-centric." Marriage was, above all, an economic arrangement between spouses. *See, e.g., Cott, Public Vows,* at 54. Whether or not there were children, the law imposed support obligations, inheritance rules, and other rights and burdens upon married men and women. Moreover, couples unwilling or unable to procreate have never been prevented from marrying. Nor was infertility generally recognized as a ground for divorce or annulment under the old fault-based regime, even though sexual impotence was. *See, e.g.,* Vernier, I § 50, II § 68.

Further, the social concept of "companionate marriage"—that is, legal marriage for companionship purposes without the possibility of children—has existed since at least the 1920s. *See* Christina Simmons, *Making Marriage Modern: Women's Sexuality from the Progressive Era to World War II* 121 (2009). The Supreme Court called on this concept when it recognized the right of married couples to use contraception in 1965. *Griswold*. *Griswold* reasoned that, with or without procreation, marriage was "an association for as noble a purpose as any." *Id.*

Same-sex marriage is thus not inherently less "child-centric" than "traditional marriage." In both versions, the couple may bear or adopt and raise children, or not.

Finally, a related notion the defendants advance, that allowing same-sex marriage will render the marriage institution "genderless," in the sense that gender roles within opposite-sex marriages will be altered, is also ahistorical. As I have explained, those roles have already been profoundly altered by social, legislative, and adjudicative changes. All these changes were adopted toward the end of eliminating the gender-role impositions that previously inhered in the legal regulation of marriage.

In short, the "child-centric"/"adult-centric" distinction is an entirely ephemeral one, at odds with the current realities of marriage as an institution. There is simply no substantial relationship between discouraging an "adult-centric" model of marriage and excluding same-sex couples.

IV. Conclusion. . . .

I do not mean, by presenting this alternative analysis, to minimize the fact that the same-sex marriage bans necessarily have their greatest effect on lesbian, gay, bisexual, and transgender individuals. Still, it bears noting that the social exclusion and state discrimination against lesbian, gay, bisexual, and transgender people reflects, in large part, disapproval of their nonconformity with gender-based expectations.[12] That is, such individuals are often discriminated against because they are not acting or speaking or dressing as "real men" or "real women" supposedly do. "[S]tereotypes about homosexuality are directly related to our stereotypes about the proper roles of men and women." *Centola v. Potter,* 183 F.Supp.2d 403, 410 (D.Mass.2002); *see also* Andrew Koppelman, "Why Discrimination Against Lesbians and Gay Men is Sex Discrimination," 69 *N.Y.U. L.Rev.* 197 (1994). The same-sex marriage prohibitions, in other words,

---

12 Although not evidently represented among the plaintiff class, transgender people suffer from similar gender stereotyping expectations. *See, e.g.,* Schwenk v. Hartford, 204 F.3d 1187, 1201–02 (9th Cir.2000) (discrimination on the basis of transgender status is also gender discrimination). [Footnote by Judge Berzon.]

impose harms on sexual orientation and gender identity minorities precisely because they impose and enforce *gender*-normative behavior.

I do recognize, however, that the gender classification rubric does not adequately capture the essence of many of the restrictions targeted at lesbian, gay, and bisexual people. Employment discrimination, housing discrimination, and peremptory strikes on the basis of sexual orientation, to name a few of the exclusions gays, lesbians, and other sexual orientation minorities have faced, are primarily motivated by stereotypes about sexual orientation; by animus against people based on their nonconforming sexual orientation; and by distaste for same-sex sexual activity or the perceived personal characteristics of individuals who engage in such behavior. See, e.g., Romer v. Evans (1996); SmithKline Beecham Corp. v. Abbott Labs., 740 F.3d 471 (2014). And those sorts of restrictions do not turn directly on gender; they do not withhold a benefit, choice, or opportunity from an individual because that individual is a man or a woman. Although the gender stereotyping so typical of sex discrimination may be present, *see generally* Koppelman, 69 *N.Y.U. L.Rev.* 197, those restrictions are better analyzed as sexual orientation discrimination, as we did in *SmithKline*.

As to the same-sex marriage bans in particular, however, the gender discrimination rubric does squarely apply. . . . [T]he concepts and standards developed in more than forty years of constitutional sex discrimination jurisprudence rest on the understanding that "[s]anctioning sex-based classifications on the grounds that men and women, simply by virtue of their gender, necessarily play different roles in the lives of their children and in their relationships with each other causes concrete harm to women and to men throughout our society." Deborah A. Widiss et al., "Exposing Sex Stereotypes in Recent Same-Sex Marriage Jurisprudence," 30 *Harv. J.L. & Gender* 461, 505 (2007). In my view, the same-sex marriage bans belie that understanding, and, for that reason as well, cannot stand.

EDITORS' NOTES

(1) What is Judge Berzon's argument that bans on same-sex marriage violate the Equal Protection Clause? How does her equal protection argument differ from that offered by Judge Posner in Baskin v. Bogan (7th Cir. 2014; reprinted above)? Which argument is more cogent?

(2) What are Berzon's arguments that laws prohibiting same-sex marriage discriminate on the basis of gender? Are these arguments persuasive? Is

discrimination on the basis of sexual orientation more analogous to racial discrimination or to gender discrimination?

(3)   How do Berzon's equal protection arguments for a right to same-sex marriage compare with the arguments in Justice Kennedy's majority opinion in *Obergefell?* For example, what role does the history—and transformation—of marriage play in Berzon's opinion? How does her analysis of marriage compare with that of Kennedy in *Obergefell?* Is her evaluation of the states' appeal to preserving "gender complementarity" in marriage and parenting persuasive?

(4)   How does Berzon's proposed form of "intermediate scrutiny" differ from what we have called "rational basis scrutiny with bite" (the standard of review evidently applied in *Romer*, *Lawrence*, *Windsor*, and *Obergefell*)? From "strict scrutiny"?

(5)   There are several available arguments for recognizing a constitutional right of gays and lesbians to marry—as we have seen in the competing liberty and equality arguments in Baker v. State (1999; reprinted above), Goodridge v. Department of Public Health (2003; reprinted above), *Obergefell*, *Baskin*, and Berzon's concurrence in *Latta*. What criteria should we use in deciding which is or are most cogent?

———

OBERGEFELL V. HODGES

576 U.S. ___, 135 S.Ct. 2584, 192 L.Ed.2d 609 (2015)

[This case, invalidating statutes in Ohio, Michigan, Kentucky, and Tennessee limiting marriage to opposite-sex couples on the grounds that they denied same-sex couples the fundamental right to marry as guaranteed by the Fourteenth Amendment, is reprinted in Chapter 1.]

CHAPTER 5

Religious Liberty v. Gay Rights

Does the protection of gay rights conflict with the religious liberty of persons who oppose gay rights on religious grounds? If so, how does the U.S. constitutional order address such conflict? Answering those questions requires taking apart the oppositional framing to examine both what the term "religious liberty" entails and what falls within the scope of "gay rights." In what ways might these rights be in conflict? On some framings, the growing protection of LGBT persons through civil rights laws—such as state and local antidiscrimination laws—as well as through the inclusion of same-sex couples in the civil law of marriage bring with them increasing threats to the religious liberty of persons who view these developments as in conflict with their beliefs about gender, sexuality, family, and marriage. Scholarly books and articles as well as religious declarations use the frame of "emerging conflicts" or "rights in conflict" to capture this tension.[1] Some religious leaders warn of threats to religious liberty and call for robust protections of "conscience"—exemptions from civil law—to reduce those threats.

This chapter examines these evident conflicts between gay rights and religious liberty, along with constitutional mechanisms for addressing them. We reprint and discuss cases in which religious individuals, religious groups, nongovernmental associations, and even for-profit businesses have challenged state and federal laws, as well as public school and university policies, as violating their First Amendment rights. These asserted rights include not only the right to the "free exercise" of religion but also the rights to freedom of speech and association. A law also violates the First Amendment by "establishing" religion, that is, by government acting in a way that favors religion in general or one religion over others. Not all of the cases in this chapter involve

---

[1] For example, *Same-Sex Marriage and Religious Liberty: Emerging Conflicts*, Douglas Laycock et al., eds. (Lanham, MD: Rowman & Littlefield, 2008); *Religious Freedom and Gay Rights: Emerging Conflicts in North America and Europe*, Timothy Shah, ed., (New York: Oxford University Press, 2016).

gay rights. Indeed, one landmark case, Reynolds v. United States (1878), involves a challenge to a federal law against polygamy. Another, Employment Division v. Smith (1990), involves a challenge brought by Native Americans to a federal law against drug trafficking and abuse. *Smith* sets out a controversial standard for reviewing free exercise claims against laws enacted for general secular purposes, like combatting the drug trade. In addition to relying upon the First Amendment, persons with religious objections to civil law also invoke state and federal "Religious Freedom Restoration Acts" ("RFRAs"), enacted to protect against "substantial burdens" on the free exercise of religion. This chapter includes Hobby Lobby v. Burwell (2013), a challenge brought under the federal RFRA to the federal Affordable Care Act ("ACA") by for-profit companies seeking a religious exemption from the ACA's requirement that insurance plans cover contraception. In the post-Obergefell v. Hodges (2015) landscape, for-profit businesses owned by persons with religious objections to marriage by two persons of the same-sex similarly invoke RFRAs or newer "freedom of conscience protection" laws in quest of exemptions from state and federal laws that protect same-sex spouses and LGBT persons from discrimination or extend governmental benefits to them. How should these conflicts be resolved?

The dissenters in *Obergefell* warned that the majority's holding that same-sex couples had a fundamental right to marry threatened religious liberty. Justice Alito pictured a future in which religious believers who "cling" to the traditional understanding of marriage could still "whisper their thoughts [only] in their recesses of their homes," fearing that "if they repeat those views in public, they will risk being labeled as bigots and treated as such by governments, employers, and schools." Alito predicted that the majority's decision "will be used to vilify Americans who are unwilling to assent to the new orthodoxy" because the majority "compares traditional marriage laws to laws that denied equal protection for African-Americans and women."

Alito's dissent encapsulates several important dimensions of the problem of evaluating claims about threats to religious liberty flowing from a new constitutional landscape protecting gay rights. First, his contrast between private and public—freedom in the privacy of one's home versus treatment as a bigot in public—puts on the table the scope of the free exercise of religion. Is religious expression in the public square at risk? What and where is the public square? Another question involves the scope of religious expression. What limits may a public authority constitutionally impose upon it? Harper v. Poway (2006), a case reprinted in this chapter, asks if a public school attempting to teach tolerance of different sexual orientations may prohibit a student from wearing a t-shirt with a biblical quotation condemning homosexuals as sinners. Other issues concern the rights of religious believers who are engaged in commerce. Does the free exercise of religion include a constitutional right to conduct one's business in the marketplace in accordance with one's religious beliefs? May a believer who opposes same-sex marriage refuse to host a same-sex wedding reception in her restaurant, refuse to bake a cake for the wedding, or refuse to photograph the event? If a state antidiscrimination law forbids bakers, photographers, and other merchants from discriminating against LGBT persons, should merchants be able to assert a sincere religious objection to obeying the law? Do such merchants have a constitutional right to religious exemptions from civil rights laws or, indeed, any laws enacted for secular purposes?

Justice Alito was concerned that analogies between racial and gender discrimination, on the one hand, and discrimination on the basis of sexual orientation, on the other, will be "exploited" to "stamp out every vestige of dissent" and brand people with traditional beliefs about marriage as "bigots." Nearly half the states in the United States now include prohibition of discrimination on the basis of sexual orientation in their antidiscrimination laws; a number also include gender identity. What values do these laws express? If, as Justice Stevens observed in dissent in Boy Scouts of America v. Dale (2000), "every state law prohibiting discrimination is designed to replace prejudice with principle," does expansion of antidiscrimination laws to protect LGBT persons imply that prejudice against them is as intolerable as racism or sexism? In present-day political battles over the scope of religious exemptions from state antidiscrimination laws, this issue of analogy among forms of prejudice—and of discrimination—is heated and contested. Participants in these debates disagree about the relevance of earlier civil rights struggles and of the lessons one should draw from them in the present.

Justice Alito's dissent in *Obergefell* refers to resistance against a "new orthodoxy." This suggests a significant difference between civil rights protection for racial minorities and civil rights protection for LGBT persons. That difference could lie in the fact that earlier civil rights laws were often defended by an appeal to majoritarian religious beliefs, specifically, that persons of all races were children of God. Well into the late twentieth century, a believer who held that gay sex is sinful and that marriage is a divinely-created union between one man and one woman could experience a basic congruence between those views and the scope and content of civil and criminal law. In Bowers v. Hardwick (1986; reprinted in Chapter 4), for example, we saw that Chief Justice Burger in concurrence referred to "millennia of moral teaching" and "Judeao-Christian moral and ethical standards" in support of a traditional moral justification for Georgia's anti-sodomy law. The *Bowers* majority also treated traditional moral disapproval as a legitimate basis for criminalizing gay sex.

By the time of Romer v. Evans (1996; reprinted in Chapter 4), a number of municipalities had taken affirmative measures to protect people against discrimination on the basis of sexual orientation. This was true in the Colorado cities of Aspen and Boulder and in the county of Denver. Amendment 2 to the Colorado Constitution halted that process by barring local civil rights protection for LGBT persons in that state. One argument provided for Amendment 2 in the ballot information given to voters was: "Granting protected status to homosexual, lesbian, and bisexual persons may compel some individuals to violate their private consciences or to face legal sanctions for failure to comply. For some individuals, homosexuality, or bisexuality conflicts with their religious values and teachings or their private moral values."[2] Similarly, a number of religious organizations filed friend of the court briefs defending Amendment 2 because it preserved traditional moral judgments about homosexuality and also avoided conflicts with religious liberty.

In *Romer*, the first of Justice Kennedy's landmark gay-rights opinions, the majority struck down Amendment 2 as lacking any rational justification. The Court held that Amendment 2 was so sweeping in scope and imposed such a "broad and undifferentiated disability on a single named group," that it seemed to be rooted in little more than hostility or "animus" against homosexuals. By contrast, the dissenters insisted that what the Court deemed animus was nothing other than traditional moral disapproval and that such disapproval should be sufficient reason to uphold Amendment 2. Religious critics of *Romer* warned that it "effectively branded as a bigot any citizen who considers homosexuality immoral."[3] Critics also echoed Justice Scalia's warning in dissent that citizens could no longer use law to express "moral and social disapprobation" of homosexuality.

Charges that religious believers would be tarred with the brush of bigotry also followed the Court's decisions in Lawrence v. Texas (2003), United States v. Windsor (2013), and *Obergefell*. Those cases further highlighted the problem of congruence and conflict between traditional moral disapproval and constitutional principles. They also represent an important shift in the Court's treatment of moral disapproval as a basis for law. In an often-quoted passage of

---

[2] Legis. Counsel of the Colo. Gen. Assemb., An Analysis of 1992 Ballot Proposals, Gen Assemb. 58–369, at 9 (1992).

[3] Charles W. Colson, "The End of Democracy? Kingdoms in Conflict," *First Things* (Nov. 1996).

her *Lawrence* concurrence, Justice O'Connor invoked *Romer* to observe that: "Moral disapproval of a group cannot be a legitimate governmental interest under the Equal Protection Clause." In her view, Texas's law singling out and criminalizing only sodomy by same-sex couples made one class of persons criminal "based solely on the State's moral disapproval of that class." This, she said, Texas could not do. By contrast, she indicated that "unlike the moral disapproval of same-sex relations ... other reasons exist to promote the institution of marriage beyond mere moral disapproval of an excluded group."[4] O'Connor thus disagreed with Scalia's warning that *Lawrence* put the Court on a slippery slope not only to recognizing a right of gays and lesbians to marry but also to "the end of all morals legislation." In subsequent battles over access by same-sex couples to marriage, proponents and opponents frequently cited these different portions of O'Connor's concurrence.

The majority in *Lawrence* stressed the need to distinguish between opinions about the morality of same-sex intimacy and the demands of the Constitution. The justices included their own moral views in this statement. A passage in *Lawrence* echoed the joint opinion in Planned Parenthood v. Casey (1992), stating that although persons have differing and conscientious views about the morality of same-sex intimacy (and abortion), the justices' "obligation is to define the liberty of all, not to mandate our own moral code."

The issue of congruence and conflict between popular moral views and law, as well as the Court's limits upon the public's moral disapproval as a permissible justification, touch upon a fundamental issue discussed in Chapters 2, 3, and 4: What counts as a reason for accepting or rejecting a claim to fairness and equality before the law? Believing that criminal and civil law should be congruent with her religious beliefs, a believer may appeal to such beliefs as a basis for upholding such a law. Thus, a believer might cite Leviticus 18:22 as authority for Colorado's Amendment 2. She would even have a First Amendment right to do so. But she would have no First Amendment right to a law that criminalizes conduct condemned in Leviticus 18:22. More generally, believers' right to believe and profess their beliefs does not entail a right to laws that are congruent with their beliefs. Indeed, the Establishment Clause of the First Amendment forbids government from enacting into law a particular religion's orthodoxy for the sake of that orthodoxy. True, for much of U.S. history, criminal laws about sexuality as well as civil law (such as certain features of family law) have been closely congruent with traditional religious morality confining sexuality to heterosexual marriage and prescribing gender hierarchy in marriage.

---

[4]   Lawrence v. Texas, 539 U.S. 558, 577 (2003) (O'Connor, J., concurring).

Nonetheless, significant areas of the civil law and religious law have been in sharp conflict. In Griswold v. Connecticut (1965), for example, by recognizing a constitutional right of a married couple to use contraception, the Court reflected a view of marriage sharply opposed to the teaching of some religious faiths about the procreative purpose of marital sex. The same holds for Eisenstadt v. Baird (1972), which, by upholding a right of unmarried couples to use contraceptives, conflicts with religions that condemn both contraception and fornication. The same is also true with respect to no-fault divorce, some form of which is available in all of the states despite its conflict with the teaching of the Catholic Church, the nation's largest religious denomination. Criminal and civil laws in the United States are thus far from congruent with religious teachings about sexuality, gender, and family. It is useful to keep this fact in mind in assessing present-day claims for exemptions from civil laws that conflict with religious beliefs.

Consider the following two quite different statements about the United States: (1) "America is a Christian nation" and (2) "What makes America distinctive is the separation of church and state and the protection of religious freedom so that people of many faiths can live together peacefully." The person who believes there should be congruence between his or her religious faith and civil law might endorse this first statement. If so, the failure of civil law to reflect "God's law" would be a reason to resist it. Consider the example of Kentucky county clerk Kim Davis, who refused to issue marriage licenses to same-sex couples: "To issue a marriage license which conflicts with God's definition of marriage, with my name affixed to the certificate, would violate my conscience. . . . It is about marriage and God's word."[5] Davis was not alone. Officials in other states also asserted that "natural marriage cannot be redefined by government."[6] These statements reflect a view not only that God's law should prevail in a conflict with civil law, but also that the definition of civil marriage should conform to a religious definition of marriage.

We emphasize that while this chapter focuses on conflicts between religious liberty and gay rights, not every religious institution perceives such a conflict. To the contrary, religious organizations have been on both sides in all four of the Court's decisions advancing the constitutional liberty and equality of gay men and lesbians. For example, countering religious arguments in support of

---

[5]   Alan Blinder and Richard Perez-Pena, "Kentucky Clerk Denies Same-Sex Marriage Licenses, Defying Court," *N.Y. Times*, Sept. 1, 2015.

[6]   Alan Blinder and Richard Fausset, "Clerk Who Said 'No' Won't Be Alone in Courts," *N.Y. Times*, Sept. 2, 2015.

Colorado's Amendment 2, some religious organizations filed amici curiae briefs in *Romer* arguing that the amendment invited discrimination that was contrary to their religious beliefs. Further, they contended that Amendment 2 was unconstitutional because it "constitutes State endorsement of one set of religious beliefs over all others."[7] Some religious amici asserted the normative good of loving homosexual relationships, describing them as "intimate to the degree of being sacred" (invoking *Griswold*'s famous description of marriage).[8] Amici also grounded their support for gay rights in the same religious teachings that inspired the civil rights movement and referred to "the civic religion of the United States" as guaranteeing "equal dignity of every person."[9]

In the Court's two marriage cases, *Windsor* and *Obergefell*, religious organizations similarly weighed in on both sides.[10] In *Windsor* some religious organizations contended that measures like the Defense of Marriage Act (DOMA) were rational responses to the increased threats to religious liberty from civil laws permitting same-sex couples to marry;[11] they warned that "redefining marriage imperils religious liberty and oftentimes requires that freedom of conscience be sacrificed to the newly regnant orthodoxy."[12] By contrast, religious amici opposing DOMA emphasized the distinction between civil and religious marriage, arguing that religious denominations were free to conduct marriages under their auspices as they wished. They also argued that appropriately crafted religious exemptions were a means of ensuring religious liberty.[13] Religious amici in *Obergefell* also supported marriage equality by emphasizing the distinction between civil and religious marriage. These amici

---

[7] Brief Amicus Curiae of the American Friends Service Committee et al. in Support of Respondents at 1, Romer v. Evans, 517 U.S. 620 (1996) (No. 94–1039).

[8] Brief for Amici Curiae of Affirmation: United Methodists for Gay, Lesbian, and Bisexual Concerns et al. As Amici Curiae in Support of Respondents at 2, Romer v. Evans, 517 U.S. 620 (1996) (No. 94–1039).

[9] Ibid., 11.

[10] For an analysis of amicus curiae briefs filed in Romer v. Evans (1996) and United States v. Windsor (2013), see Linda C. McClain, "From *Romer v. Evans* to *United States v. Windsor*: Law as a Vehicle for Moral Disapproval in Amendment 2 and the Defense of Marriage Act," 20 *Duke Journal of Gender Law & Policy* 351 (2013). On *Obergefell*, see Robert P. Jones, "Religious Americans Support Gay Marriage," *Atlantic*, April 28, 2015.

[11] Brief for Becket Fund for Religious Liberty as Amicus Curiae Supporting Hollingsworth and the Bipartisan Legal Advisory Group (on the Merits), at 29, United States v. Windsor, 133 S. Ct. 2675 (2013) (No. 12–144 and No. 12–307).

[12] Brief for Manhattan Declaration as Amicus Curiae Supporting Respondent Bipartisan Legal Advisory Group, at 3–4, United States v. Windsor, 133 S. Ct. 2675 (2013) (No. 12–307).

[13] Brief for the Bishops of the Episcopal Church in the States of California [and nine other states plus the District of Columbia], et al., as Amici Curiae Supporting Respondent Edith Schlain Windsor, at 3, United States v. Windsor, 133 S. Ct. 2675 (2013) (No. 12–307).

argued that "[e]liminating discrimination in civil marriage will not impinge upon religious doctrine, conscience, or practice."[14]

The distinction between civil and religious marriage is critical to framing the conflict between religious liberty and gay rights. This distinction enables states to extend civil marriage to same-sex couples without affecting religious marriages. It is also important to understanding the scope of religious exemptions. As the official supporting statement for New York's Marriage Equality Act says: "[T]his bill grants equal access to the government-created legal institution of civil marriage, while leaving the religious institution of marriage to its own separate, and fully autonomous sphere."[15] New York's law goes on to provide that "no member of the clergy can be compelled to perform any marriage ceremony"—a protection that few would doubt the First Amendment ensures. The law also provides that religious institutions and benevolent organizations may "choose who may use their facilities and halls for marriage ceremonies and celebrations, to whom they rent their housing accommodations, or to whom they provide religious services, consistent with their religious principles."[16] This Act does not, however, exempt public officials from issuing marriage licenses, nor does it extend exemptions to for-profit businesses that are considered "public accommodations" under state antidiscrimination laws. As examined later in this chapter, some of the most contentious issues at this writing, post-*Obergefell*, involve claims by clerks like Kim Davis and by merchants engaged in commerce who contend that, due to their religious faith, providing goods and services to a same-sex couple in connection with their wedding would make them complicit in sin. What sort of guidance does First Amendment jurisprudence provide in assessing these conflicts? How do principles of liberty and equality under the Fourteenth Amendment aid in doing so? Of what relevance are past battles over discrimination in public accommodations? Over objections to interracial marriage? As you read the cases in this chapter, keep these questions in mind.

Justice Scalia's majority opinion in *Smith* casts a cautionary pall over this discussion. If individuals can exempt themselves from generally enacted secular laws on religious grounds, Scalia warned, then each conscience will become a law unto itself. In the gay rights context, if photographers, bakers, and businesses generally can refuse service to same-sex couples on religious grounds,

---

14   Brief for President of the House of Deputies of the Episcopal Church et al., as Amicus Curiae Supporting Petitioners, at 4, Obergefell v. Hodges, 135 S. Ct. 2584 (2015).

15   A8354, "Statement in Support."

16   Ibid.; *see also* Marriage Equality Act, N.Y. Domestic Relations Law § 10–a (2016) (codifying A8354, 2011–2012 Sess. (N.Y. 2011)).

they can cite religion and refuse to employ gays and lesbians, and no law can secure general protection from discrimination in employment and public accommodations on the basis of sexual orientation (or gender identity). Indeed, such general protection would be at odds with some recently enacted state laws that instead afford expansive protection of "freedom of conscience" of religious persons and organizations from *governmental* "discrimination" for acting on their "sincerely held religious belief or moral conviction" about marriage, sexual conduct, and gender identity in numerous public and private contexts.[17] One is then left to wonder where this reasoning about free exercise of religion might stop. May some clerks invoke their religious freedom in refusing to issue not only marriage licenses but also certificates of adoption or even a registration of title in jointly owned property to gay couples, especially if other clerks were willing to perform these functions? May a police officer cite Leviticus (and Justice Thomas's statement in dissent in *Obergefell* that the Constitution guarantees no positive rights) and refuse protection to a gay man under physical assault by homophobic thugs? Government would eventually have to assert power to decide which claims of religious exemption to honor and which to reject. We can surely doubt that such a power would be consistent with the First Amendment. But then we can also doubt that Americans ever enjoyed, or in the nature of civic life could possibly have enjoyed, absolute freedom of religious exercise.

I. CONFLICTS BETWEEN GAY RIGHTS AND FREEDOMS OF ASSOCIATION AND SPEECH: CIVIL SOCIETY AND EDUCATIONAL INSTITUTIONS

"The forced inclusion of an unwanted person in a group infringes the group's freedom of expressive association if the presence of that person affects in a significant way the group's ability to advocate public or private viewpoints."—CHIEF JUSTICE REHNQUIST

"Under the majority's reasoning, an openly gay male is irreversibly affixed with the label 'homosexual.' That label, even though unseen, communicates a message that permits his exclusion wherever he goes. . . . [R]eliance on such a

---

17   The reference is to H.B. 1523, Mississippi's new law, discussed later in this Chapter.

justification is tantamount to a constitutionally prescribed symbol of inferiority."—JUSTICE STEVENS

BOY SCOUTS OF AMERICA V. DALE

530 U.S. 640, 120 S.Ct. 2446, 147 L.Ed.2d 554 (2000)

■ CHIEF JUSTICE REHNQUIST delivered the opinion of the Court.

Petitioners are the Boy Scouts of America and the Monmouth Council, a division of the Boy Scouts of America (collectively, Boy Scouts). The Boy Scouts is a private, not-for-profit organization engaged in instilling its system of values in young people. The Boy Scouts asserts that homosexual conduct is inconsistent with the values it seeks to instill. Respondent is James Dale, a former Eagle Scout whose adult membership in the Boy Scouts was revoked when the Boy Scouts learned that he is an avowed homosexual and gay rights activist. The New Jersey Supreme Court held that New Jersey's public accommodations law requires that the Boy Scouts readmit Dale. This case presents the question whether applying New Jersey's public accommodations law in this way violates the Boy Scouts' First Amendment right of expressive association. We hold that it does.

I

James Dale entered Scouting in 1978 at the age of eight by joining Monmouth Council's Cub Scout Pack 142. Dale became a Boy Scout in 1981 and remained a Scout until he turned 18. By all accounts, Dale was an exemplary Scout. In 1988, he achieved the rank of Eagle Scout, one of Scouting's highest honors.

Dale applied for adult membership in the Boy Scouts in 1989. The Boy Scouts approved his application for the position of assistant scoutmaster of Troop 73. Around the same time, Dale left home to attend Rutgers University. After arriving at Rutgers, Dale first acknowledged to himself and others that he is gay. He quickly became involved with, and eventually became the copresident of, the Rutgers University Lesbian/Gay Alliance. In 1990, Dale attended a seminar addressing the psychological and health needs of lesbian and gay teenagers. A newspaper covering the event interviewed Dale about his advocacy of homosexual teenagers' need for gay role models. In early July 1990, the newspaper published the interview and Dale's photograph over a caption identifying him as the copresident of the Lesbian/Gay Alliance.

Later that month, Dale received a letter from Monmouth Council Executive James Kay revoking his adult membership. Dale wrote to Kay requesting the reason for Monmouth Council's decision. Kay responded by letter that the Boy Scouts "specifically forbid membership to homosexuals."

In 1992, Dale filed a complaint against the Boy Scouts in the New Jersey Superior Court. The complaint alleged that the Boy Scouts had violated New Jersey's public accommodations statute and its common law by revoking Dale's membership based solely on his sexual orientation. New Jersey's public accommodations statute prohibits, among other things, discrimination on the basis of sexual orientation in places of public accommodation.

The New Jersey Supreme Court . . . held that the Boy Scouts was a place of public accommodation subject to the public accommodations law, that the organization was not exempt from the law under any of its express exceptions, and that the Boy Scouts violated the law by revoking Dale's membership based on his avowed homosexuality. . . .

II

In Roberts v. United States Jaycees (1984), we observed that "implicit in the right to engage in activities protected by the First Amendment" is "a corresponding right to associate with others in pursuit of a wide variety of political, social, economic, educational, religious, and cultural ends." This right is crucial in preventing the majority from imposing its views on groups that would rather express other, perhaps unpopular, ideas. See *ibid.* (stating that protection of the right to expressive association is "especially important in preserving political and cultural diversity and in shielding dissident expression from suppression by the majority"). . . .

The forced inclusion of an unwanted person in a group infringes the group's freedom of expressive association if the presence of that person affects in a significant way the group's ability to advocate public or private viewpoints. But the freedom of expressive association, like many freedoms, is not absolute. We have held that the freedom could be overridden "by regulations adopted to serve compelling state interests, unrelated to the suppression of ideas, that cannot be achieved through means significantly less restrictive of associational freedoms." *Roberts.*

To determine whether a group is protected by the First Amendment's expressive associational right, we must determine whether the group engages in "expressive association." . . . The Boy Scouts is a private, nonprofit organization. According to its mission statement:

It is the mission of the Boy Scouts of America to serve others by helping to instill values in young people and, in other ways, to prepare them to make ethical choices over their lifetime in achieving their full potential.

The values we strive to instill are based on those found in the Scout Oath and Law:

Scout Oath

On my honor I will do my best

To do my duty to God and my country

and to obey the Scout Law;

To help other people at all times;

To keep myself physically strong,

mentally awake, and morally straight.

Scout Law

A Scout is:

Trustworthy	Obedient
Loyal	Cheerful
Helpful	Thrifty
Friendly	Brave
Courteous	Clean
Kind	Reverent.

Thus, the general mission of the Boy Scouts is clear: "[T]o instill values in young people." The Boy Scouts seeks to instill these values by having its adult leaders spend time with the youth members, instructing and engaging them in activities like camping, archery, and fishing. During the time spent with the youth members, the scoutmasters and assistant scoutmasters inculcate them with the Boy Scouts' values—both expressly and by example. It seems indisputable that an association that seeks to transmit such a system of values engages in expressive activity.

Given that the Boy Scouts engages in expressive activity, we must determine whether the forced inclusion of Dale as an assistant scoutmaster would significantly affect the Boy Scouts' ability to advocate public or private viewpoints. This inquiry necessarily requires us first to explore, to a limited extent, the nature of the Boy Scouts' view of homosexuality.

The values the Boy Scouts seeks to instill are "based on" those listed in the Scout Oath and Law. The Boy Scouts explains that the Scout Oath and Law provide "a positive moral code for living; they are a list of 'do's' rather than 'don'ts.' " The Boy Scouts asserts that homosexual conduct is inconsistent with the values embodied in the Scout Oath and Law, particularly with the values represented by the terms "morally straight" and "clean."

Obviously, the Scout Oath and Law do not expressly mention sexuality or sexual orientation. And the terms "morally straight" and "clean" are by no means self-defining. Different people would attribute to those terms very different meanings. For example, some people may believe that engaging in homosexual conduct is not at odds with being "morally straight" and "clean." And others may believe that engaging in homosexual conduct is contrary to being "morally straight" and "clean." The Boy Scouts says it falls within the latter category.

The New Jersey Supreme Court analyzed the Boy Scouts' beliefs and found that the "exclusion of members solely on the basis of their sexual orientation is inconsistent with Boy Scouts' commitment to a diverse and 'representative' membership . . . [and] contradicts Boy Scouts' overarching objective to reach 'all eligible youth.' " . . . But our cases reject this sort of inquiry; it is not the role of the courts to reject a group's expressed values because they disagree with those values or find them internally inconsistent.

The Boy Scouts asserts that it "teach[es] that homosexual conduct is not morally straight," and that it does "not want to promote homosexual conduct as a legitimate form of behavior." We accept the Boy Scouts' assertion. . . .

We must then determine whether Dale's presence as an assistant scoutmaster would significantly burden the Boy Scouts' desire to not "promote homosexual conduct as a legitimate form of behavior." As we give deference to an association's assertions regarding the nature of its expression, we must also give deference to an association's view of what would impair its expression. That is not to say that an expressive association can erect a shield against antidiscrimination laws simply by asserting that mere acceptance of a member from a particular group would impair its message. But here Dale, by his own admission, is one of a group of gay Scouts who have "become leaders in their community and are open and honest about their sexual orientation." Dale was the copresident of a gay and lesbian organization at college and remains a gay rights activist. Dale's presence in the Boy Scouts would, at the very least, force the organization to send a message, both to the youth members and the world, that the Boy Scouts accepts homosexual conduct as a legitimate form of behavior.

Hurley v. Irish-American Gay, Lesbian and Bisexual Group of Boston, Inc. (1995) is illustrative on this point. There we considered whether the application of Massachusetts' public accommodations law to require the organizers of a private St. Patrick's Day parade to include among the marchers an Irish-American gay, lesbian, and bisexual group, GLIB, violated the parade organizers' First Amendment rights. We noted that the parade organizers did not wish to exclude the GLIB members because of their sexual orientations, but because they wanted to march behind a GLIB banner. . . .

Here, we have found that the Boy Scouts believes that homosexual conduct is inconsistent with the values it seeks to instill in its youth members; it will not "promote homosexual conduct as a legitimate form of behavior." As the presence of GLIB in Boston's St. Patrick's Day parade would have interfered with the parade organizers' choice not to propound a particular point of view, the presence of Dale as an assistant scoutmaster would just as surely interfere with the Boy Scouts' choice not to propound a point of view contrary to its beliefs. . . .

Having determined that the Boy Scouts is an expressive association and that the forced inclusion of Dale would significantly affect its expression, we inquire whether the application of New Jersey's public accommodations law to require that the Boy Scouts accept Dale as an assistant scoutmaster runs afoul of the Scouts' freedom of expressive association. We conclude that it does.

State public accommodations laws were originally enacted to prevent discrimination in traditional places of public accommodation—like inns and trains. See, *e.g., Hurley* (explaining the history of Massachusetts' public accommodations law); Romer v. Evans (1996) (describing the evolution of public accommodations laws). Over time, the public accommodations laws have expanded to cover more places.[2] New Jersey's statutory definition of " '[a] place of public accommodation' " is extremely broad. The term is said to "include, but not be limited to," a list of over 50 types of places. . . . Many on the list are what

---

[2]   Public accommodations laws have also broadened in scope to cover more groups; they have expanded beyond those groups that have been given heightened equal protection scrutiny under our cases. See *Romer*. Some municipal ordinances have even expanded to cover criteria such as prior criminal record, prior psychiatric treatment, military status, personal appearance, source of income, place of residence, and political ideology . . . . [Footnote by the Court.]

one would expect to be places where the public is invited. For example, the statute includes as places of public accommodation taverns, restaurants, retail shops, and public libraries. But the statute also includes places that often may not carry with them open invitations to the public, like summer camps and roof gardens. In this case, the New Jersey Supreme Court went a step further and applied its public accommodations law to a private entity without even attempting to tie the term "place" to a physical location.[3] As the definition of "public accommodation" has expanded from clearly commercial entities, such as restaurants, bars, and hotels, to membership organizations such as the Boy Scouts, the potential for conflict between state public accommodations laws and the First Amendment rights of organizations has increased.

We recognized in cases such as *Roberts* that States have a compelling interest in eliminating discrimination against women in public accommodations. But . . . we went on to conclude that the enforcement of these statutes would not materially interfere with the ideas that the organization sought to express. . . .

. . . We have already concluded that a state requirement that the Boy Scouts retain Dale as an assistant scoutmaster would significantly burden the organization's right to oppose or disfavor homosexual conduct. The state interests embodied in New Jersey's public accommodations law do not justify such a severe intrusion on the Boy Scouts' rights to freedom of expressive association. That being the case, we hold that the First Amendment prohibits the State from imposing such a requirement through the application of its public accommodations law.

Justice Stevens' dissent makes much of its observation that the public perception of homosexuality in this country has changed. Indeed, it appears that homosexuality has gained greater societal acceptance. But this is scarcely an argument for denying First Amendment protection to those who refuse to accept these views. The First Amendment protects expression, be it of the popular variety or not. See, e.g., Texas v. Johnson (1989); Brandenburg v. Ohio (1969). And the fact that an idea may be embraced and advocated by increasing numbers of people is all the more reason to protect the First Amendment rights of those who wish to voice a different view. . . .

We are not, as we must not be, guided by our views of whether the Boy Scouts' teachings with respect to homosexual conduct are right or wrong; public

---

[3] Four State Supreme Courts and one United States Court of Appeals have ruled that the Boy Scouts is not a place of public accommodation. No federal appellate court or state supreme court—except the New Jersey Supreme Court in this case—has reached a contrary result. [Footnote by the Court.]

or judicial disapproval of a tenet of an organization's expression does not justify the State's effort to compel the organization to accept members where such acceptance would derogate from the organization's expressive message. "While the law is free to promote all sorts of conduct in place of harmful behavior, it is not free to interfere with speech for no better reason than promoting an approved message or discouraging a disfavored one, however enlightened either purpose may strike the government." *Hurley.*

[*Reversed.*]

■ JUSTICE STEVENS, with whom JUSTICE SOUTER, JUSTICE GINSBURG, and JUSTICE BREYER join, dissenting.

Because every state law prohibiting discrimination is designed to replace prejudice with principle, Justice Brandeis' comment on the States' right to experiment with "things social" is directly applicable to this case.

> To stay experimentation in things social and economic is a grave responsibility. Denial of the right to experiment may be fraught with serious consequences to the Nation. It is one of the happy incidents of the federal system that a single courageous State may, if its citizens choose, serve as a laboratory; and try novel social and economic experiments without risk to the rest of the country. This Court has the power to prevent an experiment. We may strike down the statute which embodies it on the ground that, in our opinion, the measure is arbitrary, capricious or unreasonable. We have power to do this, because the Due Process Clause has been held by the Court applicable to matters of substantive law as well as to matters of procedure. But in the exercise of this high power, we must be ever on our guard, lest we erect our prejudices into legal principles. If we would guide by the light of reason, we must let our minds be bold. New State Ice Co. v. Liebmann (1932) (dissenting opinion).

In its "exercise of this high power" today, the Court does not accord this "courageous State" the respect that is its due.

The majority holds that New Jersey's law violates Boy Scouts of America's ["BSA"] right to associate and its right to free speech. But that law does not "impos[e] any serious burdens" on BSA's "collective effort on behalf of [its] shared goals," *Jaycees,* nor does it force BSA to communicate any message that it does not wish to endorse. New Jersey's law, therefore, abridges no constitutional right of BSA. . . .

It is plain as the light of day that neither one of [the] principles—"morally straight" and "clean"—says the slightest thing about homosexuality. Indeed, neither term in the Boy Scouts' Law and Oath expresses any position whatsoever on sexual matters. . . .

. . . [U]ntil today, we have never once found a claimed right to associate in the selection of members to prevail in the face of a State's antidiscrimination law. To the contrary, we have squarely held that a State's antidiscrimination law does not violate a group's right to associate simply because the law conflicts with that group's exclusionary membership policy. . . .

[I]n *Jaycees*, we asked whether Minnesota's Human Rights Law requiring the admission of women "impose[d] any *serious burdens*" on the group's "collective effort on behalf of [its] *shared goals*" (emphases added). Notwithstanding the group's obvious publicly stated exclusionary policy, we did not view the inclusion of women as a "serious burden" on the Jaycees' ability to engage in the protected speech of its choice. Similarly, in *Rotary Club* [1987], we asked whether California's [antidiscrimination] law would "affect in any *significant way* the existing members' ability" to engage in their protected speech, or whether the law would require the clubs "to abandon their *basic goals*" (emphases added). . . . Accordingly, it is necessary to examine what, exactly, are BSA's shared goals and the degree to which its expressive activities would be burdened, affected, or restrained by including homosexuals.

The evidence before this Court makes it exceptionally clear that BSA has, at most, simply adopted an exclusionary membership policy and has no shared goal of disapproving of homosexuality. BSA's mission statement and federal charter say nothing on the matter; its official membership policy is silent; its Scout Oath and Law—and accompanying definitions—are devoid of any view on the topic; its guidance for Scouts and Scoutmasters on sexuality declare that such matters are "not construed to be Scouting's proper area," but are the province of a Scout's parents and pastor; and BSA's posture respecting religion tolerates a wide variety of views on the issue of homosexuality. Moreover, there is simply no evidence that BSA otherwise teaches anything in this area, or that it instructs Scouts on matters involving homosexuality in ways not conveyed in the Boy Scout or Scoutmaster Handbooks. In short, Boy Scouts of America is simply silent on homosexuality. There is no shared goal or collective effort to foster a belief about homosexuality at all—let alone one that is significantly burdened by admitting homosexuals.

As in *Jaycees*, there is "no basis in the record for concluding that admission of [homosexuals] will impede the [Boy Scouts'] ability to engage in [its] protected activities or to disseminate its preferred views" and New Jersey's law "requires no change in [BSA's] creed." . . . And like *Rotary Club*, New Jersey's law "does not require [BSA] to abandon or alter any of" its activities. . . .

The majority pretermits this entire analysis. It finds that BSA in fact " 'teach[es] that homosexual conduct is not morally straight.' " This conclusion, remarkably, rests entirely on statements in BSA's briefs. Moreover, the majority insists that we must "give deference to an association's assertions regarding the nature of its expression" and "we must also give deference to an association's view of what would impair its expression." So long as the record "contains written evidence" to support a group's bare assertion, "[w]e need not inquire further." Once the organization "asserts" that it engages in particular expression, *ibid.*, "[w]e cannot doubt" the truth of that assertion.

This is an astounding view of the law. I am unaware of any previous instance in which our analysis of the scope of a constitutional right was determined by looking at what a litigant asserts in his or her brief and inquiring no further. It is even more astonishing in the First Amendment area, because, as the majority itself acknowledges, "we are obligated to independently review the factual record." It is an odd form of independent review that consists of deferring entirely to whatever a litigant claims. . . .

The majority . . . does not rest its conclusion on the claim that Dale will use his position as a bully pulpit. Rather, it contends that Dale's mere presence among the Boy Scouts will itself force the group to convey a message about homosexuality—even if Dale has no intention of doing so. . . .

The majority's argument relies exclusively on *Hurley*. Dale's inclusion in the Boy Scouts is nothing like the case in *Hurley*. His participation sends no cognizable message to the Scouts or to the world. Unlike GLIB, Dale did not carry a banner or a sign; he did not distribute any factsheet; and he expressed no intent to send any message. If there is any kind of message being sent, then, it is by the mere act of joining the Boy Scouts.

The only apparent explanation for the majority's holding . . . is that homosexuals are simply so different from the rest of society that their presence alone—unlike any other individual's—should be singled out for special First Amendment treatment. Under the majority's reasoning, an openly gay male is irreversibly affixed with the label "homosexual." That label, even though unseen, communicates a message that permits his exclusion wherever he goes. His openness is the sole and sufficient justification for his ostracism. Though unintended, reliance on such a justification is tantamount to a constitutionally prescribed symbol of inferiority. As counsel for BSA remarked, Dale "put a banner around his neck when he . . . got himself into the newspaper. . . . He created a reputation. . . . He can't take that banner off. He put it on himself and, indeed, he has continued to put it on himself." . . .

Unfavorable opinions about homosexuals "have ancient roots." Bowers v. Hardwick (1986). Like equally atavistic opinions about certain racial groups, those roots have been nourished by sectarian doctrine. *Id.* (Burger, C.J., concurring); Loving v. Virginia (1967).[27] See also Mathews v. Lucas (1976) (Stevens, J., dissenting) ("Habit, rather than analysis, makes it seem acceptable and natural to distinguish between male and female, alien and citizen, legitimate and illegitimate; for too much of our history there was the same inertia in distinguishing between black and white"). Over the years, however, interaction with real people, rather than mere adherence to traditional ways of thinking about members of unfamiliar classes, have modified those opinions. . . .

That such prejudices are still prevalent and that they have caused serious and tangible harm to countless members of the class New Jersey seeks to protect are established matters of fact that neither the Boy Scouts nor the Court disputes. That harm can only be aggravated by the creation of a constitutional shield for a policy that is itself the product of a habitual way of thinking about strangers. As Justice Brandeis so wisely advised, "we must be ever on our guard, lest we erect our prejudices into legal principles."

If we would guide by the light of reason, we must let our minds be bold. I respectfully dissent.

■ JUSTICE SOUTER, with whom JUSTICE GINSBURG and JUSTICE BREYER join, dissenting. . . .

EDITORS' NOTES

(1)   Chief Justice Rehnquist's majority opinion emphasizes the role of the Boy Scouts of America (BSA) as seeking to instill its "system of values in young people." Is Rehnquist or Justice Stevens, in dissent, more persuasive on what

---

[27] In *Loving*, the trial judge gave this explanation of the rationale for Virginia's antimiscegenation statute: "Almighty God created the races white, black, yellow, malay and red, and he placed them on separate continents. And but for the interference with his arrangement there would be no cause for such marriages. The fact that he separated the races shows that he did not intend for the races to mix." [Footnote by Justice Stevens.]

those values were with respect to homosexuality? Did the majority opinion give too much deference to the BSA's claims about the burden the New Jersey law would place on its ability to express its message and instill values? What if a white supremacist/separatist group objected to admitting blacks on the ground that doing so would impair its expression of its separatist view and would force it to send a message that association between whites and blacks is a legitimate form of behavior? Should the Court defer to that group's claims?

(2)   In opening his dissent by characterizing state antidiscrimination laws (such as the New Jersey law before the Court) as "designed to replace prejudice with principle," is Justice Stevens saying that moral disapproval of homosexuality is a form of prejudice? Can such moral convictions be prejudice even if they are rooted in sincerely-held religious beliefs? What role does the analogy to racial discrimination and opposition to interracial marriage play in Stevens's dissent?

(3)   Chief Justice Rehnquist observes that, over time, public accommodations laws have expanded to cover more places, as well as more groups, and that such expansion has led to greater potential for conflicts with First Amendment rights. You will encounter further conflicts over public accommodations laws later in this chapter, in the context of the provisions of goods and services to same-sex couples exercising their right to marry. Did you find it surprising that the BSA was considered a "public accommodation" under New Jersey's law? Commentators Andrew Koppelman and Tobias Barrington Wolff point out that BSA is not only the "largest civic youth organization in the United States," but is the "only boys' organization with quasi-official status," since it has a Congressional charter, has special permission to use military equipment, and "every president since William Howard Taft has been the BSA's honorary president." Andrew Koppelman and Tobias Barrington Wolff, *A Right to Discriminate? How the Case of* Boy Scouts of America v. James Dale *Warped the Law of Free Association* (New Haven, CT: Yale University Press, 2009), 108–11. Do these facts, combined with the BSA's message of being inclusive, "nonsectarian," and open "to all creeds, races, and classes," provide further reason to consider the BSA a public accommodation?

(4)   The majority opinion states that "[w]e recognized in cases such as *Roberts* ... that States have a compelling interest in eliminating discrimination against women in public accommodations." In *Roberts*, for example, the Court agreed with the Minnesota Supreme Court that the Jaycees local chapters were "places" (within Minnesota's statute) that offered "[l]eadership skills," "business contacts and employment promotions," and that "[a]ssuring women equal access

to such goods, privileges, and advantages clearly furthers compelling state interests." Roberts v. Jaycees (1984). Here, have the legislature and Supreme Court of New Jersey implicitly adopted the view that the state has a compelling interest in eliminating discrimination on the basis of sexual orientation in public accommodations? To what extent does the United States Supreme Court's opinion rest on a rejection of this view? Does the majority opinion give sufficient attention to the "state interests embodied in New Jersey's public accommodations law"?

(5) Justice Stevens argues that "[u]nder the majority's reasoning, an openly gay male is irreversibly affixed with the label 'homosexual.' That label, even though unseen, communicates a message that permits his exclusion wherever he goes. . . . [R]eliance on such a justification is tantamount to a constitutionally prescribed symbol of inferiority." Does Rehnquist have an adequate answer to Stevens's critique? Who has the better view concerning the implications of *Hurley* (discussed in the opinions) for this case?

(6) What are we to make of the debate concerning who has courage to take a stand against majority viewpoints that underlies the clash between Rehnquist and Stevens? On the one hand, Stevens applauds New Jersey for being a "courageous State" that dares to "experiment with 'things social'" and that is bold enough to "replace prejudice with principle." On the other hand, Rehnquist casts the Boy Scouts as a group that refuses to accept socially accepted views and dares to voice a different, unpopular, and disfavored view. Should our views on such matters affect our interpretation of the Constitution? Do Rehnquist's and Stevens's opinions reflect fundamentally different conceptions of diversity and moral pluralism? If so, what are those conceptions? And which view is more persuasive?

(7) In May 2013, the Boy Scouts of America ended its longstanding policy of excluding openly gay youths. More than 60 percent of the volunteer leaders around the country approved a measure that provided that no youth may be denied membership "on the basis of sexual orientation or preference alone." The Scouts left in place its longtime policy of not allowing openly gay scout leaders. Subsequently, on July 27, 2015, the National Executive Board of the Boy Scouts of America "ratified a resolution that removes the national restriction on openly gay adult leaders and employees," with 79% voting in favor of the resolution. This policy leaves it to local units, such as "religious chartered organizations," to "choose adult volunteer leaders whose beliefs"—including on matters of sexuality—"are consistent with their own," and also leaves it to "Scouting's members and parents to select local units, chartered to organizations

with similar beliefs, that best meet the needs of their families." Boy Scouts of America Amends Adult Leadership Policy, http://scoutingnewsroom.org/blog/boy-scouts-of-america-amends-adult-leadership-policy/.

(8) In Rumsfeld v. Forum for Academic and Institutional Rights, Inc. (2006), the Supreme Court upheld the "Solomon Amendment," a law that cuts federal financing for universities if they do not give military recruiters the same access to students that they give other potential employers. The Association of American Law Schools, which includes nearly all accredited law schools, requires adherence to a policy of nondiscrimination on the basis of sexual orientation as a condition of membership. Many law schools had complied with the Association's policy by barring military recruiters. Congress responded by passing the Solomon Amendment in 2004. A coalition of law schools argued that the Amendment imposed an "unconstitutional condition" on the universities' receipt of federal money by requiring them to surrender their First Amendment rights by forcing them to carry the government's anti-gay message. The Supreme Court rejected their arguments, stating: "The Solomon Amendment regulates conduct, not speech. . . . It affects what law schools must *do*—afford equal access to military recruiters—not what they may or may not *say*." Chief Justice Roberts pointed out that the law schools were free to disavow the military's policy. The Court also rejected the law schools' argument, by analogy to *Boy Scouts*, that the government had infringed their freedom of association. Roberts said that the analogy was incorrect: unlike Boy Scout leaders who become part of the organization, "recruiters are, by definition, outsiders who come onto campus for the limited purpose of trying to hire students—not to become members of the school's expressive association." Subsequently, in 2010, Congress repealed the "don't ask, don't tell" policy of excluding gays and lesbians from the military.

––––––

> **"In diverse contexts, our decisions have distinguished between policies that require action and those that withhold benefits. . . . Hastings, through its RSO program, is dangling the carrot of subsidy, not wielding the stick of prohibition."—JUSTICE GINSBURG**

> **"The proudest boast of our free speech jurisprudence is that we protect the freedom to express 'the thought that we hate.' Today's decision rests on a very different principle: no freedom for expression that offends prevailing standards of political**

correctness in our country's institutions of higher learning. . . ."—JUSTICE ALITO

CHRISTIAN LEGAL SOCIETY V. MARTINEZ

561 U.S. 661, 130 S.Ct. 2971, 177 L.Ed.2d 838 (2010)

■ JUSTICE GINSBURG delivered the opinion of the Court.

. . . This case concerns a novel question regarding student activities at public universities: May a public law school condition its official recognition of a student group—and the attendant use of school funds and facilities—on the organization's agreement to open eligibility for membership and leadership to all students?

In the view of petitioner Christian Legal Society (CLS), an accept-all-comers policy impairs its First Amendment rights to free speech, expressive association, and free exercise of religion by prompting it, on pain of relinquishing the advantages of recognition, to accept members who do not share the organization's core beliefs about religion and sexual orientation. From the perspective of respondent Hastings College of the Law (Hastings or the Law School), CLS seeks special dispensation from an across-the-board open-access requirement designed to further the reasonable educational purposes underpinning the school's student-organization program.

In accord with the District Court and the Court of Appeals, we reject CLS's First Amendment challenge. Compliance with Hastings' all-comers policy . . . is a reasonable, viewpoint-neutral condition on access to the student-organization forum. In requiring CLS—in common with all other student organizations—to choose between welcoming all students and forgoing the benefits of official recognition, . . . Hastings did not transgress constitutional limitations. CLS, it bears emphasis, seeks not parity with other organizations, but a preferential exemption from Hastings' policy. The First Amendment shields CLS against state prohibition of the organization's expressive activity, however exclusionary that activity may be. But CLS enjoys no constitutional right to state subvention of its selectivity.

I

. . . Through its "Registered Student Organization" (RSO) program, Hastings extends official recognition to student groups. . . . RSOs are eligible to seek financial assistance from the Law School, which subsidizes their events using funds from a mandatory student-activity fee imposed on all students. RSOs may also use Law-School channels to communicate with students: They may place announcements in a weekly Office-of-Student-Services newsletter, advertise events on designated bulletin boards, send e-mails using a Hastings-organization address, and participate in an annual Student Organizations Fair designed to advance recruitment efforts. In addition, RSOs may apply for permission to use the Law School's facilities for meetings and office space. Finally, Hastings allows officially recognized groups to use its name and logo.

In exchange for these benefits, RSOs must abide by certain conditions. Only a "non-commercial organization whose membership is limited to Hastings students may become [an RSO]." A prospective RSO must submit its bylaws to Hastings for approval. . . . Critical here, all RSOs must undertake to comply with Hastings' "Policies and Regulations Applying to College Activities, Organizations and Students."

The Law School's Policy on Nondiscrimination, which binds RSOs, states:

> [Hastings] is committed to a policy against legally impermissible, arbitrary or unreasonable discriminatory practices. All groups, including administration, faculty, student governments, [Hastings]-owned student residence facilities and programs sponsored by [Hastings], are governed by this policy of nondiscrimination. [Hasting's] policy on nondiscrimination is to comply fully with applicable law.

> [Hastings] shall not discriminate unlawfully on the basis of race, color, religion, national origin, ancestry, disability, age, sex or sexual orientation. This nondiscrimination policy covers admission, access and treatment in Hastings-sponsored programs and activities.

Hastings interprets the Nondiscrimination Policy, as it relates to the RSO program, to mandate acceptance of all comers: School-approved groups must "allow any student to participate, become a member, or seek leadership positions in the organization, regardless of [her] status or beliefs." . . . From Hastings' adoption of its Nondiscrimination Policy in 1990 until the events stirring this litigation, "no student organization at Hastings . . . ever sought an exemption from the Policy."

In 2004, CLS became the first student group to do so. At the beginning of the academic year, the leaders of a predecessor Christian organization—which had been an RSO at Hastings for a decade—formed CLS by affiliating with the national Christian Legal Society (CLS-National). CLS-National, an association of Christian lawyers and law students, charters student chapters at law schools throughout the country. CLS chapters must adopt bylaws that, *inter alia,* require members and officers to sign a "Statement of Faith" and to conduct their lives in accord with prescribed principles. Among those tenets is the belief that sexual activity should not occur outside of marriage between a man and a woman; CLS thus interprets its bylaws to exclude from affiliation anyone who engages in "unrepentant homosexual conduct." CLS also excludes students who hold religious convictions different from those in the Statement of Faith.

On September 17, 2004, CLS submitted to Hastings an application for RSO status, accompanied by all required documents, including the set of bylaws mandated by CLS-National. Several days later, the Law School rejected the application; CLS's bylaws, Hastings explained, did not comply with the Nondiscrimination Policy because CLS barred students based on religion and sexual orientation.

CLS formally requested an exemption from the Nondiscrimination Policy, but Hastings declined to grant one. "[T]o be one of our student-recognized organizations," Hastings reiterated, "CLS must open its membership to all students irrespective of their religious beliefs or sexual orientation." If CLS instead chose to operate outside the RSO program, Hastings stated, the school "would be pleased to provide [CLS] the use of Hastings facilities for its meetings and activities." CLS would also have access to chalkboards and generally available campus bulletin boards to announce its events. In other words, Hastings would do nothing to suppress CLS's endeavors, but neither would it lend RSO-level support for them.

Refusing to alter its bylaws, CLS did not obtain RSO status. It did, however, operate independently during the 2004–2005 academic year.

On October 22, 2004, CLS filed suit . . . under 42 U.S.C. § 1983 [alleging] that Hastings' refusal to grant the organization RSO status violated CLS's First and Fourteenth Amendment rights to free speech, expressive association, and free exercise of religion. The suit sought injunctive and declaratory relief.

On cross-motions for summary judgment, the U.S. District Court for the Northern District of California ruled in favor of Hastings. . . . On appeal, the Ninth Circuit affirmed. . . .

III

A

In support of the argument that Hastings' all-comers policy treads on its First Amendment rights to free speech and expressive association, CLS draws on two lines of decisions. First, . . . this Court has employed forum analysis to determine when a governmental entity, in regulating property in its charge, may place limitations on speech. Recognizing a State's right "to preserve the property under its control for the use to which it is lawfully dedicated," Cornelius v. NAACP Legal Defense & Ed. Fund, Inc. (1985), the Court has permitted restrictions on access to a limited public forum, like the RSO program here, with this key caveat: Any access barrier must be reasonable and viewpoint neutral.

Second, ... this Court has rigorously reviewed laws and regulations that constrain associational freedom. In the context of public accommodations, we have subjected restrictions on that freedom to close scrutiny; such restrictions are permitted only if they serve "compelling state interests" that are "unrelated to the suppression of ideas"—interests that cannot be advanced "through ... significantly less restrictive [means]." Roberts v. United States Jaycees (1984). See also, e.g., Boy Scouts of America v. Dale (2000). "Freedom of association," we have recognized, "plainly presupposes a freedom not to associate." *Roberts*. . . .

[T]his case fits comfortably within the limited-public-forum category, for CLS, in seeking what is effectively a state subsidy, faces only indirect pressure to modify its membership policies; CLS may exclude any person for any reason if it forgoes the benefits of official recognition. The expressive-association precedents on which CLS relies, in contrast, involved regulations that *compelled* a group to include unwanted members, with no choice to opt out. See, e.g., *Dale*. (regulation "forc[ed] [the Boy Scouts] to accept members it [did] not desire"); *Roberts* ("There can be no clearer example of an intrusion into the internal structure or affairs of an association than" forced inclusion of unwelcome participants.).

In diverse contexts, our decisions have distinguished between policies that require action and those that withhold benefits. See, e.g., Grove City College v. Bell (1984); Bob Jones Univ. v. United States (1983). . . . Hastings, through its RSO program, is dangling the carrot of subsidy, not wielding the stick of prohibition. Cf. Norwood v. Harrison (1973) ("That the Constitution may compel toleration of private discrimination in some circumstances does not mean that it requires state support for such discrimination."). . . .

C

We first consider whether Hastings' policy is reasonable taking into account the RSO forum's function and "all the surrounding circumstances." *Cornelius*.

Our inquiry is shaped by the educational context in which it arises: "First Amendment rights" . . . "must be analyzed in light of the special characteristics of the school environment." Widmar v. Vincent (1981). . . .

A college's commission—and its concomitant license to choose among pedagogical approaches—is not confined to the classroom, for extracurricular programs are, today, essential parts of the educational process. We therefore "approach our task with special caution," Healy v. James (1972), mindful that Hastings' decisions about the character of its student-group program are due decent respect.

With appropriate regard for school administrators' judgment, we review the justifications Hastings offers in defense of its all-comers requirement.[17] First, the open-access policy "ensures that the leadership, educational, and social opportunities afforded by [RSOs] are available to all students." Just as "Hastings does not allow its professors to host classes open only to those students with a certain status or belief," so the Law School may decide, reasonably in our view, "that the . . . educational experience is best promoted when all participants in the forum must provide equal access to all students." RSOs, we count it significant, are eligible for financial assistance drawn from mandatory student-activity fees; the all-comers policy ensures that no Hastings student is forced to fund a group that would reject her as a member.

Second, the all-comers requirement helps Hastings police the written terms of its Nondiscrimination Policy without inquiring into an RSO's motivation for membership restrictions. To bring the RSO program within CLS's view of the Constitution's limits, CLS proposes that Hastings permit exclusion because of *belief* but forbid discrimination due to *status*. But that proposal would impose on Hastings a daunting labor. How should the Law School go about determining whether a student organization cloaked prohibited status exclusion in belief-based garb? If a hypothetical Male-Superiority Club barred a female student from running for its presidency, . . . how could the Law School tell whether the group rejected her bid because of her sex or because, by seeking to lead the club, she manifested a lack of belief in its fundamental philosophy?

This case itself is instructive in this regard. CLS contends that it does not exclude individuals because of sexual orientation, but rather "on the basis of a conjunction of conduct and the belief that the conduct is not wrong." Our

---

[17] . . . The dissent fights the distinction between state *prohibition* and state *support*, but its real quarrel is with our limited public forum doctrine, which recognizes that distinction. CLS, it bears repetition, remains free to express whatever it will, but it cannot insist on an exemption from Hastings' embracive all-comers policy. [Footnote by the Court.]

decisions have declined to distinguish between status and conduct in this context. See Lawrence v. Texas (2003) ("When homosexual *conduct* is made criminal by the law of the State, that declaration in and of itself is an invitation to subject homosexual *persons* to discrimination." (emphasis added)).

Third, the Law School reasonably adheres to the view that an all-comers policy, to the extent it brings together individuals with diverse backgrounds and beliefs, "encourages tolerance, cooperation, and learning among students." And if the policy sometimes produces discord, Hastings can rationally rank among RSO-program goals development of conflict-resolution skills, toleration, and readiness to find common ground.

Fourth, Hastings' policy, which incorporates—in fact, subsumes—state-law proscriptions on discrimination, conveys the Law School's decision "to decline to subsidize with public monies and benefits conduct of which the people of California disapprove." State law, of course, may not *command* that public universities take action impermissible under the First Amendment. But so long as a public university does not contravene constitutional limits, its choice to advance state-law goals through the school's educational endeavors stands on firm footing.

In sum, the several justifications Hastings asserts in support of its all-comers requirement are surely reasonable in light of the RSO forum's purposes.

[W]hen access barriers are viewpoint neutral, our decisions have counted it significant that other available avenues for the group to exercise its First Amendment rights lessen the burden created by those barriers. In this case, Hastings offered CLS access to school facilities to conduct meetings and the use of chalkboards and generally available bulletin boards to advertise events. Although CLS could not take advantage of RSO-specific methods of communication, the advent of electronic media and social-networking sites reduces the importance of those channels.

Private groups, from fraternities and sororities to social clubs and secret societies, commonly maintain a presence at universities without official school affiliation. Based on the record before us, CLS was similarly situated. . . . It is beyond dissenter's license . . . constantly to maintain that nonrecognition of a student organization is equivalent to prohibiting its members from speaking.

CLS nevertheless deems Hastings' all-comers policy "frankly absurd." "There can be no diversity of viewpoints in a forum," it asserts, "if groups are not permitted to form around viewpoints." This catchphrase confuses CLS's preferred policy with constitutional limitation—the *advisability* of Hastings' policy does not control its *permissibility*.

CLS also assails the reasonableness of the all-comers policy in light of the RSO forum's function by forecasting that the policy will facilitate hostile takeovers; if organizations must open their arms to all, CLS contends, saboteurs will infiltrate groups to subvert their mission and message. This supposition strikes us as more hypothetical than real. CLS points to no history or prospect of RSO-hijackings at Hastings. . . .

RSOs, moreover, in harmony with the all-comers policy, may condition eligibility for membership and leadership on attendance, the payment of dues, or other neutral requirements designed to ensure that students join because of their commitment to a group's vitality, not its demise. . . .

Finally, CLS asserts (and the dissent repeats) that the Law School lacks any legitimate interest—let alone one reasonably related to the RSO forum's purposes—in urging "religious groups not to favor co-religionists for purposes of their religious activities." CLS's analytical error lies in focusing on the benefits it must forgo while ignoring the interests of those it seeks to fence out: Exclusion, after all, has two sides. Hastings, caught in the crossfire between a group's desire to exclude and students' demand for equal access, may reasonably draw a line in the sand permitting *all* organizations to express what they wish but *no* group to discriminate in membership.

D

We next consider whether Hastings' all-comers policy is viewpoint neutral.

Although this aspect of limited-public-forum analysis has been the constitutional sticking point in our prior decisions, . . . we need not dwell on it here. It is, after all, hard to imagine a more viewpoint-neutral policy than one requiring *all* student groups to accept *all* comers. In contrast to *Healy, Widmar,* and *Rosenberger* [v. Rector and Visitors of University of Virginia (1995)], in which universities singled out organizations for disfavored treatment because of their points of view, Hastings' all-comers requirement draws no distinction between groups based on their message or perspective. An all-comers condition on access to RSO status, in short, is textbook viewpoint neutral.

Conceding that Hastings' all-comers policy is "nominally neutral," CLS attacks the regulation by pointing to its effect: The policy is vulnerable to constitutional assault, CLS contends, because "it systematically and predictably burdens most heavily those groups whose viewpoints are out of favor with the campus mainstream." Cf. (Alito, J., dissenting) (charging that Hastings' policy favors "political[ly] correc[t]" student expression). This argument stumbles from its first step because "[a] regulation that serves purposes unrelated to the content of expression is deemed neutral, even if it has an incidental effect on some speakers or messages but not others." Ward v. Rock Against Racism (1989).

Even if a regulation has a differential impact on groups wishing to enforce exclusionary membership policies, "[w]here the [State] does not target conduct on the basis of its expressive content, acts are not shielded from regulation merely because they express a discriminatory idea or philosophy." R.A.V. v. St. Paul (1992).

Hastings' requirement that student groups accept all comers, we are satisfied, "is justified without reference to the content [or viewpoint] of the regulated speech." *Ward.* The Law School's policy aims at the *act* of rejecting would-be group members without reference to the reasons motivating that behavior: Hastings' "desire to redress th[e] perceived harms" of exclusionary membership policies "provides an adequate explanation for its [all-comers condition] over and above mere disagreement with [any student group's] beliefs or biases." Wisconsin v. Mitchell (1993). CLS's conduct—not its Christian perspective—is, from Hastings' vantage point, what stands between the group and RSO status. "In the end," as Hastings observes, "CLS is simply confusing its *own* viewpoint-based objections to . . . nondiscrimination laws (which it is entitled to have and [to] voice) with viewpoint *discrimination.*"

Finding Hastings' open-access condition on RSO status reasonable and viewpoint neutral, we reject CLS' free-speech and expressive-association claims.[27] . . .

■ JUSTICE STEVENS, concurring. . . .

In the dissent's view, by refusing to grant CLS an exemption from the Nondiscrimination Policy, Hastings violated CLS's rights, for by proscribing unlawful discrimination on the basis of religion, the policy discriminates unlawfully on the basis of religion. There are numerous reasons why this counterintuitive theory is unsound. Although the First Amendment may protect

---

[27] CLS briefly argues that Hastings' all-comers condition violates the Free Exercise Clause. Our decision in [Employment Division v. Smith (1990)] forecloses that argument. In *Smith,* the Court held that the Free Exercise Clause does not inhibit enforcement of otherwise valid regulations of general application that incidentally burden religious conduct. In seeking an exemption from Hastings' across-the-board all-comers policy, CLS, we repeat, seeks preferential, not equal, treatment; it therefore cannot moor its request for accommodation to the Free Exercise Clause. [Footnote by the Court.]

CLS's discriminatory practices off campus, it does not require a public university to validate or support them. . . .

[T]he policy [reflects] a judgment that discrimination by school officials or organizations on the basis of certain factors, such as race and religion, is less tolerable than discrimination on the basis of other factors. This approach may or may not be the wisest choice in the context of a[n] RSO program. But it is at least a reasonable choice. Academic administrators routinely employ antidiscrimination rules to promote tolerance, understanding, and respect, and to safeguard students from invidious forms of discrimination, including sexual orientation discrimination. Applied to the RSO context, these values can, in turn, advance numerous pedagogical objectives.

It is critical, in evaluating CLS's challenge to the Nondiscrimination Policy, to keep in mind that an RSO program is a *limited* forum—the boundaries of which may be *delimited* by the proprietor. When a religious association, or a secular association, operates in a wholly public setting, it must be allowed broad freedom to control its membership and its message, even if its decisions cause offense to outsiders. Profound constitutional problems would arise if the State of California tried to "demand that all Christian groups admit members who believe that Jesus was merely human." (Alito, J., dissenting). But the CLS chapter that brought this lawsuit does not want to be just a Christian group; it aspires to be a recognized student organization. The Hastings College of Law is not a legislature. And no state actor has demanded that anyone do anything outside the confines of a discrete, voluntary academic program. Although it may be the case that to some "university students, the campus is their world," it does not follow that the campus ought to be equated with the public square.

The campus is, in fact, a world apart from the public square in numerous respects, and religious organizations, as well as all other organizations, must abide by certain norms of conduct when they enter an academic community. Public universities serve a distinctive role in a modern democratic society. Like all specialized government entities, they must make countless decisions about how to allocate resources in pursuit of their role. Some of those decisions will be controversial; many will have differential effects across populations; virtually all will entail value judgments of some kind. As a general matter, courts should respect universities' judgments and let them manage their own affairs.

The RSO forum is no different. It is not an open commons that Hastings happens to maintain. It is a mechanism through which Hastings confers certain benefits and pursues certain aspects of its educational mission. . . .

In this case, petitioner excludes students who will not sign its Statement of Faith or who engage in "unrepentant homosexual conduct," The expressive association argument it presses, however, is hardly limited to these facts. Other groups may exclude or mistreat Jews, blacks, and women—or those who do not share their contempt for Jews, blacks, and women. A free society must tolerate such groups. It need not subsidize them, give them its official imprimatur, or grant them equal access to law school facilities.

■ JUSTICE KENNEDY, concurring. . . .

■ JUSTICE ALITO, with whom THE CHIEF JUSTICE [ROBERTS], JUSTICE SCALIA, and JUSTICE THOMAS join, dissenting.

The proudest boast of our free speech jurisprudence is that we protect the freedom to express "the thought that we hate." United States v. Schwimmer (1929) (Holmes, J., dissenting). Today's decision rests on a very different principle: no freedom for expression that offends prevailing standards of political correctness in our country's institutions of higher learning. . . .

I

The Court provides a misleading portrayal of this case. . . . I begin by correcting the picture.

The Court bases all of its analysis on the proposition that the relevant Hastings' policy is the so-called accept-all-comers policy. . . . Overwhelming evidence, however, shows that Hastings denied CLS's application pursuant to the Nondiscrimination Policy and that the accept-all-comers policy was nowhere to be found until it was mentioned by a former dean in a deposition taken well after this case began. . . .

The Court also distorts the record with respect to the effect on CLS of Hastings' decision to deny registration. The Court quotes a letter written by Hastings' general counsel in which she stated that Hastings " 'would be pleased to provide [CLS] the use of Hastings facilities for its meetings and activities.' " . . . Other statements in the majority opinion make it seem as if the denial of registration did not hurt CLS at all. . . . This Court does not customarily brush aside a claim of unlawful discrimination with the observation that the effects of the discrimination were really not so bad. . . .

Finally, I must comment on the majority's emphasis on funding. According to the majority, CLS is "seeking what is effectively a state subsidy". . . . In fact, funding plays a very small role in this case. Most of what CLS sought and was denied—such as permission to set up a table on the law school patio—would have been virtually cost free. . . .

IV

Analyzed under [the limited public forum] framework, Hastings' refusal to register CLS pursuant to its Nondiscrimination Policy plainly fails. [W]hen Hastings refused to register CLS, it claimed that the CLS bylaws impermissibly discriminated on the basis of religion and sexual orientation. As interpreted by Hastings and applied to CLS, both of these grounds constituted viewpoint discrimination.

Religion. The First Amendment protects the right of " 'expressive association' "—that is, "the right to associate for the purpose of speaking." Rumsfeld v. Forum for Academic and Institutional Rights, Inc. (2006) (quoting *Dale*). And the Court has recognized that "[t]he forced inclusion of an unwanted person in a group infringes the group's freedom of expressive association if the presence of that person affects in a significant way the group's ability to advocate public or private viewpoints." *Dale.*

With one important exception, the Hastings Nondiscrimination Policy respected that right. . . . Only religious groups were required to admit students who did not share their views. . . .

Sexual orientation. The Hastings Nondiscrimination Policy, as interpreted by the law school, also discriminated on the basis of viewpoint regarding sexual morality. CLS has a particular viewpoint on this subject, namely, that sexual conduct outside marriage between a man and a woman is wrongful. Hastings would not allow CLS to express this viewpoint by limiting membership to persons willing to express a sincere agreement with CLS's views. By contrast, nothing in the Nondiscrimination Policy prohibited a group from expressing a contrary viewpoint by limiting membership to persons willing to endorse that group's beliefs. A Free Love Club could require members to affirm that they reject the traditional view of sexual morality to which CLS adheres. It is hard to see how this can be viewed as anything other than viewpoint discrimination . . . .

VI

[I]t is clear that the accept-all-comers policy is not reasonable in light of the purpose of the RSO forum, and it is impossible to say on the present record that it is viewpoint neutral.

. . . Taken as a whole, the regulations plainly contemplate the creation of a forum within which Hastings students are free to form and obtain registration of essentially the same broad range of private groups that nonstudents may form off campus. That is precisely what the parties in this case stipulated: The RSO forum "seeks to promote a diversity of viewpoints *among* registered student organizations, including viewpoints on religion and human sexuality."

The accept-all-comers policy is antithetical to the design of the RSO forum for the same reason that a state-imposed accept-all-comers policy would violate the First Amendment rights of private groups if applied off campus. . . .

There can be no dispute that this standard would not permit a generally applicable law mandating that private religious groups admit members who do not share the groups' beliefs. Religious groups like CLS obviously engage in expressive association, and no legitimate state interest could override the powerful effect that an accept-all-comers law would have on the ability of religious groups to express their views. The State of California surely could not demand that all Christian groups admit members who believe that Jesus was merely human. Jewish groups could not be required to admit anti-Semites and Holocaust deniers. Muslim groups could not be forced to admit persons who are viewed as slandering Islam.

While there can be no question that the State of California could not impose such restrictions on all religious groups in the State, the Court now holds that Hastings, a state institution, may impose these very same requirements on students who wish to participate in a forum that is designed to foster the expression of diverse viewpoints. . . . [T]he justifications offered by Hastings and accepted by the Court are insufficient. . . .

[T]he Court argues that the accept-all-comers policy, by bringing together students with diverse views, encourages tolerance, cooperation, learning, and the development of conflict-resolution skills. These are obviously commendable goals, but they are not undermined by permitting a religious group to restrict membership to persons who share the group's faith. Many religious groups impose such restrictions. Such practices are not manifestations of "contempt" for members of other faiths. Cf. (opinion of Stevens, J.) (invoking groups that have "contempt for Jews, blacks, and women"). Nor do they thwart the objectives that Hastings endorses. Our country as a whole, no less than the Hastings College of Law, values tolerance, cooperation, learning, and the amicable resolution of conflicts. But we seek to achieve those goals through "[a] confident pluralism that conduces to civil peace and advances democratic consensus-building," not by abridging First Amendment rights. Brief for Gays and Lesbians for Individual Liberty as *Amicus Curiae* 35.

[T]he Court observes that Hastings' policy "incorporates—in fact, subsumes—state-law proscriptions on discrimination." Because the First Amendment obviously takes precedence over any state law, this would not justify the Hastings policy even if it were true—but it is not. The only Hastings policy considered by the Court—the accept-all-comers policy—goes far beyond any California antidiscrimination law. Neither Hastings nor the Court claims that California law demands that state entities must accept all comers. Hastings itself certainly does not follow this policy in hiring or student admissions. . . .

In sum, Hastings' accept-all-comers policy is not reasonable in light of the stipulated purpose of the RSO forum: to promote a diversity of viewpoints "*among*"—not within—"registered student organizations."

The Court is also wrong in holding that the accept-all-comers policy is viewpoint neutral. . . . The adoption of a facially neutral policy for the purpose of suppressing the expression of a particular viewpoint is viewpoint discrimination. Here, CLS has made a strong showing that Hastings' sudden adoption and selective application of its accept-all-comers policy was a pretext for the law school's unlawful denial of CLS's registration application under the Nondiscrimination Policy. . . .

In the end, the Court refuses to acknowledge the consequences of its holding. A true accept-all-comers policy permits small unpopular groups to be taken over by students who wish to change the views that the group expresses. Rules requiring that members attend meetings, pay dues, and behave politely would not eliminate this threat.

The possibility of such takeovers, however, is by no means the most important effect of the Court's holding. There are religious groups that cannot in good conscience agree in their bylaws that they will admit persons who do not share their faith, and for these groups, the consequence of an accept-all-comers policy is marginalization. . . .

* * *

I do not think it is an exaggeration to say that today's decision is a serious setback for freedom of expression in this country. Our First Amendment reflects a "profound national commitment to the principle that debate on public issues should be uninhibited, robust, and wide-open." New York Times Co. v. Sullivan (1964). Even if the United States is the only Nation that shares this commitment to the same extent, I would not change our law to conform to the international norm. I fear that the Court's decision marks a turn in that direction. Even those who find CLS's views objectionable should be concerned about the way the group has been treated—by Hastings, the Court of Appeals, and now this Court. I can only hope that this decision will turn out to be an aberration.

EDITORS' NOTES

(1) Justice Ginsburg writes: "Hastings, through its RSO program, is dangling the carrot of subsidy, not wielding the stick of prohibition." She is distinguishing between two tools that government might use in promoting anti-discrimination policies to secure the status of equal citizenship for all: (a) outright prohibition of discrimination or exclusion upon certain bases such as race, sex, or sexual orientation and (b) conditioning benefits or subsidies upon a group's not discriminating on such bases. (For fuller development of this distinction, see James E. Fleming and Linda C. McClain, *Ordered Liberty: Rights, Responsibilities, and Virtues* (Cambridge: Harvard University Press, 2013), ch. 6.) Whereas Boy Scouts of America v. Dale (2000; reprinted above) clearly involved (and rejected) tool (a), she views this case as undoubtedly involving tool (b). Does Justice Alito view it instead as involving tool (a)? Which is the sounder view?

(2) Is Justice Alito's dissent, joined by three other conservative justices, consistent with conservative justices' general acceptance of Rust v. Sullivan (1991) and Harris v. McRae (1980)? *Rust,* which upheld statutory prohibitions (within programs receiving Title X funds) upon physicians counselling, making referrals, and providing information about abortion as a form of family planning, exemplifies the general view that if one takes the government's subsidies or benefits, one "must take the bitter with the sweet" by acceding to the government's conditions. In *Rust,* the more liberal justices dissented, objecting that government was imposing unconstitutional conditions by conditioning receipt of benefits upon relinquishing "cherished freedom of speech." Have the tables turned here, with the conservatives now objecting that the government is conditioning benefits upon relinquishing cherished freedoms of expression and religion?

(3) To what extent does the disagreement between the majority and the concurrence, on the one hand, and the dissenters, on the other, reflect a disagreement between competing conceptions of diversity and moral pluralism? See Editors' Note (6) to *Boy Scouts*. Which opinion is most persuasive on the question of how best to foster such values as tolerance and such skills as conflict resolution and finding common ground? What does Justice Alito mean by "a

confident pluralism"? He quotes language from an amicus curiae (friend of the court) brief written by Gays and Lesbians for Individual Liberty, filed in support of Christian Legal Society and critical of the "all-comers policy." Whether or not the all-comers policy is constitutional, is it a wise or prudent policy? For example, some conservative religious scholars cite *CLS* as evidence that "conservative religious student groups are no longer welcome on public school campuses," and speak of "progressives" in California and elsewhere being able to "rid their campuses" of conservative religious groups "with traditional beliefs about sexuality." See John D. Inazu, "A Confident Pluralism," 88 *S. Cal. L. Rev.* 587, 587–88 (2015) (criticizing *CLS* decision). Is the effect of the majority opinion to "kick out" CLS? What status does CLS have under the all-comers policy?

(4) Justice Stevens argues that the college campus is "a world apart from the public square." How does that affect his evaluation of the constitutionality of Hastings' policy? Does either the majority opinion or Stevens's concurrence adequately address dissenting Justice Alito's argument that the Hastings policy is constitutionally impermissible viewpoint discrimination?

(5) Distinctions between status and conduct as well as between belief and conduct feature in different ways in this case. First, the majority opinion rejects CLS's argument that it is not excluding on the basis of sexual orientation but rather based on a "conjunction of conduct and the belief that the conduct is not wrong." Second, the majority argues that it is not Hastings' religious beliefs but instead its conduct in excluding certain would-be members that is the reason that Hastings does not grant it full RSO status. Is the Court's analysis of these two issues persuasive? Or is Justice Alito's dissent right that it is CLS's religious beliefs, that is, its viewpoint, against which the Nondiscrimination Policy discriminates?

(6) What role does analogy between discrimination on the basis of sexual orientation and other forms of discrimination, such as on the basis of race, sex, and religion, play in the various opinions?

(7) The majority in *CLS* states that "First Amendment rights"—such as those of the members of the student group, the Christian Legal Society—"must be analyzed in light of the special characteristics of the school environment." What are those characteristics? Concurring, Justice Stevens elaborates on the distinctive role that "public universities" serve in "a modern democratic society," and observes that they make many decisions that entail "value judgments." Reflecting such judgments, he contends, "antidiscrimination rules [are] to

promote tolerance, understanding, and respect, and to safeguard students from invidious forms of discrimination, including sexual orientation discrimination." The following case concerns the authority of a public high school to promote tolerance and the constitutional issues arising from such an effort. As you read the case, consider the sharply different views of the majority and dissent over the appropriateness of teaching tolerance.

————

"[A] school has the right to teach civic responsibility and tolerance as part of its basic educational mission; it need not as a quid pro quo permit hateful and injurious speech that runs counter to that mission."—JUDGE REINHARDT

"Tolerance is a civic virtue, but not one practiced by all members of our society toward all others. This may be unfortunate, but it is a reality we must accept in a pluralistic society. Specifically, tolerance toward homosexuality and homosexual conduct is anathema to those who believe that intimate relations among people of the same sex are immoral or sinful."—JUDGE KOZINSKI

HARPER V. POWAY UNIFIED SCHOOL DISTRICT
445 F.3d 1166 (9th Cir. 2006)

■ Before REINHARDT, KOZINSKI, and THOMAS, CIRCUIT JUDGES.

Opinion

■ REINHARDT, CIRCUIT JUDGE.

May a public high school prohibit students from wearing T-shirts with messages that condemn and denigrate other students on the basis of their sexual orientation? Appellant in this action is a sophomore at Poway High School who was ordered not to wear a T-shirt to school that read, "BE ASHAMED, OUR SCHOOL EMBRACED WHAT GOD HAS CONDEMNED" handwritten on the front, and "HOMOSEXUALITY IS SHAMEFUL" handwritten on the back. He appeals the district court's order denying his motion for a preliminary injunction. [W]e affirm the district court's order.

I.   Factual Background

Poway High School ("the School") has had a history of conflict among its students over issues of sexual orientation. In 2003, the School permitted a student group called the Gay-Straight Alliance to hold a "Day of Silence" at the School which, in the words of an Assistant Principal, is intended to "teach tolerance of others, particularly those of a different sexual orientation."[2] During the days surrounding the 2003 "Day of Silence,"[3] a series of incidents and altercations occurred on the school campus as a result of anti-homosexual comments that were made by students. One such confrontation required the Principal to separate students physically. According to David LeMaster, a teacher at Poway, several students were suspended as a result of these conflicts. Moreover, a week or so after the "Day of Silence," a group of heterosexual students informally organized a "Straight-Pride Day," during which they wore T-shirts which displayed derogatory remarks about homosexuals. According to Assistant Principal Lynell Antrim, some students were asked to remove the shirts and did so, while others "had an altercation and were suspended for their actions."

Because of these conflicts in 2003, when the Gay-Straight Alliance sought to hold another "Day of Silence" in 2004, the School required the organization to consult with the Principal to . . . find ways to reduce tensions and potential altercations. On April 21, 2004, the date of the 2004 "Day of Silence," appellant Tyler Chase Harper wore a T-shirt to school on which "I WILL NOT ACCEPT WHAT GOD HAS CONDEMNED," was handwritten on the front and "HOMOSEXUALITY IS SHAMEFUL 'Romans 1:27' " was handwritten on the back. . . .

The next day, April 22, 2004, Harper wore the same T-shirt to school, except that the front of the shirt read "BE ASHAMED, OUR SCHOOL EMBRACED WHAT GOD HAS CONDEMNED," while the back retained the same message as before, "HOMOSEXUALITY IS SHAMEFUL 'Romans 1:27.' " LeMaster, Harper's second period teacher, noticed Harper's shirt and observed "several students off-task talking about" the shirt. LeMaster, recalling the altercations that erupted as a result of "anti-homosexual speech" during the previous year's "Day of Silence," explained to Harper that he believed that the shirt was "inflammatory," that it violated the School's dress code, and that it "created a negative and hostile working environment for others." When Harper refused to remove his shirt and asked to speak to an administrator, LeMaster gave him a dress code violation card to take to the front office.

---

[2]   In his complaint, Harper alleges that he believes "the true purpose" of the "Day of Silence" was "to endorse, promote and encourage homosexual activity." [Footnote by the Court.]

[3]   On the "Day of Silence," participating students wore duct tape over their mouths to symbolize the silencing effect of intolerance upon gays and lesbians; these students would not speak in class except through a designated representative. Some students wore black T-shirts that said "National Day of Silence" and contained a purple square with a yellow equal sign in the middle. The Gay-Straight Alliance, with the permission of the School, also put up several posters promoting awareness of harassment on the basis of sexual orientation. [Footnote by the Court.]

When Harper arrived at the front office, he met Assistant Principal Antrim. She told Harper that the "Day of Silence" was "not about the school promoting homosexuality but rather it was a student activity trying to raise other students' awareness regarding tolerance in their judgement [sic] of others." Antrim believed that Harper's shirt "was inflammatory under the circumstances and could cause disruption in the educational setting." Like LeMaster, she also recalled the altercations that had arisen as a result of anti-homosexual speech one year prior. According to her affidavit, she "discussed [with Harper] ways that he and students of his faith could bring a positive light onto this issue without the condemnation that he displayed on his shirt." Harper was informed that if he removed the shirt he could return to class.

When Harper again refused to remove his shirt, the Principal, Scott Fisher, spoke with him, explaining his concern that the shirt was "inflammatory" and that it was the School's "intent to avoid physical conflict on campus." Fisher also explained to Harper that it was not healthy for students to be addressed in such a derogatory manner. According to Fisher, Harper informed him that he had already been "confronted by a group of students on campus" and was "involved in a tense verbal conversation" earlier that morning. The Principal eventually decided that Harper could not wear his shirt on campus, a decision that, he asserts, was influenced by "the fact that during the previous year, there was tension on campus surrounding the Day of Silence between certain gay and straight students."[6] Fisher proposed some alternatives to wearing the shirt, all of which Harper turned down. Harper asked two times to be suspended. Fisher "told him that [he] did not want him suspended from school, nor did [he] want him to have something in his disciplinary record because of a stance he felt strongly about." Instead, Fisher told Harper that he would be required to remain in the front office for the remainder of the school day.

Harper spent the rest of the day in the school conference room doing his homework. At some point during that day, Deputy Sheriff Norman Hubbert, who served as the school resource officer for Poway High, came in to speak with Harper. The complaint alleges that Hubbert "came to interrogate" Harper to "determine if he was a dangerous student." Hubbert, however, asserts in his

---

[6]   We note that conflicts over homosexuality at Poway High School have not been limited to the incidents surrounding a "Day of Silence." Two former students recently won a suit against the School for failing to protect them from students who harassed them because they are gay. *See* Dana Littlefield, *Two Gay Students Were Harassed, Jury Finds,* San Diego Union-Trib., June 9, 2005, at B2. During the trial, one of the students testified that Poway "students repeatedly called him names, shoved him in the hallways, threw food at him and spit on him," and "that he heard other students make disparaging remarks about gays and lesbians on a nearly daily basis." *Id.* [Footnote by the Court.]

affidavit that he and Harper had a "casual conversation concerning the content of the shirt . . . the Bible and [the] scripture reference on the shirt," and that the conversation was conducted "simpl[y out of] curiosity . . . to understand the situation."

Toward the end of the school day, Assistant Principal Ed Giles spoke with Harper. Giles had discovered earlier in the day that Harper attended the same church that he had previously attended, and that he "knew [Harper's] father personally and had attended Biblical studies that [Harper's] father led on Tuesday nights." According to Giles, he went to speak with Harper "out of respect to [Harper] and his family" and "to make sure he was alright." Giles told Harper that he understood "where he was coming from" but wished that he could "express himself in a more positive way." Giles also said that he shared the same Christian faith as Harper, but that as a school employee, he had to watch how he expressed his beliefs and that when he came to work, he had to "leave his faith in [the] car." Giles then asked Harper to "consider other alternatives that would be more positive and non-confrontational," including sponsoring activities through the campus Bible Club.

. . . . Harper was not suspended, no disciplinary record was placed in his file, and he received full attendance credit for the day. . . .

II. Procedural History

On June 2, 2004, Harper filed a lawsuit in district court against Poway Unified School District and certain named individuals in their individual and official capacities. Harper alleged . . . violations of his right to free speech, his right to free exercise of religion, the Establishment Clause, the Equal Protection Clause, and the Due Process Clause. . . . [O]n July 12, 2004, Harper filed a motion for a preliminary injunction seeking to enjoin the school from "continuing [its] violation of the constitutional rights of Plaintiff Tyler Chase Harper." On November 4, 2004 . . . the district court denied Harper's motion for a preliminary injunction. Harper then filed an interlocutory appeal from the order denying the latter motion. . . .

IV. Standard and Scope of Review

For a district court to grant a preliminary injunction, . . . the question is whether Harper demonstrated a likelihood of success on the merits as to any or all of his three First Amendment claims. . . .

V.   Analysis

1.   Freedom of Speech Claim

The district court concluded that Harper failed to demonstrate a likelihood of success on the merits of his claim that the School violated his First Amendment right to free speech because, under Tinker v. Des Moines Indep. Cmty. Sch. Dist. (1969), the evidence in the record was sufficient to permit the school officials to "reasonably . . . forecast substantial disruption of or material interference with school activities." Harper contends that the district court erred in rejecting his free speech claim on three grounds: (1) his speech is protected under the Supreme Court's holdings in *Tinker*; (2) the School's actions and policies amount to viewpoint discrimination under Rosenberger v. Rector & Visitors of Univ. of Va. (1995); and (3) the School's dress code and speech policies are overbroad. We affirm the district court's denial of the requested preliminary injunction. Although we, like the district court, rely on *Tinker*, we rely on a different provision—that schools may prohibit speech that "intrudes upon . . . the rights of other students." *Tinker*.

a.   Student Speech Under *Tinker*. . .

The courts have construed the First Amendment as applied to public schools in a manner that attempts to strike a balance between the free speech rights of students and the special need to maintain a safe, secure and effective learning environment. *See, e.g., Tinker*. . . . Although public school students do not "shed their constitutional rights to freedom of speech or expression at the schoolhouse gate," *Tinker*, the Supreme Court has declared that "the First Amendment rights of students in public schools are not automatically coextensive with the rights of adults in other settings, and must be applied in light of the special characteristics of the school environment." Hazelwood Sch. Dist. v. Kuhlmeier (1988). Thus, while Harper's shirt embodies the very sort of political speech that would be afforded First Amendment protection outside of the public school setting, his rights in the case before us must be determined "in light of [those] special characteristics." *Tinker*. . . .

In *Tinker*, the Supreme Court confirmed a student's right to free speech in public schools.[16] In balancing that right against the state interest in maintaining an ordered and effective public education system, however, the Court declared

---

16   In *Tinker*, the Supreme Court held that a public school could not ban students from wearing black armbands protesting the Vietnam war where the "silent, passive expression of opinion [was] unaccompanied by any disorder or disturbance," and there was no evidence that the display "colli[ded] with the rights of other students to be secure and to be let alone." [Footnote by the Court.]

that a student's speech rights could be curtailed under two circumstances. First, a school may regulate student speech that would "impinge upon the rights of other students." *Tinker*. Second, a school may prohibit student speech that would result in "substantial disruption of or material interference with school activities." *Id.* Because . . . the School's prohibition of the wearing of the demeaning T-shirt is constitutionally permissible under the first of the *Tinker* prongs, we conclude that the district court did not abuse its discretion in finding that Harper failed to demonstrate a likelihood of success on the merits of his free speech claim.[17]

i. The Rights of Other Students

In *Tinker,* the Supreme Court held that public schools may restrict student speech which "intrudes upon . . . the rights of other students" or "colli[des] with the rights of other students to be secure and to be let alone." Harper argues that *Tinker's* reference to the "rights of other students" should be construed narrowly to involve only circumstances in which a student's right to be free from direct physical confrontation is infringed. . . .

[T]he law does not support Harper's argument. This court has explained that vulgar, lewd, obscene, indecent, and plainly offensive speech "by definition, may well 'impinge[] upon the rights of other students,' " even if the speaker does not directly accost individual students with his remarks. *Chandler*, 978 F.2d at 529 (quoting *Tinker*). So too may other speech capable of causing psychological injury. The Tenth Circuit has held that the "display of the Confederate flag might . . . interfere with the rights of other students to be secure and let alone," even though there was no indication that any student was physically accosted with the flag, aside from its general display. West v. Derby Unified Sch. Dist., 206 F.3d 1358, 1366 (10th Cir.2000). . . .

We conclude that Harper's wearing of his T-shirt "colli[des] with the rights of other students" in the most fundamental way. *Tinker*. Public school students who may be injured by verbal assaults on the basis of a core identifying characteristic such as race, religion, or sexual orientation, have a right to be free from such attacks while on school campuses. As *Tinker* clearly states, students have the right to "be secure and to be let alone." Being secure involves not only

---

[17] The first part of our colleague's dissent is devoted to a discussion of whether there was sufficient evidence that the wearing of Harper's T-shirt caused substantial disruption, the *Tinker* prong on which the district court relied but which is not relevant to our holding. The last part of the dissent also deals with a subject we need not and do not address: what the dissent terms the School's "harassment policy." Oddly, the dissent spends only a relatively minor part of its discussion on the determinative issue here, the impermissible intrusion on the rights of gay and lesbian students. . . . [Footnote by the Court.]

freedom from physical assaults but from psychological attacks that cause young people to question their self-worth and their rightful place in society.[18] The "right to be let alone" has been recognized by the Supreme Court, of course, as " 'the most comprehensive of rights and the right most valued by civilized men.' " Hill v. Colorado (2000) (quoting Olmstead v. United States (1928) (Brandeis, J., dissenting)). Indeed, the "recognizable privacy interest in avoiding unwanted communication" is perhaps most important "when persons are 'powerless to avoid' it." *Id.* (quoting Cohen v. California (1971)). Because minors are subject to mandatory attendance requirements, the Court has emphasized "the obvious concern on the part of parents, and school authorities acting *in loco parentis,* to protect children—especially in a captive audience. . . ." *Fraser.* Although name-calling is ordinarily protected outside the school context, "[s]tudents cannot hide behind the First Amendment to protect their 'right' to abuse and intimidate other students at school." Sypniewski v. Warren Hills Reg'l Bd. of Educ., 307 F.3d 243, 264 (3rd Cir. 2002).

Speech that attacks high school students who are members of minority groups that have historically been oppressed, subjected to verbal and physical abuse, and made to feel inferior, serves to injure and intimidate them, as well as to damage their sense of security and interfere with their opportunity to learn.[19] The demeaning of young gay and lesbian students in a school environment is detrimental not only to their psychological health and well-being, but also to their educational development. Indeed, studies demonstrate that "academic underachievement, truancy, and dropout are prevalent among homosexual youth and are the probable consequences of violence and verbal and physical abuse at school." Susanne M. Stronski Huwiler and Gary Remafedi, "Adolescent Homosexuality," 33 *Rev. Jur. U.I.P.R.* 151, 164 (1999). . . . Another study confirmed that gay students had difficulty concentrating in school and feared for their safety as a result of peer harassment, and that verbal abuse led some gay students to skip school and others to drop out altogether. Human Rights Watch, Hatred in the Hallways (1999) . . . . In short, it is well established that attacks on students on the basis of their sexual orientation are harmful not only to the

---

[18]   There is nothing in *Tinker* that remotely supports the dissent's contention that the rights to "be secure and to be let alone" are limited to rights such as those that protect against "assault, defamation, invasion of privacy, extortion and blackmail." Security and privacy entail far more than freedom from those torts. . . . [Footnote by the Court.]

[19]   California law provides that "[a]ll pupils have the right to participate fully in the educational process, free from discrimination and harassment." Cal. Educ.Code § 201(a). The dissent expostulates on the meaning of the term "harassment" and speculates as to whether the California statute may be contrary to the First Amendment, all of which is irrelevant here because we do not rely on the statute in reaching our decision. [Footnote by the Court.]

students' health and welfare, but also to their educational performance and their ultimate potential for success in life.

Those who administer our public educational institutions need not tolerate verbal assaults that may destroy the self-esteem of our most vulnerable teenagers and interfere with their educational development. [T]he School had a valid and lawful basis for restricting Harper's wearing of his T-shirt on the ground that his conduct was injurious to gay and lesbian students and interfered with their right to learn.

The dissent claims that we should not take notice of the fact that gay students are harmed by derogatory messages such as Harper's because there is no "evidence" that they are in fact injured by being shamed or humiliated by their peers. It is simply not a novel concept, however, that such attacks on young minority students can be harmful to their self-esteem and to their ability to learn. [I]n Brown v. Board of Education (1954), the Supreme Court recognized that "[a] sense of inferiority affects the motivation of a child to learn." If a school permitted its students to wear shirts reading, "Negroes: Go Back To Africa," no one would doubt that the message would be harmful to young black students. So, too, in the case of gay students, with regard to messages such as those written on Harper's T-shirt. As our dissenting colleague recently concluded, "[y]ou don't need an expert witness to figure out" the self-evident effect of certain policies or messages. Jespersen v. Harrah's Operating Co. (9th Cir.2006) (Kozinski, Circuit Judge, dissenting). . . . Certainly, the California legislature had no difficulty in determining that harassment on the basis of sexual orientation adversely affects the rights of public high school students. *See* Cal. Educ.Code § 201(c).

The dissent takes comfort in the fact that there is a political disagreement regarding homosexuality in this country. We do not deny that there is, just as there was a longstanding political disagreement about racial equality that reached its peak in the 1950s . . . or [about] whether blacks or Jews should be permitted to attend private universities and prep schools, work in various industries such as banks, brokerage houses, and Wall Street law firms, or stay at prominent resorts or hotels. Such disagreements may justify social or political debate, but they do not justify students in high schools or elementary schools assaulting their fellow students with demeaning statements: by calling gay students shameful, by labeling black students inferior or by wearing T-shirts saying that Jews are doomed to Hell. Perhaps our dissenting colleague believes that one can condemn homosexuality without condemning homosexuals. If so, he is wrong. To say that homosexuality is shameful is to say, necessarily, that gays and lesbians are shameful. There are numerous locations and opportunities available to those who wish to advance such an argument. It is not necessary to do so by directly condemning, to their faces, young students trying to obtain a fair and full education in our public schools. . . .

What we hold in this opinion is a far cry from what the dissent suggests. We do not hold that schools may "define civic responsibility and then ban opposing points of view." The question of what types of assemblies schools should or may conduct regarding controversial public issues or what types of speech students may otherwise generally engage in regarding such issues is not before us. . . . We consider here only whether schools may prohibit the wearing of T-shirts on high school campuses and in high school classes that flaunt demeaning slogans, phrases or aphorisms relating to a core characteristic of particularly vulnerable students and that may cause them significant injury. We do not believe that the schools are forbidden to regulate such conduct. Nor, contrary to the dissent, do we believe that because a school sponsors or permits a "Day of Tolerance" or a "Day of Silence" minority students should be required to publicly "[c]onfront[ ]" and "refut[e]" demeaning verbal assaults on them—that they may be left with no option other than to try to justify their sexual practices to the entire student body or explain to all their fellow students why they are not inferior or evil. The First Amendment does not require that young students be subjected to such a destructive and humiliating experience.

In his declaration in the district court, the school principal justified his actions on the basis that "any shirt which is worn on campus which speaks in a derogatory manner towards an individual or group of individuals is not healthy for young people. . . ." If, by this, the principal meant that all such shirts may be banned under *Tinker*, we do not agree. T-shirts proclaiming, "Young Republicans Suck," or "Young Democrats Suck," for example, may not be very civil but they would certainly not be sufficiently damaging to the individual or the educational process to warrant a limitation on the wearer's First Amendment rights. . . .

Although we hold that the School's restriction of Harper's right to carry messages on his T-shirt was permissible under *Tinker*, we reaffirm the importance of preserving student speech about controversial issues generally and protecting the bedrock principle that students "may not be confined to the expression of those sentiments that are officially approved." *Tinker; see also Fraser* (noting students' "freedom to advocate unpopular and controversial views in schools and classrooms"). It is essential that students have the opportunity to engage in full and open political expression, both in and out of the school environment. Engaging in controversial political speech, even when it is offensive to others, is an important right of all Americans and learning the value of such freedoms is an essential part of a public school education. Indeed, the inculcation of "the fundamental values necessary to the maintenance of a democratic political system" is "truly the 'work of the schools.'" *Fraser* (quoting *Tinker*). Limitations on student speech must be narrow, and applied with sensitivity and for reasons that are consistent with the fundamental First Amendment mandate. Accordingly, we limit our holding to instances of derogatory and injurious remarks directed at students' minority status such as race, religion, and sexual orientation.[28] Moreover, our decision is based not only on the type and degree of injury the speech involved causes to impressionable young people, but on the locale in which it takes place. *See Tinker.* Thus, it is limited to conduct that occurs in public high schools (and in elementary schools). As young students acquire more strength and maturity, and specifically as they reach college age, they become adequately equipped emotionally and intellectually to deal with the type of verbal assaults that may be prohibited during their earlier years. Accordingly, we do not condone the use in public colleges or other public institutions of higher learning of restrictions similar to those permitted here.

Finally, we emphasize that the School's actions here were no more than necessary to prevent the intrusion on the rights of other students. Aside from prohibiting the wearing of the shirt, the School did not take the additional step of punishing the speaker: Harper was not suspended from school nor was the incident made a part of his disciplinary record. . . .

ii. Substantial Disruption

The district court concluded that Harper had failed to demonstrate a likelihood of success on the merits of his free speech claim because there was sufficient evidence to permit the school officials to "reasonably . . . forecast

---

[28] We do not consider here whether remarks based on gender warrant similar treatment, preferring to leave that question to another time. We recognize, however, that problems of gender discrimination remain serious and that they exist throughout learning institutions, from the public and religious schools to institutions of higher learning, not excluding the most prominent institutions in the nation. Our dissenting colleague worries that offensive words directed at majority groups such as Christians or whites will not be covered by our holding. There is, of course, a difference between a historically oppressed minority group that has been the victim of serious prejudice and discrimination and a group that has always enjoyed a preferred social, economic and political status. Growing up as a member of a minority group often carries with it psychological and emotional burdens not incurred by members of the majority. . . . We do not exclude, however, the possibility that some verbal assaults on the core characteristics of majority high school students would merit application of the *Tinker* "intrusion upon the rights of other students" prong. That question is not presently before us. [Footnote by the Court.]

substantial disruption of or material interference with school activities."
Tinker. . . .

In light of our conclusion regarding the application of the "rights of others"
prong of *Tinker*, we have no cause to decide whether the evidence would be
sufficient to warrant denial of a preliminary injunction under the "substantial
disruption" prong as well.

b.   Viewpoint Discrimination

In reaching our decision that Harper may lawfully be prohibited from
wearing his T-shirt, we reject his argument that the School's action constituted
impermissible viewpoint discrimination. The government is generally prohibited
from regulating speech "when the specific motivating ideology or the opinion or
perspective of the speaker is the rationale for the restriction." *Rosenberger.*
However, . . . speech in the public schools is not always governed by the same
rules that apply in other circumstances. *See Hazelwood.* Indeed, the Court in
Tinker held that a school may prohibit student speech, even if the consequence is
viewpoint discrimination, if the speech violates the rights of other students or is
materially disruptive. Thus, pursuant to *Tinker*, courts have allowed schools to
ban the display of Confederate flags despite the fact that such a ban may
constitute viewpoint discrimination. . . . While the Confederate flag may express
a particular viewpoint, "[i]t is not only constitutionally allowable for school
officials" to limit the expression of racially explosive views, "it is their duty to do
so." *Scott*, 324 F.3d at 1249. . . .

The dissent claims that although the School may have been justified in
banning discussion of the subject of sexual orientation altogether, it cannot
"gag[ ] only those who oppose the Day of Silence." [A]lthough *Tinker* does not
allow schools to restrict the non-invasive, non-disruptive expression of political
viewpoints, it does permit school authorities to restrict "one particular opinion"
if the expression would "impinge upon the rights of other students" or
substantially disrupt school activities. *Tinker.* Accordingly, a school may permit
students to discuss a particular subject without being required to allow them to
launch injurious verbal assaults that intrude upon the rights of other students.

"A school need not tolerate student speech that is inconsistent with its
basic educational mission, [ ] even though the government could not censor
similar speech outside the school." *Hazelwood.* Part of a school's "basic
educational mission" is the inculcation of "fundamental values of habits and
manners of civility essential to a democratic society." *Fraser.* For this reason,
public schools may permit, and even encourage, discussions of tolerance,

equality and democracy without being required to provide equal time for student or other speech espousing intolerance, bigotry or hatred. [B]ecause a school sponsors a "Day of Religious Tolerance," it need not permit its students to wear T-shirts reading, "Jews Are Christ-Killers" or "All Muslims Are Evil Doers." Such expressions would be "wholly inconsistent with the 'fundamental values' of public school education." *Id.* Similarly, a school that permits a "Day of Racial Tolerance," may restrict a student from displaying a swastika or a Confederate Flag. In sum, a school has the right to teach civic responsibility and tolerance as part of its basic educational mission; it need not as a quid pro quo permit hateful and injurious speech that runs counter to that mission.

We again emphasize that we do not suggest that all debate as to issues relating to tolerance or equality may be prohibited. [W]e consider here only the question of T-shirts, banners, and other similar items bearing slogans that injure students with respect to their core characteristics. Other issues must await another day.

2. Free Exercise of Religion Claim

Harper also contends that the district court erred because he was entitled to a preliminary injunction as a result of the School's violation of his rights under the Free Exercise Clause. He asserts that his wearing of the T-shirt was "motivated by sincerely held religious beliefs" regarding homosexuality and that the School "punished" him for expressing them, or otherwise burdened the exercise of those views. Additionally, Harper argues that the School "attempted to change" his religious views and that this effort violated both the Free Exercise Clause and the Establishment Clause.

The Free Exercise Clause of the First Amendment provides that Congress shall make no law "prohibiting the free exercise" of religion. U.S. Const. amend. I. The Clause prohibits the government from "compel[ling] affirmation of religious belief, punish[ing] the expression of religious doctrines it believes to be false, impos[ing] special disabilities on the basis of religious views or religious status, or lend[ing] its power to one or the other side in controversies over religious authority or dogma." Employment Div., Dep't of Human Res. of Oregon v. Smith (1990).

In Sherbert v. Verner (1963), the Supreme Court held that governmental actions that substantially burden a religious belief or practice must be justified by a compelling state interest and must be narrowly tailored to serve that interest. The *Sherbert* test was later largely discarded in *Smith*, which held that the "right of free exercise does not relieve an individual of the obligation to comply with a 'valid and neutral law of general applicability on the ground that the law proscribes (or prescribes) conduct that his religion prescribes (or proscribes).' " The Court held that a neutral law of general applicability need not be supported by a compelling governmental interest even though it has the incidental effect of burdening religion. *See id.; see also* Church of the Lukumi Babalu Aye, Inc. v. City of Hialeah (1993). . . .

Harper does not contend that the School's prohibition against his wearing his T-shirt was motivated by other than secular reasons or that it was applied to him because of his religious views. Nor is there anything in the record to suggest that other students wearing T-shirts similarly demeaning of gay and lesbian members of the student body would be treated differently, Christians or not. Under *Smith*, Harper's claim would surely fail. . . .

[W]hether or not *Sherbert's* strict scrutiny test applies, Harper cannot prevail here. . . .

. . . . The record simply does not demonstrate that the School's restriction regarding Harper's T-shirt imposed a substantial burden upon the free exercise of Harper's religious beliefs. There is no evidence that the School "compell[ed] affirmation of a repugnant belief," "penalize[d] or discriminate[d] against [Harper] because [he] hold[s] religious views abhorrent to the authorities," or "condition[ed] the availability of benefits upon [Harper's] willingness to violate a cardinal principle of [his] religious faith." *Sherbert.* Nor did the School "lend its power to one or the other side in controversies over religious authority or dogma," or "punish the expression of religious doctrines it believes to be false." *Smith.*

Despite Harper's allegation that the School "punished" him for expressing his religious views, the record demonstrates the contrary: the School did not punish Harper at all. It simply prohibited him from wearing the offensive and disruptive shirt and required him to refrain from attending class for a portion of a day, if he insisted on continuing to wear it. Nor did the restriction imposed on Harper's wearing of the T-shirt constitute a substantial limitation on his right to express his religious views. No one has the right to proclaim his views at all times in all manners in all places, regardless of the circumstances, and Harper does not contend that his religion suggests otherwise. Harper remains free to express his views, whatever their merits, on other occasions and in other places. The prohibition against the wearing of a T-shirt in school does not constitute a substantial burden on the exercise of his religious beliefs.

Even if a religious creed, or an individual's interpretation of that creed, could be said to require its adherents to proclaim their religious views at all times and in all places, and to do so in a manner that interferes with the rights of others, the First Amendment would not prohibit the state from banning such disruptive conduct in certain circumstances, including on a high school campus.... Schools may prohibit students and others from disrupting the educational process or causing physical or psychological injury to young people entrusted to their care, whatever the motivations or beliefs of those engaged in such conduct. Indeed, the state's interest in doing so is compelling.

Because there is no evidence that the School's restriction on Harper's wearing of his T-shirt substantially burdened a religious practice or belief, and because the School has a compelling interest in providing a proper educational environment for its students and because its actions were narrowly tailored to achieve that end, it would appear that the district court did not abuse its discretion in finding that Harper failed to demonstrate a likelihood of success on the merits as to his free exercise of religion claim. Before reaching that conclusion, however, we must deal with one final argument that Harper raises as a part of that claim. Harper asserts that the School "attempted to change" his religious views that "homosexuality is harmful to both those who practice it and the community at large." Specifically, Harper alleges that the school officials' comments that his shirt was "inflammatory," Detective Hubbert's questioning of him, and Assistant Principal Giles' statement that he leaves his Christian faith in the car when he comes to school, all were attempts by school authorities to change his religious views.

The district court rejected Harper's contention. Indeed, there is no evidence in the record that the school representatives sought to change Harper's religious beliefs. Harper's complaint avers that Detective Hubbert "proposed to [Harper] that as a member of the Christian faith, he should understand that Christianity was based on love not hate, and that [he] should not be offensive to others." Hubbert's homily did not constitute an attempt to change Harper's religious views, simply his offensive behavior.... The statements that the message on Harper's shirt was "inflammatory" and would be harmful to the educational environment were merely statements of fact that represented the School's informed judgment.... As for Giles' comments, his affidavit stated that he did not tell Harper to "leave his own faith in the car," but explained that, as a school employee, he, Giles, had to leave *his own* Christian faith in the car when he came to work. While Giles' statement might also be construed as an attempt to encourage Harper to change his conduct—to refrain, while on campus, from expressing religious views that denigrate others—it cannot be characterized as an attempt to change his views. In fact, rather than tell Harper to change his beliefs, Giles encouraged him to join the campus Bible Club so that he could become part of an "activity that would express his [Christian] opinions in a positive way on campus." . . .

Moreover, school officials' statements and any other school activity intended to teach Harper the virtues of tolerance constitute a proper exercise of a school's educational function, even if the message conflicts with the views of a particular religion. A public school's teaching of secular democratic values does not constitute an unconstitutional attempt to influence students' religious beliefs. Rather, it simply reflects the public school's performance of its duty to educate children regarding appropriate secular subjects in an appropriate secular manner. As we have reiterated earlier, "the inculcation of fundamental values necessary to the maintenance of a democratic political system" is "truly the 'work of the schools.'" *Fraser*. Public schools are not limited to teaching materials that are consistent with all aspects of the views of all religions. So long as the subject and materials are appropriate from an educational standpoint and the purpose of the instruction is secular, the school's teaching is not subject to a constitutional objection that it conflicts with a view held by members of a particular religion. There is no evidence here that the school officials' comments were associated with a religious, as opposed to a secular, purpose. Their affidavits demonstrate that the School acted in order to maintain a secure and healthy learning environment for all its students, not to advance religion.

The Constitution does not preclude school districts from teaching the essential elements of democracy or otherwise performing their proper educational mission simply because some individuals or groups may assert that their religious views are inconsistent with the lessons taught as a part of that mission. Accordingly, we affirm the district court's decision that Harper was not entitled to a preliminary injunction on the basis of his free exercise claim.

3.   Establishment Clause Claim

. . . . Harper's Establishment Clause claim as presented on appeal appears to be simply a restatement of his Free Exercise claim. . . .

. . . . [T]he district court did not abuse its discretion in finding that Harper failed to demonstrate a likelihood of success on the merits of his Establishment Clause claim. . . .

VI. Conclusion

... The Free Speech Clause permits public schools to restrict student speech that intrudes upon the rights of other students. Injurious speech that may be so limited is not immune from regulation simply because it reflects the speaker's religious views. Accordingly, we affirm the district court's denial of Harper's motion for a preliminary injunction. ...

■ KOZINSKI, CIRCUIT JUDGE, dissenting:

While I find this a difficult and troubling case, I can agree with neither the majority's rationale nor its conclusion. On the record to date, the school authorities have offered no lawful justification for banning Harper's t-shirt and the district court should therefore have enjoined them from doing so pending the outcome of this case. Harper, moreover, raised a valid facial challenge to the school's harassment policy, and the district court should have enjoined the policy as well.

The T-shirt. . . .

If the school's ban of the shirt is to be upheld, ... it must be because it "materially disrupts classwork or involves substantial disorder or invasion of the rights of others." *Tinker.*

1. School authorities may ban student speech based on the existence of "any facts which might reasonably [lead] school authorities to forecast substantial disruption." *Id.* ...

The school authorities here have shown precious little to support an inference that Harper's t-shirt would "materially disrupt[ ] classwork." One teacher, David LeMaster, said that several students in class were "off-task talking about [the] content of 'Chase's shirt' when they should have been working." Surely, however, it is not unusual in a high school classroom for students to be "off-task." The scène à faire of high school students bored or distracted in class is a cliché. LeMaster gives no indication that the distracted students refused to get back on task once they were admonished, or that the t-shirt caused a commotion or otherwise materially interfered with class activities. As this is the *only* evidence that Harper's t-shirt interfered with classroom learning, I find it ludicrously weak support for banning Harper's t-shirt on the ground that it would "materially disrupt[ ] classwork." *Tinker.*

 .... Harper's t-shirt was not an out-of-the-blue affront to fellow students who were minding their own business. Rather, Harper wore his t-shirt in response to the Day of Silence, a political activity that was sponsored or at the very least tolerated by school authorities. The Day of Silence is a protest sponsored by the Gay, Lesbian and Straight Education Network (GLSEN). According to a GLSEN press release, the Day of Silence is "an annual, national student-led effort in which participants take a vow of silence to peacefully protest the discrimination and harassment faced by lesbian, gay, bisexual and transgender (LGBT) youth in schools." The point of this protest, as I understand it, is to promote tolerance toward all students, regardless of their sexual orientation.

Tolerance is a civic virtue,[7] but not one practiced by all members of our society toward all others. This may be unfortunate, but it is a reality we must accept in a pluralistic society.[8] Specifically, tolerance toward homosexuality and homosexual conduct is anathema to those who believe that intimate relations among people of the same sex are immoral or sinful. So long as the subject is kept out of the school environment, these differences of opinion need not clash. But a visible and highly publicized political action by those on one side of the issue will provoke those on the other side to express a different point of view, if only to avoid the implication that they agree. *See* Robert Bolt, *A Man for All Seasons* act 2, at 88 (1962) ("The maxim of the law is 'Silence gives consent.' ").

Given the history of violent confrontation between those who support the Day of Silence and those who oppose it, the school authorities may have been justified in banning the subject altogether by denying both sides permission to express their views during the school day. *See, e.g., West* (10th Cir.2000) (upholding ban on items that give rise to racial tension such as Confederate flags and Malcolm X t-shirts). I find it far more problematic—and more than a little ironic—to try to solve the problem of violent confrontations by gagging only those who oppose the Day of Silence and the point of view it represents. . . .

I cannot imagine that my colleagues would approve this in other situations. Say, for example, one school group—perhaps the Young Republicans—were to organize a day of support for the war in Iraq by encouraging students to wear a yellow armband. And suppose that other students responded by wearing t-shirts

---

7   The majority waxes eloquent about the right of schools "to teach civic responsibility and tolerance as part of its basic educational mission," while suppressing other points of view. But one man's civic responsibility is another man's thought control. . . . Having public schools, and those who fund them, define civic responsibility and then ban opposing points of view, as the majority seems willing to do, may be an invitation to group-think. [Footnote by Judge Kozinski.]

8   Indeed, tolerance may not always be a virtue. Tolerating wicked conduct, bigotry or malicious gossip, for example, may not be in the least commendable. Then there is the question of whether we should tolerate intolerance, a question as imponderable as a Mobius strip. Whether tolerance is a good or a bad thing may turn on what we think about the thing being tolerated. [Footnote by Judge Kozinski.]

with messages such as "Marines are Murderers" and "U.S. Bombs Kill Babies." If a student whose brother was killed in Iraq assaulted a student wearing one of the anti-war t-shirts, would we approve a school's response that banned the t-shirts but continued to permit the yellow armbands? *See* R.A.V. v. City of Saint Paul (1992) ("[The government] has no such authority to license one side of a debate to fight freestyle, while requiring the other to follow Marquis of Queensberry rules."). . . .

2. *Tinker* does contain an additional ground for banning student speech, namely where it is an "invasion of the rights of others." The school authorities suggest that Harper's t-shirt violates California Education Code § 201(a), which provides that "[a]ll pupils have the right to participate fully in the educational process, free from discrimination and harassment." Defendants cite no California case holding that the passive display by one student of a message another student finds offensive violates this provision, and I am reluctant to so conclude on my own. . . .

Harassment law might be reconcilable with the First Amendment, if it is limited to situations where the speech is so severe and pervasive as to be tantamount to conduct. . . . The "rights of others" language in *Tinker* can only refer to traditional rights, such as those against assault, defamation, invasion of privacy, extortion and blackmail, whose interplay with the First Amendment is well established. Surely, this language is not meant to give state legislatures the power to define the First Amendment rights of students out of existence by giving others the right not to hear that speech. Otherwise, a state legislature could effectively overrule *Tinker* by granting students an affirmative right not to be offended. To the extent that state law purports to prohibit such language in the school context, it is patently unconstitutional.

Nor can I join my colleagues in concluding that Harper's t-shirt violated the rights of other students by disparaging their homosexual status. As I understand the opinion, my colleagues are saying that messages such as Harper's are so offensive and demeaning that they interfere with the ability of homosexual students to partake of the educational environment. [N]o one introduced any evidence in support of, or opposition to, this proposition. . . .

Nor do I find the proposition at the heart of the majority's opinion—that homosexual students are severely harmed by any and all statements casting aspersions on their sexual orientation—so self-evident as to require no evidentiary support. . . . We have no business assuming without proof that the educational progress of homosexual students would be stunted by Harper's statement.

I find it significant, moreover, that Harper did not thrust his view of homosexuality into the school environment as part of a campaign to demean or embarrass other students. Rather, he was responding to public statements made by others with whom he disagreed. Whatever one might think are the psychological effects of unprovoked demeaning statements by one student against another, the effects may be quite different when they are part of a political give-and-take. By participating in the Day of Silence activities, homosexual students perforce acknowledge that their status is not universally admired or accepted; the whole point of the Day of Silence, as I understand it, is to dispute views like those characterized by Harper's t-shirt. Supporters of the Day of Silence may prefer to see views such as Harper's channeled into public discourse rather than officially suppressed but whispered behind backs or scribbled on bathroom walls. Confronting—and refuting—such views in a public forum may well empower homosexual students, contributing to their sense of self-esteem.

[I] have considerable difficulty understanding the source and sweep of the novel doctrine the majority announces today. Not all statements that demean other students can be banned by schools; the majority is very clear about this. The new doctrine applies only to statements that demean students based on their "minority status such as race, religion, and sexual orientation." Is this a right created by state law? By federal law? By common law? And if interference with the learning process is the keystone to the new right, how come it's limited to those characteristics that are associated with minority status? Students may well have their self-esteem bruised by being demeaned for being white or Christian, or having bad acne or weight problems, or being poor or stupid or any one of the infinite number of characteristics that will not qualify them for minority status. Under the rule the majority announces today, schools would be able to ban t-shirts with pictures of Mohammed wearing a bomb turban but not those with pictures of a Crucifix dipped in urine—yet Muslim and Christian children, respectively, may have their learning equally disrupted.

Even the concept of minority status is not free from doubt. In defining what is a minority—and hence protected—do we look to the national community, the state, the locality or the school? In a school that has 60 percent black students and 40 percent white students, will the school be able to ban t-shirts with anti-black racist messages but not those with anti-white racist messages, or vice versa? Must a Salt Lake City high school prohibit or permit *Big Love* t-shirts?

And at what level of generality do we define a minority group? If the Pope speaks out against gay marriage, can gay students wear to school t-shirts saying "Catholics Are Bigots," or will they be demeaning the core characteristic of a religious minority? And, are Catholics part of a monolithic Christian majority, or a minority sect that has endured centuries of discrimination in America?

Finally, I have considerable difficulty with giving school authorities the power to decide that only one side of a controversial topic may be discussed in the school environment because the opposing point of view is too extreme or demeaning. . . .

The Harassment Policy

I believe we must also address Harper's claim that he is entitled to an injunction against the school's harassment policy on grounds of substantial overbreadth. . . . The majority suggests in a footnote that it need not consider whether the school's harassment policy is overbroad because it upholds the school's banning of Harper's t-shirt regardless of the policy. The policy, however, covers much more than the particular t-shirt Harper wore on the day in question. Given that the majority has effectively upheld the school's banning of that shirt, it becomes even more important for us to rule on whether and how Harper may express his views in the future. To the extent that the harassment policy limits the ways in which Harper may express himself by means *other* than his t-shirt, he is surely entitled to a ruling as to whether the district court erred in failing to enjoin the policy. . . .

The school's harassment policy seems to prohibit any student speech, whether it be in the classroom, elsewhere on campus, in connection with any school activity, going to and returning from school and quite possibly at all other times and places, if it is derogatory . . . of other students based on certain characteristics—race, ethnicity, sexual orientation, religion, sex or disability. . . .

The problems posed by the policy here . . . are not theoretical or trivial. Assuming, as we must, that on the next Day of Silence Harper will not be allowed to wear a t-shirt expressing his interpretation of Romans 1:27, what exactly *can* he say or wear? Would a t-shirt quoting Romans 1:27[14] be permissible, or is it prohibited because a homosexual student might interpret it

---

[14] "And likewise also the men, leaving the natural use of the woman, burned in their lust one toward another; men with men working that which is unseemly, and receiving in themselves that recompense of their error which was meet." Romans 1:27 (King James). [Footnote by Judge Kozinski.]

as "motivated by bias against him/her"? How about a t-shirt with the message "Straight and Proud of It"? Is this a protected "positive" message, or is it the dreaded "exalting own . . . sexual orientation" and therefore hate behavior? Indeed, is there anything at all that Harper and others of his view can say or do to distance themselves from the Day of Silence proceedings without running the risk that another student will take it personally? May Harper have a discussion at lunchtime where he says: "Homosexuality is sinful"? On his way home from school, may he tell another student a joke disparaging the movie *Brokeback Mountain*? Once he gets home, can he post criticism of the Day of Silence on his MySpace page? Given the broad language of the policy, I believe any and all of these could be punished by the school authorities as hate behavior.

Nor is Harper alone. Consider those who participate in the Day of Silence. They, of course, believe they are doing so to promote tolerance and equality. But others—like Harper—might view it as an effort to exalt homosexuality and denigrate their own sexual orientation and religious beliefs. Relying on the same overbroad policy that the school used to ban Harper's t-shirt, the school could, if it chose, easily ban the Day of Silence activities as demeaning the sexual orientation of straight students, or the religious beliefs of Christians like Harper. . . .

The types of speech that could be banned by the school authorities under the Poway High School hate policy are practically without limit. Any speech code that has at its heart avoiding offense to others gives anyone with a thin skin a heckler's veto—something the Supreme Court has not approved in the past. . . .

Conclusion

Because the *only* disputed issue before us is likelihood of success on the merits, I believe we have no choice but to reverse. I think it is highly likely that Harper will succeed on his t-shirt claim, and I have no doubt he will succeed as to his overbreadth challenge.

[I] acknowledge that the school authorities here found themselves in a difficult situation and, in light of the circumstances, acted well. Harper was not disciplined for wearing his t-shirt; the school authorities merely tried to defuse what they saw as a volatile situation.

I also have sympathy for defendants' position that students in school are a captive audience and should not be forced to endure speech that they find offensive and demeaning. There is surely something to the notion that a Jewish student might not be able to devote his full attention to school activities if the fellow in the seat next to him is wearing a t-shirt with the message "Hitler Had the Right Idea" in front and "Let's Finish the Job!" on the back. This t-shirt may well interfere with the educational experience even if the two students never come to blows or even have words about it. . . .

EDITORS' NOTES

(1)   The majority and dissent both discuss Tinker v. Des Moines Independent Community School District (1969), in which the Court famously stated that neither students nor teachers "shed their constitutional rights to freedom of speech or expression at the schoolhouse gate." In *Tinker*, a case from the era of the Vietnam War, the Court upheld the right of students to wear black armbands in protest of the war. *Tinker's* influential test for students' First Amendment rights recognized that schools may limit student speech in two situations: (1) when speech collides "with the rights of other students to be secure and to be let alone" and (2) when speech materially and substantially disrupts the work and discipline of the school. The majority in *Harper* focused primarily on the first limitation. Is the *Harper* majority's reasoning about the collision of Harper's wearing his t-shirt with the rights of other students persuasive? Was his t-shirt different from a black armband? Is the dissent's analysis more persuasive?

(2)   The majority states that "the inculcation of 'the fundamental values necessary to the maintenance of a democratic political system' is 'truly the work of the schools.' " What are those necessary values? How might schools best promote them? May schools teach such values even if they conflict with the religious views of some students?

(3)   School officials stated that the "Day of Silence" was intended to "teach tolerance." What is "tolerance"? Is it a civic virtue that schools should promote? Why does Judge Kozinski, in dissent, contend that tolerance "may not always be a virtue," particularly with respect to "homosexuality"? Does it go beyond the proper mission of a public high school to attempt to "teach tolerance"? Was Harper correct in contending that the school went beyond tolerance to promotion? Is the dissent persuasive that students like Harper might view the "Day of Silence" as "an effort to exalt homosexuality and denigrate their own sexual orientation and religious beliefs"?

(4)   The majority and dissent sharply disagree over whether the high school's prohibiting Harper from wearing his t-shirt was a form of constitutionally impermissible "viewpoint discrimination." What is the basis for

their disagreement? In justifying why schools need not provide "equal time" for student speech "espousing intolerance, bigotry, or hatred," is the majority implying that the messages on Harper's t-shirt were analogous to those of a swastika or Confederate flag (symbols which the majority contends schools may restrict)? Is the majority sound in viewing the t-shirt as a form of injurious speech that will harm gay students? If so, in what alternative ways could Harper have permissibly expressed his views? Is dissenting Judge Kozinski right that permitting "homosexual students" to view and confront t-shirts like Harper's, as part of a political give and take, is preferable to having views like Harper's "officially suppressed but whispered behind backs or scribbled on bathroom walls"?

(5) In addition to freedom of speech claims, Harper asserted a "free exercise of religion" claim, asserting that his t-shirt was "motivated by sincerely held religious beliefs." Why, according to the majority, was the sincerity of Harper's beliefs not enough to prevent the school from asking him to remove his t-shirt? What is the scope of "free exercise" in a public school? What are its limits? Did the school impose a "substantial burden" upon Harper's free exercise?

(6) The majority refers to studies about the prevalence of peer harassment and abuse of LGBT students in schools. Some of this conduct may constitute "bullying," which is defined as "unwanted, aggressive behavior among school aged children that involves a real or perceived power imbalance." In recent decades, an area of growing concern is "cyberbullying," that is, bullying that takes place using forms of electronic technology (such as computers, cell phones, and tablets) and electronic communication (such as social media cites). U.S. Dep't of Health and Human Servs., *What is Bullying?* STOPBULLYING.GOV, www.stopbullying.gov/what-is-bullying. All states have laws against bullying, which generally require school districts to adopt anti-bullying policies. Such policies generally include a definition of bullying, procedures for reporting and investigating it, disciplinary responses, and efforts to prevent bullying. U.S. Dep't of Health and Human Servs., *Policies & Laws,* STOPBULLYING.GOV. Many state laws refer to specific prohibited bases for bullying, such as race, sex, religion, national origin, and disability. Approximately nineteen states include "sexual orientation" as a prohibited basis for bullying, fourteen include "gender identity," and nine include "gender expression." *Id.*

Should state anti-bullying laws exempt from prohibition a "statement of a sincerely-held religious belief or moral conviction"? This issue arose in Michigan, when Republican lawmakers included such an exemption in the state's anti-bullying law (Matt Epling Safe School Law), enacted in 2011 after several young people (including LGBT youth) had committed suicide after being subject to bullying. See Kenneth Lythgoe, "Sleight of Hand: Michigan's Anti-Bullying Law, (Un)acceptable Exceptions, and the Reversal of Policy Making Rhetoric," 1 QED 115 (Fall 2013). After widespread criticism of this provision as a "license to bully," the Michigan legislature dropped it. "Michigan Senate Approves House Version of Anti-Bullying Bill, Drops Religious Language," *HuffPost Education* (Nov. 29, 2011), http://www.huffingtonpost.com/2011/11/29/michigan -senate-approves-_n_1119438.html. The law as enacted provides that "bullying is equally prohibited without regard to its subject matter or motivating animus." MICH. COMP. LAWS § 380.1310b (2016) (Revised School Code).

(7) Another area of conflict in public schools involves parents asserting that school efforts to teach diversity or tolerance amount to indoctrination that violates both their constitutional liberty to rear their children in accordance with their religious beliefs and their free exercise of religion. In Parker v. Hurley, 514 F.3d 87 (1st Cir. 2008), religious parents in Lexington, Massachusetts objected to including in a "Diversity Book Bag," given to children in kindergarten and first grade, books in which parents were of the same gender. They also objected to in-class reading of books featuring children with same-sex parents and a prince who marries a prince (instead of a princess). The court ruled against the parents, concluding that exposure to these books was not "systematic indoctrination" and that such curriculum was justified by the state's interest in "preventing discrimination." In addition, because Massachusetts recognized gay marriage, the court concluded that it was "rational" for the state to educate children about such families. The court also ruled that the principal could refuse the parents' request to exempt their children from such instruction. Whether or not exempting children from curriculum aimed at teaching tolerance or diversity is constitutionally required, should schools provide such exemptions?

II. CONFLICTS BETWEEN GENERAL LAWS AND RELIGIOUS LIBERTY: CLAIMS OF RELIGIOUS EXEMPTIONS IN THE POLYGAMY, PEYOTE, AND CONTRACEPTIVE MANDATE CASES

The cases in this section do not involve conflicts between gay rights and religious liberty. Instead, they concern conflicts between general laws and religious liberty and they provide important background for considering claims for religious exemptions from laws recognizing marriage for gays and lesbians and protecting LGBT persons against discrimination. The first two cases, Reynolds v. United States (1878) and Employment Division v. Smith (1990), reject constitutional claims of Mormons and Native Americans to religious exemptions to practice polygamy and to ingest peyote in religious rituals. The third, Burwell v. Hobby Lobby Stores, Inc. (2014), accepts a statutory claim to a religious exemption under the Religious Freedom Restoration Act from the Affordable Care Act's contraceptive mandate. *Reynolds* also sets the stage for considering whether, as Chief Justice Roberts suggested in dissent in *Obergefell*, recognizing a fundamental right for gays and lesbians to marry puts us on a slippery slope to protecting plural marriage or polygamy.

"So here, as a law of the organization of society under the exclusive dominion of the United States, it is provided that plural marriages shall not be allowed. Can a man excuse his practices to the contrary because of his religious belief? To permit this would be to make the professed doctrines of religious belief superior to the law of the land, and in effect to permit every citizen to become a law unto himself. Government could exist only in name under such circumstances. . . ."

REYNOLDS V. UNITED STATES
98 U.S. 145, 8 Otto 145, 25 L.Ed. 244 (1878)

[George Reynolds, a Mormon, was charged with bigamy, in violation of a law that provided: "Every person having a husband or wife living, who marries another . . . is guilty of bigamy." Reynolds argued that he was entitled to be acquitted on the ground that he married the second time because of his religious belief that it was his religious duty to do so.]

■ MR. CHIEF JUSTICE WAITE delivered the opinion of the court. . . .

On the trial, the plaintiff . . . proved that at the time of his alleged second marriage he was, and for many years before had been, a member of the Church of Jesus Christ of Latter-Day Saints, commonly called the Mormon Church, and a believer in its doctrines; that it was an accepted doctrine of that church

'that it was the duty of male members of said church, circumstances permitting, to practise polygamy; . . . that this duty was enjoined by different books which the members of said church believed to be of divine origin, and among others the Holy Bible, and also that the members of the church believed that the practice of polygamy was directly enjoined upon the male members thereof by the Almighty God, in a revelation to Joseph Smith, the founder and prophet of said church; that the failing or refusing to practise polygamy by such male members of said church, when circumstances would admit, would be punished, and that the penalty for such failure and refusal would be damnation in the life to come.'

He also proved 'that he had received permission from the recognized authorities in said church to enter into polygamous marriage; . . .'.

Upon this proof he asked the court to instruct the jury that if they found from the evidence that he 'was married as charged . . . in pursuance of and in conformity with what he believed at the time to be a religious duty, that the verdict must be 'not guilty."' This request was refused. . . .

[T]he question is raised, whether religious belief can be accepted as a justification of an overt act made criminal by the law of the land. . . .

Congress cannot pass a law . . . which shall prohibit the free exercise of religion. The first amendment to the Constitution expressly forbids such legislation. . . . The question to be determined is, whether the law now under consideration comes within this prohibition.

The word 'religion' is not defined in the Constitution. We must go elsewhere, therefore, to ascertain its meaning, and nowhere more appropriately, we think, than to the history of the times in the midst of which the provision was adopted. The precise point of the inquiry is, what is the religious freedom which has been guaranteed.

[The Court recounts some of the history regarding the First Amendment, including the following quotation from Thomas Jefferson's reply to an address by him by a committee of the Danbury Baptist Association (8 Jeff. Works. 113):]

'Believing with you that religion is a matter which lies solely between man and his God; that he owes account to none other for his faith or his worship; that the legislative powers of the government reach actions only, and not opinions,—I contemplate with sovereign reverence that act of the whole American people which declared that their legislature should 'make no law respecting an establishment of religion or prohibiting the free exercise thereof,' thus building a wall of separation between church and State. Adhering to this expression of the supreme will of the nation in behalf of the rights of conscience, I shall see with sincere satisfaction the progress of those sentiments which tend to restore man to all his natural rights, convinced he has no natural right in opposition to his social duties.'

Coming as this does from an acknowledged leader of the advocates of the measure, it may be accepted almost as an authoritative declaration of the scope and effect of the amendment thus secured. Congress was deprived of all legislative power over mere opinion, but was left free to reach actions which were in violation of social duties or subversive of good order.

Polygamy has always been odious among the northern and western nations of Europe, and, until the establishment of the Mormon Church, was almost exclusively a feature of the life of Asiatic and of African people. At common law, the second marriage was always void (2 Kent, Com. 79), and from the earliest history of England polygamy has been treated as an offence against society. . . .

By the statute of 1 James I. (c. 11), the offence, if committed in England or Wales, was made punishable in the civil courts, and the penalty was death. As this statute was limited in its operation to England and Wales, it was at a very early period re-enacted, generally with some modifications, in all the colonies. [I]t is a significant fact that on the 8th of December, 1788, after the passage of the act establishing religious freedom, and after the convention of Virginia had recommended as an amendment to the Constitution of the United States the declaration in a bill of rights that 'all men have an equal, natural, and unalienable right to the free exercise of religion, according to the dictates of conscience,' the legislature of that State substantially enacted the statute of James I., death penalty included, because, as recited in the preamble, 'it hath been doubted whether bigamy or poligamy be punishable by the laws of this Commonwealth.' 12 Hening's Stat. 691. From that day to this we think it may safely be said there never has been a time in any State of the Union when polygamy has not been an offence against society, cognizable by the civil courts and punishable with more or less severity. In the face of all this evidence, it is impossible to believe that the constitutional guaranty of religious freedom was intended to prohibit legislation in respect to this most important feature of social life. Marriage, while from its very nature a sacred obligation, is nevertheless, in most civilized nations, a civil contract, and usually regulated by law. Upon it society may be said to be built, and out of its fruits spring social relations and social obligations and duties, with which government is necessarily required to deal. In fact, according as monogamous or polygamous marriages are allowed, do we find the principles on which the government of the people, to a greater or less extent, rests. Professor, Lieber says, polygamy leads to the patriarchal principle, and which, when applied to large communities, fetters the people in stationary despotism, while that principle cannot long exist in connection with monogamy. Chancellor Kent observes that this remark is equally striking and profound. 2 Kent, Com. 81, note (e). An exceptional colony of polygamists under an exceptional leadership may sometimes exist for a time without appearing to disturb the social condition of the people who surround it; but there cannot be a doubt that, unless restricted by some form of constitution, it is within the legitimate scope of the power of every civil government to determine whether polygamy or monogamy shall be the law of social life under its dominion.

In our opinion, the statute immediately under consideration is within the legislative power of Congress. . . . This being so, the only question which remains is, whether those who make polygamy a part of their religion are excepted from the operation of the statute. If they are, then those who do not make polygamy a part of their religious belief may be found guilty and punished, while those who do, must be acquitted and go free. This would be introducing a new element into criminal law. Laws are made for the government of actions, and while they cannot interfere with mere religious belief and opinions, they may with practices. Suppose one believed that human sacrifices were a necessary part of religious worship, would it be seriously contended that the civil government under which he lived could not interfere to prevent a sacrifice? Or if a wife religiously believed it was her duty to burn herself upon the funeral pile of her dead husband, would it be beyond the power of the civil government to prevent her carrying her belief into practice?

So here, as a law of the organization of society under the exclusive dominion of the United States, it is provided that plural marriages shall not be allowed. Can a man excuse his practices to the contrary because of his religious belief? To permit this would be to make the professed doctrines of religious belief superior to the law of the land, and in effect to permit every citizen to become a law unto himself. Government could exist only in name under such circumstances. . . .

Judgment affirmed.

■ MR. JUSTICE FIELD [concurring]. . . .

EDITORS' NOTES

(1)   After same-sex marriage, is polygamy next? In *Reynolds*, the Supreme Court held that Congress (and by implication the states) may prohibit polygamy through criminal law and refuse to recognize it in civil marriage laws. Nonetheless, in Lawrence v. Texas (2003), Justice Scalia in dissent predicted that the majority's opinion signaled the "end of all morals legislation," including the ban on polygamy. In Obergefell v. Hodges (2015), Chief Justice Roberts argued in dissent that the majority's ruling immediately invites the question about whether states may retain "the definition of marriage as a union of two people." Do *Lawrence* and *Obergefell*'s protections of same-sex intimate association and marriage indeed put us on a slippery slope to protecting plural marriage? Or are there significant differences here? Stephen Macedo, for example, has rejected the slippery slope argument, contending that the two forms of marriage are on "entirely different historical trajectories"—marriage by same-sex couples is "closely associated with norms of gender equality," but polygamy "as widely practiced is a form of *hyper-traditional marriage*: gendered and patriarchal." Stephen Macedo, *Just Married: Same-Sex Marriage, Monogamy, and the Future of Marriage* (Princeton, NJ: Princeton University Press, 2015), 203.

(2)   Inspired by the Supreme Court's decision in *Obergefell* (particularly Chief Justice Roberts's dissent), Nathan Collier, legally married to Victoria Collier under Montana law, applied for a second marriage license to legally wed Christine Collier. He considered Christine his second wife and had wed her in a religious ceremony in 2007, but he did not sign a marriage license because he wanted to avoid bigamy charges. County clerk officials denied his application and he, Victoria, and Christine sued in federal district court. See "Montana Man Seeks License for Second Wife," *CBS News/AP*, July 1, 2015. The Colliers' complaint asserts that the four principles identified in the *Obergefell* majority opinion that show why marriage is "fundamental" apply equally to plural marriage. Do you agree?

In December 2015, the federal district court dismissed the Colliers' complaint on the ground that they lacked standing to challenge Montana's law, since they failed to demonstrate "injury in fact," such as a credible threat of prosecution under Montana's bigamy law. The court reasoned that the letter from the Yellowstone County Attorney's office denying the Collier's request for a second marriage license (to allow Nathan and Christine to marry), because "that act . . . would be considered bigamy in Montana," only "advised" the Colliers and did "not threaten prosecution." Findings and Recommendations of

U.S. Magistrate Judge, Collier et al. v. Fox et al., CV 15–83–BLG–SPW–CSO (D. Ct. Mont. Dec. 08, 2015). The Colliers also argued that, even without a second marriage license, Montana *might* prosecute them under its "common law marriage" statute, since common law, or informal, marriage arises without a marriage license; the court rejected that argument because there was no history of Montana using its common law marriage law against polygamists in this way. As this book goes to press, the Colliers have filed an amended complaint.

(3) In *Reynolds*, how broadly does the Supreme Court define the "free exercise of religion"? *Reynolds* grounded its rejection of the free exercise claim partly on a distinction between religious belief (which the Court said the Constitution protected) and religiously-motivated conduct (which the Court held was outside free exercise protection). What does *Reynolds* imply concerning religious exemptions from laws recognizing same-sex marriage?

(4) What justifications did *Reynolds* credit for banning polygamy? Is polygamy really "odious" in a democracy, leading to "the patriarchal principle" or "despotism"? In Brown v. Buhman, 947 F. Supp. 2d 1170 (D. Utah 2013), *vacated as moot*, 2016 WL 1399358 (10th Cir. April 11, 2016), in a challenge to Utah's bigamy law (described in Note (7)), a federal district court characterized *Reynolds* as displaying "the essence of Orientalism," with its "explicit 'distinction between Western superiority and Oriental inferiority' "—a mindset that was "entrenched" among "ruling elites" when *Reynolds* was decided. Ibid., 1183. The court contended that, in *Reynolds*, the "social harm" of polygamy was "introducing a practice perceived to be characteristic of non-European people— or non-white races—into white American society":

> Such an assessment arising from derisive societal views about race and ethnic origin prevalent in the United States at that time has no place in discourse about religious freedom, due process, equal protection or any other constitutional guarantee or right in the genuinely and intentionally racially and religiously pluralistic society that has been strengthened by the Supreme Court's twentieth-century rights jurisprudence. *Id.* at 1186–87.

The court observed, however, that while it did not view *Reynolds* as "good law," the Supreme Court—despite the "orientalist strain" in *Reynolds*—has continued to cite it on the limits of free exercise, including in our next case, Employment Division v. Smith (1990). Should the Supreme Court overrule *Reynolds*?

(5) If the *Brown* court is correct in its critique of *Reynolds*, are there nonetheless persuasive contemporary justifications for barring polygamy? Does

polygamy carry inherent harms that justify prohibiting it criminally and civilly? In 2011, the British Columbia Supreme Court upheld the constitutionality of Canada's criminal polygamy ban after an extensive trial. The court found a host of "pressing and substantial" state interests in monogamy. The court found that polygamy was linked with higher rates of domestic violence and sexual abuse for women and girls, higher rates of infant mortality, the internalization by children of "harmful gender stereotypes," and "higher levels of conflict, emotional stress and tension" arising from "rivalry and jealousy among co-wives." The court also found that Canada had international treaty obligations to take appropriate measures to eliminate polygamy. Reference re: Section 293 of the Criminal Code of Canada, 2011 BCSC 1588 (Can., B.C.). See also Susan Deller Ross, "Should Polygamy Be Permitted in the United States?," 38 *Human Rights* 20 (Spring 2011) (arguing that polygamy violates women's human right to equality in marriage and the rights of children).

(6)　Even if states have a compelling interest in preventing the types of harms noted by the British Columbia court (in Note (5)), some scholars contend those types of harms are present only in the "most extreme form of polygyny" and do not justify a complete prohibition. See Jonathan Turley, "The Loadstone Rock: The Role of Harm in the Criminalization of 'Plural Unions,'" 64 *Emory L. J.* 1905, 1909 (2015). Do you agree with Turley that such prohibition rests simply on moral disapproval? Some scholars further argue that "polyamory," by contrast with traditional polygyny, offers an example in which adults form enduring, consensual relationships with more than one partner in circumstances that are free from coercion or exploitation and that such a practice of "nonmonogamy" may share "some of its aspirations with more mainstream models of intimate relationships." Elizabeth F. Emens, "Monogamy's Law: Compulsory Monogamy and Polyamorous Existence," 29 *N.Y.U. Rev. L. & Soc. Change* 277, 283 (2004).

(7)　What are the constitutional limits on state bigamy laws? May states prohibit a legally married person from obtaining additional marriage licenses (as, for example, Montana's law does) or may they also prohibit such a legally married person from entering into a spiritual marriage with a second person or cohabiting with a second person as a spiritual spouse? This issue arose shortly after the launch of the reality television series, *Sister Wives*, featuring Kody Brown and his four wives, Meri (with whom he was in a civil marriage), and Janelle, Christine, and Robyn Brown (with whom he lived and was in marital unions based on their spiritual beliefs). After *Sister Wives* aired, Utah prosecutors began a criminal investigation. They declined to prosecute Brown and his wives, but did not rule out a future prosecution. Subsequently, in Brown v. Buhman (mentioned in Note (4)), the Browns (with the aid of law professor Jonathan Turley, mentioned above) sued in federal district court, challenging the constitutionality of Utah's bigamy law on numerous grounds, including "liberty" under the Fourteenth Amendment's Due Process Clause and the free exercise of religion under the First Amendment. They argued that Utah's law reached beyond banning entering into more than one legal union to prohibit religious "cohabitation."

In *Brown,* Utah federal district court judge Clark Waddoups deferred to *Reynolds* as "binding" with respect to entering into more than one legal union, but not as controlling on the issue of religious cohabitation. He held that the Utah bigamy statute's "cohabitation" prong violated the U.S. Constitution. Judge Waddoups acknowledged that "the state has an important interest in regulating marriage, but only insofar as marriage is understood as a legal status." This conclusion meant that the state may criminalize entry into a purported "second legal union," but it may not criminalize religious cohabitation when it does not criminalize non-religious adulterous cohabitation. 947 F. Supp.2d at 1218.

Do you agree with how Judge Waddoups resolved the challenge by Kody Brown and his four wives to Utah's bigamy statute? Did Utah's law reach too far? Contemporary social mores or norms played a role in *Brown*: Public officials admitted that they did not prosecute people engaged in "adultery or mere adulterous cohabitation," which "goes on all the time," but instead were concerned about "religious cohabitation," where a person who is legally married to one person calls the cohabiting partner a wife. Ibid., 1215. Is polygamy more troubling for society than "serial monogamy," or marrying and divorcing more than once? Than adultery?

On April 11, 2016, the Tenth Circuit vacated the lower court's opinion in *Brown*, ruling that Judge Waddoups erred by ruling on the merits of the Browns' claims about Utah's bigamy statute. The Tenth Circuit reasoned that, once the Utah County Attorney closed its investigation of the Browns and adopted a policy that the County Attorney "will bring bigamy prosecutions only against those who (1) induce a partner to marry through misrepresentation or (2) are suspected of committing a collateral crime such as fraud or abuse" (not at issue with the Browns), Judge Waddoups should have granted the County Attorney's motion to dismiss the case as moot: the Browns had no standing to sue because they no longer suffered any credible threat of prosecution. Brown v. Buhman, 2016 WL 1399358 (10th Cir. April 11, 2016). This reasoning is similar to that in *Collier*, discussed in Note (2). What are the symbolic or practical effects of leaving Utah's broad bigamy law on the books but having law enforcement authorities enforce it only in limited circumstances? Compare what the majority said in *Lawrence* (reprinted in Chapter 4) about the impact of criminal prohibitions of same-sex sodomy, even if prosecutions were rare. Would it have been preferable for the Tenth Circuit to have ruled on the merits of the Browns' claim? If so, how should they have ruled?

———

"[W]e cannot afford the luxury of deeming presumptively invalid, as applied to the religious objector, every regulation of conduct that does not protect an interest of the highest order."
—JUSTICE SCALIA

"The compelling interest test reflects the First Amendment's mandate of preserving religious liberty to the fullest extent possible in a pluralistic society. . . . [To] deem this command a 'luxury' is to denigrate '[t]he very purpose of a Bill of Rights.' "—JUSTICE O'CONNOR

"I do not believe the Founders thought their dearly bought freedom from religious persecution a 'luxury,' but an essential element of liberty."—JUSTICE BLACKMUN

EMPLOYMENT DIVISION, DEPARTMENT OF HUMAN RESOURCES OF OREGON V. SMITH
494 U.S. 872, 110 S.Ct. 1595, 108 L.Ed.2d 876 (1990)

[A private employer fired Alfred Smith and Galen Black—members of the Native American Church, working as drug and alcohol abuse rehabilitation counselors—for using peyote for sacramental purposes at religious ceremonies. Both men then claimed unemployment benefits from Oregon; the state denied the requests, saying the two had been discharged for misconduct. They sued in a state court, alleging that the denial had interfered with their free exercise of religion. Oregon's Supreme Court upheld their claims. The state obtained certiorari from the U.S. Supreme Court, which, in *Smith I* (1988), had remanded the case for a determination whether use of peyote for religious purposes violated Oregon's law. On remand, the state supreme court held that relevant statutes did forbid such use and thus violated the First Amendment's guarantee of free exercise. Oregon again obtained certiorari.]

■ JUSTICE SCALIA delivered the opinion of the Court. . . .

II

Respondents' claim for relief rests on our decisions in Sherbert v. Verner [1963], Thomas v. Review Bd. [1981], and Hobbie v. Unemployment Appeals Comm'n (1987), in which we held that a State could not condition the availability of unemployment insurance on an individual's willingness to forgo conduct required by his religion. . . .

A

The Free Exercise Clause of the First Amendment, which has been made applicable to the States by incorporation into the Fourteenth Amendment . . . means, first and foremost, the right to believe and profess whatever religious doctrine one desires. Thus, the First Amendment obviously excludes all "governmental regulation of religious beliefs as such." *Sherbert*. The government may not compel affirmation of religious belief, see Torcaso v. Watkins (1961), punish the expression of religious doctrines it believes to be false, United States v. Ballard (1944), impose special disabilities on the basis of religious views or religious status, see McDaniel v. Paty (1978); Fowler v. Rhode Island (1953); or lend its power to one or the other side in controversies over religious authority or dogma, see Presbyterian Church v. Hull Church (1969); Kedroff v. St. Nicholas Cathedral (1952); Serbian Eastern Orthodox Diocese v. Milivojevich (1976).

But the "exercise of religion" often involves not only belief and profession but the performance of (or abstention from) physical acts. . . . [A] state would be "prohibiting the free exercise [of religion]" if it sought to ban such acts or abstentions only when they are engaged in for religious reasons, or only because of the religious belief that they display. It would doubtless be unconstitutional, for example, to ban the casting of "statues that are to be used for worship purposes," or to prohibit bowing down before a golden calf. . . .

. . . [But w]e have never held that an individual's religious beliefs excuse him from compliance with an otherwise valid law prohibiting conduct that the State is free to regulate. On the contrary, the record of more than a century of our free exercise jurisprudence contradicts that proposition. As described succinctly by Justice Frankfurter in Minersville v. Gobitis (1940): "Conscientious scruples have not, in the course of the long struggle for religious toleration, relieved the individual from obedience to a general law not aimed at the promotion or restriction of religious beliefs. The mere possession of religious convictions . . . does not relieve the citizen from the discharge of political responsibilities." We first had occasion to assert that principle in Reynolds v. United States (1879), where we rejected the claim that criminal laws against polygamy could not be constitutionally applied to those whose religion commanded the practice. "Laws," we said, "are made for the government of actions, and while they cannot interfere with mere religious belief and opinions, they may with practices. . . . Can a man excuse his practices to the contrary because of his religious belief? To permit this would be to make the professed doctrines of religious belief superior to the law of the land, and in effect to permit every citizen to become a law unto himself."

Subsequent decisions have consistently held that the right of free exercise does not relieve an individual of the obligation to comply with a "valid and neutral law of general applicability on the ground that the law proscribes (or prescribes) conduct that his religion prescribes (or proscribes)." United States v. Lee (1982) (Stevens, J., concurring); see *Minersville*. . . .

The only decisions in which we have held that the First Amendment bars application of a neutral, generally applicable law to religiously motivated action have involved not the Free Exercise Clause alone, but the Free Exercise Clause in conjunction with other constitutional protections, such as freedom of speech and of the press, see Cantwell v. Connecticut (1940) . . . ; Murdock v. Penn. (1943) (invalidating a flat tax on solicitation as applied to the dissemination of religious ideas); . . . or the right of parents, acknowledged in Pierce v. Society of Sisters (1925), to direct the education of their children, see Wisconsin v. Yoder (1972). . . . Some of our cases prohibiting compelled expression, decided exclusively upon free speech grounds, have also involved freedom of religion, cf. Wooley v. Maynard (1977) (invalidating compelled display of a license plate slogan that offended individual religious beliefs); West Va. v. Barnette (1943) (invalidating compulsory flag salute statute challenged by religious objectors). . . .

The present case does not present such a hybrid situation. . . . "Our cases do not at their farthest reach support the proposition that a stance of conscientious opposition relieves an objector from any colliding duty fixed by a democratic government." Gillette v. United States (1971).

B

Respondents argue that . . . the claim for a religious exemption must be evaluated under the balancing test set forth in *Sherbert*[:] . . . governmental actions that substantially burden a religious practice must be justified by a compelling governmental interest. Applying that test we have, on three occasions, invalidated state unemployment compensation rules that conditioned the availability of benefits upon an applicant's willingness to work under conditions forbidden by his religion. We have never invalidated any governmental action on the basis of the *Sherbert* test except the denial of unemployment compensation. Although we have sometimes purported to apply the *Sherbert* test in contexts other than that, we have always found the test satisfied, see *Lee*; *Gillette*. In recent years we have abstained from applying the *Sherbert* test (outside the unemployment compensation field) at all. In Bowen v. Roy (1986), we declined to apply *Sherbert* analysis to a federal statutory scheme that required benefit applicants and recipients to provide their Social Security numbers. The plaintiffs in that case asserted that it would violate their religious beliefs to obtain and provide a Social Security number for their daughter. We held the statute's application to the plaintiffs valid regardless of whether it was necessary to effectuate a compelling interest. . . .

Even if we were inclined to breathe into *Sherbert* some life beyond the unemployment compensation field, we would not apply it to require exemptions from a generally applicable criminal law. . . . Whether or not the decisions are that limited, they at least have nothing to do with an across-the-board criminal prohibition on a particular form of conduct. Although . . . we have sometimes used the *Sherbert* test to analyze free exercise challenges to such laws, see *Lee*, *Gillette*, we have never applied the test to invalidate one. We conclude today that the sounder approach, and the approach in accord with the vast majority of our precedents, is to hold the test inapplicable to such challenges. . . . To make an individual's obligation to obey such a law contingent upon the law's coincidence with his religious beliefs, except where the State's interest is "compelling" . . . contradicts both constitutional tradition and common sense.

The "compelling government interest" requirement seems benign, because it is familiar. . . . But using it as the standard that must be met before the government may accord different treatment on the basis of race, see, e.g., Palmore v. Sidoti (1984), or before the government may regulate the content of speech, see, e.g., Sable Communications v. FCC (1989), is not remotely comparable to using it for the purpose asserted here. What it produces in those other fields—equality of treatment, and an unrestricted flow of contending speech—are constitutional norms; what it would produce here—a private right to ignore generally applicable laws—is a constitutional anomaly.

Nor is it possible to limit the impact of respondents' proposal by requiring a "compelling state interest" only when the conduct prohibited is "central" to the individual's religion. It is no more appropriate for judges to determine the "centrality" of religious beliefs before applying a "compelling interest" test in the free exercise field, than it would be for them to determine the "importance" of ideas before applying the "compelling interest" test in the free speech field. . . . Repeatedly and in many different contexts, we have warned that courts must not presume to determine the place of a particular belief in a religion or the plausibility of a religious claim. See, e.g., *Thomas; Presbyterian Church*; Jones v. Wolf (1979); *Ballard*.

If the "compelling interest" test is to be applied at all, then, it must be applied across the board, to all actions thought to be religiously commanded. Moreover, if "compelling interest" really means what it says (and watering it down here would subvert its rigor in the other fields where it is applied), many laws will not meet the test. Any society adopting such a system would be courting anarchy, but that danger increases in direct proportion to the society's diversity of religious beliefs, and its determination to coerce or suppress none of them. Precisely because "we are a cosmopolitan nation made up of people of almost every conceivable religious preference," *Braunfeld*, and precisely because we value and protect that religious divergence, we cannot afford the luxury of deeming presumptively invalid, as applied to the religious objector, every regulation of conduct that does not protect an interest of the highest order. The rule respondents favor would open the prospect of constitutionally required religious exemptions from civic obligations of almost every conceivable kind. . . .

Values that are protected against government interference through enshrinement in the Bill of Rights are not thereby banished from the political process. Just as a society that believes in the negative protection accorded to the press by the First Amendment is likely to enact laws that affirmatively foster the dissemination of the printed word, so also a society that believes in the negative protection accorded to religious belief can be expected to be solicitous of that value in its legislation as well. It is therefore not surprising that a number of States have made an exception to their drug laws for sacramental peyote use. . . . [Justice Scalia cited statutes from Arizona, Colorado, and New Mexico—**Eds.**] But to say that a nondiscriminatory religious-practice exemption is permitted, or even that it is desirable, is not to say that it is constitutionally required. . . . It may fairly be said that leaving accommodation to the political process will place at a relative disadvantage those religious practices that are not widely engaged in; but that unavoidable consequence of democratic government must be preferred to a system in which each conscience is a law unto itself or in which judges weight the social importance of all laws against the centrality of all religious beliefs.

Because respondents' ingestion of peyote was prohibited under Oregon law, and because that prohibition is constitutional, Oregon may, consistent with the Free Exercise Clause, deny respondents unemployment compensation when their dismissal results from use of the drug. . . .

■ JUSTICE O'CONNOR, with whom JUSTICE BRENNAN, JUSTICE MARSHALL, and JUSTICE BLACKMUN join as to Parts I and II, concurring in the judgment. . . .*

II

The Court today extracts from our long history of free exercise precedents the single categorical rule that "if prohibiting the exercise of religion . . . is . . . merely the incidental effect of a generally applicable and otherwise valid provision, the First Amendment has not been offended." Indeed, the Court holds that where the law is a generally applicable criminal prohibition, our usual free exercise jurisprudence does not even apply. To reach this sweeping result, however, the Court must not only give a strained reading of the First Amendment but must also disregard our consistent application of free exercise doctrine to cases involving generally applicable regulations that burden religious conduct.

A

[T]he "free exercise" of religion often, if not invariably, requires the performance of (or abstention from) certain acts. "[B]elief and action cannot be neatly confined in logic-tight compartments." *Yoder*. Because the First Amendment does not distinguish between religious belief and religious conduct, conduct motivated by sincere religious belief, like the belief itself, must therefore be at least presumptively protected by the Free Exercise Clause.

The Court today, however, interprets the Clause to permit the government to prohibit, without justification, conduct mandated by an individual's religious beliefs, so long as that prohibition is generally applicable. But a law that prohibits certain conduct—conduct that happens to be an act of worship for someone—manifestly does prohibit that person's free exercise of his religion. . . . The Court responds that generally applicable laws are "one large step" removed from laws aimed at specific religious practices. The First Amendment, however, does not distinguish between laws that are generally applicable and laws that target particular religious practices. . . . Our free exercise cases have all concerned generally applicable laws that had the effect of significantly burdening a religious practice. . . .

---

*   Although Justice Brennan, Justice Marshall, and Justice Blackmun join Parts I and II of this opinion, they do not concur in the judgment. [Footnote by Justice O'Connor.]

To say that a person's right to free exercise has been burdened, of course, does not mean that he has an absolute right to engage in the conduct. . . . [W]e have recognized that the freedom to act, unlike the freedom to believe, cannot be absolute. See, e.g., *Cantwell*; *Reynolds*. Instead, we have respected both the First Amendment's express textual mandate and the governmental interest in regulation of conduct by requiring the Government to justify any substantial burden on religiously motivated conduct by a compelling state interest and by means narrowly tailored to achieve that interest. The compelling interest test effectuates the First Amendment's command that religious liberty is an independent liberty, that it occupies a preferred position, and that the Court will not permit encroachments upon this liberty, whether direct or indirect, unless required by clear and compelling governmental interests "of the highest order," *Yoder*. . . .

The Court attempts to support its narrow reading of the Clause by claiming that "[w]e have never held that an individual's religious beliefs excuse him from compliance with an otherwise valid law prohibiting conduct that the State is free to regulate." But as the Court later notes, as it must, in cases such as *Cantwell* and *Yoder* we have in fact interpreted the Free Exercise Clause to forbid application of a generally applicable prohibition to religiously motivated conduct. Indeed, in *Yoder* we expressly rejected the interpretation the Court now adopts:

> . . . [T]o agree that religiously grounded conduct must often be subject to the broad police power of the State is not to deny that there are areas of conduct protected by the Free Exercise Clause of the First Amendment and thus beyond the power of the State to control, *even under regulations of general applicability*. . . .

> . . . A regulation neutral on its face may, in its application, nonetheless offend the constitutional requirement for government neutrality if it unduly burdens the free exercise of religion. (Emphasis added; citations omitted.)

The Court endeavors to escape from our decisions in *Cantwell* and *Yoder* by labeling them "hybrid" decisions, but there is no denying that both cases expressly relied on the Free Exercise Clause, and that we have consistently regarded those cases as part of the mainstream of our free exercise jurisprudence. Moreover, in each of the other cases cited by the Court to support its categorical rule, we rejected the particular constitutional claims before us only after carefully weighing the competing interests. That we rejected the free exercise claims in those cases hardly calls into question the applicability of First Amendment doctrine in the first place. . . .

B . . .

. . . A State that makes criminal an individual's religiously motivated conduct burdens that individual's free exercise of religion in the severest manner possible, for it "results in the choice to the individual of either abandoning his religious principle or facing criminal prosecution." *Braunfeld.* I would have thought it beyond argument that such laws implicate free exercise concerns. . . .

Legislatures, of course, have always been "left free to reach actions which were in violation of social duties or subversive of good order." *Reynolds*; see also *Yoder, Braunfeld.* Yet because of the close relationship between conduct and religious belief, "[i]n every case the power to regulate must be so exercised as not, in attaining a permissible end, unduly to infringe the protected freedom." *Cantwell.* Once . . . a government regulation or criminal prohibition burdens the free exercise of religion, we have consistently asked the Government to demonstrate that unbending application of its regulation to the religious objector "is essential to accomplish an overriding governmental interest," *Lee*, or represents "the least restrictive means of achieving some compelling state interest," *Thomas.* . . . Even if, as an empirical matter, a government's criminal laws might usually serve a compelling interest in health, safety, or public order, the First Amendment at least requires a case-by-case determination of the question, sensitive to the facts of each particular claim. . . . [W]e cannot assume, merely because a law carries criminal sanctions and is generally applicable, that the First Amendment never requires the State to grant a limited exemption for religiously motivated conduct.

Moreover, we have not "rejected" or "declined to apply" the compelling interest test in our recent cases. Recent cases have instead affirmed that test as a fundamental part of our First Amendment doctrine. . . . The cases cited by the Court signal no retreat from our consistent adherence to the compelling interest test. In . . . *Roy* . . . , for example, we expressly distinguished *Sherbert* on the ground that the First Amendment does not "require the Government *itself* to behave in ways that the individual believes will further his or her spiritual development. . . ." This distinction makes sense because "the Free Exercise Clause is written in terms of what the government cannot do to the individual, not in terms of what the individual can exact from the government." *Sherbert* (Douglas, J., concurring). . . .

The Court today gives no convincing reason to depart from settled First Amendment jurisprudence. There is nothing talismanic about neutral laws of general applicability or general criminal prohibitions, for laws neutral toward religion can coerce a person to violate his religious conscience or intrude upon his religious duties just as effectively as laws aimed at religion. Although the Court suggests that the compelling interest test, as applied to generally applicable laws, would result in a "constitutional anomaly," the First Amendment unequivocally makes freedom of religion, like freedom from race discrimination and freedom of speech, a "constitutional nor[m]," not an "anomaly." . . . As the language of the Clause itself makes clear, an individual's free exercise of religion is a preferred constitutional activity. A law that makes criminal such an activity therefore triggers constitutional concern—and heightened judicial scrutiny—even if it does not target the particular religious conduct at issue. Our free speech cases similarly recognize that neutral regulations that affect free speech values are subject to a balancing, rather than categorical, approach. . . .

Finally, the Court today suggests that the disfavoring of minority religions is an "unavoidable consequence" under our system of government and that accommodation of such religions must be left to the political process. In my view, however, the First Amendment was enacted precisely to protect the rights of those whose religious practices are not shared by the majority and may be viewed with hostility. The history of our free exercise doctrine amply demonstrates the harsh impact majoritarian rule has had on unpopular or emerging religious groups such as the Jehovah's Witnesses and the Amish. Indeed, the words of Justice Jackson in *Barnette* (overruling *Gobitis*) are apt:

> The very purpose of a Bill of Rights was to withdraw certain subjects from the vicissitudes of political controversy, to place them beyond the reach of majorities and officials and to establish them as legal principles to be applied by the courts. One's right to life, liberty, and property, to free speech, a free press, freedom of worship and assembly, and other fundamental rights may not be submitted to vote; they depend on the outcome of no elections.

The compelling interest test reflects the First Amendment's mandate of preserving religious liberty to the fullest extent possible in a pluralistic society. For the Court to deem this command a "luxury" is to denigrate "[t]he very purpose of a Bill of Rights."

III

The Court's holding today not only misreads settled First Amendment precedent; it appears to be unnecessary to this case. I would reach the same result applying our established free exercise jurisprudence. . . . [Justice O'Connor went on to argue that drug abuse was a grave problem and the state had a compelling interest in curbing the trafficking of such substances.—**Eds.**]

■ JUSTICE BLACKMUN, with whom JUSTICE BRENNAN and JUSTICE MARSHALL join, dissenting.

This Court over the years painstakingly has developed a consistent and exacting standard to test the constitutionality of a state statute that burdens the free exercise of religion. Such a statute may stand only if the law in general, and the State's refusal to allow a religious exemption in particular, are justified by a compelling interest that cannot be served by less restrictive means.

. . . I thought this was a settled and inviolate principle of this Court's First Amendment jurisprudence. The majority, however, perfunctorily dismisses it as a "constitutional anomaly." . . . [T]he majority is able to arrive at this view only by mischaracterizing this Court's precedents. The Court discards leading free exercise cases such as *Cantwell* and *Yoder*, as "hybrid." The Court views traditional free exercise analysis as somehow inapplicable to criminal prohibitions (as opposed to conditions on the receipt of benefits), and to state laws of general applicability (as opposed, presumably, to laws that expressly single out religious practices). . . . In short, it effectuates a wholesale overturning of settled law. . . .

This distorted view of our precedents leads the majority to conclude that strict scrutiny of a state law burdening the free exercise of religion is a "luxury" . . . and that the repression of minority religions is an "unavoidable consequence of democratic government." I do not believe the Founders thought their dearly bought freedom from religious persecution a "luxury," but an essential element of liberty—and they could not have thought religious intolerance "unavoidable," for they drafted the Religion Clauses precisely in order to avoid that intolerance. . . .

I

. . . It is not the State's broad interest in fighting the critical "war on drugs" that must be weighed against respondents' claim, but the State's narrow interest in refusing to make an exception for the religious, ceremonial use of peyote. . . . Failure to reduce the competing interests to the same plane of generality tends to distort the weighing process in the State's favor. See . . . [Roscoe] Pound, A Survey of Social Interests, 57 *Harv. L. Rev.* 1, 2 (1943) ("When it comes to weighing or valuing claims or demands with respect to other claims or demands, we must be careful to compare them on the same plane . . . [or else] we may decide the question in advance in our very way of putting it"). . . .

The State's interest in enforcing its prohibition, in order to be sufficiently compelling to outweigh a free exercise claim, cannot be merely abstract or symbolic. The State cannot plausibly assert that unbending application of a criminal prohibition is essential to fulfill any compelling interest, if it does not, in fact, attempt to enforce that prohibition. In this case, the State actually has not evinced any concrete interest in enforcing its drug laws against religious users of peyote. Oregon has never sought to prosecute respondents, and does not claim that it has made significant enforcement efforts against other religious users of peyote. The State's asserted interest thus amounts only to the symbolic preservation of an unenforced prohibition. But a government interest in "symbolism, even symbolism for so worthy a cause as the abolition of unlawful drugs," (Treasury Employees v. Von Raab [1989]) (Scalia, J., dissenting), cannot suffice to abrogate the constitutional rights of individuals.

Similarly, this Court's prior decisions have not allowed a government to rely on mere speculation about potential harms, but have demanded evidentiary support for a refusal to allow a religious exception. . . . In this case, the State's justification for refusing to recognize an exception to its criminal laws for religious peyote use is entirely speculative. The State . . . [offers] no evidence that the religious use of peyote has ever harmed anyone. The factual findings of other courts cast doubt on the State's assumption that religious use of peyote is harmful. . . . The Federal Government, which created the classifications of unlawful drugs from which Oregon's drug laws are derived, apparently does not find peyote so dangerous as to preclude an exemption for religious use.

The carefully circumscribed ritual context in which respondents used peyote is far removed from the irresponsible and unrestricted recreational use of unlawful drugs.[6] The Native American Church's internal restrictions on, and supervision of, its members' use of peyote substantially obviate the State's health and safety concerns. . . . The State also seeks to support its refusal to make an

---

[6]   In this respect, respondents' use of peyote seems closely analogous to the sacramental use of wine by the Roman Catholic Church. During Prohibition, the Federal Government exempted such use of wine from its general ban on possession and use of alcohol. However compelling the Government's then general interest in prohibiting the use of alcohol may have been, it could not plausibly have asserted an interest sufficiently compelling to outweigh Catholics' right to take communion. [Footnote by Justice Blackmun.]

exception for religious use of peyote by invoking its interest in abolishing drug trafficking. There is, however, practically no illegal traffic in peyote. . . .

Finally, the State argues that granting an exception for religious peyote use would erode its interest in the uniform, fair, and certain enforcement of its drug laws. The State fears that, if it grants an exemption for religious peyote use, a flood of other claims to religious exemptions will follow. . . . The State's apprehension of a flood of other religious claims is purely speculative. Almost half the States, and the Federal Government, have maintained an exemption for religious peyote use for many years, and apparently have not found themselves overwhelmed by claims to other religious exemptions. Allowing an exemption for religious peyote use would not necessarily oblige the State to grant a similar exemption to other religious groups. . . . Though the State must treat all religions equally . . . this obligation is fulfilled by the uniform application of the "compelling interest" test to all free exercise claims, not by reaching uniform results as to all claims. A showing that religious peyote use does not unduly interfere with the State's interests . . . does not mean that an exemption limited to peyote use is tantamount to an establishment of religion. . . .

II

Finally . . . I do not think this means that the courts must turn a blind eye to the severe impact of a State's restrictions on the adherents of a minority religion. . . . Respondents believe, and their sincerity has never been at issue, that the peyote plant embodies their deity, and eating it is an act of worship and communion. Without peyote, they could not enact the essential ritual of their religion. . . .

. . . This potentially devastating impact must be viewed in light of the federal policy—reached in reaction to many years of religious persecution and intolerance—of protecting the religious freedom of Native Americans. See American Indian Religious Freedom Act. . . . Congress recognized that certain substances, such as peyote, "have religious significance because they are sacred, they have power, they heal, they are necessary to the exercise of the rites of the religion, they are necessary to the cultural integrity of the tribe, and, therefore, religious survival." H. R. Rep. No. 95–1308, p. 2 (1978). . . .

EDITORS' NOTES

(1) Justice Scalia's majority opinion quotes from *Reynolds* (reprinted above) on the risk that permitting a person to use "religious belief" to excuse practices

that conflict with the law would risk permitting "every citizen to become a law unto himself." What limits, on Scalia's view, does the duty to obey the law place upon the free exercise of religion? When, if ever, does legal regulation reach too far? How do the majority and dissenting opinions differ in their understanding of the scope of the "free exercise of religion"?

(2)   The majority and dissenting opinions differ sharply about the proper test to apply to Smith's and Black's "free exercise of religion" challenge. That disagreement stems in part from their different readings of the Court's prior First Amendment cases. Is Justice Scalia's rejection of a strict scrutiny/compelling state interest test, when someone challenges a valid and neutral law of general applicability, persuasive? Or is the dissent more persuasive that the majority is taking a "distorted" view of the Court's precedents and affording less protection of religious freedom than the Constitution requires?

(3)   How do the majority and the dissenting opinions understand "tolerance" of religion? The scope of constitutional protection of religious diversity? Which approach is the most attractive?

(4)   In stressing the obligation of religious believers to obey the law notwithstanding their "conscientious scruples," Justice Scalia quotes from Justice Frankfurter's majority opinion in Minersville v. Gobitis (1940), in which the Court upheld a compulsory flag salute in public school against the free exercise claims of two children of the Jehovah's Witness faith. The Court, however, overruled *Gobitis* just three years later in West Virginia v. Barnette (1943). Indeed, Justice O'Connor (joined by three other justices) quotes the famous passage from *Barnette* about the Bill of Rights' purpose of withdrawing certain subjects from "the reach of majorities and officials." Why do you suppose Justice Scalia invoked *Gobitis*, despite its overruling by *Barnette*? In another frequently quoted passage from *Barnette*, the Court states that "[i]f there is any fixed star in our constitutional constellation, it is that no official, high or petty, can prescribe what shall be orthodox in politics, nationalism, religion, or other matters of opinion or force citizens to confess by word or act their faith therein." As you will see later in this chapter (*e.g.*, in Elane Photography v. Willock (2013)), this passage about governmental orthodoxy often features in present-day debates about the scope of religious exemptions from antidiscrimination laws protecting LGBT persons.

(5)   Justice Scalia points to examples of some states providing exemptions to their drug laws for sacramental peyote use in support of his contention that "[v]alues that are protected against government interference through

enshrinement in the Bill of Rights are not thereby banished from the political process." He also concedes, however, that "leaving accommodation to the political process will place at a relative disadvantage those religious practices that are not widely engaged in," but concludes that this "unavoidable consequence of democratic government must be preferred to a system in which each conscience is a law unto itself or in which judges weigh the social importance of all laws against the centrality of all religious beliefs." Is Scalia's approach sufficiently protective of religious minorities? Or is Justice O'Connor more persuasive that "[t]he First Amendment was enacted precisely to protect the rights of those whose religious practices are not shared by the majority and may be viewed with hostility"?

(6)   Three years after *Smith*, Church of the Lukumi Babalu v. Hialeah (1993) offered the Court an opportunity to qualify its position in *Smith*. Followers of Lukumi sacrificed animals in their religious rituals and attacked the validity of ordinances that restricted killing animals even for religious purposes. All of the justices thought that the ordinances were unconstitutional, as applied against this sect. The justices could agree, however, only on part of the justifying reasoning and produced four separate opinions. Justice Kennedy wrote an opinion that, on some points, commanded a majority. He made scant mention of *Smith* and wrote:

> if the object of a law is to infringe upon or restrict practices because of their religious motivation, the law is not neutral, see *Smith*, and it is invalid unless it is justified by a compelling interest and is narrowly tailored to advance that interest.

A paragraph later, Kennedy added that, although a law restricting religious practice must be neutral to be valid, "Facial neutrality is not determinative." Scalia wrote a brief concurrence, saying that the ordinances were not generally applicable, but applied specifically to religious activity, and thus were not neutral.

(7)   *Smith* evidences a striking division between the conservative and liberal justices on the Court at the time, with most of the other conservative justices joining Justice Scalia's majority opinion, and most of the liberals dissenting and expressing concern over what they viewed as the Court's evident retrenching on the protection of religious liberty. Justice Kennedy, who would go on to author the Court's landmark gay rights decisions, joined the majority opinion. Justice O'Connor, generally in the center of the Court, concurred in the judgment but rejected the Court's characterization of the free exercise precedents. By contrast, in present-day controversies over the evident clash between religious liberty and

laws protecting against discrimination on the basis of sexual orientation, as well as constitutional recognition of the right of gay men and lesbians to marry, Justice Scalia and other conservative justices seem to have less confidence in the political process to protect religious persons who dissent from the new "orthodoxy" (see Obergefell v. Hodges (2015)). If the Court were to apply *Smith*, how should it rule on a free exercise claim brought by a religious person that an antidiscrimination law forbidding discrimination on the basis of sexual orientation violated her conscience and that, under the First Amendment, she must be exempt from it?

(8)   Politicians from both ends of the political spectrum criticized *Smith*. One initial reaction by state legislators was that Oregon, along with several other states, decriminalized religious use of peyote—the sort of democratic protection of religious liberty that Justice Scalia indicated states were free to undertake. At the federal level, Congress reacted by passing the Religious Freedom Restoration Act of 1993 (RFRA), which sought to restore judicial use of the "compelling state interest" standard and "strict scrutiny" test any time that government "substantially burden[ed] a person's exercise of religion." 42 U.S. Code 2000bb–2000bb4, 107 Stat. 1488 Pub. Law 103–41. Among Congress's findings were that "laws 'neutral' toward religion may burden religious exercise as surely as laws intended to interfere with religious exercise" and that "the compelling interest test as set forth in prior Federal court rulings is a workable test for striking sensible balances between religious liberty and competing prior governmental interests." Subsequently, in City of Boerne v. Flores (1997), the Court, in an opinion written by Justice Kennedy, ruled that RFRA exceeded Congress's enforcement power under the Fourteenth Amendment and that its "sweeping coverage" would intrude at "every level of government" and impose a "heavy litigation burden on the States" and "curtail[ ] their traditional general regulatory power." However, since the Court invalidated RFRA only as applied to the states, RFRA remains operative as to the federal government.[18] In the next case, RFRA is the basis upon which several companies rely in asserting that the federal Affordable Care Act substantially burdens their free exercise of religion. As discussed later in this chapter, a number of states have enacted their own religious freedom restoration acts.

---

[18]   Congress subsequently responded to the Court by enacting the Religious Land Use and Institutionalized Persons Act of 2000, 42 U.S.C. Sec. 2000cc–1(a)(1)–(2), relying this time upon its authority under the spending powers and the Commerce Clauses. The law imposes a compelling state interest test on state-imposed burdens on religious exercise in two areas: land use regulation and institutionalized persons (by requiring accommodation of religious practices of institutionalized persons). The Court upheld this federal law in Cutter v. Wilkinson (2005).

———

"[R]FRA was designed to provide very broad protection for religious liberty. By enacting RFRA, Congress went far beyond what this Court has held is constitutionally required. . . . Congress provided protection for people like the Hahns and Greens by employing a familiar legal fiction: It included corporations within RFRA's definition of 'persons.' "—JUSTICE ALITO

"Free exercise in this sense implicates more than just freedom of belief. See Cantwell v. Connecticut (1940). It means, too, the right to express those beliefs and to establish one's religious (or nonreligious) self-definition in the political, civic, and economic life of our larger community. But in a complex society and an era of pervasive governmental regulation, defining the proper realm for free exercise can be difficult."—JUSTICE KENNEDY

"The Court's determination that RFRA extends to for-profit corporations is bound to have untoward effects. Although the Court attempts to cabin its language to closely held corporations, its logic extends to corporations of any size, public or private. Little doubt that RFRA claims will proliferate, for the Court's expansive notion of corporate personhood—combined with its other errors in construing RFRA—invites for-profit entities to seek religion-based exemptions from regulations they deem offensive to their faith."—JUSTICE GINSBURG

BURWELL V. HOBBY LOBBY STORES, INC.
573 U.S. ____, 134 S. Ct. 2751, 189 L.Ed. 2d 675 (2014)

■ JUSTICE ALITO delivered the opinion of the Court.

We must decide in these cases whether the Religious Freedom Restoration Act of 1993 (RFRA) permits the United States Department of Health and Human Services (HHS) to demand that three closely held corporations provide health-insurance coverage for methods of contraception that violate the sincerely held religious beliefs of the companies' owners. We hold that the regulations that impose this obligation violate RFRA, which prohibits the Federal Government from taking any action that substantially burdens the exercise of religion unless that action constitutes the least restrictive means of serving a compelling government interest

[W]e reject HHS's argument that the owners of the companies forfeited all RFRA protection when they decided to organize their businesses as corporations rather than sole proprietorships or general partnerships. The plain terms of RFRA make it perfectly clear that Congress did not discriminate in this way against men and women who wish to run their businesses as for-profit corporations in the manner required by their religious beliefs.

Since RFRA applies in these cases, we must decide whether the challenged HHS regulations substantially burden the exercise of religion, and we hold that they do. The owners of the businesses have religious objections to abortion, and according to their religious beliefs the four contraceptive methods at issue are abortifacients. If the owners comply with the HHS mandate, they believe they will be facilitating abortions, and if they do not comply, they will pay a very heavy price—as much as $1.3 million per day, or about $475 million per year, in the case of one of the companies. If these consequences do not amount to a substantial burden, it is hard to see what would.

Under RFRA, a Government action that imposes a substantial burden on religious exercise must serve a compelling government interest, and we assume that the HHS regulations satisfy this requirement. But . . . it must also constitute the least restrictive means of serving that interest, and the mandate plainly fails that test. There are other ways in which Congress or HHS could equally ensure that every woman has cost-free access to the particular contraceptives at issue here and, indeed, to all FDA-approved contraceptives.

In fact, HHS has already devised and implemented a system that seeks to respect the religious liberty of religious nonprofit corporations while ensuring that the employees of these entities have precisely the same access to all FDA-approved contraceptives as employees of companies whose owners have no religious objections to providing such coverage. The employees of these religious nonprofit corporations still have access to insurance coverage without cost sharing for all FDA-approved contraceptives; and according to HHS, this system imposes no net economic burden on the insurance companies that are required to provide or secure the coverage.

Although HHS has made this system available to religious nonprofits that have religious objections to the contraceptive mandate, HHS has provided no reason why the same system cannot be made available when the owners of for-profit corporations have similar religious objections. We therefore conclude that this system constitutes an alternative that achieves all of the Government's aims while providing greater respect for religious liberty. And under RFRA, that conclusion means that enforcement of the HHS contraceptive mandate against the objecting parties in these cases is unlawful.

As this description of our reasoning shows, our holding is very specific. We do not hold, as the principal dissent alleges, that for-profit corporations . . . can "opt out of any law (saving only tax laws) they judge incompatible with their sincerely held religious beliefs." Nor do we hold . . . that such corporations have free rein to take steps that impose "disadvantages . . . on others" or that require "the general public [to] pick up the tab." And we certainly do not hold or suggest that "RFRA demands accommodation of a for-profit corporation's religious beliefs no matter the impact that accommodation may have on . . . thousands of women employed by Hobby Lobby." The effect of the HHS-created accommodation on the women employed by Hobby Lobby and the other companies involved in these cases would be precisely zero. [T]hese women would still be entitled to all FDA-approved contraceptives without cost sharing.

I

A

Congress enacted RFRA in 1993 in order to provide very broad protection for religious liberty. RFRA's enactment came three years after this Court's decision in Employment Div., Dept. of Human Resources of Ore. v. Smith (1990), which largely repudiated the method of analyzing free-exercise claims that had been used in cases like Sherbert v. Verner (1963), and Wisconsin v. Yoder (1972). In determining whether challenged government actions violated the Free Exercise Clause of the First Amendment, those decisions used a balancing test that took into account whether the challenged action imposed a substantial burden on the practice of religion, and if it did, whether it was needed to serve a compelling government interest. . . .

In *Smith*, however, the Court rejected "the balancing test set forth in *Sherbert*." *Smith* concerned two members of the Native American Church who were fired for ingesting peyote for sacramental purposes. When they sought unemployment benefits, the State of Oregon rejected their claims on the ground that consumption of peyote was a crime, but the Oregon Supreme Court, applying the *Sherbert* test, held that the denial of benefits violated the Free Exercise Clause.

This Court then reversed, observing that use of the *Sherbert* test whenever a person objected on religious grounds to the enforcement of a generally applicable law "would open the prospect of constitutionally required religious exemptions from civic obligations of almost every conceivable kind." The Court therefore held that, under the First Amendment, "neutral, generally applicable laws may be applied to religious practices even when not supported by a compelling governmental interest." City of Boerne v. Flores (1997).

Congress responded to *Smith* by enacting RFRA. "[L]aws [that are] 'neutral' toward religion," Congress found, "may burden religious exercise as surely as laws intended to interfere with religious exercise." 42 U.S.C. § 2000bb(a)(2). In order to ensure broad protection for religious liberty, RFRA provides that "Government shall not substantially burden a person's exercise of religion even if the burden results from a rule of general applicability." If the Government substantially burdens a person's exercise of religion, under the Act that person is entitled to an exemption from the rule unless the Government "demonstrates that application of the burden to the person—(1) is in furtherance of a compelling governmental interest; and (2) is the least restrictive means of furthering that compelling governmental interest." § 2000bb–1(b).

As enacted in 1993, RFRA applied to both the Federal Government and the States, but the constitutional authority invoked for regulating federal and state agencies differed. As applied to a federal agency, RFRA is based on the enumerated power that supports the particular agency's work, but in attempting to regulate the States and their subdivisions, Congress relied on its power under Section 5 of the Fourteenth Amendment to enforce the First Amendment. In *City of Boerne,* however, we held that Congress had overstepped its Section 5 authority because "[t]he stringent test RFRA demands" "far exceed[ed] any pattern or practice of unconstitutional conduct under the Free Exercise Clause as interpreted in *Smith*."

Following our decision in *City of Boerne*, Congress passed the Religious Land Use and Institutionalized Persons Act of 2000 (RLUIPA). That statute, enacted under Congress's Commerce and Spending Clause powers, imposes the same general test as RFRA but on a more limited category of governmental actions. And . . . RLUIPA amended RFRA's definition of the "exercise of religion." . . . RFRA's definition made reference to the First Amendment. In RLUIPA, in an obvious effort to effect a complete separation from First Amendment case law, Congress deleted the reference to the First Amendment and defined the "exercise of religion" to include "any exercise of religion, whether or not compelled by, or central to, a system of religious belief." . . .

B

At issue in these cases are HHS regulations promulgated under the Patient Protection and Affordable Care Act of 2010 (ACA). ACA generally requires employers with 50 or more full-time employees to offer "a group health plan or group health insurance coverage" that provides "minimum essential coverage." [I]f a covered employer provides group health insurance but its plan fails to comply with ACA's group-health-plan requirements, the employer may be required to pay $100 per day for each affected "individual." And if the employer decides to stop providing health insurance altogether and at least one full-time employee enrolls in a health plan and qualifies for a subsidy on one of the government-run ACA exchanges, the employer must pay $2,000 per year for each of its full-time employees.

Unless an exception applies, ACA requires an employer's group health plan or group-health-insurance coverage to furnish "preventive care and screenings" for women without "any cost sharing requirements." Congress itself, however, did not specify what types of preventive care must be covered. Instead, Congress authorized the Health Resources and Services Administration (HRSA), a component of HHS, to make that important and sensitive decision. The HRSA in turn consulted the Institute of Medicine, a nonprofit group of volunteer advisers, in determining which preventive services to require.

In August 2011, based on the Institute's recommendations, the HRSA promulgated the Women's Preventive Services Guidelines. The Guidelines provide that nonexempt employers are generally required to provide "coverage, without cost sharing" for "[a]ll Food and Drug Administration [(FDA)] approved contraceptive methods, sterilization procedures, and patient education and counseling." 77 Fed.Reg. 8725. Although many of the required, FDA-approved methods of contraception work by preventing the fertilization of an egg, four of those methods . . . may have the effect of preventing an already fertilized egg from developing any further by inhibiting its attachment to the uterus.

HHS also authorized the HRSA to establish exemptions from the contraceptive mandate for "religious employers." That category encompasses "churches, their integrated auxiliaries, and conventions or associations of churches," as well as "the exclusively religious activities of any religious order." In its Guidelines, HRSA exempted these organizations from the requirement to cover contraceptive services.

In addition, HHS has effectively exempted certain religious nonprofit organizations . . . from the contraceptive mandate. An "eligible organization" means a nonprofit organization that "holds itself out as a religious organization" and "opposes providing coverage for some or all of any contraceptive services required to be covered . . . on account of religious objections." To qualify for this accommodation, an employer must certify that it is such an organization. [A] group-health-insurance issuer . . . must then exclude contraceptive coverage from the employer's plan and provide separate payments for contraceptive services for plan participants without imposing any cost-sharing requirements on the eligible organization, its insurance plan, or its employee beneficiaries. Although this procedure requires the issuer to bear the cost of these services, HHS has determined that this obligation will not impose any net expense on issuers because its cost will be less than or equal to the cost savings resulting from the services . . .

II

A

Norman and Elizabeth Hahn and their three sons are devout members of the Mennonite Church, a Christian denomination. The Mennonite Church opposes abortion and believes that "[t]he fetus in its earliest stages . . . shares humanity with those who conceived it."

Fifty years ago, Norman Hahn started a wood-working business in his garage, and since then, this company, Conestoga Wood Specialties, has grown and now has 950 employees. Conestoga is organized under Pennsylvania law as a for-profit corporation. The Hahns exercise sole ownership of the closely held business. . . .

The Hahns believe that they are required to run their business "in accordance with their religious beliefs and moral principles." 917 F.Supp.2d 394, 402 (E.D.Pa.2013). . . .

As explained in Conestoga's board-adopted "Statement on the Sanctity of Human Life," the Hahns believe that "human life begins at conception." It is therefore "against [their] moral conviction to be involved in the termination of human life" after conception, which they believe is a "sin against God to which they are held accountable." The Hahns have accordingly excluded from the group-health-insurance plan they offer to their employees certain contraceptive methods that they consider to be abortifacients.

The Hahns and Conestoga sued HHS and other federal officials and agencies under RFRA and the Free Exercise Clause of the First Amendment, seeking to enjoin application of ACA's contraceptive mandate insofar as it requires them to provide health-insurance coverage for four FDA-approved contraceptives that may operate after the fertilization of an egg. These include two forms of emergency contraception commonly called "morning after" pills and two types of intrauterine devices.

. . . The District Court denied a preliminary injunction, and the Third Circuit affirmed in a divided opinion, holding that "for-profit, secular corporations cannot engage in religious exercise" within the meaning of RFRA or the First Amendment. . . .

B

David and Barbara Green and their three children are Christians who own and operate two family businesses. Forty-five years ago, David Green started an arts-and-crafts store that has grown into a nationwide chain called Hobby Lobby. There are now 500 Hobby Lobby stores, and the company has more than 13,000 employees. Hobby Lobby is organized as a for-profit corporation under Oklahoma law. One of David's sons started an affiliated business, Mardel, which operates 35 Christian bookstores and employs close to 400 people. Mardel is also organized as a for-profit corporation under Oklahoma law. Though these two businesses have expanded over the years, they remain closely held, and David, Barbara, and their children retain exclusive control of both companies. . . .

Hobby Lobby's statement of purpose commits the Greens to "[h]onoring the Lord in all [they] do by operating the company in a manner consistent with Biblical principles." Each family member has signed a pledge to run the businesses in accordance with the family's religious beliefs and to use the family assets to support Christian ministries. . . .

Like the Hahns, the Greens believe that life begins at conception and that it would violate their religion to facilitate access to contraceptive drugs or devices that operate after that point. They specifically object to the same four contraceptive methods as the Hahns and, like the Hahns, they have no objection to the other 16 FDA-approved methods of birth control. . . .

The Greens, Hobby Lobby, and Mardel sued HHS and other federal agencies and officials to challenge the contraceptive mandate under RFRA and the Free Exercise Clause. The District Court denied a preliminary injunction. . . . The Tenth Circuit . . . reversed in a divided opinion. Contrary to the conclusion of the Third Circuit, the Tenth Circuit held that the Greens' two for-profit businesses are "persons" within the meaning of RFRA and therefore may bring suit under that law. The court then held that the corporations had established a likelihood of success on their RFRA claim. . . .

III

A

RFRA prohibits the "Government [from] substantially burden[ing] *a person's* exercise of religion even if the burden results from a rule of general applicability" unless the Government "demonstrates that application of the burden to *the person*—(1) is in furtherance of a compelling governmental interest; and (2) is the least restrictive means of furthering that compelling governmental interest." 42 U.S.C. §§ 2000bb–1(a), (b) (emphasis added). The first question . . . is whether this provision applies to regulations that govern the activities of for-profit corporations like Hobby Lobby, Conestoga, and Mardel.

HHS contends that neither these companies nor their owners can even be heard under RFRA. According to HHS, the companies cannot sue because they seek to make a profit for their owners, and the owners cannot be heard because the regulations . . . apply only to the companies and not to the owners as individuals. HHS's argument would have dramatic consequences. . . .

[R]FRA was designed to provide very broad protection for religious liberty. By enacting RFRA, Congress went far beyond what this Court has held is constitutionally required. Is there any reason to think that the Congress that enacted such sweeping protection put small-business owners to the choice that HHS suggests[: "either give up the right to seek judicial protection of their religious liberty or forgo the benefits, available to their competitors, of operating as corporations"]? An examination of RFRA's text . . . reveals that Congress did no such thing.

. . . Congress provided protection for people like the Hahns and Greens by employing a familiar legal fiction: It included corporations within RFRA's definition of "persons." [T]he purpose of this fiction is to provide protection for human beings. A corporation is simply a form of organization used by human beings to achieve desired ends. An established body of law specifies the rights and obligations of the *people* (including shareholders, officers, and employees) who are associated with a corporation in one way or another. When rights, whether constitutional or statutory, are extended to corporations, the purpose is to protect the rights of these people. For example, extending Fourth Amendment protection to corporations protects the privacy interests of employees and others associated with the company. . . . And protecting the free-exercise rights of corporations like Hobby Lobby, Conestoga, and Mardel protects the religious liberty of the humans who own and control those companies. . . .

B

1

. . . RFRA applies to "a person's" exercise of religion, and RFRA itself does not define the term "person." We therefore look to the Dictionary Act, which we must consult "[i]n determining the meaning of any Act of Congress, unless the context indicates otherwise."

Under the Dictionary Act, "the wor[d] 'person' . . . include[s] corporations, companies, associations, firms, partnerships, societies, and joint stock companies, as well as individuals." . . .

We see nothing in RFRA that suggests a congressional intent to depart from the Dictionary Act definition. . . . We have entertained RFRA and free-exercise claims brought by nonprofit corporations, see Gonzales v. O Centro Espírita Beneficente Uniao do Vegetal (2006) (RFRA); Hosanna-Tabor Evangelical Lutheran Church and School v. EEOC (2012) (Free Exercise); Church of the Lukumi Babalu Aye, Inc. v. Hialeah (1993) (Free Exercise), and HHS concedes that a nonprofit corporation can be a "person" within the meaning of RFRA.

This concession effectively dispatches any argument that the term "person" as used in RFRA does not reach the closely held corporations involved in these cases. No known understanding of the term "person" includes *some* but not all corporations. . . .

2

The principal argument advanced by HHS and the principal dissent regarding RFRA protection for Hobby Lobby, Conestoga, and Mardel focuses . . . on the phrase "exercise of religion." According to HHS and the dissent, these corporations are not protected by RFRA because they cannot exercise religion. . . .

Is it because of the corporate form? . . . HHS concedes that nonprofit corporations can be protected by RFRA. The dissent suggests that nonprofit corporations are special because furthering their religious "autonomy . . . often furthers individual religious freedom as well." But this principle applies equally to for-profit corporations. . . . In these cases, for example, allowing Hobby Lobby, Conestoga, and Mardel to assert RFRA claims protects the religious liberty of the Greens and the Hahns.

[W]hat about the profit-making objective? In Braunfeld v. Brown (1965), we entertained the free-exercise claims of individuals who were attempting to make a profit as retail merchants, and the Court never even hinted that this objective precluded their claims. . . .

If, as *Braunfeld* recognized, a sole proprietorship that seeks to make a profit may assert a free-exercise claim, why can't Hobby Lobby, Conestoga, and Mardel do the same?

Some lower court judges have suggested that RFRA does not protect for-profit corporations because the purpose of such corporations is simply to make money. This argument flies in the face of modern corporate law. "Each American jurisdiction today either expressly or by implication authorizes corporations to be formed under its general corporation act for *any lawful purpose or business*." 1 J. Cox & T. Hazen, Treatise of the Law of Corporations § 4:1, p. 224 (3d ed. 2010) (emphasis added). . . . For-profit corporations, with ownership approval, support a wide variety of charitable causes, and it is not at all uncommon for such corporations to further humanitarian and other altruistic objectives. . . . If for-profit corporations may pursue such worthy objectives, there is no apparent reason why they may not further religious objectives as well. . . .

3

. . . HHS argues that RFRA did no more than codify this Court's pre-*Smith* Free Exercise Clause precedents, and because none of those cases squarely held that a for-profit corporation has free-exercise rights, RFRA does not confer such protection. This argument has many flaws.

First, nothing in the text of RFRA as originally enacted suggested that the statutory phrase "exercise of religion under the First Amendment" was meant to be tied to this Court's pre-*Smith* interpretation of that Amendment. When first enacted, RFRA defined the "exercise of religion" to mean "the exercise of religion under the First Amendment"—not the exercise of religion as recognized only by then-existing Supreme Court precedents. . . .

Second, if the original text of RFRA was not clear enough on this point . . . the amendment of RFRA through RLUIPA surely dispels any doubt. That amendment deleted the prior reference to the First Amendment. . . . Moreover . . . the amendment went further, providing that the exercise of religion "shall be construed in favor of a broad protection of religious exercise, to the maximum extent permitted by the terms of this chapter and the Constitution." It is simply not possible to read these provisions as restricting the concept of the "exercise of religion" to those practices specifically addressed in our pre-*Smith* decisions.

Third, the one pre-*Smith* case involving the free-exercise rights of a for-profit corporation suggests ... that for-profit corporations possess such rights. . . .

Finally, the results would be absurd if RFRA merely restored this Court's pre-*Smith* decisions in ossified form and did not allow a plaintiff to raise a RFRA claim unless that plaintiff fell within a category of plaintiffs one of whom had brought a free-exercise claim that this Court entertained in the years before *Smith*. For example, we are not aware of any pre-*Smith* case in which this Court entertained a free-exercise claim brought by a resident noncitizen. Are such persons also beyond RFRA's protective reach simply because the Court never addressed their rights before *Smith*? . . .

4

Finally, HHS contends that Congress could not have wanted RFRA to apply to for-profit corporations because it is difficult as a practical matter to ascertain the sincere "beliefs" of a corporation. HHS goes so far as to raise the specter of "divisive, polarizing proxy battles over the religious identity of large, publicly traded corporations such as IBM or General Electric."

These cases, however, do not involve publicly traded corporations, and it seems unlikely that the sort of corporate giants to which HHS refers will often assert RFRA claims. [N]umerous practical restraints would likely prevent that from occurring. For example, the idea that unrelated shareholders ... would agree to run a corporation under the same religious beliefs seems improbable. In any event, we have no occasion in these cases to consider RFRA's applicability to such companies. . . .

For all these reasons, we hold that a federal regulation's restriction on the activities of a for-profit closely held corporation must comply with RFRA.

IV

Because RFRA applies in these cases, we must next ask whether the HHS contraceptive mandate "substantially burden[s]" the exercise of religion. We have little trouble concluding that it does.

A

[T]he Hahns and Greens have a sincere religious belief that life begins at conception. They therefore object on religious grounds to providing health insurance that covers methods of birth control that, as HHS acknowledges, may result in the destruction of an embryo. By requiring the Hahns and Greens and their companies to arrange for such coverage, the HHS mandate demands that they engage in conduct that seriously violates their religious beliefs.

If the Hahns and Greens and their companies do not yield to this demand, the economic consequences will be severe. If the companies continue to offer group health plans that do not cover the contraceptives at issue, they will be taxed $100 per day for each affected individual. 26 U.S.C. § 4980D. For Hobby Lobby, the bill could amount to $1.3 million per day or about $475 million per year; for Conestoga, the assessment could be $90,000 per day or $33 million per year; and for Mardel, it could be $40,000 per day or about $15 million per year. These sums are surely substantial. . . .

C

In taking the position that the HHS mandate does not impose a substantial burden on the exercise of religion, HHS's main argument (echoed by the principal dissent) is basically that the connection between what the objecting parties must do (provide health-insurance coverage for four methods of contraception that may operate after the fertilization of an egg) and the end that they find to be morally wrong (destruction of an embryo) is simply too attenuated. HHS and the dissent note that providing the coverage would not itself result in the destruction of an embryo; that would occur only if an employee chose to take advantage of the coverage and to use one of the four methods at issue.

This argument dodges the question that RFRA presents (whether the HHS mandate imposes a substantial burden on the ability of the objecting parties to conduct business in accordance with *their religious beliefs*) and instead addresses a very different question that the federal courts have no business addressing (whether the religious belief asserted in a RFRA case is reasonable). The Hahns and Greens believe that providing the coverage demanded by the HHS regulations is connected to the destruction of an embryo in a way that is sufficient to make it immoral for them to provide the coverage. This belief implicates a difficult and important question of religion and moral philosophy, namely, the circumstances under which it is wrong for a person to perform an act that is innocent in itself but that has the effect of enabling or facilitating the commission of an immoral act by another. Arrogating the authority to provide a binding national answer to this religious and philosophical question, HHS and the principal dissent in effect tell the plaintiffs that their beliefs are flawed. For good reason, we have repeatedly refused to take such a step. . . .

V

Since the HHS contraceptive mandate imposes a substantial burden on the exercise of religion, we must . . . decide whether . . . the mandate both "(1) is in furtherance of a compelling governmental interest; and (2) is the least restrictive means of furthering that compelling governmental interest." 42 U.S.C. § 2000bb–1(b).

A . . .

The objecting parties contend that HHS has not shown that the mandate serves a compelling government interest. . . . We find it unnecessary to adjudicate this issue. We will assume that the interest in guaranteeing cost-free access to the four challenged contraceptive methods is compelling within the meaning of RFRA, and we will proceed to consider . . . whether HHS has shown that the contraceptive mandate is "the least restrictive means of furthering that compelling governmental interest."

B

The least-restrictive-means standard is exceptionally demanding, see *City of Boerne*, and it is not satisfied here. HHS has not shown that it lacks other means of achieving its desired goal without imposing a substantial burden on the exercise of religion by the objecting parties in these cases.

The most straightforward way of doing this would be for the Government to assume the cost of providing the four contraceptives at issue to any women who are unable to obtain them under their health-insurance policies due to their employers' religious objections. This would certainly be less restrictive of the plaintiffs' religious liberty, and HHS has not shown that this is not a viable alternative. . . . It seems likely . . . that the cost of providing the forms of contraceptives at issue in these cases . . . would be minor when compared with the overall cost of ACA. . . . If, as HHS tells us, providing all women with cost-free access to all FDA-approved methods of contraception is a Government interest of the highest order, it is hard to understand HHS's argument that it cannot be required under RFRA to pay *anything* in order to achieve this important goal.

HHS contends that . . . "RFRA cannot be used to require creation of entirely new programs." But we see nothing in RFRA that supports this argument, and drawing the line between the "creation of an entirely new program" and the modification of an existing program (which RFRA surely allows) would be fraught with problems. We do not doubt that cost may be an important factor in the least-restrictive-means analysis, but both RFRA and its sister statute, RLUIPA, may in some circumstances require the Government to expend additional funds to accommodate citizens' religious beliefs. HHS's view that RFRA can never require the Government to spend even a small amount reflects a judgment about the importance of religious liberty that was not shared by the Congress that enacted that law.

. . . HHS itself has demonstrated that it has at its disposal an approach that is less restrictive than requiring employers to fund contraceptive methods that violate their religious beliefs. [H]HS has already established an accommodation for nonprofit organizations with religious objections. Under that accommodation, the organization can self-certify that it opposes providing coverage for particular contraceptive services. If the organization makes such a certification, the organization's insurance issuer or third-party administrator must "[e]xpressly exclude contraceptive coverage from the group health insurance coverage provided in connection with the group health plan" and "[p]rovide separate payments for any contraceptive services required to be covered" without imposing "any cost-sharing requirements . . . on the eligible organization, the group health plan, or plan participants or beneficiaries." 45 CFR § 147.131(c)(2); 26 CFR § 54.9815–2713A(c)(2).

We do not decide today whether an approach of this type complies with RFRA for purposes of all religious claims. At a minimum, however, it does not impinge on the plaintiffs' religious belief that providing insurance coverage for the contraceptives at issue here violates their religion, and it serves HHS's stated interests equally well.

The principal dissent identifies no reason why this accommodation would fail to protect the asserted needs of women as effectively as the contraceptive mandate, and there is none. . . .

C

HHS and the principal dissent argue that a ruling in favor of the objecting parties in these cases will lead to a flood of religious objections regarding a wide variety of medical procedures and drugs, such as vaccinations and blood transfusions, but HHS has made no effort to substantiate this prediction. . . .

In any event, our decision in these cases is concerned solely with the contraceptive mandate. Our decision should not be understood to hold that an insurance-coverage mandate must necessarily fall if it conflicts with an employer's religious beliefs. Other coverage requirements, such as immunizations, may be supported by different interests (for example, the need to combat the spread of infectious diseases) and may involve different arguments about the least restrictive means of providing them.

The principal dissent raises the possibility that discrimination in hiring, for example on the basis of race, might be cloaked as religious practice to escape legal sanction. Our decision today provides no such shield. The Government has a compelling interest in providing an equal opportunity to participate in the workforce without regard to race, and prohibitions on racial discrimination are precisely tailored to achieve that critical goal.

HHS also raises for the first time in this Court the argument that applying the contraceptive mandate to for-profit employers with sincere religious objections is essential to the comprehensive health-insurance scheme that ACA establishes. HHS analogizes the contraceptive mandate to the requirement to pay Social Security taxes, which we upheld in [United States v. Lee (1982)] despite the religious objection of an employer, but these cases are quite different. Our holding in *Lee* turned primarily on the special problems associated with a national system of taxation. [W]e explained that it was untenable to allow individuals to seek exemptions from taxes based on religious objections to particular Government expenditures. . . . We observed that "[t]he tax system could not function if denominations were allowed to challenge the tax system because tax payments were spent in a manner that violates their religious belief."

Lee was a free-exercise, not a RFRA, case, but if the issue in *Lee* were analyzed under the RFRA framework, the fundamental point would be that there simply is no less restrictive alternative to the categorical requirement to pay taxes. Because of the enormous variety of government expenditures funded by tax dollars, allowing taxpayers to withhold a portion of their tax obligations on religious grounds would lead to chaos. Recognizing exemptions from the contraceptive mandate is very different. . . .[43]

In its final pages, the principal dissent reveals that its fundamental objection to the claims of the plaintiffs is an objection to RFRA itself. The dissent worries about forcing the federal courts to apply RFRA to a host of claims made by

---

[43] HHS highlights certain statements in the opinion in *Lee* that it regards as supporting its position in these cases. In particular, HHS notes the statement that "[w]hen followers of a particular sect enter into commercial activity as a matter of choice, the limits they accept on their own conduct as a matter of conscience and faith are not to be superimposed on the statutory schemes which are binding on others in that activity." *Lee* was a free exercise, not a RFRA, case, and the statement to which HHS points, if taken at face value, is squarely inconsistent with the plain meaning of RFRA. Under RFRA, when followers of a particular religion choose to enter into commercial activity, the Government does not have a free hand in imposing obligations that substantially burden their exercise of religion. Rather, the Government can impose such a burden only if the strict RFRA test is met. [Footnote by the Court.]

litigants seeking a religious exemption from generally applicable laws, and the dissent expresses a desire to keep the courts out of this business. [T]he dissent reiterates a point made forcefully by the Court in *Smith* (applying the *Sherbert* test to all free-exercise claims "would open the prospect of constitutionally required religious exemptions from civic obligations of almost every conceivable kind"). But Congress, in enacting RFRA, took the position that "the compelling interest test as set forth in prior Federal court rulings is a workable test for striking sensible balances between religious liberty and competing prior governmental interests." The wisdom of Congress's judgment on this matter is not our concern. Our responsibility is to enforce RFRA as written, and under the standard that RFRA prescribes, the HHS contraceptive mandate is unlawful.

* * *

The contraceptive mandate, as applied to closely held corporations, violates RFRA. Our decision on that statutory question makes it unnecessary to reach the First Amendment claim raised by Conestoga and the Hahns. . . .

■ JUSTICE KENNEDY, concurring.

[T]he Court's opinion does not have the breadth and sweep ascribed to it by the respectful and powerful dissent. . . .

In our constitutional tradition, freedom means that all persons have the right to believe or strive to believe in a divine creator and a divine law. For those who choose this course, free exercise is essential in preserving their own dignity and in striving for a self-definition shaped by their religious precepts. Free exercise in this sense implicates more than just freedom of belief. See Cantwell v. Connecticut (1940). It means, too, the right to express those beliefs and to establish one's religious (or nonreligious) self-definition in the political, civic, and economic life of our larger community. But in a complex society and an era of pervasive governmental regulation, defining the proper realm for free exercise can be difficult. In these cases the plaintiffs deem it necessary to exercise their religious beliefs within the context of their own closely held, for-profit corporations. They claim protection under RFRA. . . .

"[T]he American community is today, as it long has been, a rich mosaic of religious faiths." Town of Greece v. Galloway (2014) (Kagan, J., dissenting). Among the reasons the United States is so open, so tolerant, and so free is that no person may be restricted or demeaned by government in exercising his or her religion. Yet neither may that same exercise unduly restrict other persons, such as employees, in protecting their own interests, interests the law deems compelling. In these cases the means to reconcile those two priorities are at hand in the existing accommodation the Government has designed, identified, and used for circumstances closely parallel to those presented here. RFRA requires the Government to use this less restrictive means. As the Court explains, this existing model, designed precisely for this problem, might well suffice to distinguish the instant cases from many others in which it is more difficult and expensive to accommodate a governmental program to countless religious claims based on an alleged statutory right of free exercise. . . .

■ JUSTICE GINSBURG, with whom JUSTICE SOTOMAYOR joins, and with whom JUSTICE BREYER and JUSTICE KAGAN join as to all but Part III-C-1, dissenting.

In a decision of startling breadth, the Court holds that commercial enterprises, including corporations, along with partnerships and sole proprietorships, can opt out of any law (saving only tax laws) they judge incompatible with their sincerely held religious beliefs. Compelling governmental interests in uniform compliance with the law, and disadvantages that religion-based opt-outs impose on others, hold no sway, the Court decides, at least when there is a "less restrictive alternative." And such an alternative, the Court suggests, there always will be whenever, in lieu of tolling an enterprise claiming a religion-based exemption, the government, *i.e.,* the general public, can pick up the tab.

The Court does not pretend that the First Amendment's Free Exercise Clause demands religion-based accommodations so extreme, for our decisions leave no doubt on that score. Instead, the Court holds that Congress, in [RFRA], dictated the extraordinary religion-based exemptions today's decision endorses. In the Court's view, RFRA demands accommodation of a for-profit corporation's religious beliefs no matter the impact that accommodation may have on third parties who do not share the corporation owners' religious faith—in these cases, thousands of women employed by Hobby Lobby and Conestoga or dependents of persons those corporations employ. Persuaded that Congress enacted RFRA to serve a far less radical purpose, and mindful of the havoc the Court's judgment can introduce, I dissent.

I

"The ability of women to participate equally in the economic and social life of the Nation has been facilitated by their ability to control their reproductive lives." Planned Parenthood of Southeastern Pa. v. Casey (1992). Congress acted on that understanding when, as part of a nationwide insurance program intended to be comprehensive, it called for coverage of preventive care responsive to women's needs. Carrying out Congress' direction, the Department of Health and

Human Services (HHS), in consultation with public health experts, promulgated regulations requiring group health plans to cover all forms of contraception approved by the Food and Drug Administration (FDA). The genesis of this coverage should enlighten the Court's resolution of these cases.

A

The ACA, in its initial form . . . left out preventive services that "many women's health advocates and medical professionals believe are critically important." 155 Cong. Rec. 28841 (2009) (statement of Sen. Boxer). To correct this oversight, Senator Barbara Mikulski introduced the Women's Health Amendment, which added to the ACA's minimum coverage requirements a new category of preventive services specific to women's health. . . .

As altered by the Women's Health Amendment's passage, the ACA requires new insurance plans to include coverage without cost sharing of "such additional preventive care and screenings . . . as provided for in comprehensive guidelines supported by the Health Resources and Services Administration [(HRSA)]," a unit of HHS. Thus charged, the HRSA developed recommendations in consultation with the Institute of Medicine (IOM). . . . Consistent with the findings of "[n]umerous health professional associations" and other organizations, the IOM experts determined that preventive coverage should include the "full range" of FDA-approved contraceptive methods. . . .

In line with the IOM's suggestions, the HRSA adopted guidelines recommending coverage of "[a]ll [FDA-]approved contraceptive methods, sterilization procedures, and patient education and counseling for all women with reproductive capacity." Thereafter, HHS, the Department of Labor, and the Department of Treasury promulgated regulations requiring group health plans to include coverage of the contraceptive services recommended in the HRSA guidelines, subject to certain exceptions. This opinion refers to these regulations as the contraceptive coverage requirement.

B

While the Women's Health Amendment succeeded, a countermove proved unavailing. The Senate voted down the so-called "conscience amendment," which would have enabled any employer or insurance provider to deny coverage based on its asserted "religious beliefs or moral convictions." 158 Cong. Rec. S539 (Feb. 9, 2012). That amendment, Senator Mikulski observed, would have "pu[t] the personal opinion of employers and insurers over the practice of medicine." Rejecting the "conscience amendment," Congress left health care decisions—including the choice among contraceptive methods—in the hands of women, with the aid of their health care providers.

II

Any First Amendment Free Exercise Clause claim Hobby Lobby or Conestoga might assert is foreclosed by this Court's decision in *Smith*. . . . The First Amendment is not offended, *Smith* held, when "prohibiting the exercise of religion . . . is not the object of [governmental regulation] but merely the incidental effect of a generally applicable and otherwise valid provision." The ACA's contraceptive coverage requirement applies generally, it is "otherwise valid," it trains on women's well being, not on the exercise of religion, and any effect it has on such exercise is incidental.

Even if *Smith* did not control, the Free Exercise Clause would not require the exemption Hobby Lobby and Conestoga seek. Accommodations to religious beliefs or observances, the Court has clarified, must not significantly impinge on the interests of third parties.[8]

The exemption sought by Hobby Lobby and Conestoga would override significant interests of the corporations' employees and covered dependents. It would deny legions of women who do not hold their employers' beliefs access to contraceptive coverage that the ACA would otherwise secure. . . .

III

A

Lacking a tenable claim under the Free Exercise Clause, Hobby Lobby and Conestoga rely on RFRA. . . . In RFRA, Congress "adopt[ed] a statutory rule comparable to the constitutional rule rejected in *Smith*." *O Centro Espírita Beneficente Uniao do Vegetal.*

RFRA's purpose is specific and written into the statute itself. The Act was crafted to "restore the compelling interest test as set forth in *Sherbert* and *Yoder* and to guarantee its application in all cases where free exercise of religion is substantially burdened." § 2000bb(b)(1).[9]

The legislative history is correspondingly emphatic on RFRA's aim. See, *e.g.,* S.Rep. No. 103–111, p. 12 (1993) (hereinafter Senate Report) (RFRA's purpose

---

[8] See *Yoder* ("This case, of course, is not one in which any harm to the physical or mental health of the child or to the public safety, peace, order, or welfare has been demonstrated or may be properly inferred.") . . . [Footnote by Justice Ginsburg.]

[9] Under *Sherbert* and *Yoder*, the Court "requir[ed] the government to justify any substantial burden on religiously motivated conduct by a compelling state interest and by means narrowly tailored to achieve that interest." *Smith* (O'Connor, J., concurring in judgment). [Footnote by Justice Ginsburg.]

was "only to overturn the Supreme Court's decision in *Smith*," not to "unsettle other areas of the law."); (statement of Sen. Kennedy) (RFRA was "designed to restore the compelling interest test for deciding free exercise claims."). In line with this restorative purpose, Congress expected courts considering RFRA claims to "look to free exercise cases decided prior to *Smith* for guidance." Senate Report 8. In short, the Act reinstates the law as it was prior to *Smith*, without "creat[ing] . . . new rights for any religious practice or for any potential litigant." 139 Cong. Rec. 26178 (statement of Sen. Kennedy). Given the Act's moderate purpose, it is hardly surprising that RFRA's enactment in 1993 provoked little controversy.

B

Despite these authoritative indications, the Court sees RFRA as a bold initiative departing from, rather than restoring, pre-*Smith* jurisprudence. . . .

"[B]y imposing a least-restrictive-means test," the Court suggests, RFRA "went beyond what was required by our pre-*Smith* decisions." (citing *City of Boerne*). But as RFRA's statements of purpose and legislative history make clear, Congress intended only to restore, not to scrap or alter, the balancing test as this Court had applied it pre-*Smith*. See also Senate Report 9 (RFRA's "compelling interest test generally should not be construed more stringently or more leniently than it was prior to *Smith*."); House Report 7 (same). . . .

C

With RFRA's restorative purpose in mind, I turn to the Act's application to the instant lawsuits. That task . . . requires consideration of several questions, each potentially dispositive of Hobby Lobby's and Conestoga's claims: Do for-profit corporations rank among "person[s]" who "exercise . . . religion"? Assuming that they do, does the contraceptive coverage requirement "substantially burden" their religious exercise? If so, is the requirement "in furtherance of a compelling government interest"? And last, does the requirement represent the least restrictive means for furthering that interest?

Misguided by its errant premise that RFRA moved beyond the pre-*Smith* case law, the Court falters at each step of its analysis.

1

RFRA's compelling interest test applies to government actions that "substantially burden *a person's exercise of religion*." 42 U.S.C. § 2000bb–1(a) (emphasis added). This reference, the Court submits, incorporates the definition of "person" found in the Dictionary Act, which extends to "corporations, companies, associations, firms, partnerships, societies, and joint stock companies, as well as individuals." The Dictionary Act's definition, however, controls only where "context" does not "indicat[e] otherwise." Here, context does so indicate. RFRA speaks of "a person's *exercise of religion*." Whether a corporation qualifies as a "person" capable of exercising religion is an inquiry one cannot answer without reference to the "full body" of pre-*Smith* "free-exercise caselaw." There is in that case law no support for the notion that free exercise rights pertain to for-profit corporations.

Until this litigation, no decision of this Court recognized a for-profit corporation's qualification for a religious exemption from a generally applicable law, whether under the Free Exercise Clause or RFRA. The absence of such precedent is just what one would expect, for the exercise of religion is characteristic of natural persons, not artificial legal entities. As Chief Justice Marshall observed nearly two centuries ago, a corporation is "an artificial being, invisible, intangible, and existing only in contemplation of law." *Trustees of Dartmouth College v. Woodward* (1819). Corporations, Justice Stevens more recently reminded, "have no consciences, no beliefs, no feelings, no thoughts, no desires." *Citizens United v. Federal Election Comm'n* (2010) (opinion concurring in part and dissenting in part).

The First Amendment's free exercise protections . . . shelter churches and other nonprofit religion-based organizations. "For many individuals, religious activity derives meaning in large measure from participation in a larger religious community," and "furtherance of the autonomy of religious organizations often furthers individual religious freedom as well." *Corporation of Presiding Bishop of Church of Jesus Christ of Latter-day Saints v. Amos* (1987) (Brennan, J., concurring in judgment). The Court's "special solicitude to the rights of religious organizations," *Hosanna-Tabor Evangelical Lutheran Church*, however, is just that. No such solicitude is traditional for commercial organizations. Indeed, until today, religious exemptions had never been extended to any entity operating in "the commercial, profit-making world." *Amos.*

The reason why is hardly obscure. Religious organizations exist to foster the interests of persons subscribing to the same religious faith. Not so of for-profit corporations. Workers who sustain the operations of those corporations commonly are not drawn from one religious community. Indeed, by law, no religion-based criterion can restrict the work force of for-profit corporations. The distinction between a community made up of believers in the same religion and one embracing persons of diverse beliefs, clear as it is, constantly escapes the Court's attention. One can only wonder why the Court shuts this key difference from sight. . . .

The Court's determination that RFRA extends to for-profit corporations is bound to have untoward effects. Although the Court attempts to cabin its language to closely held corporations, its logic extends to corporations of any size, public or private. Little doubt that RFRA claims will proliferate, for the Court's expansive notion of corporate personhood—combined with its other errors in construing RFRA—invites for-profit entities to seek religion-based exemptions from regulations they deem offensive to their faith.

2

Even if Hobby Lobby and Conestoga were deemed RFRA "person[s]," to gain an exemption, they must demonstrate that the contraceptive coverage requirement "substantially burden[s] [their] exercise of religion." . . .

[I] would conclude that the connection between the families' religious objections and the contraceptive coverage requirement is too attenuated to rank as substantial. The requirement carries no command that Hobby Lobby or Conestoga purchase or provide the contraceptives they find objectionable. Instead, it calls on the companies covered by the requirement to direct money into undifferentiated funds that finance a wide variety of benefits under comprehensive health plans. . . .

Importantly, the decisions whether to claim benefits under the plans are made not by Hobby Lobby or Conestoga, but by the covered employees and dependents, in consultation with their health care providers. Should an employee of Hobby Lobby or Conestoga share the religious beliefs of the Greens and Hahns, she is of course under no compulsion to use the contraceptives in question. . . . It is doubtful that Congress, when it specified that burdens must be "substantia[l]," had in mind a linkage thus interrupted by independent decisionmakers (the woman and her health counselor) standing between the challenged government action and the religious exercise claimed to be infringed. . . .

3

Even if one were to conclude that Hobby Lobby and Conestoga meet the substantial burden requirement, the Government has shown that the contraceptive coverage for which the ACA provides furthers compelling interests in public health and women's well being. Those interests are concrete, specific, and demonstrated by a wealth of empirical evidence. . . .

That Hobby Lobby and Conestoga resist coverage for only 4 of the 20 FDA-approved contraceptives does not lessen these compelling interests. . . . Moreover, the Court's reasoning appears to permit commercial enterprises like Hobby Lobby and Conestoga to exclude from their group health plans all forms of contraceptives. . . .

4

After assuming the existence of compelling government interests, the Court holds that the contraceptive coverage requirement fails to satisfy RFRA's least restrictive means test. But the Government has shown that there is no less restrictive, equally effective means that would both (1) satisfy the challengers' religious objections to providing insurance coverage for certain contraceptives (which they believe cause abortions); and (2) carry out the objective of the ACA's contraceptive coverage requirement, to ensure that women employees receive, at no cost to them, the preventive care needed to safeguard their health and well being. A "least restrictive means" cannot require employees to relinquish benefits accorded them by federal law in order to ensure that their commercial employers can adhere unreservedly to their religious tenets.[25]

Then let the government pay (rather than the employees who do not share their employer's faith), the Court suggests. . . .

And where is the stopping point to the "let the government pay" alternative? Suppose an employer's sincerely held religious belief is offended by health coverage of vaccines, or paying the minimum wage, see Tony and Susan Alamo Foundation v. Secretary of Labor (1985), or according women equal pay for substantially similar work, see Dole v. Shenandoah Baptist Church (C.A.4 1990)? Does it rank as a less restrictive alternative to require the government to provide the money or benefit to which the employer has a religion-based objection? Because the Court cannot easily answer that question, it proposes something else: Extension to commercial enterprises of the accommodation already afforded to nonprofit religion-based organizations. . . .

IV

Among the pathmarking pre-*Smith* decisions RFRA preserved is *Lee*. *Lee*, a sole proprietor engaged in farming and carpentry, was a member of the Old

---

[25] As the Court made clear in *Cutter,* the government's license to grant religion-based exemptions from generally applicable laws is constrained by the Establishment Clause. "[W]e are a cosmopolitan nation made up of people of almost every conceivable religious preference," *Braunfeld,* a "rich mosaic of religious faiths," *Town of Greece* (Kagan, J., dissenting). Consequently, one person's right to free exercise must be kept in harmony with the rights of her fellow citizens, and "some religious practices [must] yield to the common good." *Lee.* [Footnote by Justice Ginsburg.]

Order Amish. He sincerely believed that withholding Social Security taxes from his employees or paying the employer's share of such taxes would violate the Amish faith. This Court held that, although the obligations imposed by the Social Security system conflicted with Lee's religious beliefs, the burden was not unconstitutional. *Id.* (recognizing the important governmental interest in providing a "nationwide . . . comprehensive insurance system with a variety of benefits available to all participants, with costs shared by employers and employees"). The Government urges that *Lee* should control the challenges brought by Hobby Lobby and Conestoga. In contrast, today's Court dismisses *Lee* as a tax case. Indeed, it was a tax case and the Court in *Lee* homed in on "[t]he difficulty in attempting to accommodate religious beliefs in the area of taxation."

But the *Lee* Court made two key points one cannot confine to tax cases. "When followers of a particular sect enter into commercial activity as a matter of choice," the Court observed, "the limits they accept on their own conduct as a matter of conscience and faith are not to be superimposed on statutory schemes which are binding on others in that activity." . . . Further, the Court recognized in *Lee* that allowing a religion-based exemption to a commercial employer would "operat[e] to impose the employer's religious faith on the employees." . . . Working for Hobby Lobby or Conestoga, in other words, should not deprive employees of the preventive care available to workers at the shop next door, at least in the absence of directions from the Legislature or Administration to do so.

Why should decisions of this order be made by Congress or the regulatory authority, and not this Court? Hobby Lobby and Conestoga surely do not stand alone as commercial enterprises seeking exemptions from generally applicable laws on the basis of their religious beliefs. See, *e.g.,* Newman v. Piggie Park Enterprises, Inc., 256 F.Supp. 941, 945 (D.S.C.1966) (owner of restaurant chain refused to serve black patrons based on his religious beliefs opposing racial integration), aff'd in relevant part and rev'd in part on other grounds, 377 F.2d 433 (C.A.4 1967), aff'd and modified on other grounds, 390 U.S. 400 (1968); In re Minnesota ex rel. McClure, 370 N.W.2d 844, 847 (Minn.1985) (born-again Christians who owned closely held, for-profit health clubs believed that the Bible proscribed hiring or retaining an "individua[l] living with but not married to a person of the opposite sex," "a young, single woman working without her father's consent or a married woman working without her husband's consent," and any person "antagonistic to the Bible," including "fornicators and homosexuals"); Elane Photography, LLC v. Willock, 309 P.3d 53 [2013] (for-profit photography business owned by a husband and wife refused to photograph a lesbian couple's commitment ceremony based on the religious beliefs of the company's owners), cert. denied, 572 U.S. ___ (2014). Would RFRA require exemptions in cases of this ilk? And if not, how does the Court divine which religious beliefs are worthy of accommodation, and which are not? . . .

Would the exemption the Court holds RFRA demands for employers with religiously grounded objections to the use of certain contraceptives extend to employers with religiously grounded objections to blood transfusions (Jehovah's Witnesses); antidepressants (Scientologists); medications derived from pigs, including anesthesia, intravenous fluids, and pills coated with gelatin (certain Muslims, Jews, and Hindus); and vaccinations (Christian Scientists, among others)?[31] According to counsel for Hobby Lobby, "each one of these cases . . . would have to be evaluated on its own . . . apply[ing] the compelling interest-least restrictive alternative test." Tr. of Oral Arg. 6. Not much help there for the lower courts bound by today's decision.

The Court, however, sees nothing to worry about. Today's cases, the Court concludes, are "concerned solely with the contraceptive mandate. . . ." . . .

There is an overriding interest, I believe, in keeping the courts "out of the business of evaluating the relative merits of differing religious claims," *Lee* (Stevens, J., concurring in judgment), or the sincerity with which an asserted religious belief is held. Indeed, approving some religious claims while deeming others unworthy of accommodation could be "perceived as favoring one religion over another," the very "risk the Establishment Clause was designed to preclude." *Ibid.* The Court, I fear, has ventured into a minefield, cf. Spencer v. World Vision, Inc. (C.A.9 2010) (O'Scannlain, J., concurring), by its immoderate reading of RFRA. I would confine religious exemptions under that Act to organizations formed "for a religious purpose," "engage[d] primarily in carrying out that religious purpose," and not "engaged . . . substantially in the exchange of goods or services for money beyond nominal amounts." See *id.* (Kleinfeld, J., concurring).

* * *

---

[31] Religious objections to immunization programs are not hypothetical. See Phillips v. New York, 27 F. Supp.3d 310 (E.D.N.Y. 2014) (dismissing free exercise challenges to New York's vaccination practices); Liberty Counsel, Compulsory Vaccinations Threaten Religious Freedom (2007), available at. https://www.lc. org/memo_vaccination.pdf. [Footnote by Justice Ginsburg, with case citation and web address updated.]

For the reasons stated, I would reverse the judgment of the Court of Appeals for the Tenth Circuit and affirm the judgment of the Court of Appeals for the Third Circuit.

■ JUSTICE BREYER and JUSTICE KAGAN, dissenting.

We agree with Justice Ginsburg that the plaintiffs' challenge to the contraceptive coverage requirement fails on the merits. We need not and do not decide whether either for-profit corporations or their owners may bring claims under the Religious Freedom Restoration Act of 1993. Accordingly, we join all but Part III-C-1 of Justice GINSBURG's dissenting opinion.

EDITORS' NOTES

(1) In *Hobby Lobby*, the majority concludes that a corporation is a "person" under the Religious Freedom Restoration Act. In the controversial 5–4 decision, Citizens United v. Federal Elections Commission (2010), the Court ruled that corporations were persons for purposes of exercising First Amendment rights in political campaigns and struck down federal laws limiting corporate spending for certain forms of political speech. In dissent, Justice Stevens (joined by Justices Ginsburg, Breyer, and Sotomayor) argued that the expressive purposes underlying the protection of individuals' free speech did not apply to corporations. Is the *Hobby Lobby* majority or dissent more persuasive on whether a corporation is a "person" whose "free exercise of religion" may be burdened? Should the answer turn on whether the corporation is public or, as with Hobby Lobby, closely-held? Is the majority correct that the for-profit/non-profit line should not be determinative of corporate personhood with respect to free exercise of religion?

(2) The majority contends that the "free exercise" issue is unlikely to come up in the context of public corporations. Is this expectation sound?

(3) Many corporations have corporate mission statements. When you think about for-profit corporations, do you envision them as expressing "values"? How about religious values? If so, are corporate mission statements a good guide to determining those values? The majority recounts that the Hahns believed that they were required to run their business "in accordance with their religious beliefs and moral principles." The Greens expressed similar convictions. What beliefs did the Hahns and Greens have about contraception and how did they express them in their businesses? Was the expression of values here more explicit than that of the Boy Scouts of America in Boy Scouts of

America v. Dale (2000; reprinted above)? Is the majority's ruling, in effect, allowing Hobby Lobby and Conestoga to impose their religious values on employees who do not share those values?

(4) In interpreting the scope of "free exercise," Justice Kennedy in concurrence refers to it as essential to "dignity." Dignity is also a central concept in his landmark opinions about the liberty and equality of gay men and lesbians, such as Romer v. Evans (1996; reprinted in Chapter 4), Lawrence v. Texas (2003; reprinted in Chapter 4), United States v. Windsor (2013; reprinted in Chapter 4), and Obergefell v. Hodges (2015; reprinted in Chapter 1). Furthermore, Kennedy refers to expression and religious "self-definition" in the various areas of community life. How does Kennedy's understanding of "free exercise" of religion compare with that of the majority? With that of dissenting Justice Ginsburg? What happens, on these various views, if religious self-expression conflicts with the interests of third parties, such as the female employees of Hobby Lobby and Conestoga? What, in other words, are the limits of free exercise?

(5) The majority and dissent disagree over whether the Court's "pre-*Smith*" jurisprudence is relevant to a claim brought under RFRA. Justice Ginsburg in dissent argues that it is. How does she think that this jurisprudence should apply?

(6) How broadly should "conscience" be protected in the sphere of commerce? Do the majority and concurring opinions address the concern expressed by Justice Ginsburg and other dissenters that providing an exemption to Hobby Lobby and Conestoga will conflict with the rights of female employees under the Affordable Care Act? Which approach is more persuasive?

(7) Assuming that there is a compelling governmental interest behind the ACA's contraceptive mandate, the majority states that HHS has a "less restrictive" approach at its disposal: the accommodation procedure for nonprofit organizations with religious objections. The majority adds, however, that "we do not decide today whether an approach of this type complies with RFRA for purposes of all religious claims." In fact, at the time the majority wrote those words, a number of religious institutions had already brought lawsuits asserting that the ACA's accommodation procedure substantially violated their free exercise of religion. By contrast to the companies in *Hobby Lobby*, many religious institutions bringing such suits (for example, Catholic colleges and universities and charitable organizations) oppose all forms of contraception. Such religious organizations have argued that having to complete the paperwork for the

exemption process itself would violate their religious beliefs by making them "complicit" in facilitating contraception or abortion (in the case of abortifacients), which they view as a grave moral wrong. See Little Sisters of the Poor Home for the Aged v. Burwell, 794 F.3d 1151 (10th Cir. 2015), *cert. granted*, 136 S. Ct. 446 (Nov. 6, 2015) (No. 15–105).

Most federal courts have rejected this argument, reasoning that registering their objection is not a substantial burden and that doing so relieves them of their obligations under the ACA's contraception mandate. Moreover, the Tenth Circuit explained that "plaintiffs sincerely oppose contraception, but their religious objection cannot hamstring government efforts to ensure that plan participants and beneficiaries receive the coverage to which they are entitled under the ACA." Ibid., 1193. The Tenth Circuit, drawing on another federal appellate court decision, reasoned: "Religious objectors do not suffer substantial burdens under RFRA where the only harm to them is that they sincerely feel aggrieved by their inability to prevent what other people would do to fulfill regulatory objectives after they opt out." Ibid. (quoting Priests for Life v. U.S. Dep't Health & Human Servs., 772 F.3d 229, 246 (DC Cir. 2014)).

(8)   Shortly after *Hobby Lobby*, Wheaton College, which had brought a free exercise suit along the lines discussed in Note (7), obtained emergency relief from a majority of the Supreme Court from complying with the exemption procedure while its lawsuit was pending. In a lengthy dissent, Justice Sotomayor, joined by Justices Ginsburg and Kagan (perhaps not coincidentally the three female members of the Court), criticized the majority for its retreat from the position in *Hobby Lobby* that the ACA's accommodation provision was a way to protect religious liberty while ensuring contraceptive access. Wheaton College v. Burwell, 134 S.Ct. 2806, 2808 (2014). Sotomayor also argued that Wheaton College's claim that simply filing a "self-certification form will make it complicit in the provision of contraceptives by triggering the obligation for someone else to provide the services to which it objects" was not viable under RFRA. She reasoned that the accommodation process was "the least restrictive means of furthering the Government's compelling interests in public health and women's well-being," and that simply "*thinking* one's religious beliefs are substantially burdened—no matter how sincere or genuine that belief may be—does not make it so."

Sotomayor employed an analogy used by the Seventh Circuit (in an opinion written by Judge Richard Posner) in its rejection of the University of Notre Dame's similar RFRA claim. University of Notre Dame v. Sibelius, 743 F.3d 547 (7th Cir. 2014). Suppose that, during wartime, "there is a draft, and a Quaker is called up" and "tells the selective service system that he's a conscientious objector;" on being told "you know this means we'll have to draft someone in place of you," he "replies indignantly that if the government does that, it will be violating his religious beliefs." While counsel for Notre Dame asserted that because his refusal would "trigger" drafting that replacement and substantially burden the Quaker's religion, RFRA "would require a draft exemption for both the Quaker and his non-Quaker replacement," Judge Posner concluded that this was a "fantastic suggestion." Ibid., 566. In her dissent, Sotomayor explains that "the obligation to provide contraceptive services, like the obligation to serve in the Armed Forces, arises not from the filing of the form but from the underlying law and regulations." Thus, Wheaton's religious rights are not substantially burdened by the ACA requirement that "*some* entity provide contraceptive coverage" for its employees and students. *Wheaton College*, 134 S.Ct. at 2812–13. Likewise, Posner for the Seventh Circuit further stated that, "at bottom," what religious nonprofits object to is Congress's passing of the ACA and the contraceptive mandate; however, under RFRA, they "have no right to 'require the Government to conduct its own internal affairs in ways that comport with the religious beliefs of particular citizens' " or to "prevent other institutions, whether the government or a health insurance company, from engaging in acts" they find offensive. *University of Notre Dame*, 743 F.3d at 552, 559.

Are Justice Sotomayor's and Judge Posner's arguments persuasive? Or does the accommodation provision impose a substantial burden upon religious institutions?

(9)   On November 6, 2015, the Supreme Court granted certiorari in *Little Sisters of the Poor, University of Notre Dame,* and several other federal lawsuits in which religious institutions have challenged the ACA's accommodation provision as burdening their free exercise under RFRA. 136 S. Ct. 446 (Mem.) (2015). The Court heard oral argument on these cases, consolidated as Zubik v. Burwell, on March 24, 2016. The justices appeared to be divided 4–4, with Justice Kennedy appearing sympathetic to the challengers. Adam Liptak, "Justices Seem Split in Case on Birth Control Mandate," *N.Y. Times,* March 24, 2016. Subsequently, on March 29, 2016, in an evident effort "to avoid a 4-4 deadlock," the Court ordered the parties to provide supplemental briefs addressing "whether and how contraceptive coverage may be obtained by petitioners' employees through petitioners' insurance companies, but in a way that does not require any involvement of petitioners beyond their own decision to provide health insurance without contraceptive coverage to their employees."

Adam Liptak, "Supreme Court Order Hints at Way to Avert Deadlock on Birth Control Mandate," *N.Y. Times*, March 30, 2016, p. A10; for the Order's wording, see Zubik v. Burwell (case file), http://www.scotusblog.com/case-files/cases/zubik-v-burwell/. Whichever way the Court decides, if it addresses the moral complicity argument with respect to the ACA, its reasoning is likely to be relevant to the controversy to which we now turn: arguments that, to avoid moral complicity by acting contrary to their religious beliefs and moral convictions, religious individuals and entities should have broad religious exemptions with respect to civil laws allowing same-sex couples to marry and, more generally, to antidiscrimination laws protecting against discrimination on the basis of sexual orientation and, in some states, gender identity. For a helpful overview of these parallels, see Douglas NeJaime and Reva B. Siegel, "Conscience Wars: Complicity-Based Conscience Claims in Religion and Politics," 124 *Yale L.J.* 2516 (2015).

———

III. CONFLICTS BETWEEN GAY RIGHTS AND RELIGIOUS LIBERTY: CLAIMS OF RELIGIOUS EXEMPTIONS FROM ANTIDISCRIMINATION LAWS AND MARRIAGE LAWS

The issue of whether a corporation is a person for purposes of the free exercise of religion also arises in the context of LGBT rights, as does the issue of religious exemptions. Parallel to the "complicity" argument in the contraception context is the argument that to comply with state laws protecting LGBT rights would make religious people and institutions complicit in immorality or make them disobey God's law. As you read this section consider: If a state legislature accepts this moral complicity argument, what sorts of "conscience protection" laws might it enact? How should the impact of such laws on third parties, such as LGBT persons, limit their scope?

The next case was decided before New Mexico, pursuant to a state court decision, began to allow same-sex couples to marry (see Griego v. Oliver, 316 P.3d 865 (N.M. 2013)), and prior to the holding in *Obergefell* that same-sex couples have the fundamental right to marry in every state. The case, nonetheless, is often discussed in ongoing debates about the evident clash of rights between religious liberty and LGBT liberty and equality and provides a helpful introduction to the intensifying conflicts since *Obergefell*.

A. Claims of Religious Exemptions from Antidiscrimination Laws

"The Huguenins are free to think, to say, to believe, as they wish; they may pray to the God of their choice and follow those commandments in their personal lives wherever they lead. The Constitution protects the Huguenins in that respect and much more. But there is a price, one that we all have to pay somewhere in our civic life. In the smaller, more focused world of the marketplace, of commerce, of public accommodation, the Huguenins have to channel their conduct, not their beliefs, so as to leave space for other Americans who believe something different. That compromise is part of the glue that holds us together as a nation, the tolerance that lubricates the varied moving parts of us as a people. That sense of respect we owe others, whether or not we believe as they do, illuminates this country, setting it apart from the discord that afflicts much of the rest of the world. In short, I would say to the Huguenins, with the utmost respect: it is the price of citizenship."—JUSTICE BOSSON

ELANE PHOTOGRAPHY, LLC V. WILLOCK

309 P.3d 53 (Supreme Court of New Mexico, 2013)

Opinion

■ CHÁVEZ, JUSTICE.

By enacting the New Mexico Human Rights Act (NMHRA), NMSA 1978, §§ 28–1–1 to –13 (1969, as amended through 2007), the Legislature has made the policy decision to prohibit public accommodations from discriminating against people based on their sexual orientation. Elane Photography, which does not contest its public accommodation status under the NMHRA, offers wedding photography services to the general public and posts its photographs on a password-protected website for its customers. In this case, Elane Photography refused to photograph a commitment ceremony between two women. The questions presented are (1) whether Elane Photography violated the NMHRA when it refused to photograph the commitment ceremony, and if so, (2) whether this application of the NMHRA violates either the Free Speech or the Free Exercise Clause of the First Amendment to the United States Constitution, or

(3) whether this application violates the New Mexico Religious Freedom Restoration Act (NMRFRA), NMSA 1978, §§ 28–22–1 to –5 (2000).

First, we conclude that a commercial photography business that offers its services to the public, thereby increasing its visibility to potential clients, is subject to the antidiscrimination provisions of the NMHRA and must serve same-sex couples on the same basis that it serves opposite-sex couples. Therefore, when Elane Photography refused to photograph a same-sex commitment ceremony, it violated the NMHRA in the same way as if it had refused to photograph a wedding between people of different races.

Second, we conclude that the NMHRA does not violate free speech guarantees because the NMHRA does not compel Elane Photography to either speak a government-mandated message or to publish the speech of another. The purpose of the NMHRA is to ensure that businesses offering services to the general public do not discriminate against protected classes of people, and the United States Supreme Court has made it clear that the First Amendment permits such regulation by states. Businesses that choose to be public accommodations must comply with the NMHRA, although such businesses retain their First Amendment rights to express their religious or political beliefs. They may, for example, post a disclaimer on their website or in their studio advertising that they oppose same-sex marriage but that they comply with applicable antidiscrimination laws. We also hold that the NMHRA is a neutral law of general applicability, and as such, it does not violate the Free Exercise Clause of the First Amendment.

Finally, we hold that the NMRFRA is inapplicable in this case because the government is not a party. For these reasons, we affirm the judgment of the Court of Appeals.

BACKGROUND

The NMHRA prohibits . . . discriminatory practices against certain defined classes of people. In 2003, the NMHRA was amended to add "sexual orientation" as a class of persons protected from discriminatory treatment. "Sexual orientation" is defined in the NMHRA as "heterosexuality, homosexuality or bisexuality, whether actual or perceived." In this case, we are concerned with discrimination by a public accommodation against a person because of that person's real or perceived homosexuality—that person's propensity to experience feelings of attraction and romantic love for other members of the same sex.

"Public accommodation" is defined in the NMHRA as "any establishment that provides or offers its services, facilities, accommodations or goods to the public, but does not include a bona fide private club or other place or establishment that is by its nature and use distinctly private." Thus, a business that elects not to offer its goods or services to the public is not subject to the NMHRA.

Vanessa Willock contacted Elane Photography, LLC, by e-mail to inquire about Elane Photography's services and to determine whether it would be available to photograph her commitment ceremony[1] to another woman. Elane Photography's co-owner and lead photographer, Elaine Huguenin, is personally opposed to same-sex marriage and will not photograph any image or event that violates her religious beliefs. Huguenin responded to Willock that Elane Photography photographed only "traditional weddings." Willock e-mailed back and asked, "Are you saying that your company does not offer your photography services to same-sex couples?" Huguenin responded, "Yes, you are correct in saying we do not photograph same-sex weddings," and thanked Willock for her interest.

In order to verify Elane Photography's policy, Willock's partner, Misti Collinsworth, e-mailed Elane Photography and inquired about its willingness to photograph a wedding, without mentioning the sexes of the participants. Huguenin sent Collinsworth a list of pricing information and an invitation to meet with her and discuss her services. A few weeks later, Huguenin again e-mailed Collinsworth to follow up.

Willock filed a discrimination complaint against Elane Photography with the New Mexico Human Rights Commission for discriminating against her based on her sexual orientation in violation of the NMHRA. The Commission concluded that Elane Photography had discriminated against Willock in violation of Section 28–1–7(F), which prohibits discrimination by public accommodations on the basis of sexual orientation, among other protected classifications. . . .

Elane Photography appealed to the Second Judicial District Court for a trial de novo pursuant to Section 28–1–13(A). [T]he district court granted summary

---

[1] Willock referred to the event as a "commitment ceremony" in her e-mail to Elane Photography. However, the parties agree that the ceremony was essentially a wedding—Elane Photography emphasizes that there were vows, rings, a minister, flower girls, and a wedding dress, and Willock uses the word "wedding" to describe the ceremony in her brief. We use the terms "wedding" and "commitment ceremony" interchangeably. [Footnote by the Court.]

judgment for Willock. Elane Photography again appealed, and the Court of Appeals affirmed. We granted certiorari.

Elane Photography argues before this Court that: (1) it did not discriminate on the basis of sexual orientation, and therefore it did not violate the NMHRA; or, alternatively, (2) by requiring Elane Photography to accept clients against its will, the NMHRA violates the protection of the First Amendment against compelled speech; (3) the NMHRA violates Elane Photography's First Amendment right to freely exercise its religion; and (4) the NMHRA violates Elane Photography's right under the NMRFRA to freely exercise its religion. [W]e reject Elane Photography's arguments and affirm. . . .

I. ELANE PHOTOGRAPHY REFUSED TO SERVE WILLOCK ON THE BASIS OF HER SEXUAL ORIENTATION IN VIOLATION OF THE NMHRA

The NMHRA seeks to promote the equal rights of people within certain specified classes by protecting them against discriminatory treatment. To accomplish this goal, the NMHRA makes it unlawful for "any person in any public accommodation to make a distinction, directly or indirectly, in offering or refusing to offer its services, facilities, accommodations or goods to any person because of race, religion, color, national origin, ancestry, sex, *sexual orientation,* gender identity, spousal affiliation or physical or mental handicap." Section 28–1–7(F) (emphasis added). The Court of Appeals affirmed the district court's holding that Elane Photography was a public accommodation under Section 28–1–2(H), 284 P.3d 428, and Elane Photography did not challenge that holding in this appeal. . . .

Elane Photography argues that it did not violate the NMHRA because it did not discriminate on the basis of sexual orientation when it refused service to Willock. Instead, Elane Photography explains that it "did not want to convey through [the Huguenins'] pictures the story of an event celebrating an understanding of marriage that conflicts with [the owners'] beliefs." Elane Photography argues that it would have taken portrait photographs and performed other services for same-sex customers, so long as they did not request photographs that involved or endorsed same-sex weddings. However, Elane Photography's owners testified that they would also have refused to take photos of same-sex couples in other contexts, including photos of a couple holding hands or showing affection for each other. Elane Photography also argues in its brief that it would have turned away heterosexual customers if the customers asked for photographs in a context that endorsed same-sex marriage.

For example, Elane Photography states that it "would have declined the request even if the ceremony was part of a movie and the actors playing the same-sex couple were heterosexual." Therefore, Elane Photography reasons that it did not discriminate "because of . . . sexual orientation," but because it did not wish to endorse Willock's and Collinsworth's wedding.

The NMHRA prohibits discrimination in broad terms by forbidding "any person in any public accommodation to make a distinction, *directly or indirectly,* in offering or refusing to offer its services . . . because of . . . sexual orientation." Section 28–1–7(F) (emphasis added). Elane Photography is primarily a wedding photography business. It provides wedding photography services to heterosexual couples, but it refuses to work with homosexual couples under equivalent circumstances.

Elane Photography's argument is an attempt to distinguish between an individual's status of being homosexual and his or her conduct in openly committing to a person of the same sex. It was apparently Willock's e-mail request to have Elane Photography photograph Willock's commitment ceremony to another woman that signaled Willock's sexual orientation to Elane Photography, regardless of whether that assessment was real or merely perceived. The difficulty in distinguishing between status and conduct in the context of sexual orientation discrimination is that people may base their judgment about an individual's sexual orientation on the individual's conduct. To allow discrimination based on conduct so closely correlated with sexual orientation would severely undermine the purpose of the NMHRA.

The United States Supreme Court has rejected similar attempts to distinguish between a protected status and conduct closely correlated with that status. In Christian Legal Society Chapter of the University of California, Hastings College of the Law v. Martinez (2010), [t]he Christian Legal Society argued that "it [did] not exclude individuals because of sexual orientation, but rather on the basis of a conjunction of conduct and the belief that the conduct is not wrong." The United States Supreme Court rejected this argument, stating:

> Our decisions have declined to distinguish between status and conduct in this context. See Lawrence v. Texas (2003) ("When homosexual *conduct* is made criminal by the law of the State, that declaration in and of itself is an invitation to subject homosexual *persons* to discrimination" (emphasis added)).

Id. We agree that when a law prohibits discrimination on the basis of sexual orientation, that law similarly protects conduct that is inextricably tied to sexual orientation. Otherwise we would interpret the NMHRA as protecting same-gender couples against discriminatory treatment, but only to the extent that they do not openly display their same-gender sexual orientation.

In this case, we see no basis for distinguishing between discrimination based on sexual orientation and discrimination based on someone's conduct of publicly committing to a person of the same sex. [T]the NMHRA evinces a clear intent to prevent discrimination as it is broadly defined in Section 28–1–7(F). New Mexico has a strong state policy of promoting equality for its residents regardless of sexual orientation. [T]he NMHRA prohibits a public accommodation from refusing to serve a client based on sexual orientation, and Elane Photography violated the law by refusing to photograph Willock's same-sex commitment ceremony.

We are not persuaded by Elane Photography's argument that it does not violate the NMHRA because it will photograph a gay person (for example, in single-person portraits) so long as the photographs do not reflect the client's sexual preferences. The NMHRA prohibits public accommodations from making any distinction in the services they offer to customers on the basis of protected classifications. Section 28–1–7(F). . . . [It] does not permit businesses to offer a "limited menu" of goods or services to customers on the basis of a status that fits within one of the protected categories. Therefore, Elane Photography's willingness to offer some services to Willock does not cure its refusal to provide other services that it offered to the general public . . . Therefore, we hold that Elane Photography discriminated against Willock on the basis of sexual orientation in violation of the NMHRA.

II. THE NMHRA DOES NOT VIOLATE ELANE PHOTOGRAPHY'S FIRST AMENDMENT RIGHTS

Elane Photography challenges enforcement of the NMHRA on the grounds that enforcement of the law violates its right to free speech and the free exercise of its religion under the First Amendment to the United States Constitution. For the reasons that follow, we reject both of these arguments. . . .

A. THE NMHRA DOES NOT VIOLATE ELANE PHOTOGRAPHY'S FREE SPEECH RIGHTS

. . . Elane Photography argues that the NMHRA compels it to speak in violation of the First Amendment by requiring it to photograph a same-sex commitment ceremony, even though it is against the owners' personal beliefs. We disagree.

The First Amendment to the United States Constitution provides that "Congress shall make no law . . . abridging the freedom of speech." U.S. Const. amend. I. This prohibition applies equally to state governments.

Elane Photography observes that photography is an expressive art form and that photographs can fall within the constitutional protections of free speech. . . . [It] concludes that by requiring it to photograph same-sex weddings on the same basis that it photographs opposite-sex weddings, the NMHRA unconstitutionally compels it to "create and engage in expression" that sends a positive message about same-sex marriage not shared by its owner.

The compelled-speech doctrine on which Elane Photography relies is comprised of two lines of cases. The first . . . establishes the proposition that the government may not require an individual to "speak the government's message." Rumsfeld v. Forum for Academic & Institutional Rights, Inc. (2006). The second . . . prohibits the government from requiring a private actor "to host or accommodate another speaker's message." *Id.* Elane Photography argues that . . . the NMHRA violates both prohibitions. . . .

1. The NMHRA does not compel Elane Photography to speak the government's message

The right to refrain from speaking was established in West Virginia State Board of Education v. Barnette (1943), in which the United States Supreme Court held that the State of West Virginia could not constitutionally require students to salute the American flag and recite the Pledge of Allegiance. . . .

Similarly, in *Wooley*, the Court held that the State of New Hampshire could not constitutionally punish a man for covering the state motto ["Live Free or Die"] on the license plate of his car. . . .

Elane Photography reads *Wooley* and *Barnette* to mean that the government may not compel people "to engage in unwanted expression." However, the cases themselves are narrower. . . . [T]he respective states impermissibly required their residents to affirm or display a specific government-selected message: "Live Free or Die" in *Wooley* and allegiance to the flag in *Barnette*. Both cases stand for the proposition that the First Amendment does not permit the government to "prescribe what shall be orthodox in politics, nationalism, religion, or other matters of opinion or force citizens to confess by word or act their faith therein." *Barnette*. However, unlike th[ose] laws . . . , NMHRA does not require Elane Photography to recite or display any message. It does not even require Elane Photography to take photographs. The NMHRA only mandates that if

Elane Photography operates a business as a public accommodation, it cannot discriminate against potential clients based on their sexual orientation.

Furthermore, the laws at issue in *Wooley* and *Barnette* had little purpose other than to promote the government-sanctioned message. . . . The *Barnette* Court noted that the dissenting students' choice not to salute the flag "[did] not bring them into collision with rights asserted by any other individual." That is not the case here, where Elane Photography's asserted right not to serve same-sex couples directly conflicts with Willock's right under Section 28–1–7(F) of the NMHRA to obtain goods and services from a public accommodation without discrimination on the basis of her sexual orientation. Antidiscrimination laws have important purposes that go beyond expressing government values: they ensure that services are freely available in the market, and they protect individuals from humiliation and dignitary harm. See Daniel v. Paul (1969) (stating that the purpose of Title II of the Civil Rights Act of 1964 was "to [re]move the daily affront and humiliation involved in discriminatory denials of access to facilities ostensibly open to the general public").

. . . Elane Photography's argument here is more analogous to the claims raised by the law schools in *Rumsfeld*. In that case, a federal law made universities' federal funding contingent on the universities allowing military recruiters access to university facilities and services on the same basis as other, non-military recruiters. A group of law schools that objected to the ban on gays in the military [argued] that the law in question compelled them to speak the government's message. . . .

The United States Supreme Court held that this requirement did not constitute compelled speech. The Court observed that the federal law "neither limits what law schools may say nor requires them to say anything." Schools were compelled only to provide the type of speech-related services to military recruiters that they provided to non-military recruiters. "There [was] nothing . . . approaching a Government-mandated pledge or motto that the school [had to] endorse."

The same situation is true in the instant case. Like the law in *Rumsfeld,* the NMHRA does not require any affirmation of belief by regulated public accommodations; instead, it requires businesses that offer services to the public at large to provide those services without regard for race, sex, sexual orientation, or other protected classifications. Section 28–1–7(F). . . .

2. The NMHRA does not compel Elane Photography to host or accommodate the message of another speaker

a. State laws prohibiting discrimination by public accommodations do not constitute compelled speech

The second line of compelled-speech cases deals with situations in which a government entity has required a speaker to "host or accommodate another speaker's message." Photography argues that a same-sex wedding or commitment ceremony is an expressive event, and that by requiring it to accept a client who is having a same-sex wedding, the NMHRA compels it to facilitate the messages inherent in that event. Elane Photography argues that there are two messages conveyed by a same-sex wedding or commitment ceremony: first, that such ceremonies exist, and second, that these occasions deserve celebration and approval. Elane Photography does not wish to convey either of these messages.

The United States Supreme Court has never found a compelled-speech violation arising from the application of antidiscrimination laws to a for-profit public accommodation. In fact, it has suggested that public accommodation laws are generally constitutional. *See Hurley* ("Provisions like these are well within the State's usual power to enact when a legislature has reason to believe that a given group is the target of discrimination, and they do not, as a general matter, violate the First or Fourteenth Amendments. . . . [T]he focal point of [such statutes is] rather on the act of discriminating against individuals in the provision of publicly available goods, privileges, and services on the proscribed grounds."). The United States Supreme Court has found constitutional problems with some applications of state public accommodation laws, but those problems have arisen when states have applied their public accommodation laws to free-speech events such as privately organized parades, *id.*, and private membership organizations, Boy Scouts of Am. v. Dale (2000).[2] Elane Photography, however, is an ordinary public accommodation, a "clearly commercial entit[y]" that sells goods and services to the public. . . .

The cases in which the United States Supreme Court found that the government unconstitutionally required a speaker to host or accommodate another speaker's message are distinctly different because they involve direct government interference with the speaker's own message, as opposed to a message-for-hire. In two cases, the Court found a compelled-speech problem

---

  [2] *Dale* also was decided on freedom of association grounds. Elane Photography has not argued that its right of expressive association was violated. [Footnote by the Court.]

where the government explicitly required a publisher to distribute an opposing point of view. . . .

In [those cases], the government commandeered a speaker's means of reaching its audience and required the speaker to disseminate an opposing point of view. Nothing analogous occurred in the present case. Elane Photography is not required to print the names and addresses of rival photographers in its albums, nor does Elane Photography distribute a newsletter in which the government has required it to print someone else's ideas. Instead, the allegedly compelled message is Elane Photography's own work on behalf of its clients, which it distributes only to its clients and their loved ones. The government has not interfered with Elane Photography's editorial judgment; the only choice regulated is Elane Photography's choice of clients. . . .

b. Observers are unlikely to believe that Elane Photography's photographs reflect the views of either its owners or its employees

Elane Photography also argues that if it is compelled to photograph same-sex weddings, observers will believe that it and its owners approve of same-sex marriage. The United States Supreme Court incorporates the question of perceived endorsement into its analysis in cases that involve compulsion to host or accommodate third-party speech. *See, e.g., Hurley.* The *Hurley* Court observed that admitting GLIB or any other organization into a parade would likely be perceived as a message from the parade organizers "that [GLIB's] message was worthy of presentation and quite possibly of support as well." Therefore, the Court further observed that the government's forced inclusion of GLIB compromised the parade organizer's "right to autonomy over [its] message." . . .

Elane Photography makes an argument very similar to one rejected by the *Rumsfeld* Court:* by treating customers alike, regardless of whether they are having same-sex or opposite-sex weddings, Elane Photography is concerned that it will send the message that it sees nothing wrong with same-sex marriage. Reasonable observers are unlikely to interpret Elane Photography's photographs as an endorsement of the photographed events. It is well known to the public that wedding photographers are hired by paying customers and that a photographer may not share the happy couple's views on issues ranging from the minor (the color scheme, the hors d'oeuvres) to the decidedly major (the religious service, the choice of bride or groom). As in *Rumsfeld* and *PruneYard*, Elane Photography is free to disavow, implicitly or explicitly, any messages that

---

* *Rumsfeld* is discussed earlier in this Chapter, in Note (8) following Boy Scouts of America v. Dale (2000).—**Eds.**

it believes the photographs convey. We note that after *Rumsfeld*, many law schools published open letters expressing their continued opposition to military policies and military recruitment on campus. Elane Photography and its owners likewise retain their First Amendment rights to express their religious and political beliefs. They may, for example, post a disclaimer on their website or in their studio advertising that they oppose same-sex marriage but that they comply with applicable antidiscrimination laws. . . .

In short, we conclude that the NMHRA's prohibition on sexual-orientation discrimination does not violate Elane Photography's First Amendment right to refrain from speaking. The government has not required Elane Photography to promote the government's message, nor has the government required Elane Photography to facilitate third parties' messages, *except* to the extent that Elane Photography already facilitates third parties' messages, for hire, as part of the services that it offers as a for-profit public accommodation. Even if the services it offers are creative or expressive, Elane Photography must offer its services to customers without regard for the customers' race, sex, sexual orientation, or other protected classification.

B.   THE NMHRA DOES NOT VIOLATE ELANE PHOTOGRAPHY'S FIRST AMENDMENT FREE EXERCISE RIGHTS

Elane Photography argues that enforcement of the NMHRA against it for refusing to photograph Willock's wedding violates its First Amendment right to freely exercise its religion. *See* U.S. Const. amend. I (Congress shall make no law prohibiting the free exercise of religion).

[I]t is not necessary for this Court to address whether Elane Photography has a constitutionally protected right to exercise its religion. Assuming that Elane Photography has such rights, they are not offended by enforcement of the NMHRA.

Under established law, "the right of free exercise does not relieve an individual of the obligation to comply with a valid and neutral law of general applicability on the ground that the law proscribes (or prescribes) conduct that his religion prescribes (or proscribes)." Emp't Div., Dep't of Human Res. of Or. v. Smith (1990).[3] In order to state a valid First Amendment free exercise claim, a

---

[3]   Congress attempted to overrule *Smith* by passing the Religious Freedom Restoration Act of 1993 (USRFRA), 42 U.S.C. §§ 2000bb (2006). However, the application of the USRFRA to state and local laws was held unconstitutional in City of Boerne v. Flores (1997). The *Smith* standard continues to be good law for evaluating federal free exercise challenges to state actions. *See Christian Legal Soc'y* (applying *Smith* standard). [Footnote by the Court.]

party must show either (a) that the law in question is not a "neutral law of general applicability," *id.,* or (b) that the challenge implicates both the Free Exercise Clause and an independent constitutional protection. . . .

1. The NMHRA is a neutral law of general applicability

The United States Supreme Court elaborated on the rule concerning "law that is neutral and of general applicability" in Church of the Lukumi Babalu Aye, Inc. v. City of Hialeah (1993). A law is not neutral "if [its] object . . . is to infringe upon or restrict practices because of their religious motivation." It is not generally applicable if it "impose[s] burdens only on conduct motivated by religious belief" while permitting exceptions for secular conduct or for favored religions. *Id.* . . . If a law is neither neutral nor generally applicable, it "must be justified by a compelling governmental interest and must be narrowly tailored to advance that interest." . . . .

Elane Photography argues that the NMHRA is not generally applicable and that this Court therefore should apply strict scrutiny to the application of the NMHRA to Elane Photography. Elane Photography identifies several exemptions from the antidiscrimination provisions of the NMHRA and argues that these exemptions make it not generally applicable. Specifically, Elane Photography points to Section 28–1–9(A)(1), which exempts sales or rentals of single-family homes if the owner does not own more than three houses, and Section 28–1–9(D), which exempts owners who live in small multi-family dwellings and rent out the other units. Elane Photography argues that these exemptions, like those in *Lukumi Babalu Aye,* "impermissibly prefer the secular to the religious."

This is a misreading of Section 28–1–9. . . . [T]he exemptions in Section 28–1–9(A) and (D) apply equally to religious and secular conduct. . . . Therefore, the NMHRA does not target only religiously motivated discrimination, and these exemptions do not prevent the NMHRA from being generally applicable. These exemptions also do not indicate any animus toward religion by the Legislature that might render the law nonneutral; similar exemptions commonly appear in housing discrimination laws, including the federal Fair Housing Act.

Elane Photography also argues that the exemptions to the NMHRA for religious organizations undercut the purpose of the statute. In particular, Elane Photography highlights Section 28–1–9(B) and (C), which in its reading permits religious organizations to "decline same-sex couples as customers." . . . .

[N]either of the religious exemptions in Section 28–1–9 would permit a religious organization to take the actions that Elane Photography did in this case. Furthermore, these exemptions do not prevent the NMHRA from being generally applicable. Exemptions for religious organizations are common in a wide variety of laws, and they reflect the attempts of the Legislature to respect free exercise rights by reducing legal burdens on religion. Such exemptions are generally permissible and in some situations they may be constitutionally mandated, see Hosanna-Tabor Evangelical Lutheran Church & Sch. v. EEOC (2012) (holding that the First Amendment precludes the application of employment discrimination laws to disputes between religious organizations and their ministers).

The exemptions in the NMHRA are ordinary exemptions for religious organizations and for certain limited employment and real-estate transactions. The exemptions do not prefer secular conduct over religious conduct or evince any hostility toward religion. We hold that the NMHRA is a neutral law of general applicability, and as such it does not offend the Free Exercise Clause of the First Amendment.

[We have omitted the discussion of Elane Photography's failure to brief adequately a "hybrid rights" claim.—**Eds.**]

III. ENFORCEMENT OF THE NMHRA DOES NOT VIOLATE THE NMRFRA BECAUSE THE NMRFRA IS NOT APPLICABLE IN A SUIT BETWEEN PRIVATE PARTIES

Finally, Elane Photography argues that the Commission's enforcement of the NMHRA against it violates the New Mexico Religious Freedom Restoration Act. The NMRFRA provides:

A government agency shall not restrict a person's free exercise of religion unless:

A. the restriction is in the form of a rule of general applicability and does not directly discriminate against religion or among religions; and

B. the application of the restriction to the person is essential to further a compelling governmental interest and is the least restrictive means of furthering that compelling governmental interest.

Section 28–22–3. "Free exercise of religion" is defined as "an act or a refusal to act that is substantially motivated by religious belief." Section 28–22–2(A).

Willock argues, and the Court of Appeals held, that the NMRFRA did not protect Elane Photography's refusal to photograph Willock's wedding, even though the refusal was religiously motivated, because the NMRFRA "was not meant to apply in suits between private litigants." There is no other case law on this point in New Mexico; the Court of Appeals relied on federal cases interpreting the federal Religious Freedom Restoration Act. . . .

[T]he statute is violated only if a "government agency" restricts a person's free exercise of religion. Section 28–22–3. . . .

[W]e hold that as a matter of New Mexico law, the New Mexico Religious Freedom Restoration Act is inapplicable to disputes in which a government agency is not a party.

CONCLUSION

Elane Photography's refusal to serve Vanessa Willock violated the New Mexico Human Rights Act, which prohibits a public accommodation from refusing to offer its services to a person based on that person's sexual orientation. Enforcing the NMHRA against Elane Photography does not violate the Free Speech or the Free Exercise clause of the First Amendment or the NMRFRA. [W]e affirm the grant of summary judgment in Willock's favor.

■ WE CONCUR: Petra Jimenez Maes, Chief Justice, Charles W. Daniels, and Barbara J. Vigil, Justices.

■ Bosson, Justice, specially concurring.

In 1943 during the darkest days of World War II, the State of West Virginia required students to salute the American flag and decreed that refusal to salute would "be regarded an Act of insubordination" which could lead to expulsion for the student and criminal action against the parent. *Barnette*. Some students refused to salute, believing as Jehovah's Witnesses "that the obligation imposed by law of God is superior to that of laws enacted by temporal government." They looked for authority in the Bible, Book of Exodus, Chapter 20, verses 4 and 5: "Thou shalt not make unto thee any graven image, or any likeness of anything that is in heaven above, or that is in the earth beneath, or that is in the water under the earth: thou shalt not bow down thyself to them, nor serve them." Jehovah's Witnesses considered "the flag is an 'image' within this command," which they were bound by God not to salute.

In a ringing endorsement of the First Amendment, the United States Supreme Court struck down the West Virginia statute, noting the irony of the state's position: "To sustain the compulsory flag salute we are required to say that a Bill of Rights which guards the individual's right to speak his own mind, left it open to public authorities to compel him to utter what is not in his mind." And again, "[i]f there is any fixed star in our constitutional constellation, it is that no official, high or petty, can prescribe what shall be orthodox in politics, nationalism, religion, or other matters of opinion or force citizens to confess by word or act their faith therein." . . . Considering the times, the *Barnette* opinion stands today as an act of the utmost courage; it represents one of the Court's finest moments.

Jonathan and Elaine Huguenin see themselves in much the same position as the students in *Barnette*. As devout, practicing Christians, they believe, as a matter of faith, that certain commands of the Bible are not left open to secular interpretation; they are meant to be obeyed. Among those commands, according to the Huguenins, is an injunction against same-sex marriage. [N]o one has questioned the Huguenins' devoutness or their sincerity; their religious convictions deserve our respect. In the words of their legal counsel, the Huguenins "believed that creating photographs telling the story of that event [a same-sex wedding] would express a message contrary to their sincerely held beliefs, and that doing so would disobey God." If honoring same-sex marriage would so conflict with their fundamental religious tenets, no less than the Jehovah's Witnesses in *Barnette,* how then, they ask, can the State of New Mexico compel them to "disobey God" in this case? How indeed?

Twenty-four years later, during the zenith of the Civil Rights era, the Supreme Court provided a partial answer. In Loving v. Virginia (1967), the State of Virginia, like sixteen similarly situated states with miscegenation laws, prohibited marriage between the white and black races, making it a crime punishable by imprisonment. Such laws arose as an incident of slavery and were common in Virginia and elsewhere since early times. The Lovings, an interracial couple, had been lawfully married elsewhere and wanted to live openly as husband and wife in Virginia. For their honesty, they were prosecuted and convicted; their prison sentences were suspended on condition that they leave Virginia and not return for 25 years. The Virginia trial judge, in justifying the convictions, drew strength from his view of the Bible:

> Almighty God created the races white, black, yellow, malay and red, and he placed them on separate continents. And but for the interference with this arrangement there would be no cause for such marriages. The fact that he separated the races shows that he did not intend for the races to mix.

Id. Whatever opinion one might have of the trial judge's religious views, which mirrored those of millions of Americans of the time, no one questioned his sincerity either or his religious conviction. In affirming the Lovings' convictions,

Virginia's highest court observed the religious, cultural, historical, and moral roots that justified miscegenation laws.

The Supreme Court struck down Virginia's miscegenation statute. Observing that "[t]he freedom to marry has long been recognized as one of the vital personal rights essential in the orderly pursuit of happiness by free men," the Court held categorically that "[t]here can be no doubt that restricting the freedom to marry solely because of racial classifications violates the central meaning of the Equal Protection Clause." State laws, even those religiously inspired, may not discriminate invidiously on the basis of race.

There is a lesson here. In a constitutional form of government, personal, religious, and moral beliefs, when *acted upon* to the detriment of someone else's rights, have constitutional limits. One is free to believe, think, and speak as one's conscience, or God, dictates. But when actions, even religiously inspired, conflict with other constitutionally protected rights—in *Loving* the right to be free from invidious racial discrimination—then there must be some accommodation. Recall that *Barnette* was all about the students; their exercise of First Amendment rights did not infringe upon anyone else. The Huguenins cannot make that claim. Their refusal to do business with the same-sex couple in this case, no matter how religiously inspired, was an affront to the legal rights of that couple, the right granted them under New Mexico law to engage in the commercial marketplace free from discrimination.

But of course, the Huguenins are not trying to prohibit anyone from marrying. They only want to be left alone to conduct their photography business in a manner consistent with their moral convictions. In their view, they seek only the freedom *not* to endorse someone else's lifestyle. *Loving,* therefore, does not completely answer the question the Huguenins pose. To complete the circle, we turn to our third case.

Heart of Atlanta Motel, Inc. v. United States [1964] upheld the federal Civil Rights Act of 1964, a milestone enactment which, among other achievements, declared invidious discrimination unlawful, not just by the state but by private citizens, when providing goods and services in the sphere of public accommodations. The Act declared: " 'All persons shall be entitled to the full and equal enjoyment of the goods, services, facilities, privileges, advantages, and accommodations of any place of public accommodation, as defined in this section, without discrimination or segregation on the ground of race, color, religion or national origin.' " A watershed achievement, the Act vindicated nearly a century of frustrated effort to fulfill the promise of the Fourteenth

Amendment, to end not only slavery but all of its traces as well. And ending second-class citizenship, being denied a seat in a restaurant or a room in an inn—purely on the basis of one's race or religion—was a goal that drove the passage of the Act. *See id.*

By the time of the success of the Civil Rights Act of 1964, many states had already passed their own public accommodation laws. *See id.* Today, many states have Human Rights Acts similar to New Mexico's. Public accommodations have been expanded to preclude invidious discrimination in most every public business, including the Huguenins' photography business. Prohibited classifications have been enlarged from the historical classes—race, religion, gender, national origin—to include sexual orientation. *See, e.g.,* Douglas NeJaime, "Marriage Inequality: Same-Sex Relationships, Religious Exemptions, and the Production of Sexual Orientation Discrimination," 100 *Cal. L. Rev.* 1169, 1190 (2012) ("Twenty-one states and the District of Columbia cover sexual orientation in their antidiscrimination laws governing employment, housing, and public accommodations."). The New Mexico Legislature has made it clear that to discriminate in business on the basis of sexual orientation is just as intolerable as discrimination directed toward race, color, national origin, or religion. The Huguenins today can no more turn away customers on the basis of sexual orientation—photographing a same-sex marriage ceremony—than they could refuse to photograph African-Americans or Muslims.

All of which, I assume, is little comfort to the Huguenins, who now are compelled by law to compromise the very religious beliefs that inspire their lives. Though the rule of law requires it, the result is sobering. It will no doubt leave a tangible mark on the Huguenins and others of similar views.

On a larger scale, this case provokes reflection on what this nation is all about, its promise of fairness, liberty, equality of opportunity, and justice. At its heart, this case teaches that at some point in our lives all of us must compromise, if only a little, to accommodate the contrasting values of others. A multicultural, pluralistic society, one of our nation's strengths, demands no less. The Huguenins are free to think, to say, to believe, as they wish; they may pray to the God of their choice and follow those commandments in their personal lives wherever they lead. The Constitution protects the Huguenins in that respect and much more. But there is a price, one that we all have to pay somewhere in our civic life.

In the smaller, more focused world of the marketplace, of commerce, of public accommodation, the Huguenins have to channel their conduct, not their beliefs, so as to leave space for other Americans who believe something different. That compromise is part of the glue that holds us together as a nation, the tolerance that lubricates the varied moving parts of us as a people. That sense of respect we owe others, whether or not we believe as they do, illuminates this country, setting it apart from the discord that afflicts much of the rest of the world. In short, I would say to the Huguenins, with the utmost respect: it is the price of citizenship. I therefore concur.

EDITORS' NOTES

(1) Earlier in this chapter, in *Boy Scouts*, we saw that the New Jersey Supreme Court had ruled that the Boy Scouts of America was a "public accommodation" under New Jersey's antidiscrimination law. Elane Photography is a more typical example of a "public accommodation," since it offers services to the public. It did not challenge that it fits within the definition of a public accommodation, but instead raised various arguments about (1) why it did not violate New Mexico's law (the NMHRA) and (2) why the law itself violated its First Amendment rights. What arguments did Elane Photography make and why did the state court reject them?

(2) In *Boy Scouts*, Justice Stevens argued in dissent that "every state law prohibiting discrimination is designed to replace prejudice with principle." Applying that interpretation to the NMHRA, what principles or moral judgments does the NMHRA reflect? Of what relevance to resolving this case is the sincerity of the moral and religious beliefs of the Huguenins? Can such moral convictions, even if sincere, be prejudice?

(3) Both the majority and the concurring opinion discuss Elane Photography's invocation of West Virginia Board of Education v. Barnette (1943), which famously proclaims that the First Amendment prohibits government to "prescribe what shall be orthodox in politics, nationalism, religion, or other matters of opinion or force citizens to confess by word or act their faith therein." Is the NMHRA imposing a governmental orthodoxy upon Elane Photography? Would it be acceptable to require merchants to comply with the law but to permit them simply to display a sign in a window indicating their objection to same-sex marriage? What impact might that have on their business?

(4) Justice Bosson's concurring opinion also discusses two important civil rights-era cases, Heart of Atlanta Motel v. United States (1964) and Loving v. Virginia (1967), in arguing why Elane Photography cannot prevail on its

challenge to the NMHRA. In his concurrence, what role do racial discrimination and civil rights laws aimed at ending racial discrimination play in evaluating Elane Photography's claims? Of what relevance is historical objection, on religious grounds, to interracial marriage to present-day objections, on religious grounds, to same-sex marriage? Does Bosson, in effect, state that today, discrimination on the basis of sexual orientation is morally equivalent to that on the basis of these earlier prohibited classifications? Is this analogy persuasive? Or is racial discrimination different in some significant way from sexual orientation discrimination?

Justice Bosson observes that the trial judge's religious beliefs supporting segregation in *Loving* "mirrored those of millions of Americans at the time" and that "no one questioned his sincerity either or his religious conviction." For an examination of religious beliefs and segregation, see Fay Botham, *Almighty God Created the Races: Christianity, Interracial Marriage, & American Law* (Chapel Hill, North Carolina: The University of North Carolina Press, 2009).

(5) Elane Photography unsuccessfully raised a claim under New Mexico's RFRA, an analogue to the federal RFRA on which Hobby Lobby relied. How does the approach taken here to the "free exercise" of religion contrast with that taken in *Hobby Lobby*? Nearly half the states have RFRAs or some other constitutional or statutory provisions allowing people, churches, or nonprofit organizations to seek exemptions from state laws burdening their religious beliefs. *State Religious Exemption Laws*, MOVEMENT ADVANCEMENT PROJECT (Jan. 18, 2016), http://www.lgbtmap.org/equality-maps/non_discrimination_laws. As is explored below, the scope of those exemptions varies.

(6) Are the outcome and reasoning in *Elane Photography* persuasive? What sorts of restrictions on religious liberty are appropriate when a person engages in commerce? What does "tolerance" require? How does the idea of tolerance in the concurring opinion in *Elane Photography* compare with that of the majority and dissenting opinions in *Poway* (9th Cir. 2006; reprinted above)?

(7) Bosson observes that New Mexico's law, like those of some other states, has expanded in two ways, first, by including more "public businesses" (such as the photography business at issue in this case) within the definition of "public accommodations," and second, by enlarging the number of "prohibited classifications" from "historical classes" such as "race, religion, gender" and "national origin" to include "sexual orientation." In *Boy Scouts*, Chief Justice Rehnquist observed that this expansion increased "the potential for conflict between state public accommodations laws and the First Amendment rights of

organizations." Do these expanded antidiscrimination laws express a judgment that discrimination on the basis of sexual orientation is morally equivalent to discrimination on the basis of these earlier prohibited classifications? Do you think that public support for expanding antidiscrimination law differs depending on whether people believe that sexual orientation is immutable or a matter of choice or "preference"?

(8)   The NMRHA barred discrimination on the grounds of both "sexual orientation" and "gender identity." As of early 2016, the antidiscrimination laws of twenty-one states and the District of Columbia explicitly prohibited discrimination in public accommodations on the basis of sexual orientation. Approximately eighteen states plus the District of Columbia also bar discrimination on the basis of gender identity. Twenty-nine states do not have laws expressly preventing sexual orientation discrimination or gender identity discrimination. *See Non-Discrimination Laws*, MOVEMENT ADVANCEMENT PROJECT, (Jan. 18, 2016), http://www.lgbtmap.org/equality-maps/non_ discrimination_laws; *Race and Beyond: Expanding Protections for LGBT People Strengthens Protections for Us All*, CENTER FOR AMERICAN PROGRESS (July 30, 2015), https://www.americanprogress.org/issues/race/news/2015/07/30/118504/ expanding-protections-for-lgbt-people-strengthens-protections-for-us-all/. State antidiscrimination laws may cover public accommodations; they may also reach to areas such as employment and housing. While twenty states and the District of Columbia protect against discrimination based on sexual orientation or gender identity in employment, and two states protect based on sexual orientation but not gender identity, twenty eight states do not. *Non-discrimination Laws.*

What arguments would support protecting gender identity, so that a person who is transgender could not be refused goods or services or rejected for employment on that basis? What arguments might legislators or citizens offer against such protection? Does it matter, for example, whether one thinks of gender identity as a fixed characteristic or as a matter of choice?

If you were a state legislator considering adding "gender identity" to your antidiscrimination law, would you find it relevant that the American Psychiatric Association, in 2013, revised the Diagnostic and Statistical Manual of Mental Disorders ("DSM") V to replace the term "gender identity disorder" to describe patients whose subjective experience of gender does not match their biological sex with the term "gender dysphoria"? In 1973, the APA decided to remove homosexuality from its list of mental disorders; that shift, as you have seen, has featured in judicial opinions upholding the rights of gay men and lesbians. Is a similar shift likely in the case of gender identity?

A growing area of controversy concerns so-called "bathroom bills," laws aimed at restricting access by transgender persons to the bathrooms that correspond to the gender with which they identify by restricting access to "male" and "female" bathrooms to persons designated "male" or "female" on their birth certificates. North Carolina passed such a law (H.B. 2) applying to bathrooms in schools and public agencies. See 2016 N.C.SESS. LAWS (Sess. Law 2016–3). The North Carolina law had the effect of blocking a local ordinance intended to protect transgender persons' choice of bathrooms. Proponents of the state law alleged that the law would protect women and children from predatory men entering women's bathrooms, despite no evidence of any such threat. Several transgender persons have filed a lawsuit in federal court asserting that the law unconstitutionally "explicitly writ[es] discrimination against transgender people into state law." Complaint for Declaratory and Injunctive Relief, Carcaño v. McCrory, No. 1:16–cv–236 (M.D.N.C. Mar. 28, 2016). Some jurisdictions have rejected such proposed laws. The Virginia legislature, for example, defeated a bill that would have required transgender students at Virginia public schools to use restrooms and locker rooms corresponding to their biological sex. See Andrew Cain, "Virginia Avoids Controversy Over LGBT Legislation," *Richmond-Times Dispatch*, 2016 WLNR 9674392, March 30, 2016.

―――――

B. Post-*Obergefell* Developments: The Next Generation of Claims of Religious Exemptions

In his *Obergefell* dissent (in Chapter 1), one reason that Chief Justice Roberts faulted the majority for deciding the issue of gay men and lesbians' right to marry, rather than leaving it in "the realm of democratic decision," was that federal courts—"blunt instruments when it comes to creating rights"—lacked "the flexibility of legislatures" to address broader concerns "of parties not before the court," such as religious liberty. Roberts asserted that: "respect for sincere religious conviction has led voters and legislators in every State that has adopted same-sex marriage democratically to include accommodation for religious practice," while the majority's opinion "cannot, of course, create any such accommodation." Roberts and other dissenters seemed to predict insufficient protection of the "conscience" of persons who "cannot accept same-sex marriage." The proliferation, post-*Obergefell,* of proposed and enacted state laws to protect "conscience" and religious liberty in the wake of civil marriage equality suggests, however, that the Court's ruling has not shut down the democratic process. The sweeping scope of some of those laws even suggests resistance to *Obergefell* and efforts to blunt or nullify its impact in states that had not allowed same-sex couples to marry prior to the Court's ruling. As indicated in Editors' Note (14) to *Obergefell* in Chapter 1, some conservative thinkers have called for "constitutional resistance" to *Obergefell* by "all federal and state officeholders." American Principles Project, "Statement Calling for Constitutional Resistance to Obergefell v. Hodges."

In this final section, we provide a brief overview of some of these post-*Obergefell* legislative developments. We begin with an overview of several types of conflicts between religious liberty and LGBT rights. Consider the following contexts in which a person or entity asserts a conscientious, religiously-grounded moral objection to marriage between two men or two women. In which of these contexts do you think that a religious exemption is appropriate?

(1) A public official whose duties include issuing marriage licenses to eligible couples or a public official whose duties include performing civil marriage ceremonies;

(2) A member of the clergy who regularly performs religious marriage ceremonies for members of their religious denomination;

(3) A nonprofit religious institution that routinely provides goods or services related to marriage, for example, by making its space available for weddings or engaging in premarital counseling;

(4) A for-profit business owned by a religious person and engaged in the wedding industry, e.g., baking wedding cakes, photographing weddings, or operating a travel agency specializing in destination weddings and honeymoons.

Some of these conflicts (as in *Elane Photography*) involve the intersection of state antidiscrimination laws that include sexual orientation and state RFRAs. In states that have both of these kinds of laws, would new exemptions for religious persons and entities opposed to same-sex marriage be necessary and, if so, how far should they reach? In some instances, lawmakers opposed to same-sex marriage have proposed enhancing state RFRAS; in others, they have proposed new laws framed as "free exercise" or "conscience protection" laws with specific reference to marriage. Many states do not have antidiscrimination laws or the laws they do have do not include sexual orientation. A concern in such states was that same-sex couples might encounter difficulty obtaining access to marriage itself—if clerks refused a license or a public official refused to solemnize the marriage—as well as to goods and services—if merchants refused to provide them wedding-related services because of their religious beliefs about marriage and homosexuality.

In making sense of these contemporary controversies over religious exemptions, the understanding of the large commercial republic discussed in Chapter 2 may be helpful. As discussed below, in recent years, large businesses and business associations, sports associations, and entertainers often urge governors in conservative states to veto legislation granting religious exemptions for businesses from marriage laws or antidiscrimination laws protecting gay rights (for example, Arizona, Arkansas, Indiana, and Georgia). Thus, while Governor Nathan Deal appealed to the Bible and to First Amendment principles about separation of church and state to explain his veto of a conscience-protection law that (in his words) "allows discrimination in our state in order to protect people of faith," another relevant factor may have been that various businesses and sports organizations warned about the economic consequences of such a law.[19] A complicating dynamic of this large commercial republic at work *within* a number of Southern states is the clash between (1) cities that are diverse and economically thriving—home to national and even global employers—and pass ordinances protecting LGBT persons against discrimination and (2) rural and suburban areas within the states that are more conservative.[20] Some state legislatures, such as North Carolina and Mississippi, have passed "conscience protection" laws that bar and override such municipal ordinances, triggering economic "backlash" and also raising constitutional questions.[21] This illustrates a byproduct of the large commercial republic. The large commercial republic is religiously and morally diverse. In such a diverse society, the hope is that even though people disagree about religion and morality, they may be able to engage in commerce with one another. The further hope is that people's getting together and trading with one another may moderate their religious and moral differences. Perhaps people will see that, despite their religious and moral disagreements, they can trade with, get along with, and maybe even come to appreciate "other," different people. Seen in this light, do religious exemptions for businesses—including wedding photographers, bakers, and florists—undercut the significant, moderating influences of trade in the large commercial republic?

---

[19]   Aaron Gould Sheinin, "Deal: Reject Religious Liberty—Governor Cites New Testament to Argue Against Discrimination," *Atlanta J. and Const.*, March 4, 2016; Alan Blinder and Richard Pérez-Pena, "Georgia Governor Rejects Bill Shielding Critics of Same-sex Marriage," *N.Y. Times*, March 29, 2016, p. A12.

[20]   Campbell Robertson and Richard Fausset, "Liberal Islands in a Southern Conservative Sea," *N.Y. Times,* April 16, 2016, p. A1.

[21] Ibid.

1. Controversies Involving Public Officials and Religious Exemptions

Since *Obergefell,* the most visible example of a public official asserting that her religious beliefs provided a reason for not carrying out her duty to issue marriage licenses is Kim Davis, County Clerk for Rowan County, Kentucky (mentioned earlier in this Chapter). Within a few months of *Obergefell,* most public officials (notwithstanding their religious beliefs) were issuing marriage licenses to same-sex couples. Davis made national headlines for her decision to stop issuing *any* marriage licenses and to forbid the deputy clerks in her office from doing so.[22] Davis expressed the view that civil marriage law—if defined to include two men or two women—was "not of God" and that to issue licenses would violate her Apostolic Christian faith.[23] Gay and lesbian couples sued in federal district court, seeking an injunction ordering her to issue marriage licenses to them. Judge David Bunning, a Republican whom President George W. Bush had appointed, issued such an injunction, but Davis "willfull[ly]" refused to comply with the "lawfully issued order."[24] The court accordingly held her in "contempt of court" (the usual remedy for defying a court order). To secure compliance, the court faced a choice whether to threaten imprisonment or fines (the two most common sanctions). Because the judge concluded that fines would not be effective (since conservative organizations supporting Davis would simply pay the fines for her), he ordered her sent to county jail until she complied with the order. Eventually, the deputy clerks agreed to issue the marriage licenses to gay and lesbian couples and the judge ordered Davis released. Some opponents of same-sex marriage rallied to support Davis as a modern day civil rights heroine or appealed to the nation's long history of "accommodating conscientious objectors"; critics compared her instead to intransigent public officials fighting racial integration and argued that she was committing "official disobedience," not "civil disobedience."[25] Davis has appealed, asserting that issuing licenses infringed her rights under the United States and Kentucky Constitution and Kentucky's RFRA. Thus far, Davis has not prevailed. Kentucky's governor and its legislature have sought to change the

---

[22] Sheryl Gay Stolberg, "Kentucky Clerk Defies Court on Marriage Licenses for Gay Couples," *N.Y. Times,* Aug. 13, 2015.

[23] Alan Blinder and Tamar Lewin, "Clerk in Kentucky Chooses Jail Over Deal on Same-Sex Marriage," *N.Y. Times,* Sept. 3, 2015.

[24] Ibid.

[25] Compare Ryan T. Anderson, "We Don't Need Kim Davis to Be in Jail," *N.Y. Times,* Sept. 7, 2015, with Garrett Epps, "When Public Servants Refuse to Serve the Public," *Atlantic,* Aug. 16, 2015.

marriage license process in order to provide protection to clerks from issuing licenses that they allege violate their consciences.

North Carolina had enacted a law shortly before *Obergefell* providing magistrates "the right to recuse" from performing lawful marriages "based upon any sincerely held religious objection"; the law provides a similar right to recuse to public officials who ordinarily issue marriage licenses.[26] "If, and only if, all magistrates in a jurisdiction have recused" themselves, then a court administrator "shall ensure that a magistrate is available in that jurisdiction" to perform marriages at the normally appointed times.[27] Six plaintiffs who are North Carolina citizens, residents, and taxpayers have brought a federal constitutional challenge to the law as violating the Establishment Clause and the Due Process and Equal Protection Clauses of the Fourteenth Amendment.[28] Notably, the complaint draws an analogy to religious objections by public officials to interracial marriage even after it was legal. (Incidentally, two of the plaintiffs in the case are an interracial, opposite-sex couple whom magistrates, in 1976, refused to marry due to their "religious beliefs against interracial marriage." It took a federal court ruling, two years later, to get a magistrate to perform their marriage.[29])

As noted in Chapter 1, a number of conservative scholars and leaders have called for "constitutional resistance" to *Obergefell*; they might argue that public officials are rightfully recused from following an unconstitutional decision. How should the plaintiffs' lawsuit in North Carolina be resolved?

2.   *Members of the Clergy Authorized to Solemnize Marriages*

Both before and after *Obergefell*, as states revise their marriage laws to extend civil marriage to same-sex couples, the most commonly included exemption is one that many would argue goes without saying under the First Amendment: protecting clergy from performing a marriage ceremony that conflicts with the religious beliefs of the religious organization to which they belong. Thus, New York's Marriage Equality Act includes the "well-established constitutional and statutory principles that no member of the clergy may be compelled to perform

---

[26]   N.C. GEN. STAT. § 51–5.5 (2015).

[27]   Ibid.

[28]   Complaint in Ansley et al. v. State of North Carolina, Case No: 1:15–cv–274 (W.D. N.C.) filed Dec. 9. 2015.

[29]   Ibid., para. 2.

any marriage ceremony."[30] This protection reflects the important distinction between religious and civil marriage.

3.   Religious Institutions and Entities

Greater controversy involves the scope of exemptions for religious institutions. Prior to *Obergefell*, in New York, for example, religious exemptions were critical in securing some religious lawmakers' support for the law.[31] The law exempts religious institutions and benevolent organizations from providing "accommodations, advantages, facilities, or privileges related to the solemnization or celebration of a marriage," according them freedom to "choose who may use their facilities and halls for marriage ceremonies and celebrations, to whom they rent their housing accommodations, or to whom they provide religious services, consistent with their religious principles."[32] Other states have enacted similar exemptions, often as part of a state RFRA, or are considering doing so.[33]

Since *Obergefell,* at issue in a number of states is whether and how far religious institutions should have exemptions from implementing civil marriage for same-sex couples, and, in relevant states, from antidiscrimination laws that protect on the basis of sexual orientation and gender identity. In Georgia, Governor Nathan Deal appealed to the Bible to argue *against* proposed legislation in that state (H.B. 757), the Free Exercise Protection Act, that broadly defined "faith based organization" and exempted such organizations from providing "social, educational, or charitable services that violate such faith based organization's sincerely held religious belief."[34] Civil rights organizations and prominent leaders in the entertainment industry and the business community criticized the law for allowing discrimination. Governor Deal, a Republican, vetoed the law, suggesting that rather than asking government to confer "certain rights and protections" on the religious community, proponents of the law should instead "heed the hands-off admonition of the First Amendment of the United States Constitution."[35]

---

[30]   Supporting Statement, Marriage Equality Act.

[31]   Danny Hakim, "Exemptions Were Key to Vote on Gay Marriage," *N.Y. Times,* June 26, 2011, p. 18.

[32]   Supporting Statement, Marriage Equality Act.

[33]   See National Conference of State Legislatures, "2015 Religious Freedom Restoration Legislation."

[34]   2016 Ga. H.B. 757; Greg Bluestein and Aaron Gould Sheinin, "Reject 'Religious Liberty' Bills that Allow Discrimination," *Atlanta Journal Constitution,* March 3, 2016.

[35]   Alan Blinder and Richard Perez-Pena, "Georgia Governor Rejects Bill Shielding Critics of Same-Sex Marriage," *N.Y. Times,* March 29, 2016, p. A12.

Some federal lawmakers have proposed the "First Amendment Defense Act."[36] One spur was the oral argument in *Obergefell*. In response to a question whether, if the Court ruled that same-sex couples had a constitutional right to marry, a religious school could lose its tax-exempt status (by analogy to Bob Jones University losing such status for its opposition to interracial dating and marriage),[37] the Solicitor General for the U.S. responded that "[i]t's certainly going to be an issue." The Republican-sponsored "First Amendment Defense Act" would prohibit the federal government from taking any discriminatory action against a person (defined to include for-profit and nonprofit entities) who "believes or acts in accordance with a religious belief or moral conviction that marriage is or should be recognized as the union of one man and one woman, or that sexual relations are properly reserved to such a marriage." Discriminatory action includes altering the federal tax treatment of such a person, disallowing charitable deductions made to or by such persons, or denying any federal grant or contract.[38]

4. For-Profit Businesses Owned by Religious Persons That Provide Goods and Services to the Public

Since *Elane Photography*, a number of courts have ruled similarly that for-profit businesses open to the public, and considered public accommodations under state laws, may not discriminate against customers who seek wedding-related goods and services, notwithstanding the sincere religious belief of the owners.[39] Such judicial decisions have prompted various proposed state laws to protect such business owners. As noted above, however, such provisions have often sparked enormous criticism by large corporations and other commercial entities who warn that they send a message of discrimination; such organizations have threatened boycotts or moving out of the state. In Indiana, for example, the legislature enacted a RFRA that would include protection of for-profit businesses. Governor Pence, after an outcry, announced a "fix" that added a new provision that would clarify that the law would "not create a license to discriminate."[40] The new provision stated that the law did not permit an entity to

---

[36] H.R. 2802 (114th Cong. 1st Sess.).

[37] Bob Jones University v. United States, 461 U.S. 574 (1983).

[38] H.R. 2802.

[39] See, e.g., Gifford v. McCarthy, 23 N.Y.S. 3d 422, 2016 WL 155543 (N.Y. App. Div. 2016) (affirming Administrative Law Judge ruling that a farm that advertises wedding-related services to the public and hosts religious and secular weddings on the premises is a public accommodation and owners violated state human rights law by denying services—on the basis of their Christian beliefs—to a lesbian couple).

[40] For discussion of the controversy, see Linda C. McClain, "Conscience, Discrimination, and Marriage Equality: Are Analogies to 1964—and 1967—Inevitable?," *Cornerstone* (May 2015), http://berkleycenter.

"refuse to offer or provide services, facilities, use of public accommodations, goods, employment, or housing to any member or members of the general public on the basis of . . . sexual orientation" and "gender identity."[41] Some conservatives swiftly condemned this "fix" as leaving religious liberty unprotected.[42] Another route some legislatures are pursuing is constitutional amendment. Despite criticisms by LGBT advocates and business leaders, the Missouri legislature, after an unsuccessful filibuster by Democrats and opposition by the governor, passed a wide-ranging joint resolution that will appear as a ballot initiative before the voters in November 2016. If approved, it would bar any religious organization—including churches, corporations, schools and hospitals and their employees—from any state penalty for believing or acting "in accordance with a sincere religious belief concerning marriage between two persons of the same sex" and would also protect "religious beliefs."[43]

5.   Using the Language of "Discrimination" to Protect "Freedom of Conscience"

A recently enacted law in Mississippi, entitled the "Protecting Freedom of Conscience from Government Discrimination Act," provides all of the forms of religious exemption discussed above.[44] It is worth analyzing both for its broad scope and its use of the language of "discrimination." The law, H.B. 1523, protects a wide range of public officials and employees, religious persons and organizations, and for-profit corporations from governmental "discrimination" if they act—or refuse to act—in many spheres of society on the basis of "sincerely held religious beliefs or moral convictions" that (1) marriage "is or should be recognized as the union of one man and one woman," (2) "sexual relations are properly reserved to such a marriage," and (3) being "male" or "female" is immutably fixed at birth by one's biological sex. The implicit premise of this new law is that, without such broad protection, religious individuals and entities are vulnerable to "discriminatory" action taken against them by the state. H.B. 1523 also has the effect of nullifying ordinances adopted in several municipalities within Mississippi that "passed resolutions opposing

---

georgetown.edu/responses/conscience-discrimination-and-marriage-equality-are-analogies-to-1964-and-1967-inevitable.

[41]   Ind. Senate Enrolled Act No. 50 (effective July 1, 2015).

[42]   Sarah E. Jones, "States of Rebellion," *Church & State* (March 2016), 7, 8.

[43]   Matt Pearce, "Missouri GOP Defeats 39-Hour Filibuster to Pass Bill Criticized as Anti-Gay," *L.A. Times,* March 9, 2016.

[44]   H.B. 1523 (Reg. Sess. 2016).

discrimination against LGBT people, or protecting LGBT people from some forms of discrimination."[45]

The full implications of the Mississippi law are not yet clear, but its language expressly prohibits any state "discriminatory action" against a religious organization (which includes for-profit corporations) if it makes any "employment-related decision" concerning an individual "whose conduct or religious beliefs are inconsistent with those of the religious organization." Similar provisions against governmental discrimination address decisions concerning goods and services, adoption and foster care, and provision of "psychological, counseling, or fertility services."[46] The law, for example, appears to prevent the state from interfering "if a foster parent puts a child into conversion therapy," which is legal in Mississippi.[47] The law also defines prohibited "discriminatory action" to include altering in any way a person's "tax treatment" or eligibility for state grants, contracts, loans, scholarships, and "similar benefit"[48] that the law would protect. Governor Bryant's signing statement, issued by way of Twitter, asserts that the bill "merely reinforces the rights which currently exist to the exercise of religious freedom as stated in the First Amendment to the U.S. Constitution" and "does not limit any constitutionally protected rights or actions of any citizen of this state."[49]

EDITORS' NOTES

(1) If you were a legislator in a state considering enacting a law to protect "free exercise of religion" while also respecting LGBT rights, what sort of a law would you propose? Would it include the various forms of exemptions discussed above? Why or why not?

(2) A premise shared by the majority, concurrence, and dissent in *Hobby Lobby* (reprinted earlier in this Chapter) was that accommodation of religious belief may not be at the expense of the rights and interests of third parties. Are the laws discussed above consistent with this requirement? What is their impact

---

45 Memorandum to Interested Parties from Public Rights/Private Conscience Project about Mississippi H.B. 1523 & the Establishment Clause, 3, April 4, 2016, https://web.law.columbia.edu/sites/default/files/microsites/gender-sexuality/files/memo_regarding_ms_hb1523.pdf.

46 H.B. 1523, § 3.

47 Amber Phillips, "Mississippi's New Law Allowing Refusal of Service to LGBT People Is the Most Sweeping Yet," *Wash. Post*, April. 5, 2016.

48 H.B. 1523, §§ 3, 4.

49 *Governor Phil Bryant Releases Statement about Signing Controversial Bill*, April 5, 2016, http://www.wlox.com/story/31647579/governor-phil-bryant-releases-statement-about-signing-controversial-bill; Christina Back, *Mississippi Passes Sweeping Religious Freedom Law*, CHRISTIAN SCIENCE MONITOR, April 5, 2016.

on the rights of same-sex couples seeking to marry and LGBT persons? Which of the laws discussed above do you think would survive constitutional challenge?

(3) In including protection of sincere religious beliefs or moral convictions that "sexual relations are properly reserved" to a marriage between one man and one woman, the Mississippi law seems to permit religious persons and entities to discriminate against unmarried heterosexuals in employment, housing, and other contexts without any governmental penalty. Why do you suppose the legislature included such provisions?

(4) Do laws like Mississippi's and North Carolina's, which override municipal ordinances protecting LBGT persons against discrimination, conflict with Romer v. Evans (1996; reprinted in Chapter 4), which, two decades ago, invalidated a constitutional amendment that reversed gains made at the local level and made gay people "strangers" to the law? Do they conflict with *Obergefell*?

(5) Do laws that allow public officials to recuse themselves pose any problems under the Establishment Clause of the First Amendment?

(6) What impact do you think being part of a large commercial republic (as discussed above) will have on states like North Carolina and Mississippi? For example, responding to a reported "backlash" against North Carolina's law, Governor McCrory took some limited measures (by executive order) but has left "the most controversial provisions intact." See "North Carolina Governor Says He Wants Bathroom Law Partially Changed After Backlash," *Wash. Post,* April 12, 2016. His Executive Order begins by asserting that "North Carolina's rich legacy of inclusiveness, diversity and hospitality" have made it a "global destination for jobs, business, tourists and talent," and affirms that "it is the policy of the Executive Branch that government services be provided equally to all people." Executive Order N. 93 to Protect Privacy and Equality (Gov. Pat McCrory, April 12, 2016). The order lets private businesses "set their own rules for their own restroom, locker room and shower facilities, free from government interference," but retains the bathroom rules premised on biological sex with respect to public buildings and schools.

What's Next?

We began this book by observing that the Supreme Court's holding in Obergefell v. Hodges (2015) that same-sex couples have the fundamental right to marry marks the consummation of an important component of the gay rights revolution. "Unfinished revolution" was the theme of an opinion piece published the day after *Obergefell* by Evan Wolfson, founder of the Freedom to Marry project and a gay rights lawyer who had fought for marriage equality since the 1990s. In the editorial, "What's Next in the Fight for Gay Equality," Wolfson wrote that the Supreme Court's ruling was "a monumental and inspiring victory" worthy of celebration.[1] However, he added: "now we must get back to work," for

> securing protections from discrimination for gay, lesbian, bisexual and transgender Americans needs to be our priority. In too many parts of the country, people can still be fired, evicted, refused service or even humiliated at stores or restaurants because of their sexual orientation or gender identity—in other words, just for being who they are.

Wolfson called for "updating" federal antidiscrimination law to protect against discrimination based on sexual orientation and gender identity and for efforts at the state level as well. Mindful of the controversies over exemptions discussed in Chapter 5, Wolfson contended that "the American people know that religious freedom is protected in the Constitution and is fully compatible with civil rights." Finally, he called for a "national conversation that calls attention to gaps in civil rights law and puts a human face on discrimination through emotionally compelling storytelling."[2] Wolfson expressed faith in the "transformative power

---

[1] Evan Wolfson, "What's Next in the Fight for Gay Equality," *N.Y. Times*, June 26, 2015, http://www.nytimes.com/2015/06/27/opinion/evan-wolfson-whats-next-in-the-fight-for-gay-equality.html?_r=0.

[2] Ibid.

of seeing couples marry" as "energizing" advocates "pushing toward the more perfect union America promises."[3]

Same-sex marriage opponents, meanwhile, warned that unless *Obergefell* is reversed, other dire changes could be expected. Justice Alito, in his dissent in *Obergefell*, warned of unintended consequences. Because unintended consequences include unpredictable consequences, we don't know all that might be next in the gay rights debate. What we do know is that the Court and the country will have to confront three sets of issues (all discussed in Chapter 5) in the foreseeable future: issues related to the clash between gay rights (not only to marriage but also to protection against discrimination) and free exercise of religion; issues related to transgender rights; and issues related to plural marriages, or polygamy.[4]

Regarding the conflict between gay rights and religious liberty, the problem is framed by Justice Scalia's opinion for the Court in Employment Division v. Smith (1990): How to allow religious exemptions from civil rights laws protecting gays and lesbians without allowing like exemptions from civil rights laws protecting racial and religious minorities or, indeed, any other laws enacted for general, secular purposes—how, in brief, to avoid a situation in which "each conscience is a law unto itself"? Might we find a way out of this difficulty by allowing the nation's legislative and judicial bodies to assess the sincerity of claimants' religious beliefs, or even the plausibility (or truth?) of those beliefs? Inquiries into sincerity might sometimes be helpful, but public officials cannot pass judgment on the substance of people's religious beliefs as religious beliefs without violating the First Amendment's Establishment Clause. Another approach would be to limit freedom of religious exercise to the freedom to profess religious beliefs, but this would amount to saying that, practically speaking, free exercise can't really mean free exercise. Even under the more expansive protection of free exercise under state or federal Religious Freedom Restoration Acts ("RFRAs"), a critical—and controversial—question that courts *are* authorized to evaluate is what constitutes a "substantial" burden on religion. We can expect much acrimonious and divisive controversy in this area of the law.

---

[3]   Ibid.

[4]   In addition to these general issues, a technical question will remain what standard of review courts will use in evaluating classifications based on sexual orientation, whether in areas of family law (such as adoption or parental rights), employment, housing, or other contexts. And, in a future gay rights challenge, will the Supreme Court eventually do what it declined to do in *Obergefell* and all prior gay rights cases: formally recognize sexual orientation as a suspect (or somewhat suspicious) classification warranting, under the Equal Protection Clause, strict (or intermediate) judicial scrutiny? If the Court were to do so, it would join a number of state and federal courts that have taken this step.

With transgender rights, as this book goes to press, North Carolina has just passed a law barring transgender persons from bathrooms and locker rooms that do not match the gender on their birth certificates. The law also prohibits municipalities from creating their own antidiscrimination policies (Charlotte, the state's largest city, had recently passed an antidiscrimination ordinance providing protections based on sexual orientation, gender expression, and gender identity, including letting transgender persons use the public bathrooms that correspond with their gender identity, not gender at birth).[5] The North Carolina controversy not only previews what is next but also replays Colorado's Amendment 2, which forbade localities from protecting gays and lesbians against discrimination and which the Supreme Court struck down as a violation of the Equal Protection Clause in Romer v. Evans (1996; reprinted in Chapter 4). Shortly after passage of the North Carolina law, the Fourth Circuit Court of Appeals (which covers North Carolina) ruled for a transgender student born female who wished to use the boys' restroom at a rural Virginia high school. The Court held that Title IX—the federal law prohibiting gender discrimination in schools—protects the right of students to use the bathroom corresponding with their gender identity.[6] The North Carolina law also has triggered federal administrative responses. On May 4, 2016, the U.S. Department of Justice (DOJ) sent a letter to North Carolina Governor Pat McCrory informing him that the state's new law violates federal civil rights law by treating transgender public employees differently from other public employees and that, unless he remedies those violations, the state could lose federal funding. Title VII prohibits discrimination on the basis of "sex" in the basic terms and conditions of employment, and the DOJ interprets this to include discrimination based on "gender identity." Further, the Equal Employment Opportunity Commission has held that "equal access to restrooms" is a "significant, basic condition of employment" under Title VII and should not be denied to transgender persons.[7]

On May 9, 2016, Governor McCrory and the United States filed lawsuits against each other in federal district court in North Carolina.[8] Governor McCrory's suit, which seeks injunctive relief from the DOJ's letter, claims that, by treating transgender status as a protected class under Title VII, the DOJ is

---

[5] *See* "North Carolina Limits Bathroom Use by Birth Gender," *N.Y. Times*, Mar. 24, 2016.

[6] *See* "Appeals Court Favors Transgender Student in Virginia Restroom Case," *N.Y. Times*, Apr. 19, 2016.

[7] Eric Lichtblau and Richard Fausset, "U.S. Warns North Carolina to Change Bias Law," *N.Y. Times*, May 5, 2016, p. A1.

[8] Alan Blinder, Richard Pérez-Pena, and Eric Lichtblau, "Countersuits over North Carolina's Bias Law," *N.Y. Times*, May 10, 2016.

offering a "radical reinterpretation of Title VII" contrary to Congressional intent and the "overwhelming weight" of judicial authority; the lawsuit argues in the alternative that, even if Title VII does apply, the law's "common sense privacy policy" is not in violation of it.[9] The United States' suit seeks an order declaring that the restroom restriction discriminates on the basis of sex, in violation of Title VII, and may not be enforced.[10] In a press conference about the United States' suit, Attorney General Loretta Lynch compared the State of North Carolina's enacting the law to strike down Charlotte's antidiscrimination ordinance to past instances of "discriminatory responses to historic moments of progress for our nation," such as Jim Crow laws (including bathroom segregation), resistance to racial integration after Brown v. Board of Education (1954), and the many bills "taking aim at the LGBT community" after the rights of gay and lesbian Americans were "embedded in our Constitution." Lynch stated:

> This action is about a great deal more than just bathrooms. This is about the dignity and respect we accord our fellow citizens and the laws that we, as a people and as a country, have enacted to protect them—indeed, to protect all of us. And it's about the founding ideals that have led this country—haltingly but inexorably—in the direction of fairness, inclusion, and equality for all Americans. . . . [T]his is not a time to act out of fear. This is a time to summon our national virtues of inclusivity, diversity, compassion, and open-mindedness. . . . Instead of turning away from our neighbors, our friends, our colleagues, let us instead learn from our history and avoid repeating the mistakes of our past. . . . Let us write a different story this time.[11]

Chief Justice Roberts's dissent in *Obergefell* may have given a boost to the arguments for a right to plural unions. Not long after Roberts filed his dissent, Christine Collier, Victoria Collier, and Nathan Collier filed suit in federal district court in Montana challenging that state's failure to recognize plural unions.[12] Yet

---

[9] Complaint, McCrory et al. v. United States et al. (E.D. N.C. May 9, 2016).

[10] Complaint, United States v. State of North Carolina et al. (M.D. N.C. May 9, 2016). The complaint also alleges that the law is in violation of Title IX and the Violence Against Women Reauthorization Act of 2013.

[11] "Remarks by Attorney General Loretta Lynch at Press Conference Announcing Complaint against the State of North Carolina to Stop Discrimination Against Transgender Individuals," May 9, 2016, https://www.justice.gov/opa/speech/attorney-general-loretta-e-lynch-delivers-remarks-press-conference-announcing-complaint.

[12] *See* Complaint in Collier v. Fox, 1:15–cv–00083–SPW–CSO (D. Mont. Aug. 27, 2015). In December 2015, the federal district court dismissed the Colliers' complaint on the ground that they lacked standing to challenge Montana's law, since they failed to demonstrate a credible threat of prosecution under Montana's

research shows that the fears of Justice Scalia in dissent in Lawrence v. Texas (2003; reprinted above) and Chief Justice Roberts in dissent in *Obergefell* about the slippery slope from recognizing the right of gays and lesbians to marry to protecting a right to polygamy are ill-founded: there are rational bases for outlawing plural marriages. One basis is rooted in the concern that polygamy in its traditional form (one husband with multiple wives, or polygyny) subordinates women to men, a result offensive to the principle of gender equality in the United States and other Western democracies. Another concern is preventing harm to children in plural unions: not only the harm from the practice of polygamists taking child brides but also documented evidence of much higher rates of child abuse and conflict in such unions. And yet a third concern is that polygamy in its traditional form (virtually the only form known outside of desperately poor circumstances) disadvantages lower status males, contributing to social conflict. Some scholars and activists speculate about the rise of an egalitarian form of plural marriage, often called *polyamory*, but others point out that no such form of marriage has ever been practiced widely in any society in human history. Although federal courts have rejected the recent challenges to state bigamy laws on the ground that the plaintiffs lacked standing to sue, thus not reaching the merits, it is likely that we have not heard the end of the matter of the constitutional status of polygamy.[13]

Justice Alito may have had issues such as these in mind when he dissented in *Obergefell*. We leave the reader with a different thought. The recognition of gay rights in our time demonstrates that reason can sometimes overcome widely-held and deeply-entrenched beliefs for which scientific evidence is lacking. It vindicates Publius's faith that government by "reflection and choice" is possible and that "a blind veneration for antiquity, for custom, or for names" need not overrule the public's "own good sense."[14] Moreover, the public's acceptance of the judiciary's role in the gay rights debate manifests the sense that the right thing and the popular thing can differ and that a decent people would institutionalize a concern for the right thing. This vindication of reason and principle is cause for a measure of optimism at a time when problems like "culture war," global warming, global terrorism, and global oligarchy feed the nation's pessimism.

---

bigamy law. Findings and Recommendations of U.S. Magistrate Judge, Collier et al. v. Fox et al., CV 15–83–BLG–SPW–CSO (D. Ct. Mont. Dec. 08, 2015).

[13] *See* Stephen Macedo, *Just Married: Same-Sex Couples, Monogamy & the Future of Marriage* (Princeton, NJ: Princeton University Press, 2015), 145–203.

[14] Alexander Hamilton, John Jay, and James Madison, *The Federalist*, Jacob E. Cooke, ed. (Middletown, CT: Wesleyan University Press, 1961), 1:3; 14:88.

GLOSSARY OF LEGAL TERMS

Amicus curiae: Latin, "friend of the court"; a person or group other than a party in litigation invited or permitted by the court to state its opinion on a legal question before the court; amicus curiae briefs may be filed on behalf of one party to a litigation or on behalf of neither party.

Appeal: a request to a higher court by a losing party to review the decision of a lower court.

Appellant: the party who appeals the decision of a lower court to a higher court.

Appellee: the party against whom an appeal is made.

Brief: a formal written argument addressed to a court on why a case should be decided one way rather than another; also called "memorandum of law."

Certiorari, writ of: an order by the Supreme Court directing a lower court to send up the record of a case. A party's request that the Supreme Court issue a writ of cert. serves the same function as an "appeal," and the two ideas (appeal and certiorari) are often confounded in press reports of a case. The technical difference turns on whether the judiciary laws of Congress give the Supreme Court discretion to review the kind of case in question. Cases that reach the Supreme Court through certiorari far outnumber the cases that reach the high court on "appeal."

Circuit court: the first of two appellate levels in the federal system, the second level being occupied by one court, the Supreme Court. The lowest level of the federal system is the district court, where the initial trial occurs.

Concurring opinion: the opinion of a judge who agrees with the majority on who wins the case but who has a different view of the reasons supporting the decision or who prefers an emphasis or a tone different from the majority's.

Defendant: the person or corporation being sued in a civil case or prosecuted in a criminal case.

Dissenting opinion: the opinion of a judge who disagrees with the majority on which party should win a case.

District court: in the federal system, the lowest level of the federal system, where the initial trial or motion practice occurs.

Due process: fair procedure, as provided by law; see also **substantive due process.**

Incorporation: the process whereby the Supreme Court has made specific rights of the U.S. Constitution's first eight amendments applicable to the states of the federal union.

Injunction: a court order that prohibits a specified act or practice that is likely to cause some person or other entity permanent damage; see also **preliminary injunction**.

Judgment: the determination of a court regarding who wins and loses a civil case.

Judicial review: the power of the federal and state courts to decide whether their respective constitutions permit or forbid a challenged law or other governmental action.

Jurisdiction: the kind of cases a court is authorized to decide.

Litigant: a party to a law suit.

Litigation: the process of deciding controversies under law.

Majority opinion: a statement joined by most of the judges on a multi-judge panel setting forth the reasons for deciding who wins and who loses in a law suit or criminal prosecution.

Opinion: the written reasons by a judge or panel of judges setting forth the reasons for the decision of a case.

Ordinance: a law passed by a local government, that is, by a city council or other municipal body.

Overrule: the decision of a court to declare that a previous case was wrongly decided.

Petitioner: the party who seeks a writ of certiorari; see **certiorari, writ of**

Plaintiff: the party who initiates a law suit.

Plurality opinion: a legal opinion of a number of judges that is on the winning side of a case even though it is less than a majority of the judges on the court.

Precedent: the rule of law established by a previously decided case or the name of that previously decided case.

Preliminary injunction: a judicial order prior to trial to prevent an act or stop a practice, issued only if the court thinks the party requesting the preliminary injunction will suffer permanent damage and is likely to win at trial.

Respondent: the party against whom a party seeks a writ of certiorari.

Reverse: the decision of an appellate court to change a lower court's decision regarding winners and losers.

Standing: a requirement that a plaintiff bringing a legal action must have an actual case or controversy due to, for example, having a personal stake in the outcome. If not, then a court lacks jurisdiction to hear the case and must dismiss for lack of standing.

Substantive due process: interpretation of the commitment to "liberty" in the Due Process Clauses of the Fifth and Fourteenth Amendment to protect basic substantive liberties and to require reasons for governmental deprivations of liberty.

Stare decisis: the idea that courts should uphold the rules of previously decided cases by applying them to present cases unless there are special reasons for overruling the previously decided cases.

Statute: a law enacted by a state legislature or by Congress; also referred to as legislation.

Summary judgment: a judgment made by a court at one party's request when the parties disagree only about the meaning of applicable law, not about the facts of the case.

Vacate as moot: a ruling by a reviewing court that an opinion by a lower court should have no effect because one or both parties below lacked standing to sue and the court lacked jurisdiction to hear the case. This ruling is not a ruling on the merits of the case.

Verdict: a jury's decision about which party in a case has a true version of the facts.

Writ: a judicial order, by a trial court to a party in a case or by an appeals court to a lower court.

Index